T0391943

THE BIBLE AND THE HUMANITIES

General Editors

Hindy Najman   Elizabeth Solopova   Kirk Wetters

This series consists of scholarly monographs that re-integrate Biblical Studies into the Humanities by encouraging channels of communication from Biblical Studies into other Humanistic disciplines, and by bringing current theoretical developments to bear on biblical texts and traditions.

The Making of the Tabernacle and the Construction of Priestly Hegemony

NATHAN MACDONALD

Great Clarendon Street, Oxford, OX2 6DP,
United Kingdom

Oxford University Press is a department of the University of Oxford.
It furthers the University's objective of excellence in research, scholarship,
and education by publishing worldwide. Oxford is a registered trade mark of
Oxford University Press in the UK and in certain other countries

© Nathan MacDonald 2023

The moral rights of the author have been asserted

All rights reserved. No part of this publication may be reproduced, stored in
a retrieval system, or transmitted, in any form or by any means, without the
prior permission in writing of Oxford University Press, or as expressly permitted
by law, by licence or under terms agreed with the appropriate reprographics
rights organization. Enquiries concerning reproduction outside the scope of the
above should be sent to the Rights Department, Oxford University Press, at the
address above

You must not circulate this work in any other form
and you must impose this same condition on any acquirer

Published in the United States of America by Oxford University Press
198 Madison Avenue, New York, NY 10016, United States of America

British Library Cataloguing in Publication Data
Data available

Library of Congress Control Number: 2023935844

ISBN 978–0–19–881385–9

DOI: 10.1093/oso/9780198813859.001.0001

Printed and bound in the UK by
Clays Ltd, Elcograf S.p.A.

Links to third party websites are provided by Oxford in good faith and
for information only. Oxford disclaims any responsibility for the materials
contained in any third party website referenced in this work.

To Callum

גִּיל יָגִיל אֲבִי צַדִּיק   יוֹלֵד חָכָם וְיִשְׂמַח־בּוֹ:

καλῶς ἐκτρέφει πατὴρ δίκαιος, ἐπὶ δὲ υἱῷ σοφῷ εὐφραίνεται ἡ ψυχὴ αὐτοῦ·

(Prov 23.24)

Preface

This book originates in the summer of 2020 though parts of it had been written earlier. For the most part that summer was taken up with other concerns. At home with three children, I juggled adjusting undergraduate courses to work online with childcare and schooling. In the few spare moments I had to think about research, I re-read and tinkered with a lengthy paper that I had written a couple of years earlier on the sin of Nadab and Abihu. Unsure of what to do with something that had grown beyond the confines of a journal article, I sent copies to a few friends and colleagues asking for thoughts. Gary Anderson kindly read the paper and offered to chat about it over the phone. Gary's insights into the relationship between Exod 40 and Lev 9 helped make sense of a number of issues and at the end of the conversation I could see how various things I had been working on previously all belonged together. This book would not have existed without that conversation and I am grateful to Gary for his time and insights. His book on the tabernacle should appear a little before this one. It appears that books on the tabernacle are like London buses: you wait an age for one to appear, and then two come at once. My own book takes a different approach to Gary's, which I have had the privilege of reading pre-publication. The story is told that the puritan Thomas Manton almost gave up writing his commentary on Jude when he learned that William Jenkyn had published his own. He was eventually prevailed upon to continue with his labours, writing in the introduction, 'I consulted with my reverend brother's book, and when I found at any point at large discussed by him, I either omitted it or mentioned it very briefly; so that his labours will be necessary to supply the weakness of mine.' A remarkable claim given the length of both commentaries on such a modest biblical text. Nevertheless, Manton's observation may well assist the readers of this present volume who should also ensure they avail themselves of the wisdom to be found in *That I May Dwell among Them: The Biblical Concept of Incarnation and Atonement* (Eerdmans, forthcoming).

I owe a second debt to Hindy Najman who has been a good friend and generous encourager of my work ever since she arrived in Oxford to take up the Oriel and Laing Professorship of the Interpretation of Holy Scripture. I have benefited from several conversations with her about the book and she has been a regular source of insights and ideas. The breadth of her hermeneutical vision has challenged me on a variety of issues, and she has pushed me to think along unfamiliar lines in ways that have greatly profited this project. Her initiatives at the

viii PREFACE

boundaries of scholarship have been a constant source of inspiration, and I count it a huge privilege to have this book published in her series on the Bible and the Humanities.

A third debt is owed to Angela Erisman. For the past six years, I have had the pleasure of working together with Angie as co-chairs of the Pentateuch section at the annual meeting of the SBL. Those six years have been a true gift and the friendship with Angie has been one of the most rewarding of my academic career. Regular emails and zoom meetings during the pandemic and afterwards have encouraged me to think more carefully about what I am doing and to reflect more deeply on critical issues. Writing a book is sometimes a rather lonely business, but with Angie also completing her own book at the same time, I have felt like a runner with a companion. As a result, the entire race has been far more enjoyable.

Gary, Hindy, and Angela merit particular mention, but there are many others who have contributed to this book in ways large and small. I am grateful to Anselm Hagedorn and Noam Mizrahi for sourcing materials that were difficult to obtain during the pandemic. Also to Yitzhaq Feder, Christian Frevel, Benedikt Jürgens, Edgar Kellenberger, John B. Miller, and Christophe Nihan, for making available their essays that were otherwise inaccessible. Several colleagues were kind enough to provide me with pre-publication materials: Gary Anderson, Graham Davies, Hila Dayfani, Nancy Erickson, Christian Frevel, Jurg Hützli, Drew Longacre, Alice Mandell, Julia Rhyder, Larry Schiffman, and Sarah Schulz. I am also deeply indebted to Stefan Schorch who made available the latest version of his critical edition of the Samaritan Pentateuch for both Exodus and Numbers. Jesse Grenz, Caio Peres, and Paul Aaron Thomas kindly shared their unpublished theses or dissertations with me.

Much of this book was written during the Covid pandemic and its aftermath. Special thanks are due to the librarians at the University Library in Cambridge who provided materials through their Scan and Deliver service. Some of this book would not have been possible without the digitization of manuscripts by the Vatican Library in Rome, the Chester Beatty Library in Dublin, and the Bayerische Staatsbibliothek in Munich.

Over the last few years, various colleagues have read drafts of chapters, responded to papers presented at conferences or discussed matters in which they were specialists: James Aitken, Annie Calderbank, Graham Davies, Hila Dayfani, Marieke Dhont, Liane Feldman, Ron Hendel, Philip Jenson, Reinhard Kratz, Paul Kurtz, Mark Leuchter, Christoph Levin, Alice Mandell, Reinhard Müller, Christophe Nihan, Saul Olyan, Julia Rhyder, Harald Samuel, and James Watts. I also benefited from the questions and discussions following presentations at the Society for Old Testament Study (SOTS), the Society of Biblical Literature (SBL), Georg-August–Universität Göttingen, King's College London, Oxford University, and Edinburgh University.

Some of the arguments in this book have appeared in earlier forms. In most cases, they have been significantly revised in the process of writing this book. An early version of parts of Chapter 5 appeared as 'The Priestly Vestments', in Christoph Berner, Manuel Schäfer, Martin Schott, Sarah Schulz, and Martina Weingärtner (Eds), *Nudity and Clothing in the Hebrew Bible* (T&T Clark, 2019), 435–48. Parts of the argument of Chapter 8 were published in 'Error and Response in Leviticus 10', *Ancient Jew Review* (<https://www.ancientjewreview.com/read/2022/2/2/error-and-response-in-leviticus-10>; published 8 February 2022) and 'Whose *Ḥaṭṭāʾt*? Aaron's Enigmatic Response to Moses in Lev 10:19', *ZAW* 133 (2021): 23–36. Finally, some of Chapter 9 was published at 'The Offerings of the Tribal Leaders, the Purification of the Levites, and the Hermeneutics of Ritual Innovation', in Laura Quick and Melissa Ramos (Eds), *New Perspectives on Ritual in the Biblical World* (LHBOTS 702; T&T Clark, 2022), pp. 199–211. An early version of some of my arguments in Chapter 10 appeared as part of 'Scribalism and Ritual Innovation', *HeBAI* 7 (2018), pp. 415–29 <https://doi.org/10.1628/hebai-2018-0027>. I am grateful to *Ancient Jew Review*, de Gruyter, Mohr Siebeck Tübingen, and T&T Clark, an imprint of Bloomsbury International Plc, for permission to republish this earlier material.

I am grateful to my colleagues in the Divinity Faculty in Cambridge for permitting me to take leave during which the bulk of this book was completed. I owe a particular debt to Katharine Dell and my late - and much lamented - colleague James Aitken who covered various responsibilities in the teaching of Hebrew Bible while I was away, and also to other Cambridge colleagues including Olga Fabrikant-Burke, Alison Gray, Philip Jenson, Sophia Johnson, and Hilary Marlow. The Master and Fellows of St John's College relieved me of my college duties for the same period. I am thankful not only for that relief, but also for the extraordinary privilege to be part of such a wonderful academic community. I am particularly grateful to Simeon Zahl for looking after the theologians in St John's during my leave. That sabbatical was mostly spent in Cambridge, but I was also fortunate to spend two months in Munich as a fellow at the *Münchner Zentrum für Globalgeschichte*. Much of the time there was spent on a future project, but it did also enable me to check references and work on some aspects of the book. I am grateful to Susanne Hohler, Philipp Stockhammer, and Roland Wenzlhuemer for their hospitality. I would also like to thank Jacob Deans for the indexing and Callum for providing the cover design.

In his commentary, William Propp notes that 'the time we spend in reconstructing the Tabernacle is sacred time; the image held in our minds is sacred space'. Much of that sacred time and sacred space has been gifted to me by my family. They have been wonderfully understanding of my obsessions and gently teased the 'Tabernacle Man'. With Claire, Callum, Eilidh, and Morven, I could not be happier and more fortunate. It is a real pleasure to dedicate this book to Callum, our eldest. No parents could be prouder of the young man their son has become.

Table of Contents

List of Abbreviations	xiii
Introduction	1

PART I: THE MAKING OF THE TABERNACLE

1. Four Versions of the Tabernacle	15
2. The Tabernacle in the Late Second Temple Period	41
3. The Making of the Tabernacle Account	67

PART II: THE CONSTRUCTION OF PRIESTLY HEGEMONY

4. The Tabernacle and Its Gloriously Attired Priest	101
5. The High Priest and the Priests	129
6. Craftsmen and Community	153

PART III: THE RECAPITULATION OF PRIESTLY ORDINATION

7. Ordination, Consecration, and Inauguration	187
8. Inauguration and Violation	214
9. Leaders, Levites, and a Kingdom of Priests	240
Conclusion	269

Bibliography	275
Subject Index	293
Ancient Sources Index	296
Author Index	303

List of Abbreviations

*	an earlier layer found within the biblical text indicated
[ ]	lacuna
[text]	reconstructed text
<text>	marginal correction
א	probable letter
א	possible letter
ࠑࠑࠑ	Samaritan Pentateuch
ࠑࠑࠑᴰ	Samaritan Pentateuch (MS. Dublin Chester Beatty Library 751)
𝕲	Old Greek
𝕲ᴬ	Old Greek—Codex Alexandrinus (Royal MS 1 D.v–viii, British Library, London)
𝕲ᴮ	Old Greek—Codex Vaticanus (Vat.gr.1209, Vatican Library, Rome)
𝔏	Old Latin
𝔏ᴸ	Old Latin—Codex Lugdunensis (403 [329], Bibliothèque municipale, Lyon)
𝔏ᴹ	Old Latin—Codex Monacensis (Clm 6225, Bayerische Staatsbibliothek, Munich)
𝔐	Masoretic Text
𝔐ᴸ	Masoretic Text—Codex Leningrad (Firkovitch I, B19a, National Library of Russia, Leningrad)
AABNER	AABNER: Advances in Ancient, Biblical, and Near Eastern Research
AAWG	Abhandlungen der Akademie der Wissenschaften in Göttingen
AB	Anchor Bible
ABG	Arbeiten zur Bibel und ihrer Geschichte
ADPV	Abhandlungen des Deutschen Palästina-Vereins
AGJU	Arbeiten zur Geschichte des antiken Judentums und des Urchristentums
AGLB	Aus der Geschichte der lateinischen Bibeltexte (= Vetus Latina: die Reste der altlateinischen Bibel)
AIL	Ancient Israel and its Literature
ANEM	Ancient Near Eastern Monographs
ASOR	American Schools of Oriental Research
ATD	Das Alte Testament Deutsch
ATSAT	Arbeiten zu Text und Sprache im Alten Testament
BBB	Bonner biblische Beiträge
BEATAJ	Beiträge zur Erforschung des Alten Testaments und des antiken Judentums
BETL	Bibliotheca Ephemeridum Theologicarum Lovaniensium
BHQ	Biblia Hebraica Quinta
Bib	*Biblica*
BibInt	*Biblical Interpretation*

xiv   LIST OF ABBREVIATIONS

BJRL	*Bulletin of the John Rylands Library*
BJS	Biblical and Judaic Studies
BKAT	Biblischer Kommentar, Altes Testament
BN	*Biblische Notizen*
BRLJ	Brill Reference Library of Judaism
BWANT	Beiträge zur Wissenschaft vom Alten und Neuen Testament
BZ	*Biblische Zeitschrift*
BZABR	Beihefte zur Zeitschrift für altorientalische und biblische Rechtsgeschichte
BZAW	Beihefte zur Zeitschrift für die alttestamentliche Wissenschaft
BZNW	Beihefte zur Zeitschrift für die neutestamentliche Wissenschaft
CBC	Cambridge Bible Commentary
CBET	Contributions to Biblical Exegesis and Theology
CBQ	*Catholic Biblical Quarterly*
CC	Continental Commentaries
CHANE	Culture and History of the Ancient Near East
DJD	Discoveries in the Judaean Desert
DSD	*Dead Sea Discoveries*
ErIsr	*Eretz Israel*
ETR	*Études théologiques et religieuses*
FAT	Forschungen zum Alten Testament
FOTL	Forms of the Old Testament Literature
FRLANT	Forschungen zur Religion und Literatur des Alten und Neuen Testaments
GKC	Emil Kautzsch (ed.), *Gesenius' Hebrew Grammar*, trans. Arthur E. Cowley, 2nd edn, Oxford: Clarendon, 1910
HALOT	Ludwig Koehler, Walter Baumgartner, and Johann J. Stamm, *The Hebrew and Aramaic Lexicon of the Old Testament*, trans. and edited under the supervision of Mervyn J. Richardson, 4 vols, Leiden: Brill, 1994–99
HAR	*Hebrew Annual Review*
HAT	Handbuch zum Alten Testament
HBM	Hebrew Bible Monographs
HBS	Herders Biblische Studien
HCOT	Historical Commentary on the Old Testament
HDB	James Hastings (ed.), *A Dictionary of the Bible*, 5 vols, New York: Charles Scribner's Sons, 1898–1904
HeBAI	*Hebrew Bible and Ancient Israel*
HKAT	Handkommentar zum Alten Testament
HSS	Harvard Semitic Studies
HTKAT	Herders Theologischer Kommentar zum Alten Testament
HTR	*Harvard Theological Review*
IBC	Interpretation: A Bible Commentary for Teaching and Preaching
ICC	International Critical Commentary
IEJ	*Israel Exploration Journal*
JAJSup	Journal of Ancient Judaism, Supplement Series
JANER	*Journal of Ancient Near Eastern Religions*
JAOS	*Journal of the American Oriental Society*

JBL	*Journal of Biblical Literature*
JHebS	*Journal of the Hebrew Scriptures*
JNES	*Journal of Near Eastern Studies*
JNSL	*Journal of Northwest Semitic Languages*
JQR	*Jewish Quarterly Review*
JSCS	*Journal of Septuagint and Cognate Studies*
JSJ	*Journal for the Study of Judaism*
JSJSup	Supplements to the Journal for the Study of Judaism
JSOT	*Journal for the Study of the Old Testament*
JSOTSup	Journal for the Study of the Old Testament, Supplement Series
JSS	*Journal of Semitic Studies*
JTS	*Journal of Theological Studies*
KeHAT	Kurzgefasstes exegetisches Handbuch zum Alten Testament
KHAT	Kurzer Hand-Commentar zum Alten Testament
LASBF	*Liber Annuus Studii Biblici Franciscani*
LHBOTS	Library of Hebrew Bible/Old Testament Studies
LSTS	Library of Second Temple Studies
MdB	Le Monde de la Bible
NCB	New Century Bible
NICOT	New International Commentary on the Old Testament
NovTSup	Supplements to Novum Testamentum
NRSV	New Revised Standard Version
OBO	Orbis Biblicus et Orientalis
Or	*Orientalia*
OTL	Old Testament Library
P^g	Priestly *Grundschrift*
PEQ	*Palestine Exploration Quarterly*
Post	*Postscripts: The Journal of Sacred Texts, Cultural Histories, and Contemporary Contexts*
Proof	*Prooftexts: A Journal of Jewish Literary History*
RB	*Revue Biblique*
RBS	Resources for Biblical Study
RevQ	*Revue de Qumran*
RlA	Erich Ebeling et al. (eds.), *Reallexicon der Assyrologie*. Berlin: de Gruyter, 1928–
SBLMS	Society of Biblical Literature Monograph Series
SBT	Studies in Biblical Theology
ScrHier	Scripta Hierosolymitana
SCS	Septuagint and Cognate Studies
SemeiaSt	Semeia Studies
SJ	Studia Judaica
SJLA	Studies in Judaism in Late Antiquity
STDJ	Studies on the Texts of the Desert of Judah
Targ. Neo.	Targum Neofiti
Targ. Onq.	Targum Onqelos
ThR	*Theologische Rundschau*

xvi   LIST OF ABBREVIATIONS

TOTC	Tyndale Old Testament Commentaries
TSAJ	Texts and Studies in Ancient Judaism
TSK	*Theologische Studien und Kritiken*
UCPNES	University of California Publications, Near Eastern Studies
UTB	Uni-Taschenbücher
VT	*Vetus Testamentum*
VTSup	Supplements to Vetus Testamentum
WBC	Word Biblical Commentary
WC	Westminster Commentaries
WMANT	Wissenschaftliche Monographien zum Alten und Neuen Testament
WUNT	Wissenschaftliche Untersuchungen zum Neuen Testament
ZABR	*Zeitschrift für altorientalische und biblische Rechtsgeschichte*
ZBK	Zürcher Bibelkommentar
ZDPV	*Zeitschrift des Deutschen Palästina-Vereins*

Introduction

In the summer of 586 BCE and after a prolonged siege, Jerusalem was conquered by the army of the Babylonian king, Nebuchadnezzar. With the city's fall, the small kingdom of Judah and its native dynasty came to an end. The last king, Zedekiah, sought to flee the city, but was captured by Babylonian forces in the environs of Jericho. He was sent to appear before Nebuchadnezzar at his head-quarters in Riblah on the Orontes where he was judged and deported to Babylon to live out his remaining days in humiliating servitude.[1] Back in the city, the chief priest and his deputy, together with the temple guardians, seem to have remained at their posts. There they were captured before they too were sent to Riblah where they were flogged and executed together with other city officials. The contrasting fates of Zedekiah and his officers highlight their different status in the eyes of their captors. It was to be another four centuries before local rule was restored to this corner of the Levant when the Hasmoneans exploited divisions within the Seleucid empire to secure a measure of independence. The Hasmoneans took various titles, including governor, ethnarch, ruler, and eventually even king,[2] but their claim to hegemony stemmed from their holding the office of high priest. How did the high priesthood go from being an important, but subordinate, office in the kingdom of Judah to being the principal source of authority?

It was long believed that a significant shift in the power wielded by the high priest had occurred during the early years of the Achaemenid empire. The pro-phetic books of Haggai and Zechariah appear to suggest that the returning Jewish community was jointly led by Zerubbabel, a scion of the former royal dynasty, and Joshua, a descendant of the last chief priest Seraiah. This dyarchy of governor and priest did not endure and Zerubbabel's absence from some of Zechariah's oracles was often thought to reflect Persian fears that some of Zerubbabel's sup-porters harboured ambitions to restore the Davidic dynasty. In this view, oracles were hastily rewritten to remove references to the royal pretender with the result

---

[1] Zedekiah's end is described in Jer 52.11, but not in the parallel text of 2 Kgs 25.7. The precise implications of his imprisonment in בֵּית־הַפְּקֻדֹּת, 'house of punishment', is disputed, not least because of the Greek reading, οἰκίαν μυλῶνος, 'house of milling'. For discussion, see William McKane, *A Critical and Exegetical Commentary on Jeremiah. Volume II: Commentary on Jeremiah XXVI–LII*, ICC (Edinburgh: T&T Clark, 1996), 1365. For the fates of Zedekiah and his officials in Jeremiah, see Henk de Waard, *Jeremiah 52 in the Context of the Book of Jeremiah*, VTSup 183 (Leiden: Brill, 2020), 109–42.

[2] Josephus and Strabo disagree about which of the Hasmoneans was the first to take the title 'king' (βασιλεύς). According to Josephus it was Aristobulus I who first 'assumed the diadem' (*J.W.* 1.3.1), but Strabo credits Alexander Jannaeus with this distinction (*Geogr.* 16.2.40).

2   THE MAKING OF THE TABERNACLE

that the high priest alone bore a crown and sat upon a throne. The following decades saw the high priests consolidate their power as any lingering hopes that the Davidic dynasty would be revived faded.[3] For much recent scholarship, the historical reconstruction of the high priest's supremacy during the Persian period is belied by epigraphic and numismatic evidence which shows that the province of Yehud was ruled for most, if not all, of the period by Persian-appointed governors.[4]

Determining how the priesthood developed in the late Persian and early Hellenistic periods has been afflicted by several difficulties. Scholarship has struggled to describe well the influence wielded by the high priest during this period. Deborah Rooke, for example, makes a sharp distinction between civil and cultic leadership. In the ancient world, however, the two spheres intersected in complex ways.[5] Similar difficulties arise with Lisbeth Fried's claim that the high priests 'held little real power'.[6] Fried appears to have in mind what some would describe as coercive power, and it is true that such power was only wielded by the governor. Nevertheless, her language is intriguing, if also problematic, for it suggests there are other types of power, even if these are somehow less 'real'. Despite her headline claim, Fried recognizes that local aristocracies and priesthoods resisted encroachment on their traditional competencies, and enjoyed some influence as members of the local bureaucracy.[7] The decision of the leaders of the Elephantine community to write to the high priest and aristocrats in Jerusalem, for example, suggests that they believed the Judean community leaders could exercise some influence. In other words, they had some sort of power.

A further difficulty that afflicts any historical reconstruction of the priesthood's development is the paucity of evidence. This is true of the entire period from the ascendancy of the Persians to the Maccabean revolt, but is especially the case for

---

[3] Rooke cites some of the earlier scholarship holding this position (Deborah W. Rooke, *Zadok's Heirs: The Role and Development of the High Priesthood in Ancient Israel* [Oxford: Oxford University Press, 2000], 1–4). Grabbe maintains that there was a dyarchy in Yehud already in the late sixth century and perhaps in the following centuries (Lester L. Grabbe, *A History of the Jews and Judaism in the Second Temple Period. Vol 1: Yehud: A History of the Persian Period of Judah*, LSTS 47 [London: T&T Clark, 2004], 147–8; Lester L. Grabbe, 'The Priesthood in the Persian Period: Haggai, Zechariah, and Malachi', in *Priests and Cults in the Book of the Twelve*, ed. Lena-Sofia Tiemeyer, ANEM 14 [Atlanta: Society of Biblical Literature, 2016], 149–56). Wöhrle also argues that the earliest prophetic oracles in Haggai and Zechariah propound the idea of a dyarchy, but this was later edited to support a hierocracy (Jakob Wöhrle, 'On the Way to Hierocracy: Secular and Priestly Rule in the Books of Haggai and Zechariah', in *Priests and Cults in the Book of the Twelve*, ed. Lena-Sofia Tiemeyer, ANEM 14 [Atlanta: Society of Biblical Literature, 2016], 173–90).

[4] A table which synchronizes as far as possible the satraps of Eber-nari, the governors of Yehud and Samaria, and the high priests in Jerusalem can be found in Reinhard Achenbach, 'Satrapie, Medinah und lokale Hierokratie: Zum Einfluss der Statthalter der Achämenidenzeit auf Tempelwirtschaft und Tempelordnungen', *ZABR* 16 (2010): 111.

[5] Rooke, *Zadok's Heirs*.

[6] Lisbeth S. Fried, *The Priest and the Great King: Temple-Palace Relations in the Persian Empire*, BJS 10 (Winona Lake, IN: Eisenbrauns, 2004), 233.

[7] E.g. Fried, *Priest*, 202, 212.

INTRODUCTION   3

the late Persian and early Hellenistic periods. The consequences of this data poverty are apparent in the failure of any consensus to emerge within contemporary scholarship about how and when the high priest rose to supremacy. Did he accrue power alongside the governor so that a dyarchy emerged before giving way to a hierocracy?[8] Or was the seizure of power by the high priest sudden and driven by a specific set of events, such as the transfer of Yehud to Greek hegemony as a result of Alexander the Great's conquests[9] or the interventions of the Seleucid king Antiochus IV into the affairs of the Jerusalem temple?[10]

A final difficulty that may be observed is the significant interpretive challenge of interpreting the texts of the Hebrew Bible, our most significant and extensive collection of sources for the priesthood in Persian-period Judaism. Stated simply, our texts do not often seem to reflect the social realities of the period which they purport to describe. It is not just that we must reckon with a complex redactional history, but it is also the fact that the portrayal may reflect the ambitions of a scribal minority.[11] The biblical texts may provide some of the conditions for the priesthood's supremacy emerging in subsequent centuries, but they may not reflect the reality of their own situation. In other words, as Frevel argues for the portrayal of the priesthood in the book of Numbers, it is often the case that it was not 'the political development [that] shaped the text, but rather the other way around'.[12] Thus, the reconstruction of the priesthood's history is entangled in the question of how the ideological justification for the priesthood's supremacy developed. As a result, our sources for the history of the priesthood need to be utilized with considerable care, and, crucially, careful comparison made with the full range of available evidence.

In recent scholarship, various significant texts have benefited from incisive critical analysis, including Haggai and Zech 1–8,[13] Ezra-Nehemiah,[14] and

---

[8] Schaper, for example, argues that a dyarchy emerged in the mid-fourth century (Joachim Schaper, *Priester und Leviten im achämenidischen Juda: Studien zur Kult- und Sozialgeschichte Israels in persischer Zeit*, FAT 31 [Tübingen: Mohr Siebeck, 2000]). For the argument that the high priest progressively accrued power during the fourth century BCE see Wolfgang Oswald, 'Der Hohepriester als Ethnarch. Zur politische Organisation Judäas im 4. Jahrhundert v. Chr', *ZABR* 21 (2015): 309–20.

[9] See, e.g., James C. VanderKam, *From Joshua to Caiaphas: High Priests after the Exile* (Minneapolis: Fortress, 2004); Jeremiah W. Cataldo, *A Theocratic Yehud? Issues of Governance in a Persian Province*, LHBOTS 498 (London: Bloomsbury T&T Clark, 2009).

[10] See, e.g., Rooke, *Zadok's Heirs*; Sarah Schulz, *Joschua und Melchisedek: Studien zur Entwicklung des Jerusalemer Hohepriesteramtes vom 6. Jahrhundert v. Chr. bis zum 2. Jahrhundert v. Chr.*, BZAW (Berlin: de Gruyter, forthcoming).

[11] For detailed discussion of the possible redactional development and its significance for the history of the priesthood, see Schulz, *Joschua*.

[12] Christian Frevel, 'Leadership and Conflict: Modelling the Charisma of Numbers', in *Debating Authority: Concepts of Leadership in the Pentateuch and Former Prophets*, eds. Katharina Pyschny and Sarah Schulz, BZAW 507 (Berlin: de Gruyter, 2018), 106.

[13] Rooke, *Zadok's Heirs*, 125–51; VanderKam, *From Joshua*, 1–42; Schulz, *Joschua*.

[14] Rooke, *Zadok's Heirs*, 152–74; Fried, *Priest*; Donna Laird, *Negotiating Power in Ezra-Nehemiah*, AIL 26 (Atlanta: SBL Press, 2016).

4 THE MAKING OF THE TABERNACLE

Numbers.[15] Arguably, however, one of the most important texts is frequently overlooked: the tabernacle and ordination accounts of Exod 25–31, 35–40 and Lev 8–10. The reasons for their omission are not difficult to discern. These chapters are not a historiographic text in the way that Haggai, Zech 1–8 or Ezra-Nehemiah are. In addition, they also belong to a documentary source that is often thought to have originated before the Second Temple was established. This is true not only of the Jerusalem school that would locate the origins of the priestly literature in the monarchic period, but also for some proponents of continental criticism who would date it in the late neo-Babylonian or early Persian period. For both of these perspectives, the priestly literature forms the background for later Persian period texts.[16] In this study, however, I seek to demonstrate that the tabernacle and ordination accounts developed during the Persian period, and that they make an important contribution to our understanding of how ideological justification for the high priesthood's supremacy developed.

The Tabernacle and Social Structure

It has not always been obvious that the tabernacle account in Exodus might contribute to our understanding of priestly hegemony in early Judaism. In the middle part of the twentieth century, biblical scholarship mostly focused on how these chapters reflect Israelite ideas about divine presence and how these related to the historicity of traditions about tent shrines. The keen interest in divine presence was part of a larger focus upon the contribution that the Old Testament might make to Christian theological reflection that came about in the wake of Karl Barth.[17] It was observed that the end of the book of Exodus uses two different names for the sanctuary that God commands Moses to construct. The first title is the Hebrew term מִשְׁכָּן which has conventionally been translated into English as 'tabernacle'. The English gloss is a transliteration of the Latin *tabernaculum*, which was used to render the Greek term σκηνή, 'tent'. Whilst the Greek and Latin terms draw attention to the shrine's structural form, the Hebrew word מִשְׁכָּן is a noun formed from the verb שׁכ׳׳ן, 'to dwell', and a more suitable translation might be 'dwelling'. The second name given to the sanctuary is אֹהֶל מוֹעֵד, 'tent of meeting'. The alternative designations for the tent suggest two rather different conceptions of the divine presence. In the first God resides in the sanctuary, but in the second God encounters the people, perhaps only intermittently. Examining these two

---

[15] Reinhard Achenbach, *Die Vollendung der Tora: Studien zur Redaktionsgeschichte des Numeribuches im Kontext von Hexateuch und Pentateuch*, BZABR 3 (Wiesbaden: Harrassowitz, 2003); Katharina Pyschny, *Verhandelte Führung: Eine Analyse von Num 16–17 im Kontext der neueren Pentateuchforschung*, HBS 88 (Freiburg im Breisgau: Herder, 2017); Frevel, 'Leadership and Conflict'.

[16] Rooke, *Zadok's Heirs*.

[17] An influential example is von Rad: Gerhard von Rad, *Old Testament Theology*, 2 vols. (New York: Harper & Row, 1962), I: 234–41.

notions of divine presence and the relationship between them has occupied considerable scholarly attention which continues into the present.[18] The assessment of the different theologies of divine presence was often closely bound to claims about the antiquity of Israel's historical traditions of a tent shrine. Despite Wellhausen's famous assertion in the nineteenth century that 'the tabernacle is the copy, not the prototype, of the temple in Jerusalem',[19] various ancient parallels from Ugarit, Mari, Midian, and Egypt, were adduced to support the possibility that cultic worship in a tent was an early tradition. The quest for Near Eastern analogies has also continued in recent scholarship.[20]

The way in which the presentation of the tabernacle portrays a hierocratic society first emerges with clarity in the seminal work by Menahem Haran on temples and temple service. Haran demonstrated how increased technical workmanship and material value indicated greater sanctity. The instructions for the tabernacle envisaged a concentric structure with the small room where the ark was to be placed as the focal point and the place of greatest holiness. Moving outwards from the holy of holies resulted in diminished sanctity and material decoration. The concentric circles of holiness also determine access with only the high priest able to enter all parts of the tabernacle complex including the holy of holies. Priests, Levites, and ordinary Israelites—in that order—enjoy diminishing access and sight of the tabernacle and its furniture.[21]

The potential of thinking about the tabernacle as a space that maps Israel's social configuration was developed in a suggestive monograph by Mark George. Utilizing Henri Lefebvre's theory of space he examines how the tabernacle narratives are a cultural production expressing the priestly understanding of Israel's social organization. George worked with the Masoretic Text of Exod 25–40 which he regards as an exilic composition. The exilic context looms large in George's analysis for he argues that the tabernacle account has reappropriated royal

---

[18] See, e.g., Benjamin Sommer, 'Conflicting Constructions of Divine Presence in the Priestly Tabernacle', *BibInt* 9 (2001): 41–63. For a discussion of the issue and an account of the scholarly literature, see most recently Domenico Lo Sardo, *Post-Priestly Additions and Rewritings in Exodus 35–40*, FAT II/119 (Tübingen: Mohr Siebeck, 2020), 121–230.

[19] Julius Wellhausen, *Prolegomena to the History of Israel with a Reprint of the Article Israel from the 'Encyclopaedia Britannica'*, trans. John Sutherland Black and Allan Menzies (Edinburgh: Black, 1885), 37.

[20] See, *inter alia*, Frank Moore Cross, 'The Tabernacle: A Study from an Archaeological and Historical Approach', *BA* 10 (1947): 45–68; Richard J. Clifford, 'Tent of El and the Israelite Tent of Meeting', *CBQ* 33 (1971): 221–7; Frank Moore Cross, 'The Priestly Tabernacle in the Light of Recent Research', in *The Temple in Antiquity: Ancient Records and Modern Perspectives*, ed. Truman G. Madsen (Provo, UT: Brigham Young University Press, 1984), 91–105; Daniel E. Fleming, 'Mari's Large Public Tent and the Priestly Tent Sanctuary', *VT* 50 (2000): 484–98; Michael M. Homan, *To Your Tents, O Israel!: The Terminology, Function, Form, and Symbolism of Tents in the Hebrew Bible and the Ancient Near East*, CHANE 12 (Leiden: Brill, 2002); Madadh Richey, 'The Dwelling of ʾIlu in Baʿlu and ʾAqhatu', *JANER* 17 (2017): 149–85.

[21] Menahem Haran, *Temples and Temple-Service in Ancient Israel* (Oxford: Clarendon Press, 1978), 149–88. See also Jenson whose analysis of the spatial dimension of the tabernacle account is followed by the personal dimension because of their close correlation (Philip Peter Jenson, *Graded Holiness: A Key to the Priestly Conception of the World*, JSOTSup 106 [Sheffield: JSOT Press, 1992], 89–148).

6 THE MAKING OF THE TABERNACLE

building inscriptions and foundation deposits and attributed the monarch's role to the people. 'The Priestly writers thus democratize the king's role in royal building projects, spreading it out among the people.'[22] The notion of the tabernacle texts as democratizing sits somewhat uncomfortably alongside George's recognition that entering holier space is restricted by narrowing social criteria of descent, gender, and hereditary succession. He shows no interest in exploring this tension despite his use of the analytical framework of a Marxist theorist.

The tension between hierocratic and democratic explanations is not unique to George. It also emerges in the different analyses of the opening chapters of Leviticus by James Watts and Liane Feldman. Their divergent accounts of how power operates in the priestly literature is especially striking because they examine the same text (Leviticus) with similar methodological interests (narratological and rhetorical). Watts argues that Lev 1–16 justifies control of the cult and its perquisites by the priests. Even the story of Nadab and Abihu's infraction in Lev 10, does not serve to undermine the claims of the Aaronides, but highlights the dangers inherent in their role. They deserve the rewards that accrue to the priests because of the extraordinary risks they take.[23] Feldman, on the other hand, argues that Leviticus rests authority with the Israelites by lifting the veil on cultic affairs. It is not the priests who are addressed in Lev 1–16, but the Israelites (Lev 1.1; 4.1; 11.1; 12.1; 15.1). 'The narrator's choice to allow the reader-Israelite to hear and see the internal workings of the cult challenges the hegemony of the priesthood and centers the ordinary Israelite in the life of the cult. In many ways, this is a story of the democratization of ideas about religious practice in ancient Israel.'[24] Since Watts and Feldman can appeal to features of the text of Leviticus as well as the broader historical context to justify their understandings of the priestly literature, we return to the problem already seen with Rooke and Fried that biblical scholarship needs a more sophisticated and nuanced account of power. Only in this way will we reach a deeper and integrated understanding of the apparent hierocratic and democratic features of priestly texts.

A Theory of Power

Amongst the various theorists of power, Michel Foucault is especially useful for this study because he worked within the field of history, rather than viewing the subject through a primarily philosophical lens. Whatever is made of his specific

---

[22] Mark K. George, *Israel's Tabernacle as Social Space*, AIL 2 (Atlanta, GA: Society of Biblical Literature, 2009), 166.

[23] James W. Watts, *Ritual and Rhetoric in Leviticus: From Sacrifice to Scripture* (Cambridge: Cambridge University Press, 2007); cf. James W. Watts, 'Aaron and the Golden Calf in the Rhetoric of the Pentateuch', *JBL* 130 (2011): 417–30.

[24] Liane Marquis Feldman, *The Story of Sacrifice: Ritual and Narrative in the Priestly Source*, FAT 141 (Tübingen: Mohr Siebeck, 2020), 198.

historical arguments, he shows an attentiveness to historical particularities and the embedding of power within concrete social practices and institutions. Whilst Foucault's thinking developed over time and was never presented systematically, his writings are characterized by a distinctive set of perspectives and concerns that emerge in different forms.[25] Thus, whilst the focus on power only emerges after he published *The Archaeology of Knowledge* in 1969, earlier works can be seen to have power as their concern even if not named explicitly, as Foucault himself recognized.[26]

Much of Foucault's work was concerned with social institutions—the asylum, the clinic, the prison—and their utilization of scientific discourse.[27] Foucault argued that in the eighteenth and nineteenth centuries these institutions reflected new configurations of power and knowledge—a shift from one episteme to another. The epistemes are characterized by discursive formations that define what is intelligent and appropriate. They also set parameters for what was true, and they did so in a manner that made the previous discursive formations appear irrational or unjust. Foucault frequently began his studies juxtaposing striking examples that epitomize two epistemes. *The Birth of the Clinic* contrasts the description of how a hysteric was cured in the eighteenth century with that of a patient suffering from chronic meningitis a century later. In *Discipline and Punish*, Foucault follows an exacting account of the execution of a regicide with the disciplinary regime of a prison eighty years later. These examples illustrate how dramatically the discursive formations had changed, but also highlight continuities and discontinuities. Vaporous disorders are replaced by a scientific anatomy, whilst extreme physical torture gives way to incarceration. Yet, the earlier physician is no less attentive to description of the body's pathologies just as the executioner is no less precise in meting out punishment.[28] Foucault's earlier studies mapped out the differences between epistemes and how these were reflected in numerous fields, but with *Discipline and Punish* he also sought to explain the transformations that took place.[29]

Foucault's contributions to the understanding of power can be seen as an attempt to displace occasional displays of violent sovereignty as the main way to view the exercise of power. In modern societies, power most often takes place

---

[25] As Haugaard observes, Foucault's work forms 'a unity with differences of emphasis rather than of fundamental substance' (Mark Haugaard, *The Constitution of Power: A Theoretical Analysis of Power, Knowledge and Structure* [Manchester: Manchester University Press, 1997], 42).

[26] Michel Foucault, *The Archaeology of Knowledge* (London: Tavistock Publications, 1986). For the development of power in Foucault's thinking, see Stuart Elden, *Foucault: The Birth of Power* (Cambridge: Polity Press, 2017).

[27] Michel Foucault, *Madness and Civilization: A History of Insanity in the Age of Reason* (London: Tavistock Publications, 1967); Michel Foucault, *The Birth of the Clinic: An Archaeology of Medical Perception* (London: Tavistock Publications, 1973); Michel Foucault, *Discipline and Punish* (London: Penguin Books, 2019).

[28] Foucault, *Birth of the Clinic*, ix–xii; Foucault, *Discipline and Punish*, 3–31.

[29] In Foucault's own categories a shift from archaeology to genealogy.

8 THE MAKING OF THE TABERNACLE

through institutions and their practices of discipline. This exercise of power is ubiquitous, continuous, and diffuse. Whilst sovereign power succeeds by either coercion or destruction, Foucault emphasized the productive nature of disciplinary power. 'In fact, power produces; it produces reality; it produces domains of objects and rituals of truth.'[30] Thus, in his work on punishment, Foucault shows how power creates space and time. Prisons construct hierarchical, ordered spaces that control delinquents more effectively, whilst prison timetables ensure effective disciplining. The rearrangement of space and time also creates different people. Not only those identified as criminals, but also the entire structure of wardens, psychiatrists, educationalists. Discipline and training generate new objects to know as well as new rituals, bodily practices, and habits.[31]

The older model of sovereignty envisages power hierarchically with domination being projected downwards. For Foucault, power comes from everywhere.[32] Nor is power something that is held, instead it circulates. As such it has a dynamic quality that requires it to be constantly renegotiated. On the one hand, this allows for the possibility of resistance for consent must be granted. On the other hand, Foucault's notion of disciplinary power seems to restrict the potential for defiance. If power produces space, time, and human bodies, it also provides limits on what is thinkable.

Central to this understanding of how power works is the relationship of knowledge and power: 'power produces knowledge...power and knowledge directly imply one another'.[33] The relationship is so fundamental that Foucault spoke of 'power/knowledge'. It is consequently discourse that defines the world and what is reasonable and appropriate. Discourse does not build upon realities outside itself; rather, discourse constitutes the objects it describes. Thus, it commends itself as 'natural' to all who experience it. It is possible to see why Foucault's earlier work compared epistemes and stopped short of attempting to describe how they developed. In his later work, however, Foucault allowed that we have a 'complex and unstable process whereby a discourse can be both an instrument and an effect of power, but also a hindrance, a stumbling point of resistance and a starting point for an opposing strategy. Discourse transmits and produces power; it reinforces it, but also undermines and exposes it, renders it fragile and makes it possible to thwart.'[34] It is in these hindrances and stumbling points that the possibility for change exists.

---

[30] Foucault, *Discipline and Punish*, 194.

[31] Joseph Rouse, 'Power/Knowledge', in *The Cambridge Companion to Foucault*, ed. Gary Gutting (Cambridge: Cambridge University Press, 2005), 98.

[32] Michel Foucault, *The History of Sexuality. Volume 1, The Will to Knowledge* (London: Penguin Classics, 2020), 93.

[33] Foucault, *Discipline and Punish*, 27. Nietzsche is an important influence upon Foucault as is apparent in the close relationship for both between truth and power.

[34] Foucault, *Will to Knowledge*, 100–1.

Foucault's understanding of the encompassing nature of discourse can be seen as complementary to Antonio Gramsci's concept of 'hegemony'.[35] Gramsci uses hegemony to explain how power is exercised by rulers over the ruled not through overt displays of force or violence, but through the control of civic institutions. The values of the dominant group are propagated through these cultural vehicles such that they appear both natural and justified. Consequently, the working masses consent to the social hierarchy, conforming to its norms, and acquiescing in its inequitable distribution of resources.[36] Gramsci provides a helpful corrective to Foucault's thinking with a focus on human agency and, most noticeably, the agency of intellectuals in the formation of hegemony.

Although Foucault and Gramsci bring considerable refinement to our understanding of power and its exercise, it is not immediately obvious that their insights can be applied to the world of Persian period Judaism. Foucault is concerned with the shift from monarchic sovereignty to the modern world of bureaucratic institutions and scientific knowledge, whilst Gramsci is addressing a problem in Marxist theory. As a result, their ideas are deeply rooted in the issues facing modern societies. Nevertheless, their thinking about forms of power other than coercive rule of the state offers a potentially useful perspective for thinking about the kinds of influence the priesthood may have exercised. The priesthood was itself a bureaucratic institution with its own forms of knowledge and discipline.

Outline of This Book

The purpose of this book, then, is to contribute to the understanding of how the conditions were created for the high priesthood to assume political supremacy at some point during the early Hellenistic period. To do so, it will examine the portrayal of the priesthood in the tabernacle and ordination accounts of Exod 25–40 and related texts from elsewhere in Exodus as well as the books of Leviticus and Numbers. During the Persian period and early Hellenistic period, these chapters in the Pentateuch shaped, and were shaped by, the perception of the priesthood's powers and competencies. To examine how this occurred, this book will be divided into three parts each consisting of three chapters. The first part will seek to analyse how the tabernacle account developed working back from the extant medieval versions to the earliest priestly document. The second part will examine how the different human agents are presented through the tabernacle account's developing stages. The third part will focus on the ordination ritual and the various ways it was transformed within the books of Exodus to Numbers.

---

[35] For the intersections between the thought of Foucault and Gramsci, see David Kreps (ed.), *Gramsci and Foucault: A Reassessment* (London: Routledge, 2016).

[36] Antonio Gramsci, *Selections from the Prison Notebooks of Antonio Gramsci*, eds. Quintin Hoare and Geoffrey Nowell-Smith (London: Lawrence & Wishart, 1971), 97.

10 THE MAKING OF THE TABERNACLE

The first part examines the textual evidence for the tabernacle account and seeks to give an account of how it was that the tabernacle account survived in four distinct versions. This is to tell a story that extends over more than fifteen centuries from late medieval manuscripts back to the earliest origins of the tabernacle account in the priestly document that was composed in the early Persian period. That story begins in Chapter 1 with the four versions that were preserved in late antique and medieval manuscripts: a Masoretic, a Samaritan, an Old Greek, and an Old Latin version. Consistent with the recent turn to materiality, I will examine the best four exemplars of each version. Far too often biblical scholars work just with critical texts compiled by previous generations of scholars. There is no doubt that these are unparalleled tools and I have used them frequently during my work, but they can suggest an abstract text shorn of the many features that accompany it—better, are part of it—in actual manuscripts. Consequently, I have sought to describe the various features of these versions including those that are labelled as 'paratextual'. These are important features of how the texts were transmitted and provide an indication of how early scribes understood the tabernacle account.

The four different versions of the tabernacle account trace their origins to the late Second Temple period. How is this textual plurality to be explained and the texts related to one another? In addition to the late antique and medieval manuscripts of the tabernacle account, we also have evidence from the late Second Temple period: the manuscripts of the Dead Sea Scrolls. Chapter 2 considers this additional evidence and examines how the various textual traditions are to be related to one another. In agreement with many recent textual critics, I will argue that the Old Greek and Old Latin versions reflect a *Vorlage* or *Vorlagen* that are earlier than the text found in the Masoretic and Samaritan versions.

The extant versions exhibit the complexity of the tabernacle account in Exodus. No compositional model exists that draws upon the evidence of the various versions and accounts for their differences. In Chapter 3, I seek to close that lacuna by setting out a model for the literary-critical development of the tabernacle account which begins from the earliest priestly document and goes as far as the processes of standardization and harmonization that result in the Masoretic and Samaritan versions. The model I propose is coordinated with contemporary models in continental scholarship for how the priestly literature of the Pentateuch developed. It is worth noting that a model is precisely that: a *model*. It is a sketch of developments that seeks to account for the extant evidence. It is necessarily hypothetical, and no doubt a simplification of a process that was, in fact, much more complex. Nevertheless, as I have argued elsewhere, literary-critical models are 'good to think with'.[37] They seek to explain certain features of the text and

---

[37] Nathan MacDonald, *Priestly Rule: Polemic and Biblical Interpretation in Ezekiel 44*, BZAW 475 (Berlin: de Gruyter, 2015), 14–16.

focus attention on details that are easily overlooked in a synchronic reading. The end of such a model is not the model itself, or some putative original document, but understanding the extant forms of the text and the processes that led to them.

In the second part of this book, I take those literary-critical results and use them as a basis for examining the presentation of the tabernacle's human agents. The textual material is examined in the reverse order to that found in the first part: I begin with the earliest textual core of the tabernacle account and work, in broad terms, towards the later texts. Consequently, in Chapter 4, I examine the tabernacle as presented in the original priestly document. In common with many other contemporary scholars, I hold that this composition opened with the creation story in Gen 1 and concluded with Israel's God taking residence in the tabernacle in Exod 40. Although the sanctuary is presented as a fitting and comfortable abode for Israel's God, I will argue that the climax is not so much the tabernacle edifice as the glorious garments of Aaron. These are attributed instrumental significance that ensures that God is attentive to Israel.

Chapter 5 unfolds how the more complicated portrayal of the sanctuary and its priesthood was developed. The integration of the great atonement ritual in Lev 16 plays a significant role in creating that complexity. In particular, the perspectives of Lev 16 were incorporated in at least two distinct stages. One important consequence of these revisions is to distinguish the high priest from the rest of the priesthood.

Chapter 6 examines the roster of characters that inhabit the compliance account in Exod 35–40, including the master craftsmen and the Israelite artisans, the Israelite men and women, the leaders, and the Levites. Together, they form a complex social hierarchy which emphasizes, paradoxically, both equality within the community and the pre-eminent status of the priests. This chapter examines how the compliance account disseminates power and competencies as part of a strategy that also serves to affirm priestly supremacy.

In the third part I examine the ordination ritual and its transformation into various other rituals. The effect of literary-critical reworking is rather different in the case of a ritual than in that of a building account. As we saw in the second part, the revision of the tabernacle account in Exod 25–40 involved the envisaged structure being remodelled. Just as a physical building is repaired or extended and, because it occupies the same space, remains the same building, so also the tabernacle account was revised and continued to describe the construction of a single structure. In the case of a ritual, however, it can be altered such that when it is practiced it becomes another ritual that need not displace the original ritual. So too the instructions for the ordination ritual were reworked so that they created new rituals. In all, I will argue that there are no fewer than four different iterations of the ordination ritual in addition to the original account found in Exod 29.

In Chapter 7, I examine those original instructions for the ordination ritual in Exod 29. They describe a ceremony that is both the primary ritual and, in combining various sacrifices, the epitome of all other rituals. In the description of its fulfilment in Lev 8, however, the ordination ritual is transformed into a seven-day ritual that consecrates both priest and tabernacle. Various chronological problems arise from transforming the ordination ritual into a seven-day consecration ritual, and I will examine how these difficulties are reflected in early interpretation.

In Chapter 8, I will show how the seven-day consecration ritual was followed by a further reworking of the ordination ritual, an eighth day inauguration ritual (Lev 9). The description of this ritual, together with the description of the consequences that followed, including the offering of 'strange fire' by Nadab and Abihu, seeks to resolve tensions within the presentation of priestly rituals, but also the portrayal of the competencies of the high priest and the rest of the priesthood.

In Chapter 9, I examine two further reprises of the ordination ritual that can be found within the larger expanse of the Pentateuch. One is found in Num 7–10, where a deformation of the Pentateuch's narrative progression allows for the inauguration of the tabernacle to be retold a further time, but on this occasion with a focus on the leaders and the Levites. The dedication of the Levites echoes the ordination of the priests in several respects, but is modulated so that priests and Levites are hierarchically differentiated. The dedication of the Levites is defined principally by its differences from the ordination of the priests. The second is found in Exod 24, where a blood ritual occurred at the foot of the mountain which involved dashing the people and an altar with blood. This unusual ritual is to be related to the claim a few chapters earlier that Israel was to be a 'kingdom of priests'.

In the conclusion, I return to the issue of how the tabernacle account and the texts of the ordination ritual may have contributed to the conditions that allowed the high priests to claim supremacy in the Maccabean period.

PART I

THE MAKING OF THE TABERNACLE

1

Four Versions of the Tabernacle

Just as physical sanctuaries can be repaired and remodelled,[1] so too the tabernacle account was subject to a complex process of literary growth and rearrangement. No fewer than four versions of the tabernacle account have been substantially preserved in the manuscript tradition and are eloquent testimony to the considerable interest that these chapters evoked amongst early scribes and readers. These four versions fall into two groups with a pair of closely related versions in each group. The first group consists of the Masoretic version and the Samaritan version. Both have a Hebrew text, the language in which the tabernacle account was originally composed. Although known from medieval manuscripts, they preserve a text that was circulating in the late Second Temple period. The second group consists of two early translations: the Old Greek version and the Old Latin version preserved in a manuscript known to scholarship as Monacensis. Both versions are known from uncials that stem from the fourth or fifth century CE. They are a translation from the Hebrew in the case of the Old Greek, and a translation of a translation in the case of the Old Latin. In addition, Monacensis has survived in only fragmentary form due to the repurposing of the manuscript in the early medieval period.

In this chapter I will describe the four different versions of the tabernacle account that we encounter in the Masoretic, the Samaritan, the Old Greek, and the Old Latin. With the exception of the Old Latin text of Monacensis, each of these versions has survived in multiple copies. Rather than reconstructing an eclectic text from those multiple copies, I will select the best exemplar of each version in order to describe not only the text, but also something of the codicological features of those exemplars. Recent scholarship has insisted on the materiality of texts and has provided a useful reminder of the dangers of treating critically reconstructed texts as abstract entities. Ancient texts were transmitted with various paratextual features that aided the reading and understanding of texts. Far too often these have been discarded as meaningless husks. Instead, they should be appreciated as preserving important indications of how the text was understood, some of which may be very ancient.

---

[1] Andrew R. Davis, *Reconstructing the Temple: The Royal Rhetoric of Temple Renovation in the Ancient Near East and Israel* (New York: Oxford University Press, 2019); Peter Dubrovský, *The Building of the First Temple*, FAT 103 (Tübingen: Mohr Siebeck, 2015).

16   THE MAKING OF THE TABERNACLE

Ideally, an attention to the distinctive features of our four exemplars would require that I consider each independently of the other and only after that discuss their relationships to one another. In the case of the four editions of the tabernacle this would result in significant repetition, because the Masoretic and Samaritan versions are quite similar to one another, and the Old Greek of Exod 25–31 seems to reflect a *Vorlage* close to the Masoretic version. The Old Latin is not extant for Exod 25–31, but for Exod 35–40 it is closely related to the Old Greek. For the purposes of economy and readability, I will describe the Masoretic version more fully and then compare the Samaritan version to it. In a similar way, I will examine the Old Greek and some of its differences from the Masoretic version, before comparing the Old Latin to the Old Greek. I will try and describe the texts in a way that does not prejudge the relationship between the different texts, a matter that we will get to in the following chapter once the different versions have been described.

The Masoretic Version

The first version of the tabernacle account that I will examine is that preserved in the manuscript Firkovitch I, B 19a of the National Library of Russia, known as Codex Leningrad ($\mathfrak{M}^{L}$), a model Tiberian codex written in 1009 CE.[2] This manuscript is the oldest complete manuscript of the Hebrew Bible,[3] and has been used as the basis for several modern critical editions including the *Biblia Hebraica* from the third edition onwards.[4] Codex Leningrad was copied by Samuel ben Jacob in Cairo and within the Masoretic tradition it belongs to the Ben Asher school.[5] Like other model codices, Codex Leningrad was not used in synagogue worship, but as a tool for study and to assist in the accurate preservation of the

---

[2] A facsimile edition of Firkovitch I, B 19a is available: David Noel Freedman et al., eds., *The Leningrad Codex: A Facsimile Edition* (Grand Rapids, MI: Eerdmans, 1998).

[3] As is well known, since the fire at the central synagogue in Aleppo in 1947, the older Aleppo Codex lacks almost the entire Torah. A Pentateuch codex held by the British Library, *Or. 4445*, has been dated to the ninth or tenth century CE and contains the entire book of Exodus. For a description of the manuscript, see Christian D. Ginsburg, *Introduction to the Massoretico-Critical Edition of the Hebrew Bible* (London: Trinitarian Bible Society, 1897), 469–74; Aron Dotan, 'Reflections towards a Critical Edition of Pentateuch Codex Or. 4445', in *Estudios masoréticos (X Congreso del IOMS): En memoria de Harry M. Orlinsky*, eds. Emilia Fernández Tejero and María Teresa Ortega Monasterio (Madrid: CSIC, 1993), 39–51. The manuscript has been digitized at http://www.bl.uk/manuscripts/Viewer.aspx?ref=or_4445.

[4] For a discussion of the philosophy of the most recent edition of the *Biblia Hebraica*, *Biblia Hebraica Quinta*, and the choice of Codex Leningrad, see Adrian Schenker, 'The Edition Biblia Hebraica Quinta (BHQ)', *HeBAI* 2 (2013): 6–16.

[5] The differences between the schools of Ben Asher and Ben Naphtali were relatively minor and are catalogued at the end of Tiberian biblical manuscripts (Geoffrey Khan, *A Short Introduction to the Tiberian Masoretic Bible and Its Reading Tradition*, Gorgias Handbooks 25 [Piscataway, NJ: Gorgias Press, 2012], 4–5).

biblical text.[6] As Geoffrey Khan has reminded us, the Masoretic tradition is not simply the consonantal text, but also the various apparatus around the text. They include the text's layout, the division into paragraphs, the accents, the vocalization, as well as notes and Masoretic treatises on the text.[7] These features not only assisted in the accurate transmission of the text, but they also contributed to the interpretation of it. The antiquity of some of these features remains an area of debate, but we cannot overlook the fact that the Masoretic Text is a curated tradition. We must begin with its edition of the tabernacle account as it has been transmitted to us, and from there proceed to the critical evaluation of it.

The Leningrad codex consists of 491 vellum folios written in an oriental square script. It presents the text of Exodus in three columns. Decorative sigla in the margin mark the weekly lectionary readings for the annual cycle, the *parashot*, whilst the weekly readings for the triennial cycle,[8] the *sedarim*, are signalled by the letter *samekh* written in a different, larger hand.[9] Sense divisions are marked by *petucha* and *setuma*, the open and closed breaks.[10] In the Leningrad codex a *petucha* is marked by beginning on a new line, leaving an entire line blank if the previous line ended near the left margin. A *setuma* is marked by a space. If there was not sufficient space at the end of a line, the following line was indented.[11] Individual verses are marked by *sof pasuq*. Each of these features facilitates the liturgical reading of the Hebrew Bible, but also its study.

Instructions for the tabernacle and the account of its construction are found across five *parashot*: *Terumah* (Exod 25.1–27.19), *Tetsaveh* (27.20–30.10), *Ki Tisa* (30.11–34.35), *Vayakhel* (35.1–38.20), and *Pequde* (38.21–40.38). The tabernacle is first encountered at the beginning of the weekly reading of *Terumah* with the divine command to collect materials for the sanctuary (25.1). By the conclusion of the weekly reading of *Pequde* the tabernacle is complete and God has taken up residence: 'the cloud covered the tent of meeting and YHWH's glory filled the tabernacle' (40.34). On the basis of content and themes, the tabernacle account can

---

[6] See, esp., Khan, *Short Introduction*, 1–11.

[7] Khan, *Short Introduction*. The Masoretes also transmitted an oral reading tradition. For further discussion, see esp. Geoffrey Khan, *The Tiberian Pronunciation Tradition of Biblical Hebrew*, 2 vols., Cambridge Semitic Languages and Cultures 1 (Cambridge: Open Book Publishers, 2020).

[8] For Exod 25–40, the beginnings of *parashot* are marked at 25.1; 27.20; 30.11; 35.1; 38.21.

[9] For Exod 25–40, the beginnings of *sedarim* are indicated at Exod 25.1; 26.1, 31; 27.20; 29.1; 30.1; 31.1; 32.15; 34.1, 27; 35.30; 37.1; 38.21; 39.33. Outhwaite suggests that these were added when the manuscript changed ownership from a Babylonian Karaite community to a Palestinian one where the *sedarim* were in use (Ben Outhwaite, 'The First Owners of the Leningrad Codex: T-S 10J30.7' [2017], https://doi.org/10.17863/CAM.28071).

[10] For the use and significance of *petuchot and setumot* see, esp., Josef M. Oesch, *Petucha und Setuma: Untersuchungen zu einer überlieferten Gliederung im hebräischen Text des Alten Testaments*, OBO 27 (Freiburg im Üchtland: Universitätsverlag, 1979).

[11] In Exod 25–40, *petuchot* are found before 25.1, 23, 31; 26.7, 15; 28.6; 30.1, 11, 17, 22; 31.12; 32.7, 15; 33.12, 17; 34.27; 35.4, 30; 37.1, 10, 17, 25; 38.1; 39.2, 8, 33; 40.1, 34. *Setumot* are found before 25.10; 26.1, 31; 27.1, 9, 20; 28.1, 13, 15, 31, 36; 29.1, 38; 30.34; 31.1, 18; 33.1; 34.1; 35.1; 36.8, 14, 20; 38.8, 9, 21, 24; 39.27, 30, 32; 40.17, 20, 22, 24, 26, 28, 30, 33.

18   THE MAKING OF THE TABERNACLE

be divided into four sections. The first section, the instructions, consists of a series of divine speeches to Moses (25.1–31.17).[12] The second section does not mention the tabernacle and its construction, but describes the incident of the golden calf (31.18–34.35). The third section, the construction, describes how the tabernacle and the vestments were fabricated and brought to Moses (35.1–39.43). The fourth section, the erection, opens with divine commands to Moses to erect and anoint the sanctuary, and its subsequent assembly (40.1–38).

The Instructions (Exod 25.1–31.17)

The instructions (25.1–31.17) are presented as a series of seven speeches introduced with 'YHWH spoke to Moses' (וַיְדַבֵּר יְהוָה אֶל־מֹשֶׁה) or 'YHWH said to Moses' (וַיֹּאמֶר יְהוָה אֶל־מֹשֶׁה). The speeches concern the tabernacle, furniture vestments, and the ordination of the priests (25.1–30.10); the ransom money (30.11–16); the laver (30.17–21); the anointing oil (30.22–33); the incense (30.34–38); the craftsmen (31.1–11); and the sabbath (31.12–17).

The lengthy first speech has two main sections. The first provides instruction to Moses for the construction of the tent-sanctuary and its furniture (25.10–27.19). Throughout this section the tent-sanctuary is designated as 'the tabernacle' (הַמִּשְׁכָּן). The second section provides instructions to Moses for the vestments and ordination of the priests (28.1–29.37). Throughout this section, the tent-sanctuary is designated as 'the tent of meeting' (אֹהֶל מוֹעֵד). An introduction instructs Moses to collect the materials from the people (25.1–9). Directions about the oil for the lamp brings together the temple furniture of the first section with the priests of the second section and provides a transition between the two sections (27.20–21). A conclusion to the entire speech communicates instructions about the regular burnt offering and the promise that God will inhabit the sanctuary (29.38–46). Fittingly, the promise plays on both titles of the tent-sanctuary: 'I will meet (וְנֹעַדְתִּי) with the Israelites there...and I will dwell (וְשָׁכַנְתִּי) among the Israelites' (29.43, 45). The instructions for the altar of incense come at the end of the speech almost as an afterthought (30.1–10).[13]

The instructions about the construction of the tabernacle in 25.10–27.19 move from the innermost part of the tabernacle outwards. They are divided into four sub-sections by repeated references to the plan that Moses was given on the

---

[12] 𝔐[L.] has a *setuma* at the end of 31.17. In 31.18 the narrative action resumes and the references to Mount Sinai and the tablets of stone connect the verse to 24.12–18. The chapter division at 32.1 found in Greek and Latin Bibles, on the other hand, reflects the change in subject to the people.

[13] In his detailed discourse analysis of the first speech, Longacre identifies the instructions about the incense altar as 'post-peak' (Robert E. Longacre, 'Building for the Worship of God: Exodus 25:1–30:10', in *Discourse Analysis of Biblical Literature: What It Is and What It Offers*, ed. Walter R. Bodine, SemeiaSt [Atlanta: Scholars Press, 1995], 21–49).

FOUR VERSIONS OF THE TABERNACLE 19

mountain (25.40; 26.30; 27.8).[14] In the first sub-section, Moses is instructed about the tabernacle furniture: the construction of the ark with its atonement cover, a table, and a lampstand (25.10–40).[15] The following sub-section describes what we might call the tabernacle proper. This structure was a small oblong building. It had a wooden framework at the rear and the two long sides which supported two curtains—one of richly embroidered linen, one of goat's hair—and two covers of skin—one of rams' skins, one of leather (26.1–30). In the third sub-section, Moses is instructed about how to fabricate and hang the veil and screen through which the inner and outer sanctum are accessed, as well as where the furniture is to be erected. Instructions about the final piece of furniture, the outer altar, is also given (26.31–27.8). Finally, in the fourth sub-section there are directions about the construction of a courtyard to surround the tabernacle. This oblong space was created by linen curtains hung from pillars with a screen for a gate on the eastern side (27.9–19). Except for the opening instruction which directs the people to make the ark from acacia wood, the instructions are addressed in the second person singular to Moses alone. The style is restrained with descriptions identifying the material, dimensions, and significant features of the items to be manufactured.

The materials that the people are instructed to bring in 25.1–9 are not only to be used for the construction of the tabernacle, they are also needed for the fabrication of Aaron's vestments. The instructions about Aaron's clothing begins with the ephod, gold filigree, and breastpiece which the high priest wore on his chest,[16] before moving to the clothing for the rest of his body including the robe, the diadem, the tunic, and the sash (28.6–38). The instructions are preceded by an introduction that charges the skilled craftsmen with the task of fabrication (28.1–5) and concludes with instructions about vestments for Aaron's sons (28.39–43).

The instructions about the vestments are followed by directions for an ordination ritual that will consecrate the priests for service. Whilst in the previous chapters Moses has primarily been commanded to 'make, do' (עש״ה), he is now instructed to 'take' (לק״ח) or 'bring' (hiphil קר״ב). The sacrifices and the priests are first assembled (vv. 1–4), then Aaron and his sons are clothed in the vestments and the various sacrifices offered: a bull as a sin offering, a ram as a burnt offering, and a ram and some bread as an ordination offering (vv. 5–34). A concluding prescription requires that the sin offering is repeated every day for a week (vv. 35–37). Although the consecration ritual appears to have a different character from the preceding chapters, the entire ritual is presented at the

---

[14] Georg Steins, '"Sie sollen mir ein Heiligtum machen": Zur Struktur und Entstehung von Ex 24,12–31,18', in *Vom Sinai zum Horeb: Stationen alttestamentlicher Glaubensgeschichte*, ed. Frank-Lothar Hossfeld (Würzburg: Echter, 1989), 156–7. In 𝔐ˡ· each of these sections is marked by a *setuma*.

[15] The paragraphing of 𝔐ˡ· presents the ark and the atonement cover as a single item.

[16] 𝔐ˡ· sets the gold filigree apart as a separate paragraph. The purpose of the ephod and its stones has been described in v. 12, and, consequently, there are good grounds for seeing the golden filigree as a distinct item.

20 THE MAKING OF THE TABERNACLE

beginning and conclusion of the instructions as also an act of making or doing, עש״ה (29.1, 35). The idea that the ritual was a single 'deed' comparable to the other deeds commanded may explain the presentation of 29.1–37 uninterrupted by either *petuhot* or *setumot*. The language of 'doing' is maintained in the description of the daily offering: 'now this is what you shall do upon the altar' (וְזֶה אֲשֶׁר תַּעֲשֶׂה עַל־הַמִּזְבֵּחַ; 29.38). The final act of making in the first divine speech concerns the altar of incense (30.1–10).

It is only in 30.11 that we encounter the second speech of the instruction account. The most striking features of the organization of the speeches are the significantly greater length of the first speech and the concern of the seventh speech with the Sabbath, paralleling the seventh day of creation.[17] The organizational logic of these shorter speeches in Exod 30–31 is not always readily apparent. The anointing oil and incense clearly belong together as the 'work of a perfumer' (מַעֲשֵׂה רֹקֵחַ; 30.25, 35),[18] and the craftsmen are mentioned at the end because of their involvement in the production of all the items. The ransom money, however, has no obvious connection to the fabrication of the incense altar (30.1–10) or the laver (30.17–21).

The Incident of the Golden Calf (Exod 31.18–34.35)

In 31.18 the completion of the divine speeches is signalled and the narrative resumes with the cast of characters familiar from Exod 24. The tabernacle disappears from view and instead of constructing the sanctuary that Moses has been tasked with, the people assemble to make a golden calf. Most of the weekly reading *Ki Tisa* is taken up with the consequences of this action: the intercessions by Moses, the punishments upon the people, the debate about whether God will accompany the people, and the re-affirmation of the covenant and its terms. Throughout these chapters no mention is made of the sanctuary that Moses has been commissioned to build, except perhaps for the unexpected reference to an already standing tent of meeting (33.7–11). It is only with the weekly reading *Vayakhel* that the conditions are right for the tabernacle's construction to begin.

---

[17] Kearney's attempts to show a closer relationship between the seven speeches and the seven days of creation have not been found convincing. In contrast to the contrived connections for the other days, Kearney speaks of the way the 'seventh speech (Ex 31 12–17) effortlessly recalls the seventh day of creation' (Peter J. Kearney, 'Creation and Liturgy: The P Redaction of Ex 25–40', ZAW 89 [1977]: 378).

[18] The close connection between the two speeches is possibly indicated by the fact that the second begins with וַיֹּאמֶר יְהוָה אֶל־מֹשֶׁה rather than וַיְדַבֵּר יְהוָה אֶל־מֹשֶׁה (Rainer Albertz, Exodus 19–40, ZBK [Zurich: Theologischer Verlag, 2015], 232), and the division between the two speeches is marked by a *setuma* rather than a *petucha*.

The Construction of the Tabernacle (Exod 35.1–39.43)

The account of the tabernacle's construction, or the compliance account, has often been judged inelegant and repetitive, and consequently has been passed over quickly. It does, however, contain some distinctive perspectives and several differences from the instructions. Most noticeable are the role of the people and the master workmen, and the order of construction.

The compliance account opens with Moses relaying the instructions to the people. After a brief reprise of the Sabbath commandment (35.1–3), Moses instructs the people about what materials are required (vv. 4–9) and what is to be made (vv. 10–19). The construction is to be undertaken by 'all the wise of heart amongst you' (וְכָל־חֲכַם־לֵב בָּכֶם; v. 10). The account of the objects that are to be constructed follows a different order than that found in the instructions. The tabernacle opens the list, followed by the furniture, the courtyard, and the vestments. The alternative order has a clear logic: before the furniture is constructed, the tabernacle must be in place to house them. It should also be observed that the incense altar and the laver are mentioned in their logical place: the incense altar after the lamp and the laver after the altar of burnt offering.

The people depart and return bringing the materials required with different groups contributing distinct items. Men and women provide gold, silver, bronze, and acacia wood (vv. 22, 24), but the donation of costly fabrics is attributed to just the men (v. 23) and then to the women (v. 25). The leaders supplied precious stones as well as the oil and incense (vv. 26–27). With the materials assembled, we might have expected the construction to begin, but instead Moses informs the Israelites about the master craftsmen, Bezalel and Oholiab (35.30–36.1). Moses then calls them together with 'all the wise of heart' to receive the materials and orders the people to stop donating to the sanctuary.

The report of the construction follows the alternative order with the tabernacle made before its furniture with the incense altar and the laver in their proper places (36.8–38.20). The description of the manufacturing is fulsome and repeats many of the details from the instructions. A clear distinction is maintained between the tabernacle and the furniture. The fabrication of the tabernacle appears to be the work of 'all the wise of heart', even if the opening plural verb in 36.8 is replaced by singular verbs throughout the rest of the chapter. The furniture, however, is attributed to Bezalel alone (37.1–38.20).

After the completion of the furniture, the focus returns to the donations received from the Israelites. In the Masoretic tradition, the system of *petuchot* and *setumot* offers no clear guidance as to whether 38.21–23 should be taken with what precedes or follows, but the division into annual *parashot* and *sedarim* places 'These are the records of the tabernacle' at the beginning of a new sabbath

22   THE MAKING OF THE TABERNACLE

reading.[19] An accounting is given of the gold, silver, and bronze, both how much was collected and the use to which it was put (38.24–31). This leads to an accounting of the fabrics and then seamlessly into the fabrication of the priestly vestments. In common with the construction of the tabernacle furniture, the manufacture of the priestly vestment is relayed with considerable detail echoing the earlier instructions to Moses. There are three distinctive features. First, there is an opening summary statement about the fabrication of Aaron's vestments (v. 1). The second is the repeated insistence that everything was done 'just as the LORD had commanded Moses' (כַּאֲשֶׁר צִוָּה יְהוָה אֶת־מֹשֶׁה; 39.1, 5, 7, 21, 26, 29, 31). This creates a distinctive partitioning of the vestments which separated the ephod (vv. 2–5) from the precious stones set into it (vv. 6–7). The third distinctive feature is that there is a rearrangement of the final items of the vestments. There is no separate account of Aaron's tunic, turban, and sash (cf. 28.39), which are mentioned together with those of his sons (39.27–29), and the gold plate that is affixed to the turban is mentioned last (39.30–31) after the fabrication of the turban. The result is neater and more logical than what is found in the instructions. With tabernacle, furniture, and vestments complete, the people hand over the manufactured items to Moses in a list that corresponds to Moses' original request (39.33–43; cf. 35.10–19).

The Erection of the Tabernacle (Exod 40.1–38)

A further divine speech marks the beginning of the final section of the tabernacle account. The people fade from view and Moses is again the focus of address. The directions he receives fall into two parts. Moses is to set up the tabernacle and anoint it (vv. 2–11). He is then to attire Aaron and anoint him, and then do the same to his sons (vv. 12–15). The instructions are followed immediately by an account of their execution. The account of Moses' compliance is more detailed than the instructions. Thus, for example, where Moses is commanded to install the ark (v. 3), in the compliance account Moses is said to have placed the covenant in the ark, positioned the poles, placed the atonement cover on it and brought the ark into the tabernacle (vv. 20–21). In common with the fabrication of the vestments, each action is concluded with the formula 'just as the LORD had commanded Moses' underscored by a *setuma* (כַּאֲשֶׁר צִוָּה יְהוָה אֶת־מֹשֶׁה; vv. 19, 21, 23, 25, 27, 29, 32). Though Moses is said to have completed the task with which he was appointed (v. 32), no mention is made of the anointing of the tabernacle or the dressing and anointing of the priests. Despite these absences, the work of Moses is

---

[19] Samuel Raphael Hirsch, *The Pentateuch: Translated and Explained. Vol. II Exodus* (London: Hachinuch, 1956), 695.

met with divine approbation signalled by the divine glory taking up residence in the tent and leading the people upon their journeyings (vv. 34–38).

The Samaritan Version

Within the Samaritan community another version of the Pentateuchal text has been preserved that is second only in significance to the Masoretic tradition as a witness to the complete Hebrew text.[20] As is the case with the Masoretic Text, our earliest complete manuscripts stem from the medieval period. The discovery of pre-Samaritan texts amongst the Dead Sea Scrolls has demonstrated not only the antiquity of the textual tradition, but also the fidelity with which it has been transmitted.[21] In its medieval forms, the textual tradition shows a 'general textual uniformity...with a certain flexibility in spelling.'[22] Because of its use as the basis for the new critical edition, I will use MS. Dublin Chester Beatty Library 751 ($\underline{000}^D$), a text dating to 1225 CE.[23] The manuscript is a codex written with one column a page, and includes punctuation, vocalization, and text-critical signs.[24] Paragraphs are marked by punctuation called a *qiṣṣa*.[25] At various points the text has been copied so that repetitions in the text are arranged in ornamental columns.[26]

Although the Samaritan Pentateuch is most famous for texts that associate worship with the Samaritan holy site of Gerizim, the text of the tabernacle account contains no 'sectarian' features.[27] In comparison to the Masoretic version, the Samaritan version prefers standardized expressions, has a more exact

---

[20] Stefan Schorch, 'A Critical Editio Maior of the Samaritan Pentateuch: State of Research, Principles, and Problems', *HeBAI* 2 (2013): 100.

[21] As already remarked upon by Skehan in his publication of part of 4Q22 (4QpaleoExod^m) (Patrick W. Skehan, 'Exodus in the Samaritan Recension from Qumran', *JBL* 74 [1955]: 182–7).

[22] Schorch, 'Critical Editio Maior', 112.

[23] For the choice of this manuscript, see Schorch, 'Critical Editio Maior', 112–13. I am very grateful to Prof. Schorch for making available the critical edition of Exodus prior to its publication (Stefan Schorch [ed.], *Exodus*, Samaritan Pentateuch 2 [Boston: de Gruyter, forthcoming]). A description of the manuscript can be found at Reinhard Pummer, 'The Samaritan Manuscripts of the Chester Beatty Library', *Studies: An Irish Quarterly Review* 68 (1979): 66–8. The manuscript has been digitized and is available at: https://viewer.cbl.ie/viewer/image/Heb_751/1/.

[24] Schorch, 'Critical Editio Maior', 113–14.

[25] In Exod 25–40 *qiṣṣot* mark the start of paragraphs at 25.1, 10, 17, 23, 31; 26.1, 7, 15, 26, 31, 36 (=𝔐 30.1), 37; 27.1, 9, 20; 28.6, 15, 22, 31, 36; 29.1, 7, 15, 19, 26, 29, 38; 30.11, 17, 22, 34; 31.1, 12, 18; 32.7, 8, 15, 21, 30; 33.1, 5, 12, 17; 34.1, 10, 18, 27, 28; 35.1, 4, 20, 30; 36.2, 8, 14, 20, 31, 35; 37.1, 6, 10, 17, 25; 38.1, 9, 21, 25, 29; 39.2, 8, 15, 22, 27, 30, 32; 40.1, 9, 17, 20, 22, 24, 26, 28, 30, 33, 34.

[26] For further discussion of this feature in Samaritan manuscripts, see Edward Robertson, 'Notes and Extracts from the Semitic Manuscripts in the John Rylands Library: III Samaritan Pentateuch MSS. With a Description of Two Codices', *BJRL* 21 (1937): 248–9.

[27] For problems with labelling the Samaritan Pentateuch as 'sectarian' see, inter alia, Edmond L. Gallagher, 'Is the Samaritan Pentateuch a Sectarian Text?', *ZAW* 127 (2015): 96–107.

24   THE MAKING OF THE TABERNACLE

alignment between the instructions to Moses and their execution, and there is a handful of large-scale differences.[28]

The preference for standard expressions in comparison to the Masoretic version can be seen within the confines of a verse: in Exod 29.40 the Masoretic Text has רֶבַע and רְבִעִית, both meaning 'one-fourth', whilst the Samaritan text has the more common רבעית in both places. It can also appear across the tabernacle account: the Masoretic Text has three synonymous expressions אִישׁ אֶל־אָחִיו, אַחַת אֶל־אַחַת and אִשָּׁה אֶל־אֲחֹתָהּ meaning 'one another', where the Samaritan text has in every case אחת אל אחת.[29] Formulae that appear frequently are transmitted in the Samaritan text in a standard form. The list of textile materials used in the tabernacle, for example, is consistently reproduced as תכלת וארגמן ותולעת שני, 'blue and purple and crimson yarns',[30] though the Masoretic Text will sometimes introduce the list with a waw: וּתְכֵלֶת.[31]

The more exact alignment between instructions and compliance in the Samaritan version is seen in various small-scale differences. These include words that are not present in the Masoretic version (e.g. תעשה in 26.20; cf. 36.25), precise alignment of word order (e.g. ללאות חמשים for 𝔐^{L}'s חֲמִשִּׁים לֻלָאֹת in 26.10; cf. 36.17), the same preposition (e.g. לו for 𝔐^{L}'s עָלָיו in 25.11; cf. 37.2), or the use of precisely the same word (e.g. במחברת for 𝔐^{L}'s בַּחֹבָרֶת in 26.4; cf. 36.11).

The Samaritan version of the tabernacle account exhibits five large-scale differences from the Masoretic version. The first large-scale difference concerns the incense altar. In the Masoretic Text, the instructions for the incense altar (Exod 30.1–10) appear belatedly after the description of the priests' vestments and ordination. In the Samaritan text they occur in the main instructions for the construction of the tabernacle after the installation of the ark, the table, and the lampstand (26.34–35). The position in the Samaritan version is not without its own problems since the instructions about the manufacture of the sanctuary's sancta should logically occur in Exod 25, but none of those instructions refer to Aaron's role. It may be that the placement of the incense altar in the Samaritan tradition reflects a desire to place the incense altar adjacent to the altar of burnt offering (27.1–8).

The second large-scale difference is the presence of an instruction about the fabrication of the priestly vestments just before the instructions about the lamp (27.19b). ועשית בגדי תכלת וארגמן ותולעת שני לשרת בהם בקדש (27.20–21): The addition can be recognized as a harmonization with 39.1 where a brief summarizing statement about the fabrication of the בגדי שרד, 'the serad-vestments', immediately follows after mention of the tent pegs and prior to the detailed description of

---

[28] For further discussion see Emanuel Tov, *Textual Criticism of the Hebrew Bible*, 3rd edn. (Minneapolis, MN: Fortress, 2012), 80–7.

[29] Exod 25.20; 26.3^{2}, 5, 6, 17; 36.10^{2}, 12, 13, 22; 37.19.

[30] Exod 25.4; 26.1, 31, 36; 27.16; 28.8, 15, 33; 35.6, 23; 36.8, 35, 37; 38.18; 39.2, 5, 8, 24, 29.

[31] Exod 25.4; 26.1; 35.6; 36.8; 39.29.

Aaron's vestments.[32] The text was added by a scribe who clearly regarded these vestments as different from the high priestly garments and was disturbed by the lack of a commandment to fabricate them in Exod 25–31.[33] The Samaritan paragraph divisions, the *qiṣṣot*, potentially suggest a different understanding for a single unit is made out of 27.19b–28.5. The reference to the vestments in 27.19b now form a heading to the following section of the high priestly vestments with a brief excursus in 27.20–21 to mention the tending of the lamps. Closer inspection suggests the difference has subtle interpretive consequences. The section is framed by an *inclusio* formed by references to 'the *serad*-vestments' in 27.19b and 28.4b, 5. As a result, the instructions for the lamp are tied more closely to the priestly vestments in the Samaritan version, an association that is appropriate since Aaron and his sons are instructed to dress the lamp. In contrast, the Masoretic tradition which has a *setuma* at the end of v. 19 and one at the end of v. 21, makes the dressing of the lamp into a distinct unit.

The third and fifth large-scale differences concern the instructions for the fabrication of the Urim and Thummim and their execution (28.29; 39.21). In the Masoretic Text the Urim and Thummim are treated as familiar objects—they are *the* Urim and *the* Thummim—and they are placed in Aaron's breastpiece with no indication of how they originated.[34] The Samaritan text addresses this lacuna. These words in the Samaritan Pentateuch are unusual in having no corresponding text anywhere in the Masoretic version though they follow the pattern of other items in the tabernacle. The fourth large-scale difference is that the Samaritan text has the sprinkling of blood and oil on the vestments during the ordination ritual after the offering of the ordination sacrifice (29.28) rather than before it (29.21). This matches the order of the ritual in Lev 8.

The case of the addition of an instruction to fabricate the priestly vestments at the beginning of Exod 27.20 is a reminder that the Samaritan text not only provides an alternative consonantal tradition, but also its own division of the text. Distinctive placement of *qiṣṣot* in comparison to $\mathfrak{M}^L$ include: 25.16, which divides the ark from the atonement cover (cf. 37.5); 26.25, which separate the bars from the framework (cf. 36.30, 34); 36.1, which separates 36.1 from the repetitious 36.2; 38.24, 28 which separate the metals into gold, silver and bronze; 40.8, which separates the erection of the tabernacle from the anointing; 40.33, which connects the completion of the tabernacle to the divine appearance.

---

[32] August Klostermann, 'Die Heiligtums- und Lagerordnung', in *Der Pentateuch: Beiträge zu seinem Verständnis und seiner Entstehungsgeschichte. Neue Folge* (Leipzig: Deichert, 1907), 48.

[33] Molly M. Zahn, 'The Samaritan Pentateuch and the Scribal Culture of Second Temple Judaism', *JSJ* 46 (2015): 289–90.

[34] I am grateful to Gary Anderson for drawing my attention to Nachmanides' speculations that these oracular devices were given to Moses on Mount Sinai.

The Old Greek Version

The translation of Exodus into Greek, the Old Greek version, was probably undertaken in Egypt at some point in the third century BCE.[35] The translation is one of the best in the Greek Bible, demonstrating both a sophisticated understanding of Hebrew idiom and the ability to produce readable Greek.[36] The translator mostly preserved the word order of the Hebrew, and Wevers notes that the translation 'expands far more than contracts'.[37] The revision of the translation towards the contemporary Hebrew text seems to have begun already in the second century BCE, since two fragments amongst the Dead Sea Scrolls (7Q1 [7QpapLXXExod]) evidence a text closer to the later Masoretic Text.[38]

The best witness to the original Greek translation is Vat.gr.1209 of the Vatican Library, widely known as Codex Vaticanus ($\mathfrak{G}^B$), a fourth-century CE uncial that contained the Old and New Testaments in Greek.[39] The codex is written in small, unadorned uncials which were reinked and corrected before the eleventh century CE.[40] The text is written as *scriptio continua* and the original scribe marked each new sense unit with an *ekthesis*, the protruding of the first letter into the left margin.[41] There are additional marks indicating sense units, most notably small lines known as *paragraphoi*, but it is debated whether these were added by a

---

[35] For the orientation of the tabernacle as evidence for an Egyptian provenance, see Pierre-Maurice Bogaert, 'L'orientation du parvis du sanctuaire dans la version grecque de l'Exode (Ex., 27, 9–13 LXX)', *L'Antiquité Classique* 50 (1981): 79–85.

[36] Anneli Aejmelaeus, 'What Can We Know about the Hebrew "Vorlage" of the Septuagint?', *ZAW* 99 (1987): 71–87.

[37] John William Wevers, *Text History of the Greek Exodus*, AAWG, Philologisch-historische Klasse III/192 (Göttingen: Vandenhoeck & Ruprecht, 1992), 148.

[38] John William Wevers, 'PreOrigen Recensional Activity in the Greek Exodus', in Detlef Frankel, Udo Quast and John William Wevers (eds.), *Studien zur Septuaginta—Robert Hanhart zu Ehren: Aus Anlass seines 65 Geburtstages*, AAWG, Philologisch-historische Klasse III/190 (Göttingen: Vandenhoeck & Ruprecht, 1990), 121–39; Drew Longacre, 'A Contextualized Approach to the Hebrew Dead Sea Scrolls Containing Exodus' (Birmingham University, PhD diss., 2015).

[39] The manuscript has been digitized at: https://digi.vatlib.it/mss/detail/Vat.gr.1209. The text of $\mathfrak{G}^B$ has been reproduced and translated in Daniel M. Gurtner, *Exodus: A Commentary on the Greek Text of Codex Vaticanus*, Septuagint Commentary Series (Leiden: Brill, 2013). Gurtner's text often incorporates later scribal corrections and needs to be used in conjunction with the digitized photographs. For discussion of the date and provenance of Vaticanus, see discussion and literature cited in Jesse R Grenz, 'The Scribes and Correctors of Codex Vaticanus: A Study on the Codicology, Palaeography, and Text of B(03)' (University of Cambridge, PhD diss., 2021), 2–10; Charles Evan Hill, *The First Chapters: Dividing the Text of Scripture in Codex Vaticanus and Its Predecessors* (Oxford: Oxford University Press, 2022), 69–70.

[40] J. Keith Elliott, 'T. C. Skeat on the Dating and Origin of Codex Vaticanus', in *The Collected Biblical Writings of T.C. Skeat*, NovTSup 113 (Leiden: Brill, 2004), 293.

[41] Unfortunately the list in Gurtner, *Exodus: A Commentary on the Greek Text of Codex Vaticanus*, 6–7, is not entirely reliable. For Exod 25–40, *ektheseis* are located at 25.1; 26.1, 6, 7, 10, 11, 14, 15, 18, 26, 31; 27.4, 6, 9, 20; 28.2, 13, 15, 27, 29, 32, 36, 38; 29.1, 35, 38; 30.1, 3b, 5, 11, 17, 22, 34; 31.1, 12; 32.1, 2 (?), 7, 11, 15, 17, 19, 21, 22, 25, 26 (?), 27, 28, 31, 33, 35; 33.1, 5, 7, 11, 12, 14, 17, 21; 34.1, 4, 8, 10, 27, 28b, 35; 35.1, 4, 20, 30; 36.1, 2, 6, 8, 15, 30 (?), 33, 35, 38; 37.1, 3, 5, 7, 19; 38.1, 5, 9, 13, 18, 19, 20, 22, 23, 24, 26; 39.4, 8, 11, 14, 23; 40.1, 15, 27b.

later scribe.[42] At some point between the seventh to ninth centuries CE, the text of Exodus was divided into forty-seven numerical sections.[43] At a much later stage, the modern chapters have been indicated on the codex. When referring to the text, I will use the modern versification. Because of the differences between the Masoretic and Old Greek editions, I will indicate chapters and verses in the Old Greek with the prefix 𝕲, and chapters and verses in the Hebrew Masoretic Text with the prefix 𝔐.[44]

The Old Greek version of the instructions (Exod 25–31) can be treated briefly since its *Vorlage* appears to be similar to the Masoretic edition.[45] The most substantial difference is to be found in the instructions concerning the breastpiece. Where the Masoretic edition prescribes how the breastpiece is attached to the ephod at the top by gold chains and by blue cords at the bottom (𝔐 28.22–30), the Old Greek has the breastpiece attached by two gold tassels to small shields on the ephod (𝕲 28.22–26). Additional differences include the absence of oil and incense in the list of offerings to be brought (cf. 𝔐 25.6), the manufacture of the table from pure gold rather than acacia wood plated with gold (𝕲 25.22), the provision of a rim for the altar of burnt offering (𝕲 27.3), and the attribution of specialisms in fabrics to Bezalel (𝕲 31.4). The unit divisions in Vaticanus recognize the close connection between the lamp with the commissioning of the priests by treating 27.20–28.1 as a single unit.

In Exod 35–40, however, the Old Greek has its own distinctive edition of the tabernacle's construction. As with the Masoretic edition, the account opens with the Sabbath commandment (𝕲 35.1–3) and instructions about materials and the objects to be made (𝕲 35.4–19). Although there is no mention of oil and incense in the list of materials to be brought (cf. 𝔐 35.8), they are mentioned not once but twice in the list of objects to be manufactured (𝕲 35.14, 19), and there is no reference to the altar of incense (cf. 𝔐 35.15)! When Moses has finished speaking the people depart and return with the various materials in an account similar to that found in the Masoretic edition (𝕲 35.20–29). Moses then informs the Israelites about the master craftsmen. They collect a workforce of artisans who quickly realize that they have sufficient materials for the task and ask the people to stop donating (𝕲 35.30–36.7).

---

[42] In Exod 25–40, *paragraphoi* are found at 25.9, 17, 22; 26.26; 27.12; 29.19, 39b; 31.16; 33.8; 34.29b; 35.26; 38.6; 39.2; 40.5. A number of these correspond with the numerical sections. For discussion, see Jesse R. Grenz, 'Textual Divisions in Codex Vaticanus', *TC: A Journal of Biblical Textual Criticism* 23 (2018): 1–22; Hill, *The First Chapters*, 84–90.

[43] In Exod 25–40, numerical sections are marked at 25.17; 26.1, 26; 27.12; 28.15, 36; 29.19, 39b; 30.22; 31.16; 32.22; 33.8; 34.8, 29b; 35.26; 36.15; 37.1; 38.6; 39.2; 40.5. For the numerical sections, see further Grenz, 'Textual Divisions', 19.

[44] A further complication is that the various modern editions of the Septuagint do not agree on the versification of the text of Exodus. In particular, the versification of the Cambridge edition of Brooke-MacLean and the Göttingen edition of Wevers, which I have followed, is different from that of the *Handausgabe* of Rahlfs.

[45] For a detailed comparison see Wevers, *Text History of the Greek Exodus*, 119–25.

28 THE MAKING OF THE TABERNACLE

The account of the construction is organized according to a different kind of logic than what was seen in the Masoretic edition. The Masoretic edition envisages the tent being constructed before the furniture that is to go in it. Finally, the priestly vestments are fabricated. In the Old Greek edition, however, the construction is organized according to the materials. The objects primarily made from fabrics are manufactured first, followed by those made from metal.[46] This corresponds to the artisans involved. The fabrics are made by a group, presumably Bezalel, Oholiab, and the skilled artisans (𝕲 36.8–37.18). The metalwork, however, is attributed to Bezalel alone (𝕲 38.1–27).[47]

The first items to be constructed are the priestly vestments (𝕲 36.8–40). The description of the fabrication is comprehensive with all the details from the instructions replicated. The only omission is the description of the significance of the different components of the vestments. The correspondence between instruction and compliance is emphasized through the words 'just as the Lord instructed Moses' (καθὰ συνέταξεν κύριος τῷ Μωυσῆ; 𝕲 36.8, 12, 14, 29, 34, 37, 40). The ephod's construction describes it in accordance with the instructions found in the Masoretic Text rather than those of the shorter Old Greek text: attached by a gold braid at the top and blue material at the bottom (𝕲 36.15–29). The Old Greek text also has the tunics, turbans, undergarments, sashes, and gold plate in the same neat and logical order that is seen in the Masoretic edition.

Upon the completion of the vestments, the tent and the courtyard are fabricated. In contrast to the detailed instructions for the tent, its coverings, the frames and bars in Exod 26, the construction account is surprisingly brief with the tent described in just two verses: 'They made for the tent ten curtains. Twenty-eight cubits the length of one curtain. All were the same. Four cubits the width of one curtain' (𝕲 37.1–2). The manufacture of the veil dividing the inner and outer sanctum and the veil of the tent's entrance is then described (𝕲 37.3–6), followed by the courtyard (𝕲 37.7–18). For attentive readers of Old Greek Exodus, the orientation of the courtyard would have presented some challenges since it is different from that found in Exod 27. In its translation of Exod 27, the Old Greek had adopted an Egyptian perspective when translating the cardinal points. In the Hebrew text, the rear of the tabernacle was on the west, literally 'to the side of the sea' (לְפְאַת־יָם). The translator maintained the reference to the sea and revised the other terms in light of it, but since in Egypt the sea is to the north, the entire orientation of the tabernacle has been turned ninety degrees clockwise. Thus, in Exod 27, the entrance of the courtyard is to the south.[48] In the translation of Exod 37, however, the Palestinian orientation was maintained, and the entrance of the courtyard is to the east. The section on the fabrics concludes with a colophon that

---

[46] John William Wevers, 'The Building of the Tabernacle', *JNSL* 19 (1993): 123–31.
[47] For detailed discussions of these sections, see Wevers, *Text History of the Greek Exodus*, 129–41.
[48] Bogaert, 'L'orientation du parvis'.

acts as a pivot towards the manufacture of the metalwork by mentioning both master craftsmen (𝔊 37.19–21).

The manufacture of the metalwork is undertaken by Bezalel alone and is broadly arranged according to the metal used: gold, silver, bronze. Since the value of the metal is related to its sanctity, the material is also organized according to its holiness. Bezalel's activities begin with the tent's furniture: the ark, the atonement cover, the table, and the lampstand (𝔊 38.1–17). The descriptions of the manufacture of these items focuses on the essential items and are more compact than the corresponding instructions in Exod 25. There follow ten occurrences of the emphatic οὗτος, 'this one', listing various other metal items that Bezalel produced (𝔊 38.18–27). First, there is a brief account of the various metal items associated with the tent and the courtyard, including both gold, silver, and bronze items (𝔊 38.18–21). Second, the bronze items that will be situated in the courtyard are manufactured: the bronze altar and the laver (𝔊 38.22–24, 26–27). Unusually, the source of the bronze for both items is mentioned. The bronze altar is made from the censers used in Korah's rebellion, whilst the laver is made from the mirrors of women who fasted by the entrance of the tent. Both sources appear anachronistic since Korah's rebellion lies in the future (Num 16) and the tent has not yet been erected. Between these two bronze objects is a reference to Bezalel's manufacture of the oil and incense (𝔊 38.25). Bezalel's exertions close with an account of the metal used (𝔊 39.1–11). A concluding statement refers to the outstanding gold, which was used for utensils, and the outstanding textiles, which were used for the vestments (𝔊 39.12–13). The references to the outstanding gold and textiles have in common that both are used for ministering (λειτουργεῖν), but appear somewhat superfluous as both the utensils and the vestments have already been manufactured.

Having completed the textile work and the metalwork, the artisans deliver the items to Moses (𝔊 39.14–23). After the delivery of the vestments, the items are conveyed to Moses according to their material: first the metal items and then the fabrics (including a further mention of the vestments). In comparison to the equivalent list in the Masoretic edition, the Old Greek's list has just one altar[49] and lacks several items including the atonement cover.

Following the receipt of the tabernacle and its furniture, Moses receives instructions about its erection and anointing as well as the installation of the priests (𝔊 40.1–14). In comparison to the Masoretic edition, there is no mention

---

[49] The identification of the altar is far from straightforward. On the one hand, its location after the ark and before the lampstand and table suggests it belongs in the inner sanctum as was the case with the incense altar. In addition, the Old Greek mentions the oil of anointing and the incense of mixture immediately after it (𝔊 39.16) (Alain Le Boulluec and Pierre Sandevoir, *L'Exode: traduction du texte grec de la Septante, introduction et notes*, La Bible d'Alexandrie 2 [Paris: Cerf, 1989], 371). On the other hand, only the altar of burnt offering is said to have 'utensils' (τὰ σκεύη αὐτοῦ; 𝔊 27.3; 30.28; 38.23; 40.8) (John William Wevers, *Notes on the Greek Text of Exodus*, SCS 30 [Atlanta: Scholars Press, 1990], 640; Wevers, *Text History of the Greek Exodus*, 141).

30 THE MAKING OF THE TABERNACLE

of the laver or the screen for the courtyard (cf. 𝔐 40.7–8). On the first day of the first month of the second year, Moses erects the tabernacle and installs its furniture (𝔊 40.15–27a). In comparison to the Masoretic edition, there is no mention of the atonement cover (cf. 𝔐 40.20) or laver (cf. 𝔐 40.30–31), and no mention is made of sacrifices being offered on the altar (cf. 𝔐 40.29). The completion of Moses' endeavours is met with divine approbation. The cloud descends upon the tent and fills it with divine glory (𝔊 40.27b–32).

The Old Latin Version of Monacensis

Prior to the dominance of Jerome's Vulgate in the western church, the Bible was available in a variety of forms in Latin.[50] Translations had been made from Greek into Latin, and their readings are referred to collectively as the Old Latin or *Vetus Latina*.[51] Latin renderings are known from a number of sources, including quotations in the Latin fathers, liturgical texts and glosses in Spanish medieval manuscripts, but the principal sources of the Old Latin are five uncial codices that date from the fifth to seventh centuries CE, none of which preserves a continuous text: Lugdunensis, Vindobonensis, Ottobonianus, Wirceburgensis, and Monacensis.[52]

---

[50] Augustine famously complains about the numerous Latin renderings in *Doctr. chr.* 2.16. He contrasts unfavourably the numerous translators who took it upon themselves to translate from Greek into Latin with the legend of the seventy inspired translators of the Septuagint.

[51] For an introduction to the Old Latin translations, see Julio Trebolle Barrera, '2.5.1 Vetus Latina', in *Textual History of the Bible. Volume 1: The Hebrew Bible*, ed. Armin Lange (Leiden: Brill, 2020), 207–11.

[52] For a comprehensive description of the manuscript evidence for the Vetus Latina in Exodus see Rudolf Dietzfelbinger, 'Die Vetus Latina des Buches Exodus: Studien zur handschriftlichen Überlieferung mit Edition von Kapitel 1' (Heidelberg University, PhD diss., 1998). The text of Lugdunensis dates to the sixth century CE and was published in 1881 (Ulysses Roberts, *Pentateuchi Versio Latina antiquissima e Codice Lugdunensi* [Paris: Firmin-Didot, 1881]). The manuscript originally contained the entire Hexateuch, but only about half of Exodus survives: Exod 1.1–7.19, 21.9–36; 25.24–26.13; 27.6–40.32. The text is of a late European (Spanish) type. An examination of 34.1–35.1 by Dietzfelbinger shows that Lugdunensis has hexaplaric and byzantine readings (Dietzfelbinger, 'Vetus Latina', 36). Parts of the text of Vindobonensis were published in 1885 (Johannes Belsheim, *Palimpsestus Vindobonensis. Antiqvissimae Veteris Testamenti translationis latinae fragmenta e codice rescripto edidit* [Christianiae: P.T. Mallingi, 1885]), with Exodus and Leviticus first being published in 1986 (Bonifatius Fischer, *Beiträge zur Geschichte der lateinischen Bibeltexte*, AGLB 12 [Freiburg im Breisgau: Herder, 1986], 382–438). Vindobonensis is a palimpsest with a fifth-century CE text overwritten with various grammatical tractates. The original manuscript probably contained at least the Pentateuch, but from Exodus only 3.3–4.8; 10.27–12.3; 12.29–44 survive. The text is of a late European (Spanish) type. Ottobonianus is a seventh- or eighth-century CE Vulgate manuscript of the Heptateuch or Octateuch which was identified as preserving a number of Old Latin readings (Carlo Vercellone, *Variae lectiones Vulgatae latinae Bibliorum editionis* [Rome: Spithöver, 1860]). For Exodus the Old Latin readings are found at 10.13–15; 11.7–10; 15.1–2; 16.16–17.10; 18.18–19; 19.13, 21–24; 20.17–18; 22.3; 23.12–27.5; 29.44–45. The text-type is European (Italian). Wirceburgensis was published by Ranke in 1871 (Ernest Ranke, *Par Palimpsestorum Wirceburgensium: Antiquissimae Veteris Testamenti Versionis Latinae Fragmenta* [Vienna: William Braumüller, 1871]). The manuscript is also a palimpsest with a fifth-century CE uncial that was overwritten with Augustine's *Enarrationes in Psalmos*. Originally the text probably contained the entire Pentateuch and portions of the second half of Exodus survive: 22.7–28; 25.30–26.12; 32.15–33; 33.13–34.27; 35.13–36.1; 39.2–40.32. The text-type is also European (Italian).

The seminal work by Billen demonstrated that the texts preserved in these uncials were not of equal antiquity. He distinguished two major branches in the Old Latin tradition: an earlier African branch and a later European one.[53] Billen had already shown that some of the European texts sat closer to the African texts, and this analysis was refined by Fischer who labelled these texts as an Italian text-type that could be distinguished from a later Spanish text-type.[54] For the text of Exodus, Monacensis is particularly important because it preserves an early African text from Exod 31.15 onwards.

In common with many of the other witnesses to the Old Latin, Monacensis ($\mathfrak{L}^{M}$) has survived as a palimpsest. The underwritten text is an uncial dating from the fifth or sixth century CE probably originating in either France or Italy.[55] Originally the manuscript contained at least the entire Pentateuch written in two columns with 25 to 29 characters per column. The first letter of every column is enlarged. The text was divided into paragraphs with the new paragraph beginning on a new line with *ekthesis* and an enlarged first letter. Numbers were written with roman numerals and rubricated. The manuscript was moved at some point to the cathedral library of Freising where it was repurposed in the ninth century CE and overwritten with the Vulgate text of Job, Tobit, Judith, 1 and 2 Ezra, and Esther written by several hands in a Carolingian miniscule. The earlier uncial was a larger format than the later miniscule, and the manuscript was cut to size when it was rewritten. As a result, half of a column on each page was cut away. The palimpsest is found in folios 76–91 and 93–115 of the miniscule. Parts of every book of the underwritten Pentateuch have survived, apart from Genesis. The manuscript was held at Freising until its relocation to the Staatsbibliothek in Munich following secularization in the nineteenth century.[56] The underwritten text was published by Leo Ziegler in 1883 with an extensive introduction.[57]

The book of Exodus is preserved in some form for 9.15–10.24; 12.28–14.4; 16.10–20.5; 31.15–33.7; 36.13–40.32 [$\mathfrak{M}$ 40.38]. For the earlier part of the book, the text-type is European, but for 31.15 onwards the text-type is African. Dietzfelbinger compared Exod 31.15–33.7 with the extant Greek texts and has concluded that the Latin translation is a careful representation of a Greek

---

[53] The categorization of the Vetus Latina uncials rests primarily upon a lexicographical comparison with Latin patristic writers (A. V. Billen, *The Old Latin Texts of the Heptateuch* [Cambridge: Cambridge University Press, 1927]).

[54] Bonifatius Fischer (ed.), *Genesis*, AGLB 2 (Freiburg im Breisgau: Herder, 1951), 14*–22*.

[55] For a detailed account of the manuscript, see Dietzfelbinger, 'Vetus Latina', 61–74.

[56] The manuscript is catalogued as Clm 6225 and has been fully digitized and is available at https://daten.digitale-sammlungen.de/~db/0004/bsb00047191/images/.

[57] Leo Ziegler, *Bruchstücke einer vorhieronymianischen Übersetzung des Pentateuch: Aus einem Palimpseste der K. Hof- und Staatsbibliothek zu München zum ersten Male veröffentlicht* (Munich: Theodor Riedel, 1883).

32   THE MAKING OF THE TABERNACLE

Vorlage.[58] This is an important finding as the text of Monacensis for 36.13–40.32 diverges significantly from all known Greek manuscripts.

The tabernacle account in Monacensis is only preserved from 36.13 onwards and, because of the cutting of the manuscript when it was repurposed, many passages are damaged. For most of the damaged columns of Exod 36–40, Dold attempted a reconstruction of the lost text triangulating between the damaged manuscript, other Old Latin translations, and the Septuagint.[59] As helpful as such a reconstruction is, it must inevitably be used with considerable caution, particularly in places where the surviving text provides clear evidence that Monacensis diverges significantly from any known Greek or Latin text.

In broad terms, the structure and content of the compliance account in Monacensis is closest to that found in the Old Greek. The table on the following two pages seeks to provide an overview of those similarities, but also the key differences. The first column summarizes the content of the section. The second column identifies the lines from Monacensis. I follow Bogaert's practice of referring to the relevant section in Monacensis by the page, column and line numbers of Ziegler's diplomatic edition (e.g. $\mathfrak{L}^M$ 21/1/1 means the first line of the first column of page 21).[60] The damaged columns are indicated by underlining. The third column indicates the corresponding verses in the Old Greek. Where the text of Monacensis is a good representation of the Old Greek with any differences readily explicable as a result of translation or typical textual transmission, I have used the symbol ≈. In such cases, I have discussed the minor divergences from the Old Greek in the footnotes. Where the text of Monacensis has significant divergences from the Old Greek, I have used the symbol ~. Where the text of Monacensis has no equivalent in the Old Greek, I have used the symbol Ø. In most cases where Monacensis diverges significantly from the Old Greek or has no equivalent in the Old Greek, I will discuss the divergences in the main text that follows.

The account of the tabernacle's construction in Monacensis shows the same organizing principle as the Old Greek. The textiles, including the tent, are fabricated first ($\mathfrak{L}^M$ 21/1/1–24/2/2) followed by the objects fashioned from metal ($\mathfrak{L}^M$ 24/2/18–26/2/1). Between these two sections there is a summary that names the two master craftsmen—Beseel and Eliab—and functions as a pivot ($\mathfrak{L}^M$ 24/2/3–17). At the conclusion of the two sections there is an accounting of the materials used: first the metals and then the fabrics ($\mathfrak{L}^M$ 26/2/2–27/2/8). The final section describes how the manufactured items were delivered to Moses who erects the tabernacle on the first day of the first month of the second year ($\mathfrak{L}^M$ 26/2/2–30/2/17). Despite

---

[58] Dietzfelbinger, 'Vetus Latina', 68–74.

[59] Alban Dold, 'Versucht Neu- und Erstergänzungen zu den altlateinischen Texten im Cod. Clm 6225 der Bayer. Staatsbibliothek', *Bib* 37 (1956): 39–58.

[60] Pierre-Maurice Bogaert, 'L'importance de la Septante et du "Monacensis" de la Vetus Latina pour l'exégèse du livre de l'Exode (chap. 35–40)', in *Studies in the Book of Exodus: Redaction—Reception—Interpretation*, ed. Marc Vervenne, BETL 126 (Leuven: Leuven University Press, 1996), 404.

Table 1.1 Comparison of Codex Monacensis and the Old Greek

Priestly vestments	𝔏ᴹ 21/1/1–28; 21/2/1–22/1/27	≈ 𝔊 36.13–38[1]
Tent	𝔏ᴹ 22/2/1–23/1/24	
Tent and coverings	𝔏ᴹ 22/2/1–9	~ 𝔊 37.1–2
Entrance to the tent	𝔏ᴹ 22/2/10–23	Ø
Tent of Meeting and Holy of Holies	𝔏ᴹ 22/2/23–23/1/16	Ø
Veil	𝔏ᴹ 23/1/17–24	~ 𝔊 37.3
Courtyard	𝔏ᴹ 23/1/25–27; 23/2/1–24/1/27; 24/2/1–2	~ 𝔊 37.7–18[2]
Summary	𝔏ᴹ 24/2/3–17	~ 𝔊 37.19–21
Furniture of the tent	𝔏ᴹ 24/2/18–25/1/27; 25/2/1–8	
Ark, propitiatory, and cherubim	𝔏ᴹ 24/2/18–25/1/9	~ 𝔊 38.1–8
Table, poles, and vessels	𝔏ᴹ 25/1/10–21	≈ 𝔊 38.9–12[3]
Candlestick	𝔏ᴹ 25/1/22–27; 25/2/1–8	≈ 𝔊 38.13–17[4]
Other metal objects	𝔏ᴹ 25/2/9–26/1/27; 26/2/1	≈ 𝔊 38.18–27[5]
Accounting of the metal	𝔏ᴹ 26/2/2–27/1/26; 27/2/1–3	~ 𝔊 39.1–12
Accounting of the textiles	𝔏ᴹ 27/2/4–8	~ 𝔊 39.13
Delivery to Moses	𝔏ᴹ 27/2/9–28/1/21	~ 𝔊 39.14–23
Instructions for erection and anointing	𝔏ᴹ 28/1/22–26; 28/2/1–29/1/23	≈ 𝔊 40.1–14[6]
Erection of the tabernacle	𝔏ᴹ 29/1/24–26; 29/2/1–30/1/25; 30/2/1–2	~ 𝔊 40.15–29
Cloud and the camp	𝔏ᴹ 30/2/3–17	≈ 𝔊 40.30–32[7]

[1] In most places in Exod 36, the Latin of Monacensis has a similar text to the Old Greek. The text is shorter than the Old Greek at points, in many cases due to homoioteleuton: 𝔊 36.20 ($\chi\rho\upsilon\sigma\acute{\iota}\omega\ldots\chi\rho\upsilon\sigma\acute{\iota}\omega$; 𝔏ᴹ 21/1/24–5); 36.24 ($\chi\rho\upsilon\sigma\upsilon\hat{\varsigma}\ldots\chi\rho\upsilon\sigma\upsilon\hat{\varsigma}$; 𝔏ᴹ 21/2/5–6); 36.29 ($\dot{\epsilon}\pi\omega\mu\acute{\iota}\delta o\varsigma\ldots\dot{\epsilon}\pi\omega\mu\acute{\iota}\delta o\varsigma$; 𝔏ᴹ 21/2/15); 36.33 ($\kappa\acute{\omega}\delta\omega\nu\alpha\varsigma\ldots\kappa\acute{\omega}\delta\omega\nu\alpha\varsigma$; 𝔏ᴹ 22/1/3). There are other small omissions at 𝔊 36.18 ($\kappa\alpha\acute{\iota}$; 𝔏ᴹ 21/1/18); 36.19 ($\kappa\alpha\acute{\iota}$; 𝔏ᴹ 21/1/20); 36.20 ($\kappa\alpha\acute{\iota}$; 𝔏ᴹ 21/1/21); 36.36 ($\dot{\epsilon}\kappa\ \beta\acute{\upsilon}\sigma\sigma o\upsilon$ [x2]; 𝔏ᴹ 22/1/12–13), and probably also at 𝔊 36.21, 31, 32, but Monacensis is fragmentary at this point. The largest loss of text appears to have taken place at 36.25–29, but the fragmentary state of the text means it is difficult to determine precisely what is missing. There are also occasionally differences in number to the Greek text of Vaticanus: 𝔊 36.14 (𝔏ᴹ 21/1/2); 36.39 (𝔏ᴹ 22/1/20).

Continued

Table 1.1 *Continued*

---

2 A summary statement about the construction of the court—albeit somewhat displaced—is found in 𝔏^M 22/2/10–11: *Et fecerunt atrium extra tabernaculum* (𝔊^B read καὶ ἐποίησαν τὴν αὐλήν at 𝔊 37.7, but the parallel in 27.9 has the fuller καὶ ποιήσεις αὐλὴν τῇ σκηνῇ). Monacensis presents the sides in a different order than 𝔊^B or 𝔐^L: north, south, west, east. The description is fuller than in 𝔊^B, though in some places the precise readings are uncertain because of the fragmentary state of the text. It does, however, seem to provide the width of the hangings (Dold would restore IIII at 𝔏^M 23/2/1, 8 and 13 [Dold, 'Versucht', 46]. This seems rather perplexing since in 𝔊 37.16 [𝔐 38.18] the width of the hangings is given as five cubits, and this is presupposed in Monacensis since the length of the sides in cubits is five-times the number of columns). The pillars are identified as made from incorruptible wood and Monacensis appears to have the hangings made of hyacinth, purple, crimson and twisted linen (𝔏^M 24/1/1–4) rather than the twisted linen of the other editions. Both details make the materials used in the construction of the courtyard more akin to the tent.

3 Monacensis has no equivalent to καθαροῦ (𝔊 38.9). This could be the result of homoioteleuton, though note that in 𝔊 38.13 the lamp is said to be made of 'gold' in contrast to the 'pure gold' of 𝔐 37.17. In this case, Monacensis could preserve an earlier reading. In the description of the vessels of the table, the individual items are listed, but there is no equivalent of the opening summary expression τὰ σκεύη τῆς τραπέζης (𝔏^M 25/1/19; 𝔊 38.12; cf. 25.29).

4 Monacensis has no equivalent to 𝔊^B's ἣ φωτίζει (𝔊 38.13), though the translator may have omitted it as self-evident. Where 𝔊^B has buds (οἱ βλαστοί) projecting from the branches (ἐκ τῶν καλαμίσκων; 𝔊 38.15), Monacensis has simply the branches projecting (𝔏^M 25/1/25–7). Monacensis also lacks an equivalent to καὶ τὰς ἐπαρυστρίδας αὐτῶν χρυσᾶς (𝔊 38.17), which looks like another case of homoioteleuton (χρυσᾶς…χρυσᾶς).

5 Monacensis is explicit that the metal-worker is Beseel (reading *hic Beseel* with Ziegler, *Bruchstücke*, 25. rather than *hiebeseel* with Dold, 'Versucht', 49). There are cases where Monacensis lacks an equivalent to text found in 𝔊^B which are probably best attributed to homoioteleuton: the absence of the pillars of the veil (𝔊 38.18; 𝔏^M 25/2/13; χρυσίῳ…χρυσίῳ); the reference to only one type of clasp (𝔊 38.19; 𝔏^M 25/2/14–16; κρίκους…κρίκους); referring to the day when Moses made the laver rather than the day he pitched the tent (𝔊 38.26–7; 𝔏^M 26/1/21–2; ἔπηξεν…ἐποίησεν). There are additional places where Monacensis has a shorter text: it reads *eos* where 𝔊^B has τοὺς μοχλούς (𝔊 38.18; 𝔏^M 25/2/13); it probably lacks an equivalent to τοῖς στύλοις (𝔊 38.20; 𝔏^M 25/2/21–2), though these words are also lacking in 𝔊^A which the Göttingen critical edition follows at this point; it probably lacks an equivalent to καὶ τὴν βάσιν (𝔊 38.23; 𝔏^M 26/1/2–4); and, it lacks some words that are in 𝔊 38.27 (𝔏^M 26/1/22–3). The first two of these places where Monacensis has a shorter reading may have been an attempt by the translator to create a clear text.

6 Monacensis reads *et super eam propitiatorium* (𝔏^M 28/2/2–3) where Vaticanus has καὶ σκεπάσεις τὴν κιβωτὸν τοῦ μαρτυρίου τῷ καταπετάσματι (𝔊 40.3; other Greek texts lack τοῦ μαρτυρίου which Wevers follows in his critical edition). For further discussion of the reading in Monacensis see the main text. Monacensis refers to the *panes propositiones eius* (𝔏^M 28/2/4; examination of the photographs confirms Dold's reading of *panes* [Dold, 'Versucht', 54]) rather than Ziegler's reading of *pones* [Ziegler, Bruchstücke, 28]), where 𝔊^B has the more comprehensive, but allusive, καὶ προθήσεις τὴν πρόθεσιν αὐτῆς (v. 4). The reading in Monacensis is an assimilation to the more familiar expression (cf. 𝔊 40.23 ≈ 𝔏^M 30/1/4–5 [damaged]). Monacensis has Moses anoint the *tabernaculum testimonii* where 𝔊^B has the shorter τὴν σκηνήν (𝔏^M 28/2/8–9; 𝔊 40.7). Monacensis has probably assimilated to the fuller expression.

7 Monacensis reads *defensor* (𝔏^M 30/2/16) where 𝔊^B has ἀναζυγαῖς (𝔊 40.32).

these significant similarities, Monacensis diverges from the Old Greek at several points. I will examine these in the order they appear in the text: the fabrication of the textiles and tent ($\mathfrak{L}^M$ 21/1/1–24/2/2), the specialisms of the two master craftsmen ($\mathfrak{L}^M$ 24/2/3–17), the fabrication of the metal items ($\mathfrak{L}^M$ 24/2/18–26/2/1), the accounting of the materials used ($\mathfrak{L}^M$ 26/2/2–27/2/8) and, finally, the delivery and erection of the tabernacle ($\mathfrak{L}^M$ 27/2/9–30/2/17).

Fabrication of the Textiles and Tent ($\mathfrak{L}^M$ 21/1/1–24/2/2)

The most striking difference between Monacensis and the Old Greek is the description of the sanctuary. As we have seen, the Old Greek provides a very truncated account in comparison with the instructions to Moses mentioning only the curtains that comprise the tent, the veil that separate the two rooms of the sanctuary, the veil that served as the entrance, and the pillars upon which the two veils were hung (𝕲 37.1–6). In contrast, Monacensis has a much fuller account. After a brief report of the construction of the tent, the court, and the entrance of the tent ($\mathfrak{L}^M$ 22/2/1–23), the fabrication of the tent and its furnishings are described. In the tent of testimony, there are two seraphim, and in the holy of holies, two cherubim are found atop two pillars.

> *Et fecerunt tabernaculum testimonii in quo fuerunt sarafin duo latum[61] cubitis XX et longum […] columnae eius XUIII in lignis aseptis et bases earum XUIII aereae inargentatae et capita argentea et columnas cum capitibus deaurauerunt. Et fecerunt sanctum sanctorum in quo fuerunt cerubin duo aurea super columellas binas aureas bases argenteas et capita aurea latum cumrigore porticus mediae ab oriente in absida conuexum et columnae eius XII[62] et lignis inputribilib. deauratae.*
>
> They made the tent of testimony in which there were two seraphim, 20 cubits wide and […] long. […] their 18 columns of aseptic wood and their 18 bases of bronze covered in silver and capitals of silver, and they covered the columns with their capitals in gold. They made the holy of holies in which were two gold cherubim upon a pair of gold columns, silver bases and gold capitals, aligned towards the middle portico that leads east towards a convex apse. It had 12 columns of rot-proof wood covered with gold   ($\mathfrak{L}^M$ 22/2/24–23/1/16).

The 'tent of testimony' is clearly understood as a reference to the outer sanctum as is apparent from the description of the veil that separated it from the 'holy of holies'.

---

[61] Dold incorrectly reads here *volatum*, a modern case of dittography (Dold, 'Versucht', 45).
[62] From my examination of the digitized manuscript, Dold's reading of XII appears to be correct (Dold, 'Versucht', 45), rather than XI (Ziegler, *Bruchstücke*, 23).

36 THE MAKING OF THE TABERNACLE

Et fecerunt uelum quod diuideret inter sanctum sanctorum et tabernaculum testimonii de hiacinto et purpura et cocconeto et bysso torta[63] opus textile introitus autem eorum erat ad inuicem constitutes.

They made the veil that divided the holy of holies and tent of testimony from hyacinth, purple, scarlet, and fine linen, woven work. Their entrance was arranged correspondingly ($\mathfrak{L}^M$ 23/1/17–24).

The seraphim are not otherwise mentioned in Monacensis, but subsequent references to the cherubim reflect the same perspective that they were erected on pillars. In the account of their construction by Beseel, the cherubim are mentioned as a distinct object after the ark and the propitiatory.

Et fecit duo cerubin inaurea supra duas columnas aureas et posuit ea unum ad dextram et aliud ad sinixtram[64] in tabernaculo sancti[65] sanctorum in summum ut in umbrarent arcam testamenti et placatorium quod super eam.

He made two gold cherubim upon two gold columns, and he set them one on the right and one on the left in the holy of holies of the tent, in the highest so as to overshadow the ark of the testimony and the propitiatory which was upon it
($\mathfrak{L}^M$ 25/1/1–9).

In the delivery of the manufactured items to Moses, the cherubim are also listed separately to the ark and the propitiatory ($\mathfrak{L}^M$ 27/2/21).

In addition to the alterations in the tabernacle itself, there are some changes to the tabernacle's exterior. To the east there were eight columns of aseptic wood with bronze bases and silver capitals, the bases covered in silver, and the columns and their capitals covered in gold ($\mathfrak{L}^M$ 22/2/10–18). There were also eighteen further columns whose precise location is uncertain ($\mathfrak{L}^M$ 23/1/1–6).

The Specialisms of the Two Master Craftsmen ($\mathfrak{L}^M$ 24/2/3–17)

The pivot between the two sections on the fabrics and the metals consists of a description of the two master craftsmen, Beseel and Eliab.

Haec constitutio tabernaculi testimonii secundum quae praecepta sunt moysi. Haec fecerunt beseel filius or filii uriae de tribu iuda et eliab filius ecisame de tribu dan.

---

[63] Dold reads *et* before *opus textile* (Dold, 'Versucht', 45), but I cannot see any evidence for it in the photographs (cf. Ziegler, *Bruchstücke*, 23).

[64] Reading with Dold *sinixtram* (Dold, 'Versucht', 48), rather than Ziegler's *sinistram* (Ziegler, *Bruchstücke*, 25).

[65] Reading *sancti* with Ziegler (Ziegler, *Bruchstücke*, 25), rather than Dold's *sauctis* (Dold, 'Versucht', 48).

FOUR VERSIONS OF THE TABERNACLE   37

Hic eliab architectonizabit omne opus de ligno inputribili et fecit uela et stolas sacerdotum textiles et sutiles praemixtas uarietatem et hiacinto et purpura cocco et bysso torta.

This is the arrangement of tent of witness as instructed to Moses. Beseel son of Ur son of Uriah of the tribe of Judah and Eliab son of Ecisame of the tribe of Dan did this.

This Eliab constructed all the works of incorruptible wood and he made the curtains and the robes of the priests, woven and sown, varied mixtures from hyacinth, purple, crimson and fine linen   ($\mathfrak{L}^M$ 24/2/3–17).

The version in Monacensis has several distinctive features. First, in contrast to all the other versions we have examined, Monacensis makes no reference to the ministry of the Levites ($\mathfrak{M}$ 38.21–23; $\mathfrak{G}$ 37.19–21). Second, Beseel and Eliab are presented as equals, albeit with Beseel mentioned first. In contrast, the Old Greek edition qualifies Beseel as expressly commanded by God ($\mathfrak{G}$ 37.19), whilst the Masoretic and Samaritan editions present Oholiab as accompanying Bezalel: 'and Oholiab was with him'. Third, the distinctive responsibilities of Eliab are outlined clearly. They concern the woodwork and the fabrication of the textiles. This corresponds very well to the division of the text as we find it in Monacensis. Eliab has responsibility for the items described in the first section: the vestments and the sanctuary ($\mathfrak{L}^M$ 21/1/1–24/2/2).

Fabrication of the Metal Items ($\mathfrak{L}^M$ 24/2/18–26/2/1)

In Monacensis, the division of labour between Beseel and Eliab is underscored by the first item of the second section: the ark.

Ipse fecit arcam et inaurabit eam Beseel auro rutilo intus et foris.

This one made the ark. Beseel covered it with red gold inside and outside
($\mathfrak{L}^M$ 24/2/18–20)

In the construction of the ark, Eliab—*ipse*, 'this one'—does the woodwork and Beseel the metalwork. I have already observed that Beseel constructs the cherubim upon their pillars separately from the ark and the propitiatory ($\mathfrak{L}^M$ 25/1/1–9). For the remaining metal items, Monacensis reflects a text very close to the Old Greek.

Accounting of the Materials Used ($\mathfrak{L}^M$ 26/2/2–27/2/8)

In a similar manner to the other editions, the account of the metals in Monacensis enumerates the amount of gold, silver, and bronze used in the construction of the

38   THE MAKING OF THE TABERNACLE

sanctuary, as well as how the metal was collected and, in the case of the silver and bronze, how it was used. Despite these similarities, Monacensis differs from these other versions in several respects. First, the weights are given in talents (*talenta*), pounds (*ponda*), and shekels (*sicula*), whilst the other versions give them in talents and shekels. Second, the account includes the additional columns mentioned earlier in the fabrication of the tent:

> *Et residua talenta XXX pondi… et sicli XXXIIII miserunt in columnas atrii tabernaculi testimonii et sancti sanctorum.*
>
> *Et columnas XVIII*[66] *et fuerunt foris anianuam*[67] *ad parte occidentis.*
>
> The remaining 30 talents, ? pounds and 34 shekels they cast as columns for the atrium of the tent of testimony and the holy of holies.
>
> And 18 columns and they were outside the door to the west   ($\mathfrak{L}^M$ 26/2/22–27/1/3)

As a result, the amount of silver collected is larger than in the other versions. Third, Monacensis makes no mention of the census total of 603,550 men ($\mathfrak{L}^M$ 26/2/15–19; cf. $\mathfrak{G}$ 39.3; $\mathfrak{M}$ 38.26). Fourth, Monacensis attributes the metalwork for the columns and hooks to a plural group. Whether this is just Beseel and Eliab, or also includes the skilled Israelite workers, is not stated. It is, however, consistent with the use of the plural in the section on the fabrication of the tent ($\mathfrak{L}^M$ 22/2/1–24/2/2) and forms a contrast with the other versions that attribute all the metalwork to Bezalel alone.

The accounting of the metals ends with a brief concluding notice that the remaining gold was used to make the utensils for divine service. This observation is followed by a parallel one about how the remaining textiles were also used for ministering. Although Monacensis is fragmentary at this point, it is apparent that it has a distinctive tradition that sees the textiles being used to make the vestments of the Levites ($\mathfrak{L}^M$ 27/2/4–8), rather than the vestments of Aaron as we find in the other editions ($\mathfrak{G}$ 39.13; $\mathfrak{M}$ 39.1).

Delivery and Erection of the Tabernacle ($\mathfrak{L}^M$ 27/2/9–30/2/17)

The delivery of the tabernacle and all its furniture to Moses is, unfortunately, preserved in a paragraph that has been mutilated in the process of the manuscript being repurposed. As a result, the text of Monacensis is not entirely certain. Nevertheless, what is preserved provides clear evidence that Monacensis had a

---

[66] Both Ziegler and Dold read here CIII (Ziegler, *Bruchstücke*, 27; Dold, 'Versucht', 52), but an examination of the photographs makes me believe that the text actually reads XVIII.

[67] *Ante ianuam* is meant (see $\mathfrak{L}^M$ 27/1/18 of the same columns) (Dold, 'Versucht', 52).

text that diverges from the Old Greek. After the mention of the Levites' vestments, the tent and its cover,[68] the objects are listed working from the inside of the tent outwards: ark, propitiatory, altar, cherubim, veil, table and bread, lamps, entrance curtain (?),[69] courtyard hangings. Finally, the priestly vestments, the oil, the incense, and some other minor items including the pegs are handed over. The order is, thus, rather more like the standardized order found in the Masoretic and Samaritan editions and quite different from the Old Greek which mostly orders the items by the craftsman: first, the metals, incense, and oils that were attributed to Bezalel, and then the vestments, hanging, and covers that were attributed to Oholiab. In various other respects, this section in Monacensis aligns with the Masoretic and Samaritan traditions against the Old Greek. Monacensis mentions the propitiatory, an altar within the tabernacle itself, and various veils and screens, none of which appear in the Old Greek.

For the divine instructions to Moses to erect the tent, install its furniture and anoint them, Monacensis has a text close to the Old Greek. The most important difference is in v. 3 where Monacensis has the propitiatory, rather than the veil, covering the ark. The difference between the two readings is most likely explained as the result of a confusion of the two Hebrew terms, כפרת, 'atonement cover', and פרכת, 'veil'.

The account of the tent's erection in Monacensis is fragmentary and as a result we face some difficulties in comparing its text to the other traditions. The placement of objects in the inner sanctum is longer than in the Old Greek, but the reconstruction is uncertain. It appears that Monacensis is more precise in having the ark brought into the holy of holies, and not simply the tabernacle. This would be consistent with the differentiation between the tent of testimony and the holy of holies in 𝔏ᴹ 23/1/17–24. After the placement of the ark and its poles, Dold reconstructs *et [induxit uelum su]per eam p[osuitq. lumina]rium qu[od collocauit] e meri[die]*, 'and [he spread the veil ov]er it, a[nd placed the lam]p whi[ch stood] at the south side' (𝔏ᴹ 29/2/17–20).[70] However, both the lamp and the veil are clearly mentioned a few lines later (𝔏ᴹ 29/2/21–25; 30/1/7–13) so their appearance here is premature and repetitious. Burkitt's alternative reconstruction reads *et [inposuit su]per eam p[ropitiato]rium qu[od erat] de sup[er]* 'and [he placed ov]er it the p[ropitiato]ry whi[ch was] over it'.[71] The idea of finding a reference to the propitiatory makes more sense, but the reading of *de sup[er]* in line 20 was a speculation made without reference to the manuscript. The underwriting of

---

[68] For 𝔏ᴹ 27/2/14–16 Dold restores *Et aurea te[ctorum oper]toria de p[elle arietum] et hiacint[ina]* (Dold, 'Versucht', 53). My examination of the photographs suggests that *aurea* may have been corrected to *aulea*, perhaps by the original scribe. I would also be tempted to restore *te[gumen...* (cf. 𝔏ᴹ 28/2/11).

[69] Dold restores *[Et tabernaculu]m quod est [in testimoniu]m* (𝔏ᴹ 28/1/5–6) which would make little sense at this point (Dold, 'Versucht', 53). Elsewhere in Monacensis, *quod est* occurs in used of the various dividing veils and curtains.

[70] Dold, 'Versucht', 56.

[71] F. C. Burkitt, 'The Text of Exodus XL 17–19 in the Munich Palimpsest', *JTS* 29 (1928): 146–7.

Monacensis is quite clear at this point and Burkitt's proposal to read *de sup[er]* is simply wrong.

The account of the veil's hanging which follows in $\mathfrak{L}^M$ 29/2/21–25 is longer than in the Old Greek, and appears to describe the veil's role in dividing the tent from the holy of holies (cf. $\mathfrak{L}^M$ 23/1/17–24). The description of the installation of the lamp in Monacensis appears to have suffered from homoioteleuton at some point in transmission skipping from one occurrence of 'in the tent of witness' in $\mathfrak{G}$ 40.22 to another in $\mathfrak{G}$ 40.24. Monacensis collapses the description of the lamp and the altar of incense together and as a result lacks any reference to the altar and would have the lamp placed opposite the veil with the incense of the composition burned upon it ($\mathfrak{L}^M$ 30/1/7–13). In comparison to the Old Greek, Monacensis does not mention the erection of the courtyard, a loss that can probably be attributed to homoioteleuton.

Conclusion

In the first few centuries of the Common Era, the tabernacle account existed in at least four versions. Different tabernacles existed in the imaginations of the different communities that revered the Jewish scriptures. The existence of such a complex textual problem calls out for further examination. How are we to explain such diversity? Evidently at some point scribal interest in the arcane matters of the tabernacle's architecture led to significant reshaping of the text. And not just on one occasion. Was this the result of a Hebrew original being corrupted as the text was translated and transmitted in other communities, or is it the result of a complex history of composition? In the following chapter, we will seek to address that question.

2

The Tabernacle in the Late Second Temple Period

The manuscripts examined have shown that in late antiquity and the medieval period at least four versions of the tabernacle account were known in Jewish, Samaritan, and Christian communities. They are clearly related to one another and share a common origin in the Second Temple period. Precisely how these four versions relate to one another is the subject of this chapter. Before we turn to this topic, we must examine the evidence from the Second Temple period itself. Amongst the Dead Sea Scrolls are several texts that relate to the tabernacle account, including texts of Exodus, so-called Rewritten Pentateuch texts, and the Temple Scroll. Unfortunately, all have survived in fragmentary form. Nevertheless, they provide important evidence of the form of the tabernacle account in the late Second Temple period.

The Tabernacle Account in the Dead Sea Scrolls

The tabernacle account is preserved in ten manuscripts recovered from the caves near the Dead Sea. The fragmentary state of many of these manuscripts means that we often need to analyse them in terms of their alignment to the well-known and better-preserved literary editions from late antiquity and the medieval period. These pragmatic considerations must not obscure the fact that the text forms that survived into the medieval period due to their transmission within religious communities originated in single manuscripts from the Second Temple period. In that sense, they witness to the reading of a single text from the Second Temple period just as the biblical texts of the Dead Sea Scrolls do. In other words, we should view the Dead Sea manuscripts as individual artefacts alongside those medieval text forms and not simply as exemplars of text-types already known. In discussing these scrolls, I will examine them according to their site and the standard sequential numbering before offering a synthetic analysis.

2Q2 (2QExod[a]) has a late Herodian script that dates the scroll palaeographically to 50–68 CE, and has a fairly full orthography.[1] The scroll would appear to have

---

[1] M. Baillet, J. T. Milik, and R. de Vaux, *Les 'Petites Grottes' de Qumrân: Textes*, DJD 3 (Oxford: Clarendon Press, 1962), 49–52.

The Making of the Tabernacle and the Construction of Priestly Hegemony. Nathan MacDonald, Oxford University Press.
© Nathan MacDonald 2023. DOI: 10.1093/oso/9780198813859.003.0003

42 THE MAKING OF THE TABERNACLE

contained the continuous text of Exodus. From the tabernacle account it preserves
fragments of 26.11–13; 30.21 (?), 23–25.[2] The only variant of note is the unique
reading]לדרות[יכם at the end of 30.25, which should be judged as an assimilation
to v. 31. In the rest of the scroll, Baillet noted a number of variants that had similarities with the LXX, though Lange categorizes it as unaligned.[3]

2Q3 (2QExod[b]) has a Herodian script that dates it to the first century CE. The
orthography is full and the divine name is written in palaeo-Hebrew. There is some
uncertainty about whether the scroll contained a continuous text or excerpts
from the book of Exodus.[4] Baillet identified fragments of 27.17–19; 31.16–17, and
Longacre has recently proposed that the previously unidentified fragments
include the text of 36.3–4 and 36.33–34 (or 26.28–29).[5] The surviving text preserves a reading of ליהוה at the end of 30.16a, a variant also attested in the Peshitta.

4Q11 (4QpaleoGen–Exod[l]) is a first-century BCE scroll written in a palaeo-
Hebrew script. Whilst the surviving text includes the last verse of Genesis and
significant parts of Exodus, estimates for the scroll size mean it likely contained
the entire Pentateuch.[6] The original editors identified the following fragments
which belonged to the tabernacle account: 25.7–20; 26.29–27.1; 27.4 (?); 27.6–14;
28.33–35, 40–42; 36.34–36.[7] Dayfani, Longacre, and Perrot have recently identified additional fragments, including 25.21–22 and 28.28 (or 39.21).[8] The text of
the manuscript has some affinities with the Masoretic tradition.[9] The incense
altar is not placed after 26.34 as in the Samaritan Pentateuch and reconstructions
of the scroll's dimensions indicate that it did not have the longer Samaritan text of
Exodus.[10] Nevertheless, Dayfani, Longacre, and Perrot have argued that 4Q11 has
at least one case of systematization in common with the Samaritan Pentateuch:
the reading of אחת אל אחת at 25.20.[11]

4Q17 (4QExod–Lev[f]) has a protocursive script that Cross dated to the third
century BCE making it one of the oldest manuscripts discovered at Qumran. The
scroll was discovered in a very poor state of preservation with only parts of a few

---

[2] In addition to the fragments identified by Baillet, Longacre has plausibly proposed that frag. 12
preserves the letters אחרי from 26.12 (Longacre, 'Contextualized Approach', 102).

[3] Armin Lange, *Handbuch der Textfunde vom Toten Meer. Band I: Die Handschriften biblischer
Bücher von Qumran und den anderen Fundorten* (Tübingen: Mohr Siebeck, 2009), 57.

[4] The question about the nature of the scroll arises from the appearance of text from 19.9 before
34.10 (Baillet, Milik, and de Vaux, 'Petites Grottes', 52–5). For an up-to-date discussion of the issue, see
Longacre, 'Contextualized Approach', 103–6.

[5] Baillet, Milik, and de Vaux, 'Petites Grottes', 52–5; Longacre, 'Contextualized Approach', 103.

[6] Patrick W. Skehan, Eugene Ulrich, and Judith E. Sanderson, *Qumran Cave 4. IV: Palaeo-Hebrew
and Greek Biblical Manuscripts*, DJD 9 (Oxford: Clarendon Press, 1992), 17–50.

[7] Fragment 41 was cautiously identified as 40.15, but Longacre argues that it is 18.19–21
(Longacre, 'Contextualized Approach', 108 n. 5).

[8] Hila Dayfani, Drew Longacre, and Antony Perrot, 'New Identifications of 4QpaleoGen-Exod[l]
(4Q11) Fragments', *RevQ* 34 (2022): 137–50.

[9] Lange categorizes 4Q11 as 'semi-masoretic' (Lange, *Handbuch*, 52).

[10] Skehan, Ulrich, and Sanderson, *Qumran Cave 4. IV: Palaeo-Hebrew and Greek Biblical Manuscripts*,
23–4; Longacre, 'Contextualized Approach', 109.

[11] Dayfani, Longacre, and Perrot, 'New Identifications'. The original editors read]א.[שׁי אל אחו.

columns at the end of Exodus and the beginning of Leviticus surviving.[12] Its original extent is not certain, but given its size it could have contained the entire Pentateuch.[13] The extant text includes fragments of 38.18–22; 39.3–19, 20–24; 40.8–27. The manuscript agrees with the Masoretic and Samaritan versions against the Old Greek version in having the fabrication of the priestly vestments towards the end of the compliance account rather than at its beginning. The text is expansionistic and has justly been characterized as non-aligned.[14] Significantly, 4Q17 describes the manufacture of the Urim and Thummim in 39.21 in agreement with the Samaritan Pentateuch.[15]

4Q21 (4QExod^k) has a late Herodian or post-Herodian script that has been dated to the first century CE. It is a single fragment preserving parts of 36.9–10 which contains no significant variants.[16]

4Q22 (4QpaleoExod^m) is written in palaeo-Hebrew and has been dated palaeographically to the first century BCE. It has a fairly full orthography and major paragraph divisions are indicated by an enlarged initial *waw* ending the line. The manuscript shows a strong affinity with the text known from the Samaritan tradition. The original editors argued that almost all the major expansions of the Samaritan text are present, but not the sectarian features. Unfortunately, the columns containing the Decalogue (Exod 20) were not preserved, but the editors argued that there was not sufficient space for the commandment to build an altar on Mount Gerizim (Exod 20.17b).[17] Whilst earlier scholarship designated the text as 'proto-Samaritan', the lack of sectarian features led to a preference for describing the manuscript having a 'pre-Samaritan' text-type. In a recent article, however, Dayfani has offered a detailed reconstruction of the missing columns and demonstrated that there is sufficient space for the Gerizim commandment. As a result, 4Q22 should be identified as a proto-Samaritan text with sectarian readings.[18] In relation to the tabernacle account, the original editors identified 25.11–12, 20–29, 31–34; 26.8–15, 21–30; 30.10; 27.1–3, 9–14, 18–19; 28.3–4,

---

[12] Ulrich et al., *Qumran Cave 4. VII: Genesis to Numbers*, 133–44.

[13] Longacre, 'Contextualized Approach', 112.

[14] Armin Lange, 'The Dead Sea Scrolls and the Date of the Final Stage of the Pentateuch', in *On Stone and Scroll: Essays in Honour of Graham Ivor Davies*, eds. James K. Aitken, Katherine J. Dell, and Brian A. Mastin, BZAW 420 (Berlin: de Gruyter, 2011), 297–8. Notable expansions are found at 39.21 (reading ה[אש]ל after the first mention of האפד); 40.17 (reading ם]ממצרים לצאתם after השנית [cf. ꝑꝑꝑ^D; 𝕲^B]), 18 (reading]קרסיו אׄת after וישם), 27 (reading לקניו after סמים).

[15] This may be the reason that Cross identified the text as 'proto-Samaritan' (Ulrich et al., *Qumran Cave 4. VII: Genesis to Numbers*, 136).

[16] Ulrich et al., *Qumran Cave 4. VII: Genesis to Numbers*, 151.

[17] Skehan, Ulrich, and Sanderson, *Qumran Cave 4. IV: Palaeo-Hebrew and Greek Biblical Manuscripts*, 53–130. For more extensive discussion see Judith E. Sanderson, *An Exodus Scroll from Qumran: 4QpaleoExod^m and the Samaritan Tradition*, HSS 30 (Atlanta: Scholars Press, 1986).

[18] Hila Dayfani, '4QpaleoExod^m and the Gerizim Composition', *JBL* 141 (2022): 673–98. For a similar assessment of 4Q22 see also Stefan Schorch, 'The So-Called Gerizim Commandment in the Samaritan Pentateuch', in *The Samaritan Pentateuch and the Dead Sea Scrolls*, ed. Michael Langlois, CBET 94 (Leuven: Peeters, 2019), 77–97.

44   THE MAKING OF THE TABERNACLE

8–12, 22–24, 26–28, 30–39; 28.39–29.5, 20, 22–25, 31–34, 34–41; 30.12–18, 29–31; 30.34–31.7; 31.7–8, 13–15; 35.1; 36.21–24; 37.9–16. Longacre has sought to identify additional fragments and, if his identifications are correct, the extant text will extend to include 28.20–21; 29.12–13, 46; 30.11, 25–26, 33; 37.18. The agreement of 4Q22 with the Samaritan Pentateuch is also readily apparent in the tabernacle account. 4Q22 locates the instructions about the incense altar after 26.34 and would appear to mention the vestments before 27.20. Unfortunately, 4Q22 is not extant at the point where the Samaritan Pentateuch describes the manufacture of the Urim and Thummim. It clearly lacks mention of the priestly garments with the anointing oil after 29.20, and though the text is not extant there is sufficient space for it to be located after v. 28. There are also some places where 4Q22 shares some of the Samaritan Pentateuch's systematic tendencies. In 25.20 it reads אֹחֵז ל[א אחד and in 26.10 חמשים לֹלֹא[ות. Yet, there are various points where the text of 4Q22 agrees with the Masoretic Text rather than the Samaritan Pentateuch,[19] and places where 4Q22 has its own distinct reading.[20] This suggests that 4Q22 is not a direct ancestor of the Samaritan Pentateuch known from medieval exemplars.[21]

4Q158 (4QRP[a]) is a rewritten version of Genesis and Exodus, or perhaps just Exodus.[22] It has a Herodian script dating it to the second half of the first century BCE, and a full orthography. Only two verses from the tabernacle account are preserved: 30.32, 34. Where 𝔐[L] reads הוא קדש, 4QRP[a] has הוא קדש קדשים (30.32).

4Q364 (4QRP[b]) probably covered the entire Pentateuch. It has a Hasmonean script dating to 75–50 BCE, and a full orthography. From the tabernacle account only 25.1–2; 26.1, 33–35 are preserved. The manuscript has additional text between 24.18 and 25.1 which 'may have described what God showed Moses during the forty days and forty nights before his speech',[23] and a number of minor variants in 26.33–35. In other parts of the scroll, we find major changes that are also known from the Samaritan Pentateuch, although we do not find in the tabernacle account the characteristic Samaritan insertion of the incense altar after 26.34.

4Q365 (4QRP[c]) has a transitional late Hasmonean/early Herodian script and dates to the first-century BCE. Its text has a full orthography. It was initially classified as an example of a reworked Pentateuch.[24] Though it has been expanded at

[19] Exod 25.29, 31; 26.8, 24; 27.9, 11; 28.4, 23, 39; 29.33; 36.23.
[20] Exod 28.11 (יפתח for תפתח); 28.41 (והלבשתם for ו]הלבשת); 29.22 (היֹ[תרת for יותרת); 31.4 (לשובב]זהב for לעשות בזהב); 31.5 (]מלאכֹה for מלאכה); 31.13–14 (א ל]כם מחללֹ[יה for אֹות הֹו]א ל[כם מחלל[יה, a case of parablepsis).
[21] Cf. Sanderson, *Exodus Scroll*, 158–74.   [22] Zahn, *Rethinking Rewritten Scripture*, 25.
[23] Harold Attridge et al., *Qumran Cave 4. VIII. Parabiblical Texts, Part I*, DJD 11 (Oxford: Clarendon Press, 1994), 223.
[24] Attridge et al., *Qumran Cave 4. VIII. Parabiblical Texts, Part I*, 187–96, 255–318. The original editors, Sidnie White (Crawford) and Emanuel Tov, regarded the various examples of reworked Pentateuch—4QRP[a], 4QRP[b], 4QRP[c], 4QRP[d], 4QRP[e]—as copies of a single composition. Segal and Brooke, however, highlighted the differences between them (Michael Segal, '4QReworked Pentateuch or 4QPentateuch?', in *The Dead Sea Scrolls: Fifty Years after Their Discovery. Proceedings of the Jerusalem Congress, July 20–25, 1997*, eds. Lawrence H. Schiffman, Emanuel Tov, and James C. VanderKam

various points, the text follows the Pentateuch's narrative structure and is best regarded as a Pentateuchal text, rather than a distinct parabiblical composition.[25] The text of the tabernacle account consists of fragments of 26.34–36; 28.16–20; 29.20–22; 30.37–31.3; 35.3–5; 36.32–38; 37.29–38.7; 39.1–5, 8–19. Its closest affinities are with the Masoretic Text.[26] In particular, it lacks the characteristic changes of the Samaritan Pentateuch, such as the insertion of the incense altar after 26.34 and the placement of the sprinkling of the priestly garments with anointing oil after 29.28. There are various points of disagreement between 4Q365 and the Masoretic Text, but these are nearly always explicable as the result of the typical processes of textual transmission.[27] The only example of a systematic revision is the consistent deployment of plural verbs in 37.29–38.7, where all the other extant versions have a singular verb. Thus, the manufacture of the anointing oil and incense and the construction of the altar of burnt offering are presumably attributed to all the skilled workers, and not to Bezalel alone.

11Q19 (11QT[a]), known as the Temple Scroll, is the most challenging text that relates to the tabernacle account from amongst the Dead Sea Scrolls. Columns 3–12 detail how the temple was to be constructed, but the Temple Scroll is particularly fragmentary at this point and the extant text shows that the composer of the Temple Scroll has combined the description of the tabernacle from Exodus 25–40 with those of the Solomonic temple from 1 Kings and 2 Chronicles.[28] After brief instructions about the material with which to manufacture the furniture (col. 3), the building of the temple is described (col. 4–6) followed by the furniture

---

[Jerusalem: Israel Exploration Society, 2000], 391–9; George J. Brooke, '4Q158: Reworked Pentateuch[a] or Reworked Pentateuch A?', *DSD* 8 [2001]: 219–41). Further reflection led Tov to the same position, see Emanuel Tov, 'From 4QReworked Pentateuch To 4QPentateuch (?)', in *Authoritative Scriptures in Ancient Judaism*, ed. Mladen Popović, JSJSup 141 (Leiden: Brill, 2010), 73–91. For a detailed analysis and comparison of all the rewritten Pentateuch texts, see also Zahn, *Rethinking Rewritten Scripture*.

[25] Segal, '4QReworked Pentateuch or 4QPentateuch?'

[26] See, esp., Angela Y. Kim, 'The Textual Alignment of the Tabernacle Sections of 4Q365 (Fragments 8a–b, 9a–b i, 9b ii, 12a i, 12b iii)', *Text* 21 (2002): 45–69. White and Tov classified the text as pre-Samaritan (Attridge et al., *Qumran Cave 4. VIII. Parabiblical Texts, Part I*, 187–96), but this is partly as a result of associating 4Q365 with 4Q158 and 4Q364 which have some characteristic Samaritan Pentateuch additions. Tov later noted that 4Q365 was not as closely aligned to the Samaritan Pentateuch as initially thought (Tov, '4QReworked Pentateuch', 54). Longacre groups 4Q158, 4Q364, and 4Q365 together. In his analysis a decisive role is played by the appearance of a distinctive error in 4Q364 which he thinks was probably also found in 4Q365. At 26.34, 4Q364 has the construct form of ארון bearing the definite article: הארון העדות. At the same place 4Q365 reads]הארון (Longacre, 'Contextualized Approach', 208). Whether 4Q365 had the same error is not entirely certain, and I am inclined to give greater weight to the divergences between 4Q365 and the Samaritan Pentateuch. Lange and Davies cautiously conclude that the entire text is best regarded as non-aligned (Lange, 'Date of the Final Stage', 297; Graham I. Davies, *Exodus 1–18: A Critical and Exegetical Commentary. Volume 1: Chapters 1–10*, ICC [London: T&T Clark, 2020], 23–4).

[27] For detailed discussions of various examples, see Zahn, *Rethinking Rewritten Scripture*, 98–121; Kim, 'Textual Alignment'.

[28] For the text of 11Q19 and related manuscripts, see the new critical edition by Schiffman and Gross: Lawrence H. Schiffman and Andrew Gross, *The Temple Scroll: 11Q19, 11Q20, 11Q21, 4Q524, 5Q21 with 4Q365a and 4Q365 Frag. 23*, Dead Sea Scrolls Editions 1 (Leiden: Brill, 2021).

46 THE MAKING OF THE TABERNACLE

beginning from the holy of holies and working outwards (col. 7–10, 12).[29] In most cases, the descriptions of the furniture are briefer than those found in the extant Hebrew texts of Exodus though it is not clear that this sheds light on the known versions.[30] Several features of the Temple Scroll's descriptions of the furniture are worth noting. In the summary of the furniture, the incense altar has been fully integrated and is mentioned as the first piece of furniture after the ark (11Q19 3.10).[31] The furniture within the temple is all made from pure gold. Gold is also listed as one of the materials for the fabrication of the veil (11Q19 7.13), which is not the case in Exod 26.31. The descriptions of the table and lampstand have also incorporated Lev 24.1–9 and Num 8.1–4 into their portrayal. The challenge of bringing fire into the temple is directly addressed with references to various vessels of gold 'with which [to b]ring the fire inside' (לה]ביא בהמה אש פנימה; 11Q19 3.13). The furniture in the courtyard is to be made from 'pure bronze', a qualification distinctive to the Temple Scroll.

Viewed together, the finds from Qumran shed significant light on the textual history of Exodus. All of the texts examined show a closer alignment to the fuller texts of the later medieval Masoretic and Samaritan editions than to the shorter text of the Old Greek. 4Q11 is the most closely aligned to the Masoretic Text. 4Q365 is closer to the Masoretic version than the Samaritan, but it evidences expansion outside of the tabernacle narratives. As such, it illustrates the fluidity and pluriformity of the biblical text even in the late Second Temple period. This is

[29] For discussion, see Johann Maier, *Die Tempelrolle vom Toten Meer und das 'Neue Jerusalem': 11Q19 und 11Q20, 1Q32, 2Q24, 4Q554–555, 5Q15 und 11Q18. Übersetzung und Erläuterung*, 3rd edn, UTB 829 (Munich: Reinhardt, 1997), 74–90; Lawrence H. Schiffman, 'Architecture and Law: The Temple and Its Courtyards in the Temple Scroll', in *From Ancient Israel to Modern Judaism, Intellect in Quest of Understanding, Essays in Honor of Marvin Fox*, eds. Jacob Neusner, Ernest S. Frerichs, and Nahum M. Sarna (Atlanta: Scholars Press, 1989), 267–84; Lawrence H. Schiffman, 'The Furnishings of the Temple According to the Temple Scroll', in *The Madrid Qumran Congress Vol. 2*, eds. Julio C. Trebolle Barrera and Luis Vegas Montaner, STDJ 11 (Leiden: Brill, 1992), 621–34.

[30] In a cautious study George Brooke compares the Temple Scroll with the Old Greek of Exod 36–40 and concludes that 'some of the LXX text's principal characteristics, discernible especially in the order and brevity of its *Vorlage*, are now vaguely recognizable in part of the Temple Scroll, particularly 11QT* 3 and 10' (George J. Brooke, 'The Temple Scroll and LXX Exodus 35–40', in *Septuagint, Scrolls and Cognate Writings: Papers Presented to the International Symposium on the Septuagint and Its Relations to the Dead Sea Scrolls and Other Writings [Manchester, 1990]*, eds. George J. Brooke and Barnabas Lindars, SCS 33 [Atlanta: Scholars Press, 1992], 100–1). Brooke's comparison suggests an analogy between the tabernacle material in the Temple Scroll and the Old Greek of Exod 36–40. The instructions about the materials in col. 3 shows the same instinct to order the furniture according to their material, and the instructions concerning the furniture is often shorter than the tabernacle account in the extant Hebrew versions. What Brooke does not do is establish a link between the briefer text of the Temple Scroll and the Old Greek of Exod 36–40. Indeed, as Brooke observes the Temple Scroll shows knowledge of details that have no counterpart in the Old Greek of Exod 36–40, such as the incense altar (Brooke, 'Temple Scroll', 84–5).

[31] The description of the incense altar is not extant. The summary would suggest it must have occurred between 11Q19 7.13 and 8.4. In 7.13–14, however, the veil (הפרוכת) is described, whilst in 8.2 Schiffman and Gross read]נֹזֵח ארֹון[(Schiffman and Gross, *The Temple Scroll*, 32). This collocation is not found in the Masoretic Text, though the lampstand is said to be 'opposite' the table: וְאֶת־הַמְּנֹרָה נֹכַח הַשֻּׁלְחָן (26.35; cf. 40.24). The altar of incense was the only item, apart from the atonement cover, located with reference to the ark as it was said to have been placed לִפְנֵי אָרֹון (40.5).

evidenced still further in 4Q364, and even more so in 4Q22, which have textual features in common with the Samaritan Pentateuch. The fact that 4Q17 describes the manufacture of the Urim and Thummim (39.21) might indicate that the form of the tabernacle account that we find in the Samaritan version was already circulating in the third century BCE. At very least, at this date we seem to have a version of the tabernacle account that shows expansionistic tendencies beyond that seen in the Masoretic version.

Comparing the Four Versions

The Masoretic Version and the Samaritan Version

Although the findings at Qumran pre-date Codex Leningrad and the Chester Beatty manuscript of the Samaritan Pentateuch by about a millennium, 4Q11 and 4Q17 especially confirm that the consonantal text of Exodus has been preserved in both medieval manuscripts with a high degree of accuracy. This finding is consistent with what we know about the Hebrew and Samaritan Bibles more generally. Though the evidence is limited for the tabernacle account, the presence of non-aligned texts at Qumran also demonstrates that there was a degree of textual fluidity in the Second Temple period, whilst the reworked Pentateuch texts and the Temple Scroll show that scribal reworking of texts could be far-reaching. There is continued debate about whether the Masoretic Text tradition had already emerged as the dominant text within Judaism in the couple of centuries preceding 70 CE,[32] but the circumstances stemming from the brutal suppression of the Jewish revolt was a significant factor in the narrowing of the textual tradition.[33] Whether the same was also true of the Samaritan textual tradition is difficult to say with the current state of our knowledge.

Whilst the Samaritan text may, in isolated cases, preserve a small number of better readings than the Masoretic Text, it is, in broad terms, typologically later. The clearest indicators of this are the attempts to produce a smoother text through the standardization of formulae, and the closer alignment of the instructions and

---

[32] For a couple of contrasting views see Armin Lange, '"They Confirmed the Reading" (y. Ta'an. 4.68a): The Textual Standardization of Jewish Scriptures in the Second Temple Period', in *From Qumran to Aleppo: A Discussion with Emanuel Tov about the Textual History of Jewish Scriptures in Honor of His 65th Birthday*, eds. Matthias Weigold and József Zsengellér, FRLANT 230 (Göttingen: Vandenhoeck & Ruprecht, 2009), 29–80; Emanuel Tov, 'The Myth of the Stabilization of the Text of Hebrew Scripture', in *The Text of the Hebrew Bible: From the Rabbis to the Masoretes*, eds. Elvira Martín-Contreras and Lorena Miralles-Maciá, JAJSup 13 (Göttingen: Vandenhoeck & Ruprecht, 2014).

[33] The textual tradition was distilled further by the Masoretes, though not to the extent that complete uniformity was achieved, and the Masoretic tradition has been rightly characterized by Stuart Weeks as 'a bottleneck within a bottleneck' (Stuart Weeks, *Ecclesiastes 1–5: A Critical and Exegetical Commentary*, ICC [London: T&T Clark, 2020], 152).

48   THE MAKING OF THE TABERNACLE

their execution.[34] In the case of the large-scale differences, these are best regarded as additions or alterations in the Samaritan text away from a text similar to that preserved in the Masoretic tradition.[35] Other large-scale additions in the Samaritan tradition, such as those in the plague narratives (Exod 7–11) or the use in Exodus and Numbers of parallel stories from Deuteronomy's retelling of the wilderness wanderings (Deut 1–3) have received greater attention with scholarship.[36] They have been insightfully characterized as an attempt to create a formal correspondence between events and their description through the addition or duplication of verses from elsewhere in the Torah.[37] In the cases from the tabernacle account this is true of the reference to the fabrication of vestments in 27.19b and the relocation of the sprinkling of the blood and oil after the offering of the ordination sacrifice which aligns Exod 29 with Lev 8. The relocation of the incense altar creates as many problems as it resolves and the purposes may be more exegetical than harmonizing. The inclusion of the Urim and Thummim's manufacture is an addition that closes a textual lacuna.

The Old Greek Version and the Hebrew Versions

It is readily apparent that the Old Greek translation of Exod 25–31 sits closer to the Masoretic version than to the Samaritan version. Most of the large-scale additions in the Samaritan Pentateuch are to be found in Exod 25–31 and none of them are to be found in the Old Greek of those chapters. Where the Old Greek and the Samaritan version do agree against the Masoretic version, these can be attributed to processes of standardization and do not imply a close textual relationship between Old Greek and Samaritan versions. The situation is different for

[34]   See already Julius Popper, *Die biblische Bericht über die Stiftshütte: Ein Beitrag zur Geschichte der Composition und Diaskeue des Pentateuch* (Leipzig: Heinrich Hunger, 1862).

[35]   Commenting on the Urim and Thummim's manufacture in 4Q17 Cross suggests that their appearance 'is best taken as original in the Hebrew text, lost by parablepsis (homoioteleuton and homoiarchton) in other traditions' (Ulrich et al., *Qumran Cave 4. VII: Genesis to Numbers*, 139). This seems unlikely since it would have involved an accidental loss at both 28.26 and 39.19 (Zahn, *Rethinking Rewritten Scripture*, 139 n. 111).

[36]   See, e.g., Emanuel Tov, 'Rewritten Bible Compositions and Biblical Manuscripts, with Special Attention Paid to the Samaritan Pentateuch', in *Hebrew Bible, Greek Bible and Qumran: Collected Essays*, TSAJ 121 (Tübingen: Mohr Siebeck, 2008), 57–70; Magnar Kartveit, *The Origin of the Samaritans*, VTSup 128 (Leiden: Brill, 2009), 265–88.

[37]   These large-scale insertions have often been described as harmonizing. Michael Segal has shown that this terminology is inaccurate for cases such as when verses from Deuteronomy were inserted into Exodus and Numbers. Far from resulting in a harmony, the insertion often results in a contradiction, but it does produce a formal correspondence so that the reprise in Deuteronomy matches the earlier description. Segal observes that in these cases 'it is striking that the scribe almost always copied material in one direction, from Deuteronomy into Exodus and Numbers' (Michael Segal, 'The Text of the Hebrew Bible in Light of the Dead Sea Scrolls', *Materia Giudaica* 12 [2007]: 13) even though the problem also exists in the book of Deuteronomy. The additions merely provide a source for Deuteronomy's quotation. For the cases in the tabernacle narrative, we can observe some similarities in that the alterations are made in Exod 25–31 rather than 35–40.

the Old Greek of Exod 35–40 where the Old Greek diverges significantly from both the Masoretic and Samaritan versions, which differ from one another in only minor details. For those small differences between the two Hebrew versions, the Old Greek shows no tendency to align with one rather than the other.[38] Consequently the tabernacle account has a distinctive profile within the Pentateuch for elsewhere the Old Greek often agrees with the Samaritan Pentateuch against the Masoretic Text.[39]

The main issue that has faced interpreters is how to account for the differences between the Old Greek text and the Hebrew versions in Exod 35–40, a problem described by Wevers as 'one of the most complex mysteries in the entire Greek OT'.[40] The most conspicuous difference between the two versions is in the ordering of the material. In the Old Greek, the priestly garments are fabricated at the beginning (𝕲 36.8–38) rather than at the end (𝔐 39.1–31). The courtyard is manufactured (𝕲 37.7–18) before the furniture of the tabernacle (𝕲 38.1–26), but the reverse order is found in the Masoretic Text (𝔐 38.9–20; 37.1–38.8). The differences in order are especially to be found in 36.8–39.43 and these are represented in the table on the following page.

Besides structuring the tabernacle's construction according to a different logic, the Old Greek is also significantly shorter than the Masoretic edition. It lacks most of the details about the curtains and frames of the tent (𝕲 37.1–2; 𝔐 38.9–20) and a description of the incense altar's manufacture (𝔐 37.25–28). Some verses are shorter in the Old Greek, and others present in the Masoretic edition are entirely missing (𝔐 35.8; 37.12, 24; 38.2, 6; 39.39; 40.7, 11, 28). In a few places, however, the Old Greek edition has a text that has no parallel in the Masoretic edition: the manufacture of metal accessories in the tent and courtyard (𝕲 38.18–20), the association of the bronze altar with Korah's rebellion (𝕲 38.22b), and the manufacture of the leftover gold into utensils (𝕲 39.12).

The critical question is whether the Old Greek version provides insight into the history of the Hebrew text. If the Old Greek is a sloppy, sub-standard translation of a Hebrew *Vorlage* similar to the Masoretic Text or if its rendering of Exod

---

[38] Kyung-Rae Kim, 'Studies in the Relationship between the Samaritan Pentateuch and the Septuagint' (Hebrew University Jerusalem, PhD diss., 1994), 86–150.

[39] Tov's analysis of Genesis, Exod 1–24 and Leviticus finds a correlation between the Septuagint and Samaritan Pentateuch in secondary, harmonizing additions which he thinks suggests a common textual base (Emanuel Tov, 'The Shared Tradition of the Septuagint and the Samaritan Pentateuch', in *Die Septuaginta: Orte und Intentionen*, eds. Siegfried Kreuzer et al., WUNT 361 [Tübingen: Mohr Siebeck, 2016], 277–93; Emanuel Tov, 'From Popular Jewish LXX-SP Texts to Separate Sectarian Texts: Insights from the Dead Sea Scrolls', in *The Samaritan Pentateuch and the Dead Sea Scrolls*, ed. Michael Langlois, CBET 94 [Leuven: Peeters, 2019], 19–40).

[40] Wevers, 'The Building of the Tabernacle', 123. Unsurprisingly, the problem has been the subject of numerous technical studies. Reviews of the scholarly literature can be found in Martha Wade, *Consistency of Translation Techniques in the Tabernacle Accounts of Exodus in the Old Greek*, SCS 49 (Leiden: Brill, 2003), 4–10; Brandon E. Bruning, 'The Making of the Mishkan: The Old Greek Text of Exodus 35–40 and the Literary History of the Pentateuch' (University of Notre Dame, PhD diss., 2014), 41–101; Lo Sardo, *Post-Priestly Additions*, 11–25.

50   THE MAKING OF THE TABERNACLE

Table 2.1 Comparison of the Old Greek and Masoretic Text

Old Greek Edition	Masoretic Edition
Priestly vestments (𝕲 36.8–38)	
Tent curtains (𝕲 37.1–2)	Tent curtains (𝔐 36.8–19)
Ø	Frames and bars (𝔐 36.20–34)
Veil and veil of the entrance (𝕲 37.3–6)	Veil and screen (𝔐 36.35–38)
Courtyard (𝕲 37.7–18)	
The two workmen (𝕲 37.19–21)	
Ark (𝕲 38.1–8)	Ark (𝔐 37.1–8)
Table (𝕲 38.9–12)	Table (𝔐 37.10–16)
Lampstand (𝕲 38.13–17)	Lampstand (𝔐 37.17–24)
Small metalwork (𝕲 38.18–21)	Ø
Bronze altar (𝕲 38.22–24)	
Ø	Incense altar (𝔐 37.25–28)
Oil and incense (𝕲 38.25)	Oil and incense (𝔐 37.29)
	Altar of burnt offering (𝔐 38.1–7)
Laver (𝕲 38.26–27)	Laver (𝔐 38.8)
	Courtyard (𝔐 38.9–20)
	Summary account (𝔐 38.21–23)
Accounting of the metal (𝕲 39.1–12)	Accounting of the metal (𝔐 38.24–31)
The remaining textiles (𝕲 39.13)	The remaining textiles (𝔐 39.1)
	Priestly vestments (𝔐 39.2–31)
Delivery to Moses (𝕲 39.14–23)	Delivery to Moses (𝔐 39.32–43)

35–40 is purely an internal development within the Greek tradition without any foothold in the Hebrew, the only light it will shed is on the Greek transmission history. In a detailed study, A.H. Finn argued that an examination of the two texts showed that 'the Hebrew is consistent and natural, the Greek confused and contradictory'.[41] The errors were to be laid at the door of the translators. Forty years later, however, David Gooding considered the differences to be an aberration introduced by a later editor who revised the original Greek translation. His assessment of the results is highly pejorative: there are instances of 'deliberate carelessness', 'first-class blundering', 'glaring mistakes', 'sheer nonsense', and 'howlers'.[42] One significant difficulty with the claims of Finn and Gooding is explaining why a Greek translator or editor would have introduced such infelicities.[43] There are good reasons to assume with John Wevers that 'the product of the Alexandrian translators was throughout sensible. Their translation may not have been perfect, but it made sense to them; they did not create nonsense, and when the modern reader is puzzled the fault must lie with him or her, not with the translator.'[44] We should take a similar approach when considering the work of editors. Occasionally ancient editors did introduce errors into a work, but it is far more common to find them removing contradictions and seeking to improve the text. The evidence from the Second Temple period supports the assumption that the more consistent text is usually to be regarded as the result of editing, rather than the reverse.

The relation of the Old Greek text to a Hebrew *Vorlage* is further complicated by the question of whether the translation of Exodus 1–34 was undertaken by someone different to the translator of Exod 35–40. The possibility of a different translator was first raised by Julius Popper in his seminal study on the tabernacle narratives. Popper thought that 𝔐 36.8–38.20 was the very last section of the Hebrew text of Exodus to be composed and had not been written when the first Greek translation was made. Consequently, these chapters had to be attributed to a second translator working later to revise the Old Greek towards the expanded Hebrew text.[45] Popper's proposals were simplified when they were taken up by

---

[41] A. H. Finn, 'The Tabernacle Chapters', *JTS* 16 (1915): 466.

[42] David W. Gooding, *The Account of the Tabernacle: Translation and Textual Problems of the Greek Exodus*, Texts and Studies: Contributions to Biblical and Patristic Literature 6 (Cambridge: Cambridge University Press, 1959), 21, 26, 40, 41.

[43] Finn seems not to have considered the issue, and they pose a particular problem for his analysis because he attributes the entire book of Exodus to one and the same translator. Why would the translator who adhered closely to the Hebrew text for the first thirty-four chapters of the book suddenly alter his translation practice so significantly? Gooding recognizes the issue raised by his proposal, but has no convincing answer. He concludes his study with a consideration of the 'dates, motives and methods of the editor', but the result is entirely unsatisfactory. He simply asserts that the editor was an incompetent blunderer: 'We therefore may not expect the present Greek order to reveal some consistent, highly detailed and accurately worked out plan; such a feat was beyond the intention, if not the ability, of the editor' (Gooding, *Account*, 101).

[44] Wevers, *Greek Text of Exodus*, xv.   [45] Popper, *Die biblische Bericht*.

52 THE MAKING OF THE TABERNACLE

other historical-critical scholars at the end of the nineteenth century. On literary-critical grounds they regarded the entirety of Exod 35–40 as a later development within the priestly tradition and attributed all six chapters to a later translator. Since then, the question of whether Greek Exodus had one or more translators has been regularly discussed. A comprehensive lexical and grammatical study by Martha Wade concludes that 'it seems likely that the second tabernacle account was produced by a second translator who used the translation of the first tabernacle account as a point of reference'. Nevertheless, she also observed 'the unity of the tabernacle accounts as seen in the general style and the context-sensitive approach' and posits a close relationship between the two translators, perhaps that of a master and a student.[46] But when the similarities between the two sections are so close that we must speak in terms of a master and a student, we may wonder whether the hypothesis of two translators needs a thorough reassessment. In the aftermath of Wade's careful analysis, it is a solution without a problem.

Importantly, the evidence Wade collects points to the Old Greek of Exod 35–40 as a careful attempt to render a Hebrew *Vorlage*. Broader trends within scholarship on the Hebrew Bible also point in this direction. The discoveries of the Dead Sea Scrolls have demonstrated that biblical books were circulating in various forms in the centuries around the turn of the era and have increased the scholarly confidence that the Greek translations of the Hebrew Bible reflect an underlying Hebrew text. As a result, those who specialize in textual criticism have come to regard the Old Greek of Exod 35–40 as an important witness to an alternative form of the text of Exodus circulating when the translation was undertaken.[47] Unfortunately, this recognition has been overlooked by most commentators on the Hebrew text.[48]

---

[46] Wade, *Consistency of Translation Techniques*, 243, 245.

[47] 'The OG for Exodus 35–40 revealed, not a confused text, but an earlier edition of those chapters than the edition in the MT.' (Eugene Ulrich, 'The Developmental Composition of the Biblical Text', in *The Dead Sea Scrolls and the Developmental Composition of the Bible*, VTSup 169 [Leiden: Brill, 2015], 9); 'The LXX thus represents an earlier phase in the development of the text.' (Anneli Aejmelaeus, 'Septuagintal Translation Techniques—A Solution to the Problem of the Tabernacle Account', in *Septuagint, Scrolls and Cognate Writings: Papers Presented to the International Symposium on the Septuagint and Its Relations to the Dead Sea Scrolls and Other Writings [Manchester, 1990]*, eds. George J. Brooke and Barnabas Lindars, SCS 33 [Atlanta: Scholars Press, 1992], 398). See also Russell David Nelson, 'Studies in the Development of the Text of the Tabernacle Account' (Harvard University, PhD diss., 1986); Bruning, 'Making'; Bogaert, 'L'importance de la Septante'.

[48] William Propp provides an excursus on the LXX, but only for the purposes of setting it to one side: 'I wish to circumvent the quagmire that is the LXX version of the tabernacle construction, and will content myself with describing the problems and referring the interested reader to detailed treatments' (William Henry Propp, *Exodus 19–40: A New Translation with Introduction and Commentary*, AB 2a [New Haven: Yale University Press, 2006], 631–7, esp. 631). Thomas Dozeman merely describes the problem of the two texts and proceeds to concern himself with the Masoretic Text, except for occasional observations about Greek translation equivalents (Thomas B. Dozeman, *Commentary on Exodus* [Grand Rapids, MI: Eerdmans, 2009], 595–6). Christoph Dohmen pays no attention to the issue (Christoph Dohmen, *Exodus 19–40*, HTKAT [Freiburg im Breisgau: Herder, 2004]). Cornelis Houtman discusses the differences between the Old Greek and the Masoretic Text, and notes their importance for assessing the literary-critical development of the tabernacle account. Despite its problematic features, a brief reference to Gooding's study leads him to the conclusion that 'it is doubtful whether on the basis

Should we judge the Hebrew *Vorlage* of Old Greek Exod 35–40 as earlier or later than the Masoretic Text? The clearest evidence that the Old Greek witnesses to a typologically earlier text can be found in the account of how the tabernacle furniture was manufactured (𝕲 38.1–24 ≈ 𝔐 37.1–38.8). Two features are significant. First, the Old Greek witnesses to a text that is shorter than the Masoretic Text. Second, the additional material brings the Masoretic Text closer to the instructions given to Moses in Exod 25–31. The most compelling way of understanding these interrelationships is that something like the *Vorlage* of the Old Greek is earlier and the Masoretic Text is a revision towards the instructions given to Moses. In this way the construction of the furniture in Exod 37–38 is made to correspond more completely to the instructions given in Exod 25–31. An instructive example is the treatment of the ark of the covenant and the atonement cover as seen in the table on the next page.

In the Old Greek, the manufacture of the ark and the propitiatory is described briefly. Many of the finer details such as the measurements are omitted.[49] The same account in the Masoretic Text is much fuller with the additional details (marked with italics) bringing it in line with the instructions given to Moses in Exod 25.10–21. The only elements of Exod 25 that are not incorporated into 𝔐 37.1–9 are the instructions that the poles are to remain in the rings permanently, the placement of the atonement cover upon the ark and the depositing of the covenant into the ark (marked with underlining). None of these are actions to be completed by Bezalel. God's directions that the poles are not to be removed is not an instruction about manufacturing the ark and does not need to be repeated in Exod 37.[50] The placement of the atonement cover and the covenant will be

of B-LXX one can postulate the existence of a version of Exod. 35–40 that differs from the MT'. As a result, the Greek text rarely appears in his commentary on Exod 25–31, 35–40 except in reference to lexicographical matters. (Cornelis Houtman, *Exodus*, 4 vols., HCOT [Kampen: Kok Pharos, 1993–2002], III: 316). In contrast, Rainer Albertz's commentary provides a brief, but detailed discussion of the relevance of the Old Greek for the literary-criticism of Exodus 35–40. Whilst I disagree with his arguments, Albertz does provide a detailed reasoning against regarding the Old Greek as a witness to a Hebrew *Vorlage* that is earlier than the Masoretic Text (Albertz, *Exodus 19–40*, 342–4).

[49] In v. 2 there is no reference to the gold moulding in 𝕲^B. Wevers restores the clause in his critical edition of the Old Greek arguing that this is a result of parablepsis 'and is hardly to be taken seriously. Only an exaggerated view of B's importance as a witness could induce anyone to regard the shorter text as original' (Wevers, *Text History of the Greek Exodus*, 257). But this omission is found in several Greek witnesses as well as the Old Latin manuscripts Lugdunensis and Monacensis. The problem is not an exaggerated view of 𝕲^B's importance, but Wevers' assumption that the Old Greek translators worked from something like the Masoretic Text. The shorter text of v. 5, where 𝕲^B lacks καθαροῦ might also be original and reflect the Old Greek's *Vorlage*, though omission might have taken place due to homoioteleuton (Wevers, *Text History of the Greek Exodus*, 257). In vv. 6–7, the main text has omitted χρυσοῦς from v. 6 and χερουβ ἕνα ἐπὶ τὸ ἄκρον τοῦ ἱλαστηρίου τὸ ἓν καὶ χερουβ from the beginning of v. 7. The error was corrected in the margin.

[50] *Contra* Eichler who assumes that a compliance report is lacking in 𝔐 37.5 (Raanan Eichler, 'The Poles of the Ark: On the Ins and Outs of a Textual Contradiction', *JBL* 135 [2016]: 734). It has long been thought that there is a contradiction between the instructions for the poles to remain permanently in the ark's rings (Exod 25.15; cf. 1 Kgs 8.7–8 // 2 Chron 5.8–9) and the requirement that the poles be inserted prior to transportation (Num 4.6). Eichler makes a compelling comparison to Egyptian portable chests to argue that the poles were retractable and that the ark's feet permitted the poles to rest underneath the ark when it was stationary. The expression ושמו בדיו in Num 4.6 means 'set up the poles' rather than 'put in its poles' (Eichler, 'Poles').

Table 2.2 The ark and atonement cover in the Old Greek and Masoretic Text

Old Greek (Construction)	Masoretic Text (Construction)	Masoretic Text (Instructions)
38.1 And Beselel made the ark.	37.1 And Bezalel made the ark of acacia wood, two and a half cubits long, a cubit and a half wide, and a cubit and a half high.	25.10 They shall make an ark of acacia wood, two and a half cubits long, a cubit and a half wide, and a cubit and half high.
2 He overlaid it with pure gold, inside and outside.	2 He overlaid it with pure gold, inside and outside, and he made for it a moulding of gold around.	11 You shall overlay it with pure gold, inside and outside you shall overlay it, and you shall make for it a moulding of gold around.
3 He cast for it four gold rings, two on one side of it and two on the second side.	3 He cast for it four rings of gold for its four feet, two rings on one side of it and two rings on the second side of it.	12 You shall cast for it four rings of gold and put them on its four feet, two rings on one side of it and two rings on the second side of it.
4 wide enough for the poles so as to carry it with them.	4 He made poles of acacia wood and he overlaid them with gold.	13 You shall make poles of acacia wood and you shall overlay them with gold.
	5 He placed the poles in the rings on the side of the ark to carry the ark.	14 You shall place the poles in the rings on the side of the ark to carry the ark.
		15 The poles shall remain in the rings of the ark; they shall not be removed from it.
		16 You shall put into the ark the covenant that I shall give you.
5 And he made the propitiatory above the ark from gold	6 He made the atonement cover of pure gold, two and a half cubits long and a cubit and a half wide.	17 You shall make the atonement cover of pure gold, two and a half cubits long and a cubit and a half wide.
6 and two <gold> cheroubim.	7 He made two gold cherubim, hammered work he made them, at the two ends of the atonement cover.	18 You shall make two gold cherubim, hammered work you shall make them, at the two ends of the atonement cover.
7 <One cheroub on one end of the propitiatory and> one <cheroub> on the second end of the propitiatory	8 One cherub at this end and one cherub at that end. At the two ends of the atonement cover he made the cherubim.	19 Make one cherub at this end and one cherub at that end. At the two ends of the atonement cover you shall make the cherubim.
8 overshadowing with their wings the propitiatory (𝔊 38.1–8).	9 The cherubim were spreading their wings above, covering with their wings the atonement cover. Each one faced the other, the faces of the cherubim were towards the atonement cover (𝔐 37.1–9).	20 The cherubim shall spread their wings above, covering with their wings the atonement cover. Each one faced the other, the faces of the cherubim were towards the atonement cover.
		21 You shall place the atonement cover upon the ark, and in the ark you shall put the covenant I shall give you (25.10–21).

completed by Moses in his assembling of the tabernacle: 'He took the covenant and put it in the ark, he placed the poles upon the ark, and set the atonement cover upon the ark' (𝔐 40.20). Although the changes in the Masoretic Text bring the construction report in line with the instructions given to Moses, the redactor has also inadvertently introduced a contradiction that was not present in the Old Greek's *Vorlage*. The Old Greek's *Vorlage* had Bezalel cast rings that could accommodate the poles.[51] The Masoretic Text, however, has these poles being put in their permanent position by Bezalel and, a few chapters later, by Moses when the tabernacle is assembled![52]

Further evidence that the Old Greek represents a typological earlier stage can be seen in the various lists of items in Exod 35–40. Altogether there are four lists: one short, one medium, and two long. The short list is found in the divine instructions to Moses to erect the tabernacle and it enumerates the main items of furniture, but without their auxiliary items, together with the dividing curtains and entrances (𝔊 40.1–6 ≈ 𝔐 40.1–8).[53] The medium list is found in Moses' erection of the tabernacle and also includes the various components of the tent (𝔊 40.16–27 ≈ 𝔐 40.18–33). The long lists are Moses' instructions to the skilled workers (𝔊 35.9–19 ≈ 𝔐 35.10–19) and the delivery of the items to Moses (𝔊 39.14–21 ≈ 𝔐 39.32–41). They enumerate not only various components of the tent, the furniture and their auxiliary items, but also the vestments of the priests.

In the Old Greek, the lists exhibit a considerable amount of variation in the enumerating of the items. Some items are mentioned more than once in the same list.[54] In the Masoretic Text, however, there are no examples of duplication. The Masoretic lists also show a significant amount of consistency with items being listed in a standard order which corresponds to the description of manufacture in the Masoretic version of Exod 36–39: tent, furniture, court, vestments. The commissioning of the skilled workers in Exod 35 gives a good sense of how different the Old Greek and Masoretic Text can be.

---

[51] This argument depends on determining the Old Greek's *Vorlage*. Characteristically, Wevers assumes that the translator had the same consonantal text as found in the Masoretic Text, and he regards εὐρεῖς, 'wide', as 'a free substitute' for ויבא (Wevers, *Greek Text of Exodus*, 621). If Wevers is correct, the problem was already present in the Old Greek's *Vorlage*. Bruning speculates that the translator or an earlier copyist might have read רחב for זהב (Bruning, 'Making', 163–4 n. 251), but Aejmelaeus' comparison with 𝔊 38.10 (≈ 𝔐 37.14), בתים לבדים, 'places for the poles', is more compelling (Aejmelaeus, 'Septuagintal Translation Techniques', 392; cf. Gooding, *Account*, 55).

[52] Most interpreters understand ויבא את־הבדים (𝔐 37.5; cf. Exod 25.14) to mean that the poles were inserted into the rings. Ehrlich argues, however, that it means they were designed to fit the rings. 'Hiph von בוא ist hier rein kausativ gebraucht und bezeichnet des Ermöglichen des Hineingehens. Gemeint ist die Hineinpassung der Stangen in die Ringe.' (Arnold B. Ehrlich, *Randglossen zur Hebräischen Bibel: Textkritisches, sprachliches und sachliches. Erster Band: Genesis und Exodus* [Hildesheim: Olms, 1968], 366).

[53] A similar, short list is found in 31.6–11, but it also includes the auxiliary vessels of the table, the lamp and the altar as well as the vestments of Aaron and his sons together with the anointing oil and fragrant incense. It does not list the dividing curtains.

[54] In the instructions to the skilled workers, Moses commands that the oil of anointing and the incense be manufactured twice (𝔊 35.14, 19), whilst Exod 39 describes vestments being delivered to Moses twice (𝔊 39.14, 19).

56 THE MAKING OF THE TABERNACLE

Table 2.3 The commissioning of the skilled workers in Old Greek and Masoretic Text

Old Greek	Masoretic Text
35.9 All who are skilled in heart amongst you come and make all that the Lord instructed: 10 the tent and the stretched covers <and the coverings> and the hooks and the bars and the pillars 11 and the ark of witness and its carrying poles and its propitiatory and the veil 12 and the hangings of the court and its pillars 13 and the stones of emerald 14 and the incense and the oil of anointing 15 and the table and all its utensils 16 and the lampstand of the light and all its utensils 17 and the altar and all its utensils 18 and the holy vestments of Aaron the priest and the vestments that they will minister in 19 and the tunics of the sons of Aaron of the priesthood and the oil of anointing and the incense of composition.	35.10 All who are skilled in mind amongst you shall come and make all that YHWH commanded: 11 the tabernacle, its tent and its covering, and its clasps and its frames, its bars, its pillars and its bases, 12 the ark and its poles, the atonement cover and the veil of the screen, 13 the table and its poles and all its utensils, and the bread of the presence, 14 and the lampstand of the light and its utensils and its lamps and the oil of the light 15 and the altar of incense and its poles and the anointing oil and the fragrant incense and the screen of the entrance for the entrance of the tabernacle, 16 the altar of burnt offering and the grating of bronze that belongs to it, its poles and all its utensils, the laver and its base, 17 the hangings of the court, its pillars and its bases, and the screen of the gate of the court, 18 the pegs of the tabernacle and the pegs of the court and their cords, 19 the finely-worked vestments for ministering in the holy place, the holy vestments for Aaron the priest and the vestments of his sons to serve as priests.

The Masoretic Text is better ordered, lacks any repetitions, and is fuller than its Old Greek equivalent.[55] These are all signs of editorial activity. It can also be observed, as has already been noted, that the Masoretic Text includes the altar of incense and the laver that are absent from the Old Greek.

If the Old Greek reflects a typologically earlier Hebrew text, it is not one without deficiencies. The most important example is the truncated account of the fabrication of the tents, curtains, and the panelling of the tabernacle. In the extant Hebrew texts the Israelite craftsmen, directed by Bezalel and Oholiab, produce the ten curtains that are fastened together to make the tabernacle itself (𝔐 36.8–13), the curtains for the tent that covered the tabernacle (𝔐 36.14–19), the wooden panels that enclosed the sanctuary (𝔐 36.20–34), the veil that separated the holy of holies from the outer room of the tabernacle (𝔐 36.35–36), and the screen at the opening of the tent (𝔐 36.37–38). In the Old Greek, however, the fabrication of the ten curtains is briefly mentioned followed by the veil and screen (𝕲 37.1–6):

---

[55] The original text of $𝕲^B$ omitted καὶ τὰ καλύμματα in v. 10, probably due to homoioteleuton. It was corrected with a marginal note.

THE TABERNACLE IN THE LATE SECOND TEMPLE PERIOD   57

1 And they made for the tent ten curtains. 2 Twenty-eight cubits was the length of one curtain. All were the same. Four cubits was the width of one curtain.

3 He made the veil from blue, purple, spun scarlet and twisted linen, work of a weaver with cheroubim. 4 They placed it upon four decay-resistant pillars, gold-plated with gold. Their capitals were gold and their four bases were silver.

5 They made the veil of the entrance of the tent of witness from blue, purple, spun scarlet and twister linen, work of a weaver with the cheroubim, 6 and their five pillars and their rings and their capitals they gold-plated with gold, and their five bases were bronze.

The absence of any account of how the tent of goat's hair, the covering, the panels or the bars were fabricated is puzzling, not least because, in the Greek version just as in the Hebrew versions, the workers hand over these items to Moses (𝔊 39.14, 20) for him to assemble (𝔊 40.16–17, 27). It seems most likely, therefore, that some text has been lost in the process of transmission. Since the Old Greek translator follows the extant Hebrew text closely in the material that they have in common, it seems unlikely that the translator was responsible for the changes.[56] But why was it missing from his *Vorlage*? There is no obvious ideological reason for the omission, and accidental loss seems the best explanation. Perhaps the repetition of 'from twisted linen, blue, purple, and crimson, with skilfully worked cherubim' (𝔐 36.8, 35) led to the loss of much of the intervening text?

The brief account in the Old Greek version of the manufacture of metal accessories in the tent and courtyard (𝔊 38.18–21) has often been poorly regarded. Much of Gooding's invective about the Greek translator had these verses in view, and even Wevers, who generally takes a high view of the translator of Exodus, is dissatisfied.

That there is something wrong about vv. 18–21 seems obvious. It will be recalled that the construction of the tabernacle had except for the statement of 37.1–2 been omitted and apparently [the Old Greek of] Exod is here trying to make up in part for the deficiency by detailing some of the metal work that was involved, but if that was its purpose it has been badly done since metalwork was involved in the construction of the courtyard, and the two are not kept apart. Furthermore the translator uses a separate vocabulary of translation throughout the chapter, and one is not always certain as to which detail in the Hebrew account...is actually intended.[57]

---

[56] Le Boulluec and Sandevoir, *L'Exode*, 358. *Contra* Wevers, *Greek Text of Exodus*, 610.
[57] Wevers, *Greek Text of Exodus*, 626.

58   THE MAKING OF THE TABERNACLE

On the other hand, Wade has argued that most of these difficulties can be explicated as the result of different translations of technical terms.[58]

Regarding their positive achievement, these verses are a remarkable compendium of all the pieces of metalwork mentioned in the tabernacle account outside of the main furniture, and, in broad terms, it moves from gold to silver and bronze items.

> **18** This one silver-plated the pillars and cast gold rings for the pillar[59] and gold-plated the bars with gold and gold-plated the pillars of the veil with gold and he made the gold hooks. **19** This one made the gold clasps of the tent, and the clasps of the courtyard, and the bronze clasps to spread out the covering above. **20** This one cast the silver capitals of the tent and the bronze capitals of the door of the tent and the gate of the courtyard and he made silver hooks of the pillars upon the pillars.[60] This one silver-plated them.[61] **21** This one made the bronze pegs of the courtyard.[62]

The opening clause in v. 18 is certainly problematic since it portrays Bezalel silver-plating the frames that provided rigidity to the tabernacle building. According to Exod 26.29, however, these were to be gold-plated. The most likely explanation is that this is the result of an early inner-Greek harmonization that confused the frames of the tabernacle with the pillars of the courtyard since the Hebrew terms for the frames, קרש, and the pillars, עמוד, were both translated into Greek with στῦλος.[63] An original reference to gold-plating would also be consistent with the rest of the verse which is concerned with gold-making. Also problematic is the reference to the 'clasps of the courtyard' (τοὺς κρίκους τῆς αὐλῆς) in v. 19, not least

---

[58] Wade, *Consistency of Translation Techniques*, 222–5.

[59] 𝕲[B] reads τῷ στύλῳ. In the Göttingen edition Wevers prefers the reading τοῖς στύλοις on the grounds that 'the plural is demanded by the sense of the passage' (Wevers, *Text History of the Greek Exodus*, 201). 𝕲[B]'s reading is probably to be preferred as the *lectio difficilior*. The use of the singular of στῦλος as a collective is also found at 𝕲 26.26–27 (Wade, *Consistency of Translation Techniques*, 223).

[60] 𝕲[B]'s reading τοῖς στύλοις ἀργυρᾶς ἐπὶ τῶν στύλων is tautologous and τοῖς στύλοις may be an expansion within the Greek tradition (Wevers, *Text History of the Greek Exodus*, 250).

[61] 𝕲[B] reads αὐτάς which must refer to the hooks. Since the hooks are silver, it makes no sense for them to have been silver-plated, and Wevers persuasively suggests that this reading 'was probably created by attraction to ἀγκύλας' (Wevers, *Greek Text of Exodus*, 628). The reading αὐτούς found in other Greek manuscripts was probably the original.

[62] 𝕲[B] has a solitary reading that lacks καὶ τοὺς πασσάλους τῆς σκηνῆς, 'the pegs of the tent'. This could be an omission due to homoioteleuton, but 𝕲[B] also lacks the pegs of the tent in 𝕲 27.19 and 37.18, where the equivalent verse in the Masoretic tradition mentions the pegs (𝔐 27.19; 38.20). Although 𝕲[B] does have the pegs of the tent in 𝕲 39.9, 𝔔[M] mentions only the pegs of the court, and may preserve an earlier reading that has been corrected towards the Masoretic edition in the extant Greek texts.

[63] Wade argues that the first clause of v. 18 refers to the pillars in the courtyard, whilst the second clause refers to the frames of the tabernacle building (Wade, *Consistency of Translation Techniques*, 223 n. 143). This does not explain why the courtyard pillars are twice described as being silver-plated (vv. 18, 20), or why the gold-plating of the frames was omitted. Bruning proposes that the Old Greek's *Vorlage* simply read הוא צפה את הקרשים with no metal specified for the overlaying (Bruning, 'Making', 172 n. 267). This solution does not commend itself, because in every place that צפ"ה occurs in the Hebrew text, the metal is clearly specified.

because it interrupts two references to the clasps that held the curtains and coverings over the tabernacle building (cf. 26.6, 14). It cannot be the hooks in the courtyard, even though these are also rendered with κρίκος (e.g. ⑬ 27.10), for they will be referred to in v. 20. Most compelling is Bruning's suggestion that the translator's *Vorlage* referred to the 'clasps of the tent', and the translation with 'clasps of the courtyard' reflects the difficulties the translator faced when rendering close occurrences of אהל, 'tent', and, משכן, 'dwelling', since he used σκηνή, 'tent', to translate both.[64] The final problem occurs in v. 20 where κεφαλίς, 'head', appears to refer to the bases of the frames and the pillars. Yet, as Wevers observes, κεφαλίς is used to render the Hebrew term אדן, 'bases', and is understood in the sense of extremities. Indeed, when Exod 26.19 described the frames of the tabernacle sitting in two bases, the Greek translator has understood this to refer to the two ends of a pillar: the capital and the base.[65] Thus, despite some exegetical challenges, ⑬ 38.18–21 is far from being 'sheer nonsense' as Gooding would have it,[66] and should be regarded as an attempt to render an underlying Hebrew text. Indeed, it is harder to explain how the text could have arisen solely in the Greek tradition, because had the translator simply had the Greek text of Exod 26 before him the result would have been quite different.[67] It is also the case that the repeated οὗτος, 'this one', which Gooding describes as 'unnecessarily emphatic',[68] is explicable as a translation of הוא followed by the perfect, and more difficult to understand as a stylistic choice in Greek without a Hebrew *Vorlage*.[69]

In conclusion, there are good reasons to think that the Old Greek version reflects a Hebrew *Vorlage*. The Greek translation was not shoddy or sub-standard. Nor was the text corrupted during the procession of transmission in Greek. Many of the problematic texts within the Old Greek version can be explained and the only significant corruption was the loss of the tent coverings, frames and bars in ⑬ 37.1–6. In other respects, the Old Greek reflects a typological earlier Hebrew text with less standardization and briefer compliance accounts organized according to a different set of principles.

The Old Latin Version and the Old Greek Version

Amongst the versions that we have examined, the Old Latin sits closest to the Old Greek. Although the unique readings of Monacensis had been known since the late nineteenth century, it is only in recent decades that Bogaert has emphasized the particular importance of its readings for the textual history of the tabernacle account. In his view, Monacensis provides a witness to the original Old Greek and

---

[64] Bruning, 'Making', 174 n. 271. [65] Wevers, *Greek Text of Exodus*, 627.
[66] Gooding, *Account*, 40. [67] Lo Sardo, *Post-Priestly Additions*, 55.
[68] Gooding, *Account*, 47. [69] Aejmelaeus, 'Septuagintal Translation Techniques', 393–4.

60 THE MAKING OF THE TABERNACLE

consequently to a Hebrew *Vorlage* which would be the earliest version of the tabernacle account. Since the interior of the sanctuary in Monacensis is unlike any version of the instructions, Bogaert speculates that the book of Exodus may have originally lacked the instructions in Exod 25–31.[70] After the addition of these chapters, the divergence of the sanctuary's portrayal in the compliance account led to the removal of this material from Exod 37 resulting in the truncated account of the tabernacle building in the Old Greek.[71] Whilst Bogaert's proposals have been adopted with various degrees of caution by Nihan, Trebolle Barrera, and Lo Sardo, they have recently been questioned by Rhyder.[72]

Despite its unique readings, there are at least two reasons for thinking that Monacensis does reflect a Hebrew original, and is not simply an idiosyncratic development of the text that occurred during the text's Latin or Greek transmission. First, in several sections the Old Latin text corresponds closely to the Old Greek with the most frequent cause for divergence being homoioteleuton. Both features suggest that the Old Latin translator sought to render the Greek in a competent manner and any mistakes were accidental. Second, for Exod 40.3 Monacensis has the reading *et pones arcam testamenti et super eam propitiatorium*, 'You shall place the ark of testimony and upon it the atonement cover' ($\mathfrak{L}^M$ 28/2/1–3). Codex Vaticanus and every extant Greek witness, however, has a reference to the 'veil', $\kappa\alpha\tau\alpha\pi\acute{\epsilon}\tau\alpha\sigma\mu\alpha$. The variant in Monacensis most likely derives from an unattested Greek text which came from a Hebrew text that rea read כַּפֹּרֶת, 'atonement cover', a reading found in the Samaritan version, rather than פְּרֹכֶת, 'veil'. In other words, the variant in Monacensis reflects a different Hebrew *Vorlage* than the extant Greek manuscripts have.

The consensus amongst Septuagint scholars is that a single translation of the Torah was made into Greek and subsequently revised towards the Hebrew text as it developed. This was the position of Lagarde and stands in contrast to Kahle's alternative proposal that multiple translations were made and subsequently standardized.[73] Within the dominant Lagardian paradigm, Monacensis is best

---

[70] This part of Bogaert's theory is the most tendentious. In Monacensis the text of Exodus survives for 9.15–10.24; 12.28–14.4; 16.10–20.4; 31.15–33,7 in addition to 36.13–40.32. Ziegler was able to determine that the original codex had been produced in quaternions (Ziegler, *Bruchstücke*, iii–iv). Since Exod 25–31 would have taken approximately eight leaves, it is theoretically possible that these chapters were absent from Monacensis (Bogaert, 'L'importance de la Septante', 425).

[71] Bogaert, 'L'importance de la Septante'; Pierre-Maurice Bogaert, 'La construction de la tente (Ex 36–40) dans le Monacensis de la plus ancienne version Latine: L'autel d'or et Hébreux 9,4', in *L'enfance de la Bible hébraïque. L'histoire du texte de l'Ancien Testament à la lumière des recherches récentes*, eds. Adrian Schenker and Philippe Hugo, MdB 52 (Geneva: Labor et Fides, 2005), 62–76.

[72] Christophe Nihan, *From Priestly Torah to Pentateuch: A Study in the Composition of the Book of Leviticus*, FAT II/25 (Tübingen: Mohr Siebeck, 2007), 32; Trebolle Barrera, '2.5.1 Vetus Latina'; Lo Sardo, *Post-Priestly Additions*; Julia Rhyder, *Centralizing the Cult: The Holiness Legislation in Leviticus 17–26*, FAT 134 (Tübingen: Mohr Siebeck, 2019), 50–2.

[73] Paul de Lagarde, *Anmerkungen zur griechischen Übersetzung der Proverbien* (Leipzig: Brockhaus, 1863), 1–4; Paul Kahle, 'Untersuchungen zur Geschichte des Pentateuchtextes', *TSK* 88 (1915): 399–439; Paul Kahle, *The Cairo Geniza* (Oxford: Blackwell, 1959), 174–9. The situation with books outside the Torah is often more complex, see Natalio Fernández Marcos, *Scribes and Translators: Septuagint and Old Latin in the Books of Kings*, VTSup 54 (Leiden: Brill, 1994), 15–26.

regarded as a witness to the original old Greek translation. The text preserved in Vaticanus must have endured at least one revision. The question is whether this revision was towards a Hebrew text that was typological earlier than the one from which Monacensis was translated. Bogaert supposes that an earlier Greek text implies an earlier Hebrew text-type. But this cannot be assumed given what we know about textual plurality in the Second Temple period such that at Qumran, for example, the same work could be available in different text-types of varying ages.

The most significant divergence between the Old Latin of Monacensis and the Old Greek concerns the interior of the sanctuary. Where the Old Greek has a brief account of the sanctuary that describes the tent, the veil, and the entrance of the tent, Monacensis details two cherubim stationed on pillars in the holy of holies and two seraphim located in the outer sanctum ($\mathfrak{L}^M$ 22/2/1–23/1/24). The portrayal of the seraphim as a matching pair of divine guardians clearly draws upon Isaiah's description of the divine throne in Isaiah 6. As Bogaert recognizes, this perspective on the sanctuary's interior is also apparent in the portrayal of Beseel's fabrication of the ark, the atonement cover, and the cherubim in $\mathfrak{L}^M$ 24/2/18–25/1/9. There too the cherubim are described as mounted on pillars. The distinctive portrayal of the sanctuary has probably also influenced the accounting of the metal in $\mathfrak{L}^M$ 26/2/2–27/2/8 for additional columns are mentioned and the silver needed for the work is a greater quantity than that found in the other versions.

Although Bogaert argues that Monacensis portrays the earliest description of the tabernacle's interior, there are several reasons for regarding it as typological later. First, the portrayal in Monacensis appears to assume the truncated text witnessed in the Old Greek, rearranging it and augmenting it. Thus, the description of the tent in $\mathfrak{G}$ 37.1–2 is reproduced in $\mathfrak{L}^M$ 22/2/1–7, the veil in $\mathfrak{G}$ 37.3–4 is mentioned in $\mathfrak{L}^M$ 23/1/17–24, and the door of the tabernacle in $\mathfrak{G}$ 37.5–6 is portrayed in $\mathfrak{L}^M$ 22/2/10–18. Second, the tabernacle with the seraphim in the outer sanctum appears to be a conscious attempt to harmonize the desert sanctuary with the description of the temple in Isaiah 6. Third, as we have seen, Monacensis' vision of the sanctuary has been incorporated throughout Exod 36–40: it witnesses to a broad, thoroughgoing redaction of the tabernacle account. Its removal to produce the revised text of the Old Greek would have required extensive literary-critical intervention across Exod 36–40. Were that to have occurred, we would expect its removal to have left some literary-critical trace in the revised text of the Old Greek. But there is none. As a result, it is much easier to view the unique portrayal of Monacensis as a revision of a text similar to the Old Greek, rather than the reverse. Finally, there are places where Monacensis probably refers to architectural features that are known from the descriptions of the sanctuary in the Hebrew texts that are lacking in the Old Greek and Old Latin compliance accounts. The manufacture of metalwork is fragmentary, but refers to the 'g[old] rings' (*anulos aur[eos]*), that held the bars for the frames ($\mathfrak{L}^M$ 25/2/12; $\mathfrak{G}$ 38.18). Similarly, Moses' erection of the tent is also fragmentary, but $\mathfrak{L}^M$ 29/2/2–11 appears to follow $\mathfrak{G}$ 40.16–17 sufficiently closely that we can restore with reasonable confidence a reference to

62   THE MAKING OF THE TABERNACLE

the bars: *et inmisit s[erras]*. These seem to presuppose a tent structure such as we find in the Masoretic Text or the Old Greek of Exod 25–31.

In my view, it is most convincing to regard the unique perspective on the tabernacle's interior in Monacensis as an attempt to fill the lacuna which we see in the Old Greek of Exod 37. It is a redactional layer that augmented a text that was quite similar to the Old Greek without excising those elements that bore witness to an alternative conception of the tabernacle. The correlation of the interior of the tabernacle with that of the temple is a similar instinct to that found in the Temple Scroll (11QT). In light of this similarity to the Temple Scroll, we are probably justified in seeing this redaction having its origins in a Palestinian milieu at a stage prior to the text's translation into Greek. If the major plus in the account of the sanctuary provides sufficient evidence that Monacensis is typological later than the Old Greek, this does not mean that this is necessarily true of all its readings. Without this redactional layer, we have a text that is close to the Old Greek in its structure and contents. Nevertheless, as the example of the reading of *propitiatorium* in Exod 40.3 shows, Monacensis preserves a text that goes back to the Hebrew, even whilst disagreeing with the Old Greek. As such, it can witness to important readings that need to be evaluated alongside the other versions.

One example of where the critical utilization of Monacensis might be helpful is the vexed question about the original location of the fabrication of the priestly vestments, one of the most significant divergences between the Hebrew textual traditions and the Old Greek version. In the Masoretic and Samaritan texts the priestly vestments occur after the tabernacle has been made, whilst in the Old Greek version it occurs at the beginning. There is, however, in the Old Greek a brief reference to the fabrication of the vestments at the place where the Hebrew versions locate them:

καὶ τὴν καταλειφθεῖσαν ὑάκινθον καὶ πορφύραν καὶ τὸ κόκκινον ἐποίησαν στολὰς λειτουργικὰς Ααρων ὥστε λειτουργεῖν ἐν αὐταῖς ἐν τῷ ἁγίῳ.

And the left-over blue, purple and scarlet they made into ministry robes for Aaron so as to minister in them in the holy place (𝕲 39.13).

For those who argue that the Old Greek text is a later and corrupted version of something like the Masoretic Text, this would appear to be decisive evidence that the Masoretic Text reflects the original order. The reference to the vestments in 𝕲 39.13 is a fragment that was inadvertently left behind when the fabrication of the vestments was relocated from after the tabernacle and its furniture to before it.[74]

The corresponding Hebrew verse has indications that the matter may be more complex than it first appears.

---

[74] Gooding, *Account*, 85–98.

THE TABERNACLE IN THE LATE SECOND TEMPLE PERIOD   63

וּמִן־הַתְּכֵלֶת וְהָאַרְגָּמָן וְתוֹלַעַת הַשָּׁנִי עָשׂוּ בִגְדֵי־שְׂרָד לְשָׁרֵת בַּקֹּדֶשׁ וַיַּעֲשׂוּ אֶת־בִּגְדֵי הַקֹּדֶשׁ אֲשֶׁר לְאַהֲרֹן
כַּאֲשֶׁר צִוָּה יְהוָה אֶת־מֹשֶׁה

And from the blue, purple and crimson they made *serad*-vestments for service
in the holy place and they made the holy vestments for Aaron   (𝔐 39.1).

The meaning of שְׂרָד, *serad*, is uncertain,[75] and the repetition of the verb 'to make',
עָשׂוּ...וַיַּעֲשׂוּ, would appear to distinguish the בִגְדֵי־שְׂרָד, *serad*-vestments, from
Aaron's vestments. A number of medieval Jewish interpreters also observed that
linen was a crucial component of the high priestly vestments and its absence here
suggests that the בִּגְדֵי־שְׂרָד must be something other than Aaron's dress. Instead of
understanding the בִּגְדֵי־שְׂרָד as a reference to the high priest's apparel, they identified
them with the wrappers that covered the sacred furniture prior to their transportation, for which the term בגדים is also used (Num 4).[76]

The identification of the בִּגְדֵי־שְׂרָד with the covering cloths is an intriguing intu-
ition of the medieval interpreters, not least because on every occasion that the
בִּגְדֵי־שְׂרָד appear in the Masoretic Text they are associated with the vestments of
Aaron and his sons (𝔐 31.10; 35.19; 39.1, 41). As a result, many modern interpreters understand the בִּגְדֵי־שְׂרָד as a comprehensive term for the vestments of
Aaron and his sons.[77] Yet, there are reasons for thinking that the meaning of
בִּגְדֵי־שְׂרָד has shifted whilst the text of the tabernacle account was developing, not
least because the meaning of שְׂרָד was obscure even in the Second Temple period.[78]
Important evidence comes from the Old Greek version.[79] First, the בִּגְדֵי־שְׂרָד are made
from the blue, purple, and crimson yarns that were left over. This characterization
would be rather strange for the cultically significant items of the high priestly
vestments, but appropriate for wrappers for the tabernacle furniture. Second,
the mention of the wrappers at this point in the Old Greek version is entirely

[75] Baentsch described the term as 'ganz rätselhaft' (Bruno Baentsch, *Exodus-Leviticus-Numeri*,
HKAT I.2 [Göttingen: Vandenhoeck & Ruprecht, 1903], 266). For a brief outline of different proposals
see Othniel Margalith, 'בגדי שְׂרָד = Fine Linen from Colchis?', *ZAW* 95 (1983): 430–1.

[76] So, e.g., Rashi on Exod 31.10 writes, 'I think that the plain sense of the verse cannot possibly
understand this phrase to refer to the priestly vestments, since the continuation refers to them: "and
the garments of holiness for Aaron the priest, and the garments of his sons to minister as priests". The
בגדי שרד must be the blue, purple, and crimson covers mentioned in Num 4…My explanation is
supported by 39.1, where it is said "from the blue, purple, and crimson yarns they made בגדי שרד
for service in the holy place"—but linen is not mentioned. It would not have omitted linen from
among them, if it were speaking of the priestly vestments' (cf. Michael Carasik, *Exodus שמות*, The
Commentators' Bible: The JPS Miqra'ot Gedolot [Philadelphia: Jewish Publication Society of
America, 2005], 276–7). Ibn Ezra and Rashbam are similarly minded, but Nahmanides rejected
Rashi's proposal.

[77] E.g. Propp, *Exodus 19–40*, 490–1; Houtman, *Exodus*, III: 348–9; Haran, *Temples*, 172–3.

[78] The translators of the Old Greek render שְׂרָד with either λειτουργικός (𝔊 31.10; 39.12) or
λειτουργέω (𝔊 35.19), as though they had read שָׁרֵת (Le Boulluec and Sandevoir, *L'Exode*, 315–16). The
same interpretive tradition is reflected in the Targums which translate with שמושא. A handful of
Samaritan Pentateuch manuscripts read שרת for שרד at 31.10; whilst the Nablus 6 manuscript reads
שרת at 35.19 and 39.41 (but not at 31.10).

[79] As already perceived by Popper, *Die biblische Bericht*, 160–3.

64 THE MAKING OF THE TABERNACLE

appropriate, since the following section describes how the artisans delivered all the items to Moses (𝕲 39.14–21). To complete the delivery, the furniture would need to be covered. Third, the list of items delivered to Moses in the Old Greek mentions the 'robes', στολαί, twice: at the beginning of the list, which are the στολαί made from the left-over yarns (𝕲 39.13–14), and later in the list, where they refer to the robes of Aaron and his sons (𝕲 39.19). If the Old Greek is not simply repetitious, the στολαί refer to different items: the wrappers and the priestly vestments.

Monacensis provides further evidence that the בִּגְדֵי־שְׂרָד are wrappers for the furniture. Its equivalent for the fabrication of the wrappers is fragmentary, but has a distinctive reading:

> Et quae rem[anserant hia]cinti purp[urae et cocci] fecerunt s[tolas sacerdo]tales ad mi[nistrandum] leuuitis in [sancto].

> And what wa[s left of the hya]cinth, purp[le, and scarlet] was made into [sac]red r[obes] for the min[istry of] the Levites in [the sanctuary]   (𝔏ᴹ 27/2/4–8).[80]

Where the Old Greek refers to Aaron, Monacensis refers to the Levites. Arguably, the Hebrew versions preserve the shorter and better text which simply refers to 'ministry in the sanctuary' (לְשָׁרֵת בַּקֹּדֶשׁ). Old Greek and Monacensis attest to additions that seek to clarify what ministry is in view. Monacensis reflects an understanding that the *stolas sacredotales*, that is the בִּגְדֵי־שְׂרָד, were associated with the ministry of the Levites. In the Pentateuch, the Levites are not provided with special vestments,[81] and we should probably see in Monacensis a reference to the wrappings of Num 4. These wrappings (בגדים) were essential to the Levites' service in the sanctuary.[82]

In conclusion, the Old Latin text of Monacensis has a text that is very close to that of the Old Greek. Typologically it has a more developed account of the tabernacle with an attempt to harmonize the tent with the temple of Isaiah 6. Occasionally, however, some of its readings may preserve an earlier text than that found in the Old Greek of Vaticanus.

---

[80] For the reconstruction see Dold, 'Versucht', 53.

[81] For their part, both Bogaert and Lo Sardo think Monacensis refers to vestments worn by the Levites (Bogaert, 'L'importance de la Septante', 418–19; Lo Sardo, *Post-Priestly Additions*, 102–3).

[82] The same understanding is also found in Josephus. After an account of the high priestly vestments and before describing the anointing and consecration of the tabernacle, Josephus describes the making of the coverings for the tabernacle furniture: Ὅσα δὲ τῶν πρὸς τὴν τῆς σκηνῆς κατασκευὴν παρεσκευασμένων ἦν περιττά, ταῦτ' ἐκέλευσεν εἰς φάρση σκεπαστήρια τῆς τε σκηνῆς αὐτῆς καὶ τῆς λυχνίας καὶ τοῦ θυμιατηρίου καὶ τῶν ἄλλων σκευῶν ἀναλῶσαι. 'As for the surplus materials provided for the tent, these he ordered to be spent on protective coverings for the tent itself and the lamp and the incense altar and for the other vessels' (*Ant* 3.193–4). This appears to be a clear allusion to 𝕲 39.13.

Conclusion

Each of the late antique and medieval versions of the tabernacle account that we examined in the previous chapter have been shown to have their roots in the Second Temple period. The Old Greek and the Old Latin (without its novel account of the tabernacle's interior) are typologically the earliest versions of the tabernacle account. The two texts are clearly very close to one another, even if they do not always share identical readings. They probably shared a common ancestor rather than one being in the direct lineage of the other.

The text preserved in the Masoretic edition reflects a substantial revision away from the text witnessed to by the Old Greek and Old Latin. The construction of the tabernacle has been described according to a different logic determined not by the materials and the master craftsmen, but by the sanctity of the sanctuary and its furniture. The sanctuary must be constructed first before the furniture that will furnish it. In some respects, ordering the material in this way seems unnecessary since the individual items will be handed over to Moses who will erect the tent and install the furniture in the tabernacle. It does, however, bring the construction account into a closer alignment with the instructions, albeit with the order of furniture and tent reversed. The concern to align the instructions and the construction account is apparent in the other amendments that appear in the Masoretic edition. The vestments for the priesthood are fabricated after the tabernacle and its furniture replicating the order in Exod 25–28. The brief accounts of the fabrication of the furniture are revised with much fuller accounts that align closely with the instructions. Finally, the listing of items is standardized.

The Samaritan version's differences from the Masoretic version of the tabernacle show that it continued this process of standardization and alignment between instructions and construction. The unexplained origins of the Urim and Thummim is resolved, and the incense altar is relocated so that it finds its place amongst the other furniture of the tabernacle and as a counterpart to the altar of burnt offering.

Typologically the Samaritan version is the very latest of the four versions of the tabernacle account that we have examined. Despite that, the earliest text of the tabernacle account that has been recovered amongst the Dead Sea Scrolls, 4Q17, has a text that shows expansions beyond the Masoretic version and may correspond in significant respects with the Samaritan version. The fragmentary nature of 4Q17 means that we cannot be certain whether it had all the distinctive features of the Samaritan version. Were this to be the case, it would suggest that the development of the tabernacle account that we have traced in our four versions was complete by the third century BCE. If the earliest version of the priestly document is to be dated no earlier than the late sixth century BCE, this indicates that over the course of less than three centuries the tabernacle account was subjected to a significant degree of scribal reworking. This would be true, were we to consider only the evidence from our four different versions. But a closer examination suggests that even the earliest version of the tabernacle account, witnessed to by the Old Greek and the Old Latin, evidences a complex history of composition. It is to this history that we will turn in the next chapter.

3

The Making of the Tabernacle Account

The changing shape of the text of Exodus provides eloquent testimony to the tabernacle account's importance for Jewish scribes in the Second Temple period. The extant manuscripts show that the scribes often faced troubling textual gaps and inconsistencies that they sought to rectify in order to produce a smoother and more harmonious text. The understandable inclination of scribes to improve the text's consistency—whether for literary or theological reasons—provides an important clue for assessing the relationship of the different versions to one another. This can be readily seen in the case of the Samaritan Pentateuch where the addition or relocation of textual material clearly seeks to resolve what were perceived to be problems with a text somewhat similar to that which we find in the Masoretic version. As Popper had argued already in the nineteenth century, the very same dynamics can be seen at work in the Masoretic version when compared to the Old Greek.[1] The Masoretic version brings instructions and compliance into closer alignment and gives lists a consistent order.

In light of the evidence that scribes sought to produce a consistent and harmonious text, we are faced with the obvious conundrum of how such a problematic text arose in the first place. The most compelling explanation is that even the earliest tabernacle account witnessed to by the Old Greek and the Old Latin is not the product of a single author. Instead, it was the result of a complex process of editing and redaction. In other words, the extant versions provide only a glimpse into the final stages of the tabernacle account's journey. For the earlier stages we are reliant for the identification of compositional layers on the internal evidence of tensions and aporias.

Unfortunately, the literary-critical analysis of the tabernacle account has for far too long been deficient.[2] Too often, commentators have been content simply to attribute the instructions in Exod 30–31 together with the compliance report in Exod 35–39 and most of Exod 40 to a secondary level of the priestly literature. This tendency is already apparent in the work of Wellhausen whose primary concern was distinguishing the original priestly document from secondary material. He was certain that the secondary material in Exod 30–31, 35–39 did not belong to a

---

[1] Popper, *Die biblische Bericht*.
[2] Noted most recently by Rainer Albertz, 'Beobachtungen zur Komposition der priesterlichen Texte Ex 25–40', in *Pentateuchstudien*, ed. Jakob Wöhrle, FAT 117 (Tübingen: Mohr Siebeck, 2018), 277. Exod 25–31 has generally received more attention than 35–40.

The Making of the Tabernacle and the Construction of Priestly Hegemony. Nathan MacDonald, Oxford University Press.
© Nathan MacDonald 2023. DOI: 10.1093/oso/9780198813859.003.0004

68 THE MAKING OF THE TABERNACLE

single compositional level, but had little interest in differentiating different layers.[3] In his judgement, Exod 35–39 was probably a later composition than Exod 30–31 and was 'a mere repetition of Exod. 25–28…with a more mechanical order'.[4] Kuenen went somewhat further observing that Exod 35–39 was 'gradually elaborated' and that 'the question of the origin of Exod xxxv–xl is very difficult and involved' with 'traces of more than one hand'.[5] There have, however, been very few attempts to try and distinguish the different compositional layers.[6]

Two notable exceptions have been Baentsch and Albertz.[7] According to Baentsch the original priestly document (P) was mostly to be identified in the instruction account (Exod 25–29*) with a small number of verses from the compliance account.[8] This had been supplemented extensively with textual material especially concerned with cultic practice, including Exod 30–31; 35–36.8a*; 39.1b–40.38* (P^s). The compliance account had not originally included any description of the fabrication of the tent and its furniture, and this had been copied rather mechanically from Exod 25–27 with only verbal changes to make the instructions into actions.[9] The summary accounting of the materials (38.21–39.1) and the provision of materials by the people (35.20–29) were still later additions.[10]

Albertz identifies a number of tensions in the tabernacle account, especially in the instructions, but observes that the compliance account is better ordered. Whilst most analyses of the tabernacle account have been content to identify a handful of verses in Exod 35–40 that belonged to the original priestly document

---

[3] Julius Wellhausen, *Die Composition des Hexateuchs und der historischen Bücher des Alten Testaments*, 3rd edn (Berlin: Reimer, 1899), 135–47. Wellhausen's chief interlocuter was Nöldeke who was content to attribute both Exod 25–31 and 35–40 to the priestly *Grundschrift* (Theodor Nöldeke, *Untersuchungen zur Kritik des Alten Testaments* [Kiel: Schwers'sche Buchhandlung, 1869], 54–61).

[4] 'Eine blosse Wiederholung von Exod. 25–28…in mehr mechanischer Ordnung' (Wellhausen, *Composition*, 142).

[5] Abraham Kuenen, *An Historico-Critical Inquiry into the Origin and Composition of the Hexateuch (Pentateuch and Book of Joshua)* (London: Macmillan, 1886), 73, 76, 79.

[6] Holzinger dismissed the value of such exercises out of hand: 'Es ist ohne Interesse und aussichtlos, die Aufschichtungen in c. 35ff. unterscheiden zu wollen' (H. Holzinger, *Exodus*, KHAT 2 [Tübingen: Mohr Siebeck, 1900], 148). Like Wellhausen, he was only interested in discerning traces of P^g. These he found in Exod 25.1–27.19*; 28.1–29.35*; 31.18a; 35.4–7, 9–10, 20–29*; 36.2–3*, 8; 39.32, 43; 40.1–2, 16–17, 33b, 34 (35?) (Holzinger, *Exodus*, xix).

[7] In his commentary Galling sought to apply von Rad's identification of two priestly sources, P^A and P^B, as well as identifying supplementary material, P^s (Georg Beer and Kurt Galling, *Exodus*, HAT 3 [Tübingen: Mohr Siebeck, 1939], 128–53, 165–79). The attempt is as unsatisfactory here as it is elsewhere in the priestly corpus. Certainly it fails to do justice to what Kuenen rightly highlights as textual problems that are 'difficult and involved', and as Galling himself admits of Exod 35–40, 'die beiden Fassungen P^A und P^B sind nicht mehr intakt auf uns gekommen' (Beer and Galling, *Exodus*, 165). Interestingly, Galling's analysis departs from the consensus that Exod 30–31 was earlier than Exod 35–40. Galling attributes Exod 30–31 to P^s and most of Exod 35–40 to P^A und P^B.

[8] Exod 39.32b–33a, 42–43; 40.17, 34–35.

[9] This proposal originated with Popper, *Die biblische Bericht*.

[10] For a brief summary see Baentsch, *Exodus-Leviticus-Numeri*, 287. The Claremont dissertation by McCrory on Exod 35–40 is strongly influenced by Baentsch's analysis. McCrory attributes 35.4–9, 20–29 to the priestly *Grundschrift*, but otherwise follows Baentsch closely (Jefferson Harrell McCrory, 'The Composition of Exodus 35–40' [Claremont Graduate School, PhD diss., 1989]).

and to assume a slow accretion of material, Albertz rightly observes that such models would result in a compliance account that had aporias and tensions that betrayed its origins. As a result, Albertz reaches for a different solution. The majority of the tabernacle material was composed by a single editor incorporating at least three different sources: one sanctuary text that consisted of instructions about the tent and its furniture (Exod 25.10–27.19*); another that had instructions about the incense altar, the laver, the oil, and the incense (Exod 30*); and a developed version of the golden calf story (Exod 32–34*). These sources were incorporated with the editor's own contributions about the high priest's clothing and ordination (Exod 28–29*). In the compliance account, the editor integrated the instructions for the tabernacle, its furniture and the priestly vestments in order to present the Israelites as fully obedient to what God commanded after their egregious sin of worshipping the golden calf. This editorial composition was subject to some later redactions. The original editor envisaged only Aaron being anointed, but a subsequent redaction extended that privilege to his sons.[11] At a later stage, some additions were made that aligned the tabernacle account with the Holiness Code (Lev 17–26), including the instructions about the Sabbath that frame the story of the golden calf.[12] Somewhat later still, a number of further additions were appended that are mostly concerned with financial provision for the tabernacle and also reflect attempts to align the tabernacle account with the opening chapters of Numbers.[13]

Despite their very different approaches, both Baentsch and Albertz regard the Old Greek of Exodus 35–40 as a secondary development, and consequently set it to one side in trying to understand the compositional history of the tabernacle account.[14] This has significant consequences for their analysis, since, as we have

---

[11] Exod 28.41*; 29.21, 36b; 30.26–30; 40.1–16.

[12] Exod 27.20–21; 29.38–42; 31.12–17; 35.1b–4a. [13] Exod 29.27–30; 30.11–16; 38.21–31.

[14] Baentsch dismisses the Old Greek because of the view that Exod 35–39 was undertaken by a different translator than Exod 25–31 (Baentsch, *Exodus-Leviticus-Numeri*, xli–xlii). Even if this were the case, it hardly provides a sufficient basis to exclude the witness of the Old Greek. Albertz, in contrast, sets out his reasons for believing that the Old Greek does not go back to an older Hebrew *Vorlage* than the Masoretic Text in a detailed excursus in his commentary. I do not find his arguments compelling. First, Albertz argues that even where the Greek version deviates most substantially from the Masoretic Text it presupposes it. His first example is that in both Greek and Hebrew versions the account of the priestly vestments in the compliance account concludes with the diadem and its inscription 'Holy to ʏʜᴡʜ' (𝔊 36.38–40; 𝔐 39.30–31) rather than the linen undergarments (28.36–43). This suggests that for both versions the vestments play a climactic role in the compliance account, and presuppose the Masoretic ordering with the vestments as the final items manufactured. This argument overlooks the evidence that the reference to the undergarments is secondary in Exod 28 and, thus, both the compliance accounts of the Old Greek and the Masoretic Text reflect the earlier text of the instructions. His second example is the reference to Ithamar (𝔊 37.19–21; 𝔐 38.21–23) which relates to the record of costs that follow in 𝔐 38.24–31, but are located elsewhere in the Old Greek (𝔊 39.1–11). To my mind, Albertz rather too easily assumes that 𝔐 38.21–23 is an introduction to what follows, rather than a conclusion of what preceded. The medieval Jewish commentators already disagreed on this issue and the textual history provides some insight into these exegetical debates. His third example is the account of the making of the laver, which seems to repeat the laver's manufacture within the space of a couple of verses (𝔊 38.26–27). Albertz argues that this can be

70 THE MAKING OF THE TABERNACLE

seen, the smoothness of the compliance account is the result of systematic editing to align the instructions and their enactment, and to produce lists with a consistent order. The Old Greek of Exod 35–40 contains precisely the tensions and aporias that provide evidence of the growth of the tabernacle account, and which Albertz observes are lacking in the Masoretic Text.

Setting aside the important text-critical evidence provided by the Old Greek is an almost universal feature of critical commentaries on Exodus. In the light of the analysis by Popper, Kuenen and Wellhausen, earlier commentators pointed to the Old Greek text as evidence that the end of the book of Exodus was fluid even at the time the Pentateuch was being translated into Greek. But its value was limited to demonstrating the secondary nature of Exod 35–39.[15] Since the middle of the twentieth century, however, the technical issues raised by the Old Greek translation and the suspicion that there might be a second translator has led to a growing hesitancy amongst commentators to address the differences between the Greek and the Hebrew texts.[16] As we have seen, however, this reticence stands in striking contrast to the increasing number of text-critics who think that the Old Greek—and sometimes the Old Latin—witnesses to an earlier stage of the tabernacle account. Consequently, as Nihan observes, 'a thorough study of this problem requires a much more comprehensive approach, going beyond the isolation of a few verses to address the text- and literary-critical problems jointly. To my knowledge this has never been done.'[17] This will be the primary

---

explained by the relocation of the details about the laver's use from 𝔐 40.30–31 to 𝔊 38.27. Albertz's proposal would be rather more convincing were 𝔐 40.30–31 to have included a reference to the laver being manufactured, but it speaks only of the laver being 'set up'. Second, Albertz argues that the Old Greek version is not complete and needs the Masoretic Text to make sense. His first example is the lack of any mention of the panelling that supported the curtains of the tent (𝔊 37.1–6). The Old Greek does appear to have suffered some textual damage, not least because the items are assumed to have been manufactured in 𝔊 39.14, 20. It is not clear that this is sufficient to judge the rest of the Greek text as later. His second example is the absence of an account of the incense altar's fabrication in the Old Greek despite it being presupposed in 𝔊 39.16; 40.6, 24. In my view, the absence of the incense altar at certain points in comparison to the Masoretic Text is confirmation of the altar's late arrival in the tabernacle account and evidence that the Masoretic Text has been reworked to produce a more consistent text. The same is also true of Albertz's further examples: the laver and the gate of the court. Finally, Albertz observes that the Old Greek includes transparently later traditions such as the use of the bronze firepans of Korah's followers to plate the altar of burnt offering (𝔊 38.22). But comparably late material is also to be found in the Masoretic Text (e.g. the use of the mirrors of the women to make the laver [𝔊 38.26; 𝔐 38.8]; the account of the census [Exod 31.11–16]) and is evidence only that the tabernacle account, and especially the compliance account, continued to develop quite late in the Pentateuch's history of composition.

[15] E.g. A.H. McNeile, *The Book of Exodus: With Introduction and Notes*, 3rd edn, WC (London: Methuen, 1931), 223–6; Samuel R. Driver, *The Book of Exodus*, CBC (Cambridge: Cambridge University Press, 1911), 378–9.

[16] Childs, for example, contrasted Gooding's negative assessment of the Old Greek translation with the more positive assessment of earlier scholarship to argue for separating the literary-critical issues from the text-critical ones (Brevard Springs Childs, *Exodus: A Commentary*, OTL [London: SCM, 1974], 530). More recently, Propp and Dozeman are content to summarize the findings of Wade (Wade, *Consistency of Translation Techniques*) and on this basis ignore the textual evidence of the Old Greek (Propp, *Exodus 19–40*, 631–7; Dozeman, *Commentary on Exodus*, 595).

[17] Nihan, *Priestly Torah*, 58.

Evidence of Literary-Critical Development

There are a number of indicators that the tabernacle account has a complex history of development. These include the number and identification of fabricators, the different names of the sanctuary, the untimely appearance of the incense altar and laver, the different ways in which the fulfilment of the instructions are presented, the presence of narrative anachronisms, and the inclusion of the golden calf narrative in Exod 32–34. This is not a comprehensive list of indicators, but it is sufficient to highlight the evidence for literary growth and will provide the basis for a model of the tabernacle account's composition.

The Fabricators of the Sanctuary

The first literary problem that confronts the reader of the texts is the question of who precisely fabricates the tabernacle. In all the extant versions, the instructions are given to Moses and it is he who is directed to manufacture the tabernacle, its furniture, and the priestly vestments (Exod 25–31). In the compliance account, however, these instructions are fulfilled by the master craftsmen Bezalel and Oholiab supported by skilled artisans (Exod 35–39). The completed articles are then delivered to Moses who assembles them (Exod 40). Of course, it might not be thought entirely inappropriate that Moses might be addressed directly and commissioned to build the tabernacle, even if he did not do so himself. He was after all the appointed leader of the Israelites and the chosen recipient of divine revelation. Nevertheless, the differences between the versions show that the problem runs deeper, and early readers were not unaware of the problems in the portrayal.

For the instructions, the Masoretic version exhibits the greatest diversity. In the opening of Exod 25, God directs the people to collect the materials with which they will construct the tabernacle (vv. 1–9). The detailed instructions that follow about the fabrication open with 'they shall make' (וְעָשׂוּ; v. 10), but immediately switch to instructions to Moses alone, 'you shall overlay it' (וְצִפִּיתָ; v. 11), a perspective that is maintained for most of Exod 25–27.[18] A very similar phenomenon

---

[18] The exceptions are a second person plural in 25.19 ('from the atonement cover you shall make the cherubim upon the two ends', מִן־הַכַּפֹּרֶת תַּעֲשׂוּ אֶת־הַכְּרֻבִים עַל־שְׁנֵי קְצוֹתָיו) and a third person plural in 27.8 ('so they shall make', כֵּן יַעֲשׂוּ). At 25.19 both ⵿𝔚[D] and 𝕲[B] read the expected singular, but the plural in 𝔐[L] is to be preferred as the *lectio difficilior*. For 27.8, 𝔐[L] shifts uncomfortably from singular to plural within the space of a verse: תַּעֲשֶׂה אֹתוֹ...כֵּן יַעֲשׂוּ (cf. 𝔚[D]). 𝕲[B] has the smoother reading ποιήσεις

72 THE MAKING OF THE TABERNACLE

occurs with the fabrication of the priestly vestments in Exod 28. The majority of the instructions are directed to Moses alone (28.2, 9–43), but in vv. 3–5 Moses is to commission 'all the highly skilled' (כָּל־חַכְמֵי־לֵב) to undertake the work. In the detailed instructions, they are enjoined to construct the ephod in v. 6, but after that disappear from view. Thus, we have the same pattern for both the tabernacle and the priestly vestments. The bulk of the instructions are directed at Moses alone, but both begin with a different perspective that suggests it should, in fact, be the people who complete the task.

Whilst the Old Greek also portrays the skilled artisans being directed to fabricate the vestments in Exod 28, the opening of the instructions about the tabernacle and its furniture is directed to Moses alone. The Old Greek consistently reads a second person singular, 'you shall make' ($\pi o \iota \acute{\eta} \sigma \epsilon \iota s$) at the beginning of Exod 25 where the Masoretic version has a plural (𝕲 25.7–9; 𝔐 25.8–10). The Samaritan Pentateuch presents a mixed picture with vv. 9 and 10 in the singular, but v. 8 in the plural.

It is particularly, however, in the compliance account that complexities arise. These are already prefigured to a degree with the introduction of a further perspective at the end of the instructions (31.1–11). God informs Moses that he has chosen Bezalel ben Uri ben Hur of the tribe of Judah and Oholiab ben Ahisamach of the tribe of Dan together with all the highly skilled artisans to complete the task of constructing the tabernacle.

In the report of the tabernacle's construction, Moses is hardly to be seen and Bezalel, Oholiab, and the highly skilled artisans emerge centre-stage. Nevertheless, the oscillation between singular and plural continues in all the extant versions, but now between the individual Bezalel and the artisans. In the Hebrew of the Masoretic Text, the highly skilled workers begin the work on the tabernacle curtains (𝔐 36.8), but are quickly occluded by an unidentified individual craftsman (𝔐 36.10) who fabricates the curtains, the veil, the screen, and the frames for the courtyard. The manufacturer of the tabernacle's furniture, however, is explicitly identified as Bezalel (𝔐 38.1). As we have seen, 4Q365 attributes the oil and the altar of burnt offering to the skilled artisans rather than Bezalel. Whether the other metal items are attributed to the group is uncertain. Whilst there are occasionally singular verbs in the Masoretic Text, the vestments are portrayed primarily as the creation of the people.

$\alpha \dot{v} \tau \acute{o} \ldots o \ddot{v} \tau \omega s \ \pi o \iota \acute{\eta} \sigma \epsilon \iota s \ \alpha \dot{v} \tau \acute{o}$. The additional $\alpha \dot{v} \tau \acute{o}$ was probably a secondary assimilation to the first $\pi o \iota \acute{\eta} \sigma \epsilon \iota s \ \alpha \dot{v} \tau \acute{o}$. Other Greek manuscripts, including 𝕲[A] lack the second $\alpha \dot{v} \tau \acute{o}$. This would suggest that the Old Greek translator might have read כן תעשה at the end of the verse (cf. 26.4). Although the reading of 𝔐[L] appears to be the *lectio difficilior*, it is likely that כֵּן יַעֲשׂו was treated as an *inclusio* to 25.8–10 and experienced some of the same dynamics of revision as the construction was attributed to the Israelites. Thus, in this case, 𝕲[B] probably preserves the original reading (Baentsch, *Exodus-Leviticus-Numeri*, 234). An alternative understanding sees the third person plural as 'impersonal' (Wevers, *Greek Text of Exodus*, 434; cf. NRSV).

THE MAKING OF THE TABERNACLE ACCOUNT   73

In the Old Greek compliance account the vestments are fabricated first and are also presented primarily as the people's work.[19] The people are also involved in the making of the tents and curtains (𝕲 37.1–18), but the construction of all the tabernacle furniture and the metalwork is attributed to Bezalel (𝕲 38.1–39.10).[20] After the description of Bezalel's activities, a colophon attributes the work to the Israelites (𝕲 39.11) and the plural verbs re-emerge for a brief reference to the manufacture of the cultic vessels and the priestly vestments (𝕲 39.12–13). In the Old Latin of Monacensis a clear division of labour between Bezalel and Oholiab emerges with Bezalel responsible for the metalwork and Oholiab responsible for the textiles and woodwork.[21]

How is the attribution of the work to Moses alone in Exod 25–31 and to the people and their master craftsmen in Exod 35–39 to be squared? The two perspectives are harmonized in Exod 39–40 by distinguishing between the fabrication of the tabernacle's component parts and their erection into a functioning sanctuary. The people bring the articles they have manufactured to Moses who verified that they had been made according to the instructions he received (𝔐 39.32–42 ≈ 𝕲 39.14–23). Moses alone sets up the tabernacle and consecrates it for cultic service (Exod 40).

Different Names for the Sanctuary

The attentive reader of the Hebrew tabernacle account will observe that two different names are used for the sanctuary that Moses is to construct. The opening exhortation to Moses and the people speaks in the broadest possible terms: 'make for me a sanctuary' (25.8). The Hebrew term for sanctuary, מִקְדָּשׁ, describes something that has been consecrated as holy, קד״שׁ. After this broad exhortation the instructions fall neatly into two blocks of material using different nomenclature. In the instructions to fabricate the sanctuary and its furniture in 25.10–27.19, YHWH speaks exclusively of the 'dwelling' (הַמִּשְׁכָּן).[22] In the directions about the consecration of the priests as well as the conduct of the regular cult in 27.20–29.42, however, we encounter the expression 'the tent of meeting' (אֹהֶל מוֹעֵד).[23]

---

[19] The distribution of singular and plural verbs in the Masoretic Text and Old Greek do not correspond. In the Masoretic Text, the verbs are plural with the exception of 𝔐 39.2, 3aβ, 7, 8, 22. In the Old Greek, the verbs are plural with the exception of 𝕲 36.9, 14, 29, 39. The only case that coincides in the two versions is 𝔐 39.7 ≈ 𝕲 36.14.

[20] The sole exception is 𝕲 39.6, which Wevers describes as 'an indefinite plural' (Wevers, *Greek Text of Exodus*, 635) and is corrected towards the Hebrew in some manuscripts.

[21] Bogaert, 'L'importance de la Septante'.

[22] Exod 25.9; 26.1, 6, 7, 12, 13, 15, 17, 18, 20, 22, 23, 26, 27²; 30, 35; 27.9, 19.

[23] Exod 27.21; 28.43; 29.4, 10, 11, 30, 32, 42.

74   THE MAKING OF THE TABERNACLE

Whatever the prior history of these terms,[24] these two names for the sanctuary are understood in the Masoretic Text to reflect two different, but complementary understandings of the sanctuary's purpose as is apparent in the concluding theological reflection in Exod 29.43–46:

> **43** I will meet (וְנֹעַדְתִּי)[25] with the Israelites there and it will be sanctified by my glory. **44** I will consecrate the tent of meeting and the altar. Aaron and his sons I will also consecrate to serve me as priests. **45** I will dwell (וְשָׁכַנְתִּי)[26] among the Israelites and I will be their god. **46** They shall know that I am YHWH their god who brought them out of the land of Egypt to dwell in their midst; I am YHWH their god.

The מוֹעֵד of אֹהֶל מוֹעֵד could conceivably be a festival (i.e. an appointed time), an assembly (i.e. an appointed meeting) or a place, but is here related to the idea of two parties meeting together; the 'tent of meeting' (אֹהֶל מוֹעֵד) is the place where YHWH and the Israelites encounter one another. The term seems particularly appropriate for texts that concern the consecration of the priests. Of all the Israelites, it is the priests through their cultic service who encounter the divine. מִשְׁכָּן is related to the root שכ״ן, 'to dwell', and it is understood to mean that YHWH will dwell amongst the Israelites in the fabricated tent. Again, this term seems particularly appropriate for texts that prescribe the furniture of the sanctuary. The ark, table, lamps and altar are constructed in order to make the tabernacle a comfortable home for YHWH to occupy.

Although the two terms have been coordinated with one another as expressions of divine presence,[27] the tabernacle account also preserves evidence of a level at which the two were not related. The instructions concerning the tabernacle describe the tabernacle proper as a fabric consisting of ten curtains joined together and given shape by wooden frames (26.1–6, 15–25). Over this fabric is placed a 'tent' (אֹהֶל) consisting of eleven curtains made of goat's hair (26.7–14). This 'tent' is just one part of the 'dwelling' (הַמִּשְׁכָּן) of Exod 25–27 and distinct from the 'tent of meeting' (אֹהֶל מוֹעֵד) in Exod 28–29 which describes the entire sanctuary structure.

---

[24] There has been significant discussion about the possible history of the expression אֹהֶל מוֹעֵד. Clifford, for example, observes that at Ugarit the tent of El was envisaged as the meeting place of the divine assembly (*phr m'd*) and it is possible that this lies in the background of the tradition (Clifford, 'Tent of El').

[25] The text is somewhat uncertain. 𝔊^D reads נדרשתי and understands the tent of meeting as the place where YHWH may be consulted by oracle. 𝔊^B reads τάξομαι, 'I will appoint', and whilst the Old Greek translator does not seem to be rendering a *niphal*, it seems possible that it is seeking to translate some form of יע״ד (cf. 1 Sam 20.35; 2 Sam 20.5).

[26] 𝔊^B reads καὶ ἐπικληθήσομαι, 'I will be invoked'. Wevers thinks that the translator may be avoiding 'a somewhat overly corporeal figure' (Wevers, *Greek Text of Exodus*, 487; cf. Le Boulluec and Sandevoir, *L'Exode*, 303).

[27] Lo Sardo, *Post-Priestly Additions*, 201–30. It is necessary to hold neither that the two terms were used 'indiscriminately, without intending any difference in meaning' (Haran, *Temples*, 272) nor that they represent 'two orientations towards divine presence' that are in tension with one another (Sommer, 'Conflicting Constructions', 56).

THE MAKING OF THE TABERNACLE ACCOUNT   75

If we turn to the remaining chapters of the tabernacle account, the distribution of the two expressions is rather more complex. For the remaining instructions in Exod 30–31, only the expression 'tent of meeting' is used, and this is in keeping with Exod 28–29 for most of these instructions concern particular prerogatives of the priests. In the compliance account of Exod 36–39, the appearance of the two expressions often reflects the usage in the corresponding instructions of Exod 25–31. Thus, in Exod 36 'dwelling' (הַמִּשְׁכָּן) is used for the completion of the tent structure prescribed in Exod 26,[28] whilst in 35.21; 38.8 'tent of meeting' (אֹהֶל מוֹעֵד) is used in relation to cultic service.[29] Finally, in the deliverance of the completed articles to Moses and the erection of them into a sanctuary (39.32–40.35), the two expressions are blended into a composite expression 'the dwelling of the tent of meeting' (מִשְׁכַּן אֹהֶל מוֹעֵד [Exod 39.32; 40.2, 6, 29] or הַמִּשְׁכָּן לְאֹהֶל מוֹעֵד [Exod 39.40]), or are used as synonyms (Exod 40.22, 24, 34, 35). Finally, in 38.21 we encounter a distinctive term, מִשְׁכַּן הָעֵדֻת, 'the dwelling of the treaty', which is only otherwise found in the book of Numbers.[30]

The Old Greek version (and consequently the Old Latin) sheds only limited light on the two expressions due to the fact that both אהל, 'tent', and משכן, 'dwelling', were translated into Greek with σκηνή. At a few points the lack of differentiation presented the translator with a challenge. Thus, for example, in 26.7 where the 'tent' is a discrete component of the 'dwelling', the translator renders אֹהֶל with σκεπή, 'cover',[31] and in 𝕲 40.17, the Old Greek has τὰς αὐλαίας ἐπὶ τὴν σκηνὴν where the Masoretic Text has 'the tent over the dwelling' (אֶת־הָאֹהֶל עַל־הַמִּשְׁכָּן; 𝔐 40.19). Both examples reveal the playful sophistication of the Greek translator. In Exod 26.7 the translator forms a subtle paronomasia between σκηνή and σκεπή, whilst in 𝕲 40.17 he chooses the homologous αὐλαία to represent אֹהֶל. From the perspective of the readers of the Old Greek, however, the shift of terminology that is a noticeable feature of the Hebrew versions of Exod 25–40 was obscured: in some places, the reader encountered simply σκηνή and in other places, the longer expression σκηνὴ τοῦ μαρτυρίου, 'the tent of witness'. Since σκηνή is not a natural translation of הַמִּשְׁכָּן, the translator's rendering appears to have been informed by the synonymous usage found in Exod 39–40.[32]

The Untimely Appearance of Exod 30–31

It has long been recognized that the instructions for the incense altar (30.1–10) and the laver (30.17–21) do not appear in their logical place in the Masoretic and

---

[28] Exod 36.8, 13, 14, 20, 22, 23, 25, 27, 28, 31, 32.   [29] E.g., Exod 35.21; 38.8.
[30] Num 1.50, 53[2]; 10.11 (cf. אֹהֶל הָעֵדֻת; Num 9.15; 17.22, 23; 18.2).
[31] Wevers, Greek Text of Exodus, 415.
[32] For this translation see Larry Perkins, 'The Translation of משכן/אהל מועד and שכן in Greek Exodus', JSCS 48 (2015): 8–26.

76 THE MAKING OF THE TABERNACLE

Old Greek versions.[33] Since the incense altar is to be placed in the outer sanctum in front of the veil (30.6), its instructions should have been relayed together with the table and the lampstand in Exod 25. The laver is to be placed between the tent and the altar of burnt offering (30.18) and consequently we would have expected its instructions to have appeared together with those for the altar in Exod 27. Some discomfort with the position of the incense altar is apparent in the Samaritan version and in 4Q22, both of which place the instructions at the end of Exod 26. This does not seem an entirely satisfactory location either. It comes in the middle of instructions for the positioning of the tabernacle furniture rather than their construction. In addition, it assumes the activities of the high priest whose vestments and ordination have not yet been described.[34]

That the tabernacle was originally envisaged with just a single altar is confirmed by the frequent identification of the altar of burnt offering as 'the altar' (הַמִּזְבֵּחַ) in Exod 27–29. A single altar also appears to be presupposed in Lev 1–3, 8–9, and 16. In the compliance account in Exod 35–40, a distinction is made between two altars. They are distinguished either by the sacrifice offered on them—'the altar of incense' (מִזְבַּח הַקְּטֹרֶת), and 'the altar of burnt offering' (מִזְבַּח הָעֹלָה)[35]—or by the metal overlaid upon them—'the altar of gold' (מִזְבַּח הַזָּהָב) and the 'altar of bronze' (מִזְבַּח הַנְּחֹשֶׁת).[36]

In the Masoretic version's compliance report in 𝔐 37–38, both the incense altar and the laver appear in their expected places: the altar of incense after the lampstand (𝔐 37.25–28) and the laver after the altar of burnt offering (𝔐 38.8). The Old Greek, however, lacks any account of the altar of incense being made. It does, however, describe the construction of a 'bronze altar' (τὸ θυσιαστήριον τὸ χαλκοῦν), which seems to imply knowledge of the gold, incense altar (𝔊 38.22–24), and the laver (𝔊 38.26–27). The Old Greek version lacks the altar and laver in

---

[33] See already Wellhausen, *Composition*, 137–41. Carol Meyers has argued that the identification of the incense altar as a secondary element cannot be maintained (Carol L. Meyers, 'Realms of Sanctity: The Case of the "Misplaced" Incense Altar in the Tabernacle Texts of Exodus', in *Texts, Temples, and Traditions: A Tribute to Menahem Haran*, eds. Michael V. Fox et al. [Winona Lake, IN: Eisenbrauns, 1996], 33–46; Carol L. Meyers, 'Framing Aaron: Incense Altar and Lamp Oil in the Tabernacle Texts', in *Sacred History, Sacred Literature: Essays on Ancient Israel, the Bible, and Religion in Honor of R. E. Friedman on His Sixtieth Birthday*, ed. Shawna Dolansky [Winona Lake, IN: Eisenbrauns, 2008], 13–21). Whilst earlier critical scholars often drew the conclusion that the incense cult was a late innovation that only emerged in the Persian period, Meyers rightly observes that archaeological finds since Wellhausen's time have provided extensive evidence for small incense altars from Iron Age II like that portrayed in Exod 30.1–10. Further, Meyers' observations seek to address Wellhausen's literary-critical observations. She offers various arguments to explain the anomalous position of the incense altar. First, the altar was used for annual purgation (Exod 30.9) and not just for the daily cult. Second, it had a close relationship with the bronze altar, and the blood that was daubed on it (Lev 4–5) must have been borne in bronze basins. Consequently, the incense cult occupied a transitional position in the graduated zones of holiness. I am not convinced that either argument dispels the literary-critical observations about Exod 30–31. The first shows that Exod 30.9 had knowledge of Lev 16 which was probably not part of the Priestly *Grundschrift*. The second entails a reconstruction of the temple cult drawing on texts from across the Hebrew Bible. There are various questionable steps in Meyer's reconstruction and the resulting picture is a mosaic, rather than the tabernacle cult as imagined by the priestly writer.

[34] Albertz, 'Beobachtungen', 284–5.   [35] Exod 30.27–28; 31.8–9; 35.15–16; 38.1; 40.6, 10, 29.

[36] Exod 38.30; 39.38–39; 40.5, 26.

some of the lists where they are present in the Masoretic version:[37] it is missing from the list of items that Moses requires of the Israelites (𝕲 35.17, cf. 𝔐 35.15) and those handed over to him after their fabrication (𝕲 39.16, cf. 𝔐 39.38).[38] The incense altar is, however, named amongst the items that Moses is commanded to assemble (𝕲 40.5 ≈ 𝔐 40.5) and there is a corresponding report of Moses' compliance (𝕲 40.24 ≈ 𝔐 40.26). The laver, on the other hand, is lacking from the list of items delivered to Moses (cf. 𝔐 39.39), the items to be erected (cf. 𝔐 40.7, 30) and anointed by Moses (cf. 𝔐 40.11). In the case of both the incense altar and the laver, the Old Greek appears to witness to a stage of the text where these two items are less embedded in the compliance account. Intriguingly, however, the pattern of distribution for the incense altar is almost the inverse of the laver. With the exception of the delivery of the manufactured items to Moses, the incense altar is present where the laver is absent, and absent where the laver is present.

The Portrayal of Fulfilment

In the compliance account, the fulfilment of YHWH's instructions can be portrayed in different ways.[39] In the Masoretic version of Exod 36–38 the fabrication of the tabernacle and its furniture is represented through an almost verbatim fulfilment of the instructions of Exod 25–27, 30–31. A representative example is the instructions and manufacture of the table (Table 3.1).

Table 3.1 The table in MT: instructions and manufacture

Instructions (Exod 25.23–30)	Construction (Exod 37.10–16)
25.23 You shall make a table of acacia wood, two cubits long, one cubit wide, and a cubit and a half high. 24 And you shall overlay it with pure gold and you shall make for it a gold moulding around. 25 And you shall make for it a rim, a handbreadth around, and you shall make a gold moulding around its rim. 26 And you shall make for it four gold rings, and you	37.10 He made a table of acacia wood, two cubits long, one cubit wide, and a cubit and a half high. 11 And he overlaid it with pure gold and he made for it a gold moulding around. 12 And he made for it a rim, a handbreadth around, and he made a gold moulding around its rim. 13 And *he cast* for it four gold rings,

Continued

---

[37] An intriguing case is found in the list of items to be manufactured by the artisans in Exod 31.1–11. The Old Greek version refers to 'the altars' (τὰ θυσιαστήρια; 𝕲 31.8). The Masoretic version reads וְאֵת מִזְבַּח הַקְּטֹרֶת וְאֶת־מִזְבַּח הָעֹלָה (𝔐 31.8–9). Since there are some Greek texts that read the singular, it is worth considering whether the singular is original and the plural an early misreading or assimilation towards the developing Hebrew text.

[38] Wevers rightly observes that the altar mentioned in 𝕲 35.17 and 39.16 should probably be identified as the altar of burnt offerings (Wevers, *Greek Text of Exodus*, 580, 640; *contra* Le Boulluec and Sandevoir, *L'Exode*, 371). This is seen clearly through the reference to 'its utensils', since it is only the altar of burnt offering which is said to have 'utensils' (כלי/σκεῦος; Exod 27.3; 30.28; 𝔐 31.9; 𝔐 35.16≈ 𝕲 35.17; 𝔐 38.3≈ 𝕲 38.23; 𝔐 38.30; 𝔐 39.39; 𝔐 40.10≈ 𝕲 40.8).

[39] See already Popper, *Die biblische Bericht*, 140–65.

78 THE MAKING OF THE TABERNACLE

Table 3.1 *Continued*

Instructions (Exod 25.23–30)	Construction (Exod 37.10–16)
shall place the rings upon the four corners at its four legs. 27 The rings will be close to the rim, holders for the poles to carry the table. 28 And you shall make the poles of acacia wood, and you shall overlay them with gold. The table will be lifted by them. 29 And you shall make its dishes, and its ladles, and its jars, and its jugs with which to make libations. You shall make them of pure gold. 30 You shall place upon the table the bread of presence before me always.	and he placed the rings upon the four corners at its four legs. 14 The rings were close to the rim, holders for the poles to carry the table. 15 And he made the poles of acacia wood, and he overlaid them with gold. The table will be lifted by them. 16 And he made *the utensils that were upon the table:* its dishes, and its ladles, and its jars, and its jugs with which to make libations of pure gold.

The differences between the instructions and the manufacture of the table are very minor. For the manufacture of the rings, 37.13 uses the verb יצ״ק, 'to cast', whilst 25.26 uses עש״ה, 'to make'. The change brings the table in line with the ark which also had rings for carrying poles, and these rings were said to be 'cast', both in the instruction and the compliance account (25.12; 37.3). The instruction to make the dishes, ladles, jars, and jugs for the table has also been rephrased so as to place them under the general term הַכֵּלִים, 'the utensils'. The reason would appear to be that in the various lists of the tabernacle items, the auxiliary items that sat upon the table are summarized as 'its utensils' (31.8; 35.13; 39.36). The arranging of the bread upon the table (25.30) is absent from the construction report since it appears in the report of Moses' erection of the tabernacle (Exod 40.23).

As we have seen, it is particularly in Exod 36–38 that the Old Greek departs most conspicuously from the Masoretic version, and we have fulfilment accounts that are less detailed and do not correspond closely to the instructions in Exod 25–31. The table is fairly typical (Table 3.2).

Table 3.2 The table in OG: instructions and manufacture

Instructions (𝕲 25.22–29)	Construction (𝕲 38.9–12)
25.22 You shall make a table of pure gold, two cubits the length, one cubit the width, and a cubit and a half the height. 23 And you shall make for it twisted gold moulding around. And you shall make for it a rim, a handbreadth around, 24 and you shall make twisted moulding around its rim. 25 And you shall make for it four gold rings, and you shall place the four rings upon the four parts of its feet under the rim. 26 The rings will be cases for the poles to carry the table with them. 27 And you shall make the poles of decay-resistant wood, and you shall overlay them with pure gold. The table will be lifted by them. 28 And you shall make its bowls, and cups, and ladles, and its jugs with which to make libations. You shall make them of pure gold. 29 You shall place upon the table the bread of presence before me always.	38.9 He made the presentation table of pure gold. 10 He cast for it four rings, two on one side and two on the second side, wide enough so as to carry the poles in them. 11 He made poles of the ark and the table and gold-plated them with gold. 12 He made the utensils of the table: the bowls and the censers and the ladles and the cups with which he would pour libations from gold.

THE MAKING OF THE TABERNACLE ACCOUNT 79

Thus, the Old Greek's compliance account is considerably simpler, focusing on the main features and lacking any reference to the table's moulding and rim.

A different relationship between instructions and construction is found in the fabrication of the high priestly vestments. Despite placing the vestments at different locations, the relationship between the Masoretic version and the Old Greek version is close. In both versions the fabrication of the vestments is punctuated with the refrain 'as YHWH commanded Moses' (כַּאֲשֶׁר צִוָּה יְהוָה אֶת־מֹשֶׁה; καθὰ συνέταξεν κύριος τῷ Μωυσῇ).[40] They exhibit a greater degree of divergence between the instructions and the fabrication than can be seen in the manufacture of the furniture. A representative example is the fabrication of the robe of the ephod in the Masoretic version (Table 3.3).

Table 3.3 The robe in MT: instructions and fabrication

Instructions (Exod 28.31–35)	Fabrication (Exod 39.22–26)
28.31 You shall make the robe of the ephod, entirely of blue. **32** It shall have an opening for its head in the middle of it, and it shall have a border around the opening, woven work, like the opening of a coat of mail it shall not tear. **33** You shall make on its hem pomegranates of blue, purple, and crimson, all around the hem, and gold bells between them all around. **34** a gold bell and a pomegranate, a gold bell and a pomegranate, around the hem of the robe. **35** Aaron shall wear it for ministering and its sound shall be heard when he goes into the holy place before YHWH, and when he goes out, so that he may not die.	**39.22** He made the robe of the ephod, woven work, entirely of blue. **23** And the opening of the robe in its middle like the opening of a coat of mail, a border around the opening it shall not tear. **24** They shall make on the hem of the robe pomegranates of blue, purple, and crimson, *twisted*. **25** They shall make bells of pure gold, and they shall place the bells between the pomegranates upon the hem of the robe around, between the pomegranates; **26** a bell and a pomegranate, a bell and a pomegranate, around the hem of the robe for ministering, as YHWH commanded Moses.

With the exception of the verse explaining the purpose of the bells (28.35), almost every word of the instructions appears in the account of the fabrication, but there is considerable freedom shown in rearranging the words, even if the effect is sometimes repetitive and less elegant. There is one minor addition, where the word מָשְׁזָר, 'twisted' (𝔐 39.24), was added to the list of coloured yarns.[41]

The refrain 'as YHWH commanded Moses' is also to be found in Moses' assembly of the sanctuary in 𝔐 40.17–33 ≈ 𝔊 40.15–27.[42] The instructions that Moses fulfils are to be found in the first half of Exod 40, but the compliance report that follows often diverges from the instructions that have only just been given. A representative example is the installation of the ark in the Masoretic version.

---

[40] 𝔐 39.1, 5, 7, 21, 26, 29, 31; 𝔊 36.8, 12, 14, 29, 34 (cf. 37, 40).

[41] Since מָשְׁזָר occurs elsewhere in the stereotypical pair שֵׁשׁ מָשְׁזָר, 'twisted linen', the text in 39.24 has probably suffered from homoioteleuton. The expression שֵׁשׁ מָשְׁזָר occurs together with the coloured yarns at 26.1, 31, 36; 27.16; 28.6, 8, 15; 𝔐 36.8, 35, 37; 38.18; 39.5, 8, 29. Thus, the addition of מָשְׁזָר (שֵׁשׁ) in 39.24 assimilates to a familiar usage.

[42] Exod 40.19, 21, 23, 25, 27, 29, 32.

80   THE MAKING OF THE TABERNACLE

Table 3.4 The ark in MT: instructions and installation

Instructions (Exod 40.3)	Installation (Exod 40.20–21)
40.3 You shall place there the ark of the covenant, and screen the ark with the veil.	40.20 He took the covenant and placed it in the ark, and placed the poles upon the ark, and set the atonement cover above the ark. 21 And he brought the ark into the tabernacle, and set up the veil of the screen, and screened the ark of the covenant, as YHWH commanded Moses.

The additional actions described in 40.20–21 reflect instructions made earlier in Exod 25 and 26. Moses is commanded to place the covenant in the ark in 25.16, to place the poles upon the ark in 25.14, to set up the atonement cover upon the ark in 25.21, and to set up the veil in 26.33.

Narrative Anachronisms

A further problem we encounter in the different versions of the tabernacle account is the presence of narrative anachronisms, the anticipation of practices or individuals who will only be encountered later in the Pentateuchal text. There are several examples. The first case is found in Exod 30.11–16. God instructs Moses that the silver collected during the census of the Israelite men will be used for the tabernacle. The accounting of the metal in 𝔐 38.24–31 ≈ 𝔊 39.1–11 provides further details of how the silver was used. The tax on the 603 550 men raised a total of 100 talents and 1775 shekels of silver. The 100 talents were used for the 100 bases of the tabernacle, and the remaining silver was used for the hooks, plating the capitals, and the bands for the pillars of the courtyard. In this way account is made for every item manufactured from silver. Unfortunately, this results in two problems. The first of these is that, according to Num 1, the census is not taken until the second month of the second year, a full month after the tabernacle has been completed. The second problem is that an obligatory tax is in some tension with the idea that the Israelites donated the silver freely for the construction of the tabernacle (𝔐 35.4–9, 24 ≈ 𝔊 35.4–8, 24).[43] A second example of anachronism concerns the laver which is said to have been made from the mirrors of the women who served at the entrance of the tent of meeting (𝔐 38.8 ≈ 𝔊 38.26), rather than the bronze donated by the people. The reference to the women serving at the tent of meeting assumes that the tent, which is in the process of being constructed, already exists! Unless, of course, this tent of meeting is the tent of Exod 33.7–11. It has often been noted that the same group of women is mentioned at

---

[43] Susanne Owczarek, *Die Vorstellung vom* Wohnen Gottes inmitten seines Volkes *in der Priesterschrift: Zur Heiligtumstheologie der priesterschriftlichen Grundschrift*, Europäische Hochschulschriften. Reihe 23, Theologie 625 (Frankfurt am Main: Lang, 1998), 38.

THE MAKING OF THE TABERNACLE ACCOUNT   81

the time of Eli in 1 Sam 2.22: 'Now Eli was very old. He heard all that his sons were doing to all Israel and how they lay with the woman who served at the entrance of the tent of meeting.' A third anachronism is the appearance of the Levites. Since the roles of the Levites are not fully described until the book of Numbers, the passing allusions to them in the book of Exodus appear premature.[44] Intriguingly, they are mentioned in a couple of different places in the various versions. In the Masoretic, Samaritan, and Old Greek versions, the Levites appear in the summary account in 𝔐 38.21 ≈ 𝕲 37.19: 'These are the records of the tabernacle, the tabernacle of the covenant, that were recorded by the command of Moses, the service of the Levites under the direction of Ithamar, Aaron's son, the priest.'[45] The Levites' assistance under the oversight of Ithamar is only detailed in Num 4, and the language of 𝔐 38.21 is also characteristic of that chapter. Quite why the Levites' role in transporting the tabernacle is anticipated here is far from clear. The Old Latin of Monacensis lacks this reference to the Levites, but has a unique reference to the fabrication of vestments for the Levites in its equivalent to 𝕲 39.13: 'And what was left of the hyacinth, purple, scarlet was made into sacred robes for the ministry of the Levites in the sanctuary' (𝕷^M 27/2/4–8).[46] The fourth anachronism is that the Old Greek version describes how the altar of burnt offerings was made from the bronze censers of Korah's followers. The rebellion of Korah is not mentioned until Num 16–17 and takes place not only after the Israelites have departed from Sinai, but even after the rebellion at Kadesh Barnea.

The Insertion of the Golden Calf Incident

A final literary problem that needs to be considered is the separation of the two halves of the tabernacle account by the story concerning the sin of the golden calf (Exod 32–34). Since the nineteenth century it has been recognized that Exod 32–34 contains no priestly material. On the other hand, Exod 25–31 and 35–40 consist entirely of priestly material. As a result, it is not uncommon for the story of the golden calf and the tabernacle account to be considered entirely separately from one another.[47] Nevertheless, the appearance of the golden calf incident

---

[44] For the Levites in the book of Exodus, see Ulrich Dahmen, *Leviten und Priester im Deuteronomium: Literarkritische und redaktionsgeschichtliche Studien*, BBB 110 (Bodenheim: Philo, 1996), 74–94; Harald Samuel, *Von Priestern zum Patriarchen: Levi und die Leviten im Alten Testament*, BZAW 448 (Berlin: de Gruyter, 2014), 246–300.

[45] The Old Greek has simply ἡ σύνταξις τῆς σκηνῆς τοῦ μαρτυρίου where the Masoretic Text has פְּקוּדֵי הַמִּשְׁכָּן מִשְׁכַּן הָעֵדֻת.

[46] For discussion see Bogaert, 'L'importance de la Septante', 417–20.

[47] The detailed redaction-critical analysis of Exod 32–34 by Konkel, for example, rarely discusses its relationship with the tabernacle account. Michael Konkel, *Sünde und Vergebung: Eine Rekonstruktion der Redaktionsgeschichte der hinteren Sinaiperikope (Exodus 32–34) vor dem Hintergrund aktueller*

82   THE MAKING OF THE TABERNACLE

between the instructions and the completion of the tabernacle is an important literary-critical datum. Whilst the golden calf incident is characterized by an almost inexplicable act of disobedience,[48] the completion of the tabernacle is marked by a meticulous obedience to the instructions given to Moses. The contrast between the two portrayals could not be clearer, and the reader of the book of Exodus is left in no doubt that the repentance of the Israelites is heartfelt.

Substantive connections between the golden calf story and the tabernacle account are relatively scarce.[49] Both texts concern an act of manufacturing (עש״ה) that is intended to secure the divine presence on a permanent basis. This connection between the two is underlined by framing the golden calf story with the prohibition of 'doing' (עש״ה) work on the Sabbath (31.12–17; 35.1–3). It has often been observed that the theology of this framework as well as the language has much in common with the Holiness Code (Lev 17–26).[50] A further connection between the two accounts concerns the people's willing provision of gold for the manufacture of the sacred items. In both Exod 32.2–3 and 35.22 the men bring (hiphil בו״א) the gold earrings (נֶזֶם) of their wives.[51]

The Literary Critical Development of the Tabernacle Account

The literary problems that I have described are significant and suggest that the tabernacle account experienced a complex history of development. In what follows I will propose a model that will seek to account for the literary problems and

---

Pentateuchmodelle, FAT 58 (Tübingen: Mohr Siebeck, 2008). The same is also true of Anderson who envisages minimal editorial interventions to integrate the non-priestly material of Exod 32–34 into the priestly tabernacle account (Gary A. Anderson, *That I May Dwell among Them: The Biblical Concept of Incarnation and Atonement* [Grand Rapids: Eerdmans, forthcoming]).

[48] Nathan MacDonald, 'Aaron's Failure and the Fall of the Hebrew Kingdoms', in *The Fall of Jerusalem and the Rise of the Torah*, eds. Peter Dubrovský, Dominik Markl, and Jean-Pierre Sonnet, FAT 107 (Tübingen: Mohr Siebeck, 2016), 197–209.

[49] Nathan MacDonald, 'Recasting the Golden Calf: The Imaginative Potential of the Old Testament's Portrayal of Idolatry', in *Idolatry: False Worship in the Bible, Early Judaism, and Christianity*, ed. Stephen C. Barton (London: T&T Clark, 2007), 22–39.

[50] See, e.g., Israel Knohl, *The Sanctuary of Silence: The Priestly Torah and the Holiness School* (Minneapolis: Fortress, 1995), 63–8. Saul Olyan and Jeffrey Stackert have argued that some of the Sabbath framework belonged to the original priestly document (Saul M. Olyan, 'Exodus 31:12–17: The Sabbath According to H, or the Sabbath According to P and H?', *JBL* 124 [2005]: 201–9; Jeffrey Stackert, 'Compositional Strata in the Priestly Sabbath: Exodus 31:12–17 and 35:1–3', *JHebS* 11 [2011], https://www.jhsonline.org/index.php/jhs/article/view/16438), whilst Tucker effectively collapses H into the priestly *Grundschrift* (Paavo N. Tucker, *The Holiness Composition in the Book of Exodus*, FAT II/98 [Tübingen: Mohr Siebeck, 2017], 145–59).

[51] For the relationship see discussion in Eckart Otto, 'Die nachpriesterschriftliche Pentateuchredaktion im Buch Exodus', in *Studies in the Book of Exodus: Redaction—Reception—Interpretation*, ed. Marc Vervenne, BETL 126 (Leuven: Leuven University Press, 1996), 84–7; Helmut Utzschneider, *Das Heiligtum und das Gesetz: Studien zur Bedeutung der sinaitischen Heiligtumstexte (Ex 25–40; Lev 8–9)*, OBO 77 (Freiburg im Üchtland: Universitätsverlag, 1988), 86–7.

provide a basis for our subsequent analysis. My purpose here is to provide this model in broad outline. Some of the detailed discussion of particular passages will be best reserved for subsequent chapters.

The model I propose is simply that: a model. It seeks to provide a plausible account of the development of Exod 25–31, 35–40 that accounts for the literary evidence. If the examination of the extant textual evidence has demonstrated just how complex the literary development of the tabernacle account was in its later stages, there is no reason to think this was not true of earlier stages. A model is, therefore, necessarily a simplification and must allow for various uncertainties— and held with a corresponding degree of caution. It must be open to critical examination, but when we lack earlier texts that can provide conclusive proof (or, correspondingly, falsification), we are perhaps best to think in terms not of a model being right or wrong, but rather convincing or unconvincing.

What then is the value of literary-critical models? The proposal of literary-critical models is no different to the venturing of models in other areas of academic research. They have heuristic value; they are 'good to think with'. They provide a means of thinking about the texts that we have, how they may have come about, and what this means for how we interpret them. This means holding to redaction-critical hypotheses rather more tentatively than has sometimes been the case. It is also to recall, as proponents of final-form and canonical readings insist, that the task of the biblical interpreter is to understand and interpret the texts that we have. The value of literary-critical analyses lies ultimately in their attentiveness to the extant texts.

The Priestly *Grundschrift*

Since the work of Kuenen and Wellhausen, most scholars have agreed in seeking the origins of the tabernacle account in Exod 25–29 and that this was part of the original priestly document, the *Grundschrift*. The section finds its natural conclusion in God's promise to dwell amongst the Israelites (29.45–46; cf. 25.8). In this way the divine glory which appeared on Mount Sinai will take up permanent residence with the Israelites and accompany them on their onward journey from the mountain (24.16). If the instructions to Moses conclude at the end of Exod 29, it is apparent that Exod 30–31 are secondary. Confirmation of this is seen in the fact that both the incense altar and the laver should have appeared at earlier points in the instructions. The only partial integration of these objects in the Old Greek of Exod 35–40 and the Old Latin of Monacensis is further proof of their secondary nature.

For the most part, Exod 25–29 consists of a series of instructions addressed to Moses in the second person singular. This outlook stands in contrast to the more

84 THE MAKING OF THE TABERNACLE

complex portrayal of the tabernacle's construction in Exod 35–39, in which Bezalel, Oholiab, and the Israelite artisans undertake the work. In the case of the vestments, the attempt to harmonize the two perspectives in 28.3–5 by attributing the vestments to the skilled artisans is transparently an addition.[52] The second person plural וְעָשׂוּ (v. 6) was presumably originally a singular וְעָשִׂיתָ as we find in the remainder of the chapter. It was turned into a plural in order to assimilate the vestments into the ideal that the entire community was involved.

A rather more difficult case confronts us in 25.8–10a. The Masoretic version has three plural verbs, וְעָשׂוּ...תְּעֲשׂוּ...וְעָשׂוּ, where the Old Greek has three singular verbs, ποιήσεις ... ποιήσεις ... ποιήσεις. The Samaritan evidence is mixed with a plural verb followed by two singular verbs, ועשית...תעשה...ועשו. Each of the versions reflects the challenge of transitioning between the plural address of the Israelites in vv. 2–7 and the singular address of Moses from v. 10 onwards, and the question of to whom the programmatic statement about the construction of the sanctuary in vv. 8–9 should be directed. It could certainly be argued that the Masoretic Text preserves the *lectio difficilior* since the rest of the chapter directs Moses to make the tabernacle furniture. The similarities to Exod 28 suggest, however, that the Masoretic version has attempted to reframe the singular instructions to Moses in Exod 25–27 as a task undertaken by the entire people. The plural reference to the people in v. 8, 'I will dwell among *them*',[53] might have played a part in encouraging this pluralizing of vv. 8–9. We should, therefore, conclude that the Old Greek preserves the earlier reading. This would allow us to see the programmatic statement in vv. 8–9 as the original opening of the tabernacle account which presented Moses as the sole recipient of the instructions to construct the sanctuary.

Within Exod 25–29 we can identify three blocks of material. In chapters 25–27 we have instructions about the tabernacle and its furniture which refer exclusively to the sanctuary as the 'dwelling' (הַמִּשְׁכָּן), in chapter 28 we have instructions about the priestly vestments, and in chapter 29 there are instructions for the ordination of the priests for service in the 'tent of meeting' (אֹהֶל מוֹעֵד). The blocks are further differentiated by their approach to the significance of the items being manufactured. Exodus 25–27 provide no indication that the different parts of the tabernacle or its furniture have any distinct meaning other than contributing to the provision of a comfortable residence for YHWH. In contrast, each item of the priestly vestments is given a distinct symbolic significance in Exod 28. Perhaps unsurprisingly,

---

[52] The list of Aaron's vestments also includes the additional items listed in v. 39, which should be regarded as secondary.

[53] The reading בְּתוֹכָם, 'among them', in 𝔐^L is to be preferred, and matches the reading in 29.46. Both the Samaritan and Old Greek versions have a second person plural, which is the difference of a single letter. But in each case v. 8 reads problematically. In 𝔊^D the third person plural ועשו, 'they shall make', shifts abruptly to a second person plural, בתוככם, 'in your midst'. In 𝔊^B the second person singular ποιήσεις, 'you shall make', is followed by a second person plural, ἐν ὑμῖν, 'among you'.

THE MAKING OF THE TABERNACLE ACCOUNT   85

many recent scholars have proposed seeing Exod 28–29 as a secondary layer.[54] Nevertheless, Nihan has made the compelling observation that without Exod 28–29 'the introduction of Aaron alongside Moses in the previous Priestly narrative in Exodus remains nothing more than a blind motif'.[55] An alternative possibility was already ventured by Noth who observed that the description of the priestly vestments in Exod 29 did not correspond in every respect to the instructions for the fabrication in Exod 28.[56] Consequently, he attributed the instructions about the priestly vestments to the priestly *Grundschrift* alongside Exod 25–27. Two further observations support Noth's proposal. First, the identification of the sanctuary as the 'tent of meeting' (אֹהֶל מוֹעֵד) rather than the 'dwelling' (הַמִּשְׁכָּן) does not occur until Exod 29. Second, there is an instance of repetitive resumption in 28.41b and 29.44b, which may have been the literary means by which the instructions for the ordination rite were inserted. Thus, the original priestly document probably concluded the description of the priestly vestments with the instruction 'you shall put them on your brother Aaron' (28.41aα). With a comfortable dwelling and servants to provide for his every need, all the conditions required for YHWH to take up residence in the people's midst are present (29.45–46).

The instructions for the construction of the tabernacle and the fabrication of the priestly vestments take a very different approach to the significance of the objects produced. The different parts of the tabernacle are granted no individual significance, but they take their meaning together as the place of divine dwelling. In contrast, each part of the priestly vestments is granted its own distinctive significance. Despite their differences, Exod 28 portrays the priestly vestments being made from the same materials used in Exod 25–27—gold, linen, blue, purple, and crimson yarns—and this would appear to indicate a familiarity with the previous chapters. These differences and similarities are perhaps best explained as the result of the priestly writer utilizing an existing source on the architecture of the tabernacle, or at very least a familiar literary genre.[57] Building accounts are known in other parts of the Hebrew Bible (1 Kgs 6–8; Ezek 40–42) and are also attested elsewhere in the ancient Near East.[58]

There have been various proposals for identifying secondary elements within Exod 25–27, not all of which are equally convincing. The appearance of both a 'dwelling' (הַמִּשְׁכָּן) and a 'tent' (אֹהֶל) in Exod 26 have led a number of scholars to

---

[54] E.g. Enzo Cortese, 'The Priestly Tent (Ex 25–31.35–40): Literary Criticism and the Theology of P Today', *LASBF* 48 (1998): 11–14; Steins, 'Heiligtum', 159–67.

[55] Nihan, *Priestly Torah*, 51.

[56] Martin Noth, *Exodus: A Commentary*, trans. J. S Bowden, OTL (London: SCM, 1962), 229.

[57] Albertz, 'Beobachtungen'.

[58] Victor Hurowitz, *I Have Built You an Exalted House: Temple Building in the Bible in the Light of Mesopotamian and Northwest Semitic Writings*, JSOTSup 115 (Sheffield: JSOT Press, 1992).

86 THE MAKING OF THE TABERNACLE

suggest that we have a doublet, and to argue for excluding 26.1–6, 15–29.[59] Yet, as Nihan has persuasively argued, there is no need to regard the dwelling and the tent as doublets.[60] Similarly unconvincing are claims that the instructions concerning the entrance curtains, the altar of burnt offering, and the outer courtyard (26.36–27.19) are secondary. The basis for this argument is the idea that 26.30 is a conclusion to the instructions: 'then you shall erect the dwelling in the manner that I showed you on the mountain'.[61] It is better to regard this verse, however, as part of a series of notices that refers to the pattern shown to Moses and divides Exod 25–27 into distinct sections (25.9, 40; 26.30; 27.8).[62]

Amongst all the furniture, the instructions about the atonement cover (25.17–22) have several unusual features. First, the chain of second person singular *weqatal* instructions that characterizes Exod 25–27 is interrupted by an imperative וְעָשִׂיתָ, 'make' (25.17), and a second person plural תַּעֲשׂוּ, 'you shall make' (25.19). Second, the instructions to place the covenant inside the ark are repeated twice (25.16, 21) which could be evidence of an insertion using the technique of repetitive resumption. Third, the atonement cover is the only item of furniture in Exod 25–27 that is provided with an explanation of its function (25.22). It is likely, then, that the atonement cover should probably be seen as an expansion which entered the text under the influence of Lev 16.[63] Fourth, the tabernacle account sometimes regards the atonement cover as distinct from the ark, but at other times they are presented as a single item.[64] The inclusion of the atonement cover in Exod 25 must have occurred at a relatively early stage since the Old Greek version of the construction of the ark has both the ark and its cover (𝔊 38.1–8).

The instruction about the burning of oil on the lamp (27.20–21) has been appended at a later stage. It stands out as a commandment to the Israelites in the midst of instructions to Moses. In addition, we might naturally have expected it to have appeared together with instructions for the lampstand (25.31–40). Not only is the language of 'a perpetual ordinance throughout your generations' characteristic of the Holiness Code, but almost identical instructions appear in

---

[59] See, e.g., Manfred Görg, *Das Zelt der Begegnung: Untersuchung zur Gestalt der sakralen Zelttraditionen Altisraels*, BBB 27 (Bonn: Hanstein, 1967), 8–34; Volkmar Fritz, *Tempel und Zelt: Studien zum Tempelbau in Israel und zu dem Zeltheiligtum der Priesterschrift*, WMANT 47 (Neukirchen-Vluyn: Neukirchener Verlag, 1977), 118–21.

[60] Nihan, *Priestly Torah*, 39–41.

[61] Peter Weimar, 'Sinai und Schöpfung: Komposition und Theologie der priesterschriftlichen Sinaigeschichte', in *Studien zur Priesterschrift*, FAT 56 (Tübingen: Mohr Siebeck, 2008), 341–3.

[62] Jürg Hutzli, 'The Origins of P: Literary Profiles and Strata of the Priestly Texts in Genesis 1–Exodus 40' (Zurich University, Habilitationschrift, 2019), 230–1.

[63] Cf. J.-M. de Tarragon, 'La "kapporet" est-elle une fiction ou un élément du culte tardif?', *RB* 88 (1981): 5–12; Cortese, 'The Priestly Tent'; Peter Porzig, *Die Lade Jahwes im Alten Testament und in den Texten vom Toten Meer*, BZAW 397 (Berlin: de Gruyter, 2009), 12–18.

[64] Houtman, *Exodus*, III: 381.

THE MAKING OF THE TABERNACLE ACCOUNT   87

Lev 24.2–3. It seems likely that a redactor has introduced it into the tabernacle instructions from there.[65]

The compliance account in Exod 35–40 presents the construction of the sanctuary in two ways that are not anticipated in Exod 25–29. First, the furniture and tent are fabricated primarily by two master craftsmen with the assistance of a team of artisans (𝔐 35.10–39.31; 𝔊 35.9–39.13). Second, the completed items are then presented to Moses who assembles them (𝔐 39.32–40.15; 40.18–33; 𝔊 39.14–40.13; 40.16–27). The only part of the construction account that does not assume this perspective is to be found in 𝔐 40.16–17, 33b, 35b:

> **40.16** Moses did everything just as YHWH commanded him; so he did. **17** In the first month in the second year, on the first day of the month, the tabernacle was erected…**33**…so Moses completed the work **35**…and the glory of YHWH filled the tabernacle.

As Pola has observed, the brief account of obedience in v. 16 with its threefold structure—Moses did / just as YHWH commanded him / so he did—is consistent with other examples of command-fulfilment in the priestly *Grundschrift*.[66] The reference to Moses completing the work (v. 33b) echoes God's completion of his creation in the P creation story and indicates that the priestly writers saw the tabernacle as a reflection of the cosmos.[67]

Moses completed the work   On the seventh day God completed his work that he did

(וַיְכַל מֹשֶׁה אֶת־הַמְּלָאכָה ;40.33b).   (וַיְכַל אֱלֹהִים בַּיּוֹם הַשְּׁבִיעִי מְלַאכְתּוֹ אֲשֶׁר עָשָׂה; Gen 2.2a).

---

[65] Owczarek, *Vorstellung*, 72–3. Whilst he holds that Exod 27.20–21 is a later addition to the instructions in Exod 25–29, Nihan argues instead that Lev 24.2–4 is dependent on Exod 27.20–21. His decisive observation is that Lev 24.4 adds additional material that is not found in Exod 27.20–21 and this verse uses the plural נֵרֹת, 'lamps' rather than the collective singular נֵר, 'lamp' (v. 2) (Nihan, *Priestly Torah*, 511–12). Lev 24.4 is clearly repetitive and does nothing more than rephrase vv. 2–3 with a plural, which was clearly thought to be more appropriate for the seven lamps. It could have been appended to vv. 2–3 at any point in the transmission of the text. In other words, the fact that Exod 27.20–21 shows no knowledge of Lev 24.4 does not prove that Exod 27.20–21 is earlier than Lev 24.2–3. Two observations suggest instead that Exod 27.20–21 drew on Lev 24.2–3. First, Exod 27.20–21 has the characteristic Holiness expression חֻקַּת עוֹלָם לְדֹרֹתָם, 'a perpetual ordinance throughout your generations', which suggests it has drawn on the Holiness Code. Second, Exod 27.20–21 has Aaron and his sons 'arrange' (יַעֲרֹךְ) the lights. The distinctive usage of עֲר״ךְ for the lamp depends on Lev 24.1–9 which uses עֲר״ךְ as a way of highlighting the similarities between the bread placed on the table and the oil burnt on the lampstand.

[66] Thomas Pola, *Die ursprüngliche Priesterschrift: Beobachtungen zur Literarkritik und Traditionsgeschichte von Pg*, WMANT 70 (Neukirchen-Vluyn: Neukirchener Verlag, 1995), 116–44.

[67] For the relationship between the creation account (Gen 1.1–2.3) and the conclusion of the tabernacle account, see, *inter alia*, Joseph Blenkinsopp, 'The Structure of P', *CBQ* 38 (1976): 275–92; Kearney, 'Creation and Liturgy'. Other echoes of the creation account (Exod 39.32a // Gen 2.1; Exod 39.43a // Gen 1.31; Exod 39.43b // Gen 2.3aα) need not be part of the original tabernacle account, especially since 'strikingly clear references back to Gen. 1' are found in certain secondary texts, such as Exod 31.12–17; 35.1–3 (Reinhard Gregor Kratz, *The Composition of the Narrative Books of the Old Testament* [London: T&T Clark, 2005], 103).

88   THE MAKING OF THE TABERNACLE

The descent of the divine glory upon the tabernacle parallels the descent of the glory upon Mount Sinai in Exod 24.15–16. The two references to YHWH's glory form an *inclusio* around the entire tabernacle account and emphasizes the theological point that the God who appeared first on Mount Sinai has taken up residence in the tabernacle amongst the Israelites.[68]

Revisions in Light of Lev 1–16

The priestly literature probably experienced an extension as far as Lev 16 at an early stage, and there are some like Nihan who have argued that from its beginning the priestly *Grundschrift* included the first half of Leviticus.[69] There is a handful of places within Exod 25–28 where there are probably signs of secondary additions that seem to have the purpose of aligning the tabernacle account with the early chapters of Leviticus, and especially Lev 16. Several verses at the end of Exod 28—vv. 37–38*, 39–40, 42–43—align the instructions for the priestly vestments with the different descriptions of the vestments from Lev 16. As I have already observed, the instructions concerning the atonement cover (Exod 25.17–22) have a number of unusual features that distinguish them from the rest of the instructions in Exod 25–27. In the atoning day ritual of Leviticus 16, the atonement cover takes a central role as the place where the blood is sprinkled and has probably been introduced into Exod 25 from there. The reference to the atonement cover in 26.34 should also be regarded as a secondary addition. It is noticeable that the atonement cover is mentioned somewhat belatedly after the ark has been placed behind the veil that separates the most holy place from the holy place.[70]

It is with the mention of the atonement cover in Exod 25 that we have the first indications of an alternative conception of the tabernacle. It is not simply the place where YHWH dwells, it is also the place 'where I will meet with you' (וְנוֹעַדְתִּי לְךָ שָׁם). The language of the 'tent of meeting' is the preferred manner of talking about the tabernacle in Lev 1–16 and may have been introduced into the tabernacle account from there. The earliest appearances in the tabernacle account are in Exod 29, the ordination ritual, and the summative declaration of the tabernacle's purpose in 29.43–44. The insertion of this material has been facilitated by the use of the repetitive resumption of 'Aaron and his sons I will consecrate to serve me as priests' (Exod 29.44, cf. 28.41). In this way, the brief allusion to the ordination and consecration of the priests in 28.41 is more fully developed.

---

[68] Nihan, *Priestly Torah*, 36.   [69] Nihan, *Priestly Torah*.

[70] Propp's paraphrase of 26.34—'Moses must first set the *kappōret* on the Testimony Chest, and then put them both in the Holiness of Holiness' (Propp, *Exodus 19–40*, 419)—highlights the problem, for the ark has already been placed within the most holy place (v. 33).

The Two Workers Level

The earliest version of a detailed construction account is preserved in the Greek text of Vaticanus and the Old Latin text of Monacensis. It recounts how a plural group—'they'—made the tent and the hangings of the courtyard (𝔊 37.1–18), and then how Bezalel—'he'—made the furniture that was located in the sanctuary (𝔊 38.1–17). The division reflects the different materials that are involved: fabrics then metals. In every case the account of the construction is abbreviated in comparison to the instructions that Moses received. The abbreviation of the instructions in Exod 25–27 and rearrangement according to materials is not entirely without its problems. In particular, there is almost no reference to the wood involved. In some places, the Old Latin of Monacensis reflects a redaction that sought to rectify this omission.[71]

It seems likely that the other metal items in 𝔊 38.18–27 were appended at a subsequent stage of composition. They are distinguished from the gold items that precede them by their introduction with οὗτος, 'this one'. It seems virtually certain that the account of the making of the bronze altar (𝔊 38.22–24) is late for it presupposes the story of Korah from Num 16–17, which is recognized as a very late element within the priestly material of Numbers.[72] Somewhat less certain is whether the metal items originally included the list of small gold, silver, and bronze items that fixed the tent and hangings (𝔊 38.18–21). What is most notable about the metal items Bezalel constructs is the absence of the altar of incense. Its absence provides clear evidence that Exod 30–31 had not been appended to the instruction account at this point in the text's composition. Whilst the altar of incense is absent, the atonement cover is present. Thus, it would appear that the instructions about the tabernacle had already been coordinated with Lev 16.

Who are the plural group who fabricated the tent and the hangings of the courtyard? In all the extant versions of the text, the fabricators are Bezalel, Oholiab, and all the skilled Israelite artisans (35.30–36.7), but the mention of the Israelite artisans appears out of the blue in 36.1, and the *Vorlage* of the Old Greek of Vaticanus 36.1 reproduces 35.35 to a significant degree.[73] The difficulties with 36.1 are also apparent in the surprising appearance of the *waw*-consecutive with the perfect, וְעָשָׂה, which confused most of the early translators.[74] Consistent with

---

[71] In Bogaert's view Monacensis with its numerous references to the wood used in construction reflects a better and earlier text than that preserved in the Old Greek of Vaticanus (Bogaert, 'L'importance de la Septante'). It is very difficult to explain why a redactor would consistently remove references to wood. It is a more compelling explanation that a redactor sought to rectify what he perceived as a defective text by adding references to wood where they were lacking.

[72] Achenbach, *Die Vollendung der Tora*, 37–140; Pyschny, *Verhandelte Führung*.

[73] As Wevers observes 𝔊ᴮ 35.35 'departs considerably from MT' (Wevers, *Greek Text of Exodus*, 590). For v. 35aα, the Old Greek reads σοφίας καὶ συνέσεως διανοίας where 𝔐ᴸ has חָכְמַת־לֵב. This is close to 36.1's חָכְמָה וּתְבוּנָה. For 35aβ, the Old Greek has ποιῆσαι τὰ ἔργα τοῦ ἁγίου where 𝔐ᴸ has לַעֲשׂוֹת כָּל־מְלָאכֶת. This appears to read a text similar to 36.1's לַעֲשׂוֹת אֶת־כָּל־מְלֶאכֶת עֲבֹדַת הַקֹּדֶשׁ.

[74] Old Greek's καὶ ἐποίησεν and Vulgate's *fecit ergo* translate וְעָשָׂה as though a simple *waw* introduced the verb. The confusion led to the introduction of the chapter division at 36.1 and is

90 THE MAKING OF THE TABERNACLE

these observations, at the end of the account of the tent and the courtyard only Bezalel and Oholiab are mentioned as fabricators (𝔊 37.19–21). The inclusion of the Israelites was probably the result of a subsequent redaction.[75]

The Two Workers Level must also, therefore, have included some version of 35.30–35, which describes the calling of Bezalel and Oholiab. This passage has a close parallel in 31.1–6 which announces to Moses that God has called Bezalel and Oholiab. There are some important differences between the two passages that help us assess their relationship. First, Oholiab is introduced in an awkward manner in 35.35: וּלְהוֹרֹת נָתַן בְּלִבּוֹ הוּא וְאָהֳלִיאָב, 'and to teach he has placed in his heart, both he and Oholiab'. Grammatically, it is uncertain whether הוּא refers to Bezalel or God. In contrast, 31.6 has a smoother text: וַאֲנִי הִנֵּה נָתַתִּי אִתּוֹ אֵת אָהֳלִיאָב, 'and behold I have appointed with him Oholiab'. Second, the Israelite artisans are better integrated into the account of the two master craftsmen in 31.1–6. They are introduced simply and without repetition in 31.6: וּבְלֵב כָּל־חֲכַם־לֵב נָתַתִּי חָכְמָה וְעָשׂוּ אֵת כָּל־אֲשֶׁר צִוִּיתִךָ, 'and I have placed wisdom in the heart of all the wise-hearted, and they will make everything that I have commanded you'. The two differences suggest not only that 31.1–6 has revised and improved 35.30–35, but it helps highlight some of the difficulties in 35.30–35.[76]

Rhyder resolves the difficulties with הוּא וְאָהֳלִיאָב, 'he and Oholiab' (35.35), by arguing that Oholiab is a secondary addition and that originally Bezalel alone was the master craftsman assigned with the task of constructing the tabernacle and its furniture.[77] An alternative solution is that originally Bezalel and Oholiab were fabric workers (35.30, 34bβ) and their roles were more sharply differentiated through the insertion of 35.31–34bα:

Ex. 35.30 Then Moses said to the Israelites: See, the LORD has called by name Bezalel son of Uri son of Hur, of the tribe of Judah;

> **31** he has filled him with divine spirit, with skill, intelligence, and knowledge in every kind of craft, **32** to devise artistic designs, to work in gold, silver, and bronze, **33** in cutting stones for setting, and in carving wood, in every kind of craft. **34** And he has inspired him to teach, both him

and Oholiab son of Ahisamach, of the tribe of Dan. **35** He has filled them with skill…

---

already reflected in the sense division marked by an *ekthesis* in 𝔊[B]. In the Hebrew textual traditions, however, 𝔖𝔰[D] has a break after 36.1, and 𝔐[L] treats 35.30–36.7 as a single unit.

[75] Working with a two-source model, von Rad came to similar conclusions (Gerhard von Rad, *Die Priesterschrift im Hexateuch: Literarisch untersucht und theologisch gewertet*, BWANT 13 [Stuttgart: Kohlhammer, 1934], 64–6).

[76] Again, as already perceived by von Rad.

[77] Julia Rhyder, 'Unity and Hierarchy: North and South in the Priestly Traditions', in *Yahwistic Diversity and the Hebrew Bible: Tracing Perspectives of Group Identity from Judah, Samaria, and the Diaspora in Biblical Traditions*, eds. Benedikt Hensel, Dany Nocquet, and Bartosz Adamczewski, FAT II/120 (Tübingen: Mohr Siebeck, 2020), 109–34.

THE MAKING OF THE TABERNACLE ACCOUNT   91

The insertion of textual material drew on v. 35 to attribute to Bezalel additional skills in metalwork, stone-cutting, and woodwork.

If Bezalel is only secondarily attributed the roles of metalwork, stone-cutting, and woodwork, why is he portrayed as the one who makes the tabernacle furniture? It is a speculative suggestion, but I will argue later in this book that Bezalel was, perhaps, not the original crafter of the tabernacle furniture. Instead, Moses originally undertook the most sacred task of constructing the furniture. Bezalel and Oholiab were the חֹשֵׁב and the רֹקֵם of Exod 25–28. Whether or not Moses had the task of constructing the furniture, the Two Workers Level did not envisage Moses receiving the completed items and erecting or installing them. This notion appears only with the involvement of the entire people in the task of constructing the tabernacle (cf. 𝔊 39.11, 14, 22–23). Further confirmation can also be found in the Old Greek account of the construction of the veil, it is said that 'he made the veil...and they put it on four decay resistant pillars' (καὶ ἐποίησεν τὸ καταπέτασμα...καὶ ἐπέθηκαν αὐτὸ ἐπὶ τέσσαρας στύλους ἀσήπτους; 𝔊 37.3–4). This attributes to Bezalel and Oholiab the manufacturing of the veil *and* its installation on the pillars. In the developed account of Exod 40, the installation of the veil is envisaged as Moses' task: 'and he put on the covering of the veil' (καὶ ἐπέθηκεν τὸ κατακάλυμμα τοῦ καταπετάσματος; 𝔊 40.19). Unsurprisingly, in its version of the fabrication of the veil, the Masoretic version lacks any reference to the veil being installed on the pillars (𝔐 36.35–36).

The Israelite Artisans Level

In the Two Workers Level the tabernacle is fabricated by two master craftsmen who represent the entirety of Israel: Bezalel is a Judahite from the south and Oholiab is a Danite from the north.[78] This representative approach is incorporated into a different perspective where all the Israelites supply the items for the tabernacle and some skilled artisans from the Israelites are involved in the fabrication of the priestly vestments together with the tent and hangings. It is possible that the supply of materials for the sanctuary and the construction of the tabernacle were two distinct redactional stages, but there is little basis for separating them.

A significant feature of this redactional layer is the inclusion of the priestly vestments' fabrication (𝔊 36.8–40). As we have seen, their fabrication is relayed in a distinctive manner. There is both a detailed account of how the individual components of the vestments were fabricated together with the regular refrain 'just as YHWH instructed Moses'. It is noticeable that the description of the turban

---

[78] See, esp., Rhyder, 'Unity and Hierarchy'.

92 THE MAKING OF THE TABERNACLE

(together with the tunics, undergarments, and sashes) has been relocated to the more logical position before the gold plate that sits upon it (𝔊 36.35–40). This provides further evidence that the harmonization of Exod 25–29 with Lev 16 had already taken place by the time the Israelite Artisans Level was composed.

The account of the calling of Bezalel and Oholiab (35.30, 34b–35) was extended so that it mentioned the Israelite artisans and the people's generosity (36.1–7). The transition to this fresh textual material is achieved through a reference to the skilled artisans in 36.1 that repeats much of what is said about Bezalel and Oholiab in 35.35: 'And Bezalel and Oholiab and every man who was wise of heart (חֲכַם־לֵב, cf. חָכְמַת־לֵב; 𝔐 35.35) that YHWH had given wisdom and understanding (חָכְמָה וּתְבוּנָה, cf. σοφίας καὶ συνέσεως; 𝔊 35.35) in them to know (לָדַעַת, cf. συνιέναι; 𝔊 35.35) how to make all the work (לַעֲשׂות כָּל־מְלֶאכֶת, cf. 35.35) of the labour of the holy place (הַקֹּדֶשׁ, cf. τοῦ ἁγίου; 𝔊 35.35) did all that YHWH commanded.'[79] It was probably at this point in the compositional history that 35.31–34bα were inserted which distinguished Bezalel as someone who was uniquely filled with the spirit of God and skilled in metalwork and woodwork. The skilled Israelite artisans are merely said to have been given skill (36.1). This distinction is not observed in the secondary addition of Exod 28.3–5 which re-envisages the fabrication of the vestments originally assigned to Moses as an undertaking of all the 'wise of heart whom I have filled with the spirit of wisdom' (כָּל־חַכְמֵי־לֵב אֲשֶׁר מִלֵּאתִיו רוּחַ חָכְמָה; 28.3). These verses must have been added at a later stage than the composition of 35.30–36.1, but shows the same instincts as this redactional layer in attributing the vestments to the skilled artisans.

If my proposal that Moses was originally envisaged as the manufacturer of the furniture is correct, the attribution to Bezalel of talents in the working of metal and wood is consistent with him displacing Moses in 𝔊 37.1. Oholiab, on the other hand, retains the ability to work in fabrics (35.35) and together with Bezalel is tasked with teaching the Israelite artisans. The differentiation of Bezalel from the other craftsmen results in the rather 'unusual isolate pronoun הוא form' in 35.34.[80] Unusual as it is, it could be seen as an anticipation of the form of the pronoun הוא followed by a verb in the perfect that appears to have been in the Greek translator's *Vorlage* of 𝔊 38.18–27. Most likely then we should attribute 𝔊 38.18–21 to this redactional level. Thus, an *inclusio* is created in the account of the activities of the craftsmen opening and closing with emphatic references to Bezalel as 'he' (הוּא).

Not only do the Israelites have an enhanced role in the construction of the tabernacle, they are also involved in bringing materials that will be used. The list of materials needed is set out in the opening instructions to Moses that now

---

[79] As Rhyder observes the shift to the third person singular, וְעָשָׂה, 'he did', at the beginning of 36.1 is evidence of a literary problem (Rhyder, 'Unity and Hierarchy', 118).

[80] Wevers, *Greek Text of Exodus*, 589.

precede the directions for the tabernacle furniture (𝕲 25.2–6; cf. 𝕲 35.4–8). These further demonstrate the importance of the priestly vestments for this redaction, for, as the Old Greek version shows, the materials demanded include not only the metal and fabrics for the tabernacle and its furniture, but also the precious stones for the ephod and breastpiece.

The people's response to Moses' instruction is portrayed as overwhelming to the extent that they have to be prevented from bringing more materials (𝕲 35.20–29*; 36.2–7).[81] It should be observed that the presentation by the women of their jewellery is one of the few places where the tabernacle account and the story of the golden calf intersect.[82] It seems likely that this redactional layer is also responsible for their integration. It would explain the emphasis on the entire people, who play a significant role in the golden calf narrative, but also the insistence on the people's generosity and their punctilious obedience to the divine instructions as seen in the fabrication of the priestly vestments. Their assiduousness leaves the reader in no doubt that the lessons from the 'great sin' of the golden calf have been taken to heart and the covenant between God and the Israelites repaired.

Israel Knohl has rightly noted that the attention to the Israelites aligns Exod 35 with the holiness literature.[83] This is also true of the Sabbath legislation that now frames the golden calf narrative (31.12–18; 35.1–3) and appears to have been an important tool for inserting Exod 32–34 into the middle of the tabernacle account. Possibly the instructions about bringing oil for the lamp (27.20–21) and providing for the daily offering (29.38–42) belong to the same redactional layer. The instructions about the oil again require the Israelites to provide for the tabernacle and emphasize the close relationship between the people and the priests. The reference to the people providing for the lamp provides a neat *inclusio* with the opening of the instructions about the tabernacle and its furniture (25.2–7; 27.20–21).

Enhanced Priestly Ritual Revisions

The secondary nature of Exod 30–31 has long been recognized. The absence of the incense altar from many parts of the Old Greek version of Exod 35–40 shows that Exod 30–31 must have been composed subsequently to significant sections

---

[81] The list of items to be constructed in 𝕲 35.9–19 interrupts the connection between Moses' instructions to collect the materials (𝕲 35.4–8) and the people's offering (𝕲 35.20–29*).

[82] 'Wenn der PB¹ unter den Gewandnadeln, Fingerringen und dem rund beperlten Halsschmuck auch die goldenen Ohr- und Nasenringe (*næzæm*) erwähnt, dann wollte er damit wieder auf Ex 32 spielen, denn aus eben diesen Preziosen war das Goldene Kalb hergestellt worden (V.2–3)' (Albertz, *Exodus 19–40*, 334).

[83] Knohl, *Sanctuary of Silence*, 193.

94 THE MAKING OF THE TABERNACLE

of the compliance account. The addition of Exod 30–31 further elevates the position of Aaron as high priest, distinguishing him from his sons, and the priesthood from the people. Instructions are given to construct an incense altar and a laver. The use of the incense altar is restricted to Aaron alone. Whilst Aaron and his sons light the lamps, only Aaron is instructed to offer incense on the gold altar, and he alone is to purify it annually (30.1–10). The laver, however, is to be constructed for the use of both Aaron and his sons. Its placement between the altar of burnt offering and the tent of meeting places it beyond the point where the people may go (30.17–21). The instructions for preparing the anointing oil and the incense underscore the priesthood's unique position. Neither oil nor incense may be used for profane purposes (30.22–38).

By elevating the position of the priesthood and the high priest, Exod 30–31 could be viewed as a response to the enhanced role the people are given in the construction of the tabernacle in Exod 35–40 and in the affairs of the holy more broadly in the Holiness Code. The reassertion of the rights of the priesthood are not dissimilar to the dynamics visible in the story of Korah, where the unique call of Aaron is reasserted in the face of claims about the holiness of the people (Num 16–17). The role of the people and the master craftsmen is not eliminated. The call of Bezalel and Oholiab from Exod 35 is reproduced almost verbatim in 31.1–6,[84] together with a list of what is to be constructed in 31.7–11.

The addition of two further pieces of furniture and the rituals of anointing and offering incense required various editorial interventions across the tabernacle account which sought to integrate this novel material. That this was an ongoing challenge is apparent in some of the differences between the Old Greek and the Masoretic versions. The Old Greek version, for example, has no equivalent to the Masoretic Text's account of the incense altar's construction ($\mathfrak{M}$ 37.25–28),[85] and the laver is not mentioned in the Old Greek's account of Exod 40. As a result, it is sometimes difficult to attribute such interventions to any particular redactional level with confidence. At the beginning of the construction account, the call to donate and its realization is interrupted by instructions about what is to be constructed ($\mathfrak{G}$ 35.9–19). The list of items includes an instruction to formulate the oil and the incense ($\mathfrak{G}$ 35.14, 19).[86] Similarly, the account of how the fabricated items

---

[84] The only significant change is the replacement of the uncomfortable וּלְהוֹרֹת נָתַן בְּלִבּוֹ הוּא וְאָהֳלִיאָב (35.34) with the slightly better אֲנִי הִנֵּה נָתַתִּי אִתּוֹ אֵת אָהֳלִיאָב (31.6).

[85] Note also the inclusion of the oil and incense in the Masoretic Text (25.6; 35.8) which are absent in the Old Greek.

[86] The repetition of oil and incense in vv. 14 and 19 is clearly problematic. Arguably, $\mathfrak{G}$ 35.9–19 is one of the most difficult passages in the construction account of the Old Greek. It is perhaps best to regard the reference to the court (v. 12), the stones (v. 13) and the incense and oil of anointing (v. 14) as a later insertion. This was either inspired by the reference to the leaders donating the stones, the incense and the oil of anointing (vv. 27–28), or inserted at the same time. Without this intrusion, the order of the materials is fairly similar to that found in 31.7–11: tent, furniture, priestly vestments, oil and incense.

were delivered to Moses in ᴕ 39.14–23 refers to the oil and incense (ᴕ 39.16). The attribution of the vestments and tent to Oholiab and the Israelite artisans and the tabernacle furniture to Bezalel generates a tension with the conclusion of the tabernacle account which attributes to Moses the completion of the work. The tension is resolved through the deliverance of the completed items to Moses.

Despite their differences, the call to construct the items (ᴕ 35.9–19) and the deliverance of the completed items to Moses (ᴕ 39.14–23) probably have in common a tendency to obscure the fact that two altars were constructed. In both cases the altar is qualified as 'the altar and all its utensils' (ᴕ 35.17; 39.16), a collocation that occurs only in relation to the altar of burnt offering and not the altar of incense. Yet, in ᴕ 35.17 the altar is mentioned immediately following furniture found in the outer sanctum, whilst in ᴕ 39.16 the altar features after the ark and before the furniture of the outer sanctum, as well as in conjunction with the oil and incense. It is possible that the list of items that follow the call of Bezalel and Oholiab in 31.7–11 has similar dynamics. Unusually, the Old Greek refers to 'altars' (τὰ θυσιαστήρια; ᴕ 31.8), whilst the Masoretic Text has 'the altar of incense and the altar of burnt offering' (וְאֵת מִזְבַּח הַקְּטֹרֶת וְאֶת־מִזְבַּח הָעֹלָה; 𝔐 31.8–9). It is possible, especially when compared to ᴕ 35.17 and 39.16 that 31.8 originally referred to a single altar, which the Greek translator rendered as a plural because he was aware that the tabernacle had two altars,[87] and the Masoretic Text expanded as part of a process of standardization. If a singular וְאֵת מִזְבַּח lies behind the Old Greek's translation, we have a further example of obfuscation because the altar occurs immediately after the ark and before the furniture located in the outer sanctum. Thus, a single altar is mentioned, but it is not the altar of burnt offering, which was originally *the* altar of the tabernacle, but the altar of incense. The instructions to Moses to erect and anoint the sanctuary (ᴕ 40.1–13) and the account of the sanctuary's erection (ᴕ 40.16–27) pursue a different strategy and may have been appended subsequently. They distinguish the altar of incense from the altar of burnt offering and describe the placement of both within the sanctuary complex. The distinctive nature of Exod 40 is also indicated by its use of the composite expression מִשְׁכַּן אֹהֶל מוֹעֵד, 'tabernacle of the tent of meeting' (𝔐 40.2, 6, 29).[88]

Numbers-Influenced Additions

There also exists a collection of additions which reflects attempts to harmonize the tabernacle account with late material in the book of Numbers. A number of these concern the funding of the tabernacle. Whilst the earlier levels of the

---

[87] That this happened in ᴕ 31.8 and not in ᴕ 35.17 and 39.16 can simply be explained by the fact that 31.8 had 'altar' rather than 'altar and its utensils'.

[88] The only other appearance of מִשְׁכַּן אֹהֶל מוֹעֵד is in 𝔐 39.32.

96   THE MAKING OF THE TABERNACLE

tabernacle account envisaged the people freely donating materials for the sanctuary, Exod 30.11–16 and 𝔊 39.1–11 describe a poll tax relating to the census of the people described in Num 1–2. The first reference to the census in 30.11–16 interrupts the connection between the construction of the two pieces of sanctuary furniture, whilst in 𝔊 39.1–11 it functions as a summary of the materials used at the end of the construction account and prior to the completed items being handed over to Moses.

Further texts that show the influence of late texts in the book Numbers include the offering of precious stones as well as the oil and incense by the leaders (𝔊 35.26–27). The leaders of the Israelites are scarcely mentioned in Exodus and Leviticus, but are mentioned frequently in Numbers. Further, the construction of the altar of burnt offering (𝔊 38.22–24) refers to Korah's revolt (Num 16–17). Finally, the description of the cloud's guidance leading the people in the journey (𝔐 40.36–38 ≈ 𝔊 40.30–32) appears prematurely and summarizes the more detailed account found in Num 9.15–23.

Standardization and Harmonization

The final stages of composition that produced the consonantal texts of the Masoretic version and the Samaritan Pentateuch involved processes of standardization and harmonization. Where the compliance account departed markedly from the instructions, such as in the construction of the tent and the furniture (𝔊 37–38; 𝔐 36.8–37.24), the revision of the text entailed repurposing material from the instructions. Similarly in the account of the bronze altar, the mention of Korah's rebellion presents an anachronism that was removed by replacing the existing text with material developed from the instructions (𝔊 38.22–24; 𝔐 38.1–7). The lists of items to be constructed, delivered, or assembled that are found repeatedly in the tabernacle account are given a standard order: tent, furniture (ark, atonement cover, table, lampstand, incense altar, altar of burnt offering, laver), courtyard, vestments. This standard order had already begun to emerge in the late material of 𝔊 40 and also determined the arrangement of the entire construction account, except for the construction of the courtyard and its hangings which immediately followed that of the tent. As we have seen, many of the differences between the Masoretic Text and the Samaritan Pentateuch reflect continued efforts within the Samaritan textual tradition to harmonize and standardize the tabernacle account.

Conclusion

It has long been appreciated within critical scholarship that the tabernacle account reflects an extended history of composition. Exod 30–31 and 35–40 were identified as secondary with the compliance account composed subsequently as evidenced by its integration of the incense altar. Beyond these observations, the history of composition was rarely worked out in detail. Where this has been done, however, the text-critical evidence of the Old Greek has been omitted. When it is taken into account, a different picture emerges with the earliest layers of the compliance account preceding the composition of Exod 30–31 and with additional redactional levels in evidence in the compliance account.

In summary, my model for the composition of the tabernacle account proposes the following stages.

(1) The priestly *Grundschrift* concluded with the tabernacle account and included Exod 25.1; 25.8–28.41aα*; 29.45–46; 40.16–17, 33b, 35b.

(2) At an early stage the priestly *Grundschrift* was revised in light of Lev 16. This revision included Exod 25.17–21; 26.34; 28.37–41*; 29.1–37, 43–44. At some subsequent stage, Exod 25.22 and 28.42–43 were appended.

(3) The earliest material in the compliance account described how the tabernacle was constructed by Moses and the two workers. This compositional level consisted of 𝕲 35.30, 34bβ–35*; 37–38*.

(4) The tabernacle account was revised under the influence of the Holiness Code to include the people in the task of constructing the sanctuary. The Israelite Artisans Level included Exod 25.2–6; [28.3–5]; 31.12–17; [31.18–34.35*]; 35.1–8, 𝕲 35.20–36.40*; 38.19–21*. It possibly also included Exod 27.20–21; 29.38–42.

(5) The tabernacle account was subsequently revised to include additional rituals that emphasized the significance of the priesthood included Exod 30.1–10, 17–38; 31.1–11. Further revisions that were probably related include Exod 35.9–19*; 𝕲 39.14–23; 40.1–13, 16–27 as well as Lev 8. The closely related texts of Exod 29.21, 36–37 were probably added at a subsequent stage.

(6) Various late additions were inspired by the book of Numbers including Exod 30.11–16; 35.27–28; 𝕲 38.22–27; 39.1–13; 40.36–38. After these additions, the tabernacle account had the shape of what was the *Vorlage* of the Old Greek account. At some point, Exod 37 must have suffered some damage that led to the truncated version that we now see in Vaticanus. The Old Latin of Monacensis also reflects this impaired perspective on the construction of the tabernacle proper, but sought to repair it.

(7) The compliance account was significantly revised in light of the instructions with a concerted attempt to produce a harmonious and consistent text, not least through standardized lists. This process resulted in the textual ancestor of the Masoretic Text.

(8) This process of harmonization and standardization was continued, but with the instructions being revised in light of the compliance account. The text found in the Samaritan Pentateuch and 4Q22 reflects these scribal efforts.

98   THE MAKING OF THE TABERNACLE

In many of its stages, the proposed development of the tabernacle account can be coordinated with an understanding of the growth of the priestly literature as it has emerged over the last twenty-five years. An original priestly document that extended as far as Exod 40 was subsequently expanded as far as Lev 16. At a later stage a Holiness redaction may have created a Hexateuch that combined priestly and Deuteronomic material with the Holiness Code mediating between the two. At this point the golden calf story was inserted between the instructions and the compliance account. Finally, the various late priestly materials in the book of Numbers, which are some of the very latest pieces of the Pentateuchal composition, show an impact on the tabernacle account. Alongside these redactional layers that can be coordinated with the wider picture of the growth of the Pentateuch, there are few stages that are distinctive to the tabernacle account, including the two workers layer and the enhanced priestly rituals layer.

The resulting picture of the tabernacle account's development reveals shifting representations of the individuals and groups involved in the construction and rituals of the tabernacle. This suggests a complex process of negotiation about the structure of the ideal theocratic society within Second Temple priestly circles. In this process, different roles and responsibilities are assigned to the high priest, the priests, Levites, the leaders, as well as ordinary male and female Israelites. The task of the following chapters will be to examine the portrayal of these different groups and something of the dynamics of negotiation.

PART II

THE CONSTRUCTION OF PRIESTLY HEGEMONY

4

The Tabernacle and Its Gloriously Attired Priest

Less than three months after the exodus from Egypt, the Israelites arrive at the mountain of revelation (Exod 19.1–2). The content of the divine disclosure at the mountain reveals the central theological concerns of the major Pentateuchal traditions. In the Deuteronomistic tradition, Mount Horeb is the place where Moses received the law. In the priestly tradition, however, Mount Sinai is the place where Moses is instructed about the tabernacle. In Exodus as we now have it, these two perspectives have been juxtaposed. The legal perspective enjoys the opening position with the Decalogue and the Covenant Code, but it is the cultic view that has been given the final word, and now dominates the book of Exodus.

There is widespread agreement that the priestly source includes the itinerary in Exod 19 that delivers Israel to the wilderness of Sinai (v. 1).[1] The trail of the priestly source is not picked up again until Exod 24.15 when Moses ascends the mountain. Moses' upward movement is reciprocated with the descent of the cloud and the divine glory upon the mountain. The language is highly significant: 'YHWH's glory *settled* (וַיִּשְׁכֹּן) upon Mount Sinai' (24.16). The instructions that Moses will receive describe how a sanctuary is to be built 'so that I may *settle* (וְשָׁכַנְתִּי) amongst them' (25.8).[2] The same language is repeated in the concluding statement about the tabernacle's purpose in 29.45–46, which with its allusions to Exod 6.7 confirms that the priestly narrative finds its climax in the tabernacle's construction.[3] When the sanctuary is complete, the numinous presence of Israel's God that has descended onto the mountain in fiery splendour will be able to accompany the people permanently. No ordinary abode will suffice, and detailed

---

[1] Oswald discusses the various literary-critical issues relating to these verses and attributes vv. 1–2a to P (Wolfgang Oswald, *Israel am Gottesberg: eine Untersuchung zur Literaturgeschichte der vorderen Sinaiperikope Ex 19–24 und deren historischem Hintergrund*, OBO 159 [Freiburg im Üchtland: Universitätsverlag, 1998], 88–9). Propp attributes v. 2a to the redactor due to the rather inelegant doubling back to mention Rephidim (Propp, *Exodus 19–40*, 101).

[2] The Old Greek version reads 'I will appear among you' (καὶ ὀφθήσομαι ἐν ὑμῖν), which turns the intention into one of self-revelation (Wevers, *Greek Text of Exodus*, 395). For discussion of the text-critical and literary-critical issues in Exod 25.8–9, see also Domenico Lo Sardo, 'Ex 25:8-9 MT-LXX: Textual Differences or Different Hermeneutics? The Divine Dwelling on the *Mountain* and/or in a *Sanctuary*', *LASBF* 69 (2019): 79–98.

[3] See Matthias Ederer, *Identitätsstiftende Begegnung: Die theologische Deutung des regelmäßigen Kultes Israels in der Tora*, FAT 121 (Tübingen: Mohr Siebeck, 2018), 260–79.

The Making of the Tabernacle and the Construction of Priestly Hegemony. Nathan MacDonald, Oxford University Press.
© Nathan MacDonald 2023. DOI: 10.1093/oso/9780198813859.003.0005

102　THE MAKING OF THE TABERNACLE

instructions are provided to Moses so that he can construct a magnificent tent decked out in costly fabrics and precious metals.

In the priestly conception of the world, the tabernacle is undoubtedly important. Indeed, in many recent reconstructions, the account of the tabernacle's construction in Exod 25–31, 35–40* marks the conclusion and climax of the original priestly document, the *Grundschrift*. The priestly document opens with the creation of the world (Gen 1), and the creation finds its fulfilment in the making of the tabernacle. My claim in this chapter is that the central focus of the original priestly writer is on Aaron, the priest who serves within the tabernacle. It is not just that the tabernacle like other ancient Near Eastern sanctuaries needs servants, though this is undoubtedly true. It is rather that the tabernacle account in the original priestly document reaches its climax with Aaron's sacred vestments and ascribes to them an instrumental significance within the sanctuary (Exod 28). The priestly literature is famously reticent when it comes to the meaning of its narratives and rituals. But not so when it comes to Aaron's vestments where each item is suffused with ritual meaning.

Such an observation about the priestly vestments places a question mark against the tendency to describe Exod 25–31 and 35–40 as simply 'the tabernacle account' and downplay the significance of the vestments. Scholarship from a variety of perspectives has succumbed to this error. In their commentaries, Childs and Fretheim, prominent proponents of a final form or canonical approach to the biblical literature, say almost nothing about the priestly vestments.[4]

Taking a very different approach to the biblical text, some redactional critical analyses of the tabernacle account have removed virtually all references to the priests and their vestments from the original priestly document.[5] It can even be asked whether the labelling of this literary work as the *priestly* literature is inapt and misleading.[6] In contrast, my own literary-critical analysis will suggest a position that is diametrically opposite. The *priestly* document is no misnomer. The gloriously adorned priest is indispensable to the functioning of the tabernacle.

In this chapter, I will first examine the instructions to Moses about how to manufacture the tabernacle and its furniture (Exod 25–27), before turning to Aaron's priestly vestments (Exod 28). Examining the instructions for the tabernacle before the vestments serves two purposes. First, the tabernacle provides the context for the sacerdotal ministry of Aaron. Second, the reticence of these chapters about the purpose of the tabernacle provides a startling contrast with the animated portrayal of Aaron's vestments in which every article is suffused with meaning.

---

[4] Childs, *Exodus*, 512–52; Terence E. Fretheim, *Exodus*, IBC (Louisville, KY: John Knox Press, 1991), 263–78, 313–16.

[5] Pola, *Die ursprüngliche Priesterschrift*.

[6] See, e.g., Peter Weimar, *Studien zur Priesterschrift*, FAT 56 (Tübingen: Mohr Siebeck, 2008).

The Tabernacle

The hegemonic claims of the priestly authors are apparent in the opening instructions to Moses which insist that he is to construct the tabernacle and its furniture in accordance with the 'pattern' (תַּבְנִית) that he will be shown (25.9). The origins of the tabernacle are heavenly. There has been no little discussion about precisely what is meant by the word תַּבְנִית, 'pattern'. When Moses ascends into the cloud does he behold the heavenly archetype of which the tabernacle is but a copy? The idea that temples were mirrors of the gods' celestial dwellings was certainly common in the ancient Near East.[7] Or did Moses see a scale model of the tabernacle when he ascended into heaven? When Ahaz saw an altar in Damascus, he sent back to Jerusalem 'its pattern' (תַּבְנִיתוֹ) and it is possibly a scale model that Uriah the priest received from the king (2 Kgs 16.10).[8] Archaeological excavations in the Levant have unearthed numerous examples of temple models from the first millennium BCE.[9] Or is Moses shown a plan? When David passes on his temple plans to Solomon they are set out in writing (בִּכְתָב), which suggests something rather like a blueprint (1 Chron 29.11, 12, 19).[10] However תַּבְנִית is to be understood, the central claim is that Exod 25–27 reflects the pattern which has been revealed by God on the mountain and it is to be followed.

The importance of an exact correspondence between the pattern shown on the mountain and the tabernacle that Moses is to build is reiterated throughout Exod 25–27 with slightly variant wording.

In accordance with all that I show you, the pattern of the tabernacle (תַּבְנִית הַמִּשְׁכָּן) and the pattern of its vessels (תַּבְנִית כָּל־כֵּלָיו), so you shall make it (25.9).

See that you make them according to their pattern (בְּתַבְנִיתָם) that you are being shown on the mountain (25.40).

You shall erect the tabernacle according to its manner (כְּמִשְׁפָּטוֹ) that you were shown on the mountain (26.30).

Just as you were shown on the mountain, thus you shall make (27.8).[11]

The exhortations serve not only to emphasize the punctiliousness with which the instructions are to be followed, they also provide the instructions with a clear

---

[7] The idea goes back at least as early as the Epistle to the Hebrews, but also enjoys more recent advocates (e.g. Clifford, 'Tent of El', 226; Homan, *To Your Tents*, 34).

[8] For the possibility that the תַּבְנִית was a model with examples of Near Eastern parallels, see Hurowitz, *Exalted House*, 168–70.

[9] For a recent discussion see Christian Frevel, 'Gotteshäuser en miniature? Architekturbezug, Funktion und Medialität der sogenannten Tempelmodelle der südlichen Levante', in *Sakralarchitektur*, ed. Jens Kamlah, ADPV (Wiesbaden: Harassowitz, 2022), 153–234.

[10] Houtman, *Exodus*, III: 345–6.

[11] For this reading see footnote 18 in Chapter 3 of this volume.

104 THE MAKING OF THE TABERNACLE

four-part structure.[12] The first section describes the sanctuary furniture (25.10–39) followed by the tent itself (26.1–29), the screens, the placement of the furniture, and the construction of the altar (26.31–27.8a), and, finally, the construction of the courtyard (27.9–19). This literary structure implies a basic division between the tent sanctuary itself and the courtyard. The division within the sanctuary between the inner sanctum and the outer sanctum is not emphasized.

The correspondence between the pattern that Moses sees and the tabernacle that is to be constructed is underlined by the literary pattern of the instructions. The actions of constructing are expressed with *weqatal* formations. Nominal clauses provide further detail, especially about lengths, and *yiqtol* formations provide functional information.[13] The opening instructions for the construction of the altar provide a brief, but representative example.

> 1 You shall make (וְעָשִׂיתָ) the altar of acacia wood,
>   five cubits long and five cubits wide;
> the altar shall be (יִהְיֶה) square,
>   three cubits high.
>
> 2 You shall make (וְעָשִׂיתָ) its horns on its four corners;
>   its horns shall be (תִּהְיֶיןָ) part of it,
> you shall plate (וְצִפִּיתָ) it with bronze (27.1–2).

The literary impression is of a taut description with the focus simply on what is needed to manufacture the tabernacle and its furniture. The crisp, precise statements suggest that there is no scope for artistic licence. This sense is not negated even if a close examination of the instructions reveals various ambiguities.[14]

The Furniture in the Most Holy Place (Exod 25.10–40)

As we have seen, the instructions in Exod 25–27 describe the furniture first and then the space where the furniture is to be located. The importance of the furniture is underlined by the use of precious metals, whilst the tent and the courtyard are mostly constructed out of fabrics. The description of the furniture moves from the inside of the tabernacle outwards: first the ark, then the table, the lampstand and, finally, after the instructions for the tent, the altar.

---

[12] Steins, 'Heiligtum'.

[13] For detailed discussion of the literary pattern see Longacre, 'Building'; Utzschneider, *Das Heiligtum*, 190–4.

[14] George rightly observes that the descriptions are given from the perspective of those using the sanctuary. They are not blueprints that would have been needed by a craftsman (George, *Israel's Tabernacle*, 71).

The ark is described first and is clearly understood as the most important item within the tabernacle.[15] As the name suggests, the ark (הָאָרֹן) is a box or chest. The bones of Joseph are said to have been placed in an אָרוֹן (Gen 50.26), and the term is also used for the money chest installed at the entrance to the temple (2 Kgs 12.9–10). The tabernacle's ark is to be manufactured out of acacia wood plated in gold. It is a rectangular cuboid approximately 1.25m long, 0.75m wide, and 0.75m high. It had some form of moulding around it,[16] and was designed to be portable with gold rings that held gold-plated poles of acacia wood. Whether these rings were mounted at the top of the ark or at its bottom is unclear from the textual description.[17]

In the book of Exodus as we now have it, the ark is overshadowed—literally and literarily—by an article called the 'atonement cover' (כַּפֹּרֶת). This item is attributed considerable significance as the precise location where God meets with Moses and atonement occurs (Exod 25.22). As we have seen, however, there are good reasons for supposing that the כַּפֹּרֶת was not originally part of the description of the ark, but rather was incorporated under the influence of Lev 16. Consequently, I will examine it more closely in the following chapter. Maintaining our focus on the original priestly document, the ark is always identified as either 'the ark' (הָאָרֹן), or 'the ark of the testimony' (אֲרֹן הָעֵדֻת). The latter expression is almost entirely limited to the priestly literature.[18] But what is the testimony that is to be deposited in the ark? In the deuteronomistic tradition the ark holds the stone tablets of the Decalogue (Deut 10.1–5). It is possible that the priestly authors are familiar with this tradition and reflect it using their own distinctive idiom. Certainly, in later stages of the development of the text of Exodus, the Decalogue is equated with the testimony (Exod 31.18; 32.15; 34.28–29). In the priestly *Grundschrift*, however, there is no account of the testimony being manufactured by Moses or being received by him, nor is there any identification of what the testimony is.[19] As a result, some have speculated that the testimony may not be the Decalogue, since this reflects the Deuteronomic focus on the law, but might rather be the model of the tabernacle revealed to Moses.[20] In truth, we cannot say what the original priestly authors may have had in mind. Lest it be thought unconvincing that the priestly writer should not have provided an account of how the testimony was manufactured or what it was, the same also appears to be true of the Urim and Thummim. Thus, for some of the most sacred objects in its cultic apparatus, the priestly authors are decidedly reticent about them and their origins.

---

[15] For a detailed discussion of the ark, its form and possible significance as well as previous scholarship, see Raanan Eichler, *The Ark and the Cherubim*, FAT 146 (Tübingen: Mohr Siebeck, 2021). For literary critical issues relating to the ark, see Porzig, *Die Lade Jahwes*.

[16] The exact meaning of זֵר has occasioned considerable discussion. For a recent analysis of different proposals see Raanan Eichler, 'The Meaning of Zēr', *VT* 64 (2014): 196–210.

[17] For the problem of whether the poles were retractable, see most recently Eichler, 'Poles'.

[18] The sole exception is Josh 4.16.   [19] Utzschneider, *Das Heiligtum*, 110.

[20] E.g. George, *Israel's Tabernacle*, 170–2.

106 THE MAKING OF THE TABERNACLE

We can be certain that the ark was initially envisaged by the priestly authors as a container. Even if a later redactor augmented this picture with a novel element of atonement by providing the ark with a כַּפֹּרֶת, the idea of a lid did highlight the ark's function as a receptacle. Seow has rightly observed that this excludes any necessity for seeing the ark as either a divine throne or a footstool.[21] This seems rather surprising since by analogy with Near Eastern temples the ark occupies the location in the tabernacle where we expect the divine image to be located. In addition, the deuteronomistic literature identifies the ark with the palpable presence of YHWH. Since the tabernacle is envisaged in Exod 25–27 as the place where YHWH will dwell, the reticence of the original priestly authors about the only piece of furniture in the most holy place other than to portray it as a receptable of the testimony is rather striking. The authors avoid saying precisely *how* YHWH is resident in the sanctuary.

The remaining furniture in Exod 25 contributes to making the tabernacle a comfortable residence. Like the ark, the table is made of an acacia core that has been plated with gold. It is about 1m long, 0.50m wide, and 0.75m tall. It too had a moulding, a rim with its own moulding, and rings which held carrying poles. The table also had a dinner service consisting of various vessels for serving food and drink. The lampstand has several distinctive features. It is made entirely from gold without an acacia core, only its weight is enumerated and not its size, and no mention is made of carrying poles.[22] Envisaging what the authors intended by their description is particularly challenging in the case of the lampstand.[23] Even if they are difficult to decipher, it is particularly noticeable that there is significant use of botanical imagery to describe the various features of the lampstand: reeds (קָנֶה), flowers (פֶּרַח), almonds (מְשֻׁקָּדִים), calyxes (כַּפְתֹּר).

The significance of these two pieces of furniture has often seen interpreters take recourse to symbolism in various different ways in order to avoid the implications of anthropomorphism. The table has a significance that is transparent,[24] and the offerings that God received are often called a food gift (אִשֶּׁה) in the priestly literature.[25] This notion has often been considered problematic and has called forth a measure of apologetics. Commentators have frequently relativized its implications by noting that there are biblical texts that ridicule the idea that

---

[21] C.L Seow, 'The Designation of the Ark in Priestly Theology', *HAR* 8 (1984): 190–1.

[22] Num 4.10 seems to envisage the lamp being carried on a bar (הַמּוֹט).

[23] The discussion of this issue has been extensive, see esp. Carol L. Meyers, *The Tabernacle Menorah*, ASOR Dissertation Series 2 (Ann Arbor, MI: Scholars Press, 1976); Jens Voss, *Die Menora: Gestalt und Funktion des Leuchters im Tempel zu Jerusalem*, OBO 128 (Göttingen: Vandenhoeck & Ruprecht, 1993); Rachel Hachlili, *The Menorah, the Ancient Seven-Armed Candelabrum: Origin, Form, and Significance*, JSJSup 68 (Leiden: Brill, 2001); Rachel Hachlili, *The Menorah: Evolving into the Most Important Jewish Symbol* (Leiden: Brill, 2018).

[24] *Contra* Dozeman who writes, 'the symbolic meaning of the table is difficult to determine' (Dozeman, *Commentary on Exodus*, 616).

[25] For the meaning of אִשֶּׁה, see discussion in Jacob Milgrom, *Leviticus 1–16: A New Translation with Introduction and Commentary*, AB 3 (New York: Doubleday, 1991), 161–2. For an alternative view that retains the traditional connection to 'fire offerings', see James W. Watts, *Leviticus 1–10*, HCOT (Leuven: Peeters, 2013), 209–11.

YHWH needs nourishment (e.g. Ps 50.12–13).[26] For its part, the lampstand has been attributed symbolic meanings. Either the lampstand symbolizes the astronomical lights that are subject to YHWH and serve in attendance to him, or the lampstand represents the tree of life.[27] The difficulties in having recourse to two very different strategies for explaining the significance of the table and the lampstand is readily apparent. A more compelling solution is that the table and the lampstand provided for YHWH's comfort in his dwelling. The table provided food for nourishment and the lampstand provided light within the tent. The occasional non-cultic references to tables and lamps in the Hebrew Bible frequently occur in the context of the royal palace or the houses of the wealthy (e.g. 2 Kgs 4.10). Consequently, they were thought to be suitable furnishings for the divine dwelling.

The Sanctuary (Exod 26.1–30)

The description of the tabernacle's furniture is followed by that of tabernacle proper. It consists of two curtains and two covers of skin (26.1–14) that were supported by a solid structure of frames and bars (26.15–30). The inner curtain is identified as 'the dwelling' (הַמִּשְׁכָּן) and is to be made of fine linen with images of cherubim embroidered into it. The outer curtain is called 'the tent' (הָאֹהֶל) and is made of goat's hair. The two curtains were made in two parts with blue loops on their adjoining edges. These loops were joined together with clasps made from gold for the inner curtain and bronze for the outer curtain. We might wonder why the curtains were made in two parts, rather than one. The assumption that practical considerations—the weight of the curtain and their unwieldiness—might have been the primary issue is belied by the fact that the covers were apparently made of one piece. Albertz has observed that the boundary of loops and clasps fell at the point where the veil that separated the most holy place and the holy place would have been sited. Thus, the loops and clasps marked the liminal point between the inner and outer sanctum.[28] The inner and outer curtains fell down the sides and rear of the sanctuary but were open on the east side. These two curtains were protected by two coverings: one made of rams' skins and the other possibly of leather with beadwork (26.14).[29]

---

[26] E.g. Houtman, *Exodus*, III: 393–4.

[27] The lampstand certainly acquired additional symbolic significance in the Second Temple period, but there is nothing in Exod 25 to suggest it had acquired these when the text was composed. See esp. Hachlili, *Ancient Seven-Armed Candelabrum*; Hachlili, *Most Important Jewish Symbol*.

[28] Albertz, *Exodus 19–40*, 172–5. Cf. Haran, *Temples*, 151.

[29] The meaning of עֹרֹת תְּחָשִׁים is far from certain. Noonan provides a helpful overview of the different proposals (Benjamin J. Noonan, 'Hide or Hue? Defining Hebrew תַּחַשׁ', *Bib* 93 [2012]: 580–9). Amongst recent proposals, Dalley has argued that the word is cognate with Akkadian *duḫšu* and means 'faience beadwork' (Stephanie Dalley, 'Hebrew *Taḥaš*, Akkadian *Duḫšu*, Faience and Beadwork', *JSS* 45 [2000]: 1–19; Nathan Mastnjak, 'Hebrew *taḥaš* and the West Semitic Tent Tradition', *VT* 67

108 THE MAKING OF THE TABERNACLE

The curtains were supported by a structure that consisted of wooden frames (קְרָשִׁים). These frames were about 5m high and 0.75m wide. Pegs at the bottom fitted into silver bases which supported them. The frames were kept in position by crossbars that ran perpendicular to them. It has been observed that if the frames were made of solid wood, two problems would have arisen. First, acacia species are typically too small to produce beams of this size. Second, the resulting beams would be too heavy to transport. Kennedy famously proposed that the קְרָשִׁים were frameworks, rather than solid boards.[30] Such concerns are, perhaps, too beholden to the assumption that every aspect of the tabernacle must have been practically feasible.

The Veil and Screen, the Placement of the Furniture, and the Altar (Exod 26.31–27.8)

The following section describes the two remaining items that are required to complete the tabernacle proper: the veil (הַפָּרֹכֶת) and the screen of the tent opening (מָסָךְ לְפֶתַח הָאֹהֶל). The veil divides the sanctuary into an inner sanctum and an outer sanctum; the inner sanctum is called 'the most holy place' (קֹדֶשׁ הַקֳּדָשִׁים) and the outer sanctum is 'the holy place' (הַקֹּדֶשׁ; Exod 26.33). The screen closes off the tent sanctuary at the eastern end (26.31–33). Like the inner curtain, the veil is embroidered with cherubim so that the inner sanctum was decorated with cherubim on every side. The screen, on the other hand, was made from fine linen and coloured yarns without images. The two entrances are also differentiated by the metal from which their bases are constructed: silver for the veil and bronze for the screen. Having described the features that would complete the sanctuary structure, the priestly authors gave directions for where the furniture was to be located: the ark in the most holy place, and the table on the north side of the holy place and the lampstand on the south side (26.34–35). The arrangement of the furniture creates a corridor through the outer sanctum that would allow easy access for the priest or for YHWH himself directly into the inner sanctum through the veil.

The altar is the last item of furniture to be described, and the only one located in the courtyard (27.1–8). As has often been observed the initial instructions envisage only one altar, simply called 'the altar' (הַמִּזְבֵּחַ). It is the largest piece of furniture measuring 2.5m square and 1.5m high. The altar has an acacia core like the furniture in the sanctuary, but is overlaid with bronze rather than gold. The carrying poles are similarly covered in bronze. The priestly authors are clearly

---

[2017]: 204–12). Noonan, however, argues that the word is cognate with Egyptian *ṯḥs*, a term associated with leather (Noonan, 'Hide or Hue?').

[30] A.R.S. Kennedy, 'Tabernacle', *HDB* 4: 653–68.

THE TABERNACLE AND ITS GLORIOUSLY ATTIRED PRIEST   109

aware of the practicalities of carrying this large item were it to be solid and prescribe that it must be hollow with planks (נְבוּב לֻחֹת). Modern interpreters have often been concerned with further practical difficulties. Would such an installation have been able to withstand the temperatures that would have been needed to burn animal flesh, and how would the priests have serviced an altar that was so high?[31] We should not assume that what was described was feasible. More important was the idea that the divine need for sacrificial offerings was provided for by the existence of the altar.

The Courtyard (Exod 27.9–19)

The final section describes the courtyard which surrounds the tabernacle and in which the altar is to be located. The courtyard was an area rectangular in shape, about 50m long and 25m wide. It was shielded from view by linen sheets, 2.5m high and 2.5m wide, that were suspended from poles with silver hooks.[32] The poles sat in bronze bases. In the centre of the eastern side there was an opening protected by a screen, about 10m long. Like the screen for the entrance to the tent, it is made from fine linen and coloured yarns without images. The central placement of the entrance to the courtyard would be consistent with the assumption usually made that the tabernacle itself was located along the central axis that ran from east to west. It is unclear, however, how far forward the tabernacle itself was located. Many scholars have proposed that the entrance to the tent was halfway into the courtyard which would divide the courtyard into two equal squares with sides of 25m with the ark at the centre of one and, perhaps, the altar at the centre of the other. This would have seen the tabernacle located 10m from the north, south and west sides of the courtyard.[33] This understanding is found in the plan presented by Haran (Figure 4.1). Propp, on the other hand, suggests that the tent may have been located at the rear of the courtyard creating a larger public space in front of the tent.[34]

[31] See, e.g., Noth, *Exodus*, 215–16; Propp, *Exodus 19–40*, 499–501.

[32] For the translation of וֵ see, *inter alia*, William Johnstone, 'Biblical Hebrew *Wāwîm* in the Light of New Phoenician Evidence', *PEQ* 109 (1977): 95–102; Propp, *Exodus 19–40*, 418–19.

[33] Haran, *Temples*, 152–3; Nahum M. Sarna, *Exodus* שמות: *The Traditional Hebrew Text with the New JPS Translation*, JPS Torah Commentary (Philadelphia, PA: Jewish Publication Society of America, 1991), 155.

[34] Propp, *Exodus 19–40*, 498. If Magen's reconstruction of the Persian period temple at Mount Gerizim is correct, it would appear to have had its sanctuary at the rear of a large courtyard (Yitzhak Magen, 'The Dating of the First Phase of the Samaritan Temple on Mount Gerizim in Light of the Archaeological Evidence', in *Judah and the Judeans in the Fourth Century B.C.E.*, eds. Oded Lipschits, Gary N. Knoppers, and Rainer Albertz [Winona Lake, IN: Eisenbrauns, 2007], 157–211; Yitzhak Magen, *Mount Gerizim Excavations, Volume II. A Temple City*, Judea and Samaria Publications 8 [Jerusalem: Israel Antiquities Authority, 2008]).

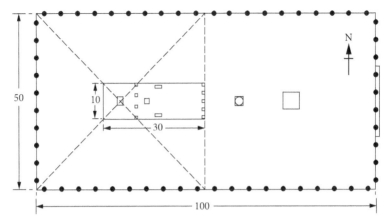

Figure 4.1 Plan of the tabernacle proposed in Menahem Haran's *Temples and Temple-Service in Ancient Israel*, 152; reproduced with permission from the Clarendon Press

The Ideology of the Tabernacle

The sanctuary that Moses is shown and instructed to make has a structure that corresponds to the symmetrical direct-axis long room temple that were common in Palestine during the second and first millennia BCE.[35] This temple type had a long room with the cella at the rear where the divine image was located. The doorway was on the opposite side of the temple to the cella and allowed direct access to the cella along the axis. There are many monumental examples of this temple type, including the temples at Tell Tayinat and Ain Dara, which have been excavated in recent decades, but the most well-known example of this temple type is, of course, the temple of Solomon which is known only from textual descriptions. The similarities between the tabernacle and the Jerusalem temple have long been recognized.

Although the biblical narrative portrays the tabernacle as a precursor to the temple, and even brought to rest within it (1 Kgs 8.4),[36] Wellhausen famously argued of the tabernacle that it is 'the copy, not the prototype, of the temple in Jerusalem'.[37] In comparison to the temple, the tabernacle is reduced in size and simplified.[38] The dimensions of the tabernacle are half of the temple. The temple

---

[35] Michael B. Hundley, *Gods in Dwellings: Temples and Divine Presence in the Ancient Near East* (Atlanta: Society of Biblical Literature, 2013), 107–14; Amihai Mazar, 'Temples of the Middle and Late Bronze Ages and the Iron Age', in *The Architecture of Ancient Israel: From the Prehistoric to the Persian Periods*, eds. Aaron Kempinski and Ronny Reich (Jerusalem: Israel Exploration Society, 1992), 161–89.

[36] For the textual relationship between Exod 25–40 and 1 Kgs 6–8 see now Rainer Albertz, 'How Jerusalem's Temple Was Aligned to Moses' Tabernacle: About the Historical Power of an Invented Myth', in *Biblical Narratives, Archaeology and Historicity: Essays in Honour of Thomas L. Thompson*, LHBOTS 680 (London: Bloomsbury, 2020), 198–209.

[37] Wellhausen, *Prolegomena*, 37.   [38] Albertz, *Exodus 19–40*, 176.

THE TABERNACLE AND ITS GLORIOUSLY ATTIRED PRIEST   111

has a footprint that is 60 cubits by 20 cubits, whilst the tabernacle is 30 by 10. The height of the temple was 30 cubits high, which is three times the height of the tabernacle. The discrepancy is probably to be explained by the fact that the height of the most holy place in the temple was 20 cubits high, twice that of the height of the tabernacle. In both the tabernacle and the temple, the most holy place was an exact cube. In the temple it was 20 cubits cubed, in the tabernacle 10 cubits cubed. Whilst the stone building of the temple could accommodate a void above the most holy place, this could not be easily replicated in the model of the tabernacle and so the entire tabernacle had the same height as the inner sanctum. All the furniture of the tabernacle can be seen as simplified versions of their temple equivalents. In Solomon's temple the free-standing cherubim are 5m high with a total wingspan of 5m; in the Masoretic, Samaritan, and Old Greek versions of the tabernacle the cherubim are smaller representations perched on the ends of the ark (1 Kgs 6.23–28). The temple has ten lampstands where the tabernacle has one (1 Kgs 7.48–50). The construction of the temple's outer altar goes unmentioned, as do its dimensions,[39] though its existence is assumed (1 Kgs 8.5, 22, 31, 54, 64).[40] There are, however, numerous other bronze items in the courtyard of the temple: the molten sea, the ten bronze stands with their lavers (1 Kgs 7.23–39).

The priestly literature's description of the tabernacle says very little about the significance of the tabernacle and its furniture. The priestly literature can be so taciturn because it shares a common Near Eastern theology. Ancient temples were understood to be the dwelling place of a deity, and the tabernacle is no different. The centrality of this idea for understanding the tabernacle is apparent in the initial instruction to Moses, 'so that I may settle (וְשָׁכַנְתִּי) amongst them' (25.8), which is repeated at the end of the instructions in 29.46, but is also implicit in the identification of the central structure as the 'tabernacle', or literally, 'the dwelling' (מִשְׁכָּן). The use of the root שׁ"כן is entirely appropriate for a temporary encampment and can be contrasted with the root יש"ב which denotes a permanent habitation.[41] The fact in no way diminishes the emphasis in Exod 25–27 on the sanctuary being constructed to be a fitting abode for Israel's God. The hangings of the courtyard and the tent structure safeguard YHWH's privacy. The altar and table ensure that his appetite is sated. The lampstand provides illumination for his dwelling place, while still guaranteeing that the most holy place is shaded behind the veil. The cherubim figures that decorate the veil and the inner curtain cater for the deity's aesthetic sensibilities, and the precious metals of the furniture ensure he is surrounded by an appropriate opulence. Haran observed that the

---

[39] According to 2 Chron 4.1, the altar was twenty cubits long, twenty cubits wide and ten cubits high. In comparison the tabernacle altar was five cubits long, five cubits wide and three cubits high. Japhet assumes that the text of 1 Kgs is corrupt and originally mentioned the altar (Sara Japhet, *I & II Chronicles: A Commentary*, OTL [Louisville, KY: Westminster John Knox, 1993], 564).

[40] See also 2 Kgs 16.14–15 where Ahaz removes the existing altar which is identified as made from bronze.

[41] For discussion see, *inter alia*, Görg, *Das Zelt der Begegnung*.

112   THE MAKING OF THE TABERNACLE

tabernacle featured what he described as a material gradation. The closer one approaches the most holy place, the more valuable the materials become. From bronze in the courtyard to gold in the tabernacle, from plain linen hangings to richly embroidered curtains with images of cherubim.[42] 'The more important the object, the more expensive and magnificent it has to be...the higher an item is on the scale of sanctity, the greater man's efforts to embellish it.'[43] As we have seen, some of the furniture, such as the lampstand and the table, may well have been enjoyed only by wealthier households in ancient Israel. The opulence of the tabernacle is, of course, unlike any other building, except perhaps the royal palace. As such the instructions in Exod 25–27 suggest a congruence between YHWH's dwelling and the royal palace that is consistent with the portrayal of royalty and divinity elsewhere in the Near East.

In Near Eastern accounts of temple building, divine and royal authority are mutually enforcing. Consistent with that, the task of building and repairing temples is usually a royal prerogative.[44] In the tabernacle account, however, there is no royal individual. Functionally, Moses receives the divine instructions and directs the work of sanctuary construction. But does Moses represent the Israelite monarchy? His descendants do not proceed to the throne of Israel or Judah. If Moses is not obviously a cipher for the monarchy, it is not the case that the high priest has displaced him. It is not Aaron who receives the instructions for how to build the sanctuary. Instead, Aaron is presented similarly to priests in other Near Eastern sanctuaries: he is a cultic servant who provides for the needs of the divine. Nevertheless, I will argue that the focus on the priestly vestments in Exod 28 suggests a role for Aaron that expands beyond that of a mere cultic servant.

The Priestly Vestments

The tabernacle like a palace needs servants to run it. In Exod 25–27 their presence is assumed for someone is needed to light the lamps, set food out on the table, and sacrifice on the altar. That priests are not mentioned is consistent with these chapters' character as building instructions and is no different to what we find in 1 Kgs 6–8 and Ezek 40–42. Unusually, however, the instructions for the tabernacle and its furniture are followed by extensive directions for the fabrication of the priestly vestments.[45] In his book on the construction of Solomon's

---

[42] Haran, *Temples*, 158–65.   [43] Haran, *Temples*, 164.

[44] For Near Eastern and biblical examples, see Hurowitz, *Exalted House*; Davis, *Reconstructing the Temple*.

[45] *Contra* Rooke who instead remarks that 'perhaps *not surprisingly*, the high priesthood is introduced by instructions for the office-holder's clothing and induction; in fact, the description of Aaron the high priest's ceremonial garments (Exod. 28:1–43; also Exod 39:1–31 and Lev. 8:5–9) is the first element of the instructions for the priesthood as a whole' (Rooke, *Zadok's Heirs*, 16; my italics). But if

temple in 1 Kgs 5–8, Hurowitz analysed numerous Near Eastern accounts of temple building and restoration from the time of the Sumerians to the Neo-Babylonian period.[46] It is notable that none of these contain a description of priestly vestments or ordination. Nor does the account of Solomon's temple in 1 Kgs 5–8. The precedent of Near Eastern temple building accounts does not prepare us for a description of the priests' garments or their ordination that we encounter in the book of Exodus. In fact, from the perspective of Near Eastern literature, the biblical description of Aaron's garments is highly unusual. As Strommenger observes of Akkadian texts, 'the regalia of the different priests and temple functionaries are rarely mentioned'.[47] The innovation that Exod 28 represents is rarely noticed, because, under the influence of Exod 28, the priestly vestments become a regular object of contemplation and wonder within Hellenistic Jewish literature. They are thematized, for example, by Aristeas, Ben Sira, Philo, and Josephus.[48] Though the importance of the vestments within Second Temple Judaism might cause us to miss its novelty, these early readers rightly direct us to the rhetorical emphasis on the vestments in the book of Exodus that has often been overlooked by modern readers.

Two Descriptions of the Priestly Vestments

Although the priestly vestments that are described in Exod 28 are the most well known and feature in most pictorial representations of Aaron's dress, there are within the broad priestly literature two different descriptions of the vestments worn by Aaron within the tabernacle. According to Exod 28, Aaron is to wear an intricate set of sacred vestments when he 'goes into the holy place before YHWH' (בְּבֹאוֹ אֶל־הַקֹּדֶשׁ לִפְנֵי יְהוָה; v. 35; cf. vv. 29–30). These include 'a breastpiece, an ephod, a robe, a chequered tunic, a turban and a sash' (v. 4) as well as a rosette (vv. 36–38) and linen undergarments (v. 42). The vestments are made from costly materials: gold, gemstones, fine linen, and yarns in blue, purple, and crimson. In contrast, Lev 16 describes the vestments that Aaron has to wear when he 'goes into the holy place' (יָבֹא אַהֲרֹן אֶל־הַקֹּדֶשׁ) to atone for Israel's sins: a tunic, undergarments, a sash,

---

we do not assume the familiar shape of the biblical text, the detailed portrayal of the priestly vestments is surprising.

[46] Hurowitz, *Exalted House*, 32–105.

[47] Eva Strommenger, 'Kleidung', *RlA* 6:27. Within biblical texts, the description of Aaron's vestments is also highly unusual. Imes rightly observes that 'this detailed treatment [in Exod 28] already distinguishes the priestly garments from any other apparel in the HB' (Carmen Joy Imes, 'Between Two Worlds: The Functional and Symbolic Significance of the High Priestly Regalia', in *Dress and Clothing in the Hebrew Bible: 'For All Her Household Are Clothed in Crimson'*, ed. Antonios Finitsis, LHBOTS 679 [London: Bloomsbury, 2019], 29).

[48] Natalio Fernández Marcos, 'Rewritten Bible or Imitatio? The Vestments of the High-Priest', in *Studies in the Hebrew Bible, Qumran, and the Septuagint*, eds. James C. VanderKam, Peter W. Flint, and Emanuel Tov, VTSup 101 (Leiden, Brill, 2006), 321–36.

114   THE MAKING OF THE TABERNACLE

and a turban (v. 4). These garments are said to be made from בַּד, another word for linen, but different from שֵׁשׁ the term that appears in Exod 28.[49] On completing the prescribed rituals within the tabernacle, Aaron is to remove his linen vestments, bathe and put on his other vestments (וְלָבַשׁ אֶת־בְּגָדָיו). In this other set of clothes he offers the burnt offerings and the fat of the sin offering on the altar (vv. 24–25).[50] It is natural for the reader of the Torah, where Lev 16 follows Exod 28, to suppose that these other clothes that Aaron dons at the end of the ritual in Lev 16 are those very same sacred vestments described in Exod 28. In this way, the two different priestly vestments fit into a harmonious whole. I will argue that a close examination of the two different portraits of the priestly vestments suggests a more complex relationship and that these were originally independent accounts of priestly clothing that have been harmonized. Discerning where this harmonization has taken place in Exod 28 will allow us to trace some of the dynamics at play amongst the writers and redactors of the chapter.

The reader who encounters Lev 16 having already read Exod 28 is likely to assume that the garments worn on the Day of Atonement are a simpler version of Aaron's full regalia. The ease with which readers relate these two accounts of the priestly vestments can partly be explained by their common elements. Exodus 28 and Lev 16 agree that the priests wore a tunic (כְּתֹנֶת), a turban (מִצְנֶפֶת), a sash (אַבְנֵט), and undergarments (מִכְנָסִים). In such a reading Aaron entered the holy of holies without the ephod (אֵפוֹד), the breastpiece (חֹשֶׁן) or the robe (מְעִיל). Unsurprisingly, readers since ancient times have regarded the divestment of Aaron's elegant garments as an act of humility in approaching God. According to the Jerusalem Talmud,

Why does he not serve in the golden vestments? Because of haughtiness. Rebbi Simon said *do not inflate yourself in front of the king* (Prov 25:6). Rebbi Levi said, because an accuser does not become a defense attorney. Yesterday it was written about them, *they made golden gods for themselves* (Exod 32:31), and today he would officiate in golden vestments?[51]

---

[49] שֵׁשׁ is an Egyptian loanword and is used of a fine linen associated with wealth and status (e.g. Gen 41.42; Ezek 16.10, 13; 27.7; Prov 31.22). בַּד's etymological origins are uncertain. It is only worn by God's human, priestly (1 Sam 2.18; 22.18; 2 Sam 6.14), or angelic attendants (Ezek 9.2, 3, 11; 10.2, 6; Dan 10.5; 12.6–7).

[50] Aaron's actions are similar to what is prescribed in Lev 6.3–4 for the treatment of the ashes of the burnt offering left behind on the altar. The priest puts on linen garments (מִדּוֹ בַד) and linen undergarments (מִכְנְסֵי־בַד) and wearing these garments moves the ashes from upon the altar to beside it. He then removes his garments (בְּגָדָיו) and puts on other garments (בְּגָדִים אֲחֵרִים) in order to transport these ashes to a clean place outside the camp.

[51] *y. Yoma* 7:3 (translation from Heinrich W. Guggenheimer, *The Jerusalem Talmud. Second Order: Mo'ed. Tractates* Pesaḥim *and* Yoma. *Edition, Translation, and Commentary*, SJ 74 [Berlin: de Gruyter, 2013], 585–6).

THE TABERNACLE AND ITS GLORIOUSLY ATTIRED PRIEST   115

Might we be better to read Lev 16 without an eye to Exod 28? Were we to do so it would be natural to suppose that Aaron dresses in priestly vestments to conduct the rituals of the Day of Atonement and that the other garments are simply his everyday clothes. Reading Lev 16 in this way is not simply wilful. It is well known that Lev 16 is an erratic within the landscape of the priestly literature: a monumental boulder significantly different from the surrounding rock.[52] Thus, for Lev 16 to have its own distinctive perspective on the priestly vestments would be in keeping with other features of the chapter, and there is a case for resisting any quick harmonization of Exod 28 and Lev 16. Although reading the change of garments as an act of humility is still found in modern commentaries,[53] such an interpretation is problematic for having transformed an act of getting dressed into an act of divesting. Leviticus 16 says nothing about Aaron removing ephod, breastpiece, and robe. Indeed, in light of what is said about those items in Exod 28, we might be surprised that Aaron would remove them. The breastpiece is worn for a 'continual remembrance before YHWH' (v. 29), and the bells and pomegranates on Aaron's robe make a sound so that Aaron does not die during his ministering in the sanctuary (v. 35). Why are they to be removed on the very day that Aaron enters the inner sanctum, the most perilous operation that he undertakes?

A closer examination of Exod 28 provides further grounds for distinguishing the two accounts of Aaron's vestments. The details about the undergarments in vv. 42–43 have the character of a loose-fitting appendix. Four observations establish the case. First, the undergarments are not mentioned in the summary of v. 4. Second, the undergarments are made from בַּד, Lev 16's preferred term for linen, rather than שֵׁשׁ, the term for linen elsewhere in Exod 28. Third, the verses begin with an imperative, וַעֲשֵׂה (v. 42), whilst the rest of the instructions have been introduced by a *weqatal* form dependent on the opening imperative in v. 1. Fourth, the previous two verses form a pleasing *inclusio* with the opening of the chapter as is apparent from the numerous repeated expressions: 'for glorious adornment' (לְכָבוֹד וּלְתִפְאָרֶת; vv. 2, 40); 'Aaron, your brother, and his sons with him'

---

[52] Most conspicuously, Lev 16 uses 'the holy place' (הַקֹּדֶשׁ) for what is elsewhere in the priestly literature called 'the holy of holies' (קֹדֶשׁ הַקֳּדָשִׁים). Also unique is its reference to the inner sanctum as מִקְדַּשׁ הַקֹּדֶשׁ (v. 33). The deployment of 'to atone' (כפ״ר) is also distinctive. Alongside the typical expression כפ״ר עַל we also find the unusual כפ״ר בְּעַד. Nowhere else is Azazel referred to, and the reference to a demonic figure is without parallel in the priestly literature. For a discussion of עֲזָאזֵל and its possible meanings, see, *inter alia*, Bernd Janowski and Gernot Wilhelm, 'Der Bock, der die Sünden hinausträgt: Zur Religionsgeschichte des Azazel-Ritus Lev 16,10.21f', in *Religionsgeschichtliche Beziehungen zwischen Kleinasien, Nordsyrien und dem Alten Testament: Internationales Symposion Hamburg, 17–21 März 1990*, eds. Bernd Janowski, Klaus Koch and Gernot Wilhelm, OBO 129 (Freiburg im Üchtland: Universitätsverlag, 1993), 109–69; Wolfgang Fauth, 'Auf den Spuren des biblischen 'Azazel (Lev 16): Einige Residuen der Gestalt oder des Namens in jüdisch-aramäischen, griechischen, koptischen, äthiopischen, syrischen und mandäischen Texten', *ZAW* 110 (1998): 514–34; Milgrom, *Leviticus 1–16*, 620–1; Nihan, *Priestly Torah*, 351–4.

[53] Milgrom, *Leviticus 1–16*, 1016; Samuel E. Balentine, *Leviticus*, IBC (Louisville, KY: Westminster John Knox Press, 2002), 126.

116   THE MAKING OF THE TABERNACLE

אֶת־אַהֲרֹן אָחִיךָ וְאֶת־בָּנָיו אִתּוֹ; vv. 1, 41); 'to serve me as priests' (לְכַהֲנוֹ־לִי; vv. 4, 41). These two verses also look forward to the following chapter with the reference to the priests' anointing and consecration. Thus, there are good reasons to identify vv. 42–43 as the work of a later editor who sought to bring the divergent accounts closer together by introducing the linen undergarments of Lev 16 into the list of priestly vestments in Exod 28.

Further evidence of a secondary attempt to harmonize the different accounts of the priestly can be found in v. 39: 'You shall weave the tunic of fine linen (וְשִׁבַּצְתָּ הַכְּתֹנֶת שֵׁשׁ), and you shall make a turban of fine linen (וְעָשִׂיתָ מִצְנֶפֶת שֵׁשׁ), and you shall make a sash of embroidered work (וְאַבְנֵט תַּעֲשֶׂה מַעֲשֵׂה רֹקֵם)'. These do not follow the pattern of the rest of Aaron's vestments, each of which begins in the same way as the instructions for the construction of the tabernacle in Exod 25–27: 'and you shall make...' (וְעָשִׂיתָ; vv. 2, 13, 15, 22, 23, 26, 27, 31, 33, 36, 39, 40).[54] The brief descriptions depart from the rest of the chapter in other respects, for they provide no insights into how the objects are to be manufactured, nor is any significance attributed to Aaron's tunic, turban, and sash. Finally, it is not clear how some of these items of clothing relate to those already mentioned.[55] How does the tunic in v. 39 relate to the robe, or even the ephod and breastpiece? Where is the sash to be wrapped?[56] The only item which stands in a clear relationship to previously made articles is the turban. According to v. 37, the gold rosette was attached to the turban, though even here we may wonder whether the turban has been added secondarily.[57] The fact that these three items are also mentioned in Lev 16.4 raises

---

[54] The only exception is, of course, v. 6, which reads וְעָשׂוּ, 'they shall make'. The verb was either altered to a plural in order to facilitate the insertion of vv. 3–5 or was changed at a subsequent stage of transmission by attraction to the third person plural in the previous verse.

[55] Noth notes their 'remarkable brevity' and the unusual formula used to describe the robe (Noth, Exodus, 226).

[56] We should also note Holzinger's concern that the sash would not be necessary if the ephod was worn (Holzinger, Exodus, 139).

[57] The reference to Aaron's headdress in Exod 28.37aβ, b appears to be premature. It is referred to as 'the turban' (הַמִּצְנֶפֶת), as though it were an object that was already well known, even though it will not be introduced until v. 39: 'you shall make a turban of linen' (וְעָשִׂיתָ מִצְנֶפֶת שֵׁשׁ). Second, the manufacture of the rosette and turban in 39.30–31 shows a number of differences from the description in 28.36–38. According to 28.37–38, 'you shall place it [the rosette] on a blue cord, and it will be upon the turban, it will be on the front of the turban, and it will be on Aaron's forehead' (וְשַׂמְתָּ אֹתוֹ עַל־פְּתִיל תְּכֵלֶת וְהָיָה עַל־הַמִּצְנָפֶת אֶל־מוּל פְּנֵי־הַמִּצְנֶפֶת יִהְיֶה: וְהָיָה עַל־מֵצַח אַהֲרֹן), but the execution in 39.30–31 has 'they fastened upon it a blue cord to fasten upon the turban above' (וַיִּתְּנוּ עָלָיו פְּתִיל תְּכֵלֶת לָתֵת עַל־הַמִּצְנֶפֶת מִלְמָעְלָה). Rashi identified two difficulties. First, is the rosette placed on the cord, or the blue cord on the rosette? Second, does the rosette rest upon the turban or Aaron's forehead? Rashi's solution was to increase the number of cords, a proposal rejected dismissively by Ramban (Rashi on Exod 28.37; Ramban on Exod 28.37 [Carasik, Exodus, 252]). The differences that Rashi identify stem from the compliance account's attempt to clarify the problematic text of Exod 28.37. The opening clause (v. 37aα) describes a pendant suspended on a blue cord, but the remainder of the verse understands the pendant as something attached to the turban (v. 37aβ, b). The compliance account of Exod 39 assumes this second understanding and revises the first accordingly: pendant is not suspended on a blue cord, but rather the blue cord attaches it to the turban. When we combine these observations with the striking duplication of וְהָיָה עַל in vv. 37aβ and 38, the most compelling solution is to regard the reference to the turban in vv. 37aβ, b as a secondary addition (cf. Holzinger, Exodus, 139). In an earlier discussion of the priestly

the possibility that they have been incorporated from there. With these additions in Exod 28.37aβb, 39, the account of the priestly vestments in Exod 28 was harmonized with the vestments in Lev 16.[58]

If the tunic, turban, and sash are to be regarded as originally independent of the ephod, breastpiece, robe, we might ask the speculative question of whether the different terms originally connoted the same items. Is what Lev 16 names the tunic (כֻּתֹּנֶת) the garment that the writer of Exod 28 labelled a robe (מְעִיל)? And when Lev 16.4 speaks of a sash (אַבְנֵט) is this the same item that the writer of Exod 28 would identify as the ephod (הָאֵפֹד)?[59] If this speculation is correct, we can gain a better picture of how the textual descriptions converge on what the priests wore in the Jerusalem sanctuary. Both texts agree that the priest wore a garment with a sash or ephod tied around his upper body.

The Vestments of Aaron and His Sons

The focus of Exod 28 is the vestments that are to be made for Aaron: 'You shall make holy vestments for Aaron your brother for glory and for splendour' (וְעָשִׂיתָ בִגְדֵי־קֹדֶשׁ לְאַהֲרֹן אָחִיךָ לְכָבוֹד וּלְתִפְאָרֶת; v. 2). The garments for Aaron's sons are mentioned only briefly at the end of the chapter with language that alludes to v. 2: 'You shall make tunics for Aaron and his sons, and you shall make sashes for them, and you shall make headdresses for them for glory and for splendour' (וְלִבְנֵי אַהֲרֹן תַּעֲשֶׂה כֻתֳּנֹת וְעָשִׂיתָ לָהֶם אַבְנֵטִים וּמִגְבָּעוֹת תַּעֲשֶׂה לָהֶם לְכָבוֹד וּלְתִפְאָרֶת; v. 40). It is immediately apparent that this verse does not follow the pattern of beginning 'and you shall make...', וְעָשִׂיתָ, found elsewhere in Exod 25–27, but that it is closely linked to the following verse which commands Moses to anoint, ordain and consecrate Aaron and his sons (27.41). The idea that Aaron's sons are anointed alongside their father is only found in a cluster of late texts. Initially there was simply one anointed priest, Aaron himself. The only other reference to the vestments of Aaron's sons is to be found in v. 4. This is part of an insertion in vv. 3–6a that attributes the

---

vestments, I proposed that the entire instructions for the rosette may have been added secondarily (Nathan MacDonald, 'The Priestly Vestments', in *Nudity and Clothing in the Hebrew Bible*, eds. Christoph Berner et al. [London: Bloomsbury, 2019], 435–48). One of my arguments—that the rosette is not listed with the other vestments at the beginning of the chapter (v. 4)—is not compelling as the rosette is made of metal and would not have been an item produced by the skilled Israelite artisans.

[58] This must have occurred before the addition of vv. 42–43, for two reasons. First, v. 4 knows of the tunic, turban and sash, but not the undergarments. Second, in Exod 29 and Lev 8 both versions of the priestly vestments have been integrated, but without mention of the undergarments. The tunic is understood as an undergarment around which is wrapped the sash. The robe is placed on top of the tunic and sash, followed by the ephod and breastpiece.

[59] It is perhaps no accident that Lev 8.7 uses the same verb חג״ר, 'to gird', of both the sash and the band of the ephod: 'He put the tunic and tied the sash around him (וַיַּחְגֹּר אֹתוֹ בָּאַבְנֵט), clothed him with the robe, and placed the ephod upon him. He tied the band of the ephod around him (וַיַּחְגֹּר אֹתוֹ בָּאַבְנֵט)'. Both are made with a distinctive craftsmanship: the ephod is 'the work of a designer' (מַעֲשֵׂה חֹשֵׁב; Exod 28.6), whilst the sash is 'the work of an embroiderer' (מַעֲשֵׂה רֹקֵם; 28.39).

118   THE MAKING OF THE TABERNACLE

fabrication of the vestments to the skilled Israelite artisans rather than to Moses. As we have seen, it is part of the strategic reframing of the instructions as communal that is also to be seen in the Masoretic version of 25.8–10 and is evidence of the secondary influence of the compliance account.

In its earliest form, then, Exod 28 was concerned with the fabrication of Aaron's vestments, and only his vestments. 'You shall make holy vestments for Aaron your brother for glory and for splendour' (v. 2) is a programmatic statement comparable to 'you shall make for me a sanctuary so that I may dwell among them' (25.8).[60] In both cases the programmatic statement is followed by instructions for the individual items presented in the same literary style. The actions of constructing are expressed with *weqatal* formations with nominal clauses providing further detail and *yiqtol* formations giving functional information. Moses is instructed to fabricate for Aaron an ephod, a breastpiece, a robe, and a gold rosette. The use of the repetitive directive 'and you shall make...' (וְעָשִׂיתָ) provides a sense of how Aaron's vestments are composed of different components:

- Ephod (vv. 6–12)
  - Filigree and chains for the ephod (vv. 13–14)
- Breastpiece (vv. 15–21, 29–30)
  - Chains for the breastpiece and ephod (v. 22)
  - Rings for the top of the breastpiece and ephod (vv. 23–25)
  - Rings for the bottom of the breastpiece and ephod (vv. 26–28 [𝔐 and 𝔊 only])
  - The Urim and Thummim (v. 30 [𝔊 only])
- Robe of the ephod (vv. 31–32, 35)
  - Pomegranates and bells on the robe (vv. 33–34)
- Rosette (vv. 36–38).

The ephod and the breastpiece are clearly thought to be the most important items of the priest's clothing. Not only are they mentioned first, but most of the chapter is taken up with describing how they are to be made and attached to one another (vv. 6–30).[61] The ephod (אֵפוֹד) was an ornate garment made from coloured yarns. It had two shoulder straps and was bound around Aaron's body with a woven band. It has traditionally been represented as an apron wrapped around the waist, though the biblical text provides nothing to confirm that

---

[60] Reading the first verb as a 2nd person singular with 𝔊[B] and 'among them', with 𝔐[L]. For discussion of the text-critical issues, see footnote 53 in Chapter 3 of this volume.

[61] For the ordering of the vestments according to their importance, see Othmar Keel, 'Die Brusttasche des Hohenpriesters als Element priesterschriftlicher Theologie', in *Das Manna fällt auch heute noch: Beiträge zur Geschichte und Theologie des Alten, Ersten Testaments. Festschrift für Erich Zenger*, ed. Frank-Lothar Hossfeld, HBS 44 (Freiburg im Breisgau: Herder, 2004), 379–91; Imes, 'Between Two Worlds'.

supposition.[62] Two onyx stones bearing the names of the sons of Israel were framed in gold and set into the shoulder straps of the ephod.[63] The breastpiece (חֹשֶׁן) is made of the same materials as the ephod.[64] The material was folded to form a square of material into which were set twelve precious stones upon which the names of the sons of Israel had been engraved. The folds produced a pocket which housed the oracular devices of the Urim and Thummim. These were presumably accessible to Aaron who could be asked to consult them (cf. Num 27.21). No account is given of the manufacture of these oracular devices in the Masoretic and Old Greek versions, though the Samaritan Pentateuch has Moses commanded to make them: 'and you shall make the Urim and Thummim' (את עשית האורים ואת התמים; v. 30). The breastpiece is attached to the ephod at the top by two gold chains and at the bottom by a blue cord.[65] The robe of the ephod (מְעִיל הָאֵפוֹד) is often assumed to be a full-length garment that was worn underneath the ephod.[66] It was made entirely from blue yarn. Its lower hem had embroidered yarns in the form of pomegranates and bells made of gold.[67] Without the turban, the rosette (צִיץ) must originally have been a pendant inscribed with the words 'holy to yhwh', which was hung by a blue cord on Aaron's forehead.[68]

The materials used to fabricate Aaron's vestments are identical to those used for the construction of the tabernacle. The ephod and breastpiece are made from coloured yarns—blue, purple, and red—together with gold and twisted linen, and their workmanship is said to be that of a designer (מַעֲשֵׂה חֹשֵׁב). The robe was made from blue yarn, the workmanship of a weaver (מַעֲשֵׂה אֹרֵג). The pomegranates that fringed it were made from blue, purple and red yarns with the bells made from

---

[62] For the limitations of the biblical description of the ephod, see esp. Hanna Liss, 'Sollen die Glöckchen wieder klingen? Die Beschreibung der Priestergewänder in Ex 28 und die Hermeneutik ihrer "alt-neuen" Rekonstruktionen', *Trumah* (2009): 4–7.

[63] In the monarchic period, the ephod was probably the characteristic garb of the priest (see 1 Sam 2.18; 14.3; 22.18; 2 Sam 6.14) (Noth, *Exodus*, 221). The term אפוד is used in a variety of ways within the Hebrew Bible—as a garment, an oracular device, and an idol. For discussion, see Propp, *Exodus 19–40*, 432–3.

[64] For discussion of the breastpiece, see Keel, 'Brusttasche'; Christophe Nihan, 'Le pectoral d'Aaron et la figure du grand prêtre dans les traditions sacerdotales du Pentateuque', in *Congress Volume Stellenbosch 2016*, eds. Louis Jonker, Gideon Kotzé, and Christl M. Maier, VTSup 177 (Leiden: Brill, 2017), 23–55.

[65] 𝕲ᴮ appears to be missing the description of how the bottom of the breastpiece was connected to the ephod. See Wevers, *Greek Text of Exodus*, 455–7.

[66] In Lev 8.7–9 the priestly vestments are described in a different order: tunic, sash, robe, ephod, breastpiece, turban, rosette (cf. Exod 29.4–6). This list includes the additional items of clothing found in 28.39 (the tunic, turban and sash) which were added secondarily. The different order for the items appears to reflect the practical order in which Aaron was dressed (see, e.g., Imes, 'Between Two Worlds').

[67] The Hebrew versions agree that there are two items on the hem. 𝕲ᴮ, however, has three: gold pomegranates, bells, and fabric pomegranates: ῥοίσκον χρυσοῦν κώδωνα καὶ ἄνθινον.

[68] For pendants on the forehead in the ancient Near East, see esp. Othmar Keel, 'Zeichen der Verbundenheit. Zur Vorgeschichte und Bedeutung der Forderungen von Deuteronomium 6,8 f. und Par.', in *Mélanges Dominique Barthélemy: Études bibliques offertes à l'occasion de son 60e anniversaire*, eds. Pierre Casetti, Othmar Keel, and Adrian Schenker, OBO 38 (Freiburg im Üchtland: Universitätsverlag, 1981), 193–212.

120 THE MAKING OF THE TABERNACLE

gold. It is the very same materials that are used to construct the inner and outer sanctum. The inner curtain (מִשְׁכָּן), the veil (פָּרֹכֶת), and the screen (מָסָךְ) are fabricated from the blue, purple, and red yarns with the workmanship of a designer. No gold thread is involved, but the furniture that the tent sanctuary housed was manufactured from gold. Not only are the same materials involved in the vestments as in the sanctuary tent, but also blue yarn and gold form the links between the different parts of both the vestment and the sanctuary. Gold chains and blue cords connect the ephod and the breastpiece. The robe is made entirely of blue yarn which provides a physical link between the ephod which sits over the robe and the robe's lower hem with its pomegranates and bells. Finally, the pendant is held on Aaron's head by blue cord. In the sanctuary too loops made of blue yarn and gold hooks mark the point in the curtains where the inner sanctum transitions to the outer sanctum.

The manufacture of Aaron's robes from the same materials as the tabernacle proper indexes the relationship between the priest and the sanctuary. When Aaron dons his priestly vestments he effectively becomes part of the tabernacle and is able to access it.[69] The tabernacle and Aaron the priest are co-constitutive. There is no tabernacle without Aaron, and no priest without the tabernacle. Consequently, the vestments identify Aaron as uniquely privileged. He, and only he, can enter the tabernacle tent. Yet, as Nihan and Rhyder observe, 'the fabrics used for Aaron's vestments do not merely symbolize his privileged access to, and unique agency within, the sanctuary: in the priestly conception, they literally enable it'.[70] They ensure that when Aaron serves in the cultic place, he blends in. The description of the vestments not only suggests a close relationship with the tabernacle, but also with YHWH himself. The programmatic statement that the vestments are 'for glory and for adornment' (לְכָבוֹד וּלְתִפְאָרֶת) indexes the divine glory (כָּבוֹד). Thus, the description of the vestments establishes a unique relationship for Aaron with both the tabernacle and YHWH.

The Significance Attributed to the Vestments

The centrality of Aaron to the ritual economy of the tabernacle is apparent in the significance granted to every item of the priestly vestments in the original priestly document.[71] No explicit meaning is attributed to the structure of the tabernacle

---

[69] That this is the case makes it unlikely that Aaron would divest these vestments in order to enter the most holy place on the day of atonement (Lev 16). It is further evidence that Exod 28 and Lev 16 do not originally belong together.

[70] Christophe Nihan and Julia Rhyder, 'Aaron's Vestments in Exodus 28 and Priestly Leadership', in *Debating Authority: Concepts of Leadership in the Pentateuch and the Former Prophets*, eds. Katharina Pyschny and Sarah Schulz, BZAW 507 (Berlin: de Gruyter, 2018), 50.

[71] Steins and Podella make a claim for the centrality of Aaron's vestments on literary grounds. In their view, Exod 28 is the centre of a chiastic arrangement found in Exod 25–31 (Steins, 'Heiligtum';

and its furniture in Exod 25–27. Instead, as we have seen, the tabernacle and its furniture are described in a manner that focuses on their physical appearance and manufacture. On the question of the symbolic significance of the resulting sanctuary and its furniture, the priestly writer is strikingly uncommunicative. Indeed, the reticence of Exod 25–27 has often been viewed as paradigmatic for the priestly text's unwillingness to explain its ritual universe.[72] But, when it comes to the vestments, the priestly text is the opposite of taciturn. Exodus 28 is replete with statements about the significance of Aaron's dress. Nevertheless, many scholars are so convinced by the conventional wisdom about the priestly literature's reticence that they look right through the chapter's explicit claims. In what is otherwise one of the most perceptive analyses of the priestly vestments in recent scholarship, Nihan and Rhyder claim that 'like other priestly ritual instructions in Exodus, Leviticus and Numbers, this text contains very few indications as to the meaning of what it describes'.[73] Quite the opposite: the text is full of meaning so that readers are left in no doubt as to how the vestments function and how significant they are to Aaron and the Israelites.

Each of the main components of the priestly vestments in the original priestly document has some significance attached to it.

- Ephod: 'Aaron shall bear their names before YHWH on his two shoulders for remembrance' (v. 12).
- Breastpiece: 'Aaron shall bear the names of the sons of Israel in the breastpiece of decision on his heart when he goes into the holy place, for a continual remembrance before YHWH' (v. 29).
- Urim and Thummim: 'Aaron shall bear the decision of the sons of Israel on his heart before YHWH continually' (v. 30).
- Robe: 'And its sound shall be heard when he goes into the holy place before YHWH, and when he comes out, so that he shall not die' (v. 35).
- Rosette: 'and Aaron shall bear any guilt incurred in the holy offering that the Israelites consecrate as their sacred donations; it shall be on his forehead continually, in order that they may find acceptance before YHWH' (v. 38).

It is striking that in each case the significance of the articles relates to Aaron's activity 'before YHWH' (לִפְנֵי יְהֹוָה). In the case of the breastpiece and the robe, the location of Aaron's activity is identified still more precisely. It is when he is 'in the holy place' (אֶל־הַקֹּדֶשׁ), the outer sanctum where the table and lampstand are to be found. This confirms what has already been observed: the priestly vestments are

---

Thomas Podella, *Das Lichtkleid JHWHs: Untersuchungen zur Gestalthaftigkeit Gottes im Alten Testament und seiner altorientalischen Umwelt*, FAT 15 [Tübingen: Mohr Siebeck, 1996], 55–60).
[72] E.g. Propp, *Exodus 19–40*, 495–8.   [73] Nihan and Rhyder, 'Aaron's Vestments', 47.

122   THE MAKING OF THE TABERNACLE

needed for Aaron to perform his cultic role within the sanctuary. It is there that
they are instrumentally effective.

The significance attributed to each article of the vestments merits being examined individually. First, by wearing the ephod, Aaron physically bears the names
of Jacob's sons, the ancestors of the Israelites, before YHWH. The idea that the sons
are to be listed 'in the order of their birth', כְּתוֹלְדֹתָם (v. 10), evokes the *toledot*-
formula that the priestly writer employs to structure his account in Genesis.[74] The
link back to the early sections of the priestly *Grundschrift* is also grounded in
the idea that the onyx stones will be 'for remembrance' (לְזִכָּרֹן). In the story of the
flood and Israel's liberation from Egypt, God is said to 'remember' (זכ״ר) Noah
and the Israelites respectively. It is God's memory, rather than the Israelites', that is
being stirred by the onyx stones in the ephod.[75] The term לְזִכְּרֹן has another resonance, since as Tigay showed, *zkrwn* was used in the Levant for votive donations.[76]
Rhyder and Nihan have also highlighted examples from Mesopotamia of
inscribed precious stones, sometimes with just the name of the donor, being
deposited at sanctuaries.[77] The idea that animates the giving of such votives is that
a physical object brought into the sanctuary might arouse the deity to action. So
also in the tabernacle, the names on the gems are visible to YHWH when Aaron
enters the sanctuary and his memory of Israel is evoked.

Second, the breastpiece is attributed a double significance. One relates to the
twelve gemstones set in the breastpiece which bear the names of the tribes of
Israel (v. 29), whilst the second relates to the Urim and Thummim (v. 30). The
existence of two explanations of the breastpiece raise obvious questions about
whether both are original, or just one. There are some reasons for thinking that
the association of the breastpiece with the Urim and Thummim is the earlier, and
the idea of the breastpiece as a receptacle for the twelve gemstones is a secondary
development. First, the full title of the breastpiece is 'the breastpiece of decision'
(חֹשֶׁן מִשְׁפָּט), which suggests a close association of the breastpiece with the Urim
and Thummim as divinatory objects.[78] According to Num. 27.21, Eleazar's role as

---

[74] In the priestly *Grundschrift* the sons of Israel are listed in Gen. 35.22–26 and then again in Exod
1.1–7. The sons are grouped by mother and listed in birth order. It may be that this is what is intended
by כְּתוֹלְדֹתָם.

[75] Willy Schottroff, *Gedenken im Alten Orient und im Alten Testament: Die Wurzel zākar im semitischen Sprachkreis*, 2nd edn, WMANT 15 (Neukirchen-Vluyn: Neukirchener Verlag, 1967), 306–12.
Contra Childs who writes, 'The memorials as cultic objects serve to insure Israel's relation to God's
order by reminding both God and Israel. Yahweh is reminded of his purpose with Israel and his
memory is equivalent to his action. Israel is reminded of the eternal order and she [sic] again relates
herself [sic] to it by cultic participation in the events which mediated the order.' (Brevard Springs
Childs, *Memory and Tradition in Israel*, SBT 37 [London: SCM, 1962], 68).

[76] Jeffrey H. Tigay, 'The Priestly Reminder Stones and Ancient Near East Votive Practices', in *Shai
Le-Sara Japhet: Studies in the Bible, Its Exegesis and Its Language*, eds. Mosheh Bar Asher et al.
(Jerusalem: Bialik Institute, 2007), 339*–55*.

[77] Nihan and Rhyder, 'Aaron's Vestments', 53.

[78] For the divinatory use of the Urim and Thummim, see *inter alia* Cornelis Houtman, 'The Urim
and Thummim: A New Suggestion', *VT* 40 (1990): 229–32; Cornelis Van Dam, *The Urim and
Thummim: A Means of Revelation in Ancient Israel* (Winona Lake, IN: Eisenbrauns, 1997).

THE TABERNACLE AND ITS GLORIOUSLY ATTIRED PRIEST   123

high priestly successor to Aaron is to inquire of YHWH how Joshua is to conduct his wars by 'the decision of the Urim' (בְּמִשְׁפַּט הָאוּרִים). Second, the breastpiece is only found within the priestly literature,[79] but it has a close relationship to the ephod, an object that is elsewhere known for its use in divination (1 Sam. 23.6–14; 30.7–10).[80] Third, the inscription of the breastpiece gemstones with the names of the sons of Israel creates a duplication with the two onyxes on the shoulder pieces of the ephod.[81] Despite the similarities, the names are not identical and reveal a different concept of what is meant by the 'names of the sons of Israel' (שְׁמֹת בְּנֵי יִשְׂרָאֵל).[82] The names inscribed on the shoulder pieces are the sons of Jacob as is confirmed by the statement that the sons are listed 'in birth order' (Exod 28.10). The twelve names include Joseph and Levi; they are not the names of the secular tribes.[83] The names inscribed on the twelve precious stones of the pectoral are the names of the Israelite tribes as is made explicit in v. 21: 'they will be according to the twelve tribes' (תִּהְיֶיןָ לִשְׁנֵי עָשָׂר שָׁבֶט). The idea of the twelve secular tribes presupposes the separation of the Levites for a cultic role, a perspective that emerges clearly only in the book of Numbers.[84] That we have here a premature reference to the twelve secular tribes finds confirmation in the fact that שֵׁבֶט is not P's term for the tribes.[85] Fourth, the Old Greek version has a variant text in which the equivalent to 𝔐 28.29 is found immediately after v. 22. The Old Greek text differs in some other respects,[86] but the floating nature of v. 29 suggests some

---

[79] Given that the breastpiece is unknown outside the tabernacle account, it is possible that it is an invention of the priestly literature as Keel suggests (Keel, 'Brusttasche'). He rejects Görg's claim that the breastpiece has Egyptian origins (Manfred Görg, 'Der Brustschmuck des Hohenpriesters', *BN* 15 [1981]: 32–4).

[80] The divinatory significance of the ephod and the Urim and Thummim eventually accumulated to the twelve gemstones too, see Philippe Guillaume, 'Aaron and the Amazing Mantic Coat', in *Studies on Magic and Divination in the Biblical World*, eds. Helen R. Jacobus, Anne Katrine de Hemmer Gudme, and Philippe Guillaume, Biblical Intersections 11 (Piscataway, NJ: Gorgias Press, 2013), 101–18.

[81] The problem of repetition in the description of the breastpiece has been noted in previous scholarship. Beer applied von Rad's theory of two priestly sources to Exod 28 and attributed v. 29 to P[B] and v. 30 to P[A] (Beer and Galling, *Exodus*, 140; von Rad, *Priesterschrift*). Noth identified two separate strands in vv. 15–16, 30 and vv. 17–21, 29 (Noth, *Exodus*, 222–4). See also Karl Elliger, 'Ephod und Choschen: Ein Beitrag zur Entwicklungsgeschichte des hohepriesterlichen Ornats', *VT* 8 (1958): 19–35; Owczarek, *Vorstellung*, 78–80.

[82] See Ederer, *Identitätsstiftende Begegnung*, 83–93.

[83] This was appreciated by the medieval interpreters, see Rashi and Ibn Ezra on Exod 28.11 (Carasik, *Exodus*, 245).

[84] The difficulties with these references to the twelve names of the sons of Israel are often overlooked in the commentaries and technical literature (e.g. Albertz, *Exodus 19–40*, 198, 200; Dozeman, *Commentary on Exodus*, 644, 646; Nihan and Rhyder, 'Aaron's Vestments', 51–2; Christian Frevel, 'On Instant Scripture and Proximal Texts: Some Insights into the Sensual Materiality of Texts and Their Ritual Roles in the Hebrew Bible and Beyond', *Post* 8 [2018]: 57–80; Podella, *Das Lichtkleid JHWHs*, 69).

[85] Samuel R. Driver, *An Introduction to the Literature of the Old Testament*, 8th edn, International Theological Library (Edinburgh: T&T Clark, 1909), 134. Ederer notes that the closest textual link is to Exod 24.4, which is itself a late text (Ederer, *Identitätsstiftende Begegnung*, 90).

[86] In addition to the rearrangement of 𝔐 28.29// 𝕲 28.23, the Old Greek knows nothing of the rings mentioned in the Masoretic Text:

> 22 And you shall make on the oracle braided tassels, chainwork of pure gold. 23 [~𝔐 v. 29] And Aaron shall take the names of the sons of Israel upon the oracle of judgement on his chest in his going into the sanctuary, a remembrance before God. 24 and you shall place

124 THE MAKING OF THE TABERNACLE

difficulties in finding a satisfactory location for it. Fifth, the statement about the gemstone's significance in v. 29 appears to be a blending of vv. 12, 30, and 35:[87]

ונשא אהרן את שמות בני ישראל בחשן המשפט על לבו בבאו אל הקדש לזכרן לפני יהוה תמיד

and Aaron will bear the names of the sons of Israel in the breastpiece of judgement upon his heart when he goes into the holy place for remembrance before yhwh continually (v. 29).

ונשא אהרן את שמותם לפני יהוה על שתי כתפיו לזכרן

and Aaron will bear their names before yhwh upon his two shoulders for remembrance (v. 12).

ונשא אהרן את משפט בני ישראל על לבו לפני יהוה תמיד

Aaron will bear the decision of the sons of Israel upon his heart before yhwh continually (v. 30).

ונשמע קולו בבאו אל הקדש לפני יהוה ובצאתו ולא ימות

and its sound shall be heard when he goes into the holy place before yhwh, and when he comes out, so that he shall not die (v. 35).

The comparison reveals that the explanation of the gemstones' significance adds nothing that has not already been mentioned in relation to the other items of Aaron's dress.

As the receptacle for the Urim and Thummim, the breastpiece is important for guiding Israel's decisions. Whilst the ephod looks back to the patriarchal period with its references to Jacob's sons and evokes the past with the word 'for remembrance' (לְזִכָּרֹן), the breastpiece anticipates a future through the word 'continuously' (תָּמִיד). The two will ultimately be united through the jewelled plaque with the polymorphous expression 'the sons of Israel' referring to both the sons of the patriarch Jacob and to their descendants, the tribes of Israel. The connection between past and future orientations is deepened by the gemstones, which are worn for 'continual remembrance before yhwh' (לְזִכָּרֹן לִפְנֵי־יְהוָה תָּמִיד; v. 29).

---

upon the oracle of judgement the tassels. You shall place the chains upon both sides of the oracle. 25 And the two small shields you shall place upon both shoulders of the ephod in the front. 26 [~ 𝔐 v. 30] And you shall place the disclosure and the truth in the oracle of judgement and it will be on Aaron's chest, whenever he enters the sanctuary before the Lord. And Aaron will bear the judgements of the sons of Israel upon his chest before the Lord forever.

Characteristically, Wevers argues that the Old Greek offers a simplified summary of the Masoretic Text (Wevers, *Greek Text of Exodus*, 455–7).

[87] Frevel, however, argues that v. 30 may have developed from v. 29, and argues that the Urim and Thummim may have been a secondary addition prompted by the reference to 'judgement' (מִשְׁפָּט) (Frevel, 'Instant Scripture', 70).

THE TABERNACLE AND ITS GLORIOUSLY ATTIRED PRIEST   125

Third, the robe is the only item where Aaron does not bear something of the Israelites before YHWH. This is to be worn as Aaron enters the holy place lest he die. In the original priestly document 'the holy place' (אֶל־הַקֹּדֶשׁ) refers to the outer sanctum as distinct from the inner sanctum, which was identified as 'the most holy place' (קֹדֶשׁ הַקֳּדָשִׁים; Exod 26.33–34).[88] Originally only Aaron had access to the outer sanctum and his attendance was required to light the lamps and arrange the bread on the table. By entering the holy place, Aaron approaches the presence of the deity and this action is fraught with danger. Consequently, Aaron's robe is hemmed with bells and pomegranates to sound as he walks into the holy place. There have been various suggestions as to who is the intended recipient of the sound made by Aaron's robe: the people, the priests, Aaron, other residents of the sanctuary such as angels, or YHWH himself. Since the other items of clothing are intended to arouse YHWH's attention, this is probably the case here too. As Houtman argues,

> by the sound of the bells (cf. Num. x 10) YHWH's attention is drawn to the high priest and his dress. YHWH must observe the high priest continuously. Thus his attention will be focussed on the names of the sons of Israel on the high priest's shoulders and breast (Ex. xxviii 12, 29) and on the text, inscribed on the plaquette, set on the high priest's turban (Ex. xxviii 36–8).[89]

Fourth, the rosette is also attributed a double significance and, consequently, raises similar questions just as the breastpiece did.[90] On the one hand, Aaron 'bears sin' (נָשָׂא אֶת־עֲוֹן) relating to the offerings (v. 38a). On the other hand, the rosette ensures Aaron finds favour before YHWH (v. 38b). There are several reasons for thinking that the reference to Aaron bearing sin was probably a secondary development.[91] First, the reference to Aaron bearing sin is surrounded by a conspicuous *Wiederaufnahme*: 'it will be upon Aaron's forehead/his forehead' (וְהָיָה עַל־מִצְחַ אַהֲרֹן / וְהָיָה עַל־מִצְחוֹ).[92] This should be seen as evidence of scribal insertion. Second, the expression נָשָׂא אֶת־עֲוֹן can be understood in several different

---

[88] Exod 35–39 uses הַקֹּדֶשׁ to refer to the large sanctuary complex, and Lev 16 uses it to refer to the area behind the veil.

[89] Cornelis Houtman, 'On the Pomegranates and the Golden Bells of the High Priest's Mantle', *VT* 40 (1990): 223–9.

[90] Houtman notices the problem but seeks to explain it away: 'The second clause introduced with והיה is not about a second purpose for the plaque. The purport of the first clause with והיה is restated with different wording. Because thanks to Aaron, Israel's iniquity does not form a barrier between YHWH and Israel, YHWH is favourably inclined toward Israel' (Houtman, *Exodus*, III: 517).

[91] The principal difficulty with this proposal is the reference to the people in לִרְצוֹן לָהֶם, 'acceptance for them' (v. 38). In the present text the referent is the בְּנֵי יִשְׂרָאֵל earlier in the verse. If this is excised, the nearest referent is the בְּנֵי יִשְׂרָאֵל in v. 30. 𝔖ᴸ has an isolated reading *acceptem ei*, 'acceptance for him'. It is perhaps the case that the entirety of v. 38 is secondary under the influence of Lev 22. The significance of the rosette would simply be its inscription: 'holy to YHWH'.

[92] In both cases, 𝔊ᴮ reads καὶ ἔσται ἐπὶ τοῦ μετώπου Ἀαρων.

126 THE MAKING OF THE TABERNACLE

ways. It can mean to 'bear away sin (i.e. forgive)' (e.g. Exod 34.7), 'to bear guilt' (e.g. Exod 28.43), 'to bear punishment' (e.g. Lev 5.1), and 'to bear responsibility' (e.g. Num 18.1). According to Lev 10 the consumption of the sacrifices by the priests is crucial for atonement to be secured, while according to Num 18.1–7 the priests bear responsibility for the sanctuary and the priesthood. Whatever the precise meaning in Exod 28.38, the notion that the priests have a role in removing sin or bearing responsibility is an idea developed in later texts in the Pentateuch. Third, the particular responsibility of the priests to protect the sacred offerings (הַקֳּדָשִׁים) is found in the Holiness Code, where it is the focus of an entire chapter (Lev 22).[93] Fourth, the notion of Aaron's rosette leading to YHWH's favourable disposition is consistent with the significance of the other vestments which are also meant to remind YHWH of his people. Concerns about punishment or responsibility for sin are absent from the other vestments, and from the rest of the original priestly tabernacle account. Fifth, the reference to the offerings of the Israelites would suggest that the rosette had a particular significance in relation to the altar which stood in the courtyard. The other items of the vestments had an association with Aaron's service in the outer sanctum. In conclusion, the original significance of the rosette was to ensure that Israel found favour with YHWH.

Each item of the vestments, then, has an instrumental role within the cultic service of the sanctuary. When Aaron approaches the altar or enters the outer sanctum, the vestments ensure that he can perform his priestly duties. As was also the case with the tabernacle, the aesthetic qualities of the vestments could, no doubt, be appreciated by the Israelites, but the primary audience for the splendid garments is YHWH. The jingling of the golden bells alerts YHWH to Aaron's presence in the sanctuary, the inscriptions ensure that he remembers the Israelites for their benefit, or assure him of the cultic propriety of Aaron. As Mandell argues, the materials that Aaron wears ensures that he blends in with the environment of the tabernacle, but also that the crucial items stand out distinctly from it.[94] Nowhere else are opals or gemstones used in the tabernacle, nor is writing publicly displayed anywhere else.[95] They stand out against the background of the tent, just as the jingling bells attract attention amidst the silence of the sanctuary.[96]

---

[93] It is possible that the opening of Lev 22 inspired a scribe to discern a relationship with the rosette. Aaron and his sons are exhorted to 'dedicate (וְיִנָּזְרוּ) the sacred donations of the Israelites so as not to profane my holy name' (v. 2). In Exod 29.6 the rosette is identified as a diadem (נֵזֶר) and according to Exod 28.36 it was engraved with the divine name. In addition, the instructions about the sacred donations (Lev 22.1–16) are followed by instructions about acceptable offerings where the expression לְרָצוֹן is frequently used (vv. 17–33). See also Ederer, *Identitätsstiftende Begegnung*, 119–20.

[94] Alice Mandell, 'Writing as a Source of Ritual Authority: The High Priest's Body as a Priestly Text in the Tabernacle-Building Story', *JBL* 141 (2022): 49–69.

[95] For the importance of writing in Exod 28, see esp. Alice Mandell, 'Aaron's Body as a Ritual Vessel in the Exodus Tabernacle Building Narrative', in *New Perspectives on Ritual in the Biblical World*, eds. Laura Quick and Melissa Ramos, LHBOTS 702 (London: Bloomsbury, 2022), 159–81.

[96] Knohl, *Sanctuary of Silence*.

THE TABERNACLE AND ITS GLORIOUSLY ATTIRED PRIEST   127

Aaron's presence in the sanctuary ensures that what YHWH perceives is Aaron in his role as representative of Israel.

Conclusion

In the original priestly document, the instructions for constructing the tabernacle and its furniture flow directly into the instructions for fabricating Aaron's vestments. They are not two distinct sets of directives, but one seamless whole. The integration of Aaron within the sanctuary is not just achieved literally, but also physically. Aaron's vestments are made from the same materials as the tabernacle. Aaron does not stand aloof from the tabernacle or enter as an alien. Instead, by wearing the vestments he is one with it. But though Aaron's vestment making him part of the sanctuary, certain articles stand out. The inscriptions and the bells announce his presence within the sanctuary to YHWH who dwells there and brings the people, whom Aaron represents, into regular remembrance.

The instrumental significance of the vestments sets Aaron's dress apart from the rest of the tabernacle account. The tabernacle provides a suitable dwelling for the deity: privacy, illumination, food. Ensconced within the holy of holies, the divine glory that appeared on Mount Sinai can dwell amongst the people assembled in the Sinai wilderness. But the significance attributed to the vestments ensures that readers recognize Aaron as indispensable for the functioning of the sanctuary. What value is there in YHWH dwelling in the midst of the Israelites, if their offerings are not accepted and if YHWH is not mindful of their concerns? By donning the priestly vestments, Aaron ensures that the cult is effective on behalf of the Israelites.

Crucial to Aaron's role is that of representation. Representation operates on two levels, implicit and explicit. First, Aaron can be understood as a cipher for a particular group within Israel. But who though is the group that Aaron represents in the original priestly *Grundschrift*? There are various possibilities. He could be the archetypal high priest. But there is no evidence that the priestly document distinguished between a high priest and other priests. As we have seen, the references to Aaron's sons should all be recognized as secondary additions. This is consistent with the rest of the original priestly document which makes no mention of Aaron's sons.[97] The instructions in Exod 25–28 simply portray a priest who serves in the tabernacle; no subordinate priests are mentioned. Alternatively, Aaron could be the eponymous representative of an Aaronide priestly sept

---

[97] Aaron's descendants are found in the genealogy of Exod 6.14–27, but this is widely recognized as a secondary addition to the text (see, e.g., Jan Christian Gertz, *Tradition und Redaktion in der Exoduserzählung: Untersuchungen zur Endredaktion des Pentateuch*, FRLANT 186 [Göttingen: Vandenhoeck & Ruprecht, 2000], 237–54).

associated with one of the traditional Israelite sanctuaries. But there is no evidence of a rival group within the priestly document. Who, then, does Aaron represent? The remaining option is that Aaron simply stands for the priesthood.

The second level on which representation operates is the text's explicit claims about Aaron's role in representing Israel. It is important not to overlook the novelty and significance of the claim being made on behalf of the priesthood. In the world of the Iron Age monarchies, the priesthood were servants of the deity and the deity's representative, the king. They did not represent the people. Nor did the people need a representative, for they were led by a king. The king of the Hebrew monarchies was a mediator with the divine, but not the people's representative. It is only in the post-monarchic imagination that the priesthood can claim the role of representing the people to the deity. At this very early stage it would be to claim far too much to characterize what is described in the priestly *Grundschrift* as either a democratic or a hierocratic vision of society. It would be true to say that the people and the priesthood emerge simultaneously as significant political entities.

5

The High Priest and the Priests

Located in the capital city and besides the royal palace, the temple in Jerusalem was already by the late Iron Age a major cultic site. Like other significant Near Eastern temples, it had begun to develop a complex bureaucracy. Although considerable caution must be exercised in utilizing the Deuteronomistic History for reconstructing the history of the Jerusalem cult, certain texts within 2 Kings suggest that by the late monarchy there were already at least a couple of tiers within the priesthood. There was an individual who was identified as the 'great priest' (הַכֹּהֵן הַגָּדוֹל; 2 Kgs 12.11; 22.4, 8; 23.4), as well as 'deputy priest(s)' (כֹּהֲנֵי הַמִּשְׁנֶה; 23.4; cf. כֹּהֵן הַמִּשְׁנֶה, Jer 52.24), and 'guardians of the threshold' (שֹׁמְרֵי הַסַּף; 2 Kgs 23.4).[1] The references are too brief to say much about the precise role of the chief priest, but he seems to have been responsible to the king for the proper running of the temple. The mention of the 'guardians of the threshold' is an indication that cultic status was linked with access to the temple space.

When we turn to the original priestly document, we find the tabernacle portrayed in ways reminiscent of the Jerusalem temple. As I argued in the last chapter, the tabernacle's priest, Aaron, is probably best understood as a cipher for the entire priesthood and its indispensability for serving the deity. But neither tabernacle nor Aaron correspond exactly with how the temple, or its priesthood, functioned in the late Judahite monarchy or the early Second Temple period. The priestly *Grundschrift* offers a simplified portrayal of the cult. The tabernacle is served by a single priest, Aaron, who can access all parts of the sanctuary. In the extant versions of the tabernacle account, however, a more complicated portrayal of the sanctuary can be found with distinctions made between high priest, priests, and people enjoying different levels of access to the holy space. In this present chapter I will examine how this more complicated picture developed and describe some of its contours.

Central to my argument in this chapter is that incorporating Lev 16, the great atonement ritual, into the presentation of tabernacle played a key role in creating a more complex portrayal of the cult. As presented in the last chapter, the original priestly document sketched a narrative arc that ran from the creation of the world in Gen 1 to the divine glory taking up residence in the tabernacle in Exod 40. At some early stage, the priestly literature was extended so that a new climax was

---

[1] For discussion of the different terminology for the high priest, see Noam Mizrahi, 'The History and Linguistic Background of Two Hebrew Titles for the High Priest', *JBL* 130 (2011): 687–705.

The Making of the Tabernacle and the Construction of Priestly Hegemony. Nathan MacDonald, Oxford University Press.
© Nathan MacDonald 2023. DOI: 10.1093/oso/9780198813859.003.0006

130 THE MAKING OF THE TABERNACLE

reached with the instructions for the great atonement ritual in Lev 16. That Lev 16 once marked the conclusion of the priestly document is evidenced by the fact that the Holiness Code (Lev 17–26) was appended immediately after Lev 16 by a redactor who also revised the existing material.

The great atonement ritual has its own history distinct from the tabernacle account and has a subtly different portrayal of Aaron. In common with the tabernacle account, the focus is entirely upon Aaron. But, the description of the great atonement ritual assumes that Aaron is the head of a family. Amongst other things, Aaron's actions secure atonement 'for himself *and for his house*' (וְכִפֶּר בַּעֲדוֹ וּבְעַד בֵּיתוֹ; vv. 6, 11). The chapters appended between the end of Exodus and Lev 16 present a picture that mediates between the perspectives of the priestly *Grundschrift* and the great atonement ritual. The sacrificial duties are not undertaken by Aaron, but by Aaron's sons (בְּנֵי־אַהֲרֹן), who are further characterized as 'the priests' (הַכֹּהֲנִים).[2] Thus, with the introduction of the first sixteen chapters of Leviticus, Aaron becomes a cipher for the high priest and Aaron's sons for the rest of the priesthood. As such, Aaron is both distinct from the rest of the priesthood as its titulary head, but also the chief representative of it.

The introduction of the great atonement ritual with its different portrayal of Aaron prompted various revisions to the original tabernacle account. The redaction of the priestly *Grundschrift* sees the reference to Aaron's house take concrete form in a place for Aaron's sons. Whilst the revision of the tabernacle account can rightly be viewed as a case of textual harmonization, the alterations to the tabernacle account also move creatively beyond both the original tabernacle account and the great atonement ritual. In particular, they allocate responsibilities and privileges in ways that contribute to a differentiation within the priesthood and the tabernacle space.

Based on the literary-critical model for the development of the tabernacle account, I will discuss the influence of Lev 16 upon Exod 25–40 in two stages. At an early stage in the history of the tabernacle account's history, some of the more obvious tensions were eliminated: instructions were given for the manufacture of the atonement cover and the differences between the portrayals of the priestly vestments were addressed. These alterations are mostly to be found at the end of Exod 28 and in Exod 29, but, in the case of the atonement cover, the redactors were willing to amend the instructions about the tabernacle furniture in Exod 25. At a much latter stage, instructions were provided for furniture and substances that are implied by Lev 16, but not explicitly named, such as the incense altar and the laver. These were appended to the original instructions in Exod 30. Before we

---

[2] Lev 1.5, 8, 11; 2.2; 3.2. In Lev 1.7 𝔐[L] reads אַהֲרֹן הַכֹּהֵן בְּנֵי, but 𝔖𝔖𝔖[D] has בני אהרן הכהנים (cf. 𝕲[B] οἱ υἱοὶ Ααρων οἱ ἱερεῖς). The plural reading in 𝔖𝔖𝔖[D] and 𝕲[B] could be regarded as a harmonization with the standard collocation elsewhere in Lev 1–3, or 𝔐[L]'s reading could be a mistaken assimilation to the common expression אַהֲרֹן הַכֹּהֵן. For discussion, see Milgrom, *Leviticus 1–16*, 157; Innocent Himbaza, *Leviticus*, BHQ 3 (Stuttgart: Deutsche Bibelgesellschaft, 2020), 58*.

THE HIGH PRIEST AND THE PRIESTS   131

turn to those two stages of development in the tabernacle account, it will be useful to examine some of the distinctive features of the great atonement ritual
of Lev 16.

The Great Atonement Ritual in Leviticus 16

The great atonement ritual is a complex ceremony that consists of several distinct
types of ritual.[3] The initial concern appears to be the question of how Aaron
might access the most sacred part of the shrine where the atonement cover and
ark are located (vv. 2–3). This requires atonement to be made for himself and for
the sanctuary through several sacrificial offerings. But atonement for the Israelite
community also needs to be achieved and this is realized through a rite of elimination in which a goat bearing the community's sin is sent into the wilderness. The
origin and development of this complex ritual remains a matter of considerable
disagreement,[4] but for my purposes the most important thing to observe is that
Lev 16 has a different origin than the tabernacle material we have been examining. The clearest evidence of this is its distinctive idiolect. In the great atonement
ritual 'the holy place' (הַקֹּדֶשׁ) is used of the inner sanctum and 'the tent of meeting'
(אֹהֶל מוֹעֵד) of the outer sanctum.[5] As we have seen the original priestly account
employs a different nomenclature. The inner sanctum is called 'the most holy
place' (קֹדֶשׁ הַקֳּדָשִׁים) and the outer sanctum is 'the holy place' (הַקֹּדֶשׁ; Exod 26.33).
The 'tent' (אֹהֶל) is used of the outer curtain that was draped over the inner curtain
and like it extended across both the inner and outer sanctum (26.7–13).

The description of the great atonement ritual has several other features that
distinguish it from what I have identified as the earliest priestly version of the
tabernacle account. First, the focus of cultic activity in Lev 16 is the atonement
cover (כַּפֹּרֶת), rather than the furniture that ensures the tabernacle is a comfortable
divine abode. The ark is mentioned briefly in v. 2, but it is merely to identify it
as the item upon which the atonement cover sat. The displacement of the ark
is particularly striking, for it is a cultic object known from other parts of the
Hebrew Bible. The כַּפֹּרֶת, however, is unknown outside the priestly literature and a
single reference in Chronicles, which has clearly been influenced by the priestly
literature.[6] The ark is often associated with the divine presence, but this role has
been subsumed by the כַּפֹּרֶת: 'I will appear in the cloud upon the atonement cover'
(בֶּעָנָן אֵרָאֶה עַל־הַכַּפֹּרֶת; v. 2).

---

[3] For the language of the 'great atonement ritual', see Martin Noth, *Leviticus: A Commentary*, trans.
J. S. Bowden, OTL (London: SCM, 1965), 115.
[4] A brief, but incisive overview of past research can be found in Nihan, *Priestly Torah*, 340–5.
[5] Milgrom, *Leviticus 1–16*, 1063.
[6] Amongst the rooms to be constructed in the temple by Solomon is the בֵּית הַכַּפֹּרֶת (1 Chron 28.11),
which is presumably a reference to the most holy place.

132 THE MAKING OF THE TABERNACLE

Second, the attention given to the atonement cover is aligned to a focus upon purification and atonement of the sanctuary, Aaron, and the entire community. Propp rightly observes that כַּפֹּרֶת is a 'richly ambivalent term',[7] but the repetition of the verb 'to atone' (כפ״ר) in Lev 16 leaves no doubt as to its importance in securing atonement.[8] In the original priestly account, the tabernacle was the glorious abode which Aaron entered bearing the names of the people's ancestors on gemstones to ensure that they were remembered. The great atonement ritual, however, emphasizes the distance between the deity and the people. They are characterized as impure because of transgressions and sins (Lev 16.16). The disparity between YHWH and the people is a mortal threat to Aaron as he approaches the inner sanctum. Without the appropriate ritual actions that provide atonement, he will die (vv. 2, 13).

Third, atonement can only be achieved by Aaron, and not by any other priest. In the original tabernacle account Aaron symbolizes the priesthood and the way that the priesthood represents the people to God. But in the great atonement ritual Aaron appears as the head of the priesthood. His actions secure atonement 'for himself *and for his house*' (וְכִפֶּר בַּעֲדוֹ וּבְעַד בֵּיתוֹ; vv. 6, 11). This observation places the opening of the ritual instructions in a new light. 'Tell your brother Aaron not to enter the sanctuary inside the veil at any time' (v. 2) is not just a temporal restriction, but also a limitation on who may perform the ritual. It is a prerogative of the high priest alone. The inner sanctum is off limits to everyone except Aaron.

Fourth, the shifting perspective on the ritual significance of the tabernacle is reflected in the different terminology for the sanctuary. In Lev 16, the sanctuary is not identified as the 'tabernacle' (מִשְׁכָּן), the place of divine abode. Instead, as we have seen, the inner sanctum is called 'the holy place' (הַקֹּדֶשׁ) and the outer sanctum 'the tent of meeting' (אֹהֶל מוֹעֵד). The sanctuary is the place where an impure people encounter a holy deity.

Finally, the vestments that Aaron wears when he performs his duties are described in subdued terms. They are a linen tunic (כְּתֹנֶת־בַּד), linen undergarments (מִכְנְסֵי־בַד), a linen sash (אַבְנֵט בַּד), and a linen turban (מִצְנֶפֶת בַּד). After Aaron has completed his activities in the inner sanctum and confessed Israel's sins over the elimination goat, he divests himself of these vestments in the outer sanctum and puts on other vestments (בְּגָדָיו) before sacrificing the burnt offerings (vv. 23–24). The sober description of the vestments used in the great atonement ritual is in keeping with the emphasis on purification and atonement, and it is a stark contrast with the glorious vestments of Exod 28. This is despite the fact that it is probably the same dress that is reflected in both descriptions.

---

[7] Propp, *Exodus 19–40*, 385.

[8] For the importance of atonement for understanding the כפרת, see esp. Bernd Janowski, *Sühne als Heilsgeschehen: Studien zur Sühnetheologie der Priesterschrift und zur Wurzel KPR im Alten Orient und im Alten Testament*, WMANT 55 (Neukirchen-Vluyn: Neukirchener Verlag, 1982).

Aaron and His Sons

The different theological emphases of the great atonement ritual have had a transformative effect on the original tabernacle account. The inclusion of the atonement cover marks a reorientation of the tabernacle's physical structure that is mirrored by an alteration in the understanding of the priesthood. These changes are incorporated into the tabernacle account in a number of different ways: the inclusion of the atonement cover into the instructions to Moses (Exod 25.16–22); alterations to the priestly vestments (Exod 28.37*, 39–40; 29.5–9); and, a climactic statement about the purpose of the tabernacle (Exod 29.43–46). I shall examine each of these in turn. The ordination ritual (Exod 29) was part of this set of changes, but it will be considered in Chapter 7.

The Atonement Cover (Exod 25.16–22)

Almost all the references to the atonement cover (כַּפֹּרֶת) are found in the tabernacle account and Lev 16. The only exceptions are Num 7.89, which is universally recognized as a rewriting of Exod 25.22, and 1 Chron 28.11 which is dependent on the priestly literature. This startling observation can be contrasted with the references to the ark of the covenant which are to be found in a number of places in the Hebrew Bible. This novel piece of sanctuary furniture takes pride of place in the great atonement ritual where it has an indispensable role in securing the purification and atonement of the sanctuary. In contrast, the initial appearance in the instructions of Exod 25 show clear signs of its secondary insertion between the ark and the table as is evidenced by the repetitive resumption 'in the ark you shall put the covenant that I shall give you' (vv. 16, 21).

The insertion in 25.16–21 prescribes the construction of the כַּפֹּרֶת. It is the same length and width as the ark, but there is no mention of its height. At the ends of the כַּפֹּרֶת, two cherubim are to be placed facing one another with wings outstretched over the כַּפֹּרֶת.[9] Although it is not explicitly stated, it is usually assumed that the two ends are those of the ark's length. The כַּפֹּרֶת is placed upon the ark. I have already observed that the close association between the כַּפֹּרֶת and the rituals that result in atonement (כפ״ר) in Lev 16 hardly seem to be coincidental. Yet it cannot be overlooked that כפ״ר also has the sense 'to cover'. Given that the length and width of the כַּפֹּרֶת correspond to those of the ark, it functions as a tight-fitting lid.[10] It is not impossible that the term was coined to play on these two distinct

---

[9] The cherubim are not mentioned in Lev 16. The composer of Exod 25.17–21 would appear to have combined the idea of the כַּפֹּרֶת with the guardian cherubim that were stationed in Solomon's temple. As some of Israel's surviving liturgical utterances demonstrate, YHWH was believed to sit enthroned above or amongst the cherubim (Pss 80.2; 99.1).

[10] Sarna, *Exodus*, 161.

134   THE MAKING OF THE TABERNACLE

nuances. Certainly, ancient readers made the association with both ideas very early as is apparent in the Old Greek's double translation ἱλαστήριον ἐπίθεμα, 'propitiation cover' (25.17).[11]

The revision of the instructions about the ark has two consequences. Most obviously, it transforms the significance of the ark. The theological meaning of the atonement cover as the place of atonement obscures the ark's original function in the priestly *Grundschrift* as a receptacle for the testimony (הָעֵדֻת; vv. 16, 21). Placed on top of the ark, the atonement cover effectively occludes it. Of even greater consequence, perhaps, is the reorientation of the tabernacle instructions. The ark and its cover are the first items for which Moses receives instructions. Radically reorientated towards the theme of atonement, the ark and its cover point not to YHWH's taking up residence in Exod 40, but to the great atonement ritual in Lev 16. They also emphasize the indispensability of Aaron. Without the high priest, atonement cannot be achieved for either the people or the sanctuary.

It is worth noting that this new perspective on the ark's significance was also itself, to some degree, displaced. According to Exod 25.22, the atonement cover received a further theological meaning expressed in a somewhat convoluted manner. 'And I will meet with you there and I will tell you all that I am commanding you for the Israelites from upon the atonement cover from between the two cherubim that are upon the ark of the covenant' (25.22). This verse sits outside the repetitive resumption (vv. 16, 21) that marked the original insertion of the atonement cover. Consequently, it should be judged a later addition and it appears to rework the climactic statement of this theology in Exod 29.42–43. But, as Utzschnieder observes, the result is a theological statement that is more prophetic than cultic. The final emphasis is not on Aaron accessing the inner sanctum to perform his crucial ritual actions, but on Moses the mediator of the divine revelation.[12] The case of the ark and the atonement cover illustrates a familiar phenomenon where important cultic objects are overlaid with multiple religious meanings. It is not entirely clear when this further modification of the atonement cover was inserted, but it does shift the focus away from Aaron to a degree.

The Vestments of Aaron and His Sons (Exod 28.37, 39–40; 29.5–9)

In the tabernacle account and the great atonement ritual we encounter two Aarons. Two Aarons that are the same *and* different. In the original account of the tabernacle, a dyarchy of Moses and Aaron build and service the tabernacle. Aaron

---

[11] Wevers, *Greek Text of Exodus*, 398.

[12] Helmut Utzschnieder, 'Tabernacle', in *The Book of Exodus: Composition, Reception, and Interpretation*, eds. Thomas B. Dozeman, Craig A. Evans, and Joel N. Lohr, VTSup 164 (Leiden: Brill, 2014), 283–5.

THE HIGH PRIEST AND THE PRIESTS   135

represents a priesthood that is undifferentiated. Yet, as we have seen, the great atonement ritual of Lev 16 presents Aaron as the head of a priestly family. Only he can access the inner sanctum to atone for himself, his house and his people. But it is not just two Aarons that we encounter, but two priestly vestments that are the same *and* different. There are broad similarities between the two accounts: Aaron wears a robe, something wrapped around his waist, and a headpiece. In other respects, they are not the same vestments. In the tabernacle account Aaron wears a glorious apparel that declares his right to enter the sanctuary and represent the Israelites. In Lev 16, Aaron's garb is plain as befits a ritual of atonement.

The harmonization of these two different perspectives is achieved by an appendix to the original instructions about the vestments in Exod 28.

> **39** You shall weave the tunic of linen and you shall make a turban of linen, and you shall make a sash, the work of an embroiderer. **40** For Aaron's sons you shall make tunics, and you shall make sashes for them and you shall make headdresses for them, for glorious adornment.

Aaron's tunic, turban, and sash are drawn from Lev 16, where it is said they were made from בַּד, 'linen'.[13] Their assimilation into the categories of the tabernacle account has been achieved by having the tunic and turban made from שֵׁשׁ, another term for linen which is found throughout Exod 28, and describing the sash as the 'work of an embroiderer' (מַעֲשֵׂה רֹקֵם), a term that appears in the instructions for the entrances to tent and court (Exod 26.36; 27.16). Strangely, no material is specified for the sash, though this lacuna is made good in the compliance account which identifies the fabrics as twisted linen, as well as blue, purple, and crimson yarns (Exod 39.29). The incorporation of the turban also led to some modification of the description of the rosette in 28.37. The description of the rosette is expanded by means of *Wiederaufnahme*: הָיָה עַל... הָיָה עַל. The rosette is understood not to be suspended on a thread resting directly upon Aaron's forehead, but is affixed upon the turban.

Aaron's sons are also provided with distinctive dress that is modelled on their father's vestments. Like him, they put on tunics and sashes, but they have a headdress (מִגְבָּעָה) instead of a turban (מִצְנֶפֶת). The precise difference between these two headpieces is unclear, not least because the מִגְבָּעָה is only mentioned in the Hebrew Bible in relation to Aaron's sons. The material out of which these

---

[13] Lev 16.4 also mentions undergarments: 'and there will be undergarments upon his body' (וּמִכְנְסֵי־בַד יִהְיוּ עַל־בְּשָׂרוֹ). The undergarments were not added to Exod 28 until a later stage (vv. 42–43). Why were the undergarments not added together with the tunic, turban, and sash? It is conceivable that the undergarments were not originally part of Lev 16.4. The other garments receive transitive verbs that describe the way that they were attached to the body (חג׳׳ר, לב׳׳ש, צנ׳׳ף), only the undergarments have the intransitive verb הי׳׳ה. The undergarments are also the only items modified with a prepositional clause. It is possible that the mention of the undergarments in Lev 16.4 came under the influence of Lev 6.3 which describe the priest placing undergarments upon his body (וּמִכְנְסֵי־בַד יִלְבַּשׁ עַל־בְּשָׂרוֹ).

136 THE MAKING OF THE TABERNACLE

vestments are fabricated is not mentioned in Exod 28. It is natural to assume that the vestments of Aaron's sons were made from the same materials as Aaron's tunic, sash, and turban. The description of the sons' vestments in the compliance account suggests that this is what one early reader inferred: 'They made the tunics, woven work of fine linen, for Aaron and his sons, and the turban of fine linen, and the headdresses of fine linen, and the linen undergarments of fine twisted linen, and the sash of fine twisted linen, blue, purple and crimson yarns, the work of an embroiderer' (𝕸 39.27–29).

The materials of these new vestments provide a subtle modification of the original portrayal of Aaron's vestments as the counterpart to the sanctuary. Aaron's additional vestments are made of linen and are 'the work of an embroiderer'. These correspond to the hangings that marked the boundary of the courtyard, which are made simply from linen (27.9, 18), and the screens that form the entrance of the tent (26.36) and the entrance to the courtyard (27.16), which are said to be 'the work of an embroiderer'. In other words, these three additional items of clothing for Aaron are indexed with the courtyard, rather than the tabernacle proper. Thus, the high priestly vestments now correspond to the *entire* sanctuary complex including the courtyard. The new items incorporated from Lev 16 are presumably thought to sit underneath the other items of Aaron's dress. This appears to be the assumption of Aaron's robing in Lev 8.7–9 where Moses first dresses Aaron in the tunic and the sash before the robe and ephod, and the turban before the rosette. If this is correct, the tabernacle space is mapped onto Aaron's costume in an inverted fashion. For the tabernacle, sanctity increases as you move into the sanctuary towards the most holy place. Aaron's vestments, however, have greater sanctity with increased externality.[14] Whilst such an assimilation of the vestments in Lev 16 does maintain the original perspective of Exod 28, which saw Aaron and the tabernacle as co-constitutive, it does present a tension with the presentation of Lev 16. Following the logic of the vestments in Exod 28, we would expect Aaron to have to wear every item in his wardrobe in order to enter the inner sanctum. In fact, the simple dress that Aaron wears in Lev 16—the linen tunic, sash, and turban—corresponds to the courtyard, rather than the inner sanctum.

Whilst Aaron's glorious vestments correspond to the *entire* sanctuary complex and allow him access to every location within it, the vestments of Aaron's sons correspond simply to the outer court.[15] Thus, the differentiation of the vestments in Exod 28.39–40 creates a hierarchy within the priesthood. Aaron is no longer a representative of the entire priesthood, but has become instead a cipher for the

---

[14] This potentially throws an interesting light on the understanding of Aaron's body. On the map of the tabernacle's sanctity, Aaron's body would sit outside with the Israelite congregation. Without the vestments that represent his office, Aaron is no different from any other Israelite.

[15] For the differing associations of the vestments, see Ederer, *Identitätsstiftende Begegnung*, 78–9.

THE HIGH PRIEST AND THE PRIESTS 137

high priest. The high priest alone can access the sanctuary proper where YHWH is present, and he is indispensable for the cultic worship of the tabernacle. The rest of the priesthood is assigned the work of attending to the altar which is the only piece of cultic furniture that sits in the courtyard. Their vestments enable them to access this part of the tabernacle complex, but no further. The notion that it was only the high priest who could enter the tent itself appears to be the assumption of the instructions about the lampstand and the table in Lev 24. Aaron is to arrange the lamps on the lampstand in the tent of meeting (vv. 1–4) and he is the one who is to arrange the bread on the table every Sabbath (vv. 5–9). The same perspective is found in Exod 30. Aaron is to offer incense on the gold altar twice a day at the same time as he attends to the lamps (vv. 7–8). In Exod 27.20–21, however, we have a different perspective. Instructions are given for the lampstand in terms that are almost identical to Lev 24, but with one crucial modification: Aaron *and his sons* will arrange the lamps.

The differentiation between the priests and the high priest is reflected in the ritual of ordination (Exod 29) which was appended to the tabernacle account immediately after the description of the priestly vestments. Like the great atonement ritual, the ordination ritual is a complex of distinct ritual actions. Moses dresses Aaron and his sons (vv. 4–9) before offering a series of sacrifices on their behalf: a sin-purification offering (vv. 10–14), a burnt offering (vv. 15–18), and an ordination offering (vv. 19–34). The purpose of the sin-purification offering appears to be to purify the altar (cf. Lev 8.15), whilst the ordination offering consecrates and atones for the priests (Exod 29.33). With its emphasis on purification and atonement, the ordination ritual strikes a similar tone to the great ordination ritual of Lev 16.

In this chapter, I will focus just on the verses in the ordination ritual where Moses dresses Aaron and his sons (Exod 29.4–9). Whilst the subsequent sacrifices unite Aaron and his sons in common ritual actions, the description of the washing and dressing creates a distinction between them. Aaron is washed and dressed first. The order of Aaron's vestments differs from Exod 28, and perhaps the most likely explanation is that they are listed in the order in which they were put on.[16] The list of articles has integrated the original list of vestments from Exod 28.6–38 as well as the short list of items from 28.39 into a single, seamless list. The only item that is missing is Aaron's sash.[17] The vestments of Aaron's sons

---

[16] Noth, however, is sceptical that this is the case (Noth, *Exodus*, 230).

[17] The sash has been included between tunic and robe in Lev 8.7. The insertion of the sash into Exod 29.5 in 𝔊ᴸ has probably been inspired by the parallel in Lev 8.7. In the Masoretic Text, Aaron's name is included rather awkwardly when the sash is listed amongst the vestments of his sons: 'You shall gird them with a sash, Aaron and his sons' (וְחָגַרְתָּ אֹתָם אַבְנֵט אַהֲרֹן וּבָנָיו; Exod 29.9). The absence of an equivalent to אַהֲרֹן וּבָנָיו in 𝔊ᴮ makes it very likely that 𝔐ᴸ's reading is a gloss that sought to make good the absence of the sash in v. 5 (Ehrlich, *Randglossen*, 377).

138 THE MAKING OF THE TABERNACLE

correspond to those listed in 28.40.[18] The difference between Aaron and his sons is expressed not only by their different vestments and the dressing of Aaron first, but also by the fact that Aaron alone is to be anointed with oil (v. 7).

Elsewhere in the Hebrew Bible, anointing with oil is associated with the assumption of kingship.[19] This led Noth to suggest that 'the act of anointing was transferred from the kingship to the high priesthood'.[20] Noth's conclusion was disputed by Fleming who observed that at Emar, as well as in Mesopotamia, the practice of anointing priests as well as kings pre-dated the existence of Israel.[21] As a result, there was no basis for assuming that anointing was originally restricted to the king and only applied to the priests in the early post-exilic period. The weakness in Fleming's argument is not just that there are no references to priests being anointed in Israelite texts earlier than the priestly literature nor that there are numerous references to the king being anointed at the time of his elevation, but that biblical texts frequently refer to the king as 'the LORD's anointed' (מְשִׁיחַ יְהוָה).[22] Such a title would appear to suggest that for Israel anointing was a distinctive feature of the monarchy whatever its connotations in other cultures of the Near East.

The royal allusions of the anointing can probably be coordinated with another feature of the list of vestments in the ordination ritual. In Exod 28 the item on Aaron's forehead is identified as a rosette (צִיץ; 28.36), but in 29.6 is called a 'holy diadem' (נֵזֶר הַקֹּדֶשׁ). It could be that נֵזֶר was chosen as a more familiar term for this item of clothing than the puzzling צִיץ, but it cannot be overlooked that נֵזֶר has clear royal connotations.[23] Connecting the rosette with royalty might have been suggested by the regal associations of the 'turban' (מִצְנֶפֶת). The only use of מִצְנֶפֶת outside the priestly literature is in Ezek 21.26 where it occurs in parallelism with עֲטָרָה, which appears to designate a ruler's crown.[24]

The regalizing of the high priest marks an important shift from the original portrayal of Aaron's vestments. None of the items that are usually identified as royal in some way—the bejewelled breastpiece, the turban, and the diadem—number amongst the original vestments. Of those articles that were part of the priestly *Grundschrift*, the ephod and the oracular breastpiece are associated with

---

[18] No mention is made of the undergarments in either the list of Aaron's or his sons' vestments. Propp attempts to clarify this omission by arguing that the undergarments were worn during the washing (Propp, *Exodus 19–40*, 457). It is more likely that the clearly secondary reference to the undergarments in 28.42–43 was not added until a later stage.

[19] Cf. 1 Sam 9.16; 10.1; 15.1, 17; 16.3, 12–13; 2 Sam 2.4, 7; 3.39; 5.3, 17; 12.7; 19.10; 1 Kgs 1.34, 39, 45; 5.15; 19.15, 16; 2 Kgs 9.3, 6, 12; 11.12; 23.30.

[20] Martin Noth, 'Office and Vocation in the Old Testament', in *The Laws in the Pentateuch and Other Studies* (Edinburgh: Oliver & Boyd, 1966), 237.

[21] Daniel E. Fleming, 'The Biblical Tradition of Anointing Priests', *JBL* 117 (1998): 401–14.

[22] Cf. 1 Sam 2.10, 35; 1 Sam 12.3; 16.6; 24.7, 11; 26.9, 11, 16, 23; 2 Sam 1.14, 16; 19.21; 22.51; 23.1; Pss 18.50; 20.6; 28.8; 84.9, 38, 51; 132.10, 17.

[23] Cf. 2 Sam 1.10; 2 Kgs 11.12 (// 2 Chron 23.11).

[24] Rooke expresses some caution noting that the single occurrence in Ezek 21.31 could be a case of a priestly status being attributed to the evil Israelite prince (Rooke, *Zadok's Heirs*, 19).

the priesthood,[25] and the robe (מְעִיל) is probably aristocratic dress and not limited to royalty.[26] It has been common to identify this appropriation of royal symbolism as a critical point in development of the Judahite priesthood where the priesthood assumes the royal office and displaces the king in Judean ideology. Since there is no evidence that the high priest possessed an authority that surpassed, or even equalled, the governor during the Persian period, such claims are probably overstated. Nevertheless, it is not coincidental that the priestly literature provides Aaron's vestments with royal associations at the same time as the high priest is being distinguished from his fellow priests. The priestly texts increasingly present the high priest as the most exalted figure within Judaism of the Persian period.

In one respect, the high priest has appropriated a distinctive role that the Judahite king was thought to exercise on behalf of the people. Some biblical texts suggest that the king's actions impacted the entire nation and that he also had a particular responsibility in securing atonement. The stories of Saul's bloodguilt from murdering the Gibeonites (2 Sam 21) and the plague that follows the census of the people (2 Sam 24) suggest the king had a particular role in effecting atonement for the kingdom. The priestly texts imagine a world before the Israelite monarchies when such atoning functions were exercised by the high priest. Consequently, they provide a blueprint for the Persian period community.

The Purpose of the Tent of Meeting (Exod 29.43–46)

The original instructions for the tabernacle ended with a climactic statement about the building's purpose as the dwelling place of YHWH. With allusions to Exod 6.7 and 16.6, the tabernacle becomes the point to which the priestly history has been leading.

> **45** I will dwell among the Israelites, and I will be their God. **46** They shall know that I am YHWH their God, who brought them out of the land of Egypt so that I might dwell amongst them. I am YHWH their God   (Exod 29.45–46).

This perspective has been recast by prefixing these verses with material that reflects the revision of the tabernacle material in light of Lev 16.[27]

---

[25] E.g. 1 Sam 2.18, 28; 22.18. The only possible exception is 2 Sam 6.14 (cf. 1 Chron 15.27) which has David wearing an ephod. Even here, the context is cultic and David is presented sacrificing as he brings up the ark to Jerusalem. That David was dressed as a cultic functionary is clearly presupposed by the Chronicler who has both David and the Levites dressed in robes of fine linen (1 Chron 15.27; Robert P. Gordon, *I & II Samuel: A Commentary* [Exeter: Paternoster Press, 1986], 233–4). As Michal points out David's conduct is far from regal (2 Sam 6.20).

[26] Cf. 1 Sam 2.19; 28.14; Ezra 9.3, 5.

[27] For revision through introduction, see Sara J. Milstein, *Tracking the Master Scribe: Revision through Introduction in Biblical and Mesopotamian Literature* (Oxford: Oxford University Press, 2016).

140   THE MAKING OF THE TABERNACLE

43 I will meet with the Israelites there and it will be sanctified by my glory. **44** I will sanctify the tent of meeting; Aaron and his sons I will sanctify to be priests for me   (Exod 29.43–44).

Just as the original statement played on the derivation of 'tabernacle' (מִשְׁכָּן) from 'to dwell' (שכ״ן), so also the prefix plays on the derivation of 'tent of meeting' (אֹהֶל מוֹעֵד) from 'to meet' (יע״ד). As the parallelism to the tabernacle makes apparent, the tent of meeting here refers to the entire tent and not just the outer sanctum as it did in Lev 16.[28]

The revised statement envisages the sanctuary as a liminal point where God and his people encounter one another. This encounter is suffused with danger for the Israelites since God is holy and they are not. The threefold repetition of 'sanctify' (קד״ש) emphasizes the necessity of purification and atonement for the functioning of the sanctuary. As a result, it is not the Israelites themselves who meet with God, but Aaron and his sons. They alone are holy. To a significant extent, then, the Israelites find themselves eased out of view. This is especially apparent if we compare vv. 45–46 and vv. 43–44. The original statement about the tabernacle emphasizes the mutuality of Israel and their God through the covenant formula and the experience of the exodus deliverance. The focus on the Israelites is consistent with the portrayal of Aaron's vestments which bear the names of the Israelite ancestors before God. The conception of the tent of meeting is quite different. Although the people are mentioned at the outset as the ones whom God will meet, they are quickly displaced and Aaron and his sons take centre stage.

High Priest, Priests, and People

The differentiation of the high priest, the priests and the people received further definition and precision at a later redactional stage through the addition of Exod 30, which provides instructions for two additional items of furniture—the incense altar and the laver—as well as two recipes—the anointing oil and the incense.[29] It has long been recognized that the instructions in this chapter are secondary, and this is especially apparent with the additional furniture. We would naturally expect instructions for the incense altar to have followed those of the ark in Exod 25, and the laver to have followed the altar of burnt offering in Exod 27. They do not belong to the original conception of the tabernacle and they have been appended after the natural conclusion of the tabernacle instructions in Exod 29.43–46.

---

[28] For the intertextual references in Exod 29.43–46, see esp. Ederer, *Identitätsstiftende Begegnung*, 249–95.

[29] As I have already noted, the reference to the census is a still later addition. It presupposes the early chapters of Numbers and interrupts the connection between the two items of furniture.

The pressure to include instructions for these additional pieces of furniture and the substances is provided by the earlier inclusion of the great atonement ritual in Lev 16. As we have seen, the obvious points of tension between the tabernacle instructions and the great atonement ritual were resolved through additions in Exod 25 and 28–29. The novel instructions in Exod 30, however, provide principally for implicit omissions. Perhaps the clearest example is the case of the laver. In the great atonement ritual, Aaron is to wash himself with water (וְרָחַץ בַּמַּיִם) before putting on his vestments (Lev 16.4). On exiting the tent, he removes his vestments and washes (וְרָחַץ אֶת־בְּשָׂרוֹ בַמַּיִם; v. 24). The precise location of his washing is not specified, merely that it is in 'a holy place' (בְּמָקוֹם קָדוֹשׁ). This washing requirement has probably influenced the ordination ritual where Aaron and his sons are washed by Moses (וְרָחַצְתָּ אֹתָם בַּמָּיִם) before being dressed (Exod 29.4). The place where the washing is to take place is specified more precisely: it is at the entrance to the tent of meeting (אֶל־פֶּתַח אֹהֶל מוֹעֵד). But how were the priests to be washed unless there is some receptacle holding water? The instructions for the laver make good this lacuna and place it between the tent of meeting and the altar.

The incense altar is a more complicated case. The great atonement ritual describes how a cloud of incense is to be produced by Aaron on his entry into the holy place. Aaron is to bring the firepan (הַמַּחְתָּה) with coals from the altar inside the veil and place two handfuls of incense upon the coals. The cloud of incense allows Aaron to step inside the holy place in order to sprinkle the sacrificial blood upon the atonement cover, but it prevents Aaron from setting eyes on the atonement cover which is no longer obscured by the veil (Lev 16.12–13). The instructions for the great atonement ritual in Lev 16 do not require a special altar for incense, for the incense was presented on a firepan. There was just one, single altar as is implicit in the references to '*the* altar' (הַמִּזְבֵּחַ) and, as with the original tabernacle instructions of Exod 25–27, this was the altar of burnt offering. This identification is consistent with the requirement that, after his atoning activities in the inner sanctum, Aaron is to 'go out' (וְיָצָא) to atone for the altar. It was this altar, then, from which the coals were collected. Since the altar of burnt offering is said to have bronze firepans amongst its paraphernalia in the tabernacle instructions (Exod 27.3), it is likely that it was one of these bronze firepans that Aaron was imagined to have taken with him when he entered into the holy place. It is easy to see how an early reader might have found such an idea incongruous. It is not just that Aaron must take the coals from outside the tent and process them through the entire outer sanctum and in through the veil to the inner sanctum, but that Aaron must bring a *bronze* firepan into the inner sanctum where otherwise only items of pure gold are permitted. The idea of a gold altar that could take its place alongside the other gold furniture in the outer sanctum avoids these incongruities.[30]

---

[30] In the Temple Scroll, reference is made to censers and perhaps other objects 'with which [to b]ring the fire inside' (לה]ביא בהמה אש בהמה פנימה; 11Q19 3.12–13). They are listed alongside objects, all of which are made from gold.

142 THE MAKING OF THE TABERNACLE

The outlining of recipes has no parallel anywhere else in the tabernacle instructions, and the inclusion of recipes for the anointing oil and the incense requires some explanation. It is perhaps for the sake of providing a balanced literary structure in Exod 30 with the two items of furniture being matched by two mixtures, and the brief collection of additions opening with the incense altar (30.1–10) and closing with the incense compound (30.34–38). The desirability of specifying a recipe for incense arises from the great atonement ritual which prescribes that Aaron offer fragrant incense (קְטֹרֶת סַמִּים) when entering the holy place (Lev 16.12). The anointing oil, on the other hand, is mentioned in the ordination ritual where it is applied on Aaron's head (Exod 29.7).

The inclusion of Exod 30 at the end of the instructions deals with these lacunae. The way that it does so, however, contributes to the portrayal of how power is distributed between the high priest, the priests and the people. These differences are mapped onto the tabernacle space in complex ways. I will examine how this occurs by examining each section of the chapter.

The Incense Altar (30.1–10)

The instructions for the construction of the incense altar blend textual material from the altar of burnt offering (Exod 27) with detail from the furniture within the sanctum (Exod 25).[31] Like the altar of burnt offering, the top surface of the altar was square with horns in the corners. In common with the sanctuary furniture, however, it was covered in gold and like the ark and the table had a gold moulding (זֵר). Unusually, the incense altar is only said to have two golden rings under the moulding in which the carrying poles were inserted. The other items of furniture carried by poles have four rings, two on each side.[32]

The new altar is identified as 'an altar, a burner of incense' (מִזְבֵּחַ מִקְטַר קְטֹרֶת; 30.1).[33] The familiarity of modern readers with the idea of an incense altar is in danger of obscuring just how incongruous the juxtaposition of מִזְבֵּחַ and מִקְטַר is and the novelty of what the author of these instructions is doing should not be overlooked. An altar (מִזְבֵּחַ) is a common term in the Hebrew Bible and as its derivation from זב״ח implies it is a place where the ritual slaughter of animals takes place. The noun מִקְטַר, on the other hand, is a hapax legomenon in the Hebrew

---

[31] See Ederer, *Identitätsstiftende Begegnung*, 300–2.

[32] The Vulgate specifies that there are two rings on each side. The incense altar was smaller than the other pieces of furniture with rings and it might have been thought sufficient for it to have one ring on each side.

[33] 𝕲[B] reads simply θυσιαστήριον θυμιάματος. Did it have a shorter text as its *Vorlage*, cf. מִזְבַּח הַקְּטֹרֶת (𝔐 37.25) or did the translator simplify the expression? Hexapla manuscripts add θυμιατήριον.

Bible, though *mqṭ* [*r*] was found inscribed on a limestone incense burner from northern Moab.[34] The prefix *m-* is probably best understood as creating a substantive of location.[35] Just as a מִזְבֵּחַ is a place of slaughter so too a מִקְטַר is a place of burning.[36] But describing an incense burner as a place of slaughter is inapt. The identification was perhaps assisted by the fact that incense burners of the late Iron Age had horns just like Israelite altars. The earliest incense burners from the Levant were terracotta models of towers, but over time these became increasingly stylized so that the horns were the outstanding feature of the burners.[37] Nevertheless, the altar and an incense burner are two distinct ritual objects which the author of Exod 30 has chosen to equate.

The location of this redesignated incense burner presents some challenges. The Masoretic Text of Exod 30.6 reads,

וְנָתַתָּה אֹתוֹ לִפְנֵי הַפָּרֹכֶת אֲשֶׁר עַל־אֲרֹן הָעֵדֻת לִפְנֵי הַכַּפֹּרֶת אֲשֶׁר עַל־הָעֵדֻת אֲשֶׁר אִוָּעֵד לְךָ שָׁמָּה

You shall place it before the veil that is upon the ark of testimony, before the atonement cover that is upon the testimony, where I will meet with you there.

But the Samaritan version preserves a shorter text,

נתתה אתו לפני הפרכת אשר על ארון העדות אשר אועד לך שמה

You shall place it before the veil that is upon the ark of the testimony, where I will meet with you there.

The same text is reflected in the Old Greek,

καὶ θήσεις αὐτὸ ἀπέναντι τοῦ καταπετάσματος τοῦ ὄντος ἐπὶ τῆς κιβωτοῦ τῶν μαρτυρίων, ἐν οἷς γνωσθήσομαί σοι ἐκεῖθεν.

You shall place it before the veil which is upon the ark of witnesses by which I will be known to you there.

---

[34] Paul E. Dion and P.M. Michèle Daviau, 'An Inscribed Incense Altar of Iron Age II at Ḥirbet El-Mudêyine (Jordan)', *ZDPV* 116 (2000): 1–13.

[35] Cf. Bruce K. Waltke and M. O'Conner, *An Introduction to Biblical Hebrew Syntax* (Winona Lake, IN: Eisenbrauns, 1990), §5.6b. So, e.g., Houtman parses it as 'place, thing upon which something is burned' (Houtman, *Exodus*, III: 558).

[36] For the meaning of קטר, see Diana Edelman, 'The Meaning of Qiṭṭêr', *VT* 35 (1985): 395–404.

[37] Seymour Gitin, 'Incense Altars from Ekron, Israel and Judah: Context and Typology', *ErIsr* 20 (1989): 52*–67*; Seymour Gitin, 'The Four-Horned Altar and Sacred Space: An Archaeological Perspective', in *Sacred Time, Sacred Place: Archaeology and the Religion of Israel*, ed. Barry M. Gittlen (Winona Lake, IN: Eisenbrauns, 2002), 95–124. The description of the incense altar in Exod 30 having a 'roof' (גג) and 'walls' (קירת) may suggest that this understanding of the burner as a miniature building endured even into the Persian period.

144 THE MAKING OF THE TABERNACLE

It is possible that the Samaritan text and the *Vorlage* of the Old Greek lost the clause לפני הכפרת אשר על־העדת due to homoioteleuton (העדת...העדת).[38] Nevertheless, the two clauses in the Masoretic Text לְפְנֵי הַכַּפֹּרֶת אֲשֶׁר עַל־הָעֵדֻת and לִפְנֵי הַפָּרֹכֶת אֲשֶׁר עַל־אֲרֹן הָעֵדֻת are almost identical and they are simply juxtaposed without coordination.[39] Consequently, they are best viewed as alternative readings with one of them being introduced into the text secondarily. The difference between the two clauses involves a transposition of letters: is the incense altar placed before the כַּפֹּרֶת or the פָּרֹכֶת: the atonement cover or the veil? The difference for the altar's location is considerable. If the incense altar is placed before the atonement cover (לִפְנֵי הַכַּפֹּרֶת), it should properly be located within the inner sanctum. But if the altar is placed before the veil (לִפְנֵי הַפָּרֹכֶת), it is located within the outer sanctum.[40] The potential for confusion is apparent in later texts. In the Masoretic version of Exod 40, for example, the incense altar is listed together with the lampstand and the table, furniture that was found in the outer sanctum (v. 5, 26), but the writer of the letter to the Hebrews understood the altar to be located within the holy of holies (Heb 9.4).

In seeking to understand how the different perspectives on the incense altar and its location might have developed, I will first begin by trying to determine which of the two expressions has the best claim to antiquity before turning to the particular case of Exod 30.6. Given their similarities, I assume that one phrase was prior to, and served as the inspiration for, the other. Three observations suggest that הַכַּפֹּרֶת אֲשֶׁר עַל־הָעֵדֻת is the earlier. First, the language of an object or person standing or being placed 'before' (לִפְנֵי) the ark is very frequent,[41] and consequently the extension of this idea to the atonement cover that sits upon the ark is understandable. But this is not the case for being before the veil. Since the veil divides the sacred space in the tabernacle into two sections, what it means to be 'before' (לִפְנֵי) the veil is ambiguous and depends upon the observer's location. It is for this reason that other texts use the language of 'outside the veil' (מִחוּץ לַפָּרֹכֶת; Exod 26.35), to describe the location of the lampstand and the table, or 'inside the veil' (מִבֵּית לַפָּרֹכֶת; Lev 16.12), to describe the location of the ark. Second, since the atonement cover sits upon the ark as a lid, it is readily apparent that the preposition עַל is appropriate to describe the atonement cover's relationship to the testimony placed within the ark. This is less the case for the veil where עַל has to be understood with the extended sense 'in front of' or 'before'. Third, in terms of redaction history, the earliest textual appearance of either of these expressions is

---

[38] Wevers, *Greek Text of Exodus*, 491. Even less likely is Dozeman's suggestion that the Samaritan text tradition 'shortened the MT by eliminating the phrase, "before the curtain [sic] that is above the testimony" (*lipnê hakkappōret ʾăšer ʾal-hāʿēdūt*)' (Dozeman, *Commentary on Exodus*, 661).

[39] Talmon notes that a copulative *waw* is found in some manuscripts (Shemaryahu Talmon, 'Synonymous Readings in the Textual Traditions of the Old Testament', in *Studies in the Bible*, ed. C. Rabin, ScrHier 8 [Jerusalem: Magnes Press, 1961], 373–4). This variant should be regarded as a case of *lectio facilior*.

[40] Holzinger, *Exodus*, 144.   [41] E.g. Josh 7.6; 1 Sam 5.3–4; 1 Kgs 3.5, 15.

THE HIGH PRIEST AND THE PRIESTS   145

found in Lev 16.13 (cf. v. 2), which mentions הַכַּפֹּרֶת אֲשֶׁר עַל־הָעֵדוּת. Apart from Exod 30.6, the only other appearance of אֲשֶׁר עַל־הָעֵדָת with reference to the פָּרֹכֶת is found in Exod 27.21, one of the latest texts in the tabernacle account.

There are strong grounds, then, for thinking that הַכַּפֹּרֶת אֲשֶׁר עַל־הָעֵדָת is the earlier expression and was already found in Lev 16.13. If we turn to Exod 30.6, however, the text-critical evidence suggests that the shorter reading לפני הפרכת אשר על ארון העדות found in the Samaritan version and confirmed by the Old Greek is the earlier text. The conclusion to draw from this must be that the author of Exod 30 coined the phrase הַפָּרֹכֶת אֲשֶׁר עַל־אָרֹן according to the pattern of Lev 16's הַכַּפֹּרֶת אֲשֶׁר עַל־הָעֵדָת. As I have already suggested, the incense altar of Exod 30 addresses the problem of how Aaron took a fire pan of coals from the altar into the inner sanctum (Lev 16.12–13). The great atonement ritual knows only one altar, the altar of burnt offering, but its fire pans were made of bronze and identifying the altar of Lev 16.12–13 with the altar of burnt offering would require Aaron to carry the fire pan full of coals the entire length of the tent. A smaller incense altar made of gold sat just outside the inner sanctum provides a neat solution, and the writer of Exod 30 has manipulated the language of his source text, Lev 16.13, to describe where this altar was to be located. The incense cloud that Aaron produces in the great atonement ritual obscures the atonement cover upon the testimony, אֶת־הַכַּפֹּרֶת אֲשֶׁר עַל־הָעֵדוּת, whilst the new altar will produce a cloud of incense that is before the veil upon the ark of testimony, לִפְנֵי הַפָּרֹכֶת אֲשֶׁר עַל־אָרֹן הָעֵדָת. The Masoretic reading with both phrases was probably the result of a scribe glossing the text or seeking to correct what he thought was an erroneous reading. For the writer of Exodus 30, 'before the veil' (לִפְנֵי הַפָּרֹכֶת) must have meant that the incense altar was to be located in the outer sanctum. This is consistent with the requirement that Aaron offer incense on it every morning and evening when he services the lamps (30.7) and the stricture that Aaron only enter the inner sanctum once a year to perform the great atonement ritual (30.10).[42]

The directions for the placement of the altar are followed by instructions about its use (vv. 7–10). Only Aaron is to offer incense on the altar. Aaron clearly stands for the institution of the high priesthood, and the narrative conceit of the tabernacle account almost disappears from view when Aaron is required to offer incense twice daily 'throughout your generations' (לְדֹרֹתֵיכֶם; v. 8), and similarly to make atonement for it annually 'throughout your generations' (לְדֹרֹתֵיכֶם; v. 10). Israel is viewed as a multi-generational reality that extends from the time of Moses to the writer's present and into the future. Thus, the Aaron who is to do

---

[42] The instructions that 'Aaron will atone upon its horns once a year' is a reference to Lev 16.18 and further evidence that Exod 30 has reinterpreted the altar of burnt offering in the great atonement ritual as the altar of incense. For an exploration of the dynamics in the re-reading of Lev 16 in light of Exod 30, see William K. Gilders, 'Is There an Incense Altar in This Ritual?', in *Writing a Commentary on Leviticus*, eds. Christian A. Eberhart and Thomas Hieke, FRLANT 276 (Göttingen: Vandenhoeck & Ruprecht, 2019), 159–70.

146   THE MAKING OF THE TABERNACLE

these things cannot be the Aaron of the narrative, but Aaron as a cipher for the high priesthood.

The assumptions of the narrative framework are also in danger of being erased with the prohibitions in v. 9: 'you shall not offer strange incense upon it, or a burnt offering, or a grain offering, nor shall you pour a libation upon it'. The plural verbs address the Israelites.[43] Since only Aaron was allowed to approach the incense altar and many of the offerings were prerogatives of the priesthood, addressing the prohibitions to the Israelites seems perplexing. One possibility is that the Israelites are charged with policing the prohibitions,[44] but it is difficult to imagine how this might have been possible since the people were not allowed into the outer sanctum. Alternatively, we might see the plural address as a recognition that the high priest numbers amongst the people. It is a correction to any perception that the hierarchy creates a class of individuals that stand outside the people. In my view, perhaps the most likely explanation is that the purpose of the prohibition is to distinguish the courtyard altar from the incense altar. Since the people could bring their various sacrifices to the altar of burnt offering, the Israelites are explicitly addressed to reinforce the fact that these common offerings are not for the incense altar.

The appearance of the incense altar in a late appendix to the tabernacle account has called forth various historical theories. Famously Wellhausen argued that the incense altar was unknown to the priestly writer and the offering of incense was introduced no earlier than the time of Jeremiah and was originally offered on firepans (Lev 10; Num 17). Further, the incense altar was a duplication of the golden table as demonstrated by Ezekiel's failure to distinguish the two: 'table is the name, altar the function'.[45] The discovery of incense burners from throughout the first millennium BCE Levant has required Wellhausen's thesis to be revised.[46] Whilst it is likely that the revival of the Arabian spice trade in the neo-Assyrian period led to an increased role for incense offerings, burners were not a novelty. Nor was the presence of one within the sanctuary as the excavations of the Judahite sanctuary at Arad show.[47] As I have argued, what is novel is to identify

---

[43] The plural verbs could be understood as a reference to Moses and Aaron, but the references to 'your generations' mean that is most likely that the entirety of Israel is meant (Houtman, *Exodus*, III: 560). In 𝕲^B the difficulties are avoided by referring to 'their generations' (εἰς γενεὰς αὐτῶν; vv. 8, 10) and rendering the verbs as singulars (ἀνοίσεις ... σπείσεις; v. 9). The plural is the *lectio difficilior* and to be preferred (*contra* Propp, *Exodus 19–40*, 357).

[44] Albertz, *Exodus 19–40*, 237.

[45] Wellhausen, *Prolegomena*, 67.

[46] For discussion of the incense cult, see Kjeld Nielsen, *Incense in Ancient Israel*, VTSup 38 (Leiden: Brill, 1986); Wolfgang Zwickel, *Räucherkult und Räuchergeräte: Exegetische und archäologische Studien zum Räucheropfer im Alten Testament*, OBO 97 (Göttingen: Vandenhoeck & Ruprecht, 1990); Paul Heger, *The Development of Incense Cult in Israel*, BZAW 245 (Berlin: de Gruyter, 1997).

[47] Yohanan Aharoni, 'Arad: Its Inscriptions and Temple', *BA* 31 (1968): 1–32. The organic residues on the incense burners from the Arad temple were recently analysed and were shown to include cannabis resin, animal dung, frankincense and animal fat (Eran Arie, Baruch Rosen, and Dvory Namdar, 'Cannabis and Frankincense at the Judahite Shrine of Arad', *TA* 47 [2020]: 5–28).

the incense burner as an *altar*. The result is that the tabernacle has two altars. In later texts, the new altar is identified as the 'altar of incense' (מִזְבַּח הַקְּטֹרֶת), 'the altar of fragrant incense' (מִזְבַּח קְטֹרֶת הַסַּמִּים), or 'the golden altar' (מִזְבַּח הַזָּהָב).[48] In contradistinction, the other altar is identified in later texts as 'the altar of burnt offering' (מִזְבַּח הָעֹלָה) or 'the bronze altar' (מִזְבַּח הַנְּחֹשֶׁת).[49] The description of them as 'bronze' or 'gold' makes explicit the hierarchical relationship between them. This hierarchy is indexed to the distinction between the high priest and the other priests. Aaron alone has access to the outer sanctum and its furniture. His daily responsibilities within the outer sanctum include not only tending to the lamps in the evening and the morning, but also offering incense on the gold altar (vv. 7–9). The remaining priests only have responsibilities related to the bronze altar. This fits neatly with the earliest priestly sacrificial instructions in Lev 1–3 where the officiants at the outer altar are identified as the 'priest' (הַכֹּהֵן) and 'Aaron's sons, the priests' (בְּנֵי אַהֲרֹן הַכֹּהֲנִים). The individual identified as the 'priest' was the chief officiant and responsibility for turning the sacrifice into smoke (הִקְטִיר הַכֹּהֵן),[50] with the remaining priests assisting him.[51] Thus, the distinction between a chief officiant and the assisting priests is already present in Lev 1–3 and the distinguishing act of the chief officiant is described with the verb קט״ר. The addition of the incense altar has identified this chief officiant more precisely as the high priest and maintained the distinction of chief officiant and assisting priests, though with only the high priest having access to the gold altar.

The Laver (30.17–21)

The instructions for the laver provide for yet another piece of furniture: one that is bronze rather than gold, and for the use of the entire priesthood and not just the high priest. Since some of the rituals required Aaron and his sons to wash themselves, there is a need for a receptacle for water. In the ordination offering, Aaron and his sons are washed before the sacrifices are offered on the altar (Exod 29.4), and, in the great atonement ritual, Aaron washed before he enters the sanctuary (Lev 16.4). Both cases are implicitly referenced in the instructions: 'When they enter the tent of meeting they shall wash with water so that they may not die or when they approach the altar to minster to make a food offering to YHWH' (Exod 30.20). The laver is placed appropriately between the tent and the altar.

---

[48] מִזְבַּח הַקְּטֹרֶת: Exod 30.27; 31.8; 35.15; 37.25; מִזְבַּח קְטֹרֶת הַסַּמִּים: Lev 4.7; מִזְבַּח הַזָּהָב: Exod 39.38; 40.5, 26; Num 4.11.

[49] מִזְבַּח הָעֹלָה: Exod 30.28; 31.9; 35.16; 38.1; 40.6, 10, 29; Lev 4.7, 10, 18, 25, 30, 34; מִזְבַּח הַנְּחֹשֶׁת: Exod 38.30; 39.39.

[50] Lev 1.9, 13, 15, 17; 2.2, 9, 16; 3.11, 16.

[51] For the issue of whether there is a distinction between a chief officiant and assisting priests in Lev 1–3 or whether the reference to Aaron's sons, the priests is the result of redaction, see Nihan, *Priestly Torah*, 200–4.

148 THE MAKING OF THE TABERNACLE

It is intriguing that the instructions about the laver assume that both Aaron and his sons can enter the tent. It aligns the instructions about the laver with some other late additions to the tabernacle narrative. In Exod 27.20–21, Aaron *and* his sons are portrayed accessing the tent and servicing the lamps. Similarly, in Exod 28.43, the late addition of instructions for the undergarments are to ensure that Aaron and his sons are appropriately attired whether they are serving in the tent or ministering at the altar.[52] As we have seen, the instructions for the incense altar seem to maintain the perspective that only Aaron did the service of the outer sanctum: he offered incense on the gold altar and tended the lamps (30.1–10). How is the discrepancy to be explained?

The problem is probably a consequence of the hierarchy of metals not entirely aligning with the concentric ordering of space. The tabernacle has a hierarchy of metals in which two feature most prominently: gold and bronze. This hierarchy is mapped onto the distinctions between high priest and the rest of the priesthood. Aaron's service is focused on the gold furniture and utensils—ark, table, lamp, and incense altar—the service of the ordinary priests is focused on the bronze furniture—the altar of burnt offering. But there is another hierarchy expressed through the concentric ordering of space. The inner sanctum has the highest level of sanctity followed by the outer sanctum and then the courtyard. Since only Aaron may access the inner sanctum, and the people may enter the area of the court known as the entrance to the tent of meeting, it is understandable that the priests are thought to have access to the outer sanctum. These two hierarchies, however, do not perfectly coincide. As a result, we have a complex picture where these hierarchies overlap. This issue is particularly apparent with the furnishings of the outer sanctum. The hierarchy of space suggests that the ordinary priest should be able to access this area, but the furniture is gold which does not suggest an association with the ordinary priest. The conflicting perspectives about whether the priests can tend the lamps (Exod 27.20–21; Lev 24.1–4) reflect different attempts to resolve this tension.

The tension between these different hierarchies results in a complex picture for the extant texts of the tabernacle. Rather than clean dividing lines between the concentric circles of sacred space, we have concentric circles with zones of liminality. The altar of incense can be seen by the ordinary priest, but he cannot do divine service upon it. Similarly, the altar of burnt offering can be seen by the Israelites, but it is only the priests who do ritual actions upon it.

---

[52] Exod 28.43 has a number of lexical links to Exod 30.17–21: בְּבֹאָם אֶל־אֹהֶל מוֹעֵד (28.43; 30.20), חָק־עוֹלָם לוֹ וּלְזַרְעוֹ (30.21 [𝔐ᴸ]); חֻקַּת עוֹלָם לוֹ וּלְזַרְעוֹ (28.43), cf. אוֹ בְגִשְׁתָּם אֶל־הַמִּזְבֵּחַ לְשָׁרֵת (28.43; 30.20); חקת עולם לו ולזרעו (30.21 [𝔊ᴰ]).

The Anointing Oil and the Incense (Exod 30.22–38)

The instructions for the production of the anointing oil and the incense share a similar literary form. First, the ingredients that are to be collected (לק״ח) are listed (vv. 23–24, 34) and then, second, they are made (עש״ה) into a blend (vv. 25, 35). Third, instructions are provided about how the compounds are to be used (vv. 26–30, 36). Fourth, there is a prohibition against any profane use (בְּמַתְכֻּנְתָּהּ לֹא תַעֲשׂוּ / וּבְמַתְכֻּנְתּוֹ לֹא תַעֲשׂוּ; vv. 31–33, 37–38).

The ingredients for both the anointing oil and the incense consist for the most part of rare and valuable aromatics that could only be obtained through long-distance trade. The anointing oil was blended from myrrh, fragrant cinnamon, fragrant cane, and *qiddah*. Myrrh (מָר־דְּרוֹר)[53] is identified as the resin of the tree *Commiphora myrrha* that grows in South Arabia, Ethiopia, and Somalia. Fragrant cinnamon (קִנְּמָן־בֶּשֶׂם) is imported from south-east Asia. Fragrant cane (קְנֵה־בֹשֶׂם) is probably an aromatic grass from India. It is identified as a distant import in Jer 6.20 and Ezek 27.19. The identification of קִדָּה is uncertain, though it is often equated with cassia. Again, Ezek 27.19 describes it being traded from far away. The incense was produced from *nāṭāp*, *šᵉḥēlet*, galbanum, and frankincense. The identification of נָטָף is uncertain, although a derivation from נט״ף, 'to drip', is often assumed. It is presumably some tree gum or resin. Similarly, שְׁחֵלֶת has no agreed identification, though the Old Greek renders with ὄνυχα, the operculum of a sea mollusc. Possible identifications with plant-based products such as ladanum and benzoin have also been suggested. Galbanum (חֶלְבְּנָה) is a resin from *Ferula glabaniflua Boisser et Buhse*, a species native to Iran and Afghanistan. Frankincense (לְבֹנָה) is the resin of *Boswellia* trees which are found in southern Arabia, Ethiopia, Somalia and India.[54] The instructions for manufacturing the oil and incense from these ingredients lack any detail and, as Nihan observes, it is rather inapt to describe them as recipes.[55] The only insight into the manufacturing process is that their production required some technical skill: they are 'blended as the work of a perfumer' (רֹקַח מַעֲשֵׂה רוֹקֵחַ /רֹקַח מִרְקַחַת מַעֲשֵׂה רֹקֵחַ; vv. 25, 35).

The oil was to be used to anoint the tent and its furniture as well as Aaron and his sons. In the earliest levels of the tabernacle account, only Aaron was anointed (Exod 29.7), and the extension to his sons occurs in secondary additions (Exod 28.41; 29.21, 36b). It is consistent with the alteration of the roles of Aaron's sons that gives them access to the outer sanctum. Anointing with oil sets the priests

---

[53] The Old Greek translator understood ראש as a construct τὸ ἄνθος σμύρνης ἐκλεκτῆς, 'the flower (i.e. the best) of choice myrrh'. The Masoretic accentuation, however, understands ראש as a modifier of the preceding word, בְּשָׂמִים.

[54] For discussion of identifications of these aromatics see, *inter alia*, Propp, *Exodus 19–40*, 481–5; Christophe Nihan, 'Une recette pour l'encens', *RTP* 149 (2017): 305–22; Nielsen, *Incense in Ancient Israel*; Houtman, *Exodus*, I: 167–71.

[55] Nihan, 'Une recette pour l'encens'.

150   THE MAKING OF THE TABERNACLE

apart from the people, but does not differentiate the priests from one another. In contrast, the incense is a high priestly prerogative. Moses is told to beat the incense fine and place it (וְנָתַתָּה) before the covenant. The language of placing the incense rather than burning it has puzzled interpreters. It is probably best understood as an allusion to Lev 16.13 where Aaron put (וְנָתַן) the incense on the censer full of coals when he entered the inner sanctum annually, rather than to the twice daily offering of incense on the altar. By alluding to the high priest's unique role in the inner sanctum during the great atonement ritual, the account of the incense emphasizes the distinction between the high priest and the priests. The prohibitions against using either the oil or the incense profanely have several similarities.[56]

32 עַל בשר אדם לא ייסך וּבְמַתְכֻנְתּוֹ לֹא תַעֲשׂוּ כמהו קדש הוא קֹדֶשׁ יִהְיֶה לָכֶם: 33 <u>אִישׁ אֲשֶׁר</u> ירקח כמהו ואשר יתן ממנו על זר <u>וְנִכְרַת מֵעַמָּיו</u>:

32 Upon human flesh it shall not be poured, a̲n̲d̲ ̲b̲y̲ ̲i̲t̲s̲ ̲c̲o̲m̲p̲o̲s̲i̲t̲i̲o̲n̲ ̲y̲o̲u̲ ̲s̲h̲a̲l̲l̲ n̲o̲t̲ ̲m̲a̲k̲e̲ anything like it. It is holy, and i̲t̲ ̲s̲h̲a̲l̲l̲ ̲b̲e̲ ̲h̲o̲l̲y̲ ̲t̲o̲ ̲y̲o̲u̲. **33** A̲n̲y̲ ̲m̲a̲n̲ ̲t̲h̲a̲t̲ compounds like it or puts it on any outsider s̲h̲a̲l̲l̲ ̲b̲e̲ ̲c̲u̲t̲ ̲o̲f̲f̲ ̲f̲r̲o̲m̲ ̲h̲i̲s̲ ̲k̲i̲n̲.

37 הקטרת אשר תעשה בְמַתְכֻנְתָּהּ לֹא תַעֲשׂוּ לכם קֹדֶשׁ תִּהְיֶה לָךְ ליהוה: 38 <u>אִישׁ אֲשֶׁר</u> יעשה כמוה להריח בה <u>וְנִכְרַת מֵעַמָּיו</u>:

37 The incense that you make b̲y̲ ̲i̲t̲s̲ ̲c̲o̲m̲p̲o̲s̲i̲t̲i̲o̲n̲ ̲y̲o̲u̲ ̲s̲h̲a̲l̲l̲ ̲n̲o̲t̲ ̲m̲a̲k̲e̲ for yourselves. I̲t̲ ̲w̲i̲l̲l̲ ̲b̲e̲ ̲h̲o̲l̲y̲ ̲t̲o̲ ̲y̲o̲u̲ for YHWH. **38** A̲n̲y̲ ̲m̲a̲n̲ ̲t̲h̲a̲t̲ makes like it to smell it s̲h̲a̲l̲l̲ ̲b̲e̲ ̲c̲u̲t̲ ̲o̲f̲f̲ ̲f̲r̲o̲m̲ ̲h̲i̲s̲ ̲k̲i̲n̲.

Despite the numerous parallels, there is an important difference. The anointing oil is 'holy to you' (קֹדֶשׁ יִהְיֶה לָכֶם). The plural 'to you' (לָכֶם) has in view the priests upon whom the oil is applied, and it distinguishes their bodies from those of others. The prohibition excludes using it on any non-priests identified here as the 'outsider' (זָר). The incense, on the other hand, is 'holy to you for YHWH' (קֹדֶשׁ תִּהְיֶה לָךְ לַיהוָה). The singular 'to you' (לָךְ) has Aaron alone in view. As the final word indicates, the beneficiary of the incense is YHWH, and consequently the following prohibition excludes anyone else from enjoying its aroma including the priests. Thus, the prohibitions for the anointing oil and the incense contribute to articulating the distinctions between high priest, the rest of the priesthood, and the non-priestly Israelites.

The prohibitions that close the instructions for the blending of the anointing oil and the incense establish a monopoly for the priesthood in the use of rare and valuable aromatics that had been brought to the Levant via long-distance trade. But they also establish subtle gradations within the priesthood between the high priest and the remaining priests. It is likely that some lay Israelites were required

---

[56] Noth, *Exodus*, 239.

THE HIGH PRIEST AND THE PRIESTS   151

to manufacture both products. Their blending was a specialist skill associated with the perfumer, and there is no indication that it could only be done by a priest. The knowledge of how to blend the aromatics is controlled with threats of divine punishment so as to maintain the priesthood's monopoly.

Conclusion

In this chapter I have examined how the original priestly instructions for the tabernacle were harmonized with the instructions for the performance of the great atonement ritual in Lev 16. To speak of harmonization can easily be understood as a process that smooths a text by eliminating differences. But the process of harmonizing texts is sometimes one of the most unexpectedly creative modes of interpretation. Such creativity takes place within the bounds of the cultural and social imagination of the text's redactors, but can also develop that cultural and social imagination in unanticipated ways.

The cases we have examined in this chapter have shown how new vestments and new furniture were created from intimations in the text. These shaped in subtle, but decisive, ways the representation of Aaron, his household and the people in the great atonement ritual into a complex hierarchical organization. The sacred space of the tabernacle and its furniture are commandeered for the purpose of providing this hierarchy with practices that articulate the differences between high priest, priesthood, and ordinary Israelites. Only Aaron can enter the inner sanctum and then only once a year. On a daily basis, however, his service is focused on offering incense upon the golden altar, a task that only he can discharge. The priests can access the outer sanctum, but their service is focused on the animal sacrifices that occur on the bronze altar in the courtyard. For their part, the people can assemble around the bronze altar as this area is known as the 'entrance of the tent of meeting'. But they cannot touch the altar, since it is holy. The result is a complex division of sacred space which indexes the social hierarchy. The space allows for different levels of the hierarchy to encounter one another. Both priests and high priest can access the outer sanctum, though incense cannot be burnt on the golden altar by the ordinary priests. Similarly, priests and people can access the entrance to the tent of meeting, but only the priests can offer the sacrifices on the altar. Despite these encounters, the rigid divisions of the hierarchy remain. No priest except Aaron may enter the inner sanctum, and the people may not enter the outer sanctum. The hierarchical divisions are protected by threats. If the priests do not wash themselves before they serve at the altar or enter the sanctuary, they will die. Those who make anointing oil or incense for profane purposes will be cut off from their kin. The violent threats protect monopolies: the high priest's monopoly over the incense, his access into the inner sanctum and service at the golden altar, and the priesthood's monopoly over the anointing oil and contact with the furniture that has been sanctified by anointing.

The priestly hierarchy that I have described in this chapter makes various claims that elevate the priesthood's status within Judaism, even if they do not infringe upon the kinds of competencies that a Persian governor may have held. Through the great atonement ritual, the high priest claimed the competence to achieve atonement, an ability that may previously have been attributed to the Judahite king. The claim to royal prerogatives is also expressed through the appropriation of some aspects of royal dress and the ritual of anointing. We do not know whether there were alterations to the physical garments that the high priest wore, or whether royal associations were simply expressed through the use of nomenclature and symbolism in the text of Exod 29. One area that could have encroached upon Persian interests is the attempt to control the incense trade. Presumably it could only have been effective within the borders of Yehud and we may wonder whether even there! The adage that prohibitions demonstrate only that the rule was being broken is as relevant as ever.

The portrayal of the priests and the high priest in the tabernacle accounts suggest some tentative steps towards appropriating some royal symbolism and prerogatives. Most of them, perhaps all, could have been borne with equanimity by the Persian authorities provided they remained within the confines of the temple cult. The overall literary portrayal, however, does envisage the priesthood, and particularly the high priest, as the apex of Israelite society. The high priest achieves atonement and represents Israel. Such claims can be kept within the confines of the cult, but they could be the basis for the accrual of power beyond it.

6

Craftsmen and Community

The tabernacle was no different from other sanctuaries in the ancient Near East in being the exclusive preserve of the priesthood. Ordinary men and women were not permitted to trespass into what was considered the deity's abode or to see the rituals that took place within it. In the earliest versions of the tabernacle account, the people are almost entirely absent. Moses receives instructions that require him to construct the tabernacle and its furniture. This expectation is communicated through the regular appearance of the command to him alone: 'you shall make' (וְעָשִׂיתָ). The same pattern is also evidenced in the instructions for the priestly vestments. True, the ancestors of the people are engraved on Aaron's epaulettes so that their descendants are represented in the tabernacle. But this is a presence that presupposes their physical absence. Even the directions for the ordination of the priests in Exod 29 makes no mention of the people assembling to witness the event in contrast to their fulfilment in Lev 8. The instructions for the anointing oil and the incense mention the people only to insist that they do not prepare a mixture similar to that which is used in holy service. Thus, the tabernacle is characterized by the people's absence from its space.

The reader's expectations that Moses is to construct the sanctuary are revised by the dramatic announcement in Exod 31 that this will be done by two master craftsmen, Bezalel and Oholiab. 'I have called by name Bezalel...and I have appointed with him Oholiab...so that they may make all that I commanded you' (vv. 1, 6). Many others will also have a role for the master craftsmen are assisted by those who described as 'everyone wise of heart' (כָּל־חֲכַם־לֵב; v. 6). Not only will the master craftsmen and Israelite artisans construct the tabernacle, they are also envisaged having a significant role in financing it. In 30.11–16 Moses is instructed to take a poll tax of half a shekel for every male over twenty years old. The levied sum will be used for 'the service of the tent of meeting' (עַל־עֲבֹדַת אֹהֶל מוֹעֵד; 30.16).

Despite their belated appearance, the craftsmen and people will go on to dominate the account of the tabernacle's construction in Exod 35–39. Once the tabernacle is erected, its furniture installed, and the entire facility consecrated in Exod 39–40, the lay Israelites will be restricted to the large open area described as the 'entrance to the tent of meeting' where the altar of burnt offering was located. In this space no differentiations are made between different classes of Israelite. All assemble together as one. The account of the tabernacle's construction, however, maps various hierarchical differences within the non-priestly community. It does so in complex ways, often deploying a rhetoric that emphasizes equality and the

The Making of the Tabernacle and the Construction of Priestly Hegemony. Nathan MacDonald, Oxford University Press.
© Nathan MacDonald 2023. DOI: 10.1093/oso/9780198813859.003.0007

154   THE MAKING OF THE TABERNACLE

participation of all the people within a holy project. In this chapter, I will examine the characterization of the master craftsmen and the Israelite artisans before turning to the portrayal of gender and class difference, and concluding with the appearances of the Levites.

The Master Craftsmen and the Israelite Artisans

The creative geniuses who superintend every aspect of the construction of the sanctuary are the two master craftsmen, Bezalel of the tribe of Judah and Oholiab of the tribe of Dan, who appear unexpectedly at the end of the instructions to Moses. The presentation of Bezalel and Oholiab in the different textual versions diverge significantly from one another and this observation suggests that the precise role of the two figures was a matter of sustained reflection and negotiation. In order to disentangle this complex history, I will first present the portrayals of the master craftsmen in the different versions, before turning to the competencies of Oholiab and the problem of the overlap with those of Bezalel. I will then address the problem of why the master craftsmen were needed at all, given that Moses was commanded to construct the sanctuary in Exod 25–30. Finally, I will examine the presentation of the Israelite artisans who assist Bezalel and Oholiab in their work.

Bezalel and Oholiab in the Versions

The Masoretic and Samaritan versions have almost identical portrayals of the two master craftsmen. Bezalel is inspired by the divine spirit which has given him insight in all manner of crafts:

3 וָאֲמַלֵּא אֹתוֹ רוּחַ אֱלֹהִים בְּחָכְמָה וּבִתְבוּנָה וּבְדַעַת וּבְכָל־מְלָאכָה: 4 לַחְשֹׁב מַחֲשָׁבֹת לַעֲשׂוֹת בַּזָּהָב וּבַכֶּסֶף וּבַנְּחֹשֶׁת: 5 וּבַחֲרֹשֶׁת אֶבֶן לְמַלֹּאת וּבַחֲרֹשֶׁת עֵץ לַעֲשׂוֹת בְּכָל־מְלָאכָה:

3 I have filled him with the divine spirit in wisdom and in understanding and in knowledge and in every work 4 to make designs, to construct in gold, silver, bronze, 5 and cutting stone for setting and in carving wood, to make every work (Exod 31.3–5).

The portrayal of Bezalel's skills in 35.31–33 is almost identical.[1] When Oholiab is first introduced in 31.6 he is attributed no specific skills, but according to

---

[1] The only divergence between the two passages is that 35.33 ends with בְּכָל־מְלֶאכֶת מַחֲשָׁבֶת (𝕸[L]) / בכל מלאכת מחשבות (𝕾𝕸[D]) and 31.5 ends with the shorter בְּכָל־מְלָאכָה. What is extant of 4Q22 suggests that it had a longer reading at 31.5: בכל מלאכ[ה, which appears to suggest a harmonizing of the two passages.

𝕸 38.23 he is described as having competencies in engraving,[2] textile designing,[3] textile embroidery, and weaving.

> וְאִתּוֹ אׇהֳלִיאָב בֶּן־אֲחִיסָמָךְ לְמַטֵּה־דָן חָרָשׁ וְחֹשֵׁב וְרֹקֵם בַּתְּכֵלֶת וּבָאַרְגָּמָן וּבְתוֹלַעַת הַשָּׁנִי וּבַשֵּׁשׁ:
>
> And with him was Oholiab son of Ahisamak of the tribe of Dan, engraver, designer, and embroiderer in blue, purple, and crimson yarns, and in fine linen (𝕸 38.23).

With the exception of engraving, these proficiencies all relate to the fabrication of textiles. The skill of engraving probably refers to the etching of the names on the two onyx stones of Aaron's vestments (28.11) and so can also be regarded as related to the fabrication of the vestments. Somewhat surprisingly, though, according to Exod 35.35, these skills are also possessed by Bezalel.

> מִלֵּא אֹתׇם חׇכְמַת־לֵב לַעֲשׂוֹת כׇּל־מְלֶאכֶת חָרָשׁ וְחֹשֵׁב וְרֹקֵם בַּתְּכֵלֶת וּבָאַרְגָּמָן בְּתוֹלַעַת הַשָּׁנִי וּבַשֵּׁשׁ
> וְאֹרֵג עֹשֵׂי כׇּל־מְלָאכָה וְחֹשְׁבֵי מַחֲשָׁבֹת:
>
> He filled them with wisdom of heart to do every work of an engraver, and a designer, and an embroiderer in blue and in purple, in crimson and in linen, and a weaver, work of every labour or skilled design   (Exod 35.35).

Bezalel and Oholiab are also entrusted with teaching the Israelite artisans. After their commissioning, the artisans, presumably under the direction of Bezalel and Oholiab, began the task of manufacturing the tent: 'And all the wise amongst the workers made the tabernacle' (וַיַּעֲשׂוּ כׇל־חֲכַם־לֵב בְּעֹשֵׂי הַמְּלָאכָה אֶת־הַמִּשְׁכָּן; 36.8). The description that follows quickly reverts to the singular, but this could be understood as an impersonal use.[4] Whilst the tent is a corporate project, the construction of the tabernacle furniture is attributed to Bezalel alone (37.1–29), and his skills also extended to the bronze work needed for the altar of burnt offering and the laver (38.1–8). Given his other elevated activities, it is surprising that the construction of the court is undertaken by him, since this is predominantly made of textiles and has a low level of sanctity. It is perhaps the metal work for the pillars that has led to the attribution of the court to him (38.9–20). The fabrication of the priestly vestments sees the involvement of all the artisans again as indicated by the return of the plural in 39.1. The singular appears sporadically throughout,

---

[2] חר״ש is used of working with wood and stone in 31.5 and 35.33. In the tabernacle account it would appear to be a skill distinct from metalwork (*contra* Houtman, *Exodus*, III: 358).

[3] חש״ב appears to be used in the tabernacle account as a general term for textile designing (Houtman, *Exodus*, III: 356). It has been argued that the term originally had a narrower meaning such as 'weaving' (e.g. Propp, *Exodus 19–40*, 406), but, even if this were so, it does not account for all the different uses in Exod 25–40.

[4] GKC §144d; Propp, *Exodus 19–40*, 664; Albertz, *Exodus 19–40*, 345. Cassuto less convincingly speaks of simpler phrasing (Umberto Cassuto, *A Commentary on the Book of Exodus* [Jerusalem: Magnes Press, 1987], 462).

156 THE MAKING OF THE TABERNACLE

often when an item is first mentioned (39.2, 7, 8, 22). As Albertz suggests, the intention could be to emphasize the cooperation between Bezalel and the Israelite artisans.[5]

In the Old Greek version, Bezalel is attributed with skills in the full range of crafts (𝕲 31.1–5; 35.30–33) and Oholiab has expertise in weaving and embroidery (𝕲 35.35; 37.20). The claim that Bezalel also has competencies in textile manufacture is found not only in 𝕲 35.35, as in the Masoretic version, but also in 31.3–5 which has a list of Bezalel's competencies that is more extensive than in the Masoretic version.

> **3** καὶ ἐνέπλησα αὐτὸν πνεῦμα θεῖον σοφίας καὶ συνέσεως καὶ ἐπιστήμης ἐν παντὶ ἔργῳ **4** διανοεῖσθαι καὶ ἀρχιτεκτονῆσαι ἐργάζεσθαι τὸ χρυσίον καὶ τὸ ἀργύριον καὶ τὸν χαλκὸν καὶ τὴν ὑάκινθον καὶ τὴν πορφύραν καὶ τὸ κόκκινον τὸ νηστὸν **5** καὶ τὰ λιθουργικὰ καὶ εἰς τὰ ἔργα τὰ τεκτονικὰ τῶν ξύλων ἐργάζεσθαι κατὰ πάντα τὰ ἔργα.

> **3** I have filled him with the divine spirit of wisdom, understanding and knowledge in every work **4** to design and construct, to work gold, silver, bronze and blue and purple and spun scarlet, **5** and cutting stone and works carved from wood, to fashion according to all the works   (𝕲 31.3–5).[6]

The longer list of Bezalel's competencies can be regarded as a counterpart to Exod 35.35 which describes God gifting both Bezalel and Oholiab with skills in textile manufacture.

It will be recalled that the Old Greek's construction account is ordered by materials with fabrics manufactured first followed by the metal objects. Thus, the structure of the Old Greek compliance account maps neatly onto the technical expertise of Bezalel and Oholiab. The Old Greek compliance account opens with the vestments which are attributed to the Israelite artisans: 'And everyone wise among the workmen made the vestments of the holy places' (καὶ ἐποίησεν πᾶς σοφὸς ἐν τοῖς ἐργαζομένοις τὰς στολὰς τῶν ἁγίων; 𝕲 36.8). In the details that follow the plural is used consistently except for the two places where the manufactured items are attached or inset into another part (𝕲 36.14, 29).[7] These were presumably thought to be the task of an individual, perhaps Oholiab. The vestments are followed by the tent and court where fabrics again feature strongly. Throughout

---

[5] Albertz, 'Beobachtungen', 281. The example he gives—'sie hämmerten das Goldblech, und er schnitt Fäden daraus' (v. 3)—is not especially compelling. The third person singular verb יְקַצֵּץ does not belong to the chain of *wayyiqtol* forms, and is probably best understood as an impersonal: 'they hammered the gold leaf and the threads were cut to work into the blue'.

[6] Many Greek manuscripts also include καὶ τὴν βύσσον τὴν κεκλωσμένην, 'and twisted linen', the standard form (cf. 25.4). Wevers prefers the longer text arguing that the additional words were lost by homoioteleuton (John William Wevers, *Exodus*, Septuaginta. Vetus Testamentum Graecum II/1 [Göttingen: Vandenhoeck & Ruprecht, 1991], 350).

[7] Wevers, however, finds the singulars perplexing (Wevers, *Greek Text of Exodus*, 600, 606).

the third person plural is used and so presumably the Israelite artisans are in view (𝔊 37.1–18). With the metal items, the shift to singular verbs is conspicuous. They are attributed entirely to Bezalel alone and arranged according to their material: gold, silver, bronze (𝔊 38.1–27).

The tabernacle account of the Old Latin of Monacensis has only survived from 𝔊 36.13 onwards and, consequently, we are not able to say how Bezalel and Oholiab were introduced in Exod 31 and 35. Where the text is extant, the vestments are attributed to a plural group as are the tent and court. Uniquely, Oholiab's responsibilities include not only the textiles, but also the woodwork: *hic eliab architectonizabit omne opus de ligno inputribili et fecit uela et stolas sacerdotum textiles et sutiles praemixtas uarietatem et hiacinto et purpura, cocco et bysso torta*, 'this Eliab made all the work of incorruptible wood and he made the curtains, the robes of the priests, woven and sown, varied mixtures from hyacinth, purple, crimson and fine linen' (𝔏^M 24/2/10–17). The attribution of the woodwork to Oholiab is understandable given how important wooden structures are to the construction of the tent and courtyard. As the craftsman responsible for wooden items, Oholiab also makes the acacia core of the ark, which Bezalel plates with gold: *ipse fecit arcam et inaurabit eam Beseel auro rutilo intus et foris*, 'this one made the ark. Beseel covered it with red gold inside and outside' (𝔏^M 24/2/18–20). The rest of the tabernacle furniture and the metalwork are attributed to Bezalel.

In all the versions, Bezalel is clearly regarded as pre-eminent amongst the master craftsmen. Whenever Bezalel and Oholiab appear together, Bezalel is always named first. He alone is said to be filled with the divine spirit, and Oholiab is depicted as his subordinate (31.6; 35.34). Except for the Old Latin of Monacensis which attributes the woodwork to Oholiab alone, it is only Bezalel that acts independently: he constructs the metal items unaided by either Oholiab or the Israelite artisans. Bezalel's pre-eminence results in a tendency to attribute increased competencies to him as is apparent in Vaticanus's version of Exod 31.4 which has a longer text than the Masoretic version of Codex Leningrad.

לַחְשֹׁב מַחֲשָׁבֹת לַעֲשׂוֹת בַּזָּהָב וּבַכֶּסֶף וּבַנְּחֹשֶׁת	διανοεῖσθαι καὶ ἀρχιτεκτονῆσαι ἐργάζεσθαι τὸ χρυσίον καὶ τὸ ἀργύριον καὶ τὸν χαλκὸν <u>καὶ τὴν ὑάκινθον καὶ τὴν πορφύραν καὶ τὸ κόκκινον τὸ νηστὸν καὶ τὴν βύσσον τὴν κεκλωσμένην</u>.
to make designs and to work in gold, silver and bronze (𝔐 31.4)	to design and construct, to work gold, silver and bronze <u>and blue and purple and spun scarlet and twisted linen</u> (𝔊 31.4)

The expansive text of Vaticanus should be regarded as secondary, not only by comparison with the Masoretic version of Leningrad, but also by comparison with Exod 35.32 which refers simply to Bezalel's abilities in gold, silver, and bronze. The addition in the Old Greek ensures that Bezalel has competencies in every kind of craft that is needed to construct the tabernacle including the manufacture of textiles, which is Oholiab's only responsibility. The tendency

158 THE MAKING OF THE TABERNACLE

to subordinate Oholiab is probably also apparent in the Masoretic Text's distinctive reading in 𝔐 38.23 of וְאִתּוֹ אָהֳלִיאָב, 'and with him Oholiab'.[8] In contrast, the equivalent verses in the Old Greek (𝔊 37.21) and Old Latin of Monacensis (𝔏^M 24/2/8–9) simply coordinate the two master craftsmen. It is not just Bezalel who contributes to Oholiab's overshadowing. With the exception of the Old Latin of Monacensis where he has responsibility for the woodwork, Oholiab always acts together with the skilled artisans. Thus, Bezalel and the skilled artisans together ensure that Oholiab has no contribution that is his own.

The Competencies of Bezalel and Oholiab

The differences between the different extant texts suggests a complex history of development. In seeking to untangle this history, our examination of the versions provides us with some important clues. First, there appears to be a tendency, especially visible in the Old Greek version of 31.1–5 in comparison to the Masoretic version, to attribute more and more competencies to Bezalel. Second, it is striking that Oholiab has no competencies that only belong to him. Third, the distinctive competencies of Bezalel and those he shares with Oholiab map precisely onto the structure of the Old Greek's construction account. Fourth, there are a couple of places which suggest Bezalel and Oholiab are more like equals. I will argue that these four observations all point in the same direction: Bezalel and Oholiab once had distinct, but complementary, competencies. Bezalel was responsible for the metalwork and Oholiab for the fabrics. They were more equal than is the case in the extant versions with Bezalel as *primus inter pares*.

I will begin by examining Oholiab's competencies. In contrast to the expansive lists of Bezalel's competencies, Oholiab's skills are clearly more circumscribed. The list in 𝔐 38.23 ≈ 𝔊 37.21 are attributed to him alone.

וְאִתּוֹ אָהֳלִיאָב בֶּן־אֲחִיסָמָךְ לְמַטֵּה־דָן חָרָשׁ וְחֹשֵׁב וְרֹקֵם בַּתְּכֵלֶת וּבָאַרְגָּמָן וּבְתוֹלַעַת הַשָּׁנִי וּבַשֵּׁשׁ	καὶ Ελιαβ ὁ τοῦ Αχισαμακ ἐκ τῆς φυλῆς Δαν, ὃς ἠρχιτεκτόνησεν τὰ ὑφαντὰ καὶ τὰ ῥαφιδευτὰ καὶ ποικιλτικὰ ὑφᾶναι τῷ κοκκίνῳ καὶ τῇ βύσσῳ
And with him Oholiab son of Achisamak from the tribe of Dan, engraver, designer, and embroiderer in blue, purple and crimson, and in fine linen (𝔐 38.23).	And Eliab the son of Achisamak from the tribe of Dan, who constructed the woven things and the needlework and the embroidered things, to weave with scarlet and linen (𝔊 37.21).

Oholiab's competencies in design (חֹשֵׁב) seems to have in view the manufacture of fabrics with some sort of artistic representation in them. The expression חֹשֵׁב is used of those fabrics where the image of cherubim has been incorporated—the tent and the veil (26.1, 31)—as well as the ephod and breastpiece (28.6, 15). It is

---

[8] Typically Wevers views the Old Greek as having omitted an original Masoretic reading (Wevers, *Greek Text of Exodus*, 618).

CRAFTSMEN AND COMMUNITY   159

perhaps the case that these parts of the high priest's vestments also bore some sort of imagery. Those parts of the sanctuary where Oholiab's skills in embroidery (רֹקֵם) were deployed did not have the same level of holiness—the screen for the entrance to the tent and the screen for the entrance to the court (26.36; 27.16). Similarly, the only item of the vestments where רֹקֵם is mentioned is the sash (28.39). Whatever was intended by the two expressions חֹשֵׁב and רֹקֵם it is likely that the former was a more technically demanding and finer piece of craftmanship than the latter.[9] Both skills are clearly related to the production of textiles, whilst the skill in engraving (חָרַשׁ) concerns the two onyx stones (28.11). The examination of the skills of Oholiab in 𝔐 38.23 ≈ 𝔊 37.21 suggests that he was not involved in the manufacture of all the fabrics, such as the various covers for the tent or the hangings of the courtyard, but only in the completion of the fine quality work.

The equivalent verse to 𝔐 38.23 ≈ 𝔊 37.21 in the Old Latin of Monacensis has a more extensive list of Oholiab's competencies:

> *Hic eliab architectonizauit omne opus de ligno inputribili et fecit uela et stolas sacerdotum textiles et sutiles praemixtas uarietate ex hiacinto et purpura cocco et bysso torta.[10]*

> This Eliab made all the work of incorruptible wood and he made the curtains, the robes of the priests, woven and sown, varied mixtures from hyacinth, purple, crimson and fine linen   ($\mathfrak{L}^M$ 24/2/10–17).

Oholiab is given responsibility for all the textiles—the vestments, the hangings of the court—but also the woodwork that provide the structure of the tent and court.

The versions disagree about which of the master craftsmen had competence for the woodwork. In the Masoretic, Samaritan, and Old Greek versions, Bezalel is attributed with skills in carving wood (31.5; 35.33). Such a competence would be vital for the construction of the sanctuary furniture since acacia wood formed the core of the ark, the table, and the poles used to carry them. The Old Latin of Monacensis, however, regards this as a specialism of Oholiab: 'this Eliab constructed all the works of incorruptible wood' (*hic eliab architectonizauit omne opus de ligno inputribili*; $\mathfrak{L}^M$ 24/2/11–12) and attributes the construction of the wooden core of the ark to Eliab ($\mathfrak{L}^M$ 24/2/18). Whilst Bogaert regards the attribution of the woodwork to Eliab in Monacensis as original,[11] it is difficult to

---

[9] For discussion, see Haran, *Temples*, 160–3.

[10] Dold reads *architectonizabit*, but my examination of the digitized manuscript would appear to confirm Ziegler's reading of *architectonizauit*.

[11] The responsibility for the woodwork is a key point of difference between Bogaert's and Rhyder's assessments of the literary history. Bogaert argues that the Old Latin of Monacensis preserves the earliest division of labour between Bezalel and Oholiab, and that Oholiab's equal standing with Bezalel was deliberately suppressed in the other versions (Bogaert, 'L'importance de la Septante', 411–16). Although I would agree with Bogaert (and against Rhyder) that Bezalel and Oholiab had a more equal standing at an earlier stage in the literary history of Exod 35–40, Rhyder rightly points out that the

160 THE MAKING OF THE TABERNACLE

explain why the references to wood would have been removed in the other textual traditions. It is rather more likely that the distinctive reading in Monacensis is an attempt to clarify what competence in 'engraving' (חש״ב) might entail. The reading *omne opus de ligno inputribili* stands in the place where the Masoretic version refers to Oholiab's competence in 'engraving' (חש״ב). This skill is attributed to Oholiab in the Old Greek and Masoretic versions of 𝔐 38.23 ≈ 𝔊 37.21 and could be applied to both wood and stone. The logic for attributing skills in woodwork to Oholiab is that the construction of the tent and the courtyard required wooden boards and pillars upon which the tent and hangings were suspended.[12] As we have seen, the Old Greek of *Vaticanus* restricts Oholiab's specialist skills to the fine embroidery work that was used for the most highly decorated parts of the tabernacle and the vestments. From this perspective חש״ב refers to the engraving of the gems on Aaron's vestments.

Unfortunately, we are not able to determine whether the Old Latin version of Monacensis had a version of Exod 31.5 // 35.33 which attributes the woodworking to Bezalel. The fact that Monacensis credits Oholiab with the woodwork suggests that it did not. If this were the case, we would have two different textual traditions: one represented in the Masoretic, Samaritan, and Old Greek traditions in which Bezalel is responsible for the woodwork and the one found in Monacensis in which Oholiab is. We have already seen that Oholiab's association with the woodwork in Monacensis is probably secondary and the same is probably also true for Bezalel. Originally, neither master craftsman was specifically tasked with the woodwork and the development of the textual traditions reflect different attempts to resolve this lacuna.

My examination of Oholiab's competencies has suggested that he was originally attributed with specialisms that related to the fine quality textile work in the tabernacle proper and the priestly vestments. These fine skills were also displayed in his work engraving the names on the precious stones that Aaron bore on his shoulders. In the Old Latin version of Monacensis, this reference to 'engraving' was understood to mean that Oholiab had particular responsibility for the woodwork, and his role was extended to all the fabrics.

---

different role of the woodworking precludes Bogaert's proposal (Rhyder, 'Unity and Hierarchy', 113–20). For Bogaert's proposal, in the Greek version known from Vaticanus, the *Vorlage* of the Old Latin must have been revised to remove references to wood, whilst in the Masoretic and Samaritan versions the expertise in wood was transferred to Bezalel. Rhyder rightly concludes that it makes more sense to hold that the Old Greek of Vaticanus reflected an earlier text than Monacensis.

[12] Rhyder expresses herself perplexed as to why Monacensis might have included a reference to Eliab as the worker of wood. She offers two speculative proposals. 'Possibly it was considered strange that YHWH should have specified two artisans to lead the construction of his sanctuary but then relegated Oholiab to a marginal role; an expansion of Oholiab's skills might, then, have been thought to produce a more coherent account of the sanctuary construction. Or perhaps it might be speculated that *Mon[acensis]* stemmed from a scribal group with particular associations with the north of Israel, which saw value in placing greater emphasis on the role that the Danite played in constructing YHWH's sanctuary' (Rhyder, 'Unity and Hierarchy', 117). Neither speculation is necessary in my view.

I now want to turn to the ways in which Bezalel's competencies overlap with Oholiab's. As we have seen, in the account of the tabernacle's construction, Bezalel is portrayed taking sole responsibility for the manufacture of the metalwork. In the extensive lists of 31.2–5 and 35.31–33, his competencies are presented as far broader and they infringe upon the areas in which Oholiab works. A careful examination of the two lists suggests some difficulty in describing how Bezalel and Oholiab relate to one another. Both lists in the Masoretic version have a reference to Oholiab attached somewhat uncomfortably. Of the two, the language of 31.6, וַאֲנִי הִנֵּה נָתַתִּי אִתּוֹ אֵת אָהֳלִיאָב, 'and behold I have given him Oholiab', appears to be an attempt to smooth the rather jarring הוּא וְאָהֳלִיאָב, 'he and Oholiab', of 35.34. This apparent smoothing of the text is one of the principal reasons for regarding the list of 35.31–33 as earlier than 31.2–5.

The difficult syntax is not the only problem with the list of Bezalel and Oholiab's skills. There is a significant degree of overlap in Exod 35 between the description of Bezalel's calling and gifting (vv. 31–34) and the joint competencies of Bezalel and Oholiab (v. 35). Both refer to the filling (מִלֵּא) of the master craftsmen with wisdom (חָכְמָה) in order to do every kind of work (לַעֲשׂוֹת כָּל־מְלֶאכֶת) including engraving (חָרַשׁ) and designing (חֹשֵׁב). It is rather perplexing that Bezalel's individual competencies are not followed by Oholiab's, but that a list of joint competencies should follow. Rhyder notes a further difficulty with Bezalel and Oholiab's appearance in Exod 35: The suffixed particle אֹתָם in v. 35—'he filled them (אֹתָם) with wisdom of heart'—is somewhat ambiguous. Does it refer to Bezalel and Oholiab or to those that are taught, the Israelite artisans?[13]

Rhyder suggests that the problems with Exod 35 result from the inclusion of Oholiab. Arguably, though, the addition of Oholiab in 35.34b–35 would only explain the doublet and provides no explanation for the appearance of אתם in v. 35. Why would a redactor follow the individual competencies of Bezalel with a list of joint competencies? A more compelling solution that would explain both problems is that the secondary material is 35.31–34a, b(הוּא).

30 וַיֹּאמֶר מֹשֶׁה אֶל־בְּנֵי יִשְׂרָאֵל רְאוּ קָרָא יְהוָה בְּשֵׁם בְּצַלְאֵל בֶּן־אוּרִי בֶן־חוּר לְמַטֵּה יְהוּדָה׃

31 וַיְמַלֵּא אֹתוֹ רוּחַ אֱלֹהִים בְּחָכְמָה בִּתְבוּנָה וּבְדַעַת וּבְכָל־מְלָאכָה׃

32 וְלַחְשֹׁב מַחֲשָׁבֹת לַעֲשֹׂת בַּזָּהָב וּבַכֶּסֶף וּבַנְּחֹשֶׁת׃

33 וּבַחֲרֹשֶׁת אֶבֶן לְמַלֹּאת וּבַחֲרֹשֶׁת עֵץ לַעֲשׂוֹת בְּכָל־מְלֶאכֶת מַחֲשָׁבֶת׃

34 וּלְהוֹרֹת נָתַן בְּלִבּוֹ הוּא

וְאָהֳלִיאָב בֶּן־אֲחִיסָמָךְ לְמַטֵּה־דָן׃

---

[13] Rhyder, 'Unity and Hierarchy', 118. Rhyder also rightly observes that there is a further difficulty in the verse that follows since there is a shift to the third person singular, 'he did' (וְעָשָׂה). As we have already argued, the texts concerned with the Israelite artisans were added at a later stage than the two master craftsmen.

162   THE MAKING OF THE TABERNACLE

30 Then Moses said to the Israelites: See, YHWH has called by name Bezalel
son of Uri son of Hur, of the tribe of Judah;

> **31** he has filled him with divine spirit, with skill, intelligence, and knowledge
> in every kind of craft, **32** to devise artistic designs, to work in gold, silver, and
> bronze, **33** in cutting stones for setting, and in carving wood, in every kind
> of craft. **34** And he has inspired him to teach, both him

and Oholiab son of Ahisamach, of the tribe of Dan.

In my proposed reconstruction, the original text had God calling both Bezalel
and Oholiab by name (35.30, 34b) and was followed in v. 35 by a description of
the work that they were equipped to do together.

The original reading of v. 35 requires some discussion because the Old Greek
and the Hebrew versions diverge from one another.

מִלֵּא אֹתָם חָכְמַת־לֵב לַעֲשׂוֹת כָּל־מְלֶאכֶת חָרָשׁ וְחֹשֵׁב וְרֹקֵם בַּתְּכֵלֶת וּבָאַרְגָּמָן בְּתוֹלַעַת הַשָּׁנִי וּבַשֵּׁשׁ וְאֹרֵג עֹשֵׂי כָּל־מְלָאכָה וְחֹשְׁבֵי מַחֲשָׁבֹת׃	ἐνέπλησεν αὐτοὺς σοφίας καὶ συνέσεως διανοίας πάντα συνιέναι ποιῆσαι τὰ ἔργα τοῦ ἁγίου καὶ τὰ ὑφαντὰ καὶ ποικιλτὰ ὑφᾶναι τῷ κοκκίνῳ καὶ τῇ βύσσῳ ποιεῖν πᾶν ἔργον ἀρχιτεκτονίας ποικιλίας.
He filled them with wisdom of heart to do every work of an engraver, and a designer, and an embroiderer in blue and in purple, in crimson and in linen, and a weaver, work of every labour or skilled design (𝔐 35.35).	He filled them with wisdom and intelligence of mind to understand all to make the works of the holy place and to weave the woven and embroidered with the scarlet and the linen to make all the work of design of embroidery (𝕲 35.35).

A critical point where the Old Greek diverges from the Masoretic Text is its
reading ποιῆσαι τὰ ἔργα τοῦ ἁγίου. The *Vorlage* of the Old Greek version was
probably לעשת מלאכת הקדש rather than Codex Leningrad's לַעֲשׂוֹת כָּל־מְלֶאכֶת חָרָשׁ.
A confusion of both ה/ח and ד/ר is readily explicable in the square script. In addition, a very similar expression to what I have suggested was the Old Greek's
Vorlage is found in the Hebrew text of the following verse: לעשת את כל מלאכת עבדת
הקדש, 'to do all the work of the labour of the sanctuary' (36.1). The result of this
divergence is that the Hebrew versions describe only those tasks which reflect
Oholiab's competencies: the engraving and textile work. In contrast, the Old
Greek has a text which refers to the 'works of the holy place' as well as the textile
fabrication. The 'works of the holy place' is, perhaps, most naturally understood
to refer to the furniture in the holy place. Thus, the Old Greek of Exod 35.35
describes Bezalel and Oholiab's joint competencies as the tabernacle furniture
and its textiles which corresponds to the Old Greek's division of the construction
into two sections: the fabrics followed by the metal. As such, the verse is an appropriate description of Bezalel and Oholiab's combined competencies, but not as a
list of their individual competencies. In other words, it is not true to say that

CRAFTSMEN AND COMMUNITY   163

Oholiab was equipped to 'make the works of the holy place', for these are the tasks undertaken by Bezalel in making the sanctuary furniture.

The competing claims of the Old Greek and the Masoretic versions are difficult to adjudicate, though it is interesting to observe that 𝕲 35.35 has similarities to both vv. 31–34a and 36.1 and may have been the inspiration for both. First, it is noticeable that the beginning of v. 35 in the Old Greek is rather close to v. 31,

καὶ ἐνέπλησεν αὐτὸν πνεῦμα θεῖον σοφίας καὶ συνέσεως καὶ ἐπιστήμης πάντων	ἐνέπλησεν αὐτοὺς σοφίας καὶ συνέσεως διανοίας πάντα συνιέναι
He filled him with a divine spirit of wisdom and intelligence and knowledge of all things (𝕲 35.31).	He filled them with wisdom and intelligence of mind to understand (𝕲 35.35).

Bezalel is also attributed with distinctive abilities. He is not just filled with wisdom, but is uniquely 'filled with divine spirit'. Bezalel's skills in gold, silver, bronze, and cutting stone and wood (35.32–33) could be seen as an explication of 'the works of the holy place' (v. 35). Second, 36.1 duplicates significant elements of 𝕲 35.35 and creates a summary statement that attributes the building of the sanctuary to Bezalel, Oholiab, and the skilled artisans.

In the Masoretic version, 𝔐 35.35 is more clearly orientated to the specialisms of Oholiab in textiles. In contrast to the Old Greek, the additional competence of weaving (וְאֹרֵג) has been added somewhat inelegantly after the list of materials. Further, הקדש was read as חרש. As a result, the verse only described Oholiab's limited remit. Nevertheless, the plural direct object, 'them' (אֹתָם) was retained. As a result, we must either assume that Bezalel's competencies also extended to the textiles—and it should be recalled that we saw a comparable extension of Bezalel's skills in the late editing of 𝕲 31.4—or we must understand that the plural אֹתָם referred to the Israelite artisans who assist Oholiab (36.8). These features suggest that we should cautiously conclude that the Hebrew version is more developed than that preserved in the Old Greek.

The textual history I have been seeking to uncover is particularly complex and it is useful to summarize its stages in sequential order. The earliest text is found in Exod 35.30, 34b, 35 (𝕲). It describes how Bezalel and Oholiab were called by God and provided with the abilities to construct the tabernacle (35.30). Their competencies are described jointly and include making the holy place and fabricating the textiles. These correspond to the division in the Old Greek compliance account between the production of the fabrics and the construction of the metal furniture. This text was revised through the insertion of 35.31–34a, b(הוה) and 36.1. The revisions sought to elevate Bezalel and provide him with distinctive skills which related particularly to the construction of the sanctum and its furniture. He was also distinguished from his co-worker Oholiab by being filled with the divine spirit. The textual inspiration for this additional material came from

164   THE MAKING OF THE TABERNACLE

35.35. The text that resulted corresponds to what was preserved in the Old Greek. The text of v. 35 continued to develop as can be seen in the Masoretic and Samaritan traditions. Through a process of dissimilation from vv. 31–34a, it lost its reference to the holy place so that the description of joint competencies only included areas where Oholiab had skills, and Bezalel was assumed to have by virtue of his role as the senior craftsman.

A similar development occurred in 𝔐 38.22–23 ≈ 𝔊 37.20–21 where Bezalel and Oholiab appear together again. I will begin by examining the Masoretic Text and Old Greek. The texts are similar, but they have some subtle differences.

22 וּבְצַלְאֵל בֶּן־אוּרִי בֶן־חוּר לְמַטֵּה יְהוּדָה עָשָׂה אֵת כָּל־אֲשֶׁר־צִוָּה יְהוָה אֶת־מֹשֶׁה: 23 וְאִתּוֹ אָהֳלִיאָב בֶּן־אֲחִיסָמָךְ לְמַטֵּה־דָן חָרָשׁ וְחֹשֵׁב וְרֹקֵם בַּתְּכֵלֶת וּבָאַרְגָּמָן וּבְתוֹלַעַת הַשָּׁנִי וּבַשֵּׁשׁ:	20 καὶ Βεσελεηλ ὁ τοῦ Ουριου ἐκ φυλῆς Ιουδα ἐποίησεν καθὰ συνέταξεν κύριος τῷ Μωυσῆ, 21 καὶ Ελιαβ ὁ τοῦ Αχισαμακ ἐκ τῆς φυλῆς Δαν, ὃς ἠρχιτεκτόνησεν τὰ ὑφαντὰ καὶ τὰ ῥαφιδευτὰ καὶ ποικιλτικὰ ὑφᾶναι τῷ κοκκίνῳ καὶ τῇ βύσσῳ.
22 Bezalel son of Uri son of Hur of the tribe of Judah made all that YHWH commanded Moses. 23 And with him was Oholiab son of Ahisamak of the tribe of Dan, engraver, designer, and embroiderer in blue, purple, and crimson yarns, and in fine linen (𝔐 38.22–23).	20 Beseleel son of Ouri from the tribe of Judah made just as the Lord commanded Moses. 21 And Eliab son of Achisamak from the tribe of Dan who designed to weave the woven things and the needlework and the embroidery with scarlet and linen (𝔊 37.20–21).

The descriptions of the two master craftsmen have some interesting features that need to be noted. First, the descriptions of their competencies are unbalanced. Bezalel is described as implementing what God commanded Moses to do, whilst Oholiab has specific competencies attributed to him. We might have expected both to have been acclaimed as those who realized the instructions to Moses, or for their specific and distinctive skills to have been outlined. Second, the Masoretic Text and the Old Greek represent two different attempts to coordinate these statements about Bezalel and Oholiab. In the Masoretic Text, Oholiab is made the subordinate party to Bezalel's activities by the brief observation that he was 'with him' (וְאִתּוֹ). The Old Greek, however, simply juxtaposes the two statements about Bezalel and Oholiab. The description of Oholiab's competencies is introduced by a relative clause that does not seem to be a translation of the text preserved in the Masoretic version.[14]

The Old Latin of Monacensis has a different reading, which can shed further light on the differences between the Masoretic and the Old Greek versions,

---

[14] Elsewhere in Exodus ἀρχιτεκτονέω renders words derived from the root חשׁב (Exod 31.4; 35.32, 35). The words ὑφαντά, ῥαφιδευτά and ποικιλτικά can translate various words for technical skills in fabric making: חשׁב, רקם and ארג. The Old Greek has three words where the Masoretic Text has only two. The expression τῷ κοκκίνῳ καὶ τῇ βύσσῳ only translates בְּתוֹלַעַת הַשָּׁנִי וּבַשֵּׁשׁ.

Haec fecerunt beseel filius or filii uriae de tribu iuda et eliab filius ecisame de tribu dan. Hic eliab architectoniuabit omne opus de ligno inputribili et fecit uela et stolas sacerdotum textiles et sutiles praemixtas uarietatem et hiacinto et purpura cocco et bysso torta.

They did this Beseel son of Or son of Uriah of the tribe of Judah and Eliab son of Ecisame of the tribe of Dan. This Eliab made all the work of incorruptible wood and he made the curtains, the robes of the priests, woven and sown, varied mixtures from hyacinth, purple, crimson and fine linen   ($𝔏^M$ 24/2/6–17).

The Old Latin is instructive in two respects. First, the Old Latin lacks any equivalent to Codex Leningrad's עָשָׂה אֵת כָּל־אֲשֶׁר־צִוָּה יְהוָה אֶת־מֹשֶׁה and Vaticanus' ἐποίησεν καθὰ συνέταξεν κύριος τῷ Μωυσῇ, 'he did all that YHWH commanded Moses'. As a result, it presents Bezalel and Oholiab as jointly constructing the tabernacle. The possibility that the clause, עָשָׂה אֵת כָּל־אֲשֶׁר־צִוָּה יְהוָה אֶת־מֹשֶׁה, was an addition would provide a simple and compelling explanation for why the Old Greek and Masoretic versions have two different ways to try and coordinate the two master craftsmen. Second, the Old Latin also has its own unique material in comparison to the Masoretic and Old Greek versions, which describes Eliab's responsibilities for the wood, the curtains, and the robe. These show the same concern that has been visible in all the versions to define Bezalel and Oholiab's distinct responsibilities more precisely and should be judged a secondary addition.

The Old Latin provides crucial evidence that $𝔐$ 38.22–23 ≈ $𝔊$ 37.20–21 underwent a similar development to Exod 35.30–35. In both cases, the earliest text appears to have described Bezalel and Oholiab sharing a common task. This was revised by the insertion of text immediately after Bezalel's ancestry and tribal affiliation which attributed to him oversight over the construction of the entire sanctuary. As a result, what had originally been the common tasks of Bezalel and Oholiab are now attributed to just Oholiab. At a subsequent stage, the Old Latin of Monacensis revised the tasks to fit its conception of Oholiab's duties just as the Masoretic version of Exod 35.35 shows a revision in comparison to the Old Greek version.

The Origins of Bezalel and Oholiab

Throughout the instructions, the reader of Exodus is justified in expecting that Moses will take the leading role in constructing the tabernacle. Those expectations are dramatically overturned in Exod 31 when God informs Moses that he has called Bezalel and Oholiab and equipped them with the skills they need. As I have demonstrated, there can be little doubt that Bezalel and Oholiab's involvement is a secondary development and that the tabernacle was originally

166   THE MAKING OF THE TABERNACLE

presented as Moses' achievement. The evidence lies to hand throughout the
tabernacle account: the secondary framing of the instructions to Moses as tasks
for the Israelite community (25.8–10*; 28.3–5), the late appearance of Bezalel and
Oholiab, and the harmonizing notion that Moses erected the items that had been
produced by the people. Given the challenges it poses to the portrayal of Moses as
the one who received God's instructions to build the tabernacle, why were Bezalel
and Oholiab introduced in the first place? The magnitude of the task involved in
building such a sanctuary provides only a partial answer. It is true that the building envisaged would far exceed the capabilities of one person, though why not
simply portray Moses directing the Israelite labourers? We might, perhaps, seek
an answer in the names, Bezalel and Oholiab. The name בְּצַלְאֵל is usually parsed as
'in the shadow of El (God)', whilst אָהֳלִיאָב means 'the father is my tent'. Both names
suit the crafters of the tabernacle and were probably chosen for their resonance.[15]
But they do not assist us in understanding why it was felt necessary to posit two
master craftsmen.

I want to suggest that the crucial clue is to be found in the earliest descriptions
of Bezalel and Oholiab's competencies in 𝕲 35.35 and 37.21. In both cases, we
have a list of skills in fabric design: καὶ τὰ ὑφαντὰ καὶ ποικιλτὰ ὑφᾶναι τῷ κοκκίνῳ
καὶ τῇ βύσσῳ, 'to weave the woven things and the embroidery with scarlet and
linen' (𝕲 35.35); τὰ ὑφαντὰ καὶ τὰ ῥαφιδευτὰ καὶ ποικιλτικὰ ὑφᾶναι τῷ κοκκίνῳ
καὶ τῇ βύσσῳ, 'to weave the woven things and the needlework and the embroidery
with scarlet and linen' (𝕲 37.21). There is sufficient alignment with the Masoretic
Text in 𝕲 35.35 to identify חשב ורקם as the *Vorlage* for τὰ ὑφαντὰ καὶ ποικιλτὰ
ὑφᾶναι. Possibly the *Vorlage* of 𝕲 37.21 also included וארג, though we might wonder
whether it is a secondary addition similar to its appearance in 𝔐 35.35. In neither
of the Old Greek texts is there a reference to חָרָשׁ, 'engraver', as we find in the
Hebrew versions. In sum, the Old Greek of Exod 35.35 and 37.21 identify Bezalel
and Oholiab as the חשב ורקם. These are two terms that have also occurred in the
instructions, but in the collocations מַעֲשֵׂה חֹשֵׁב and מַעֲשֵׂה רֹקֵם. The inspiration for
Bezalel and Oholiab is to be found in these two expressions.

When Moses receives the instructions about the tabernacle, he is commanded
to make the sanctuary himself. This is evident in the repeated 'you shall make'
(וְעָשִׂיתָ). The instructions for the fabrics do, however, make mention of several
specialized techniques. The cherubim in the inner curtains and the veil as well as
the fabrics of the ephod and the breastpiece are to be 'the work of a designer'
(מַעֲשֵׂה חֹשֵׁב); the screen of the tent and the hangings of the courtyard as well as the
sash are to be 'the work of an embroiderer' (מַעֲשֵׂה רֹקֵם). In both cases what is being
described is the particular kind of workmanship. It would appear, however, that

---

[15] Benno Jacob, *Das Buch Exodus*, ed. Schlomo Mayer (Stuttgart: Calwer, 1997), 839; Propp, *Exodus
19–40*, 486, 489.

the participles were understood as evidence that Moses was assisted by two craftsmen: a designer and an embroiderer.

The appearance of Bezalel and Oholiab in the Old Greek and the Old Latin versions is consistent with an identification of their competencies with textile manufacture. Their calling is described in Exod 35.30–36.1 immediately before the construction of the priestly vestments and the tent is begun. The two master craftsmen are mentioned again in a summary statement at the end of the tent's construction (𝕲 37.20–21). The mention of the two craftsmen form an *inclusio* around the entire section devoted to the fabrics (𝕲 36.8–37.18). But if Bezalel and Oholiab are responsible for the textiles, as the חֹשֵׁב and the רֹקֵם of Exod 25–28, what about the items made from gold, silver, and bronze? In the construction account, the metal furnishings are introduced by וַיַּעַשׂ, an expression that corresponds to וְעָשִׂיתָ of the instructions. Since the subject of the appearances of וְעָשִׂיתָ in Exod 25–28 was Moses, it is possible that this was true of the appearances of וַיַּעַשׂ in some early version of the construction account. In the extant versions, the construction of the metal furniture is undertaken by Bezalel, but this attribution depends on a single mention of Bezalel at the head of the list (𝕲 38.1; 𝔐 37.1). The ease with which this could be altered is apparent if we compare the Old Greek and the Old Latin.

1 *Καὶ ἐποίησεν Βεσελεηλ τὴν κιβωτὸν* 2 *καὶ κατεχρύσωσεν αὐτὴν χρυσίῳ καθαρῷ ἔσωθεν καὶ ἔξωθεν.*	Ipse fecit arcam et inaurabit eam beseel auro rutilo intus et foris
1 And Beseleel made the ark 2 and he plated it with pure gold inside and outside (𝕲 38.1–2).	He made the ark and Beseel plated it with rose gold inside and outside (Mon 24/2/18–20).

In the Old Greek version the furniture is attributed to Bezalel, whilst in the Old Latin of Monacensis Eliab constructs the acacia core of the ark and Beseel plates it with gold and constructs the remaining items of furniture.

In the face of no textual witness that read Moses at 𝕲 38.1; 𝔐 37.1, it may appear entirely speculative to propose that Bezalel replaced an earlier Moses. There are, however, a few pieces of evidence that support such a proposal. First, in Deut 10 Moses claims to have made the ark in which the Ten Commandments were housed. 'I made an ark of acacia wood and I carved two tablets of stone like the first…and placed the tablets in the ark I had made' (וָאַעַשׂ אֲרוֹן עֲצֵי שִׁטִּים וָאֶפְסֹל שְׁנֵי־לֻחֹת אֲבָנִים כָּרִאשֹׁנִים…וָאָשִׂם אֶת־הַלֻּחֹת בָּאָרוֹן אֲשֶׁר עָשִׂיתִי; 10.3a, 5aβ). The reference to the ark is usually recognized as one of the latest additions to Deuteronomy,[16] and the composer of these verses is evidently familiar with a developed version of the

---

[16] Otto observes that the ark has no secure foothold in the account of the golden calf and attributes its appearance to a post-exilic *Fortschreibung* (10.2b–3aα, 5aβ–11b) (Eckart Otto, *Deuteronomium 4,44–11,32*, HTKAT [Freiburg im Breisgau: Herder, 2012], 949–50).

168 THE MAKING OF THE TABERNACLE

end of Exodus where the story of the golden calf has been integrated into the tabernacle account.[17] The indebtedness to Exod 25–31, 35–40 is apparent in the idea that the ark was constructed from acacia wood, but the redactor of Deut 10.1–5 does not appear to know a version where Bezalel manufactured the ark. Second, in Num 8 it is assumed that Moses made the lampstand. 'According to the likeness YHWH showed Moses, thus he made the lampstand' (כְּמַרְאֶה אֲשֶׁר הֶרְאָה יְהוָה אֶת־מֹשֶׁה כֵּן עָשָׂה אֶת־הַמְּנֹרָה; v. 4b). Modern commentators have overlooked the implications of this verse,[18] but it was noticed by early translators and medieval commentators who sought various ways to evade its implications.[19]

North and South in the Tabernacle Account

The literary development that I have proposed suggests that Bezalel and Oholiab were originally presented as having equal responsibility for the fabrication of the textiles. Bezalel is consistently mentioned first, but he appears to be first amongst equals, rather than Oholiab's superior. Nevertheless, the development of the text of Exodus saw the competencies of both craftsmen being expanded and distinguished from one another. Bezalel was given charge over the metalwork, whilst Oholiab was given primary responsibility for the textiles and, in the Old Latin, also the woodwork. Their different accountabilities suggest a hierarchy with Bezalel constructing the furniture that is crucial for maintaining the divine presence and securing atonement, whilst Oholiab fabricates the tent that houses the furniture. Bezalel is no longer *primus inter pares*, but the leading craftsman who takes overall responsibility for the whole.

The tribal origins of the master craftsmen are an important aspect of this hierarchical ordering as Rhyder has recently argued.[20] Bezalel hails from the southern tribe of Judah and Oholiab, from the northern tribe of Dan. There are several possible reasons why the authors may have chosen a Danite and a Judahite to lead the construction of the tabernacle. These reasons are not mutually exclusive, but have the potential to shine a slightly different light on the hierarchical ordering of the two master craftsmen. The first possible reason views the tabernacle in light of

---

[17] For the cross-references between Deut 10.1–5 and texts in Exod 25–40, see Porzig, *Die Lade Jahwes*, 46–50.

[18] The issue is not observed in Baruch A. Levine, *Numbers: A New Translation with Introduction and Commentary*, 2 vols., AB 4 (New York: Doubleday, 1993–2000), I: 269–72. Milgrom translates as an impersonal third person: 'so was the lampstand made', but without commenting on the issue (Jacob Milgrom, *Numbers* במדבר: *The Traditional Hebrew Text with the New JPS Translation*, JPS Torah Commentary [Philadelphia: Jewish Publication Society of America, 1990], 60).

[19] Targum Neofiti and Pseudo-Jonathan worried about the contradiction this created and attributed the lampstand to Bezalel. Rashi explains that 'he' refers to the person who made it, and *Midr. Tanḥ* to Num 8.4 attributes the fabrication to God.

[20] Rhyder, *Centralizing the Cult*, 124–8; Rhyder, 'Unity and Hierarchy'.

CRAFTSMEN AND COMMUNITY   169

the story of the building of Solomon's temple. This account in Kings was probably composed before the tabernacle account and describes the prominent involvement of a northern craftsman. Hiram of Tyre was employed by Solomon to do the bronze work in the temple. His father was also from Tyre, but his mother was from the tribe of Naphtali.[21] The text appears to assume that the technical knowledge required to make the Jerusalem temple was lacking in Judah and needed to be imported from Phoenicia. In language reminiscent of the description of Bezalel in Exod 35.31–32, Hiram is described as 'filled with wisdom, understanding and knowledge to do all the work in bronze' (־אֶת וְאֶת־הַתְּבוּנָה אֶת־הַחָכְמָה וַיִּמָּלֵא הַדַּעַת לַעֲשׂוֹת כָּל־מְלָאכָה בַּנְּחֹשֶׁת; 1 Kgs 7.14).[22] If there are similarities between Hiram and the tabernacle craftsmen, there are also important differences. The unimpeachable ancestry of Bezalel and Oholiab could be viewed as a corrective to Hiram's mixed Tyrian-Israelite heritage. Further, the reference to Oholiab maintains a northern connection, but Bezalel is a novelty and will ultimately take on Hiram's metallurgical expertise.

Second, the association of the master craftsmen with Dan and Judah could be a reworking of the formula 'from Dan to Beer-sheba' (מִדָּן וְעַד־בְּאֵר שָׁבַע),[23] since Beersheba is a Judahite town. The formula describes the northern and southern limits of the ideal, twelve-tribe Israel and functions as a merism for the entire nation. Thus, Bezalel and Oholiab would be representatives of all Israel. It should not be overlooked that the naming of the master craftsmen reverses the order of the geographical formula which names Dan first. In this way, the superiority of Judah is subtly indexed.[24]

Third, Bezalel and Oholiab might represent the common endeavour of south and north in the construction of a pan-Israelite shrine. Since the Pentateuch came to be recognized as an authoritative text by both Judeans and Samarians, the tabernacle account offers an origin story that can be shared by the temple cults in Jerusalem and Mount Gerizim. Although the tabernacle is viewed as a collaborative effort, the predominance of a Judahite suggests that the scribes who shaped this material had a particular respect for Judahite claims. As Rhyder argues, this may not amount to an opposition to the presence of a temple on Mount Gerizim, but it does suggest that they viewed Jerusalem as the paramount Yahwistic shrine in the Persian period.[25]

Each of the three possibilities I have outlined, whether taken individually or in some combination, identify a social hierarchy within the Israelite tribes that

---

[21] Cf. 2 Chron 2.13–14 where Hiram is called Huram-abi and is the son of a Danite woman.

[22] Würthwein thought there was no relationship between the two texts, but we have merely a standardized expression, which seems unlikely (Ernst Würthwein, *Das erste Buch der Könige, Kapitel 1–16*, ATD 11,1 [Göttingen: Vandenhoeck & Ruprecht, 1977], 75).

[23] Judg 20.1; 1 Sam 3.20; 2 Sam 3.10; 17.11; 24.2, 15; 1 Kgs 4.25.

[24] Comparison can be made with the reception of the formula in the book of Chronicles where it becomes 'from Beer-sheba to Dan' (מִבְּאֵר שֶׁבַע וְעַד־דָּן).

[25] Rhyder, 'Unity and Hierarchy'.

170   THE MAKING OF THE TABERNACLE

elevates Judah above the other tribes. This hierarchy is subtly communicated through the relative ordering of the two master craftsmen, but it is expressed slightly more sharply with the revision of the tabernacle account. The hierarchy does not entirely obscure the implicit equality expressed by the ideal of the twelve tribes on Aaron's shoulders or breastpiece. Judah's precedence is relative, not absolute. In this way, the compliance account comes to express a subtly gradated hierarchy set within an ideal of tribal equality.

The Israelite Artisans

Bezalel and Oholiab are assisted in their endeavours by a company of skilled artisans. In Exod 36.1, the claim about Bezalel and Oholiab in 35.35 is reworked to portray these Israelite men as divinely endowed with the necessary skills.

וְעָשָׂה בְצַלְאֵל וְאָהֳלִיאָב וְכֹל אִישׁ חֲכַם־לֵב אֲשֶׁר נָתַן יְהוָה חָכְמָה וּתְבוּנָה בָּהֵמָּה לָדַעַת לַעֲשֹׂת
אֶת־כָּל־מְלֶאכֶת עֲבֹדַת הַקֹּדֶשׁ לְכֹל אֲשֶׁר־צִוָּה יְהוָה

Bezalel and Oholiab and every man wise of heart to whom YHWH gave wisdom and understanding in them to know and do all the work of the service of the holy place in accordance with all that YHWH commanded   (𝔐 36.1).

The revision of the compliance account makes the artisans responsible with Oholiab, and possibly also Bezalel, for the fabrication of the vestments, the tent, and the court. In the Old Greek, the verbs for the making of all these items are consistently plural. In the Hebrew versions, however, the vestments have been moved after the construction of the tabernacle furniture and present a mixed picture with both singular and plural verbs. It is not easy to determine the logic behind this oscillation of singular and plural forms. It is perhaps that Bezalel is presented as responsible for some aspects of the manufacturing. Attributing the priestly vestments to the Israelite artisans may seem surprising given the elevated presentation of the vestments in Exod 28. Surely these precious garments would be the preserve of the master craftsmen? It seems likely that the role of the artisans recognizes the close relationship that the people have with the high priestly vestments. It is through them that the people are represented before YHWH in the tabernacle.

The idea that the master craftsmen and the Israelite artisans undertook the task of manufacturing the sanctuary results in a transformation of the tabernacle account. This is most obvious in the reframing of the instructions to give the people a prominent role (25.8–10; 28.3–5), but also in the notion that after their construction the people delivered the components of the tabernacle to Moses who erected them. There are important changes to the hegemonic claims of Israel's priesthood, and we should not overlook the devolution of responsibility

CRAFTSMEN AND COMMUNITY   171

for the manufacture of the tabernacle and the vestments to the non-priestly craftsmen and artisans. Most surprising of all is that Bezalel is said to have been filled with the רוּחַ אֱלֹהִים, 'the spirit of God', something that is not said of any other figure in the tabernacle account, not even Aaron the high priest. Describing his creative abilities in this way establishes a connection between the actions of Bezalel and the divine spirit operating at the beginning of creation (Gen 1.2). On the other hand, Saul and David received the divine spirit as a result of being anointed for royal office. The filling of Bezalel, a Judahite, with the spirit of God could be seen as a transformation of this royal motif. The destiny of the tribe of Judah is realized not in a royal dynasty, but in the construction of the wilderness sanctuary. Thus, Bezalel's spirit endowment can be seen as both an unparalleled accreditation and a subordination of the royal tribe to the priestly agenda. The Davidic tribe serves the priesthood, not vice versa.

The relationship of the artisans to the priestly responsibilities also involves an element of accreditation and subordination. The labour they undertake is identified as 'all the work of the service of the sanctuary' (כָּל־מְלֶאכֶת עֲבֹדַת הַקֹּדֶשׁ; Exod 36.2). Whilst מְלָאכָה can refer to any physical work, עֲבֹדָה is frequently used in the Pentateuch of the physical service of the Levites.[26] The unrepeatable act of constructing the sanctuary creates a unique opportunity for Israelite men from the secular tribes to participate in an act of service analogous to the regular duties of the Levites. This is, however, a physical labour that is understood to be of lesser importance than the cultic activities of the priests.

This hegemonic agenda is seen even more clearly in the fact that the craftsmen and artisans have skills that the priesthood claim to lack. They are 'makers' as the regular appearance of the verb עש״ה underscores. In my literary critical analysis, I suggested it was the same redactional layer that provided the Israelite artisans with their tasks that incorporated the story of the golden calf. The abilities that the craftsmen and artisans possess to build a beautiful and worthy residence for the deity contrast with the disastrous act of manufacturing undertaken by Aaron.

> **2** Aaron said to them, 'Tear off the gold rings that are on the ears of your wives, your sons, and your daughters, and bring them to me'. **3** So all the people tore off the gold rings from their ears, and brought them to Aaron. **4** He took the gold from them, fashioned it with an engraving tool, and he made (וַיַּעֲשֵׂהוּ) an image of a calf; and they said, 'These are your gods, O Israel, who brought you up out of the land of Egypt!'   (Exod 32.2–4).

The implication is clear: the priests are not to be trusted with the business of crafting. Things go badly wrong when they get calluses on their hands. On the

---

[26] For discussion of עֲבֹדָה, see Jacob Milgrom, *Studies in Levitical Terminology: I The Encroacher and the Levite. The Term 'Aboda*, UCPNES 14 (Berkeley: University of California Press, 1970), 60–87.

172   THE MAKING OF THE TABERNACLE

one hand, this is a fascinating relinquishment of an area of competence by the priestly scribes. The capabilities of others are recognized, and the limitations of the priesthood acknowledged. There is an acceptance of the diffusion of power and knowledge. On the other hand, such a recognition assumes a hierarchy of competencies and rewards. The ability to craft is indispensable for the making of the tabernacle, but it does not bestow a right to enter the tabernacle once it is completed or enjoy the benefits that accrue to the priests. Thus, the priestly redactors give with one hand and take with the other.

Men and Women

Generosity and Gender

The non-priestly Israelites are not only involved in the manufacture of the tabernacle, but they have a crucial role in donating the necessary raw materials. The donors and the manufacturers are portrayed in similar ways: he who fabricates the tabernacle is described as someone who is 'wise of heart' (חֲכַם־לֵב; 36.1), whilst the one who donates goods is said to be 'devoting his heart' (נְדִיב לִבּוֹ; 35.5; cf. 35.21, 29). The opening of the construction account will oscillate between these two groups, suggesting their combined efforts in a common purpose. Moses calls for generous donors to bring materials (יְבִיאֶהָ; 35.5)[27] and skilled workers to come (יָבֹאוּ; 35.10). The people return with their gifts (35.21) and the artisans assemble to begin the work (36.2).

In the Hebrew versions, there is no ambiguity about the gender of those who are involved in the construction of the tabernacle.[28] Although the artisans are identified as 'everyone wise of heart amongst you' (וְכָל־חֲכַם־לֵב בָּכֶם; 35.10; cf. 36.8), they are subsequently described as 'every man wise of heart' (וְכֹל אִישׁ חֲכַם־לֵב; 36.1, 2; cf. v. 4).[29] The situation with the donors is more complicated. In some places donors include Israelites of either gender and they are described as 'all who devoted his heart' or 'every man or woman that devoted their heart' (כָּל־אִישׁ וְאִשָּׁה אֲשֶׁר נָדַב לִבָּם; 35.29), but in a few places, however, it is just men who are exhorted to give (25.2; 35.21).

The tension between these two perspectives is especially noticeable in Exod 35.20–29. The account opens with men bringing their gifts for the sanctuary

---

[27] 𝔪𝔰𝔰D reads יביא (cf. 𝕲B). See also 35.21, 22. In each case, the text critical arguments are finely balanced.

[28] The Old Greek renderings fail to identify the gender of the artisans. There are various renderings for כָּל־אִישׁ אֲשֶׁר in the tabernacle account none of which involves a precise equivalent of אִישׁ: πάντων οἷς ἂν (25.2), ἕκαστος ὧν (35.21), πάντες ὅσοι (35.22), παρ' ᾧ (35.23), πᾶς ... ᾧ (36.1), πάντας ... ᾧ (36.2). In some cases, Hexaplaric manuscripts add ἀνήρ to address the omission (35.23; 36.1).

[29] Solomon's taskforce for the Jerusalem temple was also made up of men (1 Kgs 5.27; 2 Chron 2.2).

(35.21), but it closes with a summary statement that indicates that both men and women donated (35.29). The tension is resolved in the text by subordinating the female donors to the men: 'the men came with the women' (וַיָּבֹאוּ הָאֲנָשִׁים עַל־הַנָּשִׁים; v. 22).[30] Given the similarities between v. 21 and v. 29, it is possible that we have a repetitive resumption, and the account of the donation originally consisted of vv. 20–21, and it was expanded to create a version where the donations of men and women were differentiated. The artificiality of the inclusion of women could be taken as evidence of such a reworking, for what does it mean in v. 22 to say וַיָּבֹאוּ הָאֲנָשִׁים עַל־הַנָּשִׁים? Propp rightly observes that its meaning 'is slightly obscure'.[31] The Old Greek rendered עַל with παρά, 'the men brought from the women', which understands the men to have brought the jewellery from their wives.[32] Ibn Ezra and Nachmanides, on the other hand, understood the expression to mean that the women returned to Moses earlier than the men. This was because they simply offered their jewellery which was on their person. Most likely עַל should be understood to mean 'with',[33] and the awkward phrasing is an attempt to clarify the reference to only men in the previous verse.[34]

The offering of gold consists of various pieces of jewellery—nose rings (חָח), earrings (נֶזֶם), rings (טַבַּעַת), and pendants (כּוּמָז).[35] It is presented as a joint contribution of the men and women, although it is the men that offer it (35.22).[36] The event appears to have been designed as an echo of the golden calf incident where the male Israelites bring the gold earrings of their wives and children, from which Aaron makes the golden calf. There are though some noticeable differences in Exod 35. First, the women are willing participants with the men in the offering of the gold. Second, the people offer a more extensive range of ornaments.

After the common offering of the gold, the men and the women present distinct donations. In the Hebrew texts, the men offer coloured yarns, linen, goat's hair, rams' skins and leather, as well as silver and bronze, and acacia wood (vv. 23–24). The women bring coloured yarns, linen, and goat's hair (vv. 25–26). If we are not to regard the coloured yarns, linen and goat's hair as a problematic duplication, the men's offerings include all the items that the women bring. The gendered ordering of society is expressed through men bringing what the women bring and more besides. In the Old Greek, however, the overlap is significantly reduced as the result of a different reading for v. 23.

---

[30] 𝔖𝔐[D] reads וביאו, 'they brought' (cf. 𝔊[B]).   [31] Propp, *Exodus 19–40*, 661.
[32] Wevers, *Greek Text of Exodus*, 583.   [33] *HALOT*, 827.
[34] Cf. Cassuto who writes, 'to avoid the misapprehension that the expression *every one* [literally, 'every man'] in the preceding verse refers to men only' (Cassuto, *Exodus*, 457).
[35] The precise identification of the different pieces of jewellery is uncertain. חָח is probably to be understood as a nose ring (see 2 Kgs 19.28 // Isa 37.29). For נֶזֶם as an earring see Gen 35.4; Exod 32.2; Prov 25.12, but see Gen 24.47; Ezek 16.12; Prov 11.22. כּוּמָז is only found here and Num 31.50 with neither location providing insight into the word's precise meaning.
[36] 𝔖𝔐[D], however, reads וכל אשר אשר rather than 𝔐[L]'s וְכָל־אִישׁ אֲשֶׁר. In this case and in v. 21 it is difficult to decide between the different readings of the Samaritan and Masoretic traditions.

174 THE MAKING OF THE TABERNACLE

וְכָל־אִישׁ אֲשֶׁר־נִמְצָא אִתּוֹ תְּכֵלֶת וְאַרְגָּמָן וְתוֹלַעַת שָׁנִי וְשֵׁשׁ וְעִזִּים וְעֹרֹת אֵילִם מְאָדָּמִים וְעֹרֹת תְּחָשִׁים הֵבִיאוּ	καὶ παρ' ᾧ εὑρέθη βύσσος καὶ δέρματα ὑακίνθινα καὶ δέρματα κριῶν ἠρυθροδανωμένα, ἤνεγκαν.
and every man who possessed blue, purple or crimson yarn, or linen, or goats' hair, or tanned rams' skins, or leather skins brought it (𝔐 35.23).	and everyone who possessed linen or blue skins or red-dyed ram skins brought them (𝔊 35.23).

Thus, the Old Greek lacks the coloured yarns and the goat's hair. Which reading is to be preferred? The issues are finely balanced. The Old Greek reading can claim to be the *lectio brevior*, but it could also be viewed as the *lectio facilior* with an attempt to correct an obvious duplication. The case for the latter is somewhat diminished, however, by the presence of 'linen', βύσσος, in the Old Greek, which would surely have been removed had there been a systematic attempt to remove duplication.

If the shorter reading of the Old Greek is to be preferred, we have the Israelite men and women bringing distinct donations for the sanctuary. Since the fabrics are associated with Oholiab, the second and subordinate master craftsman, and appear to be less prestigious than the metalwork associated with Bezalel, the women's donation likewise appears to be less impressive than the men's. In addition, it is striking that the women's offerings are said to have been spun at home, both the coloured yarns and linen, and the goat's hair. The proper domain of the women is implicitly the home. The public work of constructing the sanctuary, however, is associated with the two master craftsmen and the male Israelite artisans. This includes the work of design and embroidery that works the cherubim illustrations into the fabrics the women have woven. Thus, the women's offering of woven fabrics is already manufactured, but still needs further work by male artisans before it is suitable for use in the tabernacle!

Throughout the description of the donations, there is an emphasis on the people's generosity and inclusivity. Both aspects of the offering are expressed through the word כֹּל, 'all', which appears fourteen times within the space of eight verses (35.20–26, 29). The generosity of the people proves so overwhelming that the artisans have to implore Moses to stop the flow of materials: 'the people are bringing more than enough for the service of the work' (36.5). The rhetorical purpose of this scene on readers needs little exposition. The exodus generation provide a paradigm of generous provision for the cult. The limits of their generosity are determined not by their willingness to give, but by the limitations of the tabernacle itself. The people's inclusivity is seen in the fact that both men and women donate to the sanctuary. As Shectman has observed, alongside this emphasis on inclusivity, there is a hierarchical reality.[37] Women's expertise is exercised in the

---

[37] Shectman rightly criticizes Knohl for emphasizing the inclusivity of this section without also noting the differentiated valuation of the contributions of the men and the women (Knohl, *Sanctuary of Silence*, 193; Sarah Shectman, *Women in the Pentateuch: A Feminist and Source-Critical Analysis*, HBM 23 [Sheffield: Sheffield Phoenix Press, 2009], 154–5).

CRAFTSMEN AND COMMUNITY   175

home, and they contribute the less prestigious items. Though the women labour by spinning, the results are regarded as 'raw material' for which male expertise is needed to produce something suitable for the tabernacle. In Shectman's words, 'while the women's work is noted and seen as a positive aspect of the involvement of the entire community in the project, the skills of the men are nonetheless held to be of special, and higher, divinely guided status'.[38] Such observations are important, for they provide a further example of how the tabernacle account can express both inclusivity and hierarchy.

The inequitable contributions of men and women are also apparent in the poll tax (Exod 30.11–16), for it is only males over twenty that are numbered in the census and for whom an atoning payment must be made. The women make no contribution. The instructions about the census are not presented as a command-ment that is to be fulfilled, but as an instance of case law, opening with 'when you take a census' (כִּי תִשָּׂא אֶת־רֹאשׁ; v. 11). Despite the absence of a timeframe, it is clearly assumed that the census will be taken while the sanctuary is being con-structed (v. 16). Indeed, the accounting summary in 𝔐 38.24–31/𝔊 39.1–10 includes the silver from the census in the materials used for the tabernacle. The silver was cast as bases for the framework that supported the tent and the pillars of the veil as well as being used for the hooks, capitals, and bands of the pillars.

The introduction of the census into the tabernacle account results in an obvi-ous anachronism for the counting of the fighting aged men will not take place until after the tabernacle is completed in the first month of the second year (Num 1). Rashi and Ibn Ezra take recourse to the obvious harmonization that there were in fact two counts in different years, though Nahmanides already raises the obvious question about how two censuses, months apart, could result in identical totals.[39] In other respects too the poll sits uncomfortably in the tabernacle account. It dis-turbs the obvious connection between the instructions for two pieces of furniture, the incense altar and the bronze laver, and it also sits in some tension with those texts that insist the Israelites bring silver voluntarily for the sanctuary (e.g. Exod 25.3; 35.5, 24).

What contribution does the premature mention of the census make to the tab-ernacle account? On a literary level, the insertion of the census law immediately after the incense altar was probably inspired by the altar's role in atonement (כפ״ר). Aaron's application of the blood on the incense altar's horns effects atonement for it (30.10) and the payment of silver secures atonement for the people (30.15, 16).[40] The census also provides an alternative structure for Exod 30: the gold incense altar is followed by the silver of the poll tax and the bronze laver. Ideologically, the poll tax asserts an ideal of the cultic equality of non-levitical Israelites: 'The rich shall not pay more and the poor shall not pay less'

---

[38] Shectman, *Women*, 155.   [39] Carasik, *Exodus*, 267–70.   [40] Cassuto, *Exodus*, 393.

176 THE MAKING OF THE TABERNACLE

(הֶעָשִׁיר לֹא־יַרְבֶּה וְהַדַּל לֹא יַמְעִיט; 30.15). Each Israelite male contributes equally to the construction of the tabernacle.[41] There is, however, a candid admission of the economic inequality in Israelite society, an inequality that the poll tax entrenches, favouring the rich over the poor and even more so the Levites and the priests over the ordinary Israelites. Theologically, the poll tax is envisaged as a reminder to YHWH that the Israelites' lives have been ransomed (v. 16). Just as the opals on Aaron's epaulettes functioned as a memorial (זִכָּרוֹן) for the Israelites (לִבְנֵי יִשְׂרָאֵל) before YHWH (לִפְנֵי יְהוָה), so too does the silver. As already observed, the word זִכָּרוֹן was associated with votive offerings, and the accounts of the opals and the silver for the poll tax are an indication of the importance the scribes attached to bringing valuable items to the sanctuary. They communicate that the deity is worthy of such generous devotion, but they also serve to bring wealth under priestly control.

The Bronze Altar and the Bronze Laver

Much of the silver utilized in the tabernacle was visible to the Israelites in the hooks, bands, and capitals of the courtyard. Could the silver also be a memorial for the Israelites, and not just for YHWH? The language of Exod 30.16—'It will be for the Israelites a memorial before YHWH' (וְהָיָה לִבְנֵי יִשְׂרָאֵל לְזִכָּרוֹן לִפְנֵי יְהוָה)—is certainly patient of such a reading. The idea of the tabernacle furniture functioning as a reminder to Israel of their need for atonement emerges clearly with the account of the bronze altar's construction (𝔐 38.1–7 ~ 𝕲 38.22–24). The Old Greek probably preserves the earliest version, which was replaced in the Masoretic and Samaritan texts with a compliance report that corresponded more closely with the instructions in Exod 27.1–8. In the Old Greek the bronze plating of the altar stemmed from the bronze incense pans of Korah's company.

> οὗτος ἐποίησεν τὸ θυσιαστήριον τὸ χαλκοῦν ἐκ τῶν πυρείων τῶν χαλκῶν, ἃ ἦσαν τοῖς ἀνδράσιν τοῖς καταστασιάσασι μετὰ τῆς Κορε συναγωγῆς.

> This one made the bronze altar from the bronze firepans, which belonged to the men who rebelled with the assembly of Kore (𝕲 38.22).

The verse is an allusion to Num 16 and Korah's rebellion against Aaronic authority. Aaron and his 250 challengers face each other in a trial by ordeal. They place coals and incense in their firepans and assemble at the entrance of the tent of meeting (vv. 16–18). Everyone but Aaron is consumed by divine fire (v. 35). Aaron's son Eleazer is commanded to collect the bronze firepans and make them into a covering for the altar.

---

[41] Houtman, *Exodus*, III: 566.

4 וַיִּקַּח אֶלְעָזָר הַכֹּהֵן אֵת מַחְתּוֹת הַנְּחֹשֶׁת אֲשֶׁר הִקְרִיבוּ הַשְּׂרֻפִים וַיְרַקְּעוּם צִפּוּי לַמִּזְבֵּחַ: 5 זִכָּרוֹן לִבְנֵי
יִשְׂרָאֵל לְמַעַן אֲשֶׁר לֹא־יִקְרַב אִישׁ זָר אֲשֶׁר לֹא מִזֶּרַע אַהֲרֹן הוּא לְהַקְטִיר קְטֹרֶת לִפְנֵי יְהוָה וְלֹא־יִהְיֶה
כְקֹרַח

4 Eleazer the priest took the bronze firepans that had been presented by those who were burnt and they hammered them into a plating for the altar. 5 A memorial for the Israelites in order that no outsider that is not of Aaron's seed will approach to burn incense before YHWH so as not to become like Korah and his assembly   (Num 17.4–5).

The use of the censers to plate the outer altar in Num 16 is rather incongruous, since this altar was used for the offering of burnt sacrifices, not incense. We may wonder whether the story of the 250 rebels developed before the composition of Exod 30 and its novel idea of an incense altar. But even if the composer was aware of the idea of two distinct altars, the incense altar ensconced within the outer sanctum could not have served the purpose of warning the Israelites against encroaching on the prerogatives of the Aaronides. The incense altar was never seen by the ordinary Israelites. Strikingly, we have an altered sense of how a memorial (זִכָּרוֹן) is to function. Its purpose is not to remind God, rather it communicates to the Israelites. It does not bring Israel to God's attention so that he may do them good, instead it reminds Israel of the dangers of rebellion and the need to preserve the hierarchical order. Despite its brevity, the allusion to Korah probably suggests that the composer of 𝕲 38.22 intended the bronze altar to function in this way.

The rebellions associated with Korah are not given a precise chronological location in the book of Numbers, though they are placed in the wilderness wanderings not only after Sinai, but even after Kadesh Barnea. Consequently, the reference to Korah's rebellion in the Old Greek of Exodus 38 creates an obvious anachronism. The Hebrew versions resolve the problem, but in doing so create another one. The bronze altar is plated twice: once when it is manufactured at Sinai and again after the 250 pretenders to the priesthood are annihilated! The Hebrew versions do, however, remove any reference to Korah's rebellion in the construction of the tabernacle and its messaging in the tabernacle furniture of the immutability of Aaronic supremacy.

The construction of the bronze laver also contributes to understanding the role of the people in the sanctuary, but the description of it in 𝔐 38.8/𝕲 38.26 is enigmatic.

וַיַּעַשׂ אֵת הַכִּיּוֹר נְחֹשֶׁת וְאֵת כַּנּוֹ נְחֹשֶׁת בְּמַרְאֹת הַצֹּבְאֹת אֲשֶׁר צָבְאוּ פֶּתַח אֹהֶל מוֹעֵד:	οὗτος ἐποίησεν τὸν λουτῆρα χαλκοῦν καὶ τὴν βάσιν αὐτοῦ χαλκῆν ἐκ τῶν κατόπτρων τῶν νηστευσασῶν, αἳ ἐνήστευσαν παρὰ τὰς θύρας τῆς σκηνῆς τοῦ μαρτυρίου ἐν ᾗ ἡμέρᾳ ἔπηξεν αὐτήν
He made the laver of bronze with its stand of bronze, from the mirrors of the women who served at the entrance to the tent of meeting (𝔐 38.8).	This one made the bronze laver and its bronze base from the mirrors of the women who fasted by the door of the tent of meeting in the day he pitched it (𝕲 38.26).

178 THE MAKING OF THE TABERNACLE

The interpretative difficulties circle around the expression בְּמַרְאֹת הַצֹּבְאֹת אֲשֶׁר צָבְאוּ, which NRSV translates as 'from the mirrors of the women who served'. First, what is the meaning of מַרְאָה? The Old Greek translator understands מַרְאָה as mirror, a noun derived from the verb רא״ה, 'to see'. This understanding seems to be shared by the Temple Scroll, where the laver and its stand is required to made from '[pure] burnished bronze, in which one can see a f[ace]' (נְחֹשֶׁת מָרוֹק ט[הור] לראות פ[נים]; 11Q19 3.16). In the ancient world, mirrors were commonly made out of polished bronze, and Quick has pointed out the considerable evidence for the use of mirrors as votive offerings.[42] Nevertheless, all the other appearances of מַרְאָה in the Hebrew Bible refer to visions,[43] and we might translate וַיַּעַשׂ...בְּמַרְאָה with the alternative rendering, 'he made according to the visions'.[44] Second, why do we find צב״א, since this root is normally used in relation to military service? It occurs frequently in relation to the mustering of the tribes in Num 1–4. Whilst it is used of the Levites' service for the sanctuary in Num 4.23 and 8.24, this appears to be an extended sense that seeks to draw a parallel between the Levites' cultic service and the secular tribes' military service.[45] Although הַצֹּבְאֹת is usually understood to refer to women serving, צְבָאֹת is used in the priestly literature of the Israelites coming out of Egypt as military companies and mustered around the tabernacle.[46] A repointed Hebrew text could read 'according to the visions of the companies mustered at the entrance of the tent of meeting'.[47] The difficulty with this understanding of the verse is that it contradicts Exod 30.17–21 which describes Moses being instructed about the laver.

Such a reading is now excluded by 1 Sam 2.22 where those serving at the entrance to the tent of meeting appear again.

וְעֵלִי זָקֵן מְאֹד וְשָׁמַע אֵת כָּל־אֲשֶׁר יַעֲשׂוּן בָּנָיו לְכָל־יִשְׂרָאֵל וְאֵת אֲשֶׁר־יִשְׁכְּבוּן אֶת־הַנָּשִׁים הַצֹּבְאוֹת פֶּתַח אֹהֶל מוֹעֵד:

Now Eli was old. He heard all that his sons were doing to all Israel and that they were lying with the women who served at the entrance of the tent of meeting   (1 Sam 2.22).

---

[42] Laura Quick, 'Through a Glass, Darkly: Reflections on the Translation and Interpretation of Exodus 38:8', *CBQ* 81 (2019): 595–612.

[43] Gen 46.2; Num 12.6; 1 Sam 3.15; Ezek 1.1; 8.3; 40.2; 43.3; Dan 10.7, 8, 16; cf. Ezek 11.24; 9.23; Dan 10.1 (מַרְאָה).

[44] Sarah Shectman, *Women*, 156. Dohmen's translation 'im Blick' is problematic (Dohmen, *Exodus 19–40*, 384, 390). This derives בְּמַרְאֹת from מַרְאָה which is a masculine noun and whose plural construct form would be מַרְאֵי. Note, however, that Jerome translated with 'women who kept watch', *mulierum quae excubabant*.

[45] This is most apparent in Num 4.23 where לִצְבֹא צָבָא is followed by לַעֲבֹד עֲבֹדָה. The two expressions are grammatically identical—an infinitive construct with ל followed by a cognate noun—and equate the two activities. For the Levites, 'to wage war as an army' (לִצְבֹא צָבָא) means 'to do cultic service' (לַעֲבֹד עֲבֹדָה).

[46] Exod 6.26; 7.4; 12.17, 41, 51; Num 1.3, 52; 2.3, 9, 10, 15, 18, 25, 32; 10.14, 22, 28; 33.1.

[47] Dohmen interprets הַצֹּבְאֹת as a *nomen actionis* and translates 38.8 as 'dann machte er das kupferne Becken und sein kupfernes Gestell im Blick auf das Kultdienen, das am Eingang des Begegnungzseltes vollzogen wird' (Dohmen, *Exodus 19–40*, 384, cf. 390, 396–7).

CRAFTSMEN AND COMMUNITY   179

The women appear as cultic servants that are being used by Hophni and Phinehas, the sons of Eli, for their sexual gratification. The clause that describes this sexual malpractice is not present, however, in the Old Greek texts or 4Q51 (4QSamª). Since 1 Sam 2.22 is the only reference to the tent of meeting in 1 Samuel, there are good grounds for thinking that the clause is a later addition that entered the text under the influence of Exod 38, perhaps as a way of explaining the divine anger against Hophni and Phinehas.[48] Whilst 1 Sam 2.22 cannot be decisive for the original intentions of the composer of Exod 38.8, it is important evidence that at a very early stage those serving at the entrance of the tent of meeting were under-stood as women. If those assembled are women, what was the precise nature of their service at the entrance of the tent of meeting? The extended use of צב״א for the Levites' cultic responsibilities in Num 4.23 and 8.24 suggests some form of cultic activity and the early versions explored various possibilities. In the Old Greek the women are said to have fasted which is either a decision to render צב״א in a specific manner,[49] or reflects a *Vorlage* that had forms of the verb צו״ם, 'to fast', which stemmed from a *bet-mem* confusion.[50] In the Targums, the women were coming to pray.[51] We might well surmise that the possibilities of cultic service are limited by the imaginations of translators who experienced different theological orthodoxies, but that does little to help us reconstruct what the original author of Exod 38.8 might have intended about the women's religiosity. Even the compari-son to the Levites does not suggest an expansive role, for the Levites of the priestly literature are reduced to the role of guarding and porterage.

There appear to be some similarities between the cases of the bronze altar and the bronze laver. Both see the non-priestly Israelites making some contribution to the furniture that is found in the courtyard and is visible to all. They also share an anachronistic element. The plating of the bronze altar refers to an event that will take place sometime later in the priestly narrative, whilst the bronze laver assumes women serving in the gate of a tent that has not yet been erected.[52] Should we also

---

[48] For discussion, see Domenico Lo Sardo, 'The Tent of Meeting and the Women's Mirrors in 1 Sam 2:22 and Exod 38:8: A Text-Critical Inquiry of the MT, LXX, Qumran Texts and the Vetus Latina', *Text* 29 (2020): 168–92; Urs Winter, *Frau und Göttin: Exegetische und ikonographische Studien zum weiblichen Gottesbild im Alten Israel und in dessen Umwelt*, OBO 53 (Freiburg im Üchtland: Universitätsverlag, 1983), 47.

[49] Wevers understands צב״א to refer to cultic service and thinks that the reference to fasting is ingenious since fasting is 'one kind of cultic practice which anyone can perform' (Wevers, *Greek Text of Exodus*, 631).

[50] Cf. David W. Gooding, 'Two Possible Examples of Midrashic Interpretation in the Septuagint Exodus', in *Wort, Lied, und Gottesspruch: Festschrift für Joseph Ziegler. Band I: Beiträge zur Septuaginta*, ed. Josef Schreiner (Würzburg: Echter, 1972), 42–8; Albertz, *Exodus 19–40*, 358 n. 11.

[51] The text of Monacensis is damaged. Dold reads 'of those who were fasting with prayers and lam-entations at the gate of the tabernacle of testimony', *quaJe ieiunabant [orationes et plo]ratus facien[tes ad portas ta]bernaculi tes[timonii]* (𝔔ᴹ 26/1/18–21; Dold, 'Versucht', 50).

[52] The final clause in the Old Greek seeks to address this problem: 'in the day he pitched it' (ἐν ᾗ ἡμέρᾳ ἔπηξεν αὐτήν). The priestly tabernacle is never described as 'pitched', but נט״ה, 'to pitch', is used of Moses' oracular tent of meeting in Exod 33.7. It is likely that the clause was added to suggest that the service was carried out before this other tent (Gooding, 'Midrashic Interpretation', 42–3).

180 THE MAKING OF THE TABERNACLE

read across from the bronze altar and its association with the rebellion of Korah, a sinful motive behind the women's mirrors? Plenty of interpreters have sought to do so, and the original association visible in the Old Greek of Exod 38 may have animated the insertion of the women into the story of Eli's sons, though there is no textual basis for relating the mirrors to vanity or sexual misconduct. Instead, the mirrors suggest only the generosity of the women. The description of them serving may indicate a similarity to the Levites, but like everyone else other than the priests, their access is restricted to the entrance of the tent.

The Tribal Leaders and the Levites

Two further groups are mentioned once within the compliance accounts: the tribal leaders and the Levites. The leaders are mentioned in 35.27–28 contributing to the donations for the tabernacle. They bring the precious stones for Aaron's vestments, as well as the anointing oil and fragrant incense. There can be little doubt that these verses are a late addition to the chapter. First, they interrupt the focus on the gifts of the men and women in the surrounding verses. Second, these verses lack the word כֹּל, 'all', that we have already seen is the characteristic feature of the surrounding verses. Third, the leaders are rarely mentioned in Exodus and Leviticus, but become a major focus only in the book of Numbers. Fourth, the leaders' gifts include the oil and incense which are only found in the very late material of Exod 30–31.

The introduction of the leaders (הַנְּשִׂאָם) in v. 27 is an elegant play on the word for 'women' (הַנָּשִׁים) in v. 26. What is noticeable about the gifts attributed to the leaders are that they speak to the leaders' wealth and their central position within Israelite society. That the twelve leaders of the tribes could between them gift the precious stones that adorn Aaron's garment makes important assumptions about the relationship between leadership and wealth. Within the narrative world of Exodus this is by no means obvious since all the Israelites are freed slaves, and we might not have expected differentials in wealth. The Persian period world of the scribal redactors is presumably different, and the contributor of these verses assumes that the leaders number amongst the wealthiest in the tribes. In the description of Aaron's vestments in Exod 28, the onyx and the gems bear the names of the sons of Israel and ensure that the people are borne before the Lord. Yet, the attribution of these gems to the leaders displaces the tribes to some extent and forges a close connection between the leaders and the high priest. The same is also true of the association of the leaders with the oil and incense, both of which signal Aaron's unique role in the cult.

The virtual absence of the Levites from the tabernacle account is consistent with the distribution of references to them in the Pentateuch. It is only in the book of Numbers that the Levites are comprehensively introduced, and their appearances in Genesis, Exodus, and Leviticus are consistently secondary and indebted to the presentation of the Levites in Numbers.[53] Intriguingly, whilst there is a single mention of the Levites in each of the versions, they are not identical. There is a reference to the Levites in the Masoretic, Samaritan, and Old Greek versions of 𝔐 38.21/𝔊 37.19 which is absent from the Old Latin, whilst the Old Latin also mentions the fabrication of vestments for the Levites in 𝔏^M 27/2/7–8 which has no equivalent in the other versions.

The solitary reference to the Levites in the Masoretic, Samaritan, and Old Greek versions occurs in a summary statement in 𝔐 38.21/𝔊 37.19. For my purpose, it will suffice to consider the Masoretic Text,[54]

אֵלֶּה פְקוּדֵי הַמִּשְׁכָּן מִשְׁכַּן הָעֵדֻת אֲשֶׁר פֻּקַּד עַל־פִּי מֹשֶׁה עֲבֹדַת הַלְוִיִּם בְּיַד אִיתָמָר בֶּן־אַהֲרֹן הַכֹּהֵן

These are the records of the tabernacle, the tabernacle of the covenant, which were recorded by the mouth of Moses, the labour of the Levites directed by Ithamar son of Aaron the priest   (𝔐 38.21).

The phraseology of the verse is reminiscent of the book of Numbers: the verb פק״ד, occurs frequently in Number for the enrolment of the tribes in the census (Num 1–4, 26); the expression מִשְׁכַּן הָעֵדֻת, 'the tabernacle of the covenant', is only otherwise found in Numbers;[55] and, עַל־פִּי, 'by the mouth', is a favoured expression,[56] though never עַל־פִּי מֹשֶׁה. Finally, the reference to the direction of the Levites by Ithamar is a citation of Num 4.28, 33 which mention the porterage of the Gershonite and Merarite septs. Thus, there are good grounds for regarding the entirety of 𝔐 38.21/𝔊 37.19 as late and influenced by the book of Numbers.[57] In earlier versions of the compliance account, the description of the fabrication of the vestments and the tent were framed by references to the activities of Bezalel and Oholiab (35.30–35; 𝔊 37.20–21). The second of these has been reworked as a

---

[53] Outside of the tabernacle account, the Levites are mentioned in Exod 6.25; 32.25–28; Lev 25.32–33. Exod 6.25 concludes the genealogy of Moses and Aaron (6.14–25), a text that has long been recognized as intrusive and has affinities with some of the latest parts of the Pentateuch including texts in Numbers (Achenbach, *Die Vollendung der Tora*, 110–24). Similarly, the reference to the Levites in the story of the golden calf (Exod 32.25–28) has also been judged an addition. Their appearance is unanticipated and the slaughter of just 3 000 when the entire people is guilty is unexplained (for a recent examination, see Samuel, *Von Priestern*, 270–94). The reference to the Levites in the Jubilee legislation (Lev 25.32–33) presupposes the legislation about the levitical cities and is usually judged an interpolation (Nihan, *Priestly Torah*, 522 n. 503).

[54] The only significant text-critical issue is that Old Greek has τῆς σκηνῆς τοῦ μαρτυρίου for Masoretic Text's הַמִּשְׁכָּן מִשְׁכַּן הָעֵדֻת. The repetition in the Masoretic Text is suspicious and could be the result of dittography.

[55] Num 1.50, 53; 10.11.

[56] Twenty-three of the sixty-nine occurrences are found in Numbers.

[57] The Old Latin of Monacensis has the shorter reading *haec constitutio tabernaculi testimonii secundum quae praecepta sunt moysi*, 'this is the arrangement of the tabernacle of witness according to the commandments of Moses' (𝔏^M 24/2/3–6). It is possible that the Old Latin preserves the earlier reading in which case the influence of Numbers occurred in two stages through a process of *Fortschreibung*.

182   THE MAKING OF THE TABERNACLE

colophon which expresses succinctly the hierarchical order of the Israelite community. The work of the tabernacle is carried out according to the instructions Moses received. The priests have authority over the work of the Levites, and then finally the secular tribes are mentioned with Judah taking priority over Dan and, by implication, the other tribes.

The appearance of the Levites in the Old Latin of Monacensis describes how vestments were made for the Levites:

> *Et quae rem[anserant hia]cinti purp[urae et cocci] fecerunt s[tolas sacerdo]tales ad mi[nistrandum] leuuitis in [sancto].*
>
> and what was l[eft of the hya]cinth, purp[le, and scarlet] was made into s[acred rob]es for the mi[nistry] of the Levites in [the holy place]   ($\mathfrak{L}^M$ 27/2/4–8).

This would be the only place in the Pentateuch where the Levites are said to have vestments, though 2 Chron 5.12 describes the Levitical singers dressed in fine linen.[58] The medieval Jewish interpreters point to a more compelling solution for they identify the *serad*-garments (בִּגְדֵי־שְׂרָד) with the covers placed on the furniture prior to transportation (Num 4.6–13), for which the word בֶּגֶד was also used. Since the Levites transport the furniture, the association of the covers with the Levites is appropriate, and their subordination to the priests affirmed. Evidently, the precise significance of the *serad*-garments was lost to some of the scribal redactors of Exodus which led to the identification of them with the vestments of the priests in the Masoretic, Samaritan, and Old Greek versions.

Conclusion

In Exod 25–31, Moses and Aaron take centre stage in the instructions about the tabernacle. In this sacred partnership, Moses serves as mediator receiving the divine instructions for the sanctuary in which Aaron his brother will serve as priest. If people, artisans, and master craftsmen are mentioned in passing, they soon fade from view. In contrast, Exod 35–40 is populated with an extensive roster of characters. The people, both men and women, give generously for the tabernacle which is manufactured by the master craftsmen, Bezalel and Oholiab, assisted by Israelite artisans. The leaders and the Levites have walk on parts. The compliance account suggests that each of these has a place in helping to realize Moses' vision. But when the completed items are handed over to Moses, this cast of characters disappears off stage.

---

[58] Josephus complains in *Ant.* 20.216–18 that the Levitical singers requested from King Agrippa that they be allowed to wear linen vestments like the priest. For Josephus, Levitical vestments were a first-century CE innovation.

Despite only a fleeting appearance, the different members of the ensemble are presented in ways that emphasize hierarchical differences. Leaders take precedence over commoners, men over women, priests over Levites, Judah over Dan. As a result, a complex and hierarchical social landscape is described and canonized by projecting it onto the Mosaic past. It will not suffice, however, to represent the power dynamics as simply vertical. There are also significant claims about the equality of individual Israelites, tribes, and genders. All participate in this holy enterprise, and there is a recognition of the dissemination of skills. Even if the outworking of these serve to confirm the hierarchical order, we should not dismiss them as simply rhetorical. Conversely, we cannot ignore the hierarchical implications of the tabernacle account's presentation as though it were simply a celebration of democratization and equality.

In what we might label, paradoxically, a hierarchy of equals, Aaron—and, by implication, his male descendants—enjoy the highest status. These chapters in Exodus provide a justification for the prominence of the Second Temple and its priesthood. Labouring for the temple and donating to it are presented as reasonable expectations and imitations of behaviours exhibited by the Israelites of Moses' day. Not only do the aristocratic classes, represented in the text by the tribal leaders, provide for the adornment of the priesthood, but even the royal tribe of Judah is corralled into these efforts. The subservience of the royal tribe could not be clearer. Bezalel the Judahite is exalted as the master craftsmen, but his endowment with the divine spirit is simply so that he can craft for the priesthood.

PART III
THE RECAPITULATION OF PRIESTLY ORDINATION

7

Ordination, Consecration, and Inauguration

Priests are made by ritual: the ritual of ordination. At the heart of the instructions about the tabernacle, Moses is informed how the priests are to be ordained. Or, to use the Hebrew Bible's own idiom, the filling (of their hands), מִלֻּאִים. Despite the precision with which the ritual is described, scholars are uncertain whether Exod 29 describes a unique event that instituted the Aaronide priesthood in perpetuity, or whether future generations were to be ordained by a similar ritual.[1] The account of Eleazar's succession to the position of high priest only mentions the transfer of the priestly vestments (Num 20.22–29; cf. Exod 29.29–30). Whether or not the ritual was imagined as a one-off, the case I will make in the third part of this book is that we encounter repeated recapitulations of the ordination ritual throughout the books of Exodus to Numbers. The ordination ritual becomes an important site for working out Israel's theocratic structure in ways that express its complex dynamics of power.

I will begin this chapter by examining the initial instructions given to Moses about the ordination ritual in Exod 29. The fulfilment of these instructions does not occur at the end of the book of Exodus where we might have expected them. Instead, they are delayed until Lev 8. Despite the repeated claim that everything was done 'just as YHWH commanded Moses', כַּאֲשֶׁר צִוָּה יְהוָה אֶת־מֹשֶׁה, there are subtle ways in which Lev 8 has shifted the focus so as to become a ritual that consecrates priesthood and sanctuary over seven days. This week-long ritual is followed by the novel and unexpected ritual of the eighth day in Lev 9, a further reprise of the ordination ritual which highlights a number of anomalies that arise if we compare the ordination ritual of Exod 29 with the sacrificial legislation delivered to Moses in Lev 1–7. I will argue that these difficulties have arisen as a result of the development of the priestly legislation. They touch upon several significant issues all of which centre around the difference between the high priest and the rest of the priesthood.

---

[1] Milgrom, *Leviticus 1–16*, 520; Propp, *Exodus 19–40*, 532.

The Making of the Tabernacle and the Construction of Priestly Hegemony. Nathan MacDonald, Oxford University Press.
© Nathan MacDonald 2023. DOI: 10.1093/oso/9780198813859.003.0008

188   THE MAKING OF THE TABERNACLE

Instructions for the Ordination Ritual (Exod 29)

The ordination ritual is the very first ritual we encounter in the priestly literature. Originally it had the purpose of ordaining Aaron and his sons in order that they may serve in the newly constructed tabernacle as priests. The temple like a palace requires servants, and the priests are those who are appointed for the task. In the terms of van Gennep, the ordination ritual is a classic rite of passage.[2] It transforms Aaron and his sons from ordinary Israelites into sanctified priests. The extensive ritual described in Exod 29 provides directions for this rite of passage that is only briefly alluded to in 28.41, 'You shall put the vestments on your brother Aaron and on his sons with him ... and they will serve me as priests.' The repetition of this final clause in 29.44b is a textbook example of repetitive resumption. It should probably be understood as evidence that originally the brief statement in 28.41aα was followed by the concluding statement about the purpose of the tabernacle as the divine dwelling place (29.45–46). The extensive instructions that were subsequently inserted in Exod 29.1–37 explain how the ordination and sanctification of the priests is to be achieved.

The Components of the Ordination Ritual

The ordination ritual is one of the most complex rituals within the Hebrew Bible and involves several distinguishable ritual actions. After the washing and dressing of the priests (vv. 4–9), we encounter a veritable compendium of sacrifices: a sin-purification offering (חַטָּאת; vv. 10–14), a burnt offering (עֹלָה; vv. 15–18), and an ordination offering (מִלֻּאִים; vv. 19–34*), which combines features of the grain offering (מִנְחָה) with the amity offering (שְׁלָמִים). In this way the ordination ritual is not only the first ritual, but also an aggregate of the sacrificial legislation that will follow in the book of Leviticus. The description of the ordination ritual shows an awareness of this sacrificial legislation, but also that, from the perspective of the narrative, the legislation has not yet been given. The sacrificial rituals are described in detail and only at the conclusion of the description is the sacrifice identified: 'it is a sin-purification offering' (חַטָּאת הוּא; v. 14) and 'it is a burnt offering to YHWH' (עֹלָה הוּא לַיהוָה; v. 18).

The ritual is to take place at the 'entrance of the tent of meeting' (פֶּתַח אֹהֶל מוֹעֵד). There are a couple of appearances of the expression 'tent of meeting' earlier in the book of Exodus (27.21; 28.43), but these are almost certainly later additions. Thus, it is with the ritual of ordination that we are introduced to the tabernacle as a place of divine-human encounter. The importance of this new title for the

---

[2] Arnold van Gennep, *The Rites of Passage*, trans. Monika B. Vizedom and Gabrielle L. Caffee (Chicago, IL: University of Chicago Press, 1960).

ORDINATION, CONSECRATION, AND INAUGURATION   189

tabernacle is emphasized by its appearance throughout the chapter (29.4, 10, 30, 32, 42) and by the programmatic statement at the conclusion of the ritual: 'I will meet the Israelites there, and it shall be sanctified by my glory. I will sanctify the tent of meeting and the altar. Aaron and his sons I will sanctify to serve me as priests' (29.43–44).[3] This statement complements and reorientates the earlier pro-grammatic statement about the purposes of the tabernacle as the divine dwelling place (29.45–46). It foregrounds the idea of the tabernacle as a place of encounter and the crucial role of the priests.

In the initial instructions to Moses, the 'entrance of the tent of meeting' need not have been a large space, since it only needs to accommodate Moses, Aaron and his sons, and their sacrifices. The language alludes to the liminality of the location. Prior to their ordination, the priests may penetrate no further into the tabernacle complex. In the fulfilment account in Lev 8.3, however, the ritual takes place before the entire people. As a result, the 'entrance of the tent of meeting' must have been understood as a large open space, presumably the entire area of the courtyard in front of the sanctuary building.[4] Although the 'entrance of the tent of meeting' was not limited to the immediate vicinity of the courtyard screen, the notion of liminality remains. The entrance is the furthest point of the taber-nacle complex that the people may penetrate, even if it effectively incorporates the entire courtyard. It is the point of encounter between YHWH and Israel.

The instructions open with an account of what is needed to perform the ritual: a young bull, two rams, and a basket of bread products (vv. 1–3). These items are brought (וְהִקְרַבְתָּ) to the entrance followed by Aaron and his sons (תַּקְרִיב; v. 4). The use of the verb קר״ב for both the Aaronides and the sacrificial objects expresses the close relationship that will be forged between the two. The Aaronides are then washed and dressed in their vestments (vv. 4b–9). As we have already seen, the washing and outfitting of Aaron and his sons presents a clear distinction between them. Aaron is washed and dressed first. His outfit is the extensive and glorious vestment described in Exod 28 and he alone is anointed. His sons are washed and dressed together but separately from their father, and they wear simpler vest-ments and are not anointed.

Despite the distinction made between Aaron as the sole anointed priest and his sons, the sacrifices that follow involve both the father and his sons. For each sacri-fice, they collectively place their hands on the animal that is to be sacrificed. The meaning of the ritual action of laying hands on the sacrificial action has been extensively discussed within scholarship. Does the hand laying indicate

---

[3] Exod 29.43 presents a number of text-critical variants. In v. 43a 𝔊𝔊𝔊ᴰ has ונדרשתי, 'I will be con-sulted', and 𝔊ᴮ τάξομαι, 'I will order', for 𝔐¹'s ונעדתי, 'I will be met'. It is difficult to be certain what the original reading was and how the other readings arose. In v. 43b, MT has וְנִקְדַּשׁ, but 𝔊ᴮ has καὶ ἁγιασθήσομαι as though reading ונקדשתי. Most likely the Greek translator or his *Vorlage* had assimi-lated towards the first-person verbs found in the clauses that precede and follow (cf. Lev 22.32).

[4] Milgrom, *Leviticus 1–16*, 147.

190   THE MAKING OF THE TABERNACLE

ownership of the animal and the right to offer it as a sacrifice? Is the action an identification with the sacrifice, such that the sacrifice is a form of self-offering? Does the hand laying transfer sin or impurity onto the animal that is being sacrificed?[5] Whilst ritual theorists have long observed that ritual actions can have multiple meanings—and none—attributed to them by participants and observers, the issue is not identical for ritual texts like Exod 29 where a writer has already imparted some interpretive framework.[6] Nevertheless, in the case of the hand-laying ritual, no particular significance is attributed to this ritual action in the description of the ordination ritual. Perhaps the most we can say is that it creates a connection between the prospective priests and the sacrificial animals.

The first sacrifice is the sin-purification offering (vv. 10–14). A young bull is slaughtered and some of its blood smeared on the horns that protrude from the altar. The remaining blood is disposed of by pouring it into the ground at the altar's base. Some of the internal organs and fat are immolated on the altar, but the rest of the animal is burnt outside the camp. No explanation for the ritual action is given other than the final declaration that 'it is a sin-purification offering' (חַטָּאת הוּא; v. 14). The application of the bull's blood to the horns of the altar suggests that the sin-purification offering had a particular effect on the altar. This is certainly the view of the author of Lev 8. The smearing of the blood on the horns is explained with the words 'so he purified the altar' (וַיְחַטֵּא אֶת־הַמִּזְבֵּחַ; v. 15), and after the blood is poured out at the base of the altar, the writer explains 'so he consecrated it to make atonement for it' (וַיְקַדְּשֵׁהוּ לְכַפֵּר עָלָיו; v. 15). If the understanding of Lev 8 can be transferred to Exod 29, the instrumental effect of the sin-purification offering is to purify the altar. This sacrifice is necessarily prior to the others because they all require the altar to be purified in order that they can be offered. No altar, no sacrifice.

The sacrifice that follows is the whole burnt offering (vv. 15–18). A ram is slaughtered, and its blood dashed against the sides of the altar. The ram is jointed, and its rear parts washed. The animal parts are piled up on the altar and the entire animal is immolated. In this case, not only is the offering identified—'it is a burnt offering to YHWH' (עֹלָה הוּא לַיהוָה; v. 18)—but also the instrumental purpose is

---

[5] For the hand-laying ritual, see, *inter alia*, René Péter, 'L'imposition des mains dans l'Ancien Testament', *VT* 27 (1977): 48–55; David P. Wright, 'The Gesture of Hand Placement in the Hebrew Bible and in Hittite Literature', *JAOS* 106 (1986): 433–46; Milgrom, *Leviticus 1–16*, 150–3; David Calabro, 'A Reexamination of the Ancient Israelite Gesture of Hand Placement', in *Sacrifice, Cult, and Atonement in Early Judaism and Christianity: Constituents and Critique*, eds. Henrietta L. Wiley and Christian A. Eberhart, RBS 85 (Atlanta, GA: Society of Biblical Literature, 2017), 99–124. Attempts to distinguish between a single hand-laying ritual and a two hand-laying ritual founder on text-critical grounds. It is not possible to identify with confidence where one or two hands were intended because of the similarities of the singular and plural forms and the regular confusion of them in the textual traditions.

[6] The discussion by Gilders of meaning and ritual in the Hebrew Bible is both brief and incisive (William K. Gilders, *Blood Ritual in the Hebrew Bible: Meaning and Power* [Baltimore, MD: Johns Hopkins University Press, 2004], 1–12).

described. The sacrifice is a pleasing aroma to YHWH (רֵיחַ נִיחֹחַ; v. 18). The stark anthropomorphic imagery has often been glossed over or explained away, but it is consistent with what we have seen in the description of the priestly vestments. The physical senses of Israel's God are engaged in the cult's performance and YHWH can smell the aroma of the burnt offering.[7] He experiences it as pleasurable and presumably the burnt offering ensures his presence at the ordination ritual that is unfolding.

The final sacrifice is the climax of the ritual and the most complex of the offerings (vv. 19–34). On a couple of occasions this final sacrifice is identified as the ordination sacrifice (מִלֻּאִים) and is clearly understood to effect the ordination of Aaron and his sons. The sin-purification offering and the burnt offering are preparatory ritual actions that create the necessary conditions for the ordination offering. In this climactic ritual, Moses takes the remaining ram and slaughters it. He daubs some of the blood he has shed on the bodily extremities on the right-hand sides of Aaron and his sons: the ear lobe, the thumb, and the big toe. The remaining blood is then dashed against the side of the altar; in this way a relationship between the priests and the altar is indexed.[8] Moses then takes some of the internal organs and fat, the right thigh, and one of each of the bread products and places them into the hands of Aaron and his sons. They are then presented towards YHWH presumably by lifting them upwards and away from the body.[9] Moses receives the items back and places them on top of the smouldering remains of the burnt offering. Moses then takes a further part of the ram's carcass, the brisket, and presents it to YHWH by elevating it. Unlike the items elevated by Aaron and his sons, the brisket is not to be burnt, but kept by Moses as his prebend for having made the offering. The remaining meat from the ram was boiled and eaten together with the bread by Aaron and his sons. The text is insistent that they alone must eat it, and that this food atones for them, ordains and consecrates them (v. 33). Any food that remains on the following day is to be burnt. If we compare the ordination offering to the sacrificial legislation in Lev 1–5, the ordination offering appears to be a complex amalgam of the grain offering (Lev 2) and the amity offering (Lev 3). It is only in the combination of the two offerings that there is sufficient ritual efficacy to transform the Aaronides from ordinary Israelites into priests.

My account of the ordination sacrifice has omitted several details that have often been recognized as secondary additions. The first of these is the instructions to Moses to take some of the blood of the ram of the ordination offering together with the anointing oil and sprinkle it on Aaron and his sons and their vestments

---

[7] For the divine body, see now Francesca Stavrakopoulou, *God: An Anatomy* (London: Picador, 2021).

[8] For the use of blood to index relationships, see Gilders, *Blood Ritual*.

[9] For the meaning of נוּף and תְּנוּפָה see Chapter 8.

(v. 21). The practical difficulties are obvious for what blood had not been daubed on Aaron and his sons had been dashed against the altar sides. As Nihan observes, in all the other rituals of the priestly literature the application of the blood on the altar marks the end of its manipulation.[10] Nor is it clear how the blood would be collected from an altar upon which there is an offering burning. The difficulties with the instructions to Moses are apparent in the account of their enactment in Lev 8. The sprinkling with blood and oil is attached rather loosely after the actions at the altar have been completed and before the remaining flesh is consumed (Lev 8.30). In Exod 29, the versions show further variation. The Samaritan Pentateuch has the instructions after v. 28 ensuring that the instructions and their fulfilment align. The Old Greek, on the other hand, has the instructions for the oil and blood in the middle of v. 20 so that the blood is dashed against the side of the altar *after* some of it has been mixed with oil and used to anoint the priests. The readings in the Samaritan Pentateuch and Old Greek are best judged as secondary. The Samaritan Pentateuch reading is a clear attempt to harmonize Exod 29 and Lev 8, which as we have seen elsewhere is a characteristic feature of the Samaritan version. The Old Greek reading is arguably the most appropriately placed, and it is easy to discern why a scribe might have relocated it to v. 20. Consequently, there is no reason to think that the Old Greek preserves the original reading. It would also be difficult to explain how the other textual variations had arisen. For similar reasons, we should probably judge the placement in Exod 29.21 as a *lectio facilior* in comparison to Lev 8.30.[11] It places the aspersion of Aaron and his sons at the nearest mention of blood in the ritual and transposes the mention of blood and oil so as to integrate the instruction more neatly into the ritual.[12] In conclusion, the instructions about the sprinkling with blood and anointing oil are secondary and were probably initially incorporated at Lev 8.30.

The second and third additions are to be found in Exod 29.27–28 and 27.29–30. Both additions interrupt the instructions about the treatment of the meat of the ordination offering and are absent from Lev 8. The second addition has clearly been inspired by Lev 7.28–34. These verses contain instructions about the amity offering and assign the brisket to the priesthood in general and the right thigh to the officiating priest. In the ordination offering, however, the right thigh was immolated on the altar and the brisket was given to Moses as his prebend. In order to prevent any reader deducing from the distinctive features of the ordination offering that the priestly perquisites for the well-being offering could be reduced to just the brisket, Exod 29.27–28 insists that both brisket and thigh are priestly perquisites.[13] The third addition introduces the topic of Aaron's vestments

---

[10] Nihan, *Priestly Torah*, 128–9.   [11] *Contra* Noth, *Leviticus*, 72.

[12] 'The reason for mentioning the blood first in Exod 29 is contextual: it has just been dashed on the altar' (Milgrom, *Leviticus 1–16*, 532).

[13] For detailed discussion see Nihan, *Priestly Torah*, 130–2; Nathan MacDonald, 'Scribalism and Ritual Innovation', *HeBAI* 7 (2018): 420–1.

ORDINATION, CONSECRATION, AND INAUGURATION   193

and their inheritance by the son who succeeds as the anointed priest. The issue of succession interrupts the details about the ritual activities and was probably inspired by the previous verses and likewise defends the Aaronides' claim to the holy service and its rewards.

The instructions for the ordination ritual conclude in Exod 29.35–37.

> **35** You shall do to Aaron and his sons thus, just as I commanded you. Seven days you shall ordain them. **36** you shall offer a bull of sin-purification offering every day for atonement.[14] You will purify the altar when you make atonement for it, and you shall anoint it to consecrate it. **37** Seven days you shall make atonement for the altar and consecrate it. The altar will be most holy; everything touching the altar becomes holy.

As Nihan has rightly observed the insistence that atonement be made for the altar on each of the seven days (vv. 36–37) has no parallel in Lev 8 and has been appended after the natural conclusion of the ritual instruction in v. 35. The requirement that the altar be anointed is a novelty and has no counterpart in the earlier part of the chapter. It is, however, consistent with the later perspective of 30.26–29 and 40.10, which envisaged all the furniture being anointed.

The identification of vv. 36–37 as a later addition also raises questions about whether the ordination ritual was originally envisaged to have lasted seven days. With the removal of v. 30 and vv. 36–37 as later additions, the only reference to the ordination ritual lasting seven days is the concluding comment in v. 35b. There are reasons to wonder whether it too is a later addition along with vv. 36–37. First, 'you shall do to Aaron and his sons thus, just as I commanded you' (v. 35a), functions as a suitable conclusion to the entire ritual instructions. The first clause with its use of 'you shall make' (וְעָשִׂיתָ) creates a connection with the instructions for the manufacture of the tabernacle and the vestments in the previous chapters, and the second clause insists that everything was to be followed precisely as commanded. The reference to seven days attaches rather loosely at the end. Second, the ritual of ordination as prescribed in 29.1–35 describes a series of sacrifices and the consumption of bread and meat that could easily take place within a couple of hours on a single day. It is not clear what it is to happen on the other six days of the ritual. Consequently, the close connection of v. 35b to vv. 36–37 is apparent since they explain what is to happen on the remaining days of the ritual.

---

[14] 𝕲ᴮ has two distinctive readings in v. 36a. First, where 𝔐ᴸ has the indefinite פַּר חַטָּאת, 𝕲ᴮ reads τὸ μοσχάριον τῆς ἁμαρτίας. Second, 𝔐ᴸ has לַיּוֹם עַל־הַכִּפֻּרִים, 'each day for purification', which is rendered τῇ ἡμέρᾳ τοῦ καθαρισμοῦ, 'in the day of purification'. The Greek translator has understood הכפרים to be modifying the immediately preceding noun, rather than the verb (Wevers, *Greek Text of Exodus*, 482).

194 THE MAKING OF THE TABERNACLE

The Ordination Ritual and Priestly Authority

In its earliest form the ordination ritual prescribes how Aaron and his sons are to be installed as priests in the tabernacle. Prior to the performance of the rite, Aaron and his sons are no different from any other Israelite. The complex of rites purifies the altar, invoke the presence of YHWH, and provide atonement and consecration of the Aaronides. At the end of the cultic procedure, they can serve as priests. The ritual difference between the priests and the other Israelites is marked in physical space. The entrance to the tent of meeting marks a liminal point beyond which no ordinary Israelite can go. In this place, the Aaronides are ordained and afterwards they can undertake their duties in the sanctuary. Ritual and space mark out the supremacy of the priesthood in cultic matters.

The indispensability of the priesthood is communicated through the distinguishing features of the ordination ritual. It is the first ritual of the priestly literature, the *sine qua non* of the entire cultic system of P. Chronological primacy communicates the priesthood's pre-eminence. But it is not just that the ordination of the priesthood is the originary ritual, it is also the summation of the priestly literature's ritual world. The entire ordination rite requires all the sacrifices to be offered apart from the reparation offering. Whatever the different types of sacrifice may achieve individually, they are all needed to secure the ordination of the priests. Summation communicates supremacy.

It is with the installation of a priesthood that the tabernacle becomes a 'tent of meeting', and the association of this title with the ordination ritual highlights the priests' essential role in facilitating the divine and human encounter. In various ways, the ritual suggests a close relationship between the priests and sacrifice, the quintessence of worship in ancient Israel. Like the sacrifices, they are brought (קר״ב) to the sanctuary. The blood of the ordination offering is daubed on ear, thumb and toe, and the flesh eaten at the entrance of the tent of meeting. The relationship between the priests and the sacrifices applies to both Aaron and his sons. No Aaronide priests, no sacrifice. Nevertheless, the ordination rite sets Aaron apart from his sons. He alone wears the holy vestments that are described in detail in Exod 28, and he alone receives the anointing oil upon his forehead. In addition, he wears upon his head an item of clothing called 'a holy crown' which suggests some analogy between the anointed priest and royalty.

The Consecration of the Tabernacle (Lev 8)

The instructions given to Moses in Exod 25–31 are completed in Exod 35–40 with the notable exception of the ordination of Aaron and his sons. In Exod 40, Moses is instructed to set up the tabernacle (𝔐 40.1–8), to anoint it and its

ORDINATION, CONSECRATION, AND INAUGURATION   195

furniture, and to dress and anoint Aaron and his sons (𝔐 40.9–15). The second half of the chapter describes the erecting of the tabernacle and its furniture, regularly interspersed with the solemn declaration 'as YHWH commanded Moses' (כַּאֲשֶׁר צִוָּה יְהוָה אֶת־מֹשֶׁה; 𝔐 40.19, 21, 23, 25, 27, 29, 32). Yet, it conspicuously fails to describe the ordination of the priests and the consecration of the tabernacle through oil. Nevertheless, the chapter concludes with the claim that 'Moses finished the work' (וַיְכַל מֹשֶׁה אֶת־הַמְּלָאכָה; 𝔐 40.33) and YHWH's pleasure is indicated with a theophany: the divine glory fills the tabernacle (𝔐 40.34). Indeed, the attentive reader might detect something of a sleight of hand. The instructions that Aaron and his sons are consecrated for priestly service opens with the instructions to wash Aaron and his sons with water (𝔐 40.12). In the erection of the tabernacle, the final item to be mentioned is the laver. In the Masoretic Text, the laver is described as the place where Aaron and his sons washed their hands and their feet. It might easily be supposed that this has in view the ordination ritual, but it is rather a reference to the laver's permanent function: 'when they go into the tent of meeting and when they approach the altar, they will wash just as YHWH commanded Moses' (בְּבֹאָם אֶל־אֹהֶל מוֹעֵד וּבְקָרְבָתָם אֶל־הַמִּזְבֵּחַ יִרְחָצוּ כַּאֲשֶׁר צִוָּה יְהוָה אֶת־מֹשֶׁה; 𝔐 40.32). The ordination ritual is not completed until Lev 8 and is separated from the rest of the compliance account by the sacrificial legislation in Lev 1–7. As was the case with the fabrication of the vestments (𝔐 39.1–31) and the erection of the tabernacle (𝔐 40.17–33), the performance of the ordination ritual is punctuated with the claim that everything was done 'just as YHWH commanded Moses' (כַּאֲשֶׁר צִוָּה יְהוָה אֶת־מֹשֶׁה; Lev 8.4, 9, 13, 17, 21, 29).[15]

The ordination of the priests was commanded in Exod 29 and the events of Lev 8 are presented as a scrupulous implementation. At first glance it appears that there has been little deviation from Exod 29, a view reflected in some commentaries: 'practically every verse in ch. 8 is a quotation of adaptation of commands first given in Exod. 29'.[16] The rhetorical claim that everything was done exactly as God commanded Moses conceals the fact that some important changes have been made to the ordination ritual. Some of these reflect the fact that in late priestly texts all the priests are envisaged as having being anointed and not just the high priest. In addition, the ordination ritual has been transformed so that it can also serve as a ritual for consecrating the tabernacle. To see how these transformations have occurred we will need briefly to assess the relationship between Lev 8 and Exod 29 before examining how the ritual has been altered.

---

[15] Watts, *Ritual and Rhetoric*, 103–18; Frank H. Gorman, *The Ideology of Ritual: Space, Time and Status in the Priestly Theology*, JSOTSup 91 (Sheffield: JSOT Press, 1990), 103–5.

[16] Gordon J. Wenham, *The Book of Leviticus*, NICOT (London: Hodder & Stoughton, 1979), 131.

The Relationship of Lev 8 and Exod 29

The close relationship between Lev 8 and Exod 29 is immediately apparent and has led to every conceivable solution being proposed to explain the relationship: that Exod 29 borrowed from Lev 8, that Lev 8 borrowed from Exod 29, or that both Exod 29 and Lev 9 were composed by the same author. The first proposal that Lev 8 was written first and that Exod 29 was composed subsequently in order to create a series of instructions that corresponded to the ritual has no contemporary advocates.[17] It is difficult to argue for the priority of Lev 8 given the repeated references to the ritual as an act of obedience to YHWH's prior commandment to Moses. As a result, recent discussions have focused on whether both chapters were the work of a single author or whether Exod 29 was composed prior to Lev 8.

In his analysis of the two chapters, Nihan argued that by comparing the two chapters a common core of material could be identified. An examination of the places where the two chapters diverged showed that in every instance the divergent material was secondary. There was, thus, no reason to suppose that that the common core in both books had not been composed by a single author. Any differences were the result of secondary reworking.[18] Nihan's work has recently been contested by Röhrig who objects that Nihan's method of identifying a common core essentially presupposes what he seeks to prove. She makes a compelling case that the alterations to Lev 8 show a consistent theological interest and they are rather more deeply worked into the chapter than is the case for Exod 29. As a result, we should regard Lev 8 as a reworking of Exod 29 with some of the reworkings making their way back into Exod 29 secondarily.[19] To see how this takes place we need to examine Lev 8 in more detail and, as we do so, we will see how the ordination ritual has been adjusted to reflect the idea that all priests are anointed and transformed into a ritual that consecrates sanctuary and priests.

A Ritual of Consecration

In their earliest version, the instructions for the ordination rite reach their climax with the consumption of the ordination offering. The succession of sacrifices leads to this ritual action, by which the ordination and consecration of the priests is achieved (Exod 29.33). In the enactment of the ritual in Lev 8, however, the

---

[17] Karl Elliger, *Leviticus*, HAT1,4 (Tübingen: Mohr Siebeck, 1966), 106–20; Karl-Heinz Walkenhorst, *Der Sinai im liturgischen Verständnis der deuteromistischen und priesterlichen Tradition*, BBB 33 (Bonn: Hanstein, 1969).

[18] Nihan, *Priestly Torah*, 124–48.

[19] Meike J. Röhrig, *Innerbiblische Auslegung und priesterliche Fortschreibungen in Lev 8–10*, FAT II/128 (Tübingen: Mohr Siebeck, 2021), 42–91.

significance of the consumption is omitted. The efficacious ritual act is the aspersion of the priests and their vestments with the anointing oil and the blood of the ordination offering (8.30). Nor is it just the priests in their vestments who are covered with the oil and blood, so too are the tabernacle, the altar, and the laver (8.10–11). The writer's understanding of the aspersion with oil and blood is expressed on each occasion that it occurs: it consecrates (קד"ש). Thus, whilst Exod 29 was concerned with the consecration and ordination of the priesthood, Lev 8 has subtly shifted the ritual to the consecration of the priesthood and tabernacle.

As far as the priests are concerned, the results of this revision of the ordination ritual are twofold. First, it makes Aaron's sons recipients along with the high priest of the anointing oil. The earlier conception was that Aaron alone was anointed with oil, and only in later passages is the entire priesthood anointed collectively.[20] The ordination ritual is consequently being brought into line with these later texts.[21] Second, and relatedly, it imbues the vestments of Aaron's sons with a holy status that originally only Aaron's vestments had.[22]

The anointing of Aaron's sons introduces the obvious problem that the difference between Aaron and his sons has been eliminated. The composer of Lev 8 found a way to address this problem and assert Aaron's superiority. First, in comparison to Exod 29, the description of Aaron's vestments in Lev 8 has been augmented with a reference to the Urim and Thummim being placed in the breastpiece (v. 8). In this way, the oracular role of the high priest is emphasized.[23] Second, Aaron's anointing after being dressed in his vestments has been augmented by an account of the tabernacle and everything in it being anointed (Lev 8.10aβ–11). This lengthy alteration in the compliance account is clearly related to Exod 40.9–15 where God commands Moses to furnish the tabernacle and anoint it on the first day of the first month.[24] As we have already seen, Exod 40.9–15 is a very late part of the tabernacle account, demonstrated not least by its references

---

[20] Cf., e.g., Exod 28.41ba; 30.30; 40.15.

[21] See Baruch A. Levine, 'The Descriptive Tabernacle Texts of the Pentateuch', *JAOS* 85 (1965): 307–18.

[22] E.g., Exod 28.2 where Aaron's vestments are described as 'holy vestments' (בִּגְדֵי־קֹדֶשׁ).

[23] There are a couple of additional alterations to the description of Aaron's vestments in Lev 8. First, the omission of the sash in Exod 29 is made good in Lev 8, 'and he fastened the sash around him' (וַיַּחְגֹּר אֹתוֹ בָּאַבְנֵט; v. 7). Second, the ornament that is set upon the turban is described as both a 'gold rosette' and a 'holy crown' (צִיץ הַזָּהָב נֵזֶר הַקֹּדֶשׁ; v. 9). This description blends Exod 28.36 which speaks of a 'rosette of pure gold' and Exod 29.6 which speaks of a 'holy crown'. The correction of an omission and the harmonizing of two variant descriptions provide further compelling evidence that Lev 8 has been composed after Exod 29.

[24] Nihan, *Priestly Torah*, 127. This analysis is preferable to Levine's suggestion that we have 'two distinct, but combined rituals: (1) the sanctification of the tabernacle and its vessels, and of the High Priest, Aaron, by the rite of unction with the "oil of anointing" (vv. 7–12), and (2) the ordination of Aaron and his sons in their priestly office by means of sacrificial rites and a seven-day period of incubation (vv. 13–36)' (Levine, 'The Descriptive Tabernacle Texts', 311). A similar view that there were once two distinct rituals is also argued by Fleming (Fleming, 'The Biblical Tradition of Anointing Priests').

198 THE MAKING OF THE TABERNACLE

to the incense altar and the laver.[25] The anointing restores Aaron's primacy. His consecration (קד"ש) takes place prior to his sons, and he enjoys a double anointing, once together with the tabernacle, and once with his sons.[26] The anointing of both Aaron and the tabernacle forges a close relationship between the sanctuary and the high priest. This relationship is unique to him and is not shared by his sons.

The anointing of the tabernacle and its furniture is also an important component of the transformation of a rite of ordination into one that consecrates the tabernacle. A ritual which was focused on the consecration and ordination of the priesthood has become one in which the consecration of the tabernacle also plays an important role. This shift is also visible in the treatment of the sin-purification offering which is attributed additional significance that goes beyond the instructions in Exod 29. Moses' actions are said to purify (וַיְחַטֵּא) the altar, but also to consecrate (וַיְקַדְּשֵׁהוּ) and atone (לְכַפֵּר) for it (v. 15). As I suggested in my examination of Exod 29, the sin-purification offering was probably understood to achieve purification as is implicit in the sacrifice's name. It is striking though that consecration and atonement are precisely what is claimed in Exod 29 to have occurred to the priests as a result of their consuming the ordination offering. A further alteration is worth noting, for in describing the disposal of the blood at the base of the altar, Lev 8.15 uses יצ"ק rather than שפ"ך as Exod 29.12 does. The verb יצ"ק is typically used of anointing and has already appeared a few verses earlier for the pouring of oil of Aaron's head (Lev 8.12).[27] As a result, both Aaron and the altar are anointed on two occasions with some combination of oil and blood.[28] The use of יצ"ק provides further evidence both for the focus on the consecration of the tabernacle, but also for the reformulated pre-eminence of Aaron.

The shift of the ordination ritual to one focused on the consecration of both priests and sanctuary probably explains the transformation of the ritual into a seven-day affair. A significant parallel is found in Ezek 43.18–27, where a seven-day ritual is prescribed for the consecration of the altar in Ezekiel's vision of the new temple.[29] The connection of the seven-day duration with the consecration of

---

[25] Wellhausen, *Composition*, 142–3.

[26] The two anointings in 8.11–12 and 8.30 appear to be designed to create a frame around the ritual actions (Gerald A. Klingbeil, *A Comparative Study of the Ritual of Ordination as Found in Leviticus 8 and Emar 369* [Lewiston, NY: Mellen, 1998], 301). The placement of 8.30 is literary, rather than chronological, and this goes some way to explaining why Lev 8.30 was inserted where it was and why it was subsequently inserted into a place that was more chronologically suitable in Exod 29.

[27] Nihan lists the use of יצ"ק in v. 15 as one of his 'minor linguistic variants' (Nihan, *Priestly Torah*, 140), but שפ"ך is the typical word used for the disposal of blood at the base of the altar (Exod 29.12; Lev 4.7, 18, 25, 30, 34). It is also used for the pouring out of blood in Deuteronomy and the Holiness Code (Gilders, *Blood Ritual*, 28). יצ"ק is used for the pouring out of oil, and the only uses of it with blood are in 8.15 and in 9.9, which is itself dependent upon 8.15 (Nobuyoshi Kiuchi, *Leviticus*, Apollos Old Testament Commentary [Nottingham: Inter-Varsity Press, 2007], 155).

[28] Röhrig, *Innerbiblische Auslegung*, 43.

[29] For discussion, see Röhrig, *Innerbiblische Auslegung*, 64–8.

the tabernacle is not immediately apparent from Lev 8.33–35, but it is in the addition of Exod 29.35b–37, which has been inspired by Lev 8.

> You shall offer a bull as a sin-purification offering for atonement. You shall purify the altar by atoning for it, and you shall anoint it to consecrate it. Seven days you shall atone for the altar and consecrate it. The altar will be most holy, whoever touches the altar will become holy.

The ordination ritual of Exod 29 now concludes not with the consumption of the ordination sacrifice by Aaron and his sons, but with an emphasis on the consecration of the altar. As a result, the idea of ordination has been subordinated even within Exod 29.

The transformation of the ordination ritual into a tabernacle consecration ritual sheds light on the vexed question of whether the priestly Torah intended to prescribe a rite by which future generations of Aaronides could be inducted into priestly service, or was a unique occasion that needed no repetition. For Milgrom, the ordination ritual is valid for all time.[30] Presumably, though, some ceremony would have been needed to ordain those who succeeded Eleazer and Ithamar. The explanation for this tension lies in the fact that we do have an ordination ritual described in Exod 29 and Lev 8 and it presumably reflected, to a degree which we cannot now precisely ascertain, the way that priests were ordained for service in the early Second Temple period. Yet, the transformation of the ritual into a consecration ceremony for the tabernacle has given the occasion the character of a unique rite with enduring validity.

The Inauguration of the Regular Sacrificial Cult (Lev 9)

An Unexpected Ritual on the Eighth Day

Leviticus 9 describes a series of sacrifices for Aaron and the people, and the theophany that occurs as a result. The chapter opens with Moses instructing Aaron, his sons, and the elders of Israel concerning the sacrifices to be offered (vv. 1–7). Aaron first offers the sacrifices for himself: a calf as a sin-purification offering and a ram as a burnt offering. The sacrificial procedure is described in some detail (vv. 8–14). Aaron then offers the people's sacrifices: a male goat for a sin-purification offering, a calf and a lamb as a burnt offering, a grain offering, and an ox and a ram as an amity offering. The sin-purification offering and the burnt offering are summarized briefly with reference to the sacrifice Aaron just offered for himself

---

[30] Milgrom, *Leviticus 1–16*, 520. As Milgrom notes this was not the view of the Temple Scroll which prescribes an annual ritual (11Q19 15:3–16:4).

200 THE MAKING OF THE TABERNACLE

(in the case of the sin-purification offering) and sacrificial regulation (in the case of the burnt offering) (vv. 15–16). Since Aaron did not offer a grain offering or an amity offering for himself, these ritual acts are given in more detail (vv. 17–21). At the conclusion of the sacrifices, the promised theophany occurs (vv. 22–24).

For the reader of the Pentateuch the ritual of the eighth day is entirely unexpected. Every aspect of the tabernacle's construction in Exod 35–40 and the ordination of the priests in Lev 8 was set out in precise detail in YHWH's instructions to Moses on Mount Sinai in Exod 25–29. At no point was any mention made of a ritual on the eighth day to inaugurate the regular cult. Why does a previously unannounced ritual appear at this juncture, especially after a chapter that has so conspicuously emphasized that Moses obeyed YHWH's commandments? The answer to this problem is to be found in the transformation of the ordination ritual into a seven-day consecration ritual. In Exod 29, the ordination of the priests was followed by instructions for the regular burnt offering, the *tāmîd* (vv. 38–42), and an account of YHWH talking up residence in the tabernacle. Prior to the ordination ritual in Exod 29 being reshaped through the addition of the seven-day structure from Lev 8, it would have been possible—perhaps even, natural—to read Exod 29 as the order in which events would transpire on a single day. The priests would be ordained through a series of sacrifices, the first regular burnt offering would be sacrificed, and YHWH would take up residence. In the seven-day consecration ritual, however, the altar is consecrated on each day and the priests are sequestered away in the sanctuary. As a result, a further ritual was needed on the eighth day that would inaugurate the regular sacrificial cult.

We have already observed that the novel ritual in Lev 8 was an amalgam of the ordination ritual from Exod 29 and the altar consecration ritual from Ezek 43. Similar dynamics can also be observed in the inauguration ritual of Lev 9, which integrates the consecration ritual of Lev 8 with the great atonement ritual of Lev 16. The relationship between the consecration ritual of Lev 8 and the inauguration ritual of Lev 9 was observed by Wenham. Both chapters follow a similar sequence, often deploying identical language.[31] The instructions to Moses in both cases begin with the command to 'take' (לק״ח) various items (8.1–3; 9.1–4). After the instructions have been given, the congregation assembles at the entrance of the tent of meeting (8.4; 9.5). The ritual act is introduced with almost identical words from Moses: 'This is the thing that YHWH commanded to be done' (זֶה הַדָּבָר אֲשֶׁר־צִוָּה יְהוָה לַעֲשׂוֹת/תַּעֲשׂוּ; 8.5; 9.6). In the consecration ritual, the sacrifices are offered in the order sin-purification offering, burnt offering, and ordination offering, and a similar order is followed in the eighth-day ritual, but with a separate grain offering and amity offering taking the place of the ordination offering. We have already seen that the ordination offering was effectively a combination of the

---

[31] Wenham, *Leviticus*, 133. See also James D. Findlay, *From Prophet to Priest: The Characterization of Aaron in the Pentateuch*, CBET 76 (Leuven: Peeters, 2017), 179–95.

grain offering and the amity offering. The similarity between the two rituals in Lev 9 and 16 is especially apparent in the sacrifice of the sin-purification offering and the burnt offering for Aaron (Lev 9.8–11, 12–14). The description of the ritual action is almost identical to that of the sin-purification offering and the burnt offering for Aaron and his sons (Lev 8.14–17, 18–21). In addition to these similarities to Lev 8, Feldman has observed that, with separate sacrifices for the priest and the people, the inauguration ritual is very close to the sanctuary purification ritual of Lev 16.[32] 'The first four sacrifices in Lev 9 are almost identical in kind (*ḥaṭṭāʾt* or *ʿōlâ*) and ownership (Aaron or the Israelites) to Lev 16. Each chapter contains a pair of sacrifices for each group: a *ḥaṭṭāʾt* and an *ʿōlâ* for Aaron and a *ḥaṭṭāʾt* and an *ʿōlâ* for the Israelites.'[33] The similarities extend as far as the animals sacrificed with a few exceptions. In the inauguration ritual of Lev 9, Aaron offers a bull-calf as a sin-purification offering and a ram as a burnt offering for himself, and a goat as a sin-purification offering, and a calf and lamb as a burnt offering for the people. In the sanctuary purification ritual of Lev 16, Aaron offers a bull as a sin-purification offering and a ram as a burnt offering for himself, and a goat as a sin-purification offering and a ram as a burnt offering for the people. The analyses of Wenham and Feldman show that the eighth-day ritual in Lev 9 is indebted to both the consecration ritual of Lev 8 and the great atonement ritual of Lev 16. By combining both rituals together a novel ritual for the inauguration of the tabernacle has been created.

As was the case in Lev 8, the purposes of the composer of Lev 9 are not simply to create a novel ritual for an ideal wilderness sanctuary deep in Israel's mythic past. Instead, there are various issues about the competencies of the high priest and the rest of the priesthood that he wishes to address. To understand how he does this, it is necessary to examine the description of the inauguration ritual more closely and how it interacts with the existing rituals from which it borrows. I will compare the inauguration ritual in Lev 9 to the consecration ritual in Lev 8 first, before turning to the relationship of Lev 9 to the great atonement ritual of Lev 16.

The Inauguration Ritual (Lev 9) and the Consecration Ritual (Lev 8)

The most important way in which the consecration ritual and the inauguration ritual differ is in the beneficiaries of the sacrifice. During the consecration ritual, the sin-purification offering and the burnt offering were sacrificed on behalf of the priesthood—Aaron and his sons. On the eighth day, the ordination of the

---

[32] Liane Marquis Feldman, 'Ritual Sequence and Narrative Constraints in Leviticus 9:1–10:3', *JHebS* 17 (2018): 13–16. https://jhsonline.org/index.php/jhs/article/view/29375.

[33] Feldman, 'Ritual Sequence', 15.

202 THE MAKING OF THE TABERNACLE

priests and the inauguration of the tabernacle has been completed, and the regular sacrificial cult begins. As a result, the sacrifices are augmented with offerings for the people. Surprisingly, however, the sacrifices are not for the priesthood and the people, as we might have expected, but for Aaron and the people.

That the first sacrifice was for Aaron alone, and not for the entire priesthood, has often been missed by commentators.[34] But Lev 9 is at pains to identify the sacrifice as Aaron's. According to Lev 9.7, Moses instructs Aaron to approach the altar and 'sacrifice your sin offering and your burnt offering' (וַעֲשֵׂה אֶת־חַטָּאתְךָ וְאֶת־עֹלָתֶךָ). Significantly, the pronominal suffix is singular, not plural. Aaron's sons are not included. Instead, the offerings were for Aaron alone, not for the entire priesthood. Lest the import of the pronominal suffixes be missed, the point has already been made in Moses' instructions to Aaron a few verses earlier: 'take for yourself (קַח־לְךָ) a calf for a sin-purification offering and a ram for a burnt offering' (9.2). It is also reiterated in different words in the description of the sacrificial act: 'Aaron approached the altar and he sacrificed the calf of the sin offering that was for himself (אֲשֶׁר־לוֹ)' (9.8). As Rendtorff observes, 'in this entire chapter Aaron alone is the offerer of the first public sacrifice, while in the ordination of the priests in chapter 8, Aaron and his sons always performed the function of the offerer together by placing their hands on the head of the sacrificial animal'.[35]

Admittedly, the issue has been complicated by a textual variant in v. 7. Where the Masoretic version reads 'make atonement for yourself and the people' (וְכַפֵּר בַּעַדְךָ וּבְעַד הָעָם), the Old Greek reads 'make atonement for yourself and your house' (καὶ ἐξίλασαι περὶ σεαυτοῦ καὶ τοῦ οἴκου σου). There are some strong arguments that can be made in favour of the Old Greek reading. The mention of 'your people' in the Masoretic Text appears perplexing, especially since Aaron will offer sacrifices on behalf of the people which will secure atonement for them (v. 7). In

---

[34] 'Aaron soll für sich (und seine Söhne, vgl. 16,6. 11) ein Sünd- und Brandopfer darbringen' (August Dillmann, *Die Bücher Exodus und Leviticus*, 3rd edn, KeHAT [Leipzig: Hirzel, 1897], 511); 'Als Opfer sind zu bringen: a) für die Priester: 2 ein Sündopfer (Kalb, v. 8–11) und ein Brandopfer (Widder, v. 18–21)' (Alfred Bertholet, *Leviticus*, KHAT 3 [Tübingen: Mohr Siebeck, 1901], 27); 'According to ch. 9 Aaron and his sons first had to present a sin offering and a burnt offering for themselves' (Noth, *Leviticus*, 75); 'one ḥaṭṭā't calf for Aaron and his sons (9:8–11), one 'ōlâ ram for Aaron and his sons (9:12–14)' (Feldman, 'Ritual Sequence', 14); 'Aaron must offer the first sacrifices in order to atone for himself and his house' (Nihan, *Priestly Torah*, 120); 'one to effect *kippûr* for the high priest and his household and the other for the people' (Milgrom, *Leviticus 1–16*, 578); 'Moses had no qualms about the completion of the priests' purification offering of a calf (cf. 9:8–11)' (Roy E. Gane, *Cult and Character: Purification Offerings, Day of Atonement, and Theodicy* [Winona Lake, IN: Eisenbrauns, 2005], 93) Notable exceptions are Elliger (Elliger, *Leviticus*, 129) and Watts, who also prefers 𝔐[1]'s reading of 9.7 (Watts, *Leviticus 1–10*, 488–95).

[35] 'In diesem ganzen Kapitel ist Aaron allein der Darbringer der ersten öffentlichen Opfer, während bei der Einsetzung der Priester in Kap. 8 stets Aaron und seine Söhne gemeinsam die Funktion des Darbringers wahrnehmen durch das Aufstemmen der Hände auf den Kopf des Opfertieres' (Rolf Rendtorff, *Leviticus 1,1–10,20*, BKAT 3/1 [Neukirchen-Vluyn: Neukirchener Verlag, 2004], 293) Nevertheless, Rendtorff frequently elides this distinction by speaking of '[die] Zweiteilung von Opfern Aarons und seine Söhne (V. 8–14) und Opfern des Volkes (V. 15–21)' (Rendtorff, *Leviticus 1,1–10,20*, 296, cf. 291).

addition, two rituals which have a number of similarities with the eighth-day ritual in Lev 9—the seven-day ordination ceremony of Lev 8 and the great atonement ritual of Lev 16—envisage the sacrifices on Aaron's behalf benefiting both him and his family.[36] Yet, there are stronger reasons to prefer the Masoretic Text's reading. The Old Greek's reading is the *lectio facilior*, and it is easy to imagine why a scribe would alter 𝔐ᴸ's reading under the influence of Lev 8 and 16, but difficult to think of how 𝕲ᴮ's reading would have given rise to the 𝔐ᴸ's 'and the people'.[37] In addition, the idea that the anointed priest's sin-purification offering might also atone for the people is not unparalleled. According to Lev 4, when the anointed priest sins, guilt comes on the people (v. 3), and the sacrifice of the sin-purification offering presumably benefits both the anointed priest and the people.[38]

The identification of the first set of offerings with the entire priesthood has also been argued on the ground that Aaron's sons bring the blood to him (9.9, 12, 18).[39] The actions are without parallel elsewhere in the sacrificial legislation, and the vocabulary unusual,[40] and so it is difficult to ascertain the action's precise significance. Gilders rightly observes that 'Aaron's superior status in relation to his sons is enacted in their first service as consecrated priests when Aaron's sons perform the subordinate role of bringing the blood of the bull to Aaron at the altar, whilst Aaron is the one who applies it to the altar'.[41] The comparison with Lev 8 confirms Gilders' observation. In Lev 8 the commonality of Aaron and his sons is expressed through the hand-leaning ritual for the sin-purification offering, the burnt offering and the ordination offering (8.14, 18, 22), whilst in Lev 9 the attribution of distinctive ritual actions to Aaron on the one hand and his sons on the other highlights the differences between Aaron and his sons.

One unfortunate consequence of assuming that Aaron's sin-purification offering was sacrificed for himself and his family is that the ritual of the eighth day in Lev 9 is harmonized with the ordination ritual in Exod 29 and Lev 8. Since Aaron and his sons are being ordained for priestly service, it is fundamental to the ordination ceremony that the offerings are made on behalf of Aaron and his sons. The hand-leaning rite in Exod 29 leaves no doubt that the offerings are for the entire Aaronide family: together Aaron and his sons place their hands on the sacrifices prior to them being slaughtered. The contrast between the understated assumptions of Lev 8 and the rhetorical emphasis in Lev 9 provides further confirmation

---

[36] See 16.6, 11, 17, 24 (𝕲ᴮ).

[37] Similarly, Röhrig, *Innerbiblische Auslegung*, 94 n. 4; Nobuyoshi Kiuchi, *The Purification Offering in the Priestly Literature: Its Meaning and Function*, JSOTSup 56 (Sheffield: JSOT Press, 1987), 43; Rendtorff, *Leviticus 1,1–10,20*, 295–6; Himbaza, *Leviticus*, 86*.

[38] Nihan, *Priestly Torah*, 120 n. 46.

[39] E.g. Rashbam (Michael Carasik, *Leviticus ויקרא*, The Commentators' Bible: The JPS Miqra'ot Gedolot [Philadelphia, PA: Jewish Publication Society of America, 2009], 68–9); Rendtorff, *Leviticus 1,1–10,20*, 297.

[40] Rendtorff, *Leviticus 1,1–10,20*, 296–7.   [41] Gilders, *Blood Ritual*, 224 n. 111.

204 THE MAKING OF THE TABERNACLE

for my argument. With its 'take for yourself', 'your sin-purification offering and your burnt offering' and 'that was for himself', the composer of Lev 9 intends to leave us in no doubt that the sacrifices commanded in 9.2 are for Aaron alone, and not for his sons.

One effect of the division of the beneficiaries into Aaron and the people is that it brings the inauguration ritual closer to the great atonement ritual of Lev 16. A further implication, however, is that it aligns the inauguration ritual closer to the sacrificial legislation of Lev 1–7. The ordination ritual of Exod 29 envisages a sin-purification offering being sacrificed on behalf of the priesthood, Aaron and his sons. In the sacrificial legislation of Lev 4, however, sin-purification offerings are distinguished according to their offerer with distinct sacrifices for the anointed priest, the people, the chieftain, and the ordinary Israelite. No sin-purification offering is envisaged for the priesthood. As such Exod 29 does not fit into the categories of the sacrificial legislation. The adjustments in the inauguration ritual are designed to correct this deficiency.

The Inauguration Ritual (Lev 9) and the Tabernacle-Purification Ritual (Lev 16)

The most important way in which the tabernacle-purification ritual and the inauguration ritual differ is in the sacrifices offered for Aaron and the people. The similarities and differences can be seen in the table.

Table 7.1 Comparison of the sacrifices in Lev 9 and 16

	Lev 16		Lev 9	
	Sin-purification offering	*Burnt offering*	*Sin-purification offering*	*Burnt offering*
Priest	bull	ram	bull calf	ram
People	goat	ram	goat	calf and lamb

In the great atonement ritual of Lev 16 a bull is offered as a sin-purification offering for the high priest, but in Lev 9 the sin-purification offering is described as a 'bull calf'. The people's burnt offering in Lev 16 is a ram, but in Lev 16 it is a calf and a lamb. What are the reasons for these differences? Two of these appear to be related because they concern the sacrifice of a calf. In the inauguration ritual, Aaron offers as a sin-purification offering for himself a calf, עֵגֶל בֶּן־בָּקָר (9.2), whilst in the great atonement ritual Aaron offers for himself a bull, פַּר בֶּן־בָּקָר (16.3). The burnt offering for the people is a calf, עֵגֶל (9.3), whilst in the great atonement ritual, a ram, אַיִל, is offered (16.5). The mention of a calf in the rituals of the priestly literature is unusual. First, the peculiar form עֵגֶל בֶּן־בָּקָר has no parallel in any other text in the Pentateuch and has probably been formulated on the model of the regular פַּר בֶּן־בָּקָר which is found on numerous occasions in the priestly literature, Ezek 40–48, and Chronicles. Second, a calf is never otherwise mentioned as a sacrificial animal, and as Christian Frevel observes there are no other references to a 'calf' in the Pentateuch outside of Lev 9 and the golden calf story.[42] It may be that 'calf' is a literary allusion to the sin of the golden calf in Exod 32, and there are at least two plausible reasons why it may occur here. First, it could be a rather subtle signaling that the ritual of the eighth day will lead to cultic malpractice as will soon become apparent in Lev 10. Second, the original prescriptions for the ordination ritual and the regular daily sacrifice together with the promise of the divine presence occur in Exod 29 before the sin of the golden calf in Exod 32. The additional requirement in the inauguration ritual to offer sacrifices similar to what we find in the great atonement ritual in Lev 16 may suggest that the sin of the golden calf necessitates additional acts of purification that were not needed in Exod 29.

The only other difference is that the people had a second burnt offering, a lamb. As Feldman and Ederer argue, this is most likely the daily *tāmîd*.[43] There are a couple of reasons why this is the case. First, the only mention of a lamb as a burnt offering in the Pentateuch prior to Lev 9 is the *tāmîd* in Exod 29.38–42. Second, the *tāmîd* is referred to in v. 17 in the context of a handful of the grain offering being immolated on the altar. Since the altar has been used for a variety of other offerings, this cannot be a reference to an unmentioned *tāmîd* at the start of the day.[44] Instead, the offering of the *tāmîd* must have been envisaged as part of the offering of the burnt offering in the previous verse.

The appearance of the *tāmîd* within the eighth-day ritual provides an important clue for understanding Moses' puzzling assertion that 'this is the thing that YHWH commanded to be done' (Lev 9.6). In what sense had YHWH commanded the eighth-day ritual since there is no mention of a ritual to be practiced after the ordination ritual? Milgrom, one of the few commentators to notice the problem, asks 'What is the referent? None seems to exist. This situation is entirely unlike that of the previous chapter, where the same expression, *zeh haddābār* (8.5) clearly referred to the prescriptive text of Exod 29.' His own conclusion is that Lev 9.6 is nothing more than an 'editorial note explaining that Moses did not command these sacrifices on his own initiative'.[45] But the fact that what follows in Lev 9 is a ritual very like the ordination ritual into which has been integrated the

---

[42] Christian Frevel, *Mit Blick auf das Land die Schöpfung erinnern: Zum Ende der Priestergrundschrift*, HBS 23 (Freiburg im Breisgau: Herder, 2000), 178.

[43] Feldman, 'Ritual Sequence', 29–30; Ederer, *Identitätsstiftende Begegnung*, 371.

[44] *Contra* Milgrom who assumes this to be the case and consequently finds the mention of the *tāmîd* in v. 17 problematic. As a result, he regards the mention of the *tāmîd* as an interpolation (Milgrom, *Leviticus 1–16*, 584).

[45] Milgrom, *Leviticus 1–16*, 576.

206   THE MAKING OF THE TABERNACLE

tāmîd suggests that הַדָּבָר זֶה has *exactly* the same referent as it did in 8.5. It refers to the prescriptive text of Exod 29! And that includes vv. 38–46, the prescriptions for the *tāmîd* and the promise that YHWH will meet with the Israelites when the *tāmîd* is offered. As Feldman has observed, 'the establishment of the *tāmîd*, sandwiched between the ordination of the priests and the divine theophany, appears to be a necessary part of the inauguration of the tabernacle'.[46] It is for this reason that Lev 9.6 contains a final clause that Lev 8.5 lacks: 'this is the thing that YHWH commanded to be done so that YHWH's glory may appear to you (וְיֵרָא אֲלֵיכֶם כְּבוֹד יְהוָה)'.

My examination of Lev 9 demonstrates that whilst on one natural reading of the instructions given to Moses, the ritual of the eighth day had not been commanded, and was entirely unanticipated, there is another reading of Lev 9 where the ritual of the eighth day had been commanded in Exod 29. In this way, Exod 29 can be seen to provide the *script* for Lev 9. In Exod 29 Moses receives instructions that sacrifices be made for the priesthood (vv. 1–37) and for the *tāmîd* to be offered (vv. 38–42) after which YHWH will appear (vv. 43–46). In Lev 9 a series of sacrifices paralleling the ordination ritual is offered (vv. 1–21), but also incorporating the *tāmîd* (v. 17) and concluding with an appearance of the divine presence (vv. 22–24). In sum, Lev 9 is itself envisaged as a fulfilment of Exod 29.

Chronological Problems with the Inauguration of the Tabernacle

The transformation of the ordination ritual into a consecration ritual followed by inauguration sacrifices transforms the chronology of the tabernacle's first days. The sacrifices of the ordination ritual could have been completed in a couple of hours on a single day (Exod 29), but the consecration and inauguration rituals require eight days. As a result, some chronological difficulties are introduced into the Pentateuch's narrative. Most notably, we have two theophanies: one in Exod 40 and a second, seven days later, in Lev 9.

The double theophany is surprising and unexpected, especially since they both appear to be a fulfilment of the promise in Exod 29.43–46. After the initial block of instructions, Moses is promised that,

43 I will meet with the Israelites there and it will be sanctified by my glory (בִּכְבֹדִי). 44 I will sanctify the tent of meeting and the altar; Aaron and his sons I will sanctify to be priests for me. 45 I will dwell (וְשָׁכַנְתִּי) among the Israelites, and I will be their God. 46 They shall know that I am YHWH their God, who

---

[46] Feldman, 'Ritual Sequence', 11.

ORDINATION, CONSECRATION, AND INAUGURATION 207

brought them out of the land of Egypt so that I might dwell amongst them (לְשָׁכְנִי
בְתוֹכָם). I am YHWH their God (Exod 29.43–46).

It would seem natural to read this as a promise that YHWH would dwell amongst the Israelites (vv. 45–46) after the tent, altar and priests had been sanctified (v. 44). Instead, the fulfilment of this promise has been bifurcated between Exod 40 and Lev 9. In Exod 40, 'the glory of YHWH (וּכְבוֹד יְהוָה) filled the tabernacle' (vv. 34, 35) and 'the cloud settled (שָׁכַן) upon it' (Exod v. 35), whilst in Lev 9, 'the glory of YHWH (כְּבוֹד־יְהוָה) appeared to all the people' (Lev 9.23).

In a couple of recent publications, Anderson has demonstrated how premodern interpreters struggled with the chronology around the tabernacle's inauguration.[47] Some understood the final chapters of Exodus and the opening chapters of Leviticus as the presentation of a sequence of events. The tabernacle was erected by Moses on the first day of the first month and on that day the divine presence took up residence (Exod 40). In the subsequent seven days, Moses received the instructions about the sacrifices (Lev 1–7) and the priests were ordained (Lev 8). On the eighth day, the tabernacle was inaugurated, and the divine presence appeared a second time (Lev 9). Many other interpreters, however, understood there to be just one divine appearance described in two places (Exod 40.34–35; Lev 9.22–24). Thus, the events in Lev 1–9 are simultaneous with those described in the final chapters of Exodus: all occurred before a single theophanic appearance.

Anderson argues that the instinct amongst many early interpreters to read the two theophanies as one and the same event provides an important guide to how the end of Exodus and the beginning of Leviticus are to be read. Anderson notes Propp's suggestion that the creation of the tabernacle is characterized by 'an atemporal *illud tempus*' that overcomes the limits of linear time,[48] but he also argues that it allowed the authors to present material thematically: tabernacle building (Exod 25–40), altar service and the priesthood (Lev 1–10), and community organization and guidance in the wilderness (Num 1–10). 'The thematic manner of presentation...allows our author to give the several dimensions of the tabernacle the independent development that are due them.'[49] Anderson's observations are perceptive, but I will re-examine the evidence that he assembles for a different purpose. Rather than advocating for a particular way to read the text of Exodus and Leviticus, I want to suggest that the different understandings evidenced in

---

[47] Gary A. Anderson, 'The Date of the Tabernacle's Completion and Consecration', *TheTorah.Com*, 2022, https://www.thetorah.com/article/the-date-of-the-tabernacles-completion-and-consecration; Anderson, *That I May Dwell among Them*. Cf. Yoram Erder, 'The First Date in Megillat Taʿanit in Light of the Karaite Commentary on the Tabernacle Dedication', *JQR* 82 (1992): 263–83.

[48] Gary A. Anderson, 'Literary Artistry and Divine Presence', in *Contextualizing Jewish Temples*, eds. Tova Ganzel and Shalom E. Holtz, BRLJ 64 (Leiden: Brill, 2020), 98–9; Propp, *Exodus 19–40*, 692.

[49] Anderson, 'Literary Artistry', 100.

208 THE MAKING OF THE TABERNACLE

early interpretation point to the difficulties that arose from the shift of a one-day ordination rite into an eight-day ritual complex.

Josephus is one of the early interpreters who understands Exod 40–Lev 9 to describe a sequence of events. In the third book of his *Jewish Antiquities*, he describes how the work on the tabernacle was completed on the first day of Nisan. The divine approbation is signalled by God taking up residence. On the following days, sacrifices are offered to consecrate the priests, their vestments, and the tabernacle. On the eighth day, there is a feast and more sacrifices which are consumed by lightening (*Ant.* 3.201–207). It is evident that the theophanies in Exod 40 and Lev 9 are two different events for Josephus, for he describes them in distinctive ways. The first theophany sees a dense cloud of darkness descend upon the tabernacle, whilst in the second, a flash of lightning consumes the sacrifices. The Temple Scroll probably interprets the early chapters of Leviticus similarly. In its ritual calendar, an annual seven-day ordination service is placed after the arrangements for the first day of Nisan (11Q19 15:03–17:5).[50]

For a number of other interpreters, however, the descriptions of the divine appearing in Exod 40 and Lev 9 are not two distinct events, but one and the same theophany which occurred on the first day of Nisan (Exod 40.17). The *Biblical Antiquities* of Pseudo-Philo describe a single theophany which occurred after the tabernacle was complete and the priests ordained.

> And Moses hastened and did everything that God commanded him. And he went down and made the tent of meeting, and its vessels, and the ark, and the lamp, and the table, and the altar of holocausts, and the altar of incense, and the ephod and the breastplate and the precious stones and the laver and the basins and everything that was shown to him. And he arranged all the vestments of the priests, the belt and the robe and the headdress and the golden plate and the holy crown. And the oil for anointing priests and the priests themselves he consecrated. And when all this was done, the cloud covered them all (*et completis omnibus, universos eos operuit nubes*). Then Moses called to the LORD, and God spoke to him from the tent of meeting, saying, 'This is the law of the altar, according to which you will sacrifice to me...' (LAB 13.1–2).[51]

Pseudo-Philo describes the construction of the tabernacle (Exod 36–40) which is followed by the consecration of the priests (Lev 8). The divine presence appears

---

[50] Lawrence H. Schiffman, 'The Milluim Ceremony in the Temple Scroll', in *The Courtyards of the House of the Lord: Studies on the Temple Scroll*, STDJ 75 (Leiden: Brill, 2008), 315–31.

[51] Translation according to D. J. Harrington, 'Pseudo-Philo', in *The Old Testament Pseudepigrapha, Volume 2: Expansions of the 'Old Testament' and Legends, Wisdom and Philosophical Literature, Prayers, Psalms, and Odes, Fragments of Lost Judeo-Hellenistic Works*, ed. James H. Charlesworth (Garden City, NY: Doubleday, 1985), 231. For the Latin text, see Howard Jacobson, *A Commentary on Pseudo-Philo's Liber Antiquitatum Biblicarum, with Latin Text and English Translation*, AGJU 31 (Leiden: Brill, 1996).

in terms that reflect both Exod 40.34–35 and Lev 9.23–24. 'The cloud covered them all (*universos eos operuit nubes*)' (LAB 13.1) combines the reference to the cloud from Exod 40 and the reference to all the people from Lev 9.[52]

The same strategy of blending the two theophanies is also deployed by the Chronicler in his account of the inauguration of Solomon's Temple. In a description without parallel in the book of Kings, God responds to Solomon's prayer of dedication with a divine appearance that draws on Exod 40 and Lev 9:

Table 7.2 The theophanies at the inauguration of Solomon's Temple and the tabernacle

2 Chron 7.1–3	Exod 40.33–34 and Lev 9.23–24
1 When Solomon had finished praying, <u>fire descended from heaven and consumed the burnt offering and the sacrifices, and the glory of yhwh filled the temple.</u> 2 <u>The priests were not able to enter the temple of yhwh because the glory of yhwh filled the temple of yhwh.</u> **3** All the Israelites saw <u>the fire descending and the glory of yhwh upon the temple. They bowed their noses to the ground down to the pavement and worshipped.</u>	Exod 40.33 The cloud covered the tent of meeting, <u>and the glory of yhwh filled the tabernacle</u> 34 <u>Moses was not able to enter the tent of meeting because the cloud settled upon it and the glory of yhwh filled the tabernacle.</u> Lev 9.23 Moses and Aaron entered the tent of meeting. They came out and blessed the people and the glory of yhwh appeared to all the people. 24 <u>Fire came out from before yhwh and consumed the burnt offering and the fat upon the altar. All the people saw. They shouted and fell upon their faces.</u>

As Anderson observes, 'while Chronicles rewrites its source texts—Temple replaces tabernacle, kneeling and bowing replaces falling, giving thanks replaces shouting—it is essentially a pastiche, built from the passages in Exodus 40 and Leviticus 9'.[53]

Rabbinic interpreters also equated the two theophanies, and they were followed by the medieval Jewish interpreters. They understand that the seven days of the ordination ritual were completed by the first of Nisan. Consequently, the seven-day consecration ritual must have run from the twenty-third day to the twenty-ninth day of Adar. Yet, this encounters the obvious difficulty that the ordination ritual could not be performed until the tabernacle had been erected. This difficulty was countered with the proposal that Moses erected and dismantled the tabernacle on each of the seven days of the ordination ritual and so was

---

[52] Jacobson rightly observes that Pseudo-Philo departs from Exod 40.34 which describes the cloud covering the tabernacle, but admits to being perplexed. 'LAB differs somewhat and in a perplexing way... Who are LAB's *universos eos*? Does it mean the priests? Or the priests plus Moses? Or the entire people? The need for *universos* might suggest the last' (Jacobson, *Pseudo-Philo's Liber Antiquitatum Biblicarum*, 508). The puzzlement evaporates when we recognize the allusion to Lev 9.

[53] Anderson, 'Date'.

210 THE MAKING OF THE TABERNACLE

able on the first day of the first month to erect the tabernacle as described in Exod 40.2.[54]

Whilst it might be easy to dismiss such attempts to resolve the chronological problems as self-evidently absurd, Anderson has pointed out that the idea that the sanctuary was completed on the twenty-third day of Adar finds support in Ezra 6.15. Following their return to Jerusalem, the Judean exiles rebuild the temple despite considerable opposition. In 515 BCE 'this house was finished on the third day of the month of Adar' (שֵׁיצִיא בַּיְתָה דְנָה עַד יוֹם תְּלָתָה לִירַח אֲדָר; Ezra 6.15). The parallel text in 1 Esdras 7.5 preserves an alternative reading: 'the holy house was finished by the twenty-third day of the month of Adar' (συνετελέσθη ὁ οἶκος ὁ ἅγιος ἕως τρίτης καὶ εἰκάδος μηνὸς Αδαρ). It seems most likely that 1 Esdras reflects the original reading as it is easier to envisage how the word 'twenty' might have been omitted than for it to have been added.[55]

Finally, we should note that Num 7 also appears to presuppose that the priestly ordination was completed by the first of Nisan. The chapter opens with the words 'on the day when Moses completed the erection of the tabernacle', which is a clear echo of Exod 40.2, 17 and so retells the events surrounding the tabernacle's consecration. But the events it describes have not been relayed before. On that day, the first day of the first month, the leaders arrive with wagons and oxen, which are allocated to the Levites (Num 7.1–9). The leaders also bring offerings for the initiation of the altar. They apparently brought their offerings to the tabernacle together, but are instructed to present them over twelve days (7.10–88). After a brief statement about Moses' reception of revelation and the commissioning of Aaron to set the lamps (7.89–8.4), a further narrative follows that relates how the Levites were purified for service (8.5–22). In the following chapter, the focus turns to the Passover held on the fourteenth day of the month and the quandary of what to do with those who are unclean during the celebration (9.1–14).

The chronology of the leaders' offerings is not easy to square with the view that the first of Nisan is the opening day of the ritual by which sanctuary and priesthood were consecrated. YHWH's insistence that the leaders' offerings be brought on twelve separate days would result in a partial overlapping of the two rituals. For the first seven days, the priests were being ordained and the tabernacle consecrated. At the same time, the leaders of Judah, Issachar, Zebulun, Reuben, Simeon, Gad, and Ephraim presented their offerings. On the eighth day, the inauguration of the tabernacle occurred as well as the catastrophic presentation of strange fire by Nadab and Abihu. On this day, Gamaliel of Manasseh presented his offering.

---

[54] See Rashi and Ibn Ezra on Lev 9.1 (Carasik, *Leviticus*, 56), also Nachmanides on Ex 40.2 (Carasik, *Exodus*, 332–3).

[55] Zipora Talshir, *I Esdras: A Text Critical Commentary*, SCS 50 (Atlanta, GA: Society of Biblical Literature, 2001), 375; H.G.M. Williamson, *Ezra, Nehemiah*, WBC 16 (Waco, TX: Word, 1985), 72; Lisbeth S. Fried, *Ezra: A Commentary*, Critical Commentary (Sheffield: Sheffield Phoenix, 2015), 281.

ORDINATION, CONSECRATION, AND INAUGURATION   211

On the remaining days, the leaders of Benjamin, Dan, Asher, and Naphtali presented their offerings at a sanctuary that is fully functioning.[56] The scenario that we must imagine at the tabernacle is far from straightforward. For seven days, tribal leaders are turning up at a sanctuary where the priests are sequestered and the altar has not been fully consecrated. The donations would have to be handed over to Moses who presumably offered them. For the final five days, however, the newly ordained priesthood can receive and sacrifice the offerings.

It is perhaps no surprise, then, that a few scholars have concluded that the leaders' offerings did not begin until there was an ordained priesthood and consecrated tabernacle. Milgrom assumes that the leaders made their offerings between the eighth and nineteenth of Nisan. The objection that Num 7.1 dates the first offering to the first of Nisan is addressed by Milgrom in two ways. First, he argues that בְּיוֹם in 7.1 is used indefinitely. Second, he observes that the offerings were only made once the altar had been anointed and consecrated. This occurred not on one single day, but across the entire seven days of the consecration ritual. Thus, in Milgrom's view, the leaders did not bring their offerings until the altar had been fully consecrated on the eighth of Nisan.[57] The proposal that the leaders' offerings were made between the eighth and nineteenth of Nisan encounters its own problems. As Milgrom observes, Elishama of Ephraim would have offered his sacrifices on the day of Passover! To address this difficulty, Milgrom argues that the offerings were not sacrificed on the day that they were brought, they were simply donations to the public cult for use at a later date.[58] Whilst it is true that the list has the form of a temple record enumerating donations to the sanctuary,[59] the contributions of Nashon of Judah and Nethanel of Issachar are said to have been offered (*hiphil* קר״ב; Num 7.12, 18). The abbreviated form for the remaining

---

[56] Such an arrangement is set out explicitly in Gordon J. Wenham, *Numbers, an Introduction and Commentary*, TOTC 4 (Leicester: Inter-Varsity Press, 1981), 91.

[57] Milgrom, *Numbers*, 364. In her recent monograph, Feldman adopts Milgrom's proposal (Feldman, *Story*, 121–34). She argues that the beginning of the leaders' offerings on the eighth of Nisan is supported by a reference to them in Lev 9.1. There is, however, no verbal link in the Hebrew text. The tribal leaders in Num 7 are identified as נְשִׂיאֵי יִשְׂרָאֵל רָאשֵׁי בֵּית אֲבֹתָם הֵם נְשִׂיאֵי הַמַּטֹּת, 'leaders of Israel, heads of their fathers' house, leaders of the tribe' (7.2) and are twelve in number. In Lev 9.1, however, we encounter the זִקְנֵי יִשְׂרָאֵל, 'elders of Israel'. They are the same group associated with Aaron, Moses and his sons in Exod 24 and they are seventy in number (24.1; cf. Num 11). Observing the difficulties of accounting for the chronology of the events, Feldman speaks of a 'controlled chaos', and seeks to resolve some of the difficulties by insisting that there are 'multiple different activities occurring in different areas' (Feldman, *Story*, 123). Feldman attempts to harmonize the narratives in Lev 8–10 and Num 7 to create a comprehensive chronology. In particular, she distinguishes between what transpires inside the sanctuary complex—where the priests are sequestered—and what occurs outside—where the leaders assemble with their offerings (Feldman, *Story*, 123–30). But the attempt to maintain synchronous episodes in different geographical settings (cf. Shemaryahu Talmon, 'The Presentation of Synchroneity and Simultaneity in Biblical Narrative', in *Literary Studies in the Hebrew Bible* [Jerusalem: Magnes Press, 1993], 112–33) is not convincing, for all these events are occurring in the vicinity of the bronze altar.

[58] Milgrom, *Numbers*, 362–4.   [59] See, esp., Levine, *Numbers*, I: 259–66.

212   THE MAKING OF THE TABERNACLE

leaders might, perhaps, be evidence that an archival inventory was utilized,[60] but the fact that the donations were said to be offered for the first two leaders should be taken as evidence that this was assumed for the remaining ten. In addition, the leaders bring amity offerings which are not part of the public cult (cf. Num 28.1–30.1) and this also tells against Milgrom's proposal.

The attempt to combine the leaders' offerings with a seven-day consecration ritual results in torturous harmonizations. If, on the other hand, the first of Nisan was the date on which the priesthood and sanctuary were ready to begin the public cult, the chronology of Num 7 is straightforward. According to Num 7.1, the tribal leaders began their offerings on the first of Nisan, and thus their offerings ran until the twelfth of Nisan. The offering from the last leader occurs before the beginning of Passover, which occurred on the fourteenth of Nisan, and we might even imagine that the thirteenth of Nisan was available between the last offering and Passover as the day when the dedication of the Levites could have occurred (Lev 8.5–22).

In his examination of the chronology of the tabernacle's inauguration, Anderson argues that the final editor intended that the two theophanies in Exod 40 and Lev 9 be understood as the same event. This allowed the different thematic elements to be presented independently: first, the tabernacle (Exod 35–40) and then the altar (Lev 1–10).[61] What I have sought to do is not to prefer one chronological arrangement over another, but rather to show how the history of interpretation sheds unexpected light on the transformation of the ordination ritual from a one-day rite into a seven-day consecration ritual that concluded with an inauguration ritual on the eighth day.

Conclusion

The ordination ritual in Exod 29 has often been overshadowed by the descriptions of the tabernacle in the preceding chapters of Exod 25–28. Where it has been the focus of attention, questions of the textual relationship between the instructions Exod 29 and their fulfilment in Lev 8, or the similarities between biblical and Near Eastern ordination rituals have dominated. In this chapter I have attempted to take a different approach which gives attention to the way the ritual communicates the significance of the priesthood.

Within the priestly literature, the ordination ritual appears as the primary ritual. It is primary in two senses. It is the very first ritual to be performed, and it is also that which makes all subsequent rites possible. Only when the priests have

---

[60] Davies rightly cautions that this idea cannot be proven (Eryl W. Davies, *Numbers*, NCB [London: Marshall Pickering, 1995], 70).

[61] Anderson, 'Date'.

been ordained can they perform the various sacrifices. The ordination itself is a complex of distinguishable rites, and its complexity highlights its importance and marks it out as the epitome of all the sacrificial rituals. These various features of the ordination ritual emphasize the indispensability of the priests for the functioning of Israel's cult. The central figure is Aaron who is ordained wearing the holy vestments whose instrumental significance has been described in Exod 28. His sons are presented as assistants.

The transformation of the ordination ritual into one of consecration forges an even closer relationship between the priesthood and the tabernacle. Both are recipients of anointing oil and they share in the same consecration. A new set of relationships is created between the high priest and the priests. Not only Aaron, but also his sons, are anointed. Nevertheless, Aaron's superiority is reasserted since he undergoes a double anointing, with the first emphasizing the close relationship the high priest has with the sanctuary.

In the consecration and inauguration rituals, the people are given a role that they hitherto lacked. They assemble at the entrance to the tent of meeting to witness all that transpires. They are also present for the divine approbation when fire comes out and consumes the burnt offering. Thus, the people participate, but simply as observers. Their role in the consecration and inauguration rituals matches that in the cult more broadly. The people may bring gifts for the sanctuary, but the ritual activities are performed by the priests.

8
Inauguration and Violation

The story of the eighth day does not end with the theophany. Instead, it continues into Lev 10 and takes a dramatic turn of direction. The acclamation of the people as they view the divine appearance is quickly forgotten when Nadab and Abihu approach the sanctuary with 'strange fire' (אֵשׁ זָרָה) and are instantly consumed themselves (10.1–2). The sobering conversation about sacrificial remains between Aaron and Moses that follows suggests that Nadab and Abihu are not the only ones of Aaron's sons suspected of cultic malpractice. Moses discovers that the goat of the sin-purification offering has been burnt outside the camp, rather than being consumed in the sanctuary. Moses appears to hold Aaron's remaining sons, Eleazar and Ithamar, responsible for this violation. When Moses describes the act as in contradiction to 'what I commanded' (v. 18), the reader is justified in fearing that Aaron will lose all of his sons on this fateful day. Fortunately, Moses is mollified by Aaron's enigmatic reply: 'See today they have offered their sin-purification offering and their burnt offering before YHWH, but such things as this have befallen me. If I had eaten a sin-purification offering today, would it have been agreeable to YHWH?' (v. 19). This act of ritual innovation, unlike Nadab and Abihu's 'strange fire', would appear to be permissible. But why is one innovation violently rejected, and the other accepted? As Rolf Rendtorff puts it, 'there are many strange stories in the Bible, but this is one of the strangest'.[1] Unfortunately, both the nature of Nadab and Abihu's infraction and the logic of Aaron's reply are interpretive cruxes that have long resisted resolution.

The offering of strange fire by Nadab and Abihu on the final and climactic day of the priesthood's inauguration has puzzled interpreters since antiquity.[2] What was their error that led to such catastrophic consequences? If the mistake is not to

---

[1] Rolf Rendtorff, 'Nadab and Abibu', in *Reading from Right to Left: Essays on the Hebrew Bible in Honour of David J.A. Clines*, eds. J. Cheryl Exum and Hugh Godfrey Maturin Williamson, JSOTSup 373 (London: Sheffield Academic, 2003), 359.

[2] The history of interpretation has been the subject of a number of studies: Avigdor Shinan, 'The Sins of Nadab and Abihu in Rabbinic Literature', *Tarbiz* 48 (1979): 201–14; Robert Kirschner, 'The Rabbinic and Philonic Exegeses of the Nadab and Abihu Incident (Lev. 10:1–6)', *JQR* 73 (1983): 375–93; Christopher T. Begg, 'The Death of Nadab and Abihu According to Josephus', *LASBF* 59 (2009): 155–67; David Flusser, 'Nadab and Abihu According to Philo and the Rabbis', in *Judaism of the Second Temple Period. Volume 2: The Jewish Sages and Their Literature* (Grand Rapids, MI: Eerdmans, 2009), 289–96; Didier Pralon, 'L'allégorie au travail: Interprétation de Lévitique X par Philon d'Alexandrie', in *ΚΑΤΑ ΤΟΥΣ Ο: Selon les Septante*, ed. Marguerite Harl (Paris: Cerf, 1995), 483–97; Mark W. Elliott, *Engaging Leviticus: Reading Leviticus Theologically with Its Past Interpreters* (Eugene, OR: Cascade, 2012), 90–7.

The Making of the Tabernacle and the Construction of Priestly Hegemony. Nathan MacDonald, Oxford University Press.
© Nathan MacDonald 2023. DOI: 10.1093/oso/9780198813859.003.0009

be repeated, it would seem important for the early priestly readers to be able to determine the precise nature of the infraction. And yet it has proved very difficult, if not impossible, to answer this question. Edward Greenstein memorably describes the event as 'a punishment in search of a crime'.[3]

It is not that the search has lacked for leads. The expression 'strange fire' (אֵשׁ זָרָה) would appear to provide the most promising avenue to explore. The language is reminiscent of Exod 30.9, which forbids the offering of 'strange incense' (קְטֹרֶת זָרָה) on the altar of incense. The precise recipe that is to be used is described later in the same chapter (30.34–38). Was the incense offered by Nadab and Abihu prepared according to a different method? The proposal is not convincing, because the situation in Lev 10 differs from Exod 30 in two respects. First, Nadab and Abihu's offering was laid on pans, rather than on the altar of incense. Second, the expression 'strange fire' seems to indicate that the problem lay with the fire rather than the incense. This latter observation has led to an alternative proposal: that the coals for the fire were taken from somewhere other than the altar of burnt offering as required in Lev 16.12 and Num 17.11. Their strangeness is a result of their foreign provenance. Yet we might have expected this to have been made explicit at the beginning when the fire is first mentioned: 'Nadab and Abihu each took his pan and put *strange* fire in it'.[4] One further line of enquiry has observed that the offering of incense echoes the story of Korah and his followers which will occur later in the Pentateuch's storyline (Num 16–17). A trial by ordeal reveals that neither the Levites nor the Israelite chieftains have the right to offer incense, only Aaron. Christophe Nihan consequently argues that Lev 10 reiterates the perspective of Num 16–17 that the offering of incense is a monopoly of the high priest.[5] Arguably, though, this simplifies some of the ambiguities in the story of Korah. Num 17.5 excludes only non-Aaronides from offering incense: 'No stranger (אִישׁ זָר) who is not from the descendants of Aaron may approach to offer incense before YHWH'. It is possible to read Num 16–17 as an attempt to bar Levites and lay Israelites from priestly prerogatives which belong to all of Aaron's male descendants.

In the light of the difficulties that confront any proposed solution, it is perhaps unsurprising that some recent interpreters have questioned whether decoding the meaning of 'strange fire' is a fruitful approach. Eschewing attempts to determine the precise nature of the infraction, James Watts argues that the issue is that Nadab and Abihu did 'that which YHWH had not commanded them' (Lev 10.1). The story excludes *any* deviation from what Moses has instructed.[6] Greenstein, on the other hand, applies deconstruction to demonstrate the fragility of any attempt to stabilize the meaning of the passage. 'God upsets the orderliness of the

---

[3] Edward L. Greenstein, 'Deconstruction and Biblical Narrative', *Proof* 9 (1989): 56.
[4] Heger, *Incense Cult*, 80–1.   [5] Nihan, *Priestly Torah*, 582.
[6] Watts, *Leviticus 1–10*, 528.

216 THE MAKING OF THE TABERNACLE

cultic system...Lest God become altogether manipulable by the cult, the episode of Nadav and Avihu, I would suggest, subverts the orderly ritual's implication of orderliness by asserting YHWH's unpredictability and autonomy, YHWH's sheer transcendence.'[7]

Understanding the logic of Aaron's response to Moses in v. 19 and Moses' acquiescence has proved just as frustrating. One line of interpretation that goes back at least to the rabbis is that Aaron regards eating the flesh of the sin-purification offering as inappropriate on the day that Nadab and Abihu died.[8] This seems unlikely given that v. 6 forbids Aaron and his sons from mourning whilst they are serving in the tabernacle. Jacob Milgrom suggests that the deaths of Nadab and Abihu have polluted the sanctuary and that Aaron reasons that this would require the more potent form of the sin-purification offering where the entire animal is burnt outside the camp (cf. Lev 16).[9] But Aaron's response to Moses concerns what has happened to him, rather than what has happened to the sanctuary. With no agreed solution in view, Nihan has argued that what matters is not the precise reasoning that Aaron deploys, but that the high priest's interpretation of ritual practice is superior to the lawgiver himself. The episode is 'the founding legend of priestly exegesis', establishing the priests as authorized interpreters of every aspect of the ritual law.[10] In this interpretation, far from undermining the Aaronide priesthood, Moses' confrontation with Aaron ultimately establishes the priesthood's pre-eminence in ritual matters. The encounter instantiates the teaching role assigned to them in v. 11. Taking a similar view to Nihan, Watts draws the two intractable problems of vv. 1 and 19 together by regarding them both as inexplicable, but for a particular rhetorical purpose. 'To explain exactly why Nadab and Abihu's incense offering was wrong or exactly how Aaron reasoned regarding the eating of the sin offering would *spoil the mystery of priestly service.*'[11] The priestly caste's understanding of the mysteries of cultic service and their willingness to undertake what has proved to be a dangerous occupation legitimates their monopoly of the cult and its privileges.

---

[7] Greenstein, 'Deconstruction and Biblical Narrative', 63.

[8] Thus, Nihan writes, 'the formulation of v. 19 appears to suggest a much more simple [sic] explanation, namely that Aaron felt it inappropriate to eat the purification offering's flesh on the very day of his sons' death' (Nihan, *Priestly Torah*, 600–1). Although Nihan distanced his interpretation from those who saw this as due to Aaron mourning, his recent re-examination of Lev 10 sees Aaron's refusal to eat the flesh as due to his mourning: 'the most likely explanation remains that Aaron, while mourning, was not in a state to bear the community's guilt' (Christophe Nihan, 'Narrative and Exegesis in Leviticus: On Leviticus 10 and 24,10–23', in *Schriftgelehrte Fortschreibungs- und Auslegungsprozesse: Textarbeit im Pentateuch, in Qumran, Ägypten und Mesopotamien*, ed. Walter Bührer, FAT II/108 [Tübingen: Mohr Siebeck, 2019], 234). Cf. Diane M. Sharon, 'When Fathers Refuse to Eat: The Trope of Rejecting Food and Drink in Biblical Narrative', in *Food and Drink in Biblical Worlds*, eds. Athalya Brenner and Jan W. van Henten, Semeia 68 (Atlanta, GA: Society of Biblical Literature, 1999), 135–48; Michael A. Fishbane, *Biblical Interpretation in Ancient Israel* (Oxford: Clarendon Press, 1985), 226–8; Kiuchi, *Purification Offering*, 77–85.

[9] Milgrom, *Leviticus 1–16*, 635–40.   [10] Nihan, *Priestly Torah*, 598–607.

[11] Watts, *Ritual and Rhetoric*, 117.

INAUGURATION AND VIOLATION   217

Whilst Nihan and Watts have exposed some important dynamics within the chapter, Watts' appeal to the 'mystery' of priestly service feels more like a counsel of despair than a solution to the chapter's puzzles. We might suspect that such an interpretation says more about the limitations of our understanding than any intention on the parts of the text's authors to promote the priesthood's mystique. Nevertheless, by focusing on the dynamics of priestly hegemony, Nihan and Watts are seeking solutions in the right place. I will argue that the composer of Lev 10 makes some specific claims about the competencies and rights of the high priest and the rest of the priesthood. To recognize these, we need to see Lev 9–10 as a compositional whole. Some of the distinctive features of the inauguration ritual that I have identified in the previous chapter provide the solution for the two interpretive cruxes in Lev 10. First, the nature of Nadab and Abihu's transgression in v. 1 can be identified when we recognize that Lev 9 takes Exod 29 as its script. Second, the reason that Aaron's response in v. 19 mollifies Moses can be understood when we recognize that the ritual in Lev 9 has adjusted the ordination ritual to fit the categories of the sacrificial legislation in Lev 1–7. Before we turn to those problems, I will need to substantiate my claim that Lev 9–10 should be viewed as a whole since many scholars have argued that these chapters evince a complex history of composition. Finally, at the end of this chapter, I will examine the remaining issues in Lev 10 and how they shed light on the prerogatives and responsibilities of the high priest and the rest of the priesthood.

The Relationship of Lev 9 and 10

From a narratological perspective, Lev 9–10 belong together because they describe events that occur on the eighth day.[12] It has been noticed within critical

---

[12] Ruwe offers several arguments from a narratological perspective for distinguishing between Lev 8 and Lev 9–10. First, Lev 8 relates back to instructions given in the book of Exodus. Lev 9–10, by contrast, does not correspond to any prior instructions. Second, Moses is the principal actor in the ordination ceremony, but not in Lev 9–10 where Aaron and his sons emerge as the main protagonists. Third, Lev 9.1 provides the only temporal marker in the book of Leviticus. In light of the importance of temporal markers elsewhere in the priestly literature, Ruwe argues that the book of Leviticus should be divided into two parts: Lev 1.1–8.36 is part of the tabernacle texts that begin in Exod 25, whilst Lev 9.1–26.46 is the central section of the book of Leviticus. Having established the arguments for dividing Lev 9–10 from Lev 8, Ruwe offers an interpretation of the two chapters. In his view, Lev 9–10 establishes the competencies and limitations of the Aaronide priesthood in relation to the Mosaic revelation (Andreas Ruwe, 'Das Reden und Verstummen Aarons vor Mose: Levitikus 9–10 im Buch Leviticus', in *Behutsames Lesen: Alttestamentliche Exegese im interdisziplinären Methodendiskurs. Christof Hardmeier zum 65. Geburtstag*, eds. Sylke Lubs et al., ABG 28 [Leipzig: Evangelische Verlagsanstalt, 2007], 169–96). Anderson also finds a greater distance between Lev 8 and 9 than between Lev 9 and 10. He contrasts the different way the rituals are described in Lev 8 and 9. In the ordination ceremony in Lev 8 the ritual is carried out precisely as scripted in Exod 29. In contrast, the rites for the eighth day follow the general rules for sacrifice as they have been set out in Lev 1–7. In addition, Anderson observes that whilst the reader in Exod 29 might have expected the daily sacrifice, the *tāmîd*, to have followed the ordination of the priests, the rituals for the eighth day are quite unexpected, and the daily

218   THE MAKING OF THE TABERNACLE

scholarship that the chapters incorporated quite disparate material. In chapter 9, we have a narrative that recounts the performance of a ritual. Literarily, this stands in continuity with the preceding chapter. In chapter 10, however, the narrative soon gives way to legal instructions (vv. 8–11) and a discussion about legal interpretation (vv. 12–20). The earliest literary-critical examinations were sensitive to these apparent shifts in genre. Wellhausen attributed Lev 9 to the priestly writer, but Lev 10 was a more complex picture with only vv. 1–5, 12–15 belonging to P.[13] Wellhausen's analysis provides a useful vantage point from which to view subsequent developments. On the one hand, the idea that the original priestly work had some foothold within Lev 9 has been maintained by many scholars. Even Koch, who had observed that there were numerous similarities between the sacrificial terminology and descriptions in Lev 9 and the sacrificial regulations in Lev 1–7, held to the view that the concluding blessing and consumption of the sacrifices by fire (9.22–24) were part of the priestly narrative and attempted to reconstruct the bare bones of a narrative from the rest of the chapter.[14] On the other hand, more and more of Lev 10 has been attributed to later priestly revisions. Elliger, for example, argued that vv. 12–15 also reflected knowledge of the sacrificial legislation of Lev 1–7.[15]

The analysis of Achenbach and Nihan takes these two tendencies to what could be regarded as their natural conclusion.[16] Achenbach argues that the catastrophe of Nadab and Abihu's offering is completely unexpected after the ordination of

sacrifice is mentioned in an offhand remark in v. 17. Whilst Anderson speaks of the 'enormous difference between these two chapters', he, nevertheless, insists that 'chapters 8–10 remain something of a unity in my mind, notwithstanding the significant caesura between chaps. 8 and 9' (Gary A. Anderson, '"Through Those Who Are Near to Me, I Will Show Myself Holy": Nadab and Abihu and Apophatic Theology', CBQ 77 [2015]: 8 n. 17).

[13] In Wellhausen's view, vv. 6–7 must have been added later as they mistakenly assumed that the priests were still closeted in the sanctuary, and vv. 8–11 were an even later collection of instructions that were appended to vv. 6–7. Verses 16–20 assumed the regulations in Lev 1–7 which Wellhausen had argued were a later insertion between Exod 25–29 and Lev 9 (Wellhausen, Composition, 140–7; Abraham Kuenen, Historisch-kritische Einleitung in die Bücher des Alten Testaments [Leipzig: Schulze, 1885], 79). This analysis had significant influence on subsequent commentators, see Dillmann, Exodus und Leviticus, 498; Baentsch, Exodus-Leviticus-Numeri, 346–53; Bertholet, Leviticus, 27–9.

[14] For Koch, the priestly Grundschrift consisted of vv. 1, 6–7*, 22–24* (Klaus Koch, Die Priesterschrift von Exodus 25 bis Leviticus 16: Eine überlieferungsgeschichtliche und literarkritische Untersuchung, FRLANT 71 [Gottingen: Vandenhoeck & Ruprecht, 1959], 70–1). The problem with Koch's proposal is that it lacks any account of the sacrifices being offered (Nihan, Priestly Torah, 113). Elliger resolved that difficulty by incorporating the insights of von Rad who had sought to discern two distinctly priestly strands in Lev 9 as he had attempted to do elsewhere, one of which included vv. 7–14* and the other include vv. 15–22* (von Rad, Priesterschrift, 81–3). Elliger attributed vv. 3–5, 7a, 8a, 15b–21*, 22, 23b, 24b to his Pg[1] (Elliger, Leviticus, 121–8). Other attempts to recover a version of Lev 9 uncontaminated by Lev 1–7 include those by Norbert Lohfink and Peter Weimar (Norbert Lohfink, 'The Priestly Narrative and History', in Theology of the Pentateuch: Themes of the Priestly Narrative and Deuteronomy, trans. Linda M. Maloney [Edinburgh: T&T Clark, 1994], 145; Weimar, 'Sinai und Schöpfung').

[15] Elliger, Leviticus, 131–5.

[16] Their analysis already has a precursor in the work of Noth. According to him, the reference to the divine fire consuming the offerings was added secondarily. He rightly perceived that this removed an essential narrative link between chapters 9 and 10, since the destruction of Nadab and Abihu by fire

the priests. Echoing Elliger, Achenbach sees Lev 9 as a celebration of the Aaronides' supremacy.[17] But Lev 10 parades their shame and failure; it can only have stemmed from another priestly circle. In Achenbach's analysis, the links to Ezek 44 indicates a common origin amongst the Zadokites.[18] He demonstrates that the story of Nadab and Abihu is written already aware of the rebellion of the 250 men in Num 16 and argues that the idea of strange fire can be seen, in part, as a reaction to Persian religion. Consequently, Lev 10 should be regarded as one of the very latest additions to the book of Leviticus.[19] Nihan concurs with Achenbach that Lev 10 has numerous late features and that even the narrative in vv. 1–5 presupposes the Levitical genealogy of Exod 6.14–27 which has long been regarded as a late intrusion into the priestly narrative. Since the grounds for regarding the regulations in vv. 8–20 as secondary to the narrative was their dependence on Lev 6–7, Nihan is able to argue that Lev 10 is a compositional unity and draws attention to its chiastic structure.[20] In contrast to the late features of Lev 10, Nihan argues that Lev 9 belongs almost in its entirety to the priestly *Grundschrift*.[21]

---

echoes the language of fire coming out from YHWH to consume the offerings. He, therefore, concluded that no part of Lev 10 originally belonged to the priestly document (Noth, *Leviticus*, 74–88).

[17] Elliger, *Leviticus*, 121–31.

[18] For criticism of the idea that there was a distinct Zadokite priestly circle, see Alice Hunt, *Missing Priests: The Zadokites in Tradition and History*, LHBOTS 452 (New York: T&T Clark, 2006); MacDonald, *Priestly Rule*.

[19] Reinhard Achenbach, 'Das Versagen der Aaroniden: Erwägungen zum literarhistorischen Ort von Leviticus 10', in *'Basel und Bibel': Collected Communications to the XVIIth Congress of the International Organization for the Study of the Old Testament, Basel 2001*, eds. Matthias Augustin and Hermann Michael Niemann, BEATAJ 51 (Frankfurt am Main: Lang, 2004), 55–70.

[20] Nihan, *Priestly Torah*, 576–607.

[21] In Nihan's conception of the *Grundschrift*, both the theophany at the completion of the tabernacle's construction (Exod 40.34–38) and the theophany at the completion of the priesthood's ordination (Lev 9.22–24) should be envisaged as the fulfilment of the promise that both tabernacle and altar will be sanctified by the appearance of the divine glory (Exod 29.43–46). Nihan criticizes the attempts by Koch and Elliger to discern two layers in Lev 9 as a dubious attempt to remove any influence of the sacrificial legislation in Lev 1–7 which only creates textual difficulties. The only plausible solution is to accept the literary integrity of Lev 9, which together with the earliest version of the sacrificial legislation of Lev 1–3* belonged to the priestly *Grundschrift*. For their part, the supplementary regulations in Lev 10.8–20 seek to bring the ritual performance of Lev 9 in line with the subsequent development of the sacrificial legislation in Lev 4–7 (Nihan, *Priestly Torah*, 111–24).

Nihan's attempts to attribute Lev 9 almost entirely to Pg are belied by the fact that he too excises those elements of the eighth-day ritual that assume later legislation. Though his editorial interventions are far less extensive than those undertaken by Koch or Elliger, his claim to accept the 'literary coherence of Lev 9' is somewhat qualified (Nihan, *Priestly Torah*, 122). He expunges the reference to the elders of the people in v. 1 (Nihan, *Priestly Torah*, 122 n. 57), the daily sacrifice in v. 17b, which presupposes Exod 29.38–42, as well as the references to the presentation of the breast of the amity offering in v. 20a and the right thigh in v. 21aβ, which presuppose Lev 7.30, 32–34 (Nihan, *Priestly Torah*, 119–22, 156 n. 224). Feldman has also rightly observed that the reference to the daily offering is also embedded in the reference to a lamb in v. 3bβ, and consequently Nihan should arguably also excise וְכֶבֶשׂ בְּנִי־שָׁנָה (Feldman, 'Ritual Sequence', 29). To be sure, Nihan can appeal to previous scholars who have identified these parts of verses as additions, but they did so because they held to a view that Lev 9 was part of the *Grundschrift* and could not presuppose chronologically later regulations. In other words, they judged these verses as secondary for precisely the reason that Nihan wants to judge them secondary. By appealing to their literary-critical judgements to support his argument, Nihan has inadvertently embraced an argument that is circular.

220 THE MAKING OF THE TABERNACLE

The arguments by Achenbach and Nihan for separating Lev 10 from Lev 9 demand further interrogation. Moses' acceptance of Aaron's response in 10.19 undermines Achenbach's claim that the chapter stems from anti-Aaronide groups.[22] The exchange between Moses and Aaron establishes the priest's authority over the interpretation of Mosaic Torah. In Nihan's words, they are 'the founding legend of priestly exegesis'.[23] In addition, Watts has argued the death of Nadab and Abihu emphasizes the dangerous task entrusted to the priests.[24] Without his theory of rival priestly septs, Achenbach's argument is nothing more than a claim that the literary jolt as we move from Lev 9 to 10 is so great that the work of another writer must be suspected. On its own, however, this is nothing more than an aesthetic judgement that tells us more about the sensibilities of the modern reader. Yet, the story of Nadab and Abihu achieves its sobering literary effect precisely by contrasting their disobedience to what has proceeded. 'Such as he had *not* commanded them' (Lev 10.1) is so striking because it breaks the pattern 'as YHWH commanded' established in the previous two chapters.

Nihan's argument depends on his assigning Lev 9 to the original priestly document, but there are a number of reasons for thinking that the chapter belongs to a later literary layer.[25] First, although Moses claims that his instructions are a commandment from God (v. 6),[26] there is no mention of the ritual on the eighth day in the instructions given to Moses in Exod 25–29. This is significant when every aspect of the tabernacle's construction and consecration was spelt out in detail and precisely fulfilled with particular emphasis that this was done according to YHWH's commandments.[27]

Second, the presentation of the protagonists departs from the priestly *Grundschrift* in important ways. The chapter opens with Moses summoning the priests and the elders. The expression 'Moses summoned' (קָרָא מֹשֶׁה; v. 1), is not typical of P,[28] and is more at home in Deuteronomistic literature.[29] Similarly deuteronomistic is the designation of the Israelite leaders as 'the elders of Israel' (זִקְנֵי יִשְׂרָאֵל; v. 1). The elders are an important civic body in the Deuteronomic laws,[30]

---

[22] Nihan, *Priestly Torah*, 606–7.   [23] Nihan, *Priestly Torah*, 602.

[24] Watts, *Ritual and Rhetoric*, 97–129.

[25] For further arguments, see also Christian Frevel, 'Kein Ende in Sicht? Zur Priestergrundschrift im Buch Levitikus', in *Levitikus als Buch*, eds. Heinz-Josef Fabry and Hans-Winfried Jüngling, BBB 119 (Berlin: Philo, 1999), 85–123; Frevel, *Blick auf das Land*, 148–81.

[26] The expression זֶה הַדָּבָר אֲשֶׁר־צִוָּה יְהוָה occurs only eight times in the Pentateuch, and there is a compelling case for thinking that none of these belong to P^g (for discussion, see Pola, *Die ursprüngliche Priesterschrift*, 133–43; Frevel, *Blick auf das Land*, 172; Suzanne Boorer, *The Vision of the Priestly Narrative: Its Genre and Hermeneutics of Time*, AIL 27 [Atlanta: Society of Biblical Literature, 2016], 68).

[27] Exod 35.1, 4, 10, 29; 36.1, 5; 𝔐 38.22; 39.5, 7, 21, 26, 29, 42, 43; 40.16, 19, 23, 25, 27, 29, 32; Lev 8.4, 5, 9, 13, 17, 21, 29, 36.

[28] In the broad priestly corpus, it occurs only in Exod 36.2; Lev 9.1; 10.4 and Num 13.16.

[29] Deut 5.1; 29.1; 31.7.

[30] Timothy M. Willis, *The Elders of the City: A Study of the Elders-Laws in Deuteronomy*, SBLMS 55 (Atlanta, GA: Society of Biblical Literature, 2001).

but are unknown in Pg.[31] In the Tetrateuch, the elders of Israel appear frequently in the non-priestly Exodus narrative where they act as representatives of the entire people.[32] It is interesting to note that they ascend the mountain of God together with Moses, Aaron, Nadab and Abihu in Exod 24, and it is striking that the same group reappears in Lev 9–10.[33] The reference to the 'people' (הָעָם; vv. 7, 15, 18, 22, 23), and 'all the people' (כָּל־הָעָם; vv. 23, 24), are also atypical for the priestly *Grundschrift*. They are, however, frequently met in secondary P material.[34]

Third, the cultic terminology departs from that typical of the priestly *Grundschrift*.[35] The requirement to offer a calf (עֵגֶל בֶּן־בָּקָר; v. 2) is without parallel in any other text in the Pentateuch. The use of שׂוֹר is not typical of the sacrificial legislation in Lev 1–7, but of the Holiness Code and other later texts.[36] Moses instructs Aaron to 'do' (עש״ה) the sin-purification offering and the burnt offering. The language is rather unusual,[37] and only occurs in texts that are not attributed to the priestly *Grundschrift*.[38] Nor is זב״ח, 'to sacrifice' (v. 4), a P term.[39] Finally, the sacrifices are attributed an atoning significance, an idea not found elsewhere in the priestly *Grundschrift*. The expression used in Lev 9, כפ״ר בְּעַד, 'atone for', is

---

[31] Elliger, *Leviticus*, 123. The expression זִקְנֵי הָעֵדָה occurs once within the sacrificial legislation in relation to the sin-purification sacrifice for the people (Lev 4.15). Since the people as a body cannot undertake the hand-leaning act, the elders do so as the representatives of the people. As Nihan observes, 'their inclusion could well reflect the influence of the Deuteronomistic tradition' (Nihan, *Priestly Torah*, 166).

[32] E.g. Exod 3.16, 18; 4.29.

[33] Because the elders play no further role in the eighth-day ritual in Lev 9, some commentators have viewed them as a later interpolation (Bertholet, *Leviticus*, 27; Noth, *Leviticus*, 77; Nihan, *Priestly Torah*, 122 n. 57). Others, observing the appearance of the בְּנֵי יִשְׂרָאֵל in v. 3, suggest the text originally envisaged Moses addressing the priests and the people (Dillmann, *Exodus und Leviticus*, 511; Baentsch, *Exodus-Leviticus-Numeri*, 347). Both suggestions should be treated with considerable caution for the text does not betray any sign of unevenness and the proposals lack any text critical support. Indeed, זִקְנֵי יִשְׂרָאֵל is more firmly embedded in the textual traditions, for 𝔊^D reads זקני ישראל for בְּנֵי יִשְׂרָאֵל in v. 3 (cf. καὶ τῇ γερουσίᾳ Ἰσραηλ; 𝔊^B). Whilst it can be argued that this reading is a harmonization with v. 1b (Nihan, *Priestly Torah*, 122 n. 57), it can equally be argued that the Masoretic reading is a *lectio facilior* that avoids the suggestion that Aaron is to relay to the elders precisely the words that they are hearing directly from God!

[34] Frevel, *Blick auf das Land*, 177–8.

[35] 'The language of this chapter appears to be uncharacteristic in many ways, including the use of several terms that are nowhere else in P' (Naphtali S. Meshel, *The 'Grammar' of Sacrifice: A Generativist Study of the Israelite Sacrificial System in the Priestly Writings with a 'Grammar' of Σ* [Oxford: Oxford University Press, 2014], 57–8).

[36] שׂוֹר only appears in Lev 4.10 and 7.23, both relatively late texts within the sacrificial legislation. For the use in H and other texts, see 17.3; 22.23, 27; 27.26; Num. 15.11; 18.17. For discussion see Meshel, *Grammar*, 93.

[37] Rendtorff overstates the matter when he claims 'Aaron soll die Opfer "machen" oder "tun" (עשה), ein Ausdruck, der sonst nirgends den Vollzug eines Opfers bezeichnet' (Rendtorff, *Leviticus 1,1–10,20*, 295).

[38] These are the addition to the ordination ceremony in Exod 29.36, the instructions for the daily sacrifice (29.38–42), Lev 5.10, the purity laws (14.19, 30; 15.15, 30), and the ritual for Yom Kippur (16.9, 24).

[39] It does occur in the Holiness Code, see Lev 17.5; 19.5; 22.29.

222   THE MAKING OF THE TABERNACLE

characteristic of Lev 16, rather than the sacrificial legislation in Lev 1–7 which uses the preposition עַל.[40]

Fourth, the climax of the ritual through the appearance of the divine glory in vv. 23–24 is uncharacteristic of P^g.[41] Whilst the priestly narrative envisaged the glory looking like a devouring fire (Exod 24.17), the glory of yhwh and the fire are apparently distinguished in Lev 9.[42] Further, although the tabernacle account's promise that God would dwell amongst the Israelites (29.45–46) is fulfilled in the filling of the tabernacle (40.34–38), these central P^g texts do not use the language of yhwh 'appearing' to the Israelites. This idea would appear to be a later characterization of the encounter at Sinai, and is favoured in the post-priestly narratives in Numbers (14.10; 16.19; 17.7; 20.6).[43]

The strongest argument in favour of Lev 9 belonging to the priestly *Grundschrift* is the chapter's consistent reference to only one altar: הַמִּזְבֵּחַ, 'the altar'.[44] Yet, Lev 10.12 also maintains this usage despite its other conspicuous late features. Further, the similarities between the rituals in Lev 9 and Lev 8 suggest that the eighth-day ritual was modelled on the ordination ceremony and carries over its references to a single altar. Thus, the mention of just one altar cannot overturn the numerous observations that we have made against attributing Lev 9 belonging to the priestly *Grundschrift*. There are, therefore, very good reasons for regarding the eighth-day ritual as a novelty that was not anticipated in the original tabernacle narrative, since it had no foothold in the original priestly document. If this is the case, the arguments for treating Lev 9 and Lev 10 as the products of two different

---

[40] For further examples, see Meshel, *Grammar*, 58 n. 96.

[41] Nihan argues that the promise in Exod 29.43–46, which is widely accepted as belonging to the *Grundschrift*, is only completely fulfilled with both theophanies in Exod 40.34–38 and Lev 9.22–24. He offers three arguments. First, yhwh promises to consecrate tent and altar, but only the tent is mentioned in Exod 40.34–35. The altar experiences the revelation of the divine glory in Lev 9.24. Second, in Exod 40.34 yhwh is veiled by the cloud, so it is only in Lev 9.24 that the people encounter yhwh in his glory (Exod 29.43). Third, Moses' inability to enter the tabernacle (Exod 40.35) is only explicitly lifted in Lev 9.23 when Moses and Aaron enter the tabernacle together. How are such arguments to be assessed? Viewed from the vantage of Lev 9.22–24, they appear compelling. From that perspective, Lev 9.22–24 does indeed appear to supply what Exod 40.34–35 is lacking. But if we do not insist on viewing Exod 40.34–35 through the lens of Lev 9.22–24, it is not obvious that Exod 40.34–35 is defective as a fulfilment of 29.43–46. There is no reason to think that yhwh's theophany in the tent would not have been thought to have consecrated the tent itself and the altar in the court. Nor does it seem likely that the author of Exod 40.35 thought yhwh's appearance in a cloud meant that the Israelites had not encountered him in his glory. Nor is it convincing that any reader would have worried that the tabernacle had become forever off limits by the theophany. Consequently, there is no reason to regard Exod 40 as anything other than an appropriate fulfillment of the promise in Exod 29. For similar criticisms see Boorer, *Vision*, 67–9; Röhrig, *Innerbiblische Auslegung*, 117–29.

[42] Thomas Wagner, *Gottes Herrlichkeit: Bedeutung und Verwendung des Begriffs kābôd im Alten Testament*, VTSup 151 (Leiden: Brill, 2012), 100–4.

[43] The only other occurrences are to be found in Exod 16: vv. 7 and 10. Whilst many scholars would attribute one or both of these verses to P^g (e.g. Boorer, *The Vision of the Priestly Narrative*, 54–8; Ludwig Schmidt, 'Die Priesterschrift in Exodus 16', *ZAW* 119 [2007]: 483–98), the appearance of the glory at this point in the narrative is problematic. It undermines the unique distinction of the tabernacle as the place in which God deigns to dwell, if the glory had already appeared in the desert (Eckart Otto, 'Forschungen zur Priesterschrift', *TRu* 62 [1997]: 15). The sudden appearance in the context of the people's complaint is consistent, however, with the post-priestly narratives in Numbers.

[44] Lev 9.7, 8, 9, 10, 12, 13, 14, 17, 18, 20, 24.

composers have fallen away. This is not yet to have made a case that the two chapters are a compositional unity; such a case depends upon being able to offer a compelling reading of Lev 9–10.

The Failures of Aaron's Sons

The Transgression of Nadab and Abihu (Lev 10.1–2)

Within the space of a few verses, the reader of Lev 9 and 10 is moved from triumph to disaster. The people's awe at the sight of the divine glory entering the tabernacle is turned to silent horror as Aaron's eldest sons are destroyed for their cultic infraction. The relationship between the two events is marked by the expression 'fire came out from YHWH and consumed' (וַתֵּצֵא אֵשׁ מִלִּפְנֵי יְהוָה וַתֹּאכַל; 9.24; 10.2). In the first case, the sacrifices are consumed, in the second, Aaron's sons. For contemporary readers, the juxtaposition of the two events seems incongruous. As we have seen, the apparent incompatibility is sufficient that Achenbach and Nihan insist that the two chapters stem from different hands. Yet, as the repetition of 'fire came out from YHWH and consumed' demonstrates, the events are to be seen together.

I want to go further and suggest that an incense offering is to be expected at this point, if we recognize that Exod 29 has provided the script for Lev 9. In Exod 29, the ordination ritual was followed by instructions for the daily offering (the *tāmîd*) and the promise of divine presence. As we have seen, we can read Lev 9 following the same order, albeit with the daily offering integrated into the eighth-day inauguration ritual which had been modelled on the ordination ritual. But if we continue to follow the script of Exod 29, the promise of YHWH's appearance is followed by an instruction to construct the incense altar upon which a daily offering of incense is to be prepared by Aaron (30.1–10). In Lev 10, too, the theophany is followed by an offering of incense: on this occasion, Nadab and Abihu's illicit act. The literary relationship between the two passages is indicated unambiguously by the appearance of the lexemes זָרָה, 'strange, foreign', and קְטֹרֶת, 'incense', in both passages (Exod 30.9; Lev 10.1). Unfortunately, the existence of this intertextual relationship has too often been overshadowed by discussions about the difference between the 'strange incense', קְטֹרֶת זָרָה, of Exod 30.9 and the 'strange fire', אֵשׁ זָרָה, of Lev 10.1.[45] According to Exod 30, the offering of incense is not in itself an illicit act, but it would appear to be solely Aaron's prerogative: 'Aaron shall burn fragrant

---

[45] It is clearly a little puzzling that Lev 10 should use אֵשׁ זָרָה rather than signal the significance of Exod 30 more clearly by using קְטֹרֶת זָרָה. זָר is frequently used in the priestly literature to refer to unauthorized people who may not approach the sancta (Exod 29.33; 30.33; Lev 22.10, 12, 13; Num 1.51; 3.10, 38; 17.5; 18.4, 7), and Watts suggests that אֵשׁ זָרָה may have been chosen to allude to the אִישׁ זָר of Num 17.5 (Watts, *Leviticus 1–10*, 527). This would not be out of keeping with the chapter's apparent love for paronomasia, such as the play on 'consumed by fire' (9.24; 10.2) and 'those remaining over' (10.12, 16).

224   THE MAKING OF THE TABERNACLE

incense upon it. Every morning when he dresses the lamps he shall offer it, and when he sets up the lamps at twilight he shall offer it' (Exod 30.7–8).

Exodus 30 is not the only text alluded to in the Nadab and Abihu incident, there are also extensive allusions to Korah's rebellion in Num 16–17 in the first two verses of Lev 10.[46]

Table 8.1 Allusions to Korah's rebellion in Lev 10.1–2

Lev 10.1–2	Num 16.6–7, 17–18, 35
וַיִּקְחוּ בְנֵי אַהֲרֹן נָדָב וַאֲבִיהוּא אִישׁ מַחְתָּתוֹ וַיִּתְּנוּ בָהֵן אֵשׁ וַיָּשִׂימוּ עָלֶיהָ קְטֹרֶת וַיַּקְרִבוּ לִפְנֵי יְהוָה אֵשׁ זָרָה אֲשֶׁר לֹא צִוָּה אֹתָם	קְחוּ לָכֶם מַחְתּוֹת קֹרַח וְכָל עֲדָתוֹ: וּתְנוּ בָהֵן אֵשׁ וְשִׂימוּ עֲלֵיהֶן קְטֹרֶת לִפְנֵי יהוה מָחָר
'The sons of Aaron, Nadab and Abihu, <u>each took his censer</u>, and <u>they put fire in it</u> and <u>they placed incense upon it</u>, and <u>they offered before</u> YHWH strange fire that he had not commanded them'.	'<u>Take censers</u>, Korah and all his company, and <u>put fire in them</u> and <u>placed incense upon them</u> before YHWH tomorrow' (vv. 6–7).
	וּקְחוּ אִישׁ מַחְתָּתוֹ וּנְתַתֶּם עֲלֵיהֶם קְטֹרֶת וְהִקְרַבְתֶּם לִפְנֵי יהוה אִישׁ מַחְתָּתוֹ
	'Each one take his censer, and <u>place upon them</u> <u>incense</u> and <u>each one offer</u> his censer <u>before</u> YHWH' (v. 17).
	וַיִּקְחוּ אִישׁ מַחְתָּתוֹ וַיִּתְּנוּ עֲלֵיהֶם אֵשׁ וַיָּשִׂימוּ עֲלֵיהֶם קְטֹרֶת
	'Each one took his censer and <u>they placed fire in</u> <u>them</u> and <u>they put incense upon them</u>' (v. 18).
וַתֵּצֵא אֵשׁ מִלִּפְנֵי יְהוָה וַתֹּאכַל אֹתָם	וְאֵשׁ יָצְאָה מֵאֵת יהוה וַתֹּאכַל אֵת הַחֲמִשִּׁים וּמָאתַיִם אִישׁ מַקְרִיבֵי הַקְּטֹרֶת
'<u>Fire went out from before</u> YHWH and <u>consumed</u> them'.	'<u>Fire went out from</u> YHWH and <u>consumed</u> the 250 men offering incense' (v. 35).

In the story of Korah's rebellion a censer-incense rite functions as a trial by ordeal to identify who may serve as priest. Aaron stands as a representative for his family as do the 250 pretenders for theirs. The consumption of all but Aaron by fire confirms that only his descendants may hold the priestly office: 'no stranger (אִישׁ זָר) may approach to burn incense before YHWH who is not from the seed of Aaron (לֹא מִזֶּרַע אַהֲרֹן)' (17.5). The statement is ambiguous. Does 'from the seed of Aaron' bear an inclusive sense, permitting any Aaronide the right to offer incense, or an exclusive one, restricting incense offerings to the high priest?[47] The Aaron

---

[46] For the relationship between Lev 10 and Num 16–17 see the discussion in Achenbach, 'Der Versagen der Aaroniden', 56–8; Nihan, *Priestly Torah*, 582–6.

[47] Both Achenbach and Nihan think that the narrative restricts the incense offering to the high priest (Achenbach, 'Der Versagen der Aaroniden', 57; Nihan, *Priestly Torah*, 584). For Achenbach, attributing the staff ordeal (Num 17.16–26) to the same compositional level as the offering of incense

of the Korah story could represent the entire priesthood as its titulary head or just the line of the high priests. The story of Nadab and Abihu removes any possible ambiguity.

The reuse of textual material from Exod 30 and Num 16–17 accounts for almost all the lexemes in Lev 10.1–2a. The unique material provides insight into the nature of Nadab and Abihu's infraction. At the beginning of Lev 10.1, the two sons are named: 'the sons of Aaron, Nadab and Abihu', בְּנֵי־אַהֲרֹן נָדָב וַאֲבִיהוּא. The ordering of the names is unusual within the Hebrew Bible, and yet, as far as I am aware, its potential significance has not previously been observed. Where a paternal relationship is indicated, personal names usually occur prior to paternity not afterwards.[48] Reversing the order of the names would appear to be for the purpose of emphasis: Nadab and Abihu are Aaron's sons. They are not Aaron himself. At the end of the Lev 10.1 their ritual action is described as 'strange fire which he had not commanded them' (אֵשׁ זָרָה אֲשֶׁר לֹא צִוָּה אֹתָם). As Heger observes צו'׳ה is used in the priestly literature of affirmative commandments, not prohibitions, and the emphasis would appear to fall on 'them', אֹתָם.[49] It is not that the offering of incense had not been commanded, as Watts seems to suggest,[50] but that *they*—Nadab and Abihu—had not been commanded to offer it.

My reading of Lev 10.1–2 suggests that the Nadab and Abihu incident seeks to resolve an area of uncertainty within the growing Pentateuchal corpus. Was the offering of incense a high priestly prerogative, or could all priests participate? Exod 30 reads as though only Aaron could offer incense. Num 16–17 restricts incense offerings to the descendants of Aaron, though it is unclear whether this right extends to all the Aaronides or just those serving as high priest. In Lev 10, both Exod 30 and Num 16–17 are alluded to, and the story resolves the issue in favour of the view that the incense offering is a high priestly prerogative.

---

in Num 17.5 has an important role in his interpretation of the incense offering (Achenbach, *Die Vollendung der Tora*, 124–9). Nevertheless, there is a strong case for seeing the staff ordeal as a subsequent development (Pyschny, *Verhandelte Führung*, 223–66).

[48] The other exceptions are Gen 34.25; Josh 16.4; and 1 Sam 1.3. The belated mention of Simeon and Levi in Gen 34.25 has been regarded by some literary critics as a secondary insertion that provides an explanation for their condemnation in Gen 49.5–7 (Sigo Lehming, 'Zur Überlieferungsgeschichte von Gen. 34', *ZAW* 70 [1958]: 228–50; Albert de Pury, 'Genèse XXXIV et l'Histoire', *RB* 76 [1969]: 5–49; but for the contrary case, see Erhard Blum, *Die Komposition der Vätergeschichte*, WMANT 57 [Neukirchen-Vluyn: Neukirchener Verlag, 1984], 219). Alternatively, the author appears to be emphasizing that it needed just two of Jacob's sons to conquer an entire town. In Josh 16.4 the unusual order is probably because Manasseh and Ephraim are tribal identifications rather than personal names of individuals. In 1 Sam 1.3 neither Eli, Hophni nor Phinehas have been mentioned in the narrative and the reverse order probably occurs because Eli still lives, but perhaps no longer serves as a priest (A. Graeme Auld, *I & II Samuel: A Commentary*, OTL [Louisville, KY: Westminster John Knox, 2011], 27; Gordon, *I & II Samuel: A Commentary*, 73), which would be less obvious if Eli had appeared merely as a patronym (cf. 𝔊^B's Ἠλὶ καὶ οἱ δύο υἱοὶ αὐτοῦ).

[49] Heger, *Incense Cult*, 58.   [50] Watts, *Ritual and Rhetoric*, 97–129.

226 THE MAKING OF THE TABERNACLE

The Oversight of Eleazar and Ithamar (Lev 10.16–20)

The sobering conversation about sacrificial remains between Aaron and Moses that follows the destruction of Nadab and Abihu suggests that Eleazar and Ithamar are also suspected of cultic malpractice. Moses discovers that the goat of the people's sin-purification offering has been burnt outside the camp, rather than being consumed by the priests in the courtyard. Moses complains that the practice is contrary to the instructions he had given in Lev 4–7 which distinguish between two different types of sin-purification offerings: a *courtyard* sin-purification offering and a *sanctuary* sin-purification offering.[51] The blood of the courtyard sin-purification offering is placed on the horns of the altar of burnt offering in the courtyard (cf. 4.22–35), whilst the blood of the sanctuary sin-purification offering is brought into the tent of meeting and some of it is sprinkled before the veil and placed on the horns of the incense altar (cf. 4.3–21). The meat from the courtyard sin-purification offering was to be eaten by the officiating priest, whilst the meat from the sanctuary sin-purification offering was to be burnt (6.17–23). Since there is no reference to the people's sin-purification offering being brought into the sanctuary during the eighth-day ritual of Lev 9, Moses insists its meat should have been consumed,[52] and holds Aaron's remaining sons responsible for this violation. Yet, as we have seen, Moses accepts Aaron's reply: 'See today they have offered their sin-purification offering and their burnt offering before YHWH, but such things as this have befallen me. If I had eaten a sin-purification offering today, would it have been agreeable to YHWH?' (v. 19). There is an obvious puzzle that this second deviation is permissible when the first was not. Why is this the case? I will argue that it is possible to resolve the interpretive puzzle by examining an intriguing detail of Aaron's reply to Moses that has been overlooked in most examinations of Lev 10: the use of pronominal suffixes with the word חטאת, 'sin-purification offering'.

In his response to Moses, Aaron refers to the sacrifices as 'their sin-purification offering and their burnt offering' (אֶת־חַטָּאתָם וְאֶת־עֹלָתָם), that is, the sin-purification offering and the burnt offering of Eleazar and Ithamar. The sacrificial terms חַטָּאת and עֹלָה do not often take pronominal suffixes in the priestly literature,[53] and their appearance here merits further reflection. Commentators have invariably assumed that these offerings were made on behalf of the entire priesthood, and

---

[51] For further discussion of this distinction, see esp. Gane, *Cult and Character*, 45–90.

[52] As Nihan observes, 'Moses does not simply quote the law, he also comments upon it' (Nihan, *Priestly Torah*, 599). According to Moses, the sin-purification offering bears the iniquity of the congregation and its consumption appears to be an essential act in the atoning of the people.

[53] There are a handful of examples of sacrificial חַטָּאת with suffixes in the book of Numbers (6.16; 15.25; 18.9), but the only other cases in the priestly literature are to be found in Lev 9.7 and 10.19. The word עֹלָה occurs with suffixes in Num 6.16; 10.10; 23.3, 6, 15, 17; 29.39, and in Leviticus only at 9.7; 10.19; 16.24.

were to be distinguished from the offerings made on behalf of the people. To choose just one example, Milgrom informs us that '*their purification offering and burnt offering*...refers to the sacrifices that the priestly household brought on its own behalf'.[54] But if this were the case, why did Aaron not identify the offerings as '*our* sin offering and *our* burnt offering' since they were also made on his behalf? This distinction seems to be meaningful to the exchange, for Moses reproaches only Eleazar and Ithamar of failing to consume the sin-purification offering and does not include Aaron in his accusations.[55]

Aaron's disassociation from his sons' offerings has not been addressed in a satisfactory way by interpreters. Some have passed over the issue in silence,[56] or observed it without offering a solution.[57] One common explanation is to suggest that Eleazer and Ithamar were condemned because the burning of the carcass was their responsibility, not Aaron's.[58] But even if they were especially responsible for burning the carcass—and there is no evidence that they were—Aaron is surely just as responsible for failing to consume it.[59] Milgrom attributes Aaron's language to pathos. 'Aaron omits any mention of himself in order to emphasize the dimensions of the tragedy: his four newly consecrated sons had ministered for the first time and two had died in the effort.'[60] Yet, it is Moses who first accuses Aaron's sons and omits any mention of Aaron. Rendtorff follows Rashi who thought Moses' deflection was due to Aaron's honour as the high priest, though there are other passages in the Pentateuch where Moses is prepared to confront his brother (e.g. Exod 32; Num 12).[61] Nihan offers a literary justification: the accusation is made against the two remaining sons in order to enhance the parallel with the sin of Nadab and Abihu that opens the chapter.[62] This explains the problem away, rather than resolving it.

Given how infrequently חַטָּאת and עֹלָה take pronominal suffixes in the Hebrew Bible, it is striking that one of the other examples is found at the beginning of the section on the inauguration ritual. According to Lev 9.7, Moses instructs Aaron to approach the altar and 'sacrifice your sin-purification offering and your burnt offering' (וַעֲשֵׂה אֶת־חַטָּאתְךָ וְאֶת־עֹלָתֶךָ). As we have already seen, the offerings in the

---

[54] Milgrom, *Leviticus 1–16*, 626.

[55] Rendtorff rightly observes how odd it is that Moses confronts Aaron's sons rather than Aaron himself (Rendtorff, *Leviticus 1,1–10,20*, 318–19). Similarly, Mirguet thinks that Moses' complaint should be directed to Aaron in the first instance rather than his two sons: 'Moïse semble ainsi reprocher aux deux fils une faute qui en fait revient d'abord à leur pére' (Françoise Mirguet, 'Essai d'interprétation de Lévitique 10: le bouc brûlé et non mangé', *ETR* 80 [2005]: 264). This would be the case, if Aaron's offering was the same offering as his sons.

[56] Watts, *Leviticus 1–10*, 546–52.

[57] 'Aaron pointed out that "they" (this must cover Aaron's sons, including Nadab and Abihu, although Aaron himself had been the chief officiant) had indeed presented "their" offering rightly' (Noth, *Leviticus*, 88).

[58] Elliger, *Leviticus*, 138–9.   [59] Cf. Dillmann, *Exodus und Leviticus*, 517.

[60] Milgrom, *Leviticus 1–16*, 626.   [61] Rendtorff, *Leviticus 1,1–10,20*, 319.

[62] Nihan, *Priestly Torah*, 599.

228   THE MAKING OF THE TABERNACLE

inauguration ritual are for Aaron and the people. Thus, when Moses raises an issue about the offerings of Eleazar and Ithamar, it is the people's offerings that are in view. They are not Aaron's offerings. In discussing the offerings of Eleazar and Ithmar, Moses' question pursues precisely the issue that distinguishes the consecration ritual of Lev 8 from the inauguration ritual of Lev 9. In the consecration ritual, the offerings were made for the entire priesthood, and the offerings of Eleazar and Ithamar were those of Aaron. In the inauguration ritual, however, the offerings were for Aaron, on the one hand, and the people, on the other. The offerings of Eleazar and Ithamar were those of the people. Why do the two rituals depart from one another in the beneficiaries of the sacrifices?

The answer would appear to be that the inauguration ritual has been brought into dialogue with the sacrificial regulations in Lev 1–7. According to the sacrificial legislation, the precise animal sacrificed as a sin-purification offering depends on the identity of the person or group for whom it is being offered. The anointed priest or the entire congregation should offer a bull, a ruler a male goat, and an ordinary Israelite a female goat or lamb. The sin-purification offering of the ordination ritual fails to fit into the neat categories provided by Lev 4 since it is made on behalf of Aaron *and his sons*, and not simply for the individual identified as 'the anointed priest' (הַכֹּהֵן הַמָּשִׁיחַ).[63] Thus, the eighth-day ritual can be viewed as a correction of the ordination ritual that seeks to bring it into line with the sacrificial legislation.

But the matter is by no means as simple as correcting the offerer and beneficiary of the sacrifice. As we have seen, the sacrificial legislation distinguishes between two different types of sin-purification offering: a courtyard sin-purification offering and a sanctuary sin-purification offering. Both the offering for the anointed priest and the offering for the entire congregation are instances of the sanctuary sin-purification offering where the blood was sprinkled inside the outer sanctum towards the veil and placed on the horns of the incense altar (Lev 4.3–21). The suet and kidneys are offered on the altar of burnt offering, but the rest of the carcass is burnt outside the camp. No part of the animal was consumed by the priest. In contrast, the offering for the ruler and the offering for the ordinary Israelite are instances of the courtyard sin-purification offering where the blood is placed on the altar of burnt offering and is not brought within the outer sanctum. The suet is burnt, but Lev 4 provides no instructions concerning the rest of the carcass. In Lev 6, however, it is required that the meat is eaten by the priests in the courtyard (vv. 17–23).

The treatment of the sin-purification offering of the consecration ritual in Lev 8, however, fails to accord with the sacrificial legislation of Lev 1–7. The blood of Aaron and his son's sin-purification offering is placed on the horns of the altar of

---

[63] On the basis of Lev 16.32, this expression would appear to refer to the individual elsewhere identified as the 'high priest' (Milgrom, *Leviticus 1–16*, 231).

burnt offering, and is not brought into the outer sanctum. Despite the fact that the blood is only manipulated in the courtyard, the sacrificial remains are burnt outside the camp. Viewed from the perspective of Lev 1–7, the treatment of the sin-purification offering in the consecration ritual confuses the two different types of sin-purification offering that the sacrificial legislation has been at pains to distinguish. The blood is manipulated in the manner of a courtyard sin-purification offering, but the sacrificial remains are treated in the manner of a sanctuary sin-purification offering.

The ritual of the eighth day in Lev 9 replicates the consecration ritual in such a way as to highlight the ways in which the treatment of the sin-purification offering in the consecration ritual diverges from the sacrificial legislation of Lev 4. As we have seen, the equivalent to the sin-purification offering for Aaron and his sons in Lev 8 is the sin-purification offering for Aaron alone partially bringing Lev 9 in line with the sacrificial legislation of Lev 1–7. But the execution of the sin-purification offering follows the procedure of the consecration ritual. The sacrifice is performed in the manner of a courtyard sin-purification offering, and the anomaly is signalled through the placement of the words 'just as YHWH commanded Moses' (כַּאֲשֶׁר צִוָּה יְהוָה אֶת־מֹשֶׁה) prior to the burning up of the sacrificial remains. The deliberate intent of the author is apparent if we set the priesthood's sacrificial offering in the consecration ritual alongside Aaron's sacrificial offering in the eighth-day ritual:

Table 8.2 The sin-purification offering in Lev 8 and Lev 9

8.14 He brought forward the bull of the sin-purification offering. Aaron and his sons laid their hands upon the head of the bull of the sin-purification offering. **15** It was slaughtered and Moses took the blood and place it on the horns of the altar around with his finger, purifying the altar. He poured the blood out at the base of the altar. Thus he consecrated it to make atonement for it. **16** He took all the fat that was around the entrails, the lobe of the liver, and the two kidneys with their fat and Moses burned them on the altar. **17** The bull, its skins, its flesh and its dung he burned with fire outside the camp *just as YHWH commanded Moses* (8.14–17).	**9.8** Aaron approached the altar and he slaughtered the calf of the sin-purification offering that was for himself. **9** Aaron's sons presented him the blood and he dipped his finger in the blood and placed it on the horns of the altar. The blood he poured out at the base of the altar. **10** The fat and the kidneys and the lobe of the liver from the sin-purification offering he burned on the altar *just as YHWH commanded Moses.* **11** The flesh and the skin he burned with fire outside the camp (9.8–11).

The placement of the fulfilment formula in 8.17 highlights the fact that the execution of the consecration ritual in Lev 8 *does* accord with the instructions given to Moses in Exod 29, but the placement of the fulfilment formula in 9.10 highlights the fact that the eighth day ritual departs from the instructions in 6.23. Though some commentators overlook the premature placement of the fulfilment

230   THE MAKING OF THE TABERNACLE

formula in 9.10,[64] Milgrom rightly observes that 'the incineration of the animal's flesh outside the camp, actually violates God's command'.[65]

This anomaly also sheds lights on the brief descriptions of the people's sin-purification offering and burnt offering in 9.15–16. The people's sin-purification offering is said to have been offered 'as the first one' (כָּרִאשֹׁון; v. 15), that is, in the same manner as Aaron's sin-purification offering mentioned a few verses earlier, whilst the burnt offering was sacrificed 'as the regulation' (כַּמִּשְׁפָּט; v. 16). There is no reason why both offerings could not both have been described being offered 'as the first one': in the same manner as Aaron's. The use of different terms would appear to be deliberate.[66] One possibility that has been ventured is that the composer of the chapter was aware of a regulation of the burnt offering, but not of a corresponding one for the sin-purification offering.[67] It would be consistent, however, with the placement of the fulfilment formula in 9.10 if the composer of Lev 9 was yet again highlighting the fact that the offering of the people's sin-purification offering just like Aaron's sin-purification offering is not 'according to the regulation'.[68] It does, however, accord with the sin-purification offering of the ordination ritual (Exod 29; Lev 8); it is, indeed, 'as the first one'. The sacrificial legislation in Lev 1–7, however, would require that the blood of the people's sin-purification offering be brought into the outer sanctum and the carcass burned outside the camp. But, as with Aaron's sin-purification offering, the blood of the people's sin-purification offering is only manipulated in the courtyard. By implication the carcass was incinerated as was the case with Aaron's sacrifice, rather than being consumed by the priests as we would have expected for a courtyard sin-purification offering.

Having examined the relationship that the inauguration ritual of Lev 9 has with both sacrificial legislation of Lev 1–7 and the consecration ritual of Lev 8, we can now return to the disagreement between Moses and Aaron about the sacrificial remains (10.16–20). The encounter begins with Moses' enquiry about the sacrificial remains of the people's sin-purification offering. The answer is already clear from 9.15. The carcass has been burnt outside the camp, as was done with Aaron's sin-purification offering. Milgrom struggles with the question of why it is that Moses was unaware of what had happened to the carcass. 'Why did Moses need to inquire? He must have known what happened, for he had supervised Aaron and his sons during the entire sacrificial ritual! The answer might be that

---

[64] E.g. Watts, *Leviticus 1–10*, 494; Wenham, *Leviticus*, 149.   [65] Milgrom, *Leviticus 1–16*, 580.
[66] Benedikt Jürgens, *Heiligkeit und Versöhnung: Levitikus 16 in seinem literarischen Kontext*, HBS 28 (Freiburg im Breisgau: Herder, 2001), 257.
[67] See Nihan, *Priestly Torah*, 117, 154.
[68] Jürgens rightly observes that 'diese Formulierung könnte somit als subtiler Hinweis auf den in Lev 10 erzählten Konflikt zwischen Mose und Aaron gedeutet werden' (Jürgens, *Heiligkeit und Versöhnung*, 257).

Moses had left the sanctuary to summon Mishael and Elzaphan, during which time the purification carcass was burnt, or that it was not the function of the high priest (or any priest!) to burn the purification carcass.'[69] Such rationalizations are unnecessary. The literary purpose of Moses' enquiry is to draw attention to the anomaly, and as we have seen this is entirely consistent with certain features of Lev 9 including the premature fulfilment formula (9.11) and the reference to the offering of the sin-purification offering 'as the first one' rather than 'as the regulation' (9.15–16).

When he discovers the carcass had been burnt, Moses accuses Eleazar and Ithamar of failing to comply with the instructions he gave in Lev 6.17–23. In the face of this accusation of his sons, Aaron intervenes with the words, 'See today they have offered their sin-purification offering and their burnt offering before YHWH, but such things as this have befallen me. If I had eaten a sin-purification offering today, would it have been agreeable to YHWH?' (v. 19). As I have shown, Eleazar and Ithamar's offerings—'their sin-purification offering and their burnt offering'—is not a reference to sacrifices on behalf of the priesthood as scholars have usually assumed. The first set of sacrifices of the inauguration ritual were offered on behalf of Aaron alone; his sons were not included. What must be in view is the people's sacrifices that follow. But why refer to it as Eleazar and Ithamar's offerings rather than the people's? Such an identification highlights the fact that the people's offerings must also have included Aaron's sons, since Aaron's offerings were for him alone. If this is the case, precisely the same problems arise with the people's sin-purification offering as also arise with Aaron's sin-purification offering. Should it conform to the regulations in Lev 4—the sin-purification offering for the people—and its blood brought into the sanctuary or should it confirm to the instructions for the ordination ritual in Exod 29—the sin-purification offering for Aaron and his sons—and its blood placed on the altar of burnt offering? The description of the offerings as 'their sin-purification offering and their burnt offering' highlights precisely the interpretive uncertainty that 'the people's sin-purification offering and burnt offering' would not have done.

The opening sentence of Aaron's reply seems to be that, despite the atoning significance of both sacrifices, Aaron's family has still suffered YHWH's wrath. If the logic about blood not being brought into the sanctuary applies to the people's sin-purification offering, it equally applies to the high priest's sin-purification offering. Yet, Moses did not demur in Lev 9, though it was explicitly stated that the carcass of Aaron's sin-purification offering was burnt outside the camp (v. 11). Not only that, but the appearance of the divine fire at the end of the chapter would appear to signal divine approval. Aaron's reply confronts Moses with the

---

[69] Milgrom, *Leviticus 1–16*, 622.

232   THE MAKING OF THE TABERNACLE

interpretive quandary facing Aaron and his sons. In light of the fact that the existing Torah gives two contradictory rules, and God's approbation had already been indicated by the appearance of his glory, Moses is forced to express himself satisfied.

Prerogatives and Responsibilities of High Priests and Priests

Despite their differences, the two conundrums that we have examined in Lev 10 share a common element. They revolve around the question of what rules apply to the high priest alone and what apply to the whole class of priests. The story of Nadab and Abihu's destruction leaves the reader in no doubt that the offering of incense is the prerogative of the high priest alone (vv. 1–2). The discussion between Moses and Aaron about the sacrificial remains addresses an anomaly that arises from having a sin-purification offering sacrificed on behalf of the entire priesthood. The anomaly introduced by the ordination ritual is accepted, but the sacrificial legislation that distinguishes between high priest and the rest of the priesthood is affirmed as the norm (כַּמִּשְׁפָּט). An examination of the remainder of the chapter shows that it too is concerned with the prerogatives and responsibilities of the priesthood.

Beginning in v. 3, we find the author's taste for wordplay in evidence. Commenting on the deaths of Nadab and Abihu, Moses refers to a divine epigram:

Through those who are near me, I will be sanctified (בִּקְרֹבַי אֶקָּדֵשׁ)

and before all the people, I will be glorified (וְעַל־פְּנֵי כָל־הָעָם אֶכָּבֵד).[70]

Moses' claim that 'this is what YHWH said' has caused some consternation because there is no precise parallel to the statement earlier in the Pentateuch. Whilst many interpreters have construed Moses's introduction as a present tense, 'this is what YHWH is saying',[71] it is more convincing to see here a repurposing of Exod 29.43 in order to explain the dramatic punishment of Nadab and Abihu.[72]

---

[70] For the epigram as poetry see Rendtorff, *Leviticus 1,1–10,20,* 310–11; Elliger, *Leviticus,* 133. Milgrom is right to argue that this does not justify equating 'all the people' with 'those who draw near to me' (Milgrom, *Leviticus 1–16,* 601) for as Ehrlich observes 'כל העם kontrastiert mit קרובי' (Ehrlich, *Randglossen,* 34).

[71] Milgrom, *Leviticus 1–16,* 600; Ehrlich, *Randglossen,* 34; Rendtorff, *Leviticus 1,1–10,20,* 310.

[72] See, e.g., Christian Frevel, '"Und Mose hörte (es), und es war gut in seinen Augen" (Lev 10,20): Zum Verhältnis von Literargeschichte, Theologiegeschichte und innerbiblischer Auslegung am Beispiel von Lev 10', in *Gottes Name(n): Zum Gedanken an Erich Zenger,* eds. Ilse Mülner, Ludwig Schwienhorst-Schönberger, and Ruth Scoralik, HBS 71 (Freiburg im Breisgau: Herder, 2012), 116–17; Ederer, *Identitätsstiftende Begegnung,* 250–8. Nihan argues that Lev 10.3 is best understood as 'a comment reapplying the general statement of 22.32 to the priestly class' (Nihan, *Priestly Torah,* 588), but

Table 8.3 A comparison of Lev 10.3 and Exod 29.43

Lev 10.3	Exod 29.43
בקרבי <u>אקדש</u> <u>ועל־פני כל־העם אכבד</u>	ונעדתי שמה <u>לבני ישראל</u> <u>ונקדש בכבדי</u>
By those who are near me, I will be sanctified, and before all the people, I will be glorified.	I will meet with the Israelites there, And it shall be sanctified by my glory.

Thus, the two words that make up the phrase 'sanctified by my glory', וְנִקְדַּשׁ בִּכְבֹדִי are distributed amongst the bicola and the common P expression 'the sons of Israel', בְּנֵי יִשְׂרָאֵל, is replaced with 'all the people', כָּל־הָעָם, part of the distinctive diction of Lev 9–10.[73] The adjective קרוב corresponds to the notion of meeting (ונעדתי שמה). It is appropriate as a reference to the priests since they were the ones brought, קר"ב, to the sanctuary in the ordination ritual (Exod 28.1; 29.10). But the consonantal text בקרבי could be understood in a number of different ways. Should it be read with the Masoretic pointing as בִּקְרֹבַי, 'those near to me', that is the priesthood, or pointed as בִּקְרֹבִי, 'the one near to me', that is the high priest?[74] Since the distinction between the high priest and the rest of the priesthood is central to the chapter, the ambiguity in the consonantal text may be intentional.

After Moses has spoken to Aaron, he orders two cousins of Aaron, Mishael and Elzaphan, to remove the bodies of Nadab and Abihu from the sanctuary. The disposal of the bodies outside the camp appears to extend the analogy that is being made at various points in Lev 10 between the priests and the sacrificial offerings since outside the camp was the location where the remains of the sanctuary sin-purification offering (4.12, 21) and the ashes from the burnt offering (6.4) were deposited. The allusion to the same location points back to the complete consumption of Nadab and Abihu like fire in the manner of a burnt offering, but also gestures forwards to Moses's question about the disposal of the people's sin-purification offering. The removal of the corpses by means of their vestments led to considerable speculation amongst ancient and medieval interpreters about how the bodies of Nadab and Abihu could have remained intact after being consumed by fire.[75] Modern commentators have also wondered about the significance of this small detail. Watts discerns the avoidance of corpse contamination, whilst

---

the two verses are only related by an appearance of the *niphal* קד"ש, which also occurs in Exod 29.43. Problematically, Lev 22.32 occurs after Lev 10 and Moses's words appear to be alluding to an existing divine oracle.

[73] See, esp., Lev 9.23–24.

[74] The Masoretic pointing might also be understood as impersonal, 'those things near to me', that is the sacrificial offerings.

[75] See Milgrom, *Leviticus 1–16*, 606.

234   THE MAKING OF THE TABERNACLE

Milgrom argues that though the vestments had been sprinkled with oil through-out the ordination ritual (8.30), they did not share the same level of consecration as other sancta.[76] The reference to the vestments should, however, be understood as indexing Nadab and Abihu's status as common priests. In Exod 28–29 and Lev 8, the vestments of Aaron and his sons are differentiated. They are dressed in their vestments as part of the ordination ritual, but no restrictions are placed on where they may be worn. As we have seen, in Lev 16 a slightly different view of the high priest's vestments is set forth. On the occasions when Aaron is to make atone-ment in the inner sanctum, he is to wear a special set of vestments that he is to divest at the end of the ritual (vv. 4, 23–24). The fact that Nadab and Abihu can be removed from the sanctuary in their vestments highlights the fact that they are not the high priest and were not permitted to offer incense.

Moses's instructions to Aaron's remaining sons, Eleazar and Ithamar, in vv. 6–7 addresses a further problem that stems from the ordination ritual. Moses prohib-its Aaron's sons from participating in the mourning rituals for Nadab and Abihu, and forbids them from leaving the sanctuary whilst they bear the anointing oil. It has often been observed that the instructions are almost identical to 21.10–12, but with one striking difference: 'in H, this law applies to the high priest exclu-sively, whereas for the other priests the mourning custom is actually the same as for the rest of the community (cf. 21.6, and compare with 19.27–28a)'.[77] The justi-fication for these injunctions is the same in both texts: they have been anointed (10.7; 21,10). In the Holiness Code it is assumed that only one priest has been anointed with oil, and it is only to this priest that the strictures against mourning apply. Yet, according to the ordination ritual in Exod 29 and Lev 8, Aaron and his sons were anointed with oil. Both texts are harmonized by insisting that the rules of Lev 21 apply to Eleazar and Ithamar.

The divine speech that follows in vv. 8–11 is unusual for being addressed to Aaron alone. The only other place where this occurs in the Pentateuch is in Num 18, and the concern in that chapter with establishing the rights and responsibil-ities of the priests provides an important clue to the purpose of these verses in Lev 10.[78] Whilst Noth regarded the section as 'quite unrelated to this context',[79] recent scholarship has emphasized the centrality of vv. 10–11 for establishing the role of the priests as teachers of Torah.[80] These verses give Aaron and the priests the authority to rule on matters of legal interpretation as will occur in vv. 16–20, but, as Nathan Hays has recently emphasized, they also anticipate the role of the priests in the subsequent purity legislation (Lev 11–15).[81] Although the purity legislation speaks of 'the priest' (הַכֹּהֵן), the divine speech to Aaron confirms that

---

[76] Watts, *Leviticus 1–10*, 533; Milgrom, *Leviticus 1–16*, 606.   [77] Nihan, *Priestly Torah*, 589.
[78] Watts, *Leviticus 1–10*, 537.   [79] Noth, *Leviticus*, 86.
[80] See, e.g., Nihan, *Priestly Torah*, 590–3.
[81] Nathan Hays, 'The Redactional Reassertion of the Priestly Role in Leviticus 10–16', *ZAW* 130 (2018): 175–88.

this is to be understood as a generic expression for 'any priest' and not simply 'the high priest' (cf. Lev 13.2).[82] Thus, the divine speech not only binds the chapter together around the theme of the teaching authority of the priests and links it to the legislative material that follows, but also clarifies their precise responsibilities.

It has proved rather more difficult to explain why the prohibition of alcohol to the priests serving in the tabernacle should occur in v. 9. Two solutions were already proposed in rabbinic literature and find proponents even today: one is to identify drunkenness on duty as the cause of Nadab and Abihu's destruction, though there is no mention of intoxication in vv. 1–3,[83] whilst another is that alcohol is forbidden because of its association with mourning (Prov 31.6).[84] A number of literary-critical scholars, however, have observed that a similar order of prescriptions are found in Ezek 44—prohibition of mourning, prohibition of alcohol consumption, responsibility for teaching—and argued that Lev 10 has incorporated a piece of Zadokite legislation.[85] Despite its popularity, this proposal encounters a number of difficulties. First, it does not explain the order of the pre-scriptions, it merely relocates the problem to Ezek 44. Second, as we have seen, the prohibition of mourning and the instructions about priestly teaching are more at home in Lev 10. Third, Ezek 44 shows clear influence of the Holiness Code in its emphasis on the Sabbath (v. 24) and its mixture of rules are best explained not as a vestige of Zadokite legislation, but as a creative blend of Pentateuchal legislation, including Lev 10 and 21.[86]

What has not been observed, and needs some explanation, is the fact that these prohibitions against alcohol consumption only occur in two very late texts: Lev 10 and Ezek 44. Whilst an earlier text like Isa 28.7 criticizes priests and prophets for being befuddled by wine and strong drink, this is not a condemnation of any alcoholic consumption. It could even be evidence that alcoholic consumption was common in cultic ritual, but the prophet was concerned by intoxication.[87]

---

[82] The mention of Aaron and his sons in 13.2 can easily be identified as a redactional element that integrates the purity legislation into the literary context of Leviticus (Elliger, *Leviticus*, 159; Nihan, *Priestly Torah*, 270). The identification of the priest as Aaron or his sons occurs at the crucial location in 13.2 for skin disease is the first case where the priests need to make a judgement about purity. 'In other words, to any priest. There is no need to travel to a main sanctuary. To be sure, the text could simply have stated *'el-hakkōhēn* "to the priest" (vv 3, 4, 5, 6, 7, etc). But that expression might have been misinterpreted as referring to Aaron' (Milgrom, *Leviticus 1–16*, 776).

[83] Rashi on Lev 10.2 and Ramban on Lev 10.9 (Carasik, *Leviticus*, 62, 65), Kiuchi, *Leviticus*, 182. Hartley thinks that v. 9 was probably included by the final editor who thought that intoxication played some role in the transgression, though v. 1 is more concerned with the sons seeking to usurp their father (John E. Hartley, *Leviticus*, WBC 4 [Dallas, TX: Word, 1992], 133, 135).

[84] Abarbanel (Carasik, *Leviticus*, 65); Wenham, *Leviticus*, 158; Rendtorff, *Leviticus 1,1–10,20*, 314.

[85] Noth, *Leviticus*, 86; Achenbach, 'Der Versagen der Aaroniden'; Nihan, *Priestly Torah*, 590–3; Röhrig, *Innerbiblische Auslegung*, 162–7.

[86] MacDonald, *Priestly Rule*, 63–92. The strongest piece of evidence for the dependence of Lev 10 on Ezek 44 is the fact that Lev 10.9 has ושכר יין where Ezek 44.21 has just יין. Whilst the longer text would usually be evidence of a developed text, it is not difficult for a single word to have been lost in the process of transmission.

[87] Hans Wildberger, *Isaiah 28–39: A Commentary*, CC (Minneapolis, MN: Fortress, 1991), 20.

236 THE MAKING OF THE TABERNACLE

A prohibition of alcoholic consumption would also be inconsistent with the Deuteronomic encouragement to bring wine and strong drink alongside the animal offerings to the sacrificial repast (Deut 14.26).[88] If there is little to commend seeing prohibition of alcohol to priests as a traditional injunction, the opposite is true for the Nazirites. In every reference to the Nazirites in the Hebrew Bible, the renunciation of alcohol is present, frequently using the word-pair שכר–יין.[89] In the priestly regulations for the Nazirite in Num 6, we have two important links to Lev 10 which suggests that the Nazirite legislation provides the most likely explanation of the appearance of the prohibition of alcohol in Lev 10.9. First, the Nazirite legislation lays upon the Nazirite the requirement to renounce wine and strong drink, to let their hair grew long and to avoid corpses and mourning (Num. 6.2–8). These requirements parallel those required of the priests in Lev 10. Second, the requirements upon the Nazirites appear to have been composed so as to accentuate the similarities with the high priest.[90] A compelling way of explaining these two observations is that the Nazirite legislation was composed in light of the regulations concerning the high priest in Lev 21, and the requirement that the Nazirite avoid alcohol was then projected back onto the requirements for the priests. The textual trigger for this assimilation to the Nazirite's renunciation of alcohol was the injunction upon Aaron and his sons not to mourn or dishevel their hair (v. 6) and the alcohol prohibition provided a segue to the crucial emphasis on the priest's role in instructing the people about holiness and purity (vv. 10–11), based on the fear that intoxication might impair the priests' judgement.[91]

The instructions about the sacrificial remains in vv. 12–15 deal with various anomalies that arise when Lev 8 is read within the larger literary context of Leviticus. The first instructions in vv. 12–13 concern the grain offering and Moses's words reiterate the rule in Lev 6.7–11. The only deviation is the specification that the grain offering has to be consumed 'besides the altar' (אֵצֶל הַמִּזְבֵּחַ), a location that is otherwise identified as the place where the ashes from the burnt offering are placed after their removal from the altar and before their disposal outside the camp (6.3). The description of the location provides further precision about what it means to eat the grain offering 'in the court of the tent of meeting' (בַּחֲצַר אֹהֶל־מוֹעֵד; 6.9). Why was this brief and unassuming specification necessary? In the ordination ritual, Aaron and his sons also dine, but in a different location:

---

[88] 1 Sam 1.14 and Amos 2.8 could also be interpreted as evidence that alcohol was consumed at sanctuaries during cultic festivals.

[89] Num 6.3–4; 1 Sam 1.11 (LXX and 4Q51 [4QSamᵃ]); Judg 13.4, 7. Amos 2.11 is perhaps the oldest references to the Nazirite and simply refers to יין.

[90] Milgrom, *Numbers*, 44; Diether Kellermann, *Die Priesterschrift von Numeri 1,1 bis 10,10: literarkritisch und traditionsgeschichtlich untersucht*, BZAW 120 (Berlin: de Gruyter, 1970), 85–6; Horst Seebass, *Numeri 1,1–10,10*, BKAT 4/1 (Neukirchen-Vluyn: Neukirchener Verlag, 2012), 158; Achenbach, *Die Vollendung der Tora*, 510.

[91] Watts, *Leviticus 1–10*, 538.

'the entrance to the tent of meeting' (פֶּתַח אֹהֶל מוֹעֵד; 8.31). This space is entirely suited to their liminal status during the ordination rite. Nevertheless, lest it be deduced from this that the entrance to the tent of meeting was the appropriate place for the priests to consume the sacrificial remains during the ordinary running of the tabernacle cult—it was instead the place where animals were presented for offering by the lay Israelites—Moses insists that the grain offering is to be consumed 'besides the altar'.[92]

The second set of instructions in vv. 14–15 concerns the amity offering and presents a more complicated case than the grain offering. As was the case with the grain offering, Moses' words reiterate directives that he has previously given, in this case the instructions about the priestly portions of the amity offering in 7.28–34. These instructions assign the brisket to the priesthood in general and the right thigh to the priest who conducted the sacrifice. The brisket undergoes a ritual action in which it is presented (תְּנוּפָה) to the deity, whilst the right thigh is simply set aside (תְּרוּמָה) for the offering priest and does not undergo any ritual action.[93] Although v. 14 appears to maintain that distinction by referring to 'the

---

[92] My understanding of the פֶּתַח אֹהֶל מוֹעֵד differs from that of Milgrom. For Milgrom, the פתח אהל מועד encompasses the entire courtyard from the entrance of the courtyard to the entrance of the tent (Milgrom, *Leviticus 1–16*, 147). Milgrom's reasons that since the laity bring their offerings to the altar, they were not prevented from accessing any part of the court. Milgrom's arguments depend on understanding the placement of the altar of burnt offering in the centre of the court (see the plan in Milgrom, *Leviticus 1–16*, 135). As Watts rightly points out, 'no text requires such a symmetrical arrangement' (Watts, *Leviticus 1–10*, 201).

[93] Traditionally, the two manipulations were rendered into English as the 'wave offering' and the 'heave offering', translations that drew on rabbinic discussion. The decisive step in resolving the confusion was Jacob Milgrom's philological observation that whilst תְּנוּפָה was done 'before YHWH' (לִפְנֵי יהוה), the תְּרוּמָה is 'for YHWH' (ליהוה). On the basis of his observation, Milgrom argued that the תְּנוּפָה is to be understood as a ritual act that was performed in the sanctuary to objects that could be offered within the Israelite cult. Offerings subject to תְּנוּפָה include the suet and right thigh of the ordination ram together with its bread offerings (Exod 29.23; Lev 8.26–27), the brisket of the ordination ram (Exod 29.26; Lev 8.29), the brisket of the amity offering (Lev 7.30; 9.21; 10.14–15; Num 6.20; 18.18), the lamb of the skin-diseased individual's reparation offering together with its oil (Lev 14.12, 21, 24), the sheaf of the first-fruits (Lev 23.11, 15), the bread and lambs of the feast of weeks (Lev 23.17, 20), and the meal offering of the woman suspected of adultery (Num 5.25). The תְּרוּמָה, on the other hand, is not a ritual act done in the temple. Rather it is the setting aside of a donation 'for YHWH', and the donation need not be brought into the sanctuary. It can be applied to a broader range of objects. This includes not only sacrificial offerings, such as the right thigh of the consecration ram (Exod 29.27), the right thigh of the wellbeing offering (Lev 7.32, 34) and the bread of the thank-offering (Lev 7.14), but also monetary gifts, such as the census silver (Exod 30.13–15), the tithe of the tithe (Num 18.24–29) and the spoils from war (Num 31.29, 41, 52) (Jacob Milgrom, 'Hattĕnûpâ', in *Studies in Cultic Theology and Terminology*, SJLA 36 [Leiden: Brill, 1983], 139–58; Jacob Milgrom, 'The Alleged Wave-Offering in Israel and in the Ancient Near East', *IEJ* 22 [1972]: 33–8; Jacob Milgrom, 'The Šôq Hattĕrûmâ: A Chapter in Cultic History', in *Studies in Cultic Theology and Terminology*, SJLA 36 [Leiden: Brill, 1983], 159–70).

Baruch Levine translates תְּנוּפָה as 'presentation offering' (Levine, *Numbers*, I: 276). Milgrom rejects the traditional translation 'wave offering', understood as a motion back and forth, and proposed 'elevation offering'. Whilst this has become the accepted translation of תְּנוּפָה in much anglophone scholarship, Milgrom's account fails to explain why the rabbis—but not the Targumists—misunderstood the meaning of the root נו״ף and overlooks occurrences of נו״ף, such as Isa 10.15ba (with הַמַּשּׂוֹר 'the saw'), where 'elevate' makes no sense, but 'move back and forth' would. Milgrom rightly draws attention to Egyptian texts and reliefs where offerings are presented to the deity. The biblical ritual of תנופה

238 THE MAKING OF THE TABERNACLE

brisket that is presented' (חֲזֵה הַתְּנוּפָה) and 'the thigh that is set aside' (שׁוֹק הַתְּרוּמָה), the distinction is obscured in v. 15 for both portions are described as undergoing the presentation ritual. The same confusion is also present in 9.21.[94] The origins of this departure from the clear presentation of Lev 7 is again to be traced back to the ordination ceremony in Lev 8 for during the offering of the ordination offering, the bread, fat and right thigh are presented (v. 27) and the brisket is also presented (v. 29). In the ordination ritual, the right thigh is immolated, and the brisket is Moses' prebend since he functions in place of a priest. If we return to the instructions in Lev 10.14–15, we can see that their purpose is to harmonize the instructions for the ordination offering with those of the amity offering.[95] In accordance with Lev 7, the brisket is presented and the thigh set aside, but in accordance with Lev 8, both are presented. In the logic of Lev 7 this makes no sense, for the thigh is set aside and removed from the sphere of sacred offerings, whilst the brisket is subject to a rite that sees it offered to the deity in a gesture of presentation. It is part of a confusion of the rite of presentation (תְּנוּפָה) and the act of setting aside (תְּרוּמָה) that becomes common in late texts of the priestly literature.[96]

Conclusion

The story of everything that transpires on the eighth day seeks to distinguish more precisely the competencies and prerogatives of the high priest from those of the rest of the priesthood. While some of the differences between the high priest and the priesthood may have been eliminated by requiring that all priests be anointed, the incense offerings remain a task that only the high priest may perform. As we have seen, the story of Korah's rebellion generated some ambiguity on this issue by excluding any but Aaron's descendants from offering incense. The sin of Nadab and Abihu is told so as to anticipate the later rebellion and to leave no doubt that the offering incense was a high priestly prerogative.

The eighth day ritual highlights the anomalies that result from performing the ordination ritual in light of the sacrificial legislation of Lev 1–7. The ordinary priests find themselves in a liminal position. They are included with Aaron in the sacrifices for the priesthood during the seven days of consecration, but are

---

similarly seems to have involved some motion in the direction of YHWH's presence, perhaps both lifted forwards and upwards from the offerer's chest before being brought back.

[94] Milgrom rightly observes that the Hebrew text is problematic. 'Briskets' (הֶחָזוֹת) is plural as befits the act that an ox and a ram have been offered, but the 'right thigh' (שׁוֹק הַיָּמִין) is singular. A plausible explanation is that the 'right thigh' is a gloss (Milgrom, 'Šôq Hattĕrûmâ', 164).

[95] It might be thought possible for the composer of Lev 9–10 to have distinguished the ordination offering from the amity offering. It would appear, however, that the ordination offering was modelled on the amity offering and understood as a variant of it. See further Nihan, Priestly Torah, 597 n. 86.

[96] MacDonald, 'Scribalism and Ritual Innovation'.

excluded from the high priest's offering on the day of the sanctuary's inauguration. On the eighth day, the ordinary priests are numbered with the people, and Aaron stands in complete isolation. He performs all the sacrifices with the assistance of his sons. He alone blesses the people, and together he and Moses enter the tent of meeting (9.1–24). The glorious theophany is an unambiguous affirmation of the pre-eminence of Aaron the high priest. The significance of this passage was not lost on Ben Sira who echoes the scene in his paean to Simon II (Sirach 50). The destruction of Aaron's sons by fire is not a piece of anti-Aaronide polemic as Achenbach would have it. On the contrary, it communicates the high priest's superiority to any other priest.

9

Leaders, Levites, and a Kingdom of Priests

Embedded within the final chapters of Exodus and the opening chapters of Leviticus are no fewer than three iterations of the ordination ritual. The earliest of these is found in Exod 29 which prescribes a complex collection of rites that can be accomplished in an afternoon and successfully ordain the priests for cultic service. In Lev 8 this has been retold as a ritual that consecrates both priests and sanctuary over a seven-day period. Finally, in Lev 9 the ordination ritual has been reworked as an inauguration ritual on the eighth day which initiates the public cult. On the one hand, these variations upon one ritual can be seen as an attempt to harmonize differences between the ordination ritual and other ceremonies that were perceived to have a close relationship to it, such as the great atonement ritual of Lev 16 and the altar consecration ritual known from texts like Ezek 43. On the other hand, they also provide an important location for reflecting upon the rights and competencies of the high priest, the priesthood, and the other Israelites.

In this chapter, I will argue that within the larger expanse of the Pentateuch we encounter two further reprises of the ordination ritual. One is found in Num 7–10, where a deformation of the Pentateuch's narrative progression allows for the inauguration of the tabernacle to be retold with a focus on the leaders and the Levites. The dedication of the Levites parallels the ordination of the priests in several respects. The second is found in Exod 24. It does not retell the events of the tabernacle's inauguration, but has been placed so as to preface the entire priestly account of the revelation at Sinai. Consequently, it provides an interpretive lens for the tabernacle account that follows in subsequent chapters. According to Exod 24, a blood ritual occurred at the foot of the mountain which involved dashing the people and an altar with blood. This ceremony has been understood in various ways, but the similarities to the ordination ritual have increasingly been recognized. Both of these different iterations of the ordination ritual provide additional dimensions to the portrayal of the priesthood's supremacy.

Retelling the Tabernacle's Inauguration (Num 7–10)

The exchange between Moses and Aaron about the consumption of the sin-purification offering brings the dramatic narrative about the eighth day to a close (Lev 10.16–20). The chapters that follow shift to a different mode of discourse:

The Making of the Tabernacle and the Construction of Priestly Hegemony. Nathan MacDonald, Oxford University Press.
© Nathan MacDonald 2023. DOI: 10.1093/oso/9780198813859.003.0010

they provide various instructions for the people to ensure their purity and holiness. A reader would naturally assume that these regulations were delivered to Moses, or to Moses and Aaron, after the deaths of Nadab and Abihu.[1] Except for a brief narrative about a man with Egyptian and Israelite heritage who blasphemed the name (24.10–23), the narrative thread is not developed further until the book of Numbers. By this point, the reader is led to understand that a full month has passed since the tabernacle was erected: 'YHWH spoke to Moses in the wilderness of Sinai in the tent of meeting on the first day of the second month in the second year after they had come out of the land of Egypt' (Num 1.1). With the operation of the tabernacle firmly established, Moses receives instructions about the census of the people and the ordering of the wider camp (Num 1–4).

At the beginning of Num 7, however, the reader is thrust back an entire month: 'on the day Moses completed setting up the tabernacle…' (וַיְהִי בְּיוֹם כַּלּוֹת מֹשֶׁה לְהָקִים אֶת־הַמִּשְׁכָּן; v. 1). The verse clearly alludes to Exodus 40: 'in the first month on the second year, on the first day of the month, the tabernacle was set up' (וַיְהִי בַּחֹדֶשׁ הָרִאשׁוֹן בַּשָּׁנָה הַשֵּׁנִית בְּאֶחָד לַחֹדֶשׁ הוּקַם הַמִּשְׁכָּן; 40.17, cf. v. 1) the date on which 'Moses finished the work' (וַיְכַל מֹשֶׁה אֶת־הַמְּלָאכָה; v. 33). This chronological shift is maintained for a handful of chapters. The request for further directions to address the situation of some of the people being ritually unclean during the Passover must have occurred during the first month, and the description of the pillar of fire and cloud makes reference to the first day of Nisan: 'on the day the tabernacle was set up' (וּבְיוֹם הָקִים אֶת־הַמִּשְׁכָּן; 9.15). From this verse onwards, however, the book of Numbers returns to anticipating the departure of the Israelites from Sinai and their journey through the wilderness and the original chronological sequence of the book is clearly resumed with the departure of the Israelites from the wilderness of Sinai on the twentieth day of the second month (Num 10.11).

The chronological shift found in Num 7.1–10.11 is unusual within the Pentateuch. From its majestic opening lines in Gen 1 until the death of Moses in Deut 34, the Pentateuch typically sets forth a narrative that moves forward through time. Retrospects may be offered by characters within the narrative, most notably by Moses in Deuteronomy, but these are portrayed as recollections and remain within the chronological framework. As we have seen, however, a plausible case can be made for seeing the events of Lev 1–10 as the result of a similar chronological shift, retelling the events leading up to and occurring on the first of Nisan. The effect of Num 7.1–10.11 is to revisit the events around the erection and consecration of the tabernacle a further time, but with very different emphases.

---

[1] In the case of the instructions about the day of atonement in Lev 16 this is made explicit: 'YHWH spoke to Moses after the death of the two sons of Aaron when they approached YHWH and died. YHWH said to Moses…' (vv. 1–2).

Explaining the Chronological Shift

The unusual shift in chronology in Num 7.1–10.11 has long been observed and various solutions have been proposed. Dillmann argued that the offerings of the leaders originally belonged either at the end of Exod 40 or Lev 10, and had been relocated to the book of Numbers in the final redaction of the Pentateuch.[2] One difficulty with this proposal is that the offerings of the leaders presuppose Num 1, and consequently Dillmann has to argue that the account was reworked at the same time as it was relocated. A second difficulty is that Dillmann provides no explanation for why the final redactor should have chosen to relocate the account of the leaders' offerings from its natural chronological location. Levine also reaches for a redactional solution, but he argues that Num 9.1 with its reference to the first month must have 'appeared in the text of Numbers before the opening caption of the book was added'.[3] This does not resolve the problem, it merely relocates it: why would an author or editor have mentioned the second month in Num 1.1, if there was a reference to the first month a few chapters later? Milgrom proposes that בְּיוֹם in 7.1 should be understood as indefinite, and a suitable English translation would be a vaguer 'when Moses finished setting up the tabernacle'.[4] This proposal was already anticipated by Gray, who rightly observed that despite 'when' being a legitimate translation of בְּיוֹם the allusions to the specific occasion of Exod 40 preclude such an indefinite rendering.[5] Davies regards the dating as evidence of an inattentive editor.[6] However, the importance of dates within the book of Numbers and the insistence with which the composer of Num 7–10 dates these events prior to Num 1–4 suggests that this is no accident.[7] Kellermann argues that although the material in Num 7–10 naturally belongs in Exodus or Leviticus, the text of those books was already fixed and consequently these

---

[2] August Dillmann, *Die Bücher Numeri, Deuteronomium und Josua*, KeHAT (Leipzig: Hirzel, 1886), 39. The same problem is also encountered in the account of the first remembrance of Passover. Whilst Dillmann entertains the possibility that the same dynamics of textual rearrangement were also found in Num 9, he judges it more probable that the final redactor chose to locate here a short account of a Passover in the second month for those who had been impure in the first month (Dillmann, *Numeri*, 46).

[3] Levine, *Numbers*, I: 295. Levine appears to view the reference in 7.1 as less problematic, regarding it as a vague reference to the time after the consecration of the tabernacle. 'This chapter carries forward the chronology of Exodus 40 and of Numbers 1. It dates the events it records in the second year after the Exodus, though it is not entirely clear in which month of that year.' (Levine, *Numbers*, I: 247, cf. 253).

[4] Milgrom, *Numbers*, 53, 362–4. For the case of 9.1, Milgrom argues that 'the chronology is not out of joint'. Instead, the focus is on the observance of the additional Passover held in the second month with the incorporation of a 'flashback' to the first Passover (Milgrom, *Numbers*, 67).

[5] George Buchanan Gray, *Numbers*, ICC (Edinburgh: T&T Clark, 1903), 75.

[6] Davies, *Numbers*, 71.

[7] Sturdy shows a better literary sensitivity than Davies. 'This is a flashback. It is not an instance of carelessness, for this earlier date comes again in 9:1 and 9:15' (John Sturdy, *Numbers*, CBC [Cambridge: Cambridge University Press, 1976], 56).

chapters had to be placed in the book of Numbers.[8] As we have seen, Exod 35–40 has sections that have been added under the influence of late priestly texts in Numbers, and, consequently, there is no basis for claiming that the text of Exodus was unalterable at this early stage. This rebuttal can be made more broadly on the basis of the textual evidence from Qumran. As Chavel observes,

> the idea that the interpolator could not add it somewhere in Exodus or Leviticus because these scrolls were somehow closed, namely, seen to be in a kind of final form that should not be tampered with, must be discounted at the very outset as fundamentally anachronistic; the idea is totally belied by the wide range of revisionary activity attested in the scrolls found at Qumran, in which one encounters all manner of manipulation of received text, from small insertions to large-scale excerpting to comprehensive recomposition.[9]

The alternative to these solutions is that the composer of Num 7.1–10.10 consciously chose to rewind the chronology and add further details to the story of the tabernacle's completion. As Wenham observes of the offering by the leaders,

> It would no doubt have been possible to have included the material in Numbers 7–9 at appropriate points in the main narrative of Exodus 40 to Numbers 1. But the present arrangement makes for a clearer exposition of the main themes of Leviticus and at the same time permits the reader to see the full significance of the tribal gifts to the altar. Had the narrative in Leviticus been interrupted by twelve notices of tribal gifts on twelve consecutive days, it would have obscured the focus of that book on the sacrifices and the ordination of Aaron.[10]

It is not just the synchronizing of the leaders' offerings that would have had to have been integrated into the text of Exodus and Leviticus. The account of the leaders' offerings in Num 7 presupposes not only the names of the tribal leaders from Num 1, but also the arrangement of the tribes around the tabernacle in Num 2. Further, the allocation of the carts brought by the leaders assumes the assigning of physical labour to the levitical tribes. The Levites are almost entirely absent from the first three books of the Pentateuch,[11] and it is only with Num 3–4 that they are properly introduced. The dedication of the Levites in Num 8 also develops aspects of the assignment of the Levites to the priests described in Num 3. These examples further underscore Wenham's point that the composer of these chapters sacrifices a consistent chronological progression for literary elegance. It

---

[8] Kellermann, *Priesterschrift*, 99.

[9] Simeon Chavel, *Oracular Law and Priestly Historiography in the Torah*, FAT II/71 (Tübingen: Mohr Siebeck, 2014), 116.

[10] Wenham, *Numbers*, 92. A similar point is made in Anderson, 'Literary Artistry'.

[11] See footnote 52 in Chapter 6.

244 THE MAKING OF THE TABERNACLE

is possible to envisage the Levites being introduced earlier and the rite of levitical dedication incorporated into Exodus or Leviticus, but the focus on the priests in Lev 8–10 and the Levites in Num 3 and 8 is simple and effective.

It is apparent, then, that the leaders' offerings and dedication of the Levites could not have been placed earlier than the end of Num 4. It is more difficult to account for why the diverse legislation of Num 5–6 should intervene before the account of the leaders' offerings. Achenbach revives Ibn Ezra's suggestion that the appearance of the priestly blessing in Num 6.22–27 brought to mind Aaron's blessing of the people in Lev 9.22,[12] and in the absence of any other convincing proposal this is an attractive idea.

We have already examined how the chronology of these chapters was probably understood by its composer. The twelve days of offerings by the tribal leaders began on the first of Nisan and concluded on the twelfth (Num 7.1–88). This would have allowed one day for the dedication of the Levites (8.5–22) before the Passover began (9.1–14). It is apparent that the author of these chapters created an intricate and elegant chronology. It is strikingly different from the chronological problems that result from the transformation of the one-day ordination ritual into an eight-day consecration and ordination complex in Lev 8–10. Since the chronology of the leaders' offerings is coherent without the seven-day ritual of consecration, it is worth considering whether Num 7–10 was ignorant of it. In other words, did the reworking of the ordination ritual as a seven-day consecration ritual occur after the composition of Num 7–10? The evidence does not seem to support this possibility. As we have seen, the presentation of the leaders and the Levites presupposes Num 1–4. These chapters already know about Nadab and Abihu's death (3.1–4) and must presuppose the story of the eighth day in Lev 9–10.[13] In addition, if Num 7–10 was inserted at this point in the Pentateuchal narrative because the priestly blessing in Num 6.22–27 suggested an association with Aaron blessing the people in Lev 9.22, a further feature of the narrative of Lev 9–10 would appear to be presupposed.

Elegant though the rewinding of time is, the author's purpose is not simply the introduction of new, previously unanticipated themes in an elegant manner. Instead, it is to provide new insights on the earlier account of the tabernacle's erection and inauguration. Numbers 7–10 are meant to be read in parallel with Exod 40–Lev 10 with the texts shedding light on one another. Most importantly,

---

[12] Achenbach, *Die Vollendung der Tora*, 529. 'After the blessing of the priests, this is how it happened. On the day that Aaron lifted his hands to the people and blessed them, the initiation of the altar began' (Ibn Ezra on Num 7.1 [Michael Carasik, *Numbers* במדבר, The Commentators' Bible: The JPS Miqra'ot Gedolot (Philadelphia, PA: Jewish Publication Society of America, 2011), 44]). It is also the case that the events of that day had already been referred to earlier in the summary of Aaron's lineage and family (Num 3.1–4).

[13] As Samuel has shown, there is no basis for arguing that Num 3.1–4 is secondary to Num 1–4. These verses are certainly secondary to Pg, but this is a feature they share with the surrounding chapters (Samuel, *Von Priestern*, 161).

The Offering of the Leaders (Num 7.1–88)

The tribal leaders (נשׂיאים) emerge as significant figures in Israelite society only in the book of Numbers. At the beginning of the second month, they are appointed (קְרִיאֵי הָעֵדָה; 1.16) from the heads of households with the task of counting the number of adult males in their tribe. Prior to Num 1, the leaders are scarcely mentioned.[14] Nevertheless, there was an attempt to project them back into the events surrounding the consecration of the tabernacle even though they had not been appointed at that time. As we have already seen, the leaders are attributed with bringing gems, incense, and oil in Exod 35.27–28. In Num 7, they provide gifts for the tabernacle and the altar on the day that the tabernacle is erected. The tribal leaders provide two sets of gifts. The first gifts are six wagons, each drawn by two oxen. They will be given to the Levites to assist in transporting the tabernacle and are consequently said to have been brought 'before the tabernacle' (לִפְנֵי הַמִּשְׁכָּן; 7.3). The second gifts are sacrifices and utensils needed for their offering. They provide for the initiation of the altar (חֲנֻכַּת הַמִּזְבֵּחַ; 7.10),[15] and are consequently said to have been brought 'before the altar' (לִפְנֵי הַמִּזְבֵּחַ; 7.10).[16]

Do the tribal leaders provide gifts on their own behalf, or do they do so as representatives of the tribes? Already in Josephus we find the assumption that the offerings were provided by the tribes.

> The tabernacle having now been consecrated and all arrangements relating to the priests, the people, assured of God's fellowship with them in the tent, gave themselves up to the offering of sacrifices… and, tribe by tribe, they offered gifts, whether public or private, to God. Thus the tribal leaders came two and two, each pair bringing a wagon and two oxen… (*Ant* III.219–20).

---

[14] In some cases, נָשִׂיא may be a general term for a prominent figure (e.g. Exod 22.28; Lev 4.22), but in other cases, it would appear that the twelve appointed tribal leaders have been projected back by redactional activity (e.g. Exod 16.22 and Exod 34.31). (See also Achenbach, *Die Vollendung der Tora*, 466 n. 89.)

[15] For the translation of חֲנֻכָּה, see Stefan C. Reif, 'Dedicated to חנך', *VT* 22 (1972): 495–501. The term חֲנֻכָּה only appears in late texts (see Ps 30.1; Neh 12.27; 2 Chron 7.9).

[16] *Contra* Levine, *Numbers*, I: 255–6. In Levine's view vv. 1–9 are an introduction to what follows. He observes that the locations 'before the tabernacle' (לִפְנֵי הַמִּשְׁכָּן; 7.3) and 'before the altar' (לִפְנֵי הַמִּזְבֵּחַ; 7.10) are essentially indistinguishable, though that raises the question of why the composer should have referred to the same location with different terminology. In his view, the altar is *pars pro toto* for the entire tabernacle complex. In contrast, Knierim and Coats rightly divide vv. 2–88 into two sections: gifts for the tabernacle (vv. 2–9) and gifts for the initiation of the altar (vv. 10–88) (Rolf P. Knierim and George W. Coats, *Numbers*, FOTL 4 [Grand Rapids, MI: Eerdmans, 2005], 97–102).

246 THE MAKING OF THE TABERNACLE

The same idea is sometimes reflected in modern commentators as when Budd writes about 'the community's commitment to the priestly theocracy' and 'the separate offerings of each tribe' or Levine refers to 'the participation of all twelve tribes of Israel'.[17] Two considerations suggest that this assumption is incorrect. First, amongst the offerings that each leader brought is a male goat for a sin-purification offering. This is the sacrifice prescribed for an individual leader to offer should they sin (Lev 4.22–26).[18] Should the entire people transgress, the prescribed sacrifice is a bull and the *elders* of the congregation (זִקְנֵי הָעֵדָה) act as representatives for the people placing their hands on the head of the bull before it is slaughtered (Lev 4.13–21). Secondly, the offerings are identical for each leader and do not reflect the fact that the tribes varied in size.[19]

Kuenen complains that nowhere else are the priestly writings as 'monotonous and tediously wearisome' as in Num 7.[20] But, the rhetorical purpose is clear; the meticulous repetition of the sacrificial offerings emphasizes the equality of each of the tribal leaders. The leaders are not only equals, but they are also presented as involved in a common enterprise. They arrive initially as a cohort with all their offerings assembled, and they cooperate in pairs to provide a cart and oxen.[21] The rhetoric of equality needs to be qualified in two respects. First, the divine instructions that only one tribal leader present their sacrifice on each day suggests the primacy of Judah. In Num 1 the leaders are named in the birth order of Jacob's sons with the sons of Jacob's wives listed first followed by the sons of his concubines. The leaders offer their gifts according to their encampments of the tribes around the sanctuary. In this arrangement, Nahshon of Judah takes the lead on the first day; he and his tribe are *primus inter pares*.[22] Second, Num 7 assumes that the tribal leaders have the means to provide offerings on such an extravagant scale. Political influence and wealth are understood to be co-constitutive in the same way as occurred in Exod 35.27–28 when the leaders offered precious stones, incense and oil for the tabernacle. The equality of the tribal leaders can be seen as a realization of the principle expressed in Exod 30.15 that 'the rich shall not give more, and the poor shall not give less'. The leader of one tribe does donate exactly the same as the leaders of the others. But with their own special offerings for the altar, the rich leaders *do* give more than other Israelites and the requirement of a daily ritual that communally marks their generosity ensures that they are seen to give more.

---

[17] Philip J. Budd, *Numbers*, WBC 5 (Waco, TX: Word, 1984), 78, 84; Levine, *Numbers*, I: 247.

[18] Kellermann, *Priesterschrift*, 106.   [19] Knierim and Coats, *Numbers*, 99.

[20] Kuenen, *Historico-Critical Inquiry*, 94.

[21] It is sometimes suggested that the carts transported the offerings to the tabernacle (e.g. Levine, *Numbers*, I: 247). However, the wagons and the sacrificial gifts are treated separately, and the wagons are allocated to the levitical tribes before the sacrifices are presented.

[22] Judg 1 has a similar picture of Judah and the other tribes and may be contemporaneous with Num 7.

The generosity of the tribal leaders is divinely affirmed not least because it is intended as an example as Kuenen already recognized. The passage introduces 'the heads of tribes...as models of liberality towards the sanctuary which his own contemporaries would do well to copy'.[23] This liberality is seen as spontaneous and unexpected.[24] When the leaders arrive, Moses needs to seek divine guidance about whether they can be accepted and how to treat the offerings. The extravagance of the offerings is characteristic of the late layers of Numbers, most especially the list of annual offerings in Num 28.1–30.1. Unlike those public sacrifices, however, the offerings of the leaders include amity offerings. As such, they are better compared to the sacrifices that were offered as part of the consecration ritual (Lev 8). There too we find burnt offerings, grain offerings, amity offerings and sin-purification offerings. In addition, the leaders also bring incense. Consequently, the leaders supply their equivalents to all the sacrifices offered in Lev 8–10.

The narrative simultaneity encourages readers to understand the leaders' offerings in light of the events of Lev 8–10. The offerings in Num 7 establish a close relationship between the leaders and the altar. Without them, the altar would not be initiated. As we have seen, the consecration ritual establishes a close relationship between the priesthood and the altar, but one that is necessarily prior to that between the leaders and the altar. Both underscore the privileged position of priests and leaders, whilst also implying a connection between the two (Exod 35.27–28). It is also possible to contrast the unanticipated offering of the leaders with the unrequested offering of incense by Nadab and Abihu. Both are examples of ritual innovation. Whilst arrogating the high priestly prerogative of offering incense is punished with instant death, the generosity of the tribal leaders is regarded as appropriate. In this way, the narrative encourages a degree of freedom within the cult to express gratitude.

The Functioning Sanctuary (Num 7.89–8.4)

The twelve days of offerings leave one day before the Passover is celebrated on the fourteenth day. It is possible that the composer imagined that the dedication of the Levites would occur on that thirteenth day. But before describing how the Levites were purified, the composer provides two vignettes that relate to the sanctuary building and its functioning: the first describes how Moses was able to enter the tent of meeting and hear God's instructions (Num 7.89) and the second concerns the setting up of the lamps (8.1–4). Both have close parallels in the tabernacle account and are examples of textual rewriting and interpretation.

---

[23] Kuenen, *Historico-Critical Inquiry*, 94.   [24] Knierim and Coats, *Numbers*, 103.

248   THE MAKING OF THE TABERNACLE

It has often been observed that the first vignette in Num 7.89 is an 'isolated fragment'.[25] It is not clear how it relates to the surrounding texts, it does not identify to whom Moses is speaking,[26] and it is natural to expect a divine speech after the words 'and he spoke to him' (וַיְדַבֵּר אֵלָיו). It is possible that it once belonged elsewhere and has been displaced, but attempts to identify its original location are speculative. We can say that it is a fulfilment of Exod 25.22 which promises that God will meet Moses and speak to him from above the atonement cover. It is also possible that the verse addresses the statement in Exod 40.35 that Moses was not able to enter the tent of meeting because the divine glory had descended on it. At no point in the subsequent narrative was it specified when or how Moses regained access to the tent of meeting. The opening of the book of Leviticus which presents God speaking to Moses 'from the tent of meeting' (מֵאֹהֶל מוֹעֵד; Lev 1.1) could quite legitimately be understood to mean that Moses stood outside the tent whilst God spoke from its midst, but at the opening of the book of Numbers God spoke to Moses a month later 'in the tent of meeting' (בְּאֹהֶל מוֹעֵד; Num 1.1). Thus, Num 7.89 resolves an issue created by 1.1 and suggests that after the dedication of the altar, Moses was again able to enter the tabernacle proper.[27]

The second vignette concerns Aaron's activity in the outer sanctum (Num 8.1–4). The seven lamps on the lampstand were to be 'set up' (hiphil על״ה) so that they cast their light into the centre of the room. The insistence that Aaron set up the lamps seeks to resolve a tension in the priestly materials of Exodus and Leviticus that had resulted from their redactional development. In Exod 40.4, Moses is tasked with 'setting up the lamps' (וְהַעֲלֵיתָ אֶת־נֵרֹתֶיהָ) as part of the erection of the sanctuary (cf. 40.25). This is most naturally understood as a unique task associated with the initial installation of the lampstand. The regular tending of the lamps by Aaron is described as 'arranging the lamps' (יַעֲרֹךְ אֶת־הַנֵּרֹת; Lev 24.4), utilizing the same verb that is used for displaying the loaves on the table (Lev 24.5–9).[28] This picture is complicated, however, by Exod 30.8 which indicates that Aaron 'set up' the lamps every evening (וּבְהַעֲלֹת אַהֲרֹן אֶת־הַנֵּרֹת בֵּין הָעַרְבַּיִם). A late addition to the original instructions about the construction of the lampstand reflects this ambiguity and avoids identifying who sets up the lamps: 'the lamps shall be set up and illuminate the space before it' (וְהֶעֱלָה אֶת־נֵרֹתֶיהָ וְהֵאִיר עַל־עֵבֶר פָּנֶיהָ; Exod 25.37).[29]

---

[25] Gray, Numbers, 77.

[26] Moses is simply said 'to speak with him' (לְדַבֵּר אִתּוֹ), He hears 'the voice' (הַקּוֹל) which echoes the language of Deuteronomy (e.g. Deut 5.22–26). 𝔊[B] reads 'the voice of the Lord' (τὴν φωνὴν κυρίου) which provides additional clarity.

[27] Cf. Milgrom, Numbers, 59, who refers to the seven-day ordination ceremony of the priests instead.

[28] In 𝔐 39.37, the lamps are described as the 'lamps of the arrangement' (נֵרֹת הַמַּעֲרָכָה). The purpose of this qualification appears to be to identify them with Aaron's cultic activities in the sanctuary (cf. Lev 24.1–4), rather than indicating that they were already arranged when delivered to Moses (contra Propp, Exodus 19–40, 670).

[29] The intrusive nature of v. 37b has often been observed. First, the pattern of second person singular verbs in Exod 25–27 is broken by the third person verbs וְהֶעֱלָה and וְהֵאִיר. וְהֶעֱלָה must be understood

In Num 8.1–4, however, Aaron is portrayed as fulfilling this requirement to illuminate the outer sanctum.[30]

Taken together, the two vignettes in Num 7.89–8.4 fulfil instructions in Exod 25 that were perceived to have been left incomplete in the previous books. They underscore not only that the instructions about the tabernacle in Exod 25–31 are fully realized, but also that the regular cultic service in the tabernacle had now begun. In Lev 8–10 the regular cultic service begins once the altar has been consecrated and the priests ordained. In Num 7–8, however, the regular cult commences only once the leaders have brought their offerings for the initiation of the altar. It is a striking insistence on the importance of the tribal leaders for the functioning of Israel's cult.

The Dedication of the Levites (Num 8.5–22)

The two brief vignettes in Num 7.89–8.4 are followed by an account of the dedication of the Levites (8.5–22). The precise date for their dedication is not specified in Num 8. If we accept the claim in Num 7.1 that the offerings of the leaders were begun on the first day of Nisan, the offerings are not only completed before the celebration of Passover, which is described in Num 9.1–14, but there is also a single day, the thirteenth of the month, as the occasion for the dedication of the

---

as an impersonal use of the third person, and the subject of וְהֵאִיר is presumably the lampstand (v. 34), rather than the more proximate lamps (v. 37). Whilst 𝔐[D] has a reading והעלית את נרתיה והאירו אל חבר פניה (cf. 𝕲[B] καὶ ἐπιθήσεις τοὺς λύχνους, καὶ φανοῦσιν ἐκ τοῦ ἑνὸς προσώπου), this is best understood as a secondary correction. Second, the intrusion of v. 37b leaves וּמַלְקָחֶיהָ וּמַחְתֹּתֶיהָ זָהָב טָהוֹר (v. 38) lacking a verb. 𝕲[B]'s smoother reading καὶ τὸν ἐπαρυστῆρα αὐτῆς καὶ τὰ ὑποθέματα αὐτῆς ἐκ χρυσίου καθαροῦ ποιήσεις highlights the difficulties with v. 38. Finally, the manufacture of the lampstand in 𝔐 37.23 (// 𝕲 38.17) lacks any reference to the setting up of the lamps and their illumination, and, consequently, avoids the difficulties I have noted. Kellermann has argued that Exod 27.37b was inserted under the influence of Num 8.1–4, rather than Exod 27.37b influencing Num 8 (Kellermann, *Priesterschrift*, 111–15). The difficulty with this proposal is that אֶל־מוּל פְּנֵי הַמְּנֹרָה (Num 8.3) appears to be a clarification of the unusual עַל־עֵבֶר פָּנֶיהָ (Exod 25.37). The expression אֶל־עֵבֶר with the preposition אֶל rather than עַל occurs in Exod 28.26 and 39.19 (cf. Deut 30.13; Josh 22.11; Ezek 1.9, 12; 10.22). Achenbach rightly describes 25.37 as an 'etwas kryptischen Text' (Achenbach, *Die Vollendung der Tora*, 539). For other occurrences of אֶל־מוּל פְּנֵי see Exod 26.9; 28.26, 37; 39.18; Lev 8.9.

[30] The translators of Greek Exodus and Leviticus appear to have been cognizant of the problems with the uses of על'ה and ער'ך. The Old Greek version distinguishes between the initial act of setting up the lamps and the kindling of them. For the former, the verb ἐπιτίθημι translates על'ה. Moses is commanded to set up the lamps (Exod 25.37; 40.4) and does so (Exod 40.25). For the latter, the verb καίω is used and relates to Aaron and his sons. In some of these cases, the extant Hebrew texts have על'ה (Exod 27.20; Lev 24.1) and in other cases, they have ער'ך (Exod 27.21; 𝕲 39.16 [//𝔐 39.37]; Lev 24.3, 4). In Exod 30.8 ἐξάπτω is used with a similar meaning where the Hebrew text has על'ה. (The translator of Greek Numbers, on the other hand, appears to be unaware of this distinction for Aaron is the subject of both ἐπιτίθημι [Num 8.2] and ἐξάπτω [8.3]. In both cases, the extant Hebrew texts have על'ה). The attempts of ancient interpreters such as the translators of the Old Greek to provide harmonizations of the different texts about the lamps provides no secure basis to argue that the verb על'ה should bear the meaning 'to kindle' (*contra* Jacob Milgrom, *Leviticus 23–27: A New Translation with Introduction and Commentary*, AB 3B [New York: Doubleday, 2001], 2087).

250 THE MAKING OF THE TABERNACLE

Levites. Not only does the chronology lack the complications that result from assuming the offerings began on the eighth of Nisan, but it places the dedication of the Levites the day before the first anniversary of the Passover. It is hard to see this as coincidental for the Levites are designated as an acceptable substitute for the firstborn of the Israelites whose lives were redeemed at Passover. Against this, we can observe that the text never identifies the precise date when the dedication ritual occurred other than being around the time when Moses finished erecting the tabernacle (7.1; 9.15).

Whatever the precise date, Moses received instructions about how the Levites were to be dedicated for sanctuary service (vv. 5–14). There appear to be three main aspects to this dedication ceremony. First, the Levites are to be purified. This is effected through sprinkling the Levites with the water of purification, shaving them with a razor, and them washing their clothes (v. 7).[31] Second, the Israelite congregation are instructed to lay their hands on the Levites as though they were a sacrificial offering and 'Aaron presented the Levites as a presentation' (וְהֵנִיף אַהֲרֹן אֶת־הַלְוִיִּם תְּנוּפָה) before YHWH. The instruction about a presentation is repeated twice. On the first occasion Aaron presents the Levites (v. 11), and the second time Moses is instructed to do so (v. 13). The duplication may reflect the idea that the Levites are both a gift to God and a gift to the priests (cf. vv. 15–19).[32] Third, a sin-purification offering, a burnt offering, and its grain offering are to be offered by the Levites and these offerings are said to secure atonement for them (vv. 8, 12).

As we might expect from the other instructions that concerned the preparation of the tabernacle for ritual service, the dedication of the Levites is completed in accordance with the divine instructions (vv. 20–22). Unusually, the connection between instructions and fulfilment is interrupted by a continuation of the divine speech that explains the significance of the dedication rite. No other ritual is explained in such detail elsewhere in the priestly literature. The explanation draws upon various images. The Levites are understood as substitutes for the firstborn

---

[31] Num 8.7 refers to 'the waters of purification' (מֵי חַטָּאת). This is often thought to be identical with the waters produced as a result of the red cow ritual in Num 19 though they are referred to as 'the waters of cleansing' (מֵי־הַנִּדָּה; vv. 9, 13, 20, 21). Gray identifies the two (Gray, *Numbers*, 79), whilst Levine regards their equation as 'improbable' (Levine, *Numbers*, I: 274, 464) and Davies is cautious (Davies, *Numbers*, 77). Stökl argues that shaving was important in Mesopotamian ordination rituals for diagnosing physical purity (Jonathan Stökl, 'Innovating Ordination', *HeBAI* 7 [2018]: 483–99). Erickson, on the other hand, sees shaving as a demeaning rite (Nancy Erickson, 'Shaving It All Off: A Demeaning Priestly Prescription for the Levites in Numbers 8', *AABNER* [*forthcoming*]). It is striking that priests are prohibited from various acts of shaving (Lev 21.5; Ezek 44.20), whilst Levites must undergo a shaving rite. It provides a further point of contrast between the two groups and might be intended to leave no doubt that the Levites cannot serve as priests.

[32] Alternatively, this duplication could necessitate a literary-critical solution (e.g. Kellermann, *Priesterschrift*, 115–24).

who were saved at Passover; they are the part of a sacrificial offering that is ritually presented to God; they are a gift to the priests (vv. 15–19).

It has long been appreciated that the explanation of the ritual in Num 8.14–19 is indebted to 3.11–13 and that the dedication ceremony is a ritualization of the instructions to set apart the Levites for assisting the priesthood in the sanctuary.[33] The portrayal of this ritual has not enjoyed the esteem of biblical scholarship and critical scholarship of the nineteenth century was particularly harsh in its judgements. The chapter was rightly perceived to have a close relationship with Num 3, but Julius Wellhausen saw the ritualization in Num 8 as 'frivolous' and a 'mechanical historicization on the basis of legal conceptions', whilst Kuenen described it as a 'tasteless repetition and exaggeration' of Num 3.[34] Such pejorative assessments are characteristic of their age and are rarer in contemporary scholarly discourse. Nevertheless, the levitical dedication ritual has rarely received attention outside the commentaries, and the interpretive skill of the priestly authors deserves great recognition.[35]

The ritualization of Num 3 in Num 8 is achieved by amalgamating various existing ritual texts. First, the purification has several similarities to the requirements laid on those who are purified after suffering from a skin ailment. They are purified by washing their clothes, shaving, and bathing (Lev 14.8). Though the terminology used of the Levites is different, and sprinkling with the water of purification replaces the need to bathe, Lev 14 and Num 8 are the only places in the priestly corpus where the *hithpael* of טה״ר is used.

Second, the gifting of the Levites is effected by adopting the priestly instructions for the treatment of the amity offerings. When an amity offering is sacrificed, the brisket was presented before YHWH (Lev 7.28–34). The ritual action when applied to sacrificial portions involved some motion in the direction of YHWH's presence, perhaps both vertically and horizontally. We should, perhaps, imagine the priest moving the sacrificial portion from chest height upwards and away from his chest before bringing it back.[36] The idea that the Levites were subjected to this ritual action may have been inspired by textual exegesis. The description of the Levites in Num 3.9 has a number of similarities with the description of the presentation portion in Lev 7.34.

---

[33] For the relationships between the two passages, see especially Christian Frevel, ' "…dann gehören die Leviten mir": Anmerkungen zum Zusammenhang von Num 3; 8 und 18', in *Kulte, Priester, Rituale: Beiträge zu Kult und Kultkritik im Alten Testament und Alten Orient*, eds. Stephanie Ernst and Maria Häusl, ATSAT 89 (St Ottilien: EOS Verlag, 2010), 133–58.

[34] 'In einer so frivolen Weise ist die einfache Idee 3,5–13 hier auf Grund gesetzlicher Vorstellungen mechanisch vergeschichtlicht, noch einen Schritt über 3,14–51 hinaus' (Wellhausen, *Composition*, 178); 'It is an insipid repetition and exaggeration of the account of the separation of the Levites for the service of the sanctuary in *Num*. iii. and iv' (Kuenen, *Historico-Critical Inquiry*, 93).

[35] One notable exception is the recent article by Stökl, 'Innovating Ordination'.

[36] For discussion of תְּנוּפָה and תְּרוּמָה, see footnote 93 in Chapter 8.

252 THE MAKING OF THE TABERNACLE

ונתתה את־הלוים לאהרן ולבניו נתונם המה לו מאת בני ישראל

You shall give the Levites to Aaron and his sons. They are entirely given to him from the Israelites (Num 3.9).

כי את־חזה התנופה ואת שוק התרומה לקחתי מאת בני־ישראל מזבחי שלמיהם ואתן אתם לאהרן

הכהן ולבניו לחק־עולם מאת בני ישראל

For I have taken the brisket of the presentation portion and the thigh that is reserved from the Israelites from their amity offerings, and I have given them to Aaron the priest and his sons as a perpetual due from the Israelites (Lev 7.34).

As a result of these similarities, the composer of Num 8 has deduced that the Levites were offered as a presentation portion. There are two significant features about the presentation portion that have been developed in its utilization for the Levites' dedication ritual. First, the sacrificial portion that was presented before YHWH was not the entire animal, but a choice part. Second, the presentation portion was assigned to the priesthood as a whole for their use. The rite of presenting the Levites distinguishes from the other Israelites (8.14) and provides them to Aaron and his sons for service (8.19). The idea of the Levites being subject to a ritual action of presentation comparable to that which sacrificial portions underwent is admittedly incongruous. How were the Levites to be lifted towards the deity?[37] The difficulty in imagining a ritual action is presumably what animated Wellhausen's complaint about the rite's 'mechanical historicization'. It appears that we have a literary ritual rather than a literal one.[38]

Third, the extensive list of sacrificial offerings is reminiscent of the offerings for the ordination of the priests in Lev 8. Both passages feature a burnt offering, a grain offering, and a sin-purification offering. The result of the sacrifices in both cases is the same: they effect atonement (Lev 8.34; Num 8.12). Unsurprisingly, in comparison to the ordination ritual, the dedication of the Levites lacks the ordination offering. As we have seen in the previous chapter, the ordination offering was a form of amity offering with a portion presented to YHWH. The levitical dedication ritual has its own equivalent, for the Levites themselves are presented. They are a portion of the amity offering!

There are further links between the texts portraying the dedication of the Levites and the ordination of the priests that suggest the priestly composers of Num 8 intended their readers to compare the two rituals. First, both the priests and the Levites are said to have been taken 'from the midst of the sons of Israel'

---

[37] Levine is amongst a number of commentators that observe that the 'usage here is more figurative than literal' (Levine, *Numbers*, I: 276; cf. Martin Noth, *Das Vierte Buch Mose: Numeri*, 4th edn, ATD 7 [Göttingen: Vandenhoeck & Ruprecht, 1982], 62; Davies, *Numbers*, 78; Milgrom, *Numbers*, 62; Seebass, *Numeri 1,1–10,10*, 217).

[38] For further discussion of the issue of scribal rituals, see MacDonald, 'Scribalism and Ritual Innovation'.

(מִתּוֹךְ בְּנֵי יִשְׂרָאֵל; Exod 28.1; Num 8.6).[39] Second, both sets of instructions begin with something like 'this is what you shall do to them', even if precise expressions are different in each case. Num 8.7. reads וְכֹה־תַעֲשֶׂה לָהֶם while Exod 29.1 has וְזֶה הַדָּבָר אֲשֶׁר־תַּעֲשֶׂה לָהֶם. Third, in both rituals a bull is offered as a sin offering, though one or other ritual may reflect the instructions of Lev 4 that require a bull to be offered by the congregation. Both rituals share references to the laying of hands upon the sacrifice, but this is a feature of many pieces of sacrificial legislation. Fourth, in both cases Moses is required to bring those being ordained or purified to the same location at the entrance of the tent of meeting. In both cases the *hiphil* of קר״ב is used. The description of the location is not quite identical. Num 8.9 speaks of 'before the tent of meeting' (לִפְנֵי אֹהֶל מוֹעֵד), whilst Exod 29.4 speaks of the entrance of the tent of meeting (אֶל־פֶּתַח אֹהֶל מוֹעֵד). Fifth, both rituals are performed in the presence of the entire people. In both cases the entire congregation (כָּל־הָעֵדָה) is assembled (קה״ל) (Exod 29.4–5; Num 8.9). Sixth, both rituals occur around the time that Moses erected the tabernacle. It is striking that most of the similarities between the dedication ritual and the ordination ritual are to be found in the framing of the rituals: they occur around the same time, in the same place, with the same audience. As a result, it is justified to compare the two rituals, but as Levine observes a comparison serves 'to pinpoint significant differences between the two groups'.[40]

The first difference is the intended effect of the ritual. The purpose of the ritual for the priests is to 'consecrate them' (לְקַדֵּשׁ אֹתָם; Exod 29.1). In this way they can serve in the sanctuary by offering sacrifices. In contrast the Levites are only 'purified' (לְטַהֲרָם; Num 8.7). This key difference is expressed most directly by the sprinkling rites. The priests together with their vestments are sprinkled (נז״ה) with the blood of the burnt offering and the anointing oil (Lev 8.30). This oil has also been used to anoint the tabernacle and the altar and indexes the close relationship the priests have with the tabernacle and the altar (8.11).[41] The Levites, however, are sprinkled (נז״ה) with the 'water of purification' (מֵי חַטָּאת; Num 8.7). The priestly authors' decision to identify the Levites as no more than 'purified' is striking as they are substitutes for the Israelite firstborn who are described in Num 3.13 as 'consecrated for me' (הִקְדַּשְׁתִּי לִי).

The second difference is the intended role of the priests and Levites within the cult. According to Exod 29.1, the consecration takes place in order that Aaron and his sons might be YHWH's priests. The priestly role is indexed by the priestly vestments that are given significant levels of instrumental meaning in Exod 28. In contrast, the Levites are purified in order to 'do the service of YHWH' (לַעֲבֹד אֶת־עֲבֹדַת יְהוָה; Num 8.11). With one exception, the term עֲבֹדָה is used consistently of

---

[39] This expression מִתּוֹךְ בְּנֵי יִשְׂרָאֵל is only found in Exod 28 and in Num 3, 8, and 18.
[40] Levine, *Numbers*, I: 273; cf. Davies, *Numbers*, 76; Budd, *Numbers*, 92; Milgrom, *Numbers*, 61.
[41] Gilders, *Blood Ritual*, 103.

254 THE MAKING OF THE TABERNACLE

levitical service in Numbers,[42] which consists of various tasks such as guarding the sanctuary and carrying the tabernacle. It does not include altar service or any activities in the sanctuary tent itself. As a result, the Levites do not require any change of garments, only that theirs be washed.

Finally, the Levites are described in sacrificial terms, rather than as those who offer sacrifices. The people lay their hands on the Levites as they would a bovine or caprovine, and the Levites are given as a presentation portion before YHWH. As we have seen, the application of the presentation portion to the Levites indexes the presentation of the brisket in Lev 7. After the ritual of presentation was performed, the brisket belongs to the priesthood as a whole. The Levites are given to the priesthood from the entirety of the people of Israel just as the brisket was given to the priesthood from the entirety of the sacrifice.[43]

Ordaining a Kingdom of Priests

In the consecration ritual, Aaron and his sons are daubed with the blood of the ordination offering. The blood that remained was dashed against the altar. In this way a close relationship is forged between the priests and the altar. For readers of the Pentateuch, however, this is not the first occasion that individuals and an altar have had blood applied to them. Immediately before the instructions about the tabernacle, Moses erects an altar and the entire people of Israel were dashed with blood at the foot of Mount Sinai. 'Moses took half of the blood and placed it in basins, and half the blood he dashed against the altar ... Moses took the blood and he dashed it upon the people' (Exod 24.6, 8). Unlike the ordination ritual where different verbs are used for applying the blood to the altar and the Aaronides, here the same verb, זר״ק, 'to dash', is used of both the application of the blood on the altar and the blood on the people.[44] Consequently, the passage suggests an even closer correspondence between the people and the altar than was the case for the priests and the altar in the consecration ritual.

The use of זר״ק of blood splashed on the people is particularly striking because this verb is typically used in the priestly literature of dashing the blood against the altar. Only in the red heifer ritual, itself a late text in the priestly tradition, is זר״ק used of a liquid being splashed over an individual and there it is used of the water for cleansing (Num 19.13, 20).[45] Nor is it the only feature of the ritual on Mount

---

[42] In speaking of the priesthood, Num 18.7 reads עֲבֹדַת מַתָּנָה אֶתֵּן אֶת־כְּהֻנַּתְכֶם, 'as a service of gift, I give your priesthood'. The text is awkward and contains an unresolved textual crux. Since the previous clause concluded with וַעֲבַדְתֶּם, the simplest solution is to regard עֲבֹדַת as a case of dittography.

[43] For this reason מֵאֵת בְּנֵי יִשְׂרָאֵל in Num 8.11 should probably be translated as 'from the Israelites' and not as 'on behalf of the Israelites' (contra Levine, Numbers, I: 270).

[44] For the translation of זר״ק see Gilders, Blood Ritual, 25–7.

[45] Reinhard Achenbach, 'Verunreinigung durch die Berührung Toter: Zum Ursprung einer altisraelitischen Vorstellung', in Tod und Jenseits im Alten Israel und in seiner Umwelt: Theologische,

Sinai that diverges from the priestly literature. These divergences have led to very different assessments of the significance of the ritual at the foot of Mount Sinai and its relationship to the rituals of the priestly literature. As many recent scholars have recognized, to understand the ritual in Exod 24.3–8, we need to see it together with Exod 19.3–8 as part of a framing of the Sinai revelation. Both texts stem from the same redactional hand and shed light upon each other. We will then be able to reflect upon the different possible ways of understanding the ritual in Exod 24 in relation to the ordination rituals that follow in the books of Exodus and Leviticus.

The Framing of the Sinai Narrative (Exod 19–24)

On the third month after their departure from Egypt, the people of Israel arrive at Mount Sinai. This mountain will prove to be the place of revelation with God descending on the mountain to address Moses. In Exod 19.9, Moses receives a divine communication that God is going to appear on Mount Sinai and, consequently, the people need to sanctify themselves in preparation. Somewhat prematurely, however, Moses is called to ascend the mountain (vv. 3–8). Apparently, God is already present on Sinai and wishes to address Moses. The description of God's message to Moses and Moses's relaying it to the people has a striking aesthetic quality. In his commentary Brevard Childs remarks, 'It has been generally recognized that these verses have a compositional integrity of their own. Indeed, the unit is a remarkable example of poetic symmetry and artistic beauty.'[46] The artistry is seen especially in the neat vertical descent of divine speech matched by the ascending response from the people. God speaks to Moses (vv. 3–6), who relays the words to the people (v. 7). They respond to Moses (v. 8a) who conveys their reply to God (v. 8b). The literary structure focuses attention on the words that descend from God and the response that ascends from the Israelites.

> **3** The YHWH called to him from the mountain, 'Thus you shall say to the house of Jacob and declare to the Israelites, **4** "You have seen what I have done to Egypt and I lifted you upon eagle's wings and I brought you to myself. **5** Now, therefore, if you obey my voice and keep my covenant, you will be a treasured possession from all the nations, for the whole earth is mine. **6** You will be a kingdom of priests and a holy nation." These are the words that you will speak to the

---

religionsgeschichtliche, archäologische und ikonographische Aspekte, eds. Angelika Berlejung and Bernd Janowski, FAT 64 (Tübingen: Mohr Siebeck, 2009), 347–69; Nathan MacDonald, 'The Hermeneutics and Genesis of the Red Cow Ritual', *HTR* 105 (2012): 351–71.

[46] Childs, *Exodus*, 360. For further discussion of some of the literary features, see John A. Davies, *A Royal Priesthood: Literary and Intertextual Perspectives on an Image of Israel in Exodus 19.6*, JSOTSup 395 (London: T&T Clark, 2004), 36–8.

256 THE MAKING OF THE TABERNACLE

Israelites.' **7** Moses came and summoned the elders of the people. He set before them all these words that YHWH had commanded him. **8** All the people answered in unity. They said, 'All that YHWH has spoken, we will do.' Moses relayed the people's word to YHWH   (Exod 19.3–8).

The divine words are the focus of the passage and move from God's past actions in bringing the people out of Egypt, the impending experience at Sinai of hearing God's words to a promise about Israel's future. Uniting past and future are the obligations being placed before the Israelites at Sinai. The Israelites' response corresponds to those obligations: united they agree to do them.

After the giving of the Ten Commandments and the ordinances of Exod 21–23, the elders of Israel are commanded to approach YHWH together with Moses, Aaron and his sons (vv. 1–2). An altar is set up at the foot of the mountain and oxen sacrificed. Moses collects the blood in basins and tosses half of it against the altar, and half of it over the people (vv. 3–8). At the conclusion of the ritual, the elders ascend the mountain where they behold God and feast in his presence (vv. 9–11). It has long been suggested that Exod 24 combines two distinct episodes as revealed by their different characters and locations.[47] The revelation atop of the mountain involves Moses, Aaron and his sons, and the elders, whilst the ritual at the foot of the mountain has a different cast consisting of Moses, the young men, and the people. The blood ritual in vv. 3–8 appears to interrupt the divine instructions to Moses in vv. 1–2 from their fulfilment in vv. 9–11.[48]

3 Moses came and recounted to the people all YHWH's words and all the ordinances. The people answered with one voice, and they said, 'All the words that YHWH has said, we will do.' **4** Moses wrote all YHWH's words. He rose early in the morning and built an altar at the foot of the mountain and twelve pillars for the twelve tribes of Israel. **5** He sent the young Israelite men and they offered burnt offerings and sacrificed oxen as amity offerings to YHWH. **6** Moses took half of the blood and placed it in basins, and half the blood he dashed against the altar. **7** He took the book of the covenant and read it to the people, and they said, 'All that YHWH has said we will do and obey.' **8** Moses took the blood and he dashed it upon the people, and he said 'Look the blood of the covenant that YHWH has made with you according to all these words.'   (Exod 24.3–8).

The divine words are no less important than they were in Exod 19.3–8, but in Exod 24.3–8 they have been integrated into a ritual.

---

[47] Wellhausen, *Composition*, 87–9.
[48] See, e.g., Ernest Wilson Nicholson, *God and His People: Covenant and Theology in the Old Testament* (Oxford: Clarendon Press, 1986), 11–13, 121–33.

LEADERS, LEVITES, AND A KINGDOM OF PRIESTS   257

The exchange between YHWH, Moses, and the people in Exod 19.3–8 has a number of similarities with the ritual at the foot of the mountain in Exod 24.3–8. First, in both passages Moses comes to the people with instructions from God which he relays to then (Exod 19.7; 24.3). Second, both passages emphasize that the people were united in agreement to obey the words. According to Exod 19.8, 'the people answered as one' (וַיַּעֲנוּ כָל־הָעָם יַחְדָּו), whilst in Exod 24.3, 'all the people answered with one voice' (וַיַּעַן כָּל־הָעָם קוֹל אֶחָד). Third, in both cases the people agreed to do what is commanded with almost identical language. In Exod 19.8, they respond 'all that YHWH has said, we will do' (כֹּל אֲשֶׁר־דִּבֶּר יְהוָה נַעֲשֶׂה) and in Exod 24.3, they reply 'all the words that YHWH has spoken, we will do' (כָּל־הַדְּבָרִים אֲשֶׁר־דִּבֶּר יְהוָה נַעֲשֶׂה).[49] Finally, both passages refer to Israel's covenant with God (Exod 19.5; 24.7–8). With the exception of Exod 23.32, these are the only references to the covenant in the Sinai pericope. On the basis of these similarities, Ludwig Schmidt argued that the passages stemmed from the same authorial hand.[50]

On the other hand, Adrian Schenker argued that we should not overlook the differences between the two passages. First, Exod 19 has a global perspective. The whole earth is God's, but he has chosen Israel. This wider perspective is absent from Exod 24. Second, Exod 19 is concerned with the obedience of the divine words, and there is no rite as there is in Exod 24. Third, in Exod 19 holiness is achieved by keeping the covenant, whilst in Exod 24 holiness is secured by application of a blood rite.[51] It must be questioned though whether these are simply differences in emphasis in the two passages that do not require positing different authors. The ritual in Exod 24 is not a precise repetition of the dialogues in Exod 19. Thus, the absence of a global perspective in Exod 24 should not be seen as a decisive problem. The other two objections are rather problematic as they imply a dichotomy between divine word and ritual that is alien to ancient Israel. This is especially apparent in Exod 24 which is no less concerned with the divine instructions. Exod 19 does not, of course, refer to a ritual, but as we shall see the sanctification of the people in Exod 24 can be regarded as a fulfilment of the promise in Exod 19 that Israel will be a 'kingdom of priests'. Thus, we should almost certainly regard Exod 19.3–8 and 24.3–8 as the product of the same hand and designed to produce an interpretive framework around the Sinai narrative.[52]

---

[49] The two texts are closer in 𝕲ᴮ which has ποιήσομεν καὶ ἀκουσόμεθα where 𝔐ᴸ has נַעֲשֶׂה (cf. 24.7).

[50] Ludwig Schmidt, 'Israel und das Gesetz: Ex 19,3b–8 und 24,3–8 als literarischer und theologischer Rahmen für das Bundesbuch', ZAW 113 (2001): 167–85.

[51] Adrian Schenker, 'Drei Mosaiksteinchen: "Königreich von Priestern", "Und ihre Kinder gehen weg", "Wir tun und wir hören" (Exodus 19,6; 21,22; 24,7)', in Studies in the Book of Exodus: Redaction—Reception—Interpretation, ed. Marc Vervenne, BETL 126 (Leuven: Leuven University Press, 1996), 367–80.

[52] Christoph Berner, 'The Redaction History of the Sinai Pericope (Exod 19–24) and Its Continuation in 4Q158', DSD 20 (2013): 402.

The Date of the Framework

Within critical scholarship, the blood ritual was long regarded as a very ancient element. In his influential volume, *Origins and History of the Oldest Sinai Traditions*, Walter Beyerlin offered two proofs of its antiquity. First, the two-fold splashing of blood is without parallel in the Old Testament. Second, the sacrifices are offered by young men rather than by priests.[53] The first argument assumes that uniqueness was a sign of antiquity, and has often been deployed in the study of Israelite ritual. The dangers of this kind of argument are not only its obvious subjectivity, but also its implicit assumptions about the steady rationalization of religious practice and belief. In the case of Exod 24, Beyerlin's claim about the uniqueness of the twofold manipulation of sacrificial blood is only true if we insist that the single verb זר״ק be applied in a ritual on two different objects. As we have seen, the ordination ritual in Exod 29 envisages blood being manipulated and applied to Aaron and his sons and to the altar, albeit using two different verbs, זר״ק and נת״ן. The second argument is rather weightier and was first advanced by Steuernagel. Some texts seem to require that the act of sacrificing was restricted to cultic officials in the Second Temple period, but this does not seem to have been the case in earlier periods.[54] In particular, Steuernagel pointed to Judg 17–18, the story of the Levite from Bethlehem, and 1 Sam 2, the story of Samuel and his sons, as evidence that 'young men' (נְעָרִים) functioned as cultic officials in the dying days of the pre-monarchic period.[55] In the middle of the twentieth century this apparent clue to the dating of the ritual was combined with theories about covenant renewal ceremonies in the amphicytony to argue that the blood sprinkling ritual was part of a ritual complex that was celebrated at either Shechem or Gilgal.[56]

For several reasons, however, many contemporary scholars argue that Exod 19.3–8 and Exod 24.3–8 are to be dated considerably later and should be regarded as post-deuteronomistic and post-priestly texts.[57] First, and most obviously, the

---

[53] Walter Beyerlin, *Herkunft und Geschichte der ältesten Sinaitraditionen* (Tübingen: Mohr, 1961).

[54] According to Ezek 44.10–11, the slaughter of the animals was a levitical responsibility, but in Ezra 6.20 and 2 Chron 35.6, 11 the priests and the Levites together slaughter the Passover lambs. On the other hand, 2 Chron 30.17 could imply that levitical slaughtering was only necessary if the offerer had not purified themselves.

[55] Carl Steuernagel, 'Der jehovitische Bericht über den Bundesschluss am Sinai', *TSK* 72 (1899): 319–50.

[56] For covenant ceremonies at Shechem and Gilgal, see *inter alia*, Eduard Nielsen, *Shechem: A Traditio-Historical Investigation* (Copenhagen: G.E.C. Gad, 1959); Eckart Otto, *Das Mazzotfest in Gilgal*, BWANT 107 (Stuttgart: Kohlhammer, 1975).

[57] The exceptions include neo-documentarians who attribute 24.3–8 to the Elohist (e.g. Baruch J. Schwartz, 'The Priestly Account of the Theophany and Lawgiving at Sinai', in *Texts, Temples, and Traditions: A Tribute to Menahem Haran*, ed. Michael V. Fox [Winona Lake, IN: Eisenbrauns, 1996], 121; Jeffrey Stackert, *A Prophet like Moses: Prophecy, Law, and Israelite Religion* [Oxford: Oxford University Press, 2014], 75–82; Samuel L. Boyd, 'Applied Ritual: The Application of Blood and Oil on Bodies in the Pentateuchal Sources', *BibInt* 29 [2020]: 120–47). As in a number of other places in the

fact that the two passages frame the entire Sinai pericope is evidence that they were composed after most of the intervening text. Second, integral to both passages are references to the covenant. Since the work of Perlitt, Nicholson and others, the older critical view that covenant is a late concept has been firmly re-established.[58] In some models, covenant theology first emerges only in the context of Assyrian imperialism.[59] Third, the late idea of an Israel consisting of twelve tribes is assumed in the ritual (24.4). Fourth, the language and theology of these passages is often redolent of Deuteronomy, but not identical with it. Prominent in both passages is a divine word theology similar to what is found in Deuteronomy. God is represented as speaking, the people are exhorted to listen to God's voice, and the people agree to do what God commands. The content of the divine communication is described as 'all the words' (כָּל־הַדְּבָרִים; 19.6; 24.3, 8) or 'these are the words' (אֵלֶּה הַדְּבָרִים; 19.6).[60] The election theology of 19.3–8 is also reminiscent of Deuteronomy. Israel is described as a 'treasured possession from the nations', סְגֻלָּה מִכָּל־הָעַמִּים (v. 5). Deuteronomy speaks instead of Israel as a 'treasured people', עַם סְגֻלָּה מִכֹּל הָעַמִּים (Deut 7.6; 14.2; cf. 26.18).[61] According to Exod 19.6, Israel is to be a 'holy nation', גּוֹי קָדוֹשׁ, whilst Deuteronomy uses the language of עַם קָדוֹשׁ (Deut 7.6; 14.2, 21; 26.19; 28.9). The distillation of terminology similar to that which we find scattered throughout the Deuteronomic literature suggests that such vocabulary is post-deuteronomistic rather than pre-deuteronomistic.[62] Fifth, in a similar way, although Exod 24.3–8 uses language that is not typical of the priestly literature, it also appears to be familiar with priestly diction. We have already observed the unusual use of זר״ק, 'to dash', with humans as objects of the blood. We can add to this the basins that Moses uses to hold the blood. The term אַגָּנֹת is not found within the priestly literature which prefers מִזְרָק (e.g. Exod 27.3).[63] On the other hand, the use of זְבָחִים שְׁלָמִים in v. 5 appears to show familiarity with priestly literature. The compound expression זֶבַח שְׁלָמִים is probably a coinage of the priestly literature and only appears in relatively late texts that show the influence

---

Pentateuch, neodocumentarians have resolved what earlier proponents of the documentary hypothesis found to be more intractable problems. For discussion, see Axel Graupner, 'Exodus 24 und die Frage nach dem Ursprung der Bundestheologie im Alten Testament mit einem Ausblick auf die Herrenmahlsüberlieferung im Neuen Testament', in *Beiträge zur urchristlichen Theologiegeschichte*, ed. Wolfgang Kraus, BZNW 163 (Berlin: de Gruyter, 2009), 129–48.

[58] Lothar Perlitt, *Bundestheologie im Alten Testament*, WMANT 36 (Neukirchen-Vluyn: Neukirchener Verlag, 1969); Nicholson, *God and His People*.

[59] See esp. the work of Otto, e.g., Eckart Otto, *Das Deuteronomium: Politische Theologie und Rechtsreform in Juda und Assyrien*, BZAW 284 (Berlin: de Gruyter, 1999).

[60] Perlitt, *Bundestheologie im Alten Testament*, 181–90.

[61] 𝕲[B] reads λαὸς περιούσιος an assimilation to the Deuteronomistic expression either in the *Vorlage* or by the translator.

[62] See, further Jean-Louis Ska, 'Exode 19,3b–6 et l'identité de l'Israël post-exilique', in *Studies in the Book of Exodus: Redaction—Reception—Interpretation*, ed. Marc Vervenne, BETL 126 (Leuven: Leuven University Press, 1996), 293–8.

[63] The only uses elsewhere in the Hebrew Bible are Isa 22.24 and Songs 7.2. In the latter case, it holds wine.

260 THE MAKING OF THE TABERNACLE

of the priestly literature.[64] The form זְבָחִים שְׁלָמִים with its ungrammatical juxtaposition of two nouns is a further development of the priestly idiom.[65] The indebtedness to priestly idiolect and differences from it are best seen as evidence of a post-priestly author. In conclusion, a close examination of the two passages provides sufficient grounds to recognize the framework as a post-priestly and post-deuteronomistic composition.

More precision about the dating can perhaps be provided by examining the relationship of 24.3–8 to 24.1–2, 9–11. It is almost universally accepted that the account of the blood rite in 24.3–8 has been inserted into the narrative about the theophany on Mount Sinai (24.1–2, 9–11), though Römer has questioned whether there are substantial grounds for distinguishing two layers of material.[66] Either way, the account of the blood ritual is no earlier than the theophany material which refers to the ascent of Nadab, Abihu, and the seventy elders upon Mount Sinai. The reference to the seventy elders would appear to have in view the story of Num 11, when the elders receive the spirit of prophecy from Moses. The reference to Nadab and Abihu is often seen as an allusion to the incident in Lev 10. It is striking that only these two of Aaron's sons are mentioned, not least because we might have expected all four of Aaron's sons to be named since they were all ordained alongside him according to Exod 29. The natural conclusion to draw is that the theophany on Mount Sinai in Exod 24 provides a positive counterpart to the destruction of Nadab and Abihu in Lev 10. The contrast between the two occasions throws Lev 10 into even starker relief, performing a similar function to the theophany in Lev 9.22–24. Nadab and Abihu's presumption appears even more shocking given their witnessing of the theophany on Mount Sinai. If this is correct, it would appear that Exod 24.1–2, 9–11 is later even than Lev 10.[67]

---

[64] The only possible exceptions are 1 Sam 10.8 and 11.15. In both cases, Rendtorff argues that שְׁלָמִים was original (Rolf Rendtorff, *Studien zur Geschichte des Opfers im Alten Israel*, WMANT 24 [Neukirchen-Vluyn: Neukirchener Verlag, 1967], 150–1). 1 Sam 10.8 is usually thought to interrupt vv. 7, 9 and anticipates 13.8–15 (Ludwig Schmidt, *Menschlicher Erfolg und Jahwes Initiative: Studien zu Tradition, Interpretation und Historie in Überlieferungen von Gideon, Saul und David*, WMANT 38 [Neukirchen-Vluyn: Neukirchener Verlag, 1970], 102), whilst 1 Sam 11.15 is somewhat overfull (e.g. the repeated שׁם) and the verse as a whole has sometimes been judged as unnecessary. (For the most detailed discussion, see Reinhard Müller, *Königtum und Gottesherrschaft: Untersuchungen zur alttestamentlichen Monarchiekritik*, FAT II/3 [Tübingen: Mohr Siebeck, 2004], 149–58).

[65] Otherwise only 1 Sam 11.15. The alternative is to understand either זְבָחִים or שְׁלָמִים as a secondary addition (cf. Rendtorff, *Geschichte des Opfers*, 98–9). Several Samaritan Pentateuch manuscripts have the easier זבחי שלמים, though the majority, including 𝔊[D], have the same consonantal text as the Masoretic Text (see Schorch [ed.], *Exodus*).

[66] Thomas Römer, 'Provisorische Überlegungen zur Entstehung von Exodus 18–24', in '*Gerechtigkeit und Recht zu üben*' (Gen 18,19): *Studien zur altorientalischen und biblischen Rechtsgeschichte, zur Religionsgeschichte Israels und zur Religionssoziologie. Festschrift für Eckart Otto zum 65. Geburtstag*, eds. Reinhard Achenbach and Martin Arneth, BZABR 13 (Wiesbaden: Harrassowitz, 2009), 128–54.

[67] Albertz regards 24.1–2, 9–11 as part of his *Exoduskomposition* (K[EX]), which forces him to regard 'Nadab and Abihu' as a late gloss (PB[5]) (Albertz, *Exodus 19–40*, 107, 134).

The Framing as an Interpretive Key for the Sinai Narrative

The framing of the Sinai narrative in Exod 19.3–8 and 24.3–8 is clearly designed to provide an interpretive lens through which to view the revelation at Sinai. Most obviously, the framing understands the entire Sinai revelation as a covenant between God and Israel. The idea of a covenant is almost entirely absent from the Sinai pericope with the exception of 23.32, an instruction not to make covenants with the Canaanites or their gods. In Exod 19.5–6 the terms of the covenant are outlined with the briefest sketch of the obligations and benefits. The people are to obey God's voice and keep the covenant, and if they do so, they will enjoy an exalted position amongst the nations. The people's agreement is secured with the words 'everything that YHWH has spoken we will do' (כֹּל אֲשֶׁר־דִּבֶּר יְהוָה נַעֲשֶׂה; v. 8). The implications of that commitment are only fully apparent in 24.3 when they are repeated in the context of Moses reporting all the instructions that God has delivered to him on Mount Sinai. The people reaffirm their commitment of 19.8 in almost identical wording—'all the words that YHWH has spoken we will do' (כָּל־הַדְּבָרִים אֲשֶׁר־דִּבֶּר יְהוָה נַעֲשֶׂה; 24.3)—but the 'words' are now the Decalogue and the ordinances of Exod 21–23. These words are now understood to be the content of the covenant. When Moses writes them down, they are identified as the 'book of the covenant'. Thus, it is through the addition of the frame that Sinai is turned into a covenant between God and Israel.

The frame not only defines the significance of the encounter at Mount Sinai, but also places it into the larger narrative flow of the book of Exodus. The opening in 19.3–8 looks forwards to the Sinai revelation, but it also looks backwards to the previous chapters. The story of the exodus is rehearsed in the briefest way possible. Israel has experienced what God did to Egypt and the care shown to the Israelites. They were borne on eagle's wings, an image perhaps intended to describe the divine protection.[68] Thus, 19.3–8 can be regarded not simply as part of the framing of the Sinai pericope, but also as a hinge between two parts of the book of Exodus. Arguably, the same can also be said of Exod 24.3–8. The integration of word and rite looks back to the instructions delivered to Moses, but also forward to the tabernacle account. The construction of an altar, and a ritual act that involves the aspersion of blood on an altar and individuals, anticipates the construction of the tabernacle and the ordination of its priests. The notion of a hinge is especially apparent in the distinctive terminology 'blood of the covenant' (דַּם־הַבְּרִית; Exod 24.8), which unites the interpretation of Sinai as a covenant with the sanctifying role of blood in the tabernacle account.

---

[68] The use of an eagle as an image of divine care is also found in Deut 32.10–11. For God carrying Israel in the wilderness, see Deut 1.31.

The Blood Ritual in Exod 24

The significance of the blood ritual in Exod 24 has been the subject of extensive discussion. Three distinct interpretations have been proposed. First, the blood is a symbol of an imprecatory oath.[69] Self-imprecation is an effective explanation of the divided animals in Jer 34, and there are many other examples from the ancient Near East.[70] In such cases, however, the oath of imprecation is explicit, and this is not the case in Exod 24.3–8.

The second proposal is that the blood establishes a bond of covenant. In favour of this view we can note the fact that the blood is identified as the 'blood of the covenant', דַּם־הַבְּרִית, in v. 8. This expression is found only here and in Zech 9.11, which appears to be dependent on Exod 24. William Gilders argues that the blood is sprinkled on the two parties and represents the bond between them.[71] If that were the case, the altar would represent God. The problem with this proposal is that there is nowhere else in the Hebrew Bible where the altar represents God.[72] In addition, as Nicholson observes, there is no parallel to blood being understood in this way elsewhere in the Hebrew Bible.[73]

In the third interpretation the sprinkling of the people with blood is understood as an act that sanctifies both altar and people similar to what we find in the ordination and consecration rituals (Exod 29; Lev 8). These are the only rites in the Hebrew Bible where blood from the same sacrifice is applied to both an altar and a group of individuals. They bring the Israelites into relationship with the altar for the purpose of priestly service. As Nicholson puts it, 'those over whom the blood of Yahweh's sacrifices is cast now belong peculiarly to him, and are thereby also solemnly commissioned to his service, just as the consecration of priests was a commissioning to the office of priests.'[74]

Gilders rejects this third interpretation because Exod 24 and Lev 8 'are not identical in form or purpose' and do not occur in the same source.[75] Such objections are not compelling. We may deal briefly with his observation that they do not occur in the same source, and cannot be used to interpret each other. Gilders' source critical assessment has limited value because it is so blunt. He simply

---

[69] See, e.g., Ernst Kutsch, 'Das sog. Bundesblut in Ex 24:8 und Sach 9:11', *VT* 23 (1973): 25–30.

[70] Theodore J. Lewis, 'Covenant and Blood Rituals: Understanding Exodus 24:3–8 in Its Ancient Near Eastern Context', in *Confronting the Past: Archaeological and Historical Essays on Ancient Israel in Honor of William G. Dever*, eds. Seymour Gitin, J. Edward Wright, and J.P. Dessel (University Park, PA: Pennsylvania State University Press, 2006), 344.

[71] The idea that sacrificial blood creates a bond between two parties is found already in the work of William Robertson Smith, *Lectures on the Religion of the Semites. First Series: The Fundamental Institutions*, 2nd edn (London: Black, 1894). See also Cassuto, *Exodus*, 312.

[72] Ronald S. Hendel, 'Sacrifice as a Cultural System: The Ritual Symbolism of Exodus 24:3–8', *ZAW* 101 (1989): 388.

[73] Ernest Wilson Nicholson, 'The Covenant Ritual in Exodus 24:3–8', *VT* 32 (1982): 82.

[74] Nicholson, *God and His People*, 172.

[75] Gilders, *Blood Ritual*, 39.

identifies Exod 24 as non-P. But if Exod 24.3–8 is a late, post-priestly composition, as I have argued and is accepted by many contemporary scholars, there is
no reason to exclude the possibility that its scribal authors were aware of the
ordination ritual in Lev 8 and consciously modelled the blood ritual on it.
Nevertheless, Gilders is right to identify differences between Exod 24 and Lev 8.
Blood is applied to an altar and individuals in both accounts, but the ritual in Lev
8 includes anointing with oil and uses different terminology for the blood application. In Lev 8 the blood is dashed (זר״ק) against the altar, but placed (נת״ן) on
the priest's bodily extremities and sprinkled (הז״ה) on Aaron and his sons. In Exod
24 the blood is dashed (זר״ק) on altar and people. It is possible that Exod 24 has
overlooked or ignored the fine technical distinctions of the priestly instructions
and in doing so emphasized the equivalence of the blood application to the altar
and people. The second important difference is, of course, the role of the young
men in offering the sacrifices. In Lev 9 it is Moses that offers the sacrifices. As we
have already seen, the appearance of the 'young men' (נְעָרִים) has long been something of an interpretive crux. There is some evidence that נְעָרִים was sometimes
used as a technical term designating subordinate cultic officials, rather than
young men with no cultic status.[76] Consequently, Steuernagel's argument that this
terminology pointed to an early tradition in which any young male could serve as
priest is no longer compelling.[77] Rather, the appearance of נְעָרִים illustrates the
subtlety of the late scribal author. The use of 'young men' alludes to the occasional
cultic use of the terminology, but is literarily appropriate to Exod 24, which
occurs many chapters before the Aaronide priesthood will be ordained. In addition, the 'young men' at the foot of the mountain may have been chosen as a
counterpart to the 'elders' assembled on its summit (v. 1).[78]

The Kingdom of Priests

The proposal that the blood ritual sanctifies the people for the purpose of ordaining them as priests must also be seen in relation to the promise that 'you will be

---

[76] Nicholson, 'Covenant Ritual', 81. See already Ehrlich, *Randglossen*, 362–3. For further evidence
of נְעָרִים as a technical term within the cult, see Brian Peckham, 'Notes on a Fifth-Century Phoenician
Inscription from Kition, Cyprus (CIS 86)', *Or* 37 (1968): 304–24. In some Ugaritic texts *nʿr* seems to
be a cultic profession, such as when it appears alongside *khn* and *qdš* (KTU 9.436). For further discussion of נער, see John MacDonald, 'The Status and Role of the Naʿar in Israelite Society', *JNES* 35
(1976): 147–70.

[77] The acceptance of Steuernagel's argument created some difficulties for Perlitt, who had rightly
recognized that covenant was not an ancient tradition in the Hebrew Bible. Perlitt identified a fragment of an ancient tradition in vv. 4aβ–6 (Perlitt, *Bundestheologie im Alten Testament*, 190–203). It is
difficult to explain, however, why the blood was divided in half and only one half of it used. Perlitt has
been forced into this unattractive proposal by the need to explain the supposed antiquity of נְעָרִים.

[78] Dohmen, *Exodus 19–40*, 202. For the word-pair נער and זָקֵן, see Gen 19.4; Exod 10.9; Deut 28.50;
Josh 6.21; Isa 3.5; 20.4; 65.20; Jer 51.22; Ps 148.12; Lam 2.21; Esth 3.13 (cf. Ps 37.25; Prov 22.6).

264 THE MAKING OF THE TABERNACLE

for me a kingdom of priests, a holy nation' (תִּהְיוּ־לִי מַמְלֶכֶת כֹּהֲנִים וְגוֹי קָדוֹשׁ) in Exod 19.6. The expression מַמְלֶכֶת כֹּהֲנִים, 'kingdom of priests', which is found nowhere else in the Hebrew Bible, is a famous exegetical crux.[79] In Exodus 19 it occurs in conjunction with several expressions that have their inspiration in Deuteronomistic idioms, but מַמְלֶכֶת כֹּהֲנִים stands out for lacking this heritage. The challenges in interpreting מַמְלֶכֶת כֹּהֲנִים begin with the word מַמְלֶכֶת, which is best understood as the construct form of an abstract noun formed from מֶלֶךְ, 'king'. It can be used of the dominion ruled by a king, his kingdom (e.g. Num 32.33), or the concept of ruling, his kingship (e.g. 1 Sam 13.13). These two possible meanings of מַמְלֶכֶת provide two very different interpretations of the expression מַמְלֶכֶת כֹּהֲנִים,[80] and two different understandings of the relationship between מַמְלֶכֶת כֹּהֲנִים and the following expression גוֹי קָדוֹשׁ, 'a holy nation.'[81] If מַמְלֶכֶת means 'kingship' what is envisaged is that Israel will be a nation ruled by priests. The following expression 'holy nation' is not a parallel expression, but something that flows from the rulership exercised by the priests. The theocratic leadership results in a society characterized by holiness.[82] It has rightly been objected that we do not see a theocracy of this sort in Israel until the Hasmonean period, which would be far too late for the composition of Exod 19.[83] If מַמְלֶכֶת means 'kingdom', however, the idea is that the entire nation will be priests. The following words 'holy nation' express the same notion in a different way.[84] The priestly vocation of every Israelite necessarily requires that the entire nation is holy.

When 'kingdom of priests' is understood to mean that the entire nation of Israelites serve as priests, it clearly corresponds to the ritual in Exod 24. Having heard the divine commandments and committed themselves to obey them, the ritual realizes God's covenantal agreement. By sprinkling the altar and the Israelites with sacrificial blood, the Israelites become the 'kingdom of priests'. The notion that the entire nation might be priests is not unknown in the Persian period. In Isa 61.6 a future is envisaged where the Israelites are called 'priests of YHWH' and 'ministers of our God'. What Trito-Isaiah envisions as a future utopia, Exod 24 has

---

[79] There was clearly considerable uncertainty already in antiquity about how to understand the expression. The Old Greek of Vaticanus reads βασίλειον ἱεράτευμα, 'royal priesthood'. Israel is envisaged as a priesthood from kingly stock (Wevers, *Greek Text of Exodus*, 295). The Targ. Onq. has the two words in apposition 'kingdom, priests' (מלכין כהנין), whilst Targ. Neo. has the two joined by a conjunction 'kingdom and priests' (מלכין וכהנין).

[80] Cf. Ska, 'Exode 19,3b–6', 290; Propp, *Exodus 19–40*, 157.

[81] Georg Steins, 'Priesterherrschaft, Volk von Priestern oder was sonst? Zur Interpretation von Ex 19,6', *BZ* 45 (2001): 23.

[82] Ska argues for the same idea on different lines. He compares the uses of the construct form of מַמְלֶכֶת elsewhere in the Hebrew Bible and observes that the most common form is with a proper noun of the ruler. On this basis he proposes that the priests are the rulers: 'a kingdom ruled by priests' (Ska, 'Exode 19,3b–6').

[83] E.g. Steins, 'Priesterherrschaft', 26–8.

[84] מַמְלֶכֶת and גוי appear in poetic parallelism in Isa 13.4; Jer 29.18; 51.20, 27; Ezek 37.22; Nah 3.5; Zeph 3.8; Pss 46.6; 79.6; 105.13 (// 1 Chron 16.20) and as a pair in 1 Kgs 18.10; Isa 60.12; Jer 1.10; 18.7, 9; 27; Hag 2.22; 2 Chron 32.15 (cf. Ezek 29.15).

projected into Israel's mythic past. In both cases we appear to have scribal speculations whose precise relationship to Persian period cultic practice is difficult to
determine. The ritual at the foot of Mount Sinai is not only presented as a unique
historical moment, it is difficult to envisage how it could be realized. The impedi-
ments to actual practice of the ritual have long been observed. How were the
entire people to be dashed with sacrificial blood? Notwithstanding such problems, were attempts ever made to realize the ritual? There is no evidence, so far as
I am aware, of the ritual being practised in the Second Temple period. As in the
case of the dedication of the Levites, the existence of a ritual that is a scribal
invention raises the intriguing possibility of textual speculation giving rise to
ritual, rather than the text reflecting ritual practice. Even if, as in this case, it is
likely that a rite of priestly ordination lies in the background of Exod 24.

As we have seen, the exchange between God, Moses and the people in Exod
19.3–8 and the blood sprinkling ritual in Exod 24.3–8 provide an interpretive
framework for the Sinai revelation. The divine instructions are understood to be
the terms of the covenant that Israel is to keep. But the framework also provides
an interpretation of the texts that surround the Sinai pericope. This is readily
apparent in Exod 19.3–8, where the exodus events are portrayed as an act of res-
cue and protection, but it is also the case in Exod 24.3–8 where the consecration
of the entire nation of Israel as priests forms the text that immediately precedes
the tabernacle account.

But what kind of effect was intended by the insertion of the blood rite in Exod
24.3–8? It could be seen as a major qualification of the claims about the Aaronide
priests made in the tabernacle account.[85] Rather than having a distinctive and
privileged role in the Israelite cult, the Aaronides are, in fact, no better than any
other Israelite. The entire nation is holy and all have been sprinkled with blood
that ordains them as priests. Even allowing for the ritual as an interpretive lens for
all that follows in Exodus to Numbers, it is difficult to see how the account of this
one ritual could displace the overwhelming impression of Aaronide pre-eminence
in the Pentateuch. This understanding is also precluded by the way that the blood
ritual is framed by the events on top of Mount Sinai (vv. 1–2, 9–11). Moses,
Aaron, Nadab and Abihu, and the seventy elders do not ascend the mountain
until after the blood ritual has been performed. Consequently, they receive the
sanctifying blood, but they are also distinguished from the ordinary Israelites.
They ascend the mountain, see God, and eat and drink before him! The theocratic

---

[85] In contrast, understanding מַמְלֶכֶת כֹּהֲנִים as 'kingship of priests' is rather more easily aligned with
the theology of the priestly literature. For reflections from this perspective see Ska, 'Exode 19,3b–6'.
Ska notes two differences between Exod 19.3–8 and the priestly *Grundschrift*. First, in Exod 19 an
important role is played by the Sinai covenant. In the priestly document there are covenants with
Noah and Abraham, but not a Sinai covenant. Within the development of the priestly literature, it is
only with the Holiness Code that we find the notion of a Sinai covenant. Second, the idea of the nation
as holy is not an idea found in the priestly literature, and is closer to the theology of the Holiness Code.

266   THE MAKING OF THE TABERNACLE

structures that have been articulated in earlier iterations of the ordination ritual are not dissolved by a ritual that establishes Israel as a 'kingdom of priests'. This kingdom of priests has a priestly family who enjoy cultic pre-eminence as well as communal leaders, both groups receive divine approbation in Exod 24. Thus, far from qualifying the claims of the Aaronide priests, the notion of a kingdom of priests suggests a favoured group within a favoured nation. As Dozeman puts it, 'the ideal vision of the Israelites in a priestly role to the nations does not eliminate the role of the priesthood within the Israelite cult. Rather it demands it.'[86]

If the entire nation has not displaced the cultic role of the Aaronides, what does it mean to call the Israelites a 'kingdom of priests' and to splash sacrificial blood upon them? One possibility is that the language should simply be understood metaphorically and bears no cultic implications. Thus, it could be understood as an expression of Israel's sanctity in comparison to the nations. We might imagine concentric circles of sanctity with Aaron in the centre as high priest surrounded by the remaining priests occupying a circle of lower sanctity. The people have a still lower level of sanctity, but they are holy in comparison to the nations. But could this not simply have been expressed by calling Israel a 'holy nation'?

The parallel in Isa 61.5–6 may provide some insight into what kinds of hopes were attached to the idea of a 'kingdom of priests':

> 5 Strangers shall stand and feed your flocks,
>   And foreigners will be your ploughmen and vinedressers
> 6 But you will be called YHWH's priests,
>   You will be named minister of our God;
>   You will consume the wealth of nations,
>   And you will be fattened by their abundance.

In Trito-Isaiah, the hope of being YHWH's priests brings with it some specific, material benefits. The cultic service of the Israelites contrasts with the agricultural labours of the nations, which they will do on behalf of Israel (v. 5). The Israelites escape the toil in the fields but enjoy its fruits. The benefits are material and specific: the Israelites *eat* (תֹּאכֵלוּ) the wealth of nations and are *fattened* (תִּתְיַמָּרוּ)[87] on their abundance (v. 6). As texts like Lev 1–7, Num 18, and 1 Sam 2 demonstrate, the priesthood enjoyed a privileged access to the agricultural produce of the land. The sacrificial economy ensured that the priests were well supplied with the best cuts of meat and the first fruits of the harvest. Trito-Isaiah's vision of the future

---

[86] Dozeman, *Commentary on Exodus*, 446.

[87] The interpretation of the *hapax legomenon* תִּתְיַמָּרוּ is difficult. The translation 'and you will be fattened' assumes the word derives from a by-form of מר״א. This has the advantage of providing a suitable parallel with אכ״ל in the previous colon. For discussion and other proposals, see Shalom M. Paul, *Isaiah 40-66: Translation and Commentary*, Eerdmans Critical Commentary (Grand Rapids, MI: Eerdmans, 2012), 544; John Goldingay, *Isaiah 56-66*, ICC (London: Bloomsbury, 2014), 287–8.

sees the Israelites acting as priesthood for the world with the best agricultural produce coming to them.

The covenantal promises to Israel in Exod 19 are not as explicit as in Isa 61, though they do emphasize Israel's favoured state. The language of a 'treasured possession' or a 'kingdom' refers to those assembled at Mount Sinai, rather than the benefits they accrue. Nevertheless, the language of privilege and benefit is implicit in the description of Israel's exalted status and unique relationship with YHWH. Beyond that, the enjoyment of agricultural bounty is the point at which the blessings of the covenant and the benefits of priestly status overlap. Thus, post-deuteronomistic covenant theology and post-priestly cultic ritual converge around the material issue of food distribution.

Conclusion

In this chapter we have examined two further iterations of the ordination ritual, though one is, in some sense, more like a photographic negative: the dedication of the Levites is *not* an ordination. These two iterations move in very different directions, yet they both show ways in which Pentateuchal texts continue to be a site of negotiations about the power of the priesthood in relation to other groups in Israel.

In the book of Numbers readers meet a theocratic community that they have not encountered in the previous books. Not only is there a tabernacle served by priests, but a lower clergy assist them and defend the sanctuary from incursion by outsiders. Beyond the settlements of the Levites encamp the twelve secular tribes, each with their own tribal leader. This theocratic vision of the people of Israel is set out in the opening chapters of Numbers. In Num 7–10, later priestly writers incorporate that new theocratic vision into the earlier narrative by turning the clock back a month. The story of the tabernacle's erection and consecration is retold with a place for the tribal leaders and the Levites. Rather than revising the texts of Exod 40 and Lev 8–10, these later priestly authors simply provide their own account of rituals that integrate the tribal leaders and the Levites into the story of the tabernacle. The intention is not simply that it leaves the difficult work of establishing a coherent chronology to the reader—though it is not clear this can be achieved in any satisfactory way—but also that it encourages the reader to reflect on the rituals in light of one another. The story of the tribal leaders' offerings reminds the reader of the ritual innovations of Aaron's sons, but the tribal leaders are not destroyed by fire. Their offering proves acceptable to YHWH. It does not encroach on the prerogatives of the established priestly hierarchy. The offerings of the leaders show that there is an appropriate avenue for those who desire to do something novel for the sanctuary. The account of the Levites' dedication has many similarities to the ordination ritual, but it is not a retelling of it. Instead, Num 8 emphasizes the differences: most importantly, the Levites are purified, not consecrated. For both the leaders and the Levites, their involvement in the opening days of the tabernacle grants them a legitimacy and authority not shared by ordinary Israelites. They have a distinguished relationship to the tabernacle. But, they do not displace the priests and are adopted into the existing hierarchy in a subordinate position below the priest and the high priest.

Perhaps the latest iteration of the ordination ritual in the Pentateuch is to be found in Exod 24. It is given an interpretive priority through its narrative location at the end of the non-priestly Sinai pericope and prior to the tabernacle account. The claim that Israel is a 'kingdom of priests' that undergoes its own ritual of ordination does not displace the ritual competencies of the Aaronide priests. The theocratic order that has been outlined in the book of Numbers remains in place: Moses, Aaron, his sons and the seventy elders enjoy the privilege of seeing God and eating in his presence. The rest of the people remain at the foot of the mountain. As a result, the Aaronide priests maintain their role as the principal ritual actors in the books that follow. If anything, the power of the priesthood is enhanced. Only priests can truly represent and lead a 'kingdom of priests'. Thus, Exod 19 and 24 do not mean that ordinary Israelites start exercising priestly functions. These chapters do, however, envisage a world where Israel enjoys an exalted status due to its covenantal relationship with YHWH. As a result of which, the Israelites too will experience the material benefits that accrue to the priests.

Conclusion

This examination of the tabernacle account began with the late antique and medieval exemplars of the book of Exodus and sought to move from there to the earliest version composed by the priestly writer in the early Persian period. The medieval encounter with the Bible was quite unlike the modern one. It is not just that Bibles were unusual and precious artefacts in the Middle Ages. Nor that literacy was the preserve of a small caste. Nor that Bibles were owned by monasteries, and occasionally bishops or kings. It is also that readers of the Bible encountered the wilderness tabernacle in a manner unlike that experienced by modern readers. Many contemporary readers of the Bible are spared exposure to the tabernacle. Devotional reading schemes and Christian lectionaries steer around what is regarded as one of the most unappealing parts of the Bible to the modern palate. The medieval reader of the Bible, however, was confronted by images of the tabernacle furniture which accompanied the biblical text. In a medieval Hebrew Bible these were often placed at the codex's beginning and end, or between the Torah, the prophets, and the writings. In this way an analogy was signalled between text and tabernacle: the Scriptures were imagined as a virtual sanctuary. In the words of the Catalan Profiat Duran, 'God intentionally prepared the Torah for Israel in its time of exile, after the destruction of the temple, precisely so that it could serve as a little sanctuary, within whose pages God's presence might be found just as his presence formally dwelled within the Temple's four walls.'[1]

Amongst Christian codices of the Bible a stunning example of a tabernacle illumination is found in Codex Amiatinus, the earliest surviving complete Vulgate Bible.[2] The codex is a monumental achievement, one of three pandects produced

---

[1] Theodor Dunkelgrün, 'Tabernacles of Text: A Brief Visual History of the Hebrew Bible', in *Impagination—Layout and Materiality of Writing and Publication: Interdisciplinary Approaches from East and West*, eds. Ku-Ming Chang, Anthony Grafton, and Glenn W. Most (Berlin: de Gruyter, 2021), 74. The 'little sanctuary' (מקדש מעט) is a reference to Ezek 11.16, a famous *crux interpretum*. For an extensive discussion of this iconographic tradition, especially in medieval Spain, see Katrin Kogman-Appel, *Jewish Book Art between Islam and Christianity: The Decoration of Hebrew Bibles in Medieval Spain* (Leiden: Brill, 2004). In contrast to the Jewish traditions of illustrating biblical codices with tabernacle furniture and implements, there are no illuminated Samaritan Torah manuscripts. For the sixteenth century onwards representations of the tabernacle exist as self-standing pieces of religious art (J.D. Purvis, 'The Tabernacle in Samaritan Iconography and Thought', in *Uncovering Ancient Stones: Essays in Memory of H.N. Richardson*, ed. L.M. Hopfe [Winona Lake, IN: Eisenbrauns, 1994]; Reinhard Pummer, 'Samaritan Tabernacle Drawings', *Numen* 45 [1998]: 30–68).

[2] There is an extensive literature devoted to Codex Amiatinus, its history and significance. For recent discussion and earlier bibliography, see Jane Hawkes and Meg Boulton, eds., *All Roads Lead to Rome: The Creation, Context and Transmission of the Codex Amiatinus*, Studia Traditionis Theologiae 31

by the twin monasteries of Wearmouth-Jarrow under the leadership of their abbot Ceolfrith (688–716 CE). Now held in the Laurentian Library in Florence, Codex Amiatinus was gifted to the bishop of Rome by Ceolfrith. Whether it made it to Rome is uncertain, as are the circumstances that led to it becoming the possession of San Salvatore at Monte Amiata, from which it took its name. There is no doubt, however, that the codex was an extravagant gift. Written in a clear Roman uncial script, the entire manuscript numbers over 2000 pages and is just over 25cm thick. Arguably the most stunning feature of Codex Amiatinus is the opening quire which consists of a verse dedication by Ceolfrith, three schemas of the divisions of Scripture, a cross diagram of the Pentateuch, and two illuminations portraying Ezra and the tabernacle. The precise order originally intended for these features of the opening quire cannot be determined with certainty as the pages have been rearranged on at least three occasions during the codex's history, and modern scholars have offered various proposals for the original order.[3] It seems likely, however, that the tabernacle illumination occupied the central position in the quire, since it is the only illustration to extend over two pages.[4]

Codex Amiatinus offers a bird's-eye view of the entire tabernacle complex with the furniture portrayed in three dimensions as though viewed from the southeast corner.[5] The various architectural features are depicted with a frontal view. When combined with the bird's-eye perspective of the furniture, this gives the impression that the pillars, boards, and veils are lying flat on the ground. The architectural features and the furniture of the courtyard—the altar of burnt offering and the basin—are outlined in black, whilst the sanctuary furniture—the lampstand, table, incense altar, and ark—are outlined in red. The furniture is identified in Latin with white uncials. So, too, is the sanctuary entrance, which is marked by a small red cross. The cardinal points are given with Greek names— *dysis, arctos, mesembria, anatol*—in a large, outline lettering in black.[6]

What is particularly striking about the tabernacle illumination of Codex Amiatinus is that the theocratic structure of the wilderness camp is also

---

(Turnhout: Brepols, 2019); Celia Chazelle, *The Codex Amiatinus and Its 'Sister' Bibles: Scripture, Liturgy, and Art in the Milieu of the Venerable Bede*, Commentaria 10 (Leiden: Brill, 2019).

[3] For discussion, see Paul Meyvaert, 'Bede, Cassiodorus, and the Codex Amiatinus', *Speculum* 71 (1996): 827–83; Sabina Magrini, 'Per difetto del legatore: Storia delle rilegature della Bibbia Amiatina in Laurenziana', *Quinio* 3 (2001): 137–67; Celia Chazelle, 'Ceolfrid's Gift to St Peter: The First Quire of *Codex Amiatinus* and the Evidence of Its Roman Destination', *Early Medieval Europe* 12 (2003): 129–58; Chazelle, *Codex Amiatinus*, 315–19.

[4] Chazelle notes the rarity of illuminations that spread over two pages in the early medieval period (Chazelle, 'Ceolfrid's Gift', 136).

[5] The south-east projection is also apparent from the boards of the tabernacle since the boards of the north and west are portrayed. In addition, the writing is orientated so as to be read either from the south or the east.

[6] For the possible significance of the Greek names for the cardinal points, see Jennifer O'Reilly, *Early Medieval Text and Image 2: The Codex Amiatinus, the Book of Kells and Anglo-Saxon Art*, Variorum Collected Studies Series (London: Routledge, 2019), 38–40.

CONCLUSION 271

represented.[7] The names and numbers of the three Levitical septs are written in a white uncial script at their assigned locations around the sanctuary with the names and numbers of the twelve Israelite tribes placed outside the courtyard in the places identified as their encampment by the book of Numbers. Finally, the names of Moses and Aaron are placed prominently besides the basin and underneath the altar of burnt offering in a slightly larger, red script. Throughout the entire illumination, the use of different colour inks and larger or small scripts provide subtle clues to the relationships between different elements. The red ink indexes the names of Moses and Aaron with the cross of the entrance and the furniture within the sanctuary as does the placement of the names close to the entrance. The illumination subtly, but determinedly, emphasizes that only Moses and Aaron may enter the sanctuary itself. They play a critical role in the Old Testament cultus. The other illumination of Codex Amiatinus also alludes to the importance of the priesthood for it portrays Ezra as both a biblical scholar and a Jewish high priest. Ezra sits writing in a codex with a table before him and the tools of the scriptorium on the floor besides him. Dominating the picture is an open cupboard which holds nine volumes of the Scriptures. Although the pose and writing tools are those of an evangelist of Late Antique portraiture, Ezra also bears the breastplate and gold headband of the high priest. The role of Ezra in restoring the Scriptures is communicated in the caption above the picture: 'After the sacred codices were incinerated in the enemy devastation, Esdra, burning for God, repaired this work.'[8]

In her comprehensive study of Codex Amiatinus, Chazelle has argued compellingly that the focus on the priestly hierarchy was deliberate in light of the book's intended function as a gift to the Pope in Rome.[9] The illuminations highlight the priesthood's crucial role within the divine economy. If the Christian Bible is the current locus of the divine presence, the typological fulfilment of the ancient wilderness tabernacle, the priests are the indispensable means by which to access it. Despite a millennium separating Codex Amiatinus and the composition of the tabernacle account, the pandect's illuminations understood that the tabernacle expressed the cultic power of the priesthood.

---

[7] The distinctiveness of Codex Amiatinus is apparent if, as is often suggested, its representation of the tabernacle has as its precursor Cosmas Indicopleustes' *Christian Topography*.

[8] Chazelle, *Codex Amiatinus*, 320.

[9] The dedication poem originally read: *corpus ad eximii merito / uenerabile Petri // quem caput ecclesiae / dedicat alta fides // Ceolfridus Anglorum / extremis de finibus abbas // deuoti affectus / pignora mitto mei // meque meosque optans / tanti inter gaudia patris // in caelis memorem / semper habere locum.* 'To the deservedly venerable body of the outstanding Peter, whom deep faith dedicates head of the church, I Ceolfrith, of the Angles, abbot from the farthest ends, send tokens of my devoted affection, desiring that my men and I, among the joys of such a father, may forever have a remembered place in heaven' (Chazelle, *Codex Amiatinus*, 319).

The Priestly Hierarchy and the Tabernacle Account

In each of the extant versions that survived into late antiquity and the medieval period, the tabernacle account and its related texts in the Pentateuch portrayed a complex, hierarchical society. They reflect an extended history of composition in which the texts were an important site where the power of the priesthood and of other groups were negotiated. This process was not straightforward, nor did it progress in a linear direction. The distribution of power was never a settled affair. At one stage, for example, the high priest alone is anointed with oil, a privilege that may have originally been reserved for the king, but this was later enjoyed by all priests. Nevertheless, as the tabernacle account developed the high priesthood accrued significant privileges. From the earliest priestly document, the high priest was portrayed representing Israel, and his indispensability for the performance of the cult accrued additional features over time: without the high priest no atonement could be made for the tabernacle and no incense offered on the gold altar in the outer sanctum.

The hierarchy of the priestly literature can easily be imagined as a social pyramid. At the bottom are the ordinary Israelites, above whom are the Levites. Above them are the priests and at the pinnacle is the high priest himself. As we move up the pyramid, the groups are progressively smaller, accrue greater holiness, and lay claim to enhanced material benefits. Certainly, there is a great deal to this idea, though it needs to be qualified. Whilst such a hierarchy maps onto the tabernacle space to some extent, the portrait of the society is itself a composite. The depiction of the tabernacle in Exodus does show that proximity to the ark and the inner sanctum communicates privilege with the screens and veils restricting access and preventing sight of the holy furniture. The ordinary Israelites cannot move beyond the entrance to the tent of meeting, the priests may enter the outer sanctum, but only Aaron can penetrate the veil and step into the inner sanctum. The Levites, however, have no role in the tabernacle's space and we need to augment its portrayal with that of the camp in the early chapters of Numbers. It is only with the assignment of encampments in Num 1–4 that the Levites are assigned their place, settled closer to the tabernacle than the remaining tribes, but with the families of Moses and Aaron encamped on the eastern side by the entrance.

To this picture we should also add the various nested hierarchies introduced primarily within Exod 35–40: male and female, Judah and non-Judah, leader and led. In most cases, these can be introduced into the hierarchy, leaving its basic structure untouched. On the other hand, priestly and Levitical women are unmentioned. Are they included in the women who offer for the sanctuary and contribute to the fabrication of materials? In the case of the leaders, the hierarchical layers are cut across by forging a relationship between the high priest and the leaders. The tribal chiefs provide for the most valuable parts of Aaron's vestments. Arguably, they enjoy a closer relationship with him than the ordinary priests or the Levites.

The contestation and renegotiation of the tabernacle's space further complicates the portrayal of the hierarchy. The entrance to the tent of meeting initially depicts the liminal zone at the edge of the courtyard. The priests cannot enter until they have been consecrated. This space is quite modest when it need only accommodate Moses, Aaron, and his four sons. A different concept is required when the Israelites witness the ritual and commentators have not surprisingly imagined an 'entrance' that incorporates a significant portion of the courtyard. In a similar way, it seems likely that the outer sanctum was once envisaged as off-limits to the ordinary priests and was serviced by Aaron alone, but subsequent developments allow the priests to service the table and lampstand, leaving only the incense altar to the high priest's attentions. Thus, the division of tabernacle space into inner and outer sanctum and courtyard does not map onto the hierarchical divisions in the community, and more complicated liminal zones are created.

The development of the tabernacle account not only gave rise to complexities in the portrayal of hierarchy, but also created power. The multiplication of rituals and the complex gradation of space generates additional levels of hierarchy and, simultaneously, domains of knowledge and control. The original tabernacle featured only Aaron as representative of the priesthood, the sole official within the sanctuary. The multi-layered hierarchy in the extant versions bestows rights and responsibilities to further groups: the ordinary priests, the Levites, the artisans, the tribal leaders. Far from diminishing the power and pre-eminence of the high priest, such generation and diffusion of power further enhances it. Allowing the people into the courtyard to witness the consecration of the tabernacle and the priesthood affirms the distinctive calling of the priests. Similarly, affirming the Israelite artisans as capable manufacturers—in contrast to the fashioning of a golden calf by Aaron—attributes significant creative authority to them, whilst also subordinating crafting expertise to ritual competence. Or, to choose another example, the insistence that Israel is a 'kingdom of priests' does not undermine the stature of the Aaronic priesthood. Instead, it makes priests central to Israel's meaningfulness as a community.

Paradoxical though it may initially appear, the tabernacle account and description of the ordination rituals make both hierarchical and egalitarian claims. The tribal leaders bring identical offerings, though Judah takes the leading position. Similarly, the half-shekel tax is raised from each Israelite male. It goes unmentioned that such revenue raising is determined by class and gender, and that the Levites and priests do not contribute. In the tabernacle account, all Israelites are equal, but some are more equal than others. Similarly, whilst the biblical text presents the cult benefiting the community by ensuring the divine presence and securing atonement, the community also benefits the cult and its officials. Indeed, the original priestly document orientates history and the entirety of God's creation to the tabernacle. The pre-eminence of the cult is matched spatially in later developments by orientating the camp around the sanctuary, and through the

274   THE MAKING OF THE TABERNACLE

organization of labour with the entire community employed in the tabernacle's construction. All are granted a place and a role, but the sanctuary and its priests are at the centre.

Our discussion of the priestly hierarchy and the tabernacle account has, to this point, been simply on a literary level. The tabernacle, its space, its priesthood, and its Israelite community exist as textual realities. The nature of their relationship to historical institutions is difficult to ascertain with confidence. Whilst the composition of the tabernacle account and the related texts about ordination mostly took place within the Persian period, its relationship to any temple or priesthood of that time is not straightforward. The tabernacle was, in Hanna Liss' words, an imaginary sanctuary.[10] It is set outside the time and space of the Hebrew kingdoms and the later Persian provinces. It need not reflect the cultic worship in Jerusalem, and, from the beginning, reading the text was an exercise in hermeneutics. Inevitably, we return to Frevel's observation that it was not 'the political development [that] shaped the text, but rather the other way around'.[11] It is from this perspective that we must view the question of how the high priest came to exercise coercive power. As the scribal illustrators of Codex Amiatinus rightly perceived priesthood, power, and writing are tightly bound together.

There is little basis for the idea that the high priests laid claim to the king's right to sovereignty. The authority that the priest exercised was focused entirely on the cult. As we have seen, the inclusion of an ordination ritual within the tabernacle account involved the appropriation of some royal symbolism. The high priest was anointed with oil, which in monarchic Israel and Judah appears to have been an exclusively royal distinction. The headdress of the high priest was identified as a 'crown'. Such brief allusions do not seem to have been cultivated further in subsequent redactions. In other respects, the portrayal of the high priest developed new resonances that, in retrospect, created the conditions for the high priest's political ascendancy. The tabernacle account from its earliest stages presents a priesthood at the apex of history: Israel and the world's. The subsequent developments place the high priest at the centre of Israel's community. He represents the tribes through his vestments and he atones for Israel by his actions. By what they do and what they are (and are not), the people, priests, craftsmen, leaders constantly index the high priest. The original priestly document of the early Persian period created an ideal sanctuary in the desert safe from imperial aggression and human failure, by the end of the Persian period the extant versions of the Pentateuch portray an ideal community without an imperial governor and with the high priest at its apex. The conditions for the high priest's assumption of coercive power were firmly established.

---

[10]   Hanna Liss, 'The Imaginary Sanctuary: The Priestly Code as an Example of Fictional Literature in the Hebrew Bible', in *Judah and the Judeans in the Persian Period*, eds. Oded Lipschits and Manfred Oeming (Winona Lake, IN: Eisenbrauns, 2006), 663–89.

[11]   Frevel, 'Leadership and Conflict', 106.

Bibliography

Achenbach, Reinhard, 'Das Versagen der Aaroniden: Erwägungen zum literarhistorischen Ort von Leviticus 10', in Matthias Augustin and Hermann Michael Niemann (Eds), 'Basel und Bibel': Collected Communications to the XVIIth Congress of the International Organization for the Study of the Old Testament, Basel 2001, BEATAJ 51 (Frankfurt am Main: Lang, 2004), 55–70.

Achenbach, Reinhard, Die Vollendung der Tora: Studien zur Redaktionsgeschichte des Numeribuches im Kontext von Hexateuch und Pentateuch, BZABR 3 (Wiesbaden: Harrassowitz, 2003).

Achenbach, Reinhard, 'Satrapie, Medinah und lokale Hierokratie: Zum Einfluss der Statthalter der Achämenidenzeit auf Tempelwirtschaft und Tempelordnungen', ZABR 16 (2010): 105–44.

Achenbach, Reinhard, 'Verunreinigung durch die Berührung Toter: Zum Ursprung einer altisraelitischen Vorstellung', in Angelika Berlejung and Bernd Janowski (Eds), Tod und Jenseits im Alten Israel und in seiner Umwelt: Theologische, religionsgeschichtliche, archäologische und ikonographische Aspekte, FAT 64 (Tübingen: Mohr Siebeck, 2009), 347–69.

Aejmelaeus, Anneli, 'Septuagintal Translation Techniques—A Solution to the Problem of the Tabernacle Account', in George J. Brooke and Barnabas Lindars (Eds), Septuagint, Scrolls and Cognate Writings: Papers Presented to the International Symposium on the Septuagint and Its Relations to the Dead Sea Scrolls and Other Writings (Manchester, 1990), SCS 33 (Atlanta, GA: Scholars Press, 1992), 381–402.

Aejmelaeus, Anneli, 'What Can We Know about the Hebrew "Vorlage" of the Septuagint?', ZAW 99 (1987): 58–89.

Aharoni, Yohanan, 'Arad: Its Inscriptions and Temple', BA 31 (1968): 1–32.

Albertz, Rainer, 'Beobachtungen zur Komposition der priesterlichen Texte Ex 25–40', in Jakob Wöhrle (Ed.), Pentateuchstudien, FAT 117 (Tübingen: Mohr Siebeck, 2018), 277–95.

Albertz, Rainer, Exodus 19–40, ZBK (Zurich: Theologischer Verlag, 2015).

Albertz, Rainer, 'How Jerusalem's Temple Was Aligned to Moses' Tabernacle: About the Historical Power of an Invented Myth', in Emanuel Pfoh and Lukasz Niesiolowski-Spanò (Eds), Biblical Narratives, Archaeology and Historicity: Essays in Honour of Thomas L. Thompson, LHBOTS 680 (London: Bloomsbury, 2020), 198–209.

Anderson, Gary A., 'Literary Artistry and Divine Presence', in Tova Ganzel and Shalom E. Holtz (Eds), Contextualizing Jewish Temples. BRLJ 64 (Leiden: Brill, 2020), 85–102.

Anderson, Gary A., That I May Dwell among Them: The Biblical Concept of Incarnation and Atonement (Grand Rapids: Eerdmans, forthcoming).

Anderson, Gary A., 'The Date of the Tabernacle's Completion and Consecration', TheTorah. Com, 2022. https://www.thetorah.com/article/the-date-of-the-tabernacles-completion-and-consecration.

Anderson, Gary A., '"Through Those Who Are Near to Me, I Will Show Myself Holy": Nadab and Abihu and Apophatic Theology', CBQ 77 (2015): 1–19.

276 BIBLIOGRAPHY

Arie, Eran, Baruch Rosen, and Dvory Namdar, 'Cannabis and Frankincense at the Judahite Shrine of Arad', *TA* 47 (2020): 5–28.

Attridge, Harold, Torleif Elgvin, Jozef Milik, Saul Olyan, and John Strugnell, *Qumran Cave 4. VIII. Parabiblical Texts, Part I*, DJD 11 (Oxford: Clarendon Press, 1994).

Auld, A. Graeme, *I & II Samuel: A Commentary*, OTL (Louisville, KY: Westminster John Knox, 2011).

Baentsch, Bruno, *Exodus-Leviticus-Numeri*, HKAT I.2 (Göttingen: Vandenhoeck & Ruprecht, 1903).

Baillet, M., J.T. Milik, and R. de Vaux, *Les 'Petites Grottes' de Qumrân: Textes*, DJD 3 (Oxford: Clarendon Press, 1962).

Balentine, Samuel E., *Leviticus*, IBC (Louisville, KY: Westminster John Knox Press, 2002).

Beer, Georg, and Kurt Galling, *Exodus*, HAT 3 (Tübingen: Mohr Siebeck, 1939).

Begg, Christopher T., 'The Death of Nadab and Abihu According to Josephus', *LASBF* 59 (2009): 155–67.

Belsheim, Johannes, *Palimpsestus Vindobonensis. Antiqvissimae Veteris Testamenti translationis latinae fragmenta e codice rescripto eruit et primum edidit* (Christianiae: P.T. Mallingi, 1885).

Berner, Christoph, 'The Redaction History of the Sinai Pericope (Exod 19–24) and Its Continuation in 4Q158', *DSD* 20 (2013): 378–409.

Bertholet, Alfred, *Leviticus*, KHAT 3 (Tübingen: Mohr Siebeck, 1901).

Beyerlin, Walter, *Herkunft und Geschichte der ältesten Sinaitraditionen* (Tübingen: Mohr, 1961).

Billen, A. V., *The Old Latin Texts of the Heptateuch* (Cambridge: Cambridge University Press, 1927).

Blenkinsopp, Joseph, 'The Structure of P', *CBQ* 38 (1976): 275–92.

Blum, Erhard, *Die Komposition der Vätergeschichte*, WMANT 57 (Neukirchen-Vluyn: Neukirchener Verlag, 1984).

Bogaert, Pierre-Maurice, 'La construction de la tente (Ex 36–40) dans le Monacensis de la plus ancienne version Latine: L'autel d'or et Hébreux 9,4', in Adrian Schenker and Philippe Hugo (Eds), *L'enfance de la Bible hébraïque. L'histoire du texte de l'Ancien Testament à la lumière des recherches récentes*, MdB 52 (Geneva: Labor et Fides, 2005), 62–76.

Bogaert, Pierre-Maurice, 'L'importance de la Septante et du 'Monacensis' de la Vetus Latina pour l'exégèse du livre de l'Exode (chap. 35–40)', in Marc Vervenne (Ed.), *Studies in the Book of Exodus: Redaction—Reception—Interpretation*, BETL 126 (Leuven: Leuven University Press, 1996), 399–428.

Bogaert, Pierre-Maurice, 'L'orientation du parvis du sanctuaire dans la version grecque de l'Exode (Ex., 27, 9–13 LXX)', *L'Antiquité Classique* 50 (1981): 79–85.

Boorer, Suzanne, *The Vision of the Priestly Narrative: Its Genre and Hermeneutics of Time*, AIL 27 (Atlanta, GA: Society of Biblical Literature, 2016).

Boyd, Samuel L., 'Applied Ritual: The Application of Blood and Oil on Bodies in the Pentateuchal Sources', *BibInt* 29 (2020): 120–47.

Brooke, George J., '4Q158: Reworked Pentateuch[a] or Reworked Pentateuch A?' *DSD* 8 (2001): 219–41.

Brooke, George J., 'The Temple Scroll and LXX Exodus 35–40', in George J. Brooke and Barnabas Lindars (Eds), *Septuagint, Scrolls and Cognate Writings: Papers Presented to the International Symposium on the Septuagint and Its Relations to the Dead Sea Scrolls and Other Writings (Manchester, 1990)*, SCS 33 (Atlanta, GA: Scholars Press, 1992), 81–106.

Bruning, Brandon E., 'The Making of the Mishkan: The Old Greek Text of Exodus 35–40 and the Literary History of the Pentateuch' (PhD diss., University of Notre Dame, 2014).

Budd, Philip J., *Numbers*, WBC 5 (Waco, TX: Word, 1984).

Burkitt, F. C., 'The Text of Exodus XL 17–19 in the Munich Palimpsest', *JTS* 29 (1928): 146–7.

Calabro, David, 'A Reexamination of the Ancient Israelite Gesture of Hand Placement', in Henrietta L. Wiley and Christian A. Eberhart (Eds), *Sacrifice, Cult, and Atonement in Early Judaism and Christianity: Constituents and Critique*, RBS 85 (Atlanta, GA: Society of Biblical Literature, 2017), 99–124.

Carasik, Michael, *Exodus* שמות, *The Commentators' Bible: The JPS Miqra'ot Gedolot* (Philadelphia, PA: Jewish Publication Society of America, 2005).

Carasik, Michael, *Leviticus* ויקרא, *The Commentators' Bible: The JPS Miqra'ot Gedolot* (Philadelphia, PA: Jewish Publication Society of America, 2009).

Carasik, Michael, *Numbers* במדבר, *The Commentators' Bible: The JPS Miqra'ot Gedolot* (Philadelphia, PA: Jewish Publication Society of America, 2011).

Cassuto, Umberto, *A Commentary on the Book of Exodus* (Jerusalem: Magnes Press, 1987).

Cataldo, Jeremiah W., *A Theocratic Yehud? Issues of Governance in a Persian Province*, LHBOTS 498 (London: Bloomsbury T&T Clark, 2009).

Chavel, Simeon, *Oracular Law and Priestly Historiography in the Torah*, FAT II/71 (Tübingen: Mohr Siebeck, 2014).

Chazelle, Celia, 'Ceolfrid's Gift to St Peter: The First Quire of Codex Amiatinus and the Evidence of Its Roman Destination', *Early Medieval Europe* 12 (2003): 129–58.

Chazelle, Celia, *The Codex Amiatinus and Its "Sister" Bibles: Scripture, Liturgy, and Art in the Milieu of the Venerable Bede*, Commentaria 10 (Leiden: Brill, 2019).

Childs, Brevard Springs, *Memory and Tradition in Israel*, SBT 37 (London: SCM, 1962).

Childs, Brevard Springs, *Exodus: A Commentary*, OTL (London: SCM, 1974).

Clifford, Richard J., 'Tent of El and the Israelite Tent of Meeting', *CBQ* 33 (1971): 221–7.

Cortese, Enzo, 'The Priestly Tent (Ex 25–31.35–40): Literary Criticism and the Theology of P Today', *LASBF* 48 (1998): 9–30.

Cross, Frank Moore, 'The Priestly Tabernacle in the Light of Recent Research', in Truman G. Madsen (Ed.), *The Temple in Antiquity: Ancient Records and Modern Perspectives* (Provo, UT: Brigham Young University Press, 1984), 91–105.

Cross, Frank Moore, 'The Tabernacle: A Study from an Archaeological and Historical Approach', *BA* 10 (1947): 45–68.

Dahmen, Ulrich, *Leviten und Priester im Deuteronomium: Literarkritische und redaktionsgeschichtliche Studien*, BBB 110 (Bodenheim: Philo, 1996).

Dalley, Stephanie, 'Hebrew Taḥaš, Akkadian Duhšu, Faience and Beadwork', *JSS* 45 (2000): 1–19.

Davies, Eryl W., *Numbers*, NCB (London: Marshall Pickering, 1995).

Davies, Graham I., *Exodus 1–18: A Critical and Exegetical Commentary. Volume 1: Chapters 1–10*, ICC (London: T&T Clark, 2020).

Davies, John A., *A Royal Priesthood: Literary and Intertextual Perspectives on an Image of Israel in Exodus 19.6*, JSOTSup 395 (London: T&T Clark, 2004).

Davis, Andrew R., *Reconstructing the Temple: The Royal Rhetoric of Temple Renovation in the Ancient Near East and Israel* (New York: Oxford University Press, 2019).

Dayfani, Hila, '4QpaleoExod^m and the Gerizim Composition', *JBL* 141 (2022): 673–98.

Dayfani, Hila, Drew Longacre, and Antony Perrot, 'New Identifications of 4QpaleoGen-Exod^L (4Q11) Fragments', *RevQ* 34(2022): 137–50.

Dietzfelbinger, Rudolf, 'Die Vetus Latina des Buches Exodus: Studien zur handschriftlichen Überlieferung mit Edition von Kapitel 1' (PhD diss., Heidelberg University, 1998).

Dillmann, August, *Die Bücher Exodus und Leviticus*, 3rd edn, KeHAT (Leipzig: Hirzel, 1897).

278 BIBLIOGRAPHY

Dillmann, August, *Die Bücher Numeri, Deuteronomium und Josua*, KeHAT (Leipzig: Hirzel, 1886).

Dion, Paul E., and P.M. Michèle Daviau, 'An Inscribed Incense Altar of Iron Age II at Ḥirbet El-Mudēyine (Jordan)', *ZDPV* 116 (2000): 1–13.

Dohmen, Christoph, *Exodus 19–40*, HTKAT (Freiburg im Breisgau: Herder, 2004).

Dold, Alban, 'Versucht Neu- und Erstergänzungen zu den altlateinischen Texten im Cod. Clm 6225 der Bayer. Staatsbibliothek', *Bib* 37 (1956): 39–58.

Dotan, Aron, 'Reflections towards a Critical Edition of Pentateuch Codex Or. 4445', in Emilia Fernández Tejero and María Teresa Ortega Monasterio (Eds), *Estudios masoréticos (X Congreso del IOMS): en memoria de Harry M. Orlinsky* (Madrid: CSIC, 1993), 39–51.

Dozeman, Thomas B., *Commentary on Exodus* (Grand Rapids, MI: Eerdmans, 2009).

Driver, Samuel R., *An Introduction to the Literature of the Old Testament*, 8th edn, International Theological Library (Edinburgh: T&T Clark, 1909).

Driver, Samuel R., *The Book of Exodus*, CBC (Cambridge: Cambridge University Press, 1911).

Dubrovský, Peter, *The Building of the First Temple*, FAT 103 (Tübingen: Mohr Siebeck, 2015).

Dunkelgrün, Theodor, 'Tabernacles of Text: A Brief Visual History of the Hebrew Bible', in Ku-Ming Chang, Anthony Grafton, and Glenn W. Most (Eds), *Impagination—Layout and Materiality of Writing and Publication: Interdisciplinary Approaches from East and West* (Berlin: de Gruyter, 2021), 47–92.

Edelman, Diana, 'The Meaning of Qiṭṭēr', *VT* 35 (1985): 395–404.

Ederer, Matthias, *Identitätsstiftende Begegnung: Die theologische Deutung des regelmäßigen Kultes Israels in der Tora*, FAT 121 (Tübingen: Mohr Siebeck, 2018).

Ehrlich, Arnold B., *Randglossen zur Hebräischen Bibel: Textkritisches, sprachliches und sachliches. Erster Band: Genesis und Exodus* (Hildesheim: Olms, 1968).

Eichler, Raanan, *The Ark and the Cherubim*, FAT 146 (Tübingen: Mohr Siebeck, 2021).

Eichler, Raanan, 'The Meaning of Zēr', *VT* 64 (2014): 196–210.

Eichler, Raanan, 'The Poles of the Ark: On the Ins and Outs of a Textual Contradiction', *JBL* 135 (2016): 733–41.

Elden, Stuart, *Foucault: The Birth of Power* (Cambridge: Polity Press, 2017).

Elliger, Karl, 'Ephod und Choschen: Ein Beitrag zur Entwicklungsgeschichte des hohepriesterlichen Ornats', *VT* 8 (1958): 19–35.

Elliger, Karl, *Leviticus*, HAT 1,4 (Tübingen: Mohr Siebeck, 1966).

Elliott, J. Keith, 'T. C. Skeat on the Dating and Origin of Codex Vaticanus', in *The Collected Biblical Writings of T.C. Skeat*, NovTSup 113 (Leiden: Brill, 2004), 281–94.

Elliott, Mark W., *Engaging Leviticus: Reading Leviticus Theologically with Its Past Interpreters* (Eugene, OR: Cascade, 2012).

Erder, Yoram, 'The First Date in Megillat Taʿanit in Light of the Karaite Commentary on the Tabernacle Dedication', *JQR* 82 (1992): 263–83.

Erickson, Nancy, 'Shaving It All Off: A Demeaning Priestly Prescription for the Levites in Numbers 8', *AABNER* (forthcoming).

Fauth, Wolfgang, 'Auf den Spuren des biblischen 'Azazel (Lev 16): Einige Residuen der Gestalt oder des Namens in jüdisch-aramäischen, griechischen, koptischen, äthiopischen, syrischen und mandäischen Texten', *ZAW* 110 (1998): 514–34.

Feldman, Liane Marquis, *The Story of Sacrifice: Ritual and Narrative in the Priestly Source*, FAT 141 (Tübingen: Mohr Siebeck, 2020).

Feldman, Liane Marquis, 'Ritual Sequence and Narrative Constraints in Leviticus 9:1–10:3', *JHebS* 17 (2018). https://jhsonline.org/index.php/jhs/article/view/29375.

Fernández Marcos, Natalio, *Scribes and Translators: Septuagint and Old Latin in the Books of Kings*, VTSup 54 (Leiden: Brill, 1994).

Fernández Marcos, Natalio, 'Rewritten Bible or Imitatio? The Vestments of the High-Priest', in James C. VanderKam, Peter W. Flint, and Emanuel Tov (Eds), *Studies in the Hebrew Bible, Qumran, and the Septuagint*, VTSup 101 (Leiden: Brill, 2006), 321–36.

Findlay, James D., *From Prophet to Priest: The Characterization of Aaron in the Pentateuch*, CBET 76 (Leuven: Peeters, 2017).

Finn, A. H., 'The Tabernacle Chapters', *JTS* 16 (1915): 449–82.

Fischer, Bonifatius, *Beiträge zur Geschichte der lateinischen Bibeltexte*, AGLB 12 (Freiburg im Breisgau: Herder, 1986).

Fischer, Bonifatius (Ed.), *Genesis*, AGLB 2 (Freiburg im Breisgau: Herder, 1951).

Fishbane, Michael A., *Biblical Interpretation in Ancient Israel* (Oxford: Clarendon Press, 1985).

Fleming, Daniel E., 'The Biblical Tradition of Anointing Priests', *JBL* 117 (1998): 401–14.

Fleming, Daniel E., 'Mari's Large Public Tent and the Priestly Tent Sanctuary', *VT* 50 (2000): 484–98.

Flusser, David, 'Nadab and Abihu According to Philo and the Rabbis', in *Judaism of the Second Temple Period. Volume 2: The Jewish Sages and Their Literature* (Grand Rapids, MI: Eerdmans, 2009), 289–96.

Foucault, Michel, *Discipline and Punish* (London: Penguin Books, 2019).

Foucault, Michel, *Madness and Civilization: A History of Insanity in the Age of Reason* (London: Tavistock Publications, 1967).

Foucault, Michel, *The Archaeology of Knowledge* (London: Tavistock Publications, 1986).

Foucault, Michel, *The Birth of the Clinic: An Archaeology of Medical Perception* (London: Tavistock Publications, 1973).

Foucault, Michel, *The History of Sexuality. Volume 1, The Will to Knowledge* (London: Penguin Classics, 2020).

Freedman, David Noel, Astrid B. Beck, Bruce Zuckerman, and Marilyn J. Lundberg (Eds), *The Leningrad Codex: A Facsimile Edition* (Grand Rapids, MI: Eerdmans, 1998).

Fretheim, Terence E., *Exodus*, IBC (Louisville, KY: John Knox Press, 1991).

Frevel, Christian, '"…dann gehören die Leviten mir": Anmerkungen zum Zusammenhang von Num 3; 8 und 18', in Stephanie Ernst and Maria Häusl (Eds), *Kulte, Priester, Rituale: Beiträge zu Kult und Kultkritik im Alten Testament und Alten Orient*, ATSAT 89 (St Ottilien: EOS Verlag, 2010), 133–58.

Frevel, Christian, 'Gotteshäuser en miniature? Architekturbezug, Funktion und Medialität der sogenannten Tempelmodelle der südlichen Levante', in Jens Kamlah (Ed.), *Sakralarchitektur*, ADPV (Wiesbaden: Harassowitz, 2022), 153–234.

Frevel, Christian, 'Kein Ende in Sicht? Zur Priestergrundschrift im Buch Levitikus', in Heinz-Josef Fabry and Hans-Winfried Jüngling (Eds), *Levitikus als Buch*, BBB 119 (Berlin: Philo, 1999), 85–123.

Frevel, Christian, 'Leadership and Conflict: Modelling the Charisma of Numbers', in Katharina Pyschny and Sarah Schulz (Eds), *Debating Authority: Concepts of Leadership in the Pentateuch and Former Prophets*, BZAW 507 (Berlin: de Gruyter, 2018), 89–114.

Frevel, Christian, *Mit Blick auf das Land die Schöpfung erinnern: Zum Ende der Priestergrundschrift*, HBS 23 (Freiburg im Breisgau: Herder, 2000).

Frevel, Christian, 'On Instant Scripture and Proximal Texts: Some Insights into the Sensual Materiality of Texts and Their Ritual Roles in the Hebrew Bible and Beyond', *Post* 8 (2018): 57–80.

Frevel, Christian, '"Und Mose hörte (es), und es war gut in seinen Augen" (Lev 10,20): Zum Verhältnis von Literargeschichte, Theologiegeschichte und innerbiblischer Auslegung am Beispiel von Lev 10', in Ilse Mülner, Ludwig Schwienhorst-Schönberger, and Ruth Scoralik (Eds), *Gottes Name(n): Zum Gedanken an Erich Zenger*, HBS 71 (Freiburg im Breisgau: Herder, 2012), 104–36.

280 BIBLIOGRAPHY

Fried, Lisbeth S., *Ezra: A Commentary*, Critical Commentary (Sheffield: Sheffield Phoenix, 2015).

Fried, Lisbeth S., *The Priest and the Great King: Temple-Palace Relations in the Persian Empire*, BJS 10 (Winona Lake, IN: Eisenbrauns, 2004).

Fritz, Volkmar, *Tempel und Zelt: Studien zum Tempelbau in Israel und zu dem Zeltheiligtum der Priesterschrift*, WMANT 47 (Neukirchen-Vluyn: Neukirchener Verlag, 1977).

Gallagher, Edmond L., 'Is the Samaritan Pentateuch a Sectarian Text?' *ZAW* 127 (2015): 96–107.

Gane, Roy E., *Cult and Character: Purification Offerings, Day of Atonement, and Theodicy* (Winona Lake, IN: Eisenbrauns, 2005).

Gennep, Arnold van, *The Rites of Passage*, trans. Monika B. Vizedom and Gabrielle L. Caffee (Chicago, IL: University of Chicago Press, 1960).

George, Mark K., *Israel's Tabernacle as Social Space*, AIL 2 (Atlanta, GA: Society of Biblical Literature, 2009).

Gertz, Jan Christian, *Tradition und Redaktion in der Exoduserzählung: Untersuchungen zur Endredaktion des Pentateuch*, FRLANT 186 (Göttingen: Vandenhoeck & Ruprecht, 2000).

Gilders, William K., *Blood Ritual in the Hebrew Bible: Meaning and Power* (Baltimore, MD: Johns Hopkins University Press, 2004).

Gilders, William K., 'Is There an Incense Altar in This Ritual?', in Christian A. Eberhart and Thomas Hieke (Eds), *Writing a Commentary on Leviticus*, FRLANT 276 (Göttingen: Vandenhoeck & Ruprecht, 2019), 159–70.

Ginsburg, Christian D., *Introduction to the Massoretico-Critical Edition of the Hebrew Bible* (London: Trinitarian Bible Society, 1897).

Gitin, Seymour, 'Incense Altars from Ekron, Israel and Judah: Context and Typology', *ErIsr* 20 (1989): 52*–67*.

Gitin, Seymour, 'The Four-Horned Altar and Sacred Space: An Archaeological Perspective', in Barry M. Gittlen (Ed.), *Sacred Time, Sacred Place: Archaeology and the Religion of Israel* (Winona Lake, IN: Eisenbrauns, 2002), 95–124.

Goldingay, John, *Isaiah 56–66*, ICC (London: Bloomsbury, 2014).

Gooding, David W., *The Account of the Tabernacle: Translation and Textual Problems of the Greek Exodus*, Texts and Studies: Contributions to Biblical and Patristic Literature 6 (Cambridge: Cambridge University Press, 1959).

Gooding, David W., 'Two Possible Examples of Midrashic Interpretation in the Septuagint Exodus', in Josef Schreiner (Ed.), *Wort, Lied, und Gottesspruch: Festschrift für Joseph Ziegler. Band I: Beiträge zur Septuaginta* (Würzburg: Echter, 1972), 39–48.

Gordon, Robert P., *I & II Samuel: A Commentary* (Exeter: Paternoster Press, 1986).

Görg, Manfred, *Das Zelt der Begegnung: Untersuchung zur Gestalt der sakralen Zelttraditionen Altisraels*, BBB 27 (Bonn: Hanstein, 1967).

Görg, Manfred, 'Der Brustschmuck des Hohenpriesters', *BN* 15 (1981): 32–4.

Gorman, Frank H., *The Ideology of Ritual: Space, Time and Status in the Priestly Theology*, JSOTSup 91 (Sheffield: JSOT Press, 1990).

Grabbe, Lester L., *A History of the Jews and Judaism in the Second Temple Period. Vol 1: Yehud: A History of the Persian Period of Judah*, LSTS 47 (London: T&T Clark, 2004).

Grabbe, Lester L., 'The Priesthood in the Persian Period: Haggai, Zechariah, and Malachi', in Lena-Sofia Tiemeyer (Ed.), *Priests and Cults in the Book of the Twelve*, ANEM 14 (Atlanta, GA: Society of Biblical Literature, 2016), 149–56.

Gramsci, Antonio, *Selections from the Prison Notebooks of Antonio Gramsci* (Eds). Quintin Hoare and Geoffrey Nowell-Smith (London: Lawrence & Wishart, 1971).

Graupner, Axel, 'Exodus 24 und die Frage nach dem Ursprung der Bundestheologie im Alten Testament mit einem Ausblick auf die Herrenmahlsüberlieferung im Neuen

Testament', in Wolfgang Kraus (Ed.), *Beiträge zur urchristlichen Theologiegeschichte*, BZNW 163 (Berlin: de Gruyter, 2009), 129–48.

Gray, George Buchanan, *Numbers*, ICC (Edinburgh: T&T Clark, 1903).

Greenstein, Edward L., 'Deconstruction and Biblical Narrative', *Proof* 9 (1989): 43–71.

Grenz, Jesse R., 'Textual Divisions in Codex Vaticanus', *TC: A Journal of Biblical Textual Criticism* 23 (2018): 1–22.

Grenz, Jesse R., 'The Scribes and Correctors of Codex Vaticanus: A Study on the Codicology, Palaeography, and Text of B(03)' (PhD diss., University of Cambridge, 2021).

Guggenheimer, Heinrich W., *The Jerusalem Talmud. Second Order: Mo'ed. Tractates Pesaḥim and Yoma. Edition, Translation, and Commentary*, SJ 74 (Berlin: de Gruyter, 2013).

Guillaume, Philippe, 'Aaron and the Amazing Mantic Coat', in Helen R. Jacobus, Anne Katrine de Hemmer Gudme, and Philippe Guillaume (Eds), *Studies on Magic and Divination in the Biblical World*, Biblical Intersections 11 (Piscataway, NJ: Gorgias Press, 2013), 101–18.

Gurtner, Daniel M., *Exodus: A Commentary on the Greek Text of Codex Vaticanus*, Septuagint Commentary Series (Leiden: Brill, 2013).

Hachlili, Rachel, *The Menorah: Evolving into the Most Important Jewish Symbol* (Leiden: Brill, 2018).

Hachlili, Rachel, *The Menorah, the Ancient Seven-Armed Candelabrum: Origin, Form, and Significance*, JSJSup 68 (Leiden: Brill, 2001).

Haran, Menahem, *Temples and Temple-Service in Ancient Israel* (Oxford: Clarendon Press, 1978).

Harrington, D. J., 'Pseudo-Philo', in James H. Charlesworth (Ed.), *The Old Testament Pseudepigrapha, Volume 2: Expansions of the 'Old Testament' and Legends, Wisdom and Philosophical Literature, Prayers, Psalms, and Odes, Fragments of Lost Judeo-Hellenistic Works* (Garden City, NY: Doubleday, 1985), 297–377.

Hartley, John E., *Leviticus*, WBC 4 (Dallas: Word, 1992).

Haugaard, Mark, *The Constitution of Power: A Theoretical Analysis of Power, Knowledge and Structure* (Manchester: Manchester University Press, 1997).

Hawkes, Jane, and Meg Boulton (Eds), *All Roads Lead to Rome: The Creation, Context and Transmission of the Codex Amiatinus*, Studia Traditionis Theologiae 31 (Turnhout: Brepols, 2019).

Hays, Nathan, 'The Redactional Reassertion of the Priestly Role in Leviticus 10–16', *ZAW* 130 (2018): 175–88.

Heger, Paul, *The Development of Incense Cult in Israel*, BZAW 245 (Berlin: de Gruyter, 1997).

Hendel, Ronald S., 'Sacrifice as a Cultural System: The Ritual Symbolism of Exodus 24:3–8', *ZAW* 101 (1989): 366–90.

Hill, Charles Evan, *The First Chapters: Dividing the Text of Scripture in Codex Vaticanus and Its Predecessors* (Oxford: Oxford University Press, 2022).

Himbaza, Innocent, *Leviticus*, BHQ 3 (Stuttgart: Deutsche Bibelgesellschaft, 2020).

Hirsch, Samuel Raphael, *The Pentateuch: Translated and Explained. Vol. II Exodus* (London: Hachinuch, 1956).

Holzinger, H., *Exodus*, KHAT 2 (Tübingen: Mohr Siebeck, 1900).

Homan, Michael M., *To Your Tents, O Israel!: The Terminology, Function, Form, and Symbolism of Tents in the Hebrew Bible and the Ancient Near East*, CHANE 12 (Leiden: Brill, 2002).

Houtman, Cornelis, 'On the Pomegranates and the Golden Bells of the High Priest's Mantle', *VT* 40 (1990): 223–9.

Houtman, Cornelis, 'The Urim and Thummim: A New Suggestion', *VT* 40 (1990): 229–32.

Houtman, Cornelis, *Exodus*, 4 vols., HCOT (Kampen: Kok Pharos, 1993–2002).

282 BIBLIOGRAPHY

Hundley, Michael B., *Gods in Dwellings: Temples and Divine Presence in the Ancient Near East* (Atlanta, GA: Society of Biblical Literature, 2013).

Hunt, Alice, *Missing Priests: The Zadokites in Tradition and History*, LHBOTS 452 (New York: T&T Clark, 2006).

Hurowitz, Victor, *I Have Built You an Exalted House: Temple Building in the Bible in the Light of Mesopotamian and Northwest Semitic Writings*, JSOTSup 115 (Sheffield: JSOT Press, 1992).

Hutzli, Jürg, 'The Origins of P: Literary Profiles and Strata of the Priestly Texts in Genesis 1–Exodus 40' (Habilitationschrift, Zurich University, 2019).

Imes, Carmen Joy, 'Between Two Worlds: The Functional and Symbolic Significance of the High Priestly Regalia', in Antonios Finitsis (Ed.), *Dress and Clothing in the Hebrew Bible: 'For All Her Household Are Clothed in Crimson'*, LHBOTS 679 (London: Bloomsbury, 2019), 63–86.

Jacob, Benno, *Das Buch Exodus*, ed. Schlomo Mayer (Stuttgart: Calwer, 1997).

Jacobson, Howard, *A Commentary on Pseudo-Philo's Liber Antiquitatum Biblicarum, with Latin Text and English Translation*, AGJU 31 (Leiden: Brill, 1996).

Janowski, Bernd, *Sühne als Heilsgeschehen: Studien zur Sühnetheologie der Priesterschrift und zur Wurzel KPR im Alten Orient und im Alten Testament*, WMANT 55 (Neukirchen-Vluyn: Neukirchener Verlag, 1982).

Janowski, Bernd, and Gernot Wilhelm, 'Der Bock, der die Sünden hinausträgt: Zur Religionsgeschichte des Azazel-Ritus Lev 16,10.21f', in Bernd Janowski, Klaus Koch, and Gernot Wilhelm (Eds), *Religionsgeschichtliche Beziehungen zwischen Kleinasien, Nordsyrien und dem Alten Testament: Internationales Symposion Hamburg, 17–21 März 1990*, OBO 129 (Freiburg im Üchtland: Universitätsverlag, 1993), 109–69.

Japhet, Sara, *I & II Chronicles: A Commentary*, OTL (Louisville, KY: Westminster John Knox, 1993).

Jenson, Philip Peter, *Graded Holiness: A Key to the Priestly Conception of the World*, JSOTSup 106 (Sheffield: JSOT Press, 1992).

Johnstone, William, 'Biblical Hebrew Wâwîm in the Light of New Phoenician Evidence', *PEQ* 109 (1977): 95–102.

Jürgens, Benedikt, *Heiligkeit und Versöhnung: Levitikus 16 in seinem literarischen Kontext*, HBS 28 (Freiburg im Breisgau: Herder, 2001).

Kahle, Paul, *The Cairo Geniza* (Oxford: Blackwell, 1959).

Kahle, Paul, 'Untersuchungen zur Geschichte des Pentateuchtextes', *TSK* 88 (1915): 399–439.

Kartveit, Magnar, *The Origin of the Samaritans*, VTSup 128 (Leiden: Brill, 2009).

Kearney, Peter J., 'Creation and Liturgy: The P Redaction of Ex 25–40', *ZAW* 89 (1977): 375–87.

Keel, Othmar, 'Die Brusttasche des Hohenpriesters als Element priesterschriftlicher Theologie', in Frank-Lothar Hossfeld (Ed.), *Das Manna fällt auch heute noch: Beiträge zur Geschichte und Theologie des Alten, Ersten Testaments. Festschrift für Erich Zenger*, HBS 44 (Freiburg im Breisgau: Herder, 2004), 379–91.

Keel, Othmar, 'Zeichen der Verbundenheit. Zur Vorgeschichte und Bedeutung der Forderungen von Deuteronomium 6,8 f. und Par', in Pierre Casetti, Othmar Keel, and Adrian Schenker (Eds), *Mélanges Dominique Barthélemy: Études bibliques offertes à l'occasion de son 60e anniversaire*, OBO 38 (Freiburg im Üchtland: Universitätsverlag, 1981), 159–240.

Kellermann, Diether, *Die Priesterschrift von Numeri 1,1 bis 10,10: literarkritisch und traditionsgeschichtlich untersucht*, BZAW 120 (Berlin: de Gruyter, 1970).

Kennedy, A.R.S., 'Tabernacle', *HDB* 4: 653–68.

Khan, Geoffrey, *A Short Introduction to the Tiberian Masoretic Bible and Its Reading Tradition*, Gorgias Handbooks 25 (Piscataway, NJ: Gorgias Press, 2012).

Khan, Geoffrey, *The Tiberian Pronunciation Tradition of Biblical Hebrew*, 2 vols., Cambridge Semitic Languages and Cultures 1 (Cambridge: Open Book Publishers, 2020).

Kim, Angela Y., 'The Textual Alignment of the Tabernacle Sections of 4Q365 (Fragments 8a–b, 9a–b i, 9b ii, 12a i, 12b iii)', *Text* 21 (2002): 45–69.

Kim, Kyung-Rae, 'Studies in the Relationship between the Samaritan Pentateuch and the Septuagint' (PhD diss., Hebrew University Jerusalem, 1994).

Kirschner, Robert, 'The Rabbinic and Philonic Exegeses of the Nadab and Abihu Incident (Lev. 10:1–6)', *JQR* 73 (1983): 375–93.

Kiuchi, Nobuyoshi, *The Purification Offering in the Priestly Literature: Its Meaning and Function*, JSOTSup 56 (Sheffield: JSOT Press, 1987).

Kiuchi, Nobuyoshi, *Leviticus*, Apollos Old Testament Commentary (Nottingham: Inter-Varsity Press, 2007).

Klingbeil, Gerald A., *A Comparative Study of the Ritual of Ordination as Found in Leviticus 8 and Emar 369* (Lewiston, NY: Mellen, 1998).

Klostermann, August, 'Die Heiligtums- und Lagerordnung', in *Der Pentateuch: Beiträge zu seinem Verständnis und seiner Entstehungsgeschichte. Neue Folge* (Leipzig: Deichert, 1907), 42–153.

Knierim, Rolf P., and George W. Coats, *Numbers*, FOTL 4 (Grand Rapids, MI: Eerdmans, 2005).

Knohl, Israel, *The Sanctuary of Silence: The Priestly Torah and the Holiness School* (Minneapolis, MN: Fortress, 1995).

Koch, Klaus, *Die Priesterschrift von Exodus 25 bis Leviticus 16: Eine überlieferungsgeschichtliche und literarkritische Untersuchung*, FRLANT 71 (Gottingen: Vandenhoeck & Ruprecht, 1959).

Kogman-Appel, Katrin, *Jewish Book Art between Islam and Christianity: The Decoration of Hebrew Bibles in Medieval Spain* (Leiden: Brill, 2004).

Konkel, Michael, *Sünde und Vergebung: Eine Rekonstruktion der Redaktionsgeschichte der hinteren Sinaiperikope (Exodus 32–34) vor dem Hintergrund aktueller Pentateuchmodelle*, FAT 58 (Tübingen: Mohr Siebeck, 2008).

Kratz, Reinhard Gregor, *The Composition of the Narrative Books of the Old Testament* (London: T&T Clark, 2005).

Kreps, David (Ed.), *Gramsci and Foucault: A Reassessment* (London: Routledge, 2016).

Kuenen, Abraham, *An Historico-Critical Inquiry into the Origin and Composition of the Hexateuch (Pentateuch and Book of Joshua)* (London: Macmillan, 1886).

Kuenen, Abraham, *Historisch-kritische Einleitung in die Bücher des Alten Testaments* (Leipzig: Schulze, 1885).

Kutsch, Ernst, 'Das sog. Bundesblut in Ex 24:8 und Sach 9:11', *VT* 23 (1973): 25–30.

de Lagarde, Paul, *Anmerkungen zur griechischen Übersetzung der Proverbien* (Leipzig: Brockhaus, 1863).

Laird, Donna, *Negotiating Power in Ezra-Nehemiah*, AIL 26 (Atlanta, GA: SBL Press, 2016).

Lange, Armin, *Handbuch der Textfunde vom Toten Meer. Band I: Die Handschriften biblischer Bücher von Qumran und den anderen Fundorten* (Tübingen: Mohr Siebeck, 2009).

Lange, Armin, 'The Dead Sea Scrolls and the Date of the Final Stage of the Pentateuch', in James K. Aitken, Katherine J. Dell, and Brian A. Mastin (Eds), *On Stone and Scroll: Essays in Honour of Graham Ivor Davies*, BZAW 420 (Berlin: de Gruyter, 2011), 269–85.

Lange, Armin, '"They Confirmed the Reading" (y. Ta'an. 4.68a): The Textual Standardization of Jewish Scriptures in the Second Temple Period', in Matthias Weigold and József Zsengellér (Eds), *From Qumran to Aleppo: A Discussion with Emanuel Tov about the Textual History of Jewish Scriptures in Honor of His 65th Birthday*, FRLANT 230 (Göttingen: Vandenhoeck & Ruprecht, 2009), 29–80.

Le Boulluec, Alain, and Pierre Sandevoir, *L'Exode: traduction du texte grec de la Septante, introduction et notes*, La Bible d'Alexandrie 2 (Paris: Cerf, 1989).

Lehming, Sigo, 'Zur Überlieferungsgeschichte von Gen. 34', *ZAW* 70 (1958): 228–50.

Levine, Baruch A., *Numbers: A New Translation with Introduction and Commentary*, 2 vols., AB 4 (New York: Doubleday, 1993–2000).

Levine, Baruch A., 'The Descriptive Tabernacle Texts of the Pentateuch', *JAOS* 85 (1965): 307–18.

Lewis, Theodore J., 'Covenant and Blood Rituals: Understanding Exodus 24:3–8 in Its Ancient Near Eastern Context', in Seymour Gitin, J. Edward Wright, and J.P. Dessel (Eds), *Confronting the Past: Archaeological and Historical Essays on Ancient Israel in Honor of William G. Dever* (University Park, PA: Pennsylvania State University Press, 2006), 341–50.

Liss, Hanna, 'The Imaginary Sanctuary: The Priestly Code as an Example of Fictional Literature in the Hebrew Bible', in Oded Lipschits and Manfred Oeming (Eds), *Judah and the Judeans in the Persian Period* (Winona Lake, IN: Eisenbrauns, 2006), 663–89.

Liss, Hanna, 'Sollen die Glöckchen wieder klingen? Die Beschreibung der Priestergewänder in Ex 28 und die Hermeneutik ihrer "alt-neuen" Rekonstruktionen', *Trumah* (2009): 1–22.

Lo Sardo, Domenico, 'Ex 25:8-9 MT-LXX: Textual Differences or Different Hermeneutics? The Divine Dwelling on the Mountain and/or in a Sanctuary', *LASBF* 69 (2019): 79–98.

Lo Sardo, Domenico, *Post-Priestly Additions and Rewritings in Exodus 35–40*, FAT II/119 (Tübingen: Mohr Siebeck, 2020).

Lo Sardo, Domenico, 'The Tent of Meeting and the Women's Mirrors in 1 Sam 2:22 and Exod 38:8: A Text-Critical Inquiry of the MT, LXX, Qumran Texts and the Vetus Latina', *Text* 29 (2020): 168–92.

Lohfink, Norbert, 'The Priestly Narrative and History', in *Theology of the Pentateuch: Themes of the Priestly Narrative and Deuteronomy*, trans. Linda M. Maloney (Edinburgh: T&T Clark, 1994), 136–72.

Longacre, Drew, 'A Contextualized Approach to the Hebrew Dead Sea Scrolls Containing Exodus' (PhD diss., Birmingham University, 2015).

Longacre, Robert E., 'Building for the Worship of God: Exodus 25:1–30:10', in Walter R. Bodine (Ed.), *Discourse Analysis of Biblical Literature: What It Is and What It Offers*, SemeiaSt (Atlanta, GA: Scholars Press, 1995), 21–49.

MacDonald, John, 'The Status and Role of the Naʿar in Israelite Society', *JNES* 35 (1976): 147–70.

MacDonald, Nathan, 'Aaron's Failure and the Fall of the Hebrew Kingdoms', in Peter Dubrovský, Dominik Markl, and Jean-Pierre Sonnet (Eds), *The Fall of Jerusalem and the Rise of the Torah*, FAT 107 (Tübingen: Mohr Siebeck, 2016), 197–209.

MacDonald, Nathan, *Priestly Rule: Polemic and Biblical Interpretation in Ezekiel 44*, BZAW 475 (Berlin: de Gruyter, 2015).

MacDonald, Nathan, 'Recasting the Golden Calf: The Imaginative Potential of the Old Testament's Portrayal of Idolatry', in Stephen C. Barton (Ed.), *Idolatry: False Worship in the Bible, Early Judaism, and Christianity* (London: T&T Clark, 2007), 22–39.

MacDonald, Nathan, 'Scribalism and Ritual Innovation', *HeBAI* 7 (2018): 415–29.

MacDonald, Nathan, 'The Hermeneutics and Genesis of the Red Cow Ritual', *HTR* 105 (2012): 351–71.

MacDonald, Nathan, 'The Priestly Vestments', in Christoph Berner, Manuel Schäfer, Martin Schott, Sarah Schulz, and Martina Weingärtner (Eds), *Nudity and Clothing in the Hebrew Bible* (London: Bloomsbury, 2019), 435–48.

Magen, Yitzhak, *Mount Gerizim Excavations, Volume II. A Temple City*, Judea and Samaria Publications 8 (Jerusalem: Israel Antiquities Authority, 2008).

BIBLIOGRAPHY 285

Magen, Yitzhak, 'The Dating of the First Phase of the Samaritan Temple on Mount Gerizim in Light of the Archaeological Evidence', in Oded Lipschits, Gary N. Knoppers, and Rainer Albertz (Eds), *Judah and the Judeans in the Fourth Century B.C.E.* (Winona Lake, IN: Eisenbrauns, 2007), 157–211.

Magrini, Sabina, 'Per difetto del legatore: Storia delle rilegature della Bibbia Amiatina in Laurenziana', *Quinio* 3 (2001): 137–67.

Maier, Johann, *Die Tempelrolle vom Toten Meer und das 'Neue Jerusalem': 11Q19 und 11Q20, 1Q32, 2Q24, 4Q554-555, 5Q15 und 11Q18. Übersetzung und Erläuterung*, 3rd edn, UTB 829 (Munich: Reinhardt, 1997).

Mandell, Alice, 'Aaron's Body as a Ritual Vessel in the Exodus Tabernacle Building Narrative', in Laura Quick and Melissa Ramos (Eds), *New Perspectives on Ritual in the Biblical World*, LHBOTS 702 (London: Bloomsbury, 2022), 159–81.

Mandell, Alice, 'Writing as a Source of Ritual Authority: The High Priest's Body as a Priestly Text in the Tabernacle-Building Story', *JBL* 141 (2022): 49–69.

Margalith, Othniel, 'בגדי שֵׁרָד = Fine Linen from Colchis?' *ZAW* 95 (1983): 430–31.

Mastnjak, Nathan, 'Hebrew taḥaš and the West Semitic Tent Tradition', *VT* 67 (2017): 204–12.

Mazar, Amihai, 'Temples of the Middle and Late Bronze Ages and the Iron Age', in Aaron Kempinski and Ronny Reich (Eds), *The Architecture of Ancient Israel: From the Prehistoric to the Persian Periods* (Jerusalem: Israel Exploration Society, 1992), 161–89.

McCrory, Jefferson Harrell, 'The Composition of Exodus 35–40' (PhD diss., Claremont Graduate School, 1989).

McKane, William, *A Critical and Exegetical Commentary on Jeremiah. Volume II: Commentary on Jeremiah XXVI–LII*, ICC (Edinburgh: T&T Clark, 1996).

McNeile, A.H., *The Book of Exodus: With Introduction and Notes*, 3rd edn, WC (London: Methuen, 1931).

Meshel, Naphtali S., *The 'Grammar' of Sacrifice: A Generativist Study of the Israelite Sacrificial System in the Priestly Writings with a 'Grammar' of Σ* (Oxford: Oxford University Press, 2014).

Meyers, Carol L., 'Framing Aaron: Incense Altar and Lamp Oil in the Tabernacle Texts', in Shawna Dolansky (Ed.), *Sacred History, Sacred Literature: Essays on Ancient Israel, the Bible, and Religion in Honor of R. E. Friedman on His Sixtieth Birthday* (Winona Lake, IN: Eisenbrauns, 2008), 13–21.

Meyers, Carol L., 'Realms of Sanctity: The Case of the "Misplaced" Incense Altar in the Tabernacle Texts of Exodus', in Michael V. Fox, Victor Hurowitz, Avi Hurvitz, Michael L. Klein, Baruch J. Schwartz, and Nili Shupak (Eds), *Texts, Temples, and Traditions: A Tribute to Menahem Haran* (Winona Lake, IN: Eisenbrauns, 1996), 33–46.

Meyers, Carol L., *The Tabernacle Menorah*, ASOR Dissertation Series 2 (Ann Arbor, MI: Scholars Press, 1976).

Meyvaert, Paul, 'Bede, Cassiodorus, and the Codex Amiatinus', *Speculum* 71 (1996): 827–83.

Milgrom, Jacob, 'Hattĕnûpâ', in *Studies in Cultic Theology and Terminology*, SJLA 36 (Leiden: Brill, 1983), 139–58.

Milgrom, Jacob, *Leviticus 1–16: A New Translation with Introduction and Commentary*, AB 3 (New York: Doubleday, 1991).

Milgrom, Jacob, *Leviticus 23–27: A New Translation with Introduction and Commentary*, AB 3B (New York: Doubleday, 2001).

Milgrom, Jacob, *Numbers* במדבר: *The Traditional Hebrew Text with the New JPS Translation*, JPS Torah Commentary (Philadelphia, PA: Jewish Publication Society of America, 1990).

Milgrom, Jacob, *Studies in Levitical Terminology: I The Encroacher and the Levite. The Term 'Aboda*, UCPNES 14 (Berkeley, CA: University of California Press, 1970).

286 BIBLIOGRAPHY

Milgrom, Jacob, 'The Alleged Wave-Offering in Israel and in the Ancient Near East', *IEJ* 22 (1972): 33–38.

Milgrom, Jacob, 'The Šôq Hattĕrûmâ: A Chapter in Cultic History', in *Studies in Cultic Theology and Terminology*, SJLA 36 (Leiden: Brill, 1983), 159–70.

Milstein, Sara J., *Tracking the Master Scribe: Revision through Introduction in Biblical and Mesopotamian Literature* (Oxford: Oxford University Press, 2016).

Mirguet, Françoise, 'Essai d'interprétation de Lévitique 10: Le bouc brûlé et non mangé', *ETR* 80 (2005): 261–71.

Mizrahi, Noam, 'The History and Linguistic Background of Two Hebrew Titles for the High Priest', *JBL* 130 (2011): 687–705.

Müller, Reinhard, *Königtum und Gottesherrschaft: Untersuchungen zur alttestamentlichen Monarchiekritik*, FAT II/3 (Tübingen: Mohr Siebeck, 2004).

Nelson, Russell David, 'Studies in the Development of the Text of the Tabernacle Account' (PhD diss., Harvard University, 1986).

Nicholson, Ernest Wilson, *God and His People: Covenant and Theology in the Old Testament* (Oxford: Clarendon Press, 1986).

Nicholson, Ernest Wilson, 'The Covenant Ritual in Exodus 24:3–8', *VT* 32 (1982): 74–86.

Nielsen, Eduard, *Shechem: A Traditio-Historical Investigation* (Copenhagen: G.E.C. Gad, 1959).

Nielsen, Kjeld, *Incense in Ancient Israel*, VTSup 38 (Leiden: Brill, 1986).

Nihan, Christophe, 'Narrative and Exegesis in Leviticus: On Leviticus 10 and 24,10–23', in Walter Bührer (Ed.), *Schriftgelehrte Fortschreibungs- und Auslegungsprozesse: Textarbeit im Pentateuch, in Qumran, Ägypten und Mesopotamien*, FAT II/108 (Tübingen: Mohr Siebeck, 2019), 207–42.

Nihan, Christophe, *From Priestly Torah to Pentateuch: A Study in the Composition of the Book of Leviticus*, FAT II/25 (Tübingen: Mohr Siebeck, 2007).

Nihan, Christophe, 'Le pectoral d'Aaron et la figure du grand prêtre dans les traditions sacerdotales du Pentateuque', in Louis Jonker, Gideon Kotzé, and Christl M. Maier (Eds), *Congress Volume Stellenbosch 2016*, VTSup 177 (Leiden: Brill, 2017), 23–55.

Nihan, Christophe, 'Une recette pour l'encens', *RTP* 149 (2017): 305–22.

Nihan, Christophe, and Julia Rhyder, 'Aaron's Vestments in Exodus 28 and Priestly Leadership', in Katharina Pyschny and Sarah Schulz (Eds), *Debating Authority: Concepts of Leadership in the Pentateuch and the Former Prophets*, BZAW 507 (Berlin: de Gruyter, 2018), 45–67.

Nöldeke, Theodor, *Untersuchungen zur Kritik des Alten Testaments* (Kiel: Schwers'sche Buchhandlung, 1869).

Noonan, Benjamin J., 'Hide or Hue? Defining Hebrew תַּחַשׁ', *Bib* 93 (2012): 580–89.

Noth, Martin, *Das Vierte Buch Mose: Numeri*, 4th edn, ATD 7 (Göttingen: Vandenhoeck & Ruprecht, 1982).

Noth, Martin, *Exodus: A Commentary*, trans. J.S. Bowden, OTL (London: SCM, 1962).

Noth, Martin, *Leviticus: A Commentary*, trans. J.S. Bowden, OTL (London: SCM, 1965).

Noth, Martin, 'Office and Vocation in the Old Testament', in *The Laws in the Pentateuch and Other Studies* (Edinburgh: Oliver & Boyd, 1966), 229–49.

Oesch, Josef M., *Petucha und Setuma: Untersuchungen zu einer überlieferten Gliederung im hebräischen Text des Alten Testaments*, OBO 27 (Freiburg im Üchtland: Universitätsverlag, 1979).

Olyan, Saul M., 'Exodus 31:12–17: The Sabbath According to H, or the Sabbath According to P and H?', *JBL* 124 (2005): 201–9.

O'Reilly, Jennifer, *Early Medieval Text and Image 2: The Codex Amiatinus, the Book of Kells and Anglo-Saxon Art*, Variorum Collected Studies Series (London: Routledge, 2019).

Oswald, Wolfgang, 'Der Hohepriester als Ethnarch. Zur politische Organisation Judäas im 4. Jahrhundert v. Chr', *ZABR* 21 (2015): 309–20.

Oswald, Wolfgang, *Israel am Gottesberg: eine Untersuchung zur Literaturgeschichte der vorderen Sinaiperikope Ex 19–24 und deren historischem Hintergrund*, OBO 159 (Freiburg im Üchtland: Universitätsverlag, 1998).

Otto, Eckart, *Das Deuteronomium: Politische Theologie und Rechtsreform in Juda und Assyrien*, BZAW 284 (Berlin: de Gruyter, 1999).

Otto, Eckart, *Das Mazzotfest in Gilgal*, BWANT 107 (Stuttgart: Kohlhammer, 1975).

Otto, Eckart, *Deuteronomium 4,44–11,32*, HTKAT (Freiburg im Breisgau: Herder, 2012).

Otto, Eckart, 'Die nachpriesterschriftliche Pentateuchredaktion im Buch Exodus', in Marc Vervenne (Ed.), *Studies in the Book of Exodus: Redaction—Reception—Interpretation*, BETL 126 (Leuven: Leuven University Press, 1996), 61–111.

Otto, Eckart, 'Forschungen zur Priesterschrift', *TRu* 62 (1997): 1–50.

Outhwaite, Ben, 'The First Owners of the Leningrad Codex: T-S 10J30.7' (2017). https://doi.org/10.17863/CAM.28071.

Owczarek, Susanne, *Die Vorstellung vom Wohnen Gottes inmitten seines Volkes in der Priesterschrift: Zur Heiligtumstheologie der priesterschriftlichen Grundschrift*, Europäische Hochschulschriften. Reihe 23, Theologie 625 (Frankfurt am Main: Lang, 1998).

Paul, Shalom M., *Isaiah 40–66: Translation and Commentary*, Eerdmans Critical Commentary (Grand Rapids, MI: Eerdmans, 2012).

Peckham, Brian, 'Notes on a Fifth-Century Phoenician Inscription from Kition, Cyprus (CIS 86)', *Or* 37 (1968): 304–24.

Perkins, Larry, 'The Translation of מועד אהל/משכן and שכן in Greek Exodus', *JSCS* 48 (2015): 8–26.

Perlitt, Lothar, *Bundestheologie im Alten Testament*, WMANT 36 (Neukirchen-Vluyn: Neukirchener Verlag, 1969).

Péter, René, 'L'imposition des mains dans l'Ancien Testament', *VT* 27 (1977): 48–55.

Podella, Thomas, *Das Lichtkleid JHWHs: Untersuchungen zur Gestalthaftigkeit Gottes im Alten Testament und seiner altorientalischen Umwelt*, FAT 15 (Tübingen: Mohr Siebeck, 1996).

Pola, Thomas, *Die ursprüngliche Priesterschrift: Beobachtungen zur Literarkritik und Traditionsgeschichte von Pg*, WMANT 70 (Neukirchen-Vluyn: Neukirchener Verlag, 1995).

Popper, Julius, *Die biblische Bericht über die Stiftshütte: Ein Beitrag zur Geschichte der Composition und Diaskeue des Pentateuch* (Leipzig: Heinrich Hunger, 1862).

Porzig, Peter, *Die Lade Jahwes im Alten Testament und in den Texten vom Toten Meer*, BZAW 397 (Berlin: de Gruyter, 2009).

Pralon, Didier, 'L'allégorie au travail: Interprétation de Lévitique X par Philon d'Alexandrie', in Marguerite Harl (Ed.), *ΚΑΤΑ ΤΟΥΣ Ο: Selon les Septante* (Paris: Cerf, 1995), 483–97.

Propp, William Henry, *Exodus 19–40: A New Translation with Introduction and Commentary*, AB 2a (New Haven, CT: Yale University Press, 2006).

Pummer, Reinhard, 'Samaritan Tabernacle Drawings', *Numen* 45 (1998): 30–68.

Pummer, Reinhard, 'The Samaritan Manuscripts of the Chester Beatty Library', *Studies: An Irish Quarterly Review* 68 (1979): 66–75.

Purvis, J.D., 'The Tabernacle in Samaritan Iconography and Thought', in L.M. Hopfe (Ed.), *Uncovering Ancient Stones: Essays in Memory of H.N. Richardson* (Winona Lake, IN: Eisenbrauns, 1994), 223–36.

de Pury, Albert, 'Genèse XXXIV et l'Histoire', *RB* 76 (1969): 5–49.

Pyschny, Katharina, *Verhandelte Führung: Eine Analyse von Num 16–17 im Kontext der neueren Pentateuchforschung*, HBS 88 (Freiburg im Breisgau: Herder, 2017).

288 BIBLIOGRAPHY

Quick, Laura, 'Through a Glass, Darkly: Reflections on the Translation and Interpretation of Exodus 38:8', *CBQ* 81 (2019): 595–612.

von Rad, Gerhard, *Die Priesterschrift im Hexateuch: Literarisch untersucht und theologisch gewertet*, BWANT 13 (Stuttgart: Kohlhammer, 1934).

von Rad, Gerhard, *Old Testament Theology*, 2 vols. (New York: Harper & Row, 1962).

Ranke, Ernest, *Par palimpsestorum Wirceburgensium: Antiquissimae Veteris Testamenti versionis latinae fragmenta* (Vienna: William Braumüller, 1871).

Reif, Stefan C., 'Dedicated to חנך', *VT* 22 (1972): 495–501.

Rendtorff, Rolf, *Leviticus 1,1–10,20*, BKAT 3/1 (Neukirchen-Vluyn: Neukirchener Verlag, 2004).

Rendtorff, Rolf, 'Nadab and Abibu', in J. Cheryl Exum and Hugh Godfrey Maturin Williamson (Eds), *Reading from Right to Left: Essays on the Hebrew Bible in Honour of David J.A. Clines*, JSOTSup 373 (London: Sheffield Academic, 2003), 359–63.

Rendtorff, Rolf, *Studien zur Geschichte des Opfers im Alten Israel*, WMANT 24 (Neukirchen-Vluyn: Neukirchener Verlag, 1967).

Rhyder, Julia, *Centralizing the Cult: The Holiness Legislation in Leviticus 17–26*, FAT 134 (Tübingen: Mohr Siebeck, 2019).

Rhyder, Julia, 'Unity and Hierarchy: North and South in the Priestly Traditions', in Benedikt Hensel, Dany Nocquet, and Bartosz Adamczewski (Eds), *Yahwistic Diversity and the Hebrew Bible: Tracing Perspectives of Group Identity from Judah, Samaria, and the Diaspora in Biblical Traditions*, FAT II/120 (Tübingen: Mohr Siebeck, 2020), 109–34.

Richey, Madadh, 'The Dwelling of ʾIlu in Baʿlu and ʾAqhatu', *JANER* 17 (2017): 149–85.

Roberts, Ulysses, *Pentateuchi versio latina antiquissima e codice Lugdunensi* (Paris: Firmin-Didot, 1881).

Robertson, Edward, 'Notes and Extracts from the Semitic Manuscripts in the John Rylands Library: III Samaritan Pentateuch MSS. With a Description of Two Codices', *BJRL* 21 (1937): 244–72.

Röhrig, Meike J., *Innerbiblische Auslegung und priesterliche Fortschreibungen in Lev 8–10*, FAT II/128 (Tübingen: Mohr Siebeck, 2021).

Römer, Thomas, 'Provisorische Überlegungen zur Entstehung von Exodus 18–24', in Reinhard Achenbach and Martin Arneth (Eds), *'Gerechtigkeit und Recht zu üben' (Gen 18,19): Studien zur altorientalischen und biblischen Rechtsgeschichte, zur Religionsgeschichte Israels und zur Religionssoziologie. Festschrift für Eckart Otto zum 65. Geburtstag*, BZABR 13 (Wiesbaden: Harrassowitz, 2009), 128–54.

Rooke, Deborah W., *Zadok's Heirs: The Role and Development of the High Priesthood in Ancient Israel* (Oxford: Oxford University Press, 2000).

Rouse, Joseph, 'Power/Knowledge', in Gary Gutting (Ed.), *The Cambridge Companion to Foucault* (Cambridge: Cambridge University Press, 2005), 95–122.

Ruwe, Andreas, 'Das Reden und Verstummen Aarons vor Mose: Levitikus 9–10 im Buch Leviticus', in Sylke Lubs, Louis Jonker, Andreas Ruwe, and Uwe Weise (Eds), *Behutsames Lesen: Alttestamentliche Exegese im interdisziplinären Methodendiskurs. Christof Hardmeier zum 65. Geburtstag*, ABG 28 (Leipzig: Evangelische Verlagsanstalt, 2007), 169–96.

Samuel, Harald, *Von Priestern zum Patriarchen: Levi und die Leviten im Alten Testament*, BZAW 448 (Berlin: de Gruyter, 2014).

Sanderson, Judith E., *An Exodus Scroll from Qumran: 4QpaleoExod^m and the Samaritan Tradition*, HSS 30 (Atlanta, GA: Scholars Press, 1986).

Sarna, Nahum M., *Exodus* שמות: *The Traditional Hebrew Text with the New JPS Translation*, JPS Torah Commentary (Philadelphia, PA: Jewish Publication Society of America, 1991).

Schaper, Joachim, *Priester und Leviten im achämenidischen Juda: Studien zur Kult- und Sozialgeschichte Israels in persischer Zeit*, FAT 31 (Tübingen: Mohr Siebeck, 2000).

Schenker, Adrian, 'Drei Mosaiksteinchen: "Königreich von Priestern", "Und ihre Kinder gehen weg", "Wir tun und wir hören" (Exodus 19,6; 21,22; 24,7)', in Marc Vervenne (Ed.), *Studies in the Book of Exodus: Redaction—Reception—Interpretation*, BETL 126 (Leuven: Leuven University Press, 1996), 367–80.

Schenker, Adrian, 'The Edition Biblia Hebraica Quinta (BHQ)', *HeBAI* 2 (2013): 6–16.

Schiffman, Lawrence H., 'Architecture and Law: The Temple and Its Courtyards in the Temple Scroll', in Jacob Neusner, Ernest S. Frerichs, and Nahum M. Sarna (Eds), *From Ancient Israel to Modern Judaism, Intellect in Quest of Understanding, Essays in Honor of Marvin Fox* (Atlanta, GA: Scholars Press, 1989), 267–84.

Schiffman, Lawrence H., 'The Furnishings of the Temple According to the Temple Scroll', in Julio C. Trebolle Barrera and Luis Vegas Montaner (Eds), *The Madrid Qumran Congress, Vol. 2*. STDJ 11 (Leiden: Brill, 1992), 621–34.

Schiffman, Lawrence H., 'The Milluim Ceremony in the Temple Scroll', in *The Courtyards of the House of the Lord: Studies on the Temple Scroll*, STDJ 75 (Leiden: Brill, 2008), 315–31.

Schiffman, Lawrence H., and Andrew Gross, *The Temple Scroll: 11Q19, 11Q20, 11Q21, 4Q524, 5Q21 with 4Q365a and 4Q365 Frag. 23*, Dead Sea Scrolls Editions 1 (Leiden: Brill, 2021).

Schmidt, Ludwig, 'Israel und das Gesetz: Ex 19,3b–8 und 24,3–8 als literarischer und theologischer Rahmen für das Bundesbuch', *ZAW* 113 (2001): 167–85.

Schmidt, Ludwig, *Menschlicher Erfolg und Jahwes Initiative: Studien zu Tradition, Interpretation und Historie in Überlieferungen von Gideon, Saul und David*, WMANT 38 (Neukirchen-Vluyn: Neukirchener Verlag, 1970).

Schorch, Stefan, 'A Critical Editio Maior of the Samaritan Pentateuch: State of Research, Principles, and Problems', *HeBAI* 2 (2013): 100–20.

Schorch, Stefan, 'The So-Called Gerizim Commandment in the Samaritan Pentateuch', in Michael Langlois (Ed.), *The Samaritan Pentateuch and the Dead Sea Scrolls*, CBET 94 (Leuven: Peeters, 2019), 77–97.

Schorch, Stefan (Ed.), *Exodus, Samaritan Pentateuch 2* (Boston, MA: de Gruyter, forthcoming).

Schottroff, Willy, *Gedenken im Alten Orient und im Alten Testament: Die Wurzel zākar im semitischen Sprachkreis*, 2nd edn, WMANT 15 (Neukirchen-Vluyn: Neukirchener Verlag, 1967).

Schulz, Sarah, *Joschua und Melchisedek: Studien zur Entwicklung des Jerusalemer Hohepriesteramtes vom 6. Jahrhundert v. Chr. bis zum 2. Jahrhundert v. Chr*, BZAW (Berlin: de Gruyter, forthcoming).

Schwartz, Baruch J., 'The Priestly Account of the Theophany and Lawgiving at Sinai', in Michael V. Fox (Ed.), *Texts, Temples, and Traditions: A Tribute to Menahem Haran* (Winona Lake, IN: Eisenbrauns, 1996), 109–34.

Seebass, Horst, *Numeri 1,1–10,10*, BKAT 4/1 (Neukirchen-Vluyn: Neukirchener Verlag, 2012).

Segal, Michael, '4QReworked Pentateuch or 4QPentateuch?', in Lawrence H. Schiffman, Emanuel Tov, and James C. VanderKam (Eds), *The Dead Sea Scrolls: Fifty Years after Their Discovery. Proceedings of the Jerusalem Congress, July 20–25, 1997* (Jerusalem: Israel Exploration Society, 2000), 391–9.

Segal, Michael, 'The Text of the Hebrew Bible in Light of the Dead Sea Scrolls', *Materia Giudaica* 12 (2007): 5–20.

Seow, C.L., 'The Designation of the Ark in Priestly Theology', *HAR* 8 (1984): 185–98.

Sharon, Diane M., 'When Fathers Refuse to Eat: The Trope of Rejecting Food and Drink in Biblical Narrative', in Athalya Brenner and Jan W. van Henten (Eds), *Food and Drink in Biblical Worlds*, Semeia 68 (Atlanta, GA: Society of Biblical Literature, 1999), 135–48.

Shectman, Sarah, *Women in the Pentateuch: A Feminist and Source-Critical Analysis*, HBM 23 (Sheffield: Sheffield Phoenix, 2009).

Shinan, Avigdor, 'The Sins of Nadab and Abihu in Rabbinic Literature', *Tarbiz* 48 (1979): 201–14.

Ska, Jean-Louis, 'Exode 19,3b–6 et l'identité de l'Israël post-exilique', in Marc Vervenne (Ed.), *Studies in the Book of Exodus: Redaction—Reception—Interpretation*, BETL 126 (Leuven: Leuven University Press, 1996), 289–318.

Skehan, Patrick W., 'Exodus in the Samaritan Recension from Qumran', *JBL* 74 (1955): 182–7.

Skehan, Patrick W., Eugene Ulrich, and Judith E. Sanderson. *Qumran Cave 4. IV: Palaeo-Hebrew and Greek Biblical Manuscripts*, DJD 9 (Oxford: Clarendon Press, 1992).

Smith, William Robertson, *Lectures on the Religion of the Semites. First Series: The Fundamental Institutions*, 2nd edn (London: Black, 1894).

Sommer, Benjamin, 'Conflicting Constructions of Divine Presence in the Priestly Tabernacle', *BibInt* 9 (2001): 41–63.

Stackert, Jeffrey, *A Prophet like Moses: Prophecy, Law, and Israelite Religion* (Oxford: Oxford University Press, 2014).

Stackert, Jeffrey, 'Compositional Strata in the Priestly Sabbath: Exodus 31:12–17 and 35:1–3', *JHebS* 11 (2011). https://www.jhsonline.org/index.php/jhs/article/view/16438.

Stavrakopoulou, Francesca, *God: An Anatomy* (London: Picador, 2021).

Steins, Georg, 'Priesterherrschaft, Volk von Priestern oder was sonst? Zur Interpretation von Ex 19,6', *BZ* 45 (2001): 20–36.

Steins, Georg, '"Sie sollen mir ein Heiligtum machen": Zur Struktur und Entstehung von Ex 24,12– 31,18', in Frank-Lothar Hossfeld (Ed.), *Vom Sinai zum Horeb: Stationen alttestamentlicher Glaubensgeschichte* (Würzburg: Echter, 1989), 145–67.

Steuernagel, Carl, 'Der jehovitische Bericht über den Bundesschluss am Sinai', *TSK* 72 (1899): 319–50.

Stökl, Jonathan, 'Innovating Ordination', *HeBAI* 7 (2018): 483–99.

Strommenger, Eva, 'Kleidung', *RlA* 6: 18–38.

Sturdy, John, *Numbers*, CBC (Cambridge: Cambridge University Press, 1976).

Talmon, Shemaryahu, 'Synonymous Readings in the Textual Traditions of the Old Testament', in C. Rabin (Ed.), *Studies in the Bible*, ScrHier 8 (Jerusalem: Magnes Press, 1961), 335–83.

Talmon, Shemaryahu, 'The Presentation of Synchroneity and Simultaneity in Biblical Narrative', in *Literary Studies in the Hebrew Bible* (Jerusalem: Magnes Press, 1993), 112–33.

Talshir, Zipora, *I Esdras: A Text Critical Commentary*, SCS 50 (Atlanta, GA: Society of Biblical Literature, 2001).

de Tarragon, J.-M., 'La "kapporet" est-elle une fiction ou un élément du culte tardif?', *RB* 88 (1981): 5–12.

Tigay, Jeffrey H., 'The Priestly Reminder Stones and Ancient Near East Votive Practices', in Mosheh Bar Asher, Dalit Rom-Shiloni, Emanuel Tov, and Nili Wazana (Eds), *Shai Le-Sara Japhet: Studies in the Bible, Its Exegesis and Its Language* (Jerusalem: Bialik Institute, 2007), 339*–355*.

Tov, Emanuel, 'From 4QReworked Pentateuch to 4QPentateuch (?)', in Mladen Popović (Ed.), *Authoritative Scriptures in Ancient Judaism*, JSJSup 141 (Leiden: Brill, 2010), 73–91.

Tov, Emanuel, 'From Popular Jewish LXX-SP Texts to Separate Sectarian Texts: Insights from the Dead Sea Scrolls', in Michael Langlois (Ed.), *The Samaritan Pentateuch and the Dead Sea Scrolls*, CBET 94 (Leuven: Peeters, 2019), 19–40.

Tov, Emanuel, 'Rewritten Bible Compositions and Biblical Manuscripts, with Special Attention Paid to the Samaritan Pentateuch', in *Hebrew Bible, Greek Bible and Qumran: Collected Essays*, TSAJ 121 (Tübingen: Mohr Siebeck, 2008), 57–70.

Tov, Emanuel, *Textual Criticism of the Hebrew Bible*, 3rd edn (Minneapolis: Fortress, 2012).

Tov, Emanuel, 'The Myth of the Stabilization of the Text of Hebrew Scripture', in Elvira Martín-Contreras and Lorena Miralles-Maciá (Eds), *The Text of the Hebrew Bible: From the Rabbis to the Masoretes*, JAJSup 13 (Göttingen: Vandenhoeck & Ruprecht, 2014).

Tov, Emanuel, 'The Shared Tradition of the Septuagint and the Samaritan Pentateuch', in Siegfried Kreuzer, Martin Meiser, Marcus Sigismund, Martin Karrer, and Wolfgang Kraus (Eds), *Die Septuaginta: Orte und Intentionen*, WUNT 361 (Tübingen: Mohr Siebeck, 2016), 277–93.

Trebolle Barrera, Julio, '2.5.1 Vetus Latina', in Armin Lange (Ed.), *Textual History of the Bible. Volume 1: The Hebrew Bible* (Leiden: Brill, 2020), 207–11.

Tucker, Paavo N., *The Holiness Composition in the Book of Exodus*, FAT II/98 (Tübingen: Mohr Siebeck, 2017).

Ulrich, Eugene, 'The Developmental Composition of the Biblical Text', in *The Dead Sea Scrolls and the Developmental Composition of the Bible*, VTSup 169 (Leiden: Brill, 2015), 1–14.

Ulrich, Eugene, Frank Moore Cross, James R. Davila, Nathan Jastram, Judith E. Sanderson, Emanuel Tov, and John Strugnell, *Qumran Cave 4. VII: Genesis to Numbers*, DJD 12 (Oxford: Clarendon Press, 1994).

Utzschneider, Helmut, *Das Heiligtum und das Gesetz: Studien zur Bedeutung der sinaitischen Heiligtumstexte (Ex 25–40; Lev 8–9)*, OBO 77 (Freiburg im Üchtland: Universitätsverlag, 1988).

Utzschneider, Helmut, 'Tabernacle', in Thomas B. Dozeman, Craig A. Evans, and Joel N. Lohr (Eds), *The Book of Exodus: Composition, Reception, and Interpretation*, VTSup 164 (Brill: Leiden, 2014), 267–301.

Van Dam, Cornelis, *The Urim and Thummim: A Means of Revelation in Ancient Israel* (Winona Lake, IN: Eisenbrauns, 1997).

VanderKam, James C., *From Joshua to Caiaphas: High Priests after the Exile* (Minneapolis: Fortress, 2004).

Vercellone, Carlo, *Variae lectiones Vulgatae latinae Bibliorum editionis* (Rome: Spithöver, 1860).

Voss, Jens, *Die Menora: Gestalt und Funktion des Leuchters im Tempel zu Jerusalem*, OBO 128 (Göttingen: Vandenhoeck & Ruprecht, 1993).

de Waard, Henk, *Jeremiah 52 in the Context of the Book of Jeremiah*, VTSup 183 (Leiden: Brill, 2020).

Wade, Martha, *Consistency of Translation Techniques in the Tabernacle Accounts of Exodus in the Old Greek*, SCS 49 (Leiden: Brill, 2003).

Wagner, Thomas, *Gottes Herrlichkeit: Bedeutung und Verwendung des Begriffs kābôd im Alten Testament*, VTSup 151 (Leiden: Brill, 2012).

Walkenhorst, Karl-Heinz, *Der Sinai im liturgischen Verständnis der deuteromistischen und priesterlichen Tradition*, BBB 33 (Bonn: Hanstein, 1969).

Waltke, Bruce K., and M. O'Conner, *An Introduction to Biblical Hebrew Syntax* (Winona Lake, IN: Eisenbrauns, 1990).

Watts, James W., 'Aaron and the Golden Calf in the Rhetoric of the Pentateuch', *JBL* 130 (2011): 417–30.

Watts, James W., *Leviticus 1–10*, HCOT (Leuven: Peeters, 2013).

Watts, James W., *Ritual and Rhetoric in Leviticus: From Sacrifice to Scripture* (Cambridge: Cambridge University Press, 2007).

292 BIBLIOGRAPHY

Weeks, Stuart, *Ecclesiastes 1–5: A Critical and Exegetical Commentary*, ICC (London: T&T Clark, 2020).

Weimar, Peter, 'Sinai und Schöpfung: Komposition und Theologie der priesterschriftlichen Sinaigeschichte', in *Studien zur Priesterschrift*, FAT 56 (Tübingen: Mohr Siebeck, 2008), 269–317.

Weimar, Peter, *Studien zur Priesterschrift*, FAT 56 (Tübingen: Mohr Siebeck, 2008).

Wellhausen, Julius, *Die Composition des Hexateuchs und der historischen Bücher des Alten Testaments*, 3rd edn (Berlin: Reimer, 1899).

Wellhausen, Julius, *Prolegomena to the History of Israel with a Reprint of the Article Israel from the 'Encyclopaedia Britannica'*, trans. John Sutherland Black and Allan Menzies (Edinburgh: Black, 1885).

Wenham, Gordon J., *Numbers, an Introduction and Commentary*, TOTC 4 (Leicester: Inter-Varsity Press, 1981).

Wenham, Gordon J., *The Book of Leviticus*, NICOT (London: Hodder & Stoughton, 1979).

Wevers, John William, *Exodus, Septuaginta. Vetus Testamentum Graecum II/1* (Göttingen: Vandenhoeck & Ruprecht, 1991).

Wevers, John William, *Notes on the Greek Text of Exodus*, SCS 30 (Atlanta, GA: Scholars Press, 1990).

Wevers, John William, 'PreOrigen Recensional Activity in the Greek Exodus', in Detlef Frankel, Udo Quast and John William Wevers (Eds), *Studien zur Septuaginta—Robert Hanhart zu Ehren: Aus Anlass seines 65 Geburtstages*. AAWG, Philologisch-historische Klasse III/190 (Göttingen: Vandenhoeck & Ruprecht, 1990), 121–39.

Wevers, John William, *Text History of the Greek Exodus*, AAWG, Philologisch-historische Klasse III/192 (Göttingen: Vandenhoeck & Ruprecht, 1992).

Wevers, John William, 'The Building of the Tabernacle', *JNSL* 19 (1993): 123–31.

Wildberger, Hans, *Isaiah 28–39: A Commentary*, CC (Minneapolis: Fortress, 1991).

Williamson, H. G. M., *Ezra, Nehemiah*, WBC 16 (Waco, TX: Word, 1985).

Willis, Timothy M., *The Elders of the City: A Study of the Elders-Laws in Deuteronomy*, SBLMS 55 (Atlanta, GA: Society of Biblical Literature, 2001).

Winter, Urs, *Frau und Göttin: Exegetische und ikonographische Studien zum weiblichen Gottesbild im Alten Israel und in dessen Umwelt*, OBO 53 (Freiburg im Üchtland: Universitätsverlag, 1983).

Wöhrle, Jakob, 'On the Way to Hierocracy: Secular and Priestly Rule in the Books of Haggai and Zechariah', in Lena-Sofia Tiemeyer (Ed.), *Priests and Cults in the Book of the Twelve*, ANEM 14 (Atlanta, GA: Society of Biblical Literature, 2016), 173–90.

Wright, David P., 'The Gesture of Hand Placement in the Hebrew Bible and in Hittite Literature', *JAOS* 106 (1986): 433–46.

Würthwein, Ernst, *Das erste Buch der Könige, Kapitel 1–16*, ATD 11,1 (Göttingen: Vandenhoeck & Ruprecht, 1977).

Zahn, Molly M., *Rethinking Rewritten Scripture: Composition and Exegesis in the 4QReworked Pentateuch Manuscripts*, STDJ 95 (Leiden: Brill, 2011).

Zahn, Molly M., 'The Samaritan Pentateuch and the Scribal Culture of Second Temple Judaism', *JSJ* 46 (2015): 285–313.

Ziegler, Leo, *Bruchstücke einer vorhieronymianischen Übersetzung des Pentateuch: Aus einem Palimpseste der K. Hof- und Staatsbibliothek zu München zum ersten Male veröffentlicht* (Munich: Theodor Riedel, 1883).

Zwickel, Wolfgang, *Räucherkult und Räuchergeräte: Exegetische und archäologische Studien zum Räucheropfer im Alten Testament*, OBO 97 (Göttingen: Vandenhoeck & Ruprecht, 1990).

Subject Index

For the benefit of digital users, indexed terms that span two pages (e.g., 52–53) may, on occasion, appear on only one of those pages.

Aaronide priesthood 6, 127–8, 177, 187, 189, 191–4, 199, 203–4, 215–16, 217n.12, 218–20, 224–5, 238–9, 254, 262–3, 265–6, 268

Aaron, sons of (*see* Nadab and Abihu; Eleazar and Ithamar)

Achaemenid empire (*see* Persian empire)

alcohol 235–6

altar (מִזְבֵּחַ)
  of incense (מִזְבַּח הַקְּטֹרֶת) 18–21, 24, 27, 29, 40, 42–50, 56, 65, 68–71, 75–7, 83, 89, 93–7, 130–1, 140–50, 175–7, 197–8, 208, 215, 223–4, 226, 228, 270, 273
  of burnt offering (מִזְבַּח הָעֹלָה) 11, 21, 27, 44–5, 50, 56, 65, 72, 75–7, 96, 140–2, 145–8, 153–6, 215, 226, 228–9, 231, 270–1

anointing oil 18, 20, 43–5, 55n.53, 56, 93–4, 140, 142, 149–51, 153, 180, 191–2, 194, 196–7, 213, 234, 253

Antiochus IV 2–3

ark, the (אֲרוֹן) 33, 36–40, 50, 53–6, 60, 80, 86, 105–6, 131, 133–4, 143–5, 167–8, 272

Assyrian empire 146–7, 258–60

atonement cover (כַּפֹּרֶת) 18–19, 22–3, 25, 29–30, 39, 53–6, 60–1, 80, 86, 88–9, 96, 105, 130–4, 141, 143–5, 248

Babylonian exile, period 3–6, 17, 113–14, 210, 269

Ben Sira 118–19, 238–9

Bezalel and Oholiab, Beseel and Eliab 21, 27–9, 32–9, 44–5, 53–6, 58–9, 71–3, 83–4, 89–95, 153–72, 174, 181–3

breastpiece (חֹשֶׁן) 25, 27, 115–26, 138–9, 158–9, 166–7, 169–70, 197–8

census 38, 80–1, 95–6, 139, 140n.29, 175–6, 181–2, 240–1

cherubim (כְּרֻבִים) 33, 35–9, 54, 57, 61, 71–2, 105n.15, 107–8, 110–12, 133–4, 158–9, 166–7, 174

Codex Leningrad 16–17, 47, 157, 162–3, 165

compliance account 21–2, 32, 42–3, 60, 68–70, 72–3, 75–9, 87, 93–4, 96–8, 116n.57, 117–18, 135–6, 156–7, 163–4, 169–70, 181–2, 194–5, 197–8

Covenant Code 101–2

Dan, tribe of 36–7, 72, 90, 154–5, 158, 162, 164–5, 168–9, 181–3, 210–11

David 103, 139n.25, 170–1

Dead Sea Scrolls 10, 23, 26, 41–7, 52, 65–6, 242–3

Decalogue 43–4, 101, 105, 261

Deuteronomic, Deuteronomistic 98, 101, 105–6, 129, 220–1, 235–6, 258–60, 263–4

divine presence 4–5, 74, 82, 131, 204–9, 223–4, 271, 273–4

dwelling (מִשְׁכָּן) 4–5, 59, 73–5, 84–6, 106–7, 111–12, 127, 139, 188–9

dyarchy 1–2, 134–5

earrings (נֶזֶם) 82, 173

Egypt, Egyptian 4–5, 26, 28–9, 53n.50, 74, 101, 107n.29, 114n.49, 122, 123n.79, 139, 171, 178, 206–7, 237n.93, 240–1, 255–6, 261

Eleazar and Ithamar 69n.14, 80–1, 122–4, 181, 187, 214, 226–32, 234

Elephantine 2

Ephod (אֵפֹד) 19, 21–2, 27–8, 71–2, 79, 92–3, 113–24, 136, 138–9, 139n.25, 158–9, 166–7, 208

Ephraim, tribe of 210–12, 225n.48

exile, exilic (*see* Babylonian exile)

final form/canonical reading 83, 102

gender 5–6, 153–4, 172–6, 183, 273–4

Gerizim, Mount 23–4, 43–4, 109n.34, 169

glory (כָּבוֹד) 17–18, 21–3, 83, 87–8, 101–2, 117–18, 120, 127, 129–30, 140, 188–9, 194–5, 205–7, 209, 222–3, 229, 231–3, 248

golden calf 17–18, 20, 68–9, 71, 81–2, 93, 98, 167–8, 167n.16, 171, 173, 181n.53, 204–5, 273

294 SUBJECT INDEX

Hasmoneans 1
Hasmonean period 12, 44–5, 263–4
hegemony 1–2, 4–6, 9, 103, 170–1, 217
Hellenistic period 2–3, 9, 112–13
Hexateuch 98
Holiness Code (H) 69–70, 82, 86–7, 87n.65,
    93–4, 97–8, 125–6, 129–30, 198n.27,
    221–2, 234–5
Holy of holies (קֹדֶשׁ הַקֳּדָשִׁים) 5, 33, 35–6, 38–40,
    45–6, 56, 115n.52, 127, 144
Horeb, Mount 101
hierocracy 2–3

Jacob 122–4, 246, 255–6
Jerusalem (*see also* Temple, Second; Temple,
    Solomon's) 1–5, 103, 110–11, 117, 129,
    154–69, 210, 274
Josephus 1n.2, 64n.82, 113–14, 182n.58, 208, 245
Judah
    kingdom of 1, 112, 129, 139, 152, 168–9, 274
    tribe of 37, 72, 90–1, 154, 162, 164–5, 168–71,
        181–3, 210–12, 246, 272–4
    province of (*see* Yehud)
Judaism 3–5, 9, 47, 113–14, 138–9, 152

Korah 29, 49, 80–1, 89, 94, 96, 176–7, 179–80,
    215, 224–5, 238

Lamp, lampstand (מְנוֹרָה) 18–19, 21, 24–5, 27, 29,
    39–40, 45–6, 50, 55–6, 75–7, 86–7, 87n.65,
    93, 96, 104, 106–8, 111–12, 136–7, 144, 148,
    167–8, 208, 248–9, 270, 273
laver (כִּיּוֹר) 18, 20–1, 29–30, 50, 56, 68–9, 69n.14,
    71, 75–7, 80–1, 83, 93–6, 110–11, 130–1,
    140–1, 147–9, 155–6, 175–80, 194–8, 208
Levites 5, 11–12, 37–9, 64, 80–1, 98, 122–4,
    139n.25, 153–4, 171, 175–6, 178–83, 210,
    212, 215, 240, 243–5, 247, 249–54, 258n.54,
    264–5, 267–8, 272–3
linen (בַּד, שֵׁשׁ) 57, 63, 79n.41, 85, 113–17,
    132, 135–6

Maccabean revolt 2–3
Maccabean period (*see* Hasmonean period)
Mari 4–5
Midian 4–5
Monarchic period (*see* Judah, kingdom of)

Nadab and Abihu 6, 12, 210–11, 214–27, 232–5,
    238, 240–1, 244, 247, 260, 265–6
Nebuchadnezzar 1

offering (*see also* sacrifice)
    amity (שְׁלָמִים) 188, 191–3, 199–201, 211–12,
        237–8, 247, 251–2, 256

burnt (עֹלָה) 18–20, 113–14, 137, 146, 188,
    190–1, 199–205, 209, 213–14, 221–2,
    226–31, 233–4, 236–7, 250, 252–3
daily (תָּמִיד) 19–20, 93, 149–50,
    219n.21, 223–4
grain (מִנְחָה) 146, 188, 191, 199–201, 205,
    236–8, 250, 252
ordination (מִלֻּאִים) 19–20, 137, 147, 188,
    191–4, 196–8, 200–1, 203, 237–8, 252, 254
sin-purification (חַטָּאת) 137, 188, 190–1, 193,
    198–205, 214, 216, 221–2, 226–34, 240–1,
    246, 250, 252
votive 113–14, 175–6, 178

Palestine, the Levant 1, 103, 110, 122, 142–3,
    146–7, 150–1
Passover 210–12, 241, 242n.2, 244, 247,
    249–51, 258
Persian empire 1–3, 152, 274
Persian period 1–4, 9–10, 138–9, 169–70, 180,
    264–5, 269, 274
Peshitta 42
Philo (*see also* Pseudo-Philo) 112–13
poll tax, half shekel tax 95–6, 153, 175–6,
    273–4
post-priestly 222, 258–60, 262–3, 267
Priestly *Grundschrift* 68nn.3,10, 76n.33, 83–8,
    97, 102, 105, 122, 127–30, 134, 138–9,
    218n.14, 220–3, 265n.85
Pseudo-Philo 208–9

Qumran (*see* Dead Sea Scrolls)

Rambam 116n.57
ransom money 18, 20
Rashi 63n.76, 116n.57, 123n.83, 168n.19, 175,
    210n.54, 227
Rewritten Pentateuch 41, 44n.24
rings (טַבַּעַת) 53–5, 77–8, 105, 118, 142, 171, 173
robe (מְעִיל) 19, 79, 114–22, 125, 134–6,
    138–9, 165
rosette (צִיץ) 115–16, 116n.57, 118–19, 121,
    125–6, 135, 138, 169n.23

Sabbath 18, 20–2, 27, 68–9, 82, 93, 136–7, 235
sacrifice (*see also* altar; offering) 11–12, 19–20,
    25, 29–30, 47–8, 112–13, 125–6, 147,
    151–2, 189–94, 196–208, 210–13, 217–18,
    221–3, 226–8, 230–2, 237–9, 243–7, 252–4,
    256, 258, 262–3
Samaritan Pentateuch 10–11, 15–16, 23–6,
    37, 39, 42–9, 60, 62, 63n.78, 65–7, 72,
    75–6, 80–1, 84–5, 96–7, 110–11,
    118–19, 143–5, 159–60, 166–7, 180–2,
    191–2, 260n.64

SUBJECT INDEX 295

Samaritan temple (*see* Gerizim, Mount)
sanctuary, consecration of 194–9, 201–4,
 267–8, 273
sanctuary, purification and atonement of
 (*see also* atonement cover; offering,
 sin-purification) 129–34, 140, 200–1, 216,
 226, 228–9
Second Temple Period 10, 15, 41, 46–7, 51–2,
 60–1, 63–5, 67, 112–13, 129, 138, 199,
 258, 265
Seleucids 1–3
Seraphim 35–6, 61–2
Sinai, Mount 18n.12, 80–1, 83, 88, 101–2,
 127, 175, 200, 222, 240–1, 254–62,
 264–8
Solomon 103, 110, 131n.6, 168–9, 209
strange fire (אֵשׁ זָרָה) 12, 210–11, 214–19,
 223–5

Talmud 114
Temple, Second 3–4, 98, 183
Temple, Solomon's 45–6, 110–13, 131n.6,
 133n.9, 168–9, 209
Temple Scroll 41, 45–7, 62, 141n.30, 178,
 199n.30, 208

tent of meeting (אֹהֶל מוֹעֵד) 4–5, 20, 33, 73–5,
 80–1, 131, 139–41, 179, 188–9, 194, 236–7,
 248, 252–3, 272–3
theocracy 3n.9, 98, 187, 246, 263–8, 270–1
theophany 194–5, 199–200, 206–9, 212, 214,
 219n.21, 222n.41, 223–4, 238–9, 260
tribes 122–4, 169–71, 178, 180–2, 243–6, 256,
 258–60, 267–8, 274

Ugarit 4–5, 74n.24, 263n.76
Urim and Thummim (תֻּמִּים, אוּרִים) 25, 42–4,
 46–8, 65, 105–6, 118–19, 121–4

vestments 17–22, 24–5, 28–9, 33, 37–9, 42–4,
 47–8, 50, 62–5, 69n.14, 71–3, 79–81, 83–5,
 88, 91–5, 102, 120–7, 132, 134–41, 151–3,
 155–60, 170–1, 180–2, 193, 196–8, 272, 274
 for consecration 187–9, 191–4, 196–8,
 212–13, 233–4, 253–4
 serad vestments (בִּגְדֵי־שְׂרָד) 24–5, 63, 182
Vulgate 30–1, 89n.74, 142n.32, 269–70

Yehud, province of 1–3, 152

Zadokite 218–19, 235

Ancient Sources Index

Versification follows the Masoretic Text. Where there is a notable divergence from the Old Greek, the Old Greek versification is noted in parentheses. For the Old Latin, see Codex Monacensis, below.

For the benefit of digital users, indexed terms that span two pages (e.g., 52–53) may, on occasion, appear on only one of those pages.

Hebrew Bible

Genesis
 2.2 87
 50.26 105

Exodus
 1–34 51–2
 6.7 101–2
 6.14–27 218–19
 16.7–10 222n.43
 19 268
 19.1–2 101–2
 19.3–8 254–61, 265
 19.6 166–7
 19.9 255
 24 220–1, 268
 24.1–2 256, 260, 265–6
 24.3–8 254–66
 24.6 254
 24.8 254
 24.9–11 255, 260, 265–6
 24.15–16 88, 101–2
 24.17 222
 25 24, 53–5, 88, 106, 140
 25–27 67–86, 103, 106, 120–1
 25–28 127–8, 167
 25–29 68, 83–5, 220
 25–31 24–5, 53, 62, 81–2, 102, 167–8,
   182, 249
 25.1–9 19, 71–2
 25.1–31.17 18–20
 25.2 172
 25.2–7 (𝕲 25.2–6) 92–3
 25.8 101–2, 111–12, 118
 25.8–10 (𝕲 25.7–9) 72, 84, 117–18,
   165–6, 170–1
 25.9 85–6, 103
 25.10 71–2
 25.10–21 53–5
 25.10–40 103–7
 25.10–27.19 18–19, 73–4
 25.11 71–2
 25.16 133–4
 25.16–22 85–6, 88, 133–4
 25.17 133–4
 25.19 43n.18
 25.21 133–4
 25.22 134, 248
 25.26 78
 25.31–40 86–7
 25.37 248–9
 25.40 85–6, 103
 26 28–9, 75–6, 85–6
 26.1–6 85–6
 26.7–13 131
 26.1 158–9
 26.1–14 107
 26.1–30 107–8
 26.7 75
 26.15–30 85–6, 107
 26.26 135
 26.30 85–6, 103
 26.31 158–9
 26.31–33 108
 26.31–27.8 108–9
 26.33–34 125
 26.34 88
 26.34–35 108
 26.36 136, 158–9
 26.36–26.19 85–6
 27 28–9, 75–6, 140
 27–29 76
 27.1–2 104
 27.1–8 108–9, 176
 27.8 43n.18, 85–6, 103
 27.9 136
 27.9–19 109–10
 27.16 135–6, 158–9
 27.18 136
 27.20 25

ANCIENT SOURCES INDEX 297

27.20–21 24–5, 86–7, 93, 136–7, 148
27.20–29.42 73
27.21 144, 188–9
28 113–16, 120–1, 253–4
28–29 75, 84–5, 233–4
28.1 233, 252–3
28.1–29.37 18
28.2 71–2, 117–18
28.3–5 71–2, 83–4, 92, 165–6, 170–1
28.4 113–18
28.6 71–2, 83–4, 158–9
28.6–30 118–19
28.6–39 118, 137–8
28.7 137–8
28.9–43 71–2
28.10 122–4
28.11 155, 158–9
28.12 121, 124
28.15 158–9
28:21 122–4
28.22–30 27
28.24–25 113–14
28.29 (❦ 28.23) 25, 95–6, 115, 121–4
28.30 95–6, 118–19, 121–4
28.35 95–6, 115, 121
28.36 138
28.36–38 113–14, 125–6
28.37–42 88
28.37 116–17, 134–9
28.38 121
28.39 116–17, 137–8, 158–9
29.39–40 134–9
28.40 117–18, 137–8
28.41 84–5, 88, 115–18, 149–50, 188
28.42–43 115–16
28.43 148, 188–9
29 88, 137, 153, 188, 197–9, 204–6, 217, 217n.12, 223, 229–31, 262
29.1 252–4
29.4–5 252–3
29.4–9 137–8
29.4–34 137, 188–91
29.5–9 134–9
29.6 138
29.7 142, 149–50
29.10 233
29.21 25, 149–50, 191–2
29.27–28 192–3
29.28 25
29.29–30 192–3
29.33 137, 196–7
29.35–37 193
29.36 149–50

29.38 19–20
29.38–42 93, 95, 205
29.40 24
29.42–43 134
29.43–44 88, 140, 188–9, 219n.21, 222n.41, 232n.72, 233
29.43–46 74, 139–40, 206–7
29.44 84–5, 188
29.45 83, 222
29.45–46 84–5, 101–2, 188–9
30 140, 225
30–31 67–8, 75–7, 83, 93–4, 96–7
30.1 142–3
30.1–10 24, 75–6, 93–4, 142–8
30.6 75–6, 143–5
30.7–10 145–6, 223–4
30.8 145–6, 248–9
30.9 146, 215, 223–4
30.10 145–6, 175–6
30.11 20
30.11–16 (❦ 39.1–11) 80–1, 95–6, 153, 175
30.15 175–6
30.16 176
30.17–21 75–6, 93–4, 147–9
30.18 75–6
30.20 147
30.22–38 93–4, 149–51
30.32–38 150
30.34–38 142, 215
31.1 153
31.1–6 90, 93–4
31.1–11 72
31.2–5 154, 161
31.4 (❦ 31.4) 157, 163
31.5 154n.1, 155n.2, 159–60
31.6 153–5, 157, 161
31.7–11 93–4
31.8–9 94–5
31.12 81–2
31.12–18 93
31.18 20, 105
31.18–34.35 20
32–34 81–2
32.2–4 81–2, 171
32.15 105
33.7 179n.52
33.7–11 20, 80–1
34.28–29 105
35–39 67–8, 70–1, 153–4
35–40 27, 49–53, 55, 68–70, 76, 81–2, 87, 96–7, 102, 167–8, 182, 272
35.1–3 81–2, 93
35.1–5 156, 158

298 ANCIENT SOURCES INDEX

Exodus (*cont.*)
35.1–39.43 (𝕲 35.1–39.23) 21–2
35.3–5 156
35.4–9 (𝕲 35.4–8) 80–1
35.5 172
35.10 (𝕲 35.9) 172
35.10–19 (𝕲 35.9–19) 55–6, 94–5
35.10–39.31 (𝕲 35.9–39.13) 87
35.13 (𝕲 35.12) 78
35.18 (𝕲 35.17) 76–7
35.20–29 93, 172–5
35.21 75
35.22 81–2
35.24 80–1
35.26–27 96
35.27–28 180
35.30 163–4
35.30–33 156
35.30–35 90–2, 161–4
35.30–36.1 92, 167
35.30–36.7 89–90
35.31 163
35.31–34 154–5, 161, 163–4
35.32 157–8, 163
35.33 155n.2, 159–60, 163
35.34 157, 161, 163–4
35.34–35 92, 161
35.35 155–6, 161–6, 170
36–39 75
36–40 61–2, 208–9
36.1 89–90, 162–4, 170, 172
36.1–7 92
36.2 171–2
36.2–7 93
36.5 174–5
36.8 155–6, 163
36.8b (𝕲 37.1) 92
36.8b–9 (𝕲 37.1–2) 57, 61–2
36.8b–20 (𝕲 37.1–18) 73, 89, 156–7
36.8–37.24 (37–38) 96
38.8b–38 (𝕲 37.1–6) 35, 56–7, 69n.14
36.8–38.20 51–2
36.13–38 (𝕲 37.2–6) 56–7
36.21–23 (𝕲 37.19–21) 89–90
36.35–36 (𝕲 37.3–4) 91
37–38 53, 76–7
37.1–2 (𝕲 38.1–2) 167–8
37.1–9 (𝕲 38.1–8) 53–5, 86
37.1–23 (𝕲 38.1–17) 89
37.1–29 155–6
37.1–38.8 (𝕲 38.1–26) 49, 53, 156–7
𝕲 38.18–20 49
𝕲 38.18–21 57–9, 89, 92
𝕲 38.18–27 89, 92
37.25–28 49, 76–7, 94–5

38.1–4 (𝕲 38.22–24) 76–7, 89, 96
𝕲 38.22b 49
38.1–7 (𝕲 38.22–24) 96, 176–7
38.1–8 153
38.8 (𝕲 38.26) 75–7, 80–1, 177, 179
𝕲 38.26–27 76–7
38.9–20 (𝕲 37.1–2) 49, 155–6
38.21(𝕲 37.19) 80–1, 180–2
38.21–23 (𝕲 37.19–21) 37
38.22 (𝕲 37.20) 156
38.22–23 (𝕲 37.20–21) 164–5, 167
38.23 (𝕲 37.21) 154–5, 157–60, 166
38.24–31 (𝕲 39.1–11) 80–1, 175
39.1 (𝕲 39.13) 24–5, 62–4
39.1–31 (𝕲 36.8–38) 49
39.2–31 (𝕲 36.8–40) 28, 91–2
39.6 (𝕲 36.13) 157
39.7 (𝕲 36.14) 156–7
39.9–20 (𝕲 37.7–18) 49
39.21 (𝕲 36.29) 25, 156–7
39.27–29 135–6
39.32–41 (𝕲 39.14–21) 55
39.32–40.15 (𝕲 39.14–40.13) 87
39.32–40.35 75
𝕲 39.12 49
39.33–43 (𝕲 39.14–23) 94–5
39.38 (𝕲 39.16) 76–7
40.1–8 (𝕲 40.1–6) 55
40.1–15 (𝕲 40.1–13) 95
40.1–33 194–5
40.1–38 22–3
40.2 95, 209–10
40.4 248–9
40.5 76–7, 144
40.6 95
40.9–15 194–5, 197–8
40.16–17 87
40.17 208, 241
40.17–33 (𝕲 40.15–27) 79, 95
40.18–33 (𝕲 40.16–27) 55, 87
40.19 (𝕲 40.17) 75
40.20–21 80
40.21 (𝕲 40.19) 91
40.26 (𝕲 40.24) 76–7, 144
40.29 95
40.33 87, 241
40.34–35 207, 209
40.34–38 219n.21, 222n.41
40.35 87, 248
40.36–38 (𝕲 40.30–32) 96

Leviticus
1–3 146–7, 219n.21
1–7 187, 204, 217–18, 219n.21, 221–2,
  228–30, 266–7
1–10 207–8

ANCIENT SOURCES INDEX 299

1–16 6, 88–9
1.1 6
1.1–8.36 217n.12
2 191
3 191
4 204, 228
4–5 76n.33
4–7 219n.21
4.1 6
4.3 202–3
4.10 221n.36
4.15 221n.31
5.10 221n.38
7 237–8
7.23 221n.36
7.28–34 192–3
7.30 219n.21
7.32–34 219n.21
7.34 251–2
8 25, 47–8, 97, 187, 191–204, 217n.12, 222–3,
   227–31, 236–8, 262–3
8–9 243–4
8–10 244, 249, 267–8
8.1–3 200–1
8.1–5 200–1
8.4 200–1
8.5 200–1, 205–6
8.5–22 212
8.7 117n.59, 137n.17
8.7–9 118–19
8.10–11 196–8
8.12 198
8.14 203, 252
8.14–17 140, 200–1, 229
8.15 198
8.18 203
8.18–21 200–1
8.19 252
8.22 203
8.30 191–2, 198n.26, 233–4
8.33–35 198–9
8.34 252
9 199–208, 217–23, 227–31, 262–3
9–10 217–18, 220–4, 238n.95, 244
9.1 211n.57, 217n.12, 220–1
9.1–6 200–1
9.1–7 199–200, 222–3
9.1–21 206
9.2 202–5, 221–2
9.3 204–5
9.5 200–1
9.6 200–1, 205–6, 220
9.7 202–3, 220–1, 227–8
9.8–11 200–1, 229
9.8–14 199–201

9.9 203
9.10 230
9.11 230–1
9.12 203
9.12–14 200–1
9.15 220–1, 230–1
9.15–16 199–200, 230–1
9.17 206
9.17–21 199–200
9.18 203, 220–1
9.21 237–8
9.22 220–1, 244
9.22–24 199–200, 206–9, 222n.41, 260
9.23 207, 220–1, 222n.41
9.23–24 222
9.24 220–1, 222n.41, 223
10 6, 125–6, 204–5, 214–15, 217–24, 235–6,
   242–3, 260
10.1 215–17, 220, 223–5
10.1–2 225
10.2 223
10.3 232–3
10.6–7 234
10.8–11 217–18, 234–6
10.8–20 219n.21
10.9 235–6, 235n.86
10.12 222–3
10.12–15 236–8
10.12–20 217–18
10.14–15 237–8
10.16–20 230–1
10.19 216, 220
11.1 6
12.1 6
14.8 251
15.1 6
16 11, 76n.33, 86, 88–9, 91–2, 97–8, 105,
   113–17, 120n.69, 129–37, 139–41, 200–1,
   204–6, 221–2
16.2 131–2
16.2–3 131
16.3 204–5
16.4 113–14, 116–17, 135n.13, 141,
   147, 233–4
16.5 204–5
16.6 130, 132
16.11 130, 132
16.12 144–5, 215
16.12–13 141, 145
16.13 132, 144–5
16.16 132
16.23–25 113–14, 132
16.32 228n.63
17–26 68–9, 82
21 235–6

300 ANCIENT SOURCES INDEX

Leviticus (*cont.*)
  21.10–12 234
  22 125–6
  22.32 232n.72
  24.1–9 45–6, 136–7
  24.2–4 86–7

Numbers
  1 80–1, 175, 243–4, 246
  1–4 178, 181–2, 240–3, 272
  1–5 191
  1–10 207–8
  1.1 240–3
  1.16 245
  2 243–4
  3 243–4, 251
  3–4 243–4
  3.1–4 244
  3.9 251–2
  3.11–13 251
  3.13 253
  4 63–4, 80–1, 244
  4.6 53n.50
  4.6–13 182
  4.10 106n.22
  4.23 178–9
  4.28 181–2
  4.33 181–2
  5–6 244
  6 235–6
  6.2–8 235–6
  6.22–27 244
  7 210, 211n.57, 212, 243–7
  7–8 249
  7–9 240–54
  7–10 12, 242–4, 267–8
  7.1–10.10 241–3
  7.1–88 210, 244–7
  7.1–9 210
  7.1 211–12, 241, 249–50
  7.3 245
  7.10 245
  7.12 211–12
  7.18 211–12
  7.89 133, 247–8
  7.89–8.4 210, 247–50
  8 243–4, 248n.29, 251–2, 267–8
  8.1–4 46–7, 247–9, 248n.29
  8.2–3 248n.29
  8.3 189
  8.4 167–8
  8.5–14 250
  8.5–22 210, 244, 249–54
  8.6 252–3
  8.7 250, 253
  8.9 252–3

  8.11 253–4
  8.12 252
  8.14 252
  8.14–19 251
  8.15 190
  8.19 252
  8.20–22 250–1
  8.24 178–9
  9 187, 242n.2
  9.1 242–3
  9.1–14 210
  9.15 241, 249–50
  10.11 241
  11 260
  16 29, 176–7, 218–19
  16–17 80–1, 89, 94–6, 215, 224–5
  16.6–7 224
  16.17–18 224
  17.4–5 177
  17.5 223n.45, 224n.47
  17.11 215
  17.15 215
  17.16–26 224n.47
  18 234–5, 266–7
  18.1–7 125–6
  18.17 254n.42
  19 250n.31
  19.13 254–5
  19.20 254–5
  20.22–29 187
  25.32–33 181n.53
  26 181–2
  27.21 122–4
  28.1–30.1 247

Deuteronomy
  1–3 47–8
  1.31 261n.68
  7.6 258–60
  10.1–5 105, 167–8
  10.3–5 167–8
  14.2 258–60
  14.21 258–60
  14.26 236–7
  26.19 258–60
  28.9 258–60
  32.10–11 261n.68

Joshua
  16.4 225n.48

Judges
  1 246n.22
  17–18 258

1 Samuel
  1.3 225n.48
  1.14 236n.88

ANCIENT SOURCES INDEX 301

2 258, 266–7
2.22 80–1, 178–9
10.8 260n.64
11.15 260nn.64,65
23.6–14 122–4
30.7–10 122–4

2 Samuel
21 139
24 139

1 Kings
6–8 85, 112–13
6.23–28 110–11
7.23–29 110–11
8.4 110–11

2 Kings
12.9–10 105
16.10 103

Isaiah
28.7 235–6
61.5–6 266
61.6 264–5

Jeremiah
6.20 149
34 262
52.11 1n.1

Ezekiel
11.16 269n.1
21.21, 26 138–9
27.19 149
40–42 85, 112–13
40–48 204–5
43 240
43.18–27 198–9
44 218–19, 235–6
44.10–11 258n.54
44.20 250n.31

Amos
2.8 236n.88

Zechariah
1–8 3–4

Psalms
50.12–13 106–7
80.2 133n.9
99.1 133n.9

Ezra
6.15 210
6.20 258n.54

1 Chronicles
15.27 139n.25
28.11 133
29.11 103

29.12 103
29.19 103

2 Chronicles
2.13–14 169n.21
4.1 111n.39
5.12 182
30.17 258n.54
35.6 258n.54
35.11 258n.54

Apocrypha

1 Esdras
7.5 210

Sirach
50 238–9

Codex Monacensis ($\mathfrak{L}^{M}$)

Exodus
21/1/1–24/2/2 (𝕲 36.13–37.18) 35–7
22/2/1–7 (𝕲 37.1–2) 61–2
22/2/1–23 35
22/2/1–23/1/24 (𝕲 37.1–3) 61
22/2/10–18 (𝕲 37.5–6) 61–2
22/2/24–23/1/16 35
23/1/17–24 (𝕲 37.3–4) 35–6, 39–40, 61–2
24/2/3–6 (𝕲 37.19) 181n.57
24/2/3–17 (𝕲 37.19–21) 36–7
24/2/6–17 (𝕲 37.20–21) 164–5
24/2/8–9 (𝕲 37.21) 157–8
24/2/10–17 (𝕲 37.20–21) 157, 159
24/2/11–12 (𝕲 37.21) 159–60
24/2/18 (𝕲 38.1) 159–60
24/2/18–20 (𝕲 38.1) 157
24/2/18–25/1/9 (𝕲 38.1–8) 61
24/2/18–26/2/1 (𝕲 38.1–27) 37
25/1/1–9 36
25/2/12 (𝕲 38.18) 61–2
26/2/22–27/1/3 (𝕲 39.1–12) 38
26/2/2–27/2/8 (𝕲 39.1–13) 37–8, 61
27/2/4–8 (𝕲 39.13) 64, 80–1, 182
27/2/7–8 (𝕲 39.13) 180–1
27/2/9–30/2/17 (𝕲 38.14) 38–40
28/2/1–3 (𝕲 40.3) 60
29/2/2–11 (𝕲 40.16–17) 61–2
29/2/21–25 (𝕲 40.19) 40
30/1/7–13 (𝕲 40.22–24) 40

Qumran

2Q2 (2QExod^{a})
30.25 41–2

302 ANCIENT SOURCES INDEX

2Q3 (2QExod[b])
30.16 42

4Q11 (4QpaleoGen-Exod[1])
25.20 42
26.34 42

4Q17
39.21 42–3, 46–7, 48n.34

4Q22 (4QpaleoExod[m])
25.20 43–4
26.34 43–4, 75–6, 97
27.20 43–4
29.20 43–4
31.5 154n.1

4Q158 (QRP[a])
30.32 44

4Q364 (4QRP[b])
24.18–25.1 44
26.33–35 44
26.34 44, 45n.26

4Q365 (4QRP[c])
26.34 44–5
29.28 44–5
37.29–28.7 44–5, 72

11Q19 (11QT[a])
3–12 45–6

3.10 45–6
3.13 45–6
3.16 178
7.13 45–6
15.3–16.4 199n.30
15.3–17.5 208

Pseudo-Philo

Biblical Antiquities (LAB)
13.1 208–9
13.1–2 208

Josephus

Jewish War (J.W.)
1.3.1 1n.2

Antiquities (Ant.)
3.193–4 64n.82
3.201–207 208
3.219–20 245
20.216–18 182n.58

Strabo

Geography (Geogr.)
16.2.40 1n.2

Author Index

For the benefit of digital users, indexed terms that span two pages (e.g., 52–53) may, on occasion, appear on only one of those pages.

Achenbach, Reinhard 2n.4, 4n.15, 89n.72, 181n.53, 218–20, 223, 224nn.46, 47, 234n.80, 235n.85, 238–9, 244, 245n.14, 248n.29, 254n.45, 260n.66
Aejmelaeus, Anneli 26n.36, 52n.47, 55n.51, 59n.69
Aharoni, Yohanan 146n.47
Albertz, Rainer 20n.18, 52n.48, 67n.2, 68–70, 76n.34, 85n.57, 93n.82, 107, 109n.34, 110nn.36, 38, 123n.84, 146n.44, 155–6, 179n.50, 260n.67
Anderson, Gary A. 25n.34, 81n.47, 188, 207, 209–10, 212, 217n.12, 243n.10
Arie, Eran 146n.47
Attridge, Harold 44n.23, 45n.26
Auld, A. Graeme 225n.48

Baentsch, Bruno 63n.75, 68–70, 71n.18, 218n.13, 221n.33
Baillet, M. 41–2
Balentine, Samuel E. 115n.53
Beer, Georg 68n.7, 123n.81
Begg, Christopher T. 214n.2
Belsheim, Johannes 30n.52
Berner, Christoph 116n.57, 257n.52
Bertholet, Alfred 202n.34, 218n.13, 221n.33
Beyerlin, Walter 258
Billen, A. V. 30–1
Blenkinsopp, Joseph 87n.67
Blum, Erhard 225n.48
Bogaert, Pierre-Maurice 26n.35, 28n.48, 32, 52n.47, 59–62, 64n.81, 73n.21, 81n.46, 89n.71, 159–60
Boorer, Suzanne 220n.26, 222n.41
Boulton, Meg 269n.2
Boyd, Samuel L. 258n.57
Brooke, George J. 44n.24, 46n.29, 52n.47
Bruning, Brandon E. 49n.40, 52n.47
Budd, Philip J. 246, 253n.40
Burkitt, F. C. 39–40

Calabro, David 190n.5
Carasik, Michael 63n.76, 116n.57, 123n.83, 175n.39, 203n.39, 210n.54, 235nn.83–84, 244n.12

Cassuto, Umberto 155n.4, 173n.34, 175n.40, 262n.71
Cataldo, Jeremiah W. 3n.9
Chavel, Simeon 242–3
Chazelle, Celia 269nn.2–4
Childs, Brevard Springs 70n.16, 102, 122n.75, 255
Clifford, Richard J. 5n.20, 74n.24, 103n.7
Coats, George W. 245n.16, 246n.19, 247n.24
Cortese, Enzo 85n.54, 86n.63
Cross, Frank Moore 5n.20, 42–3, 43n.15, 48n.35

Dahmen, Ulrich 81n.44
Dalley, Stephanie 107n.29
Daviau, P.M. Michèle 143n.34
Davies, Eryl W. 212n.60, 242–3, 250n.31, 252n.37, 253n.40
Davies, Graham I., 45n.26
Davies, John A. 255n.46
Davis, Andrew R. 15n.1, 112n.44
Dayfani, Hila 42–4
Dietzfelbinger, Rudolf 30n.52, 31–2
Dillmann, August 202n.34, 218n.13, 221n.33, 227n.59, 242–3
Dion, Paul E. 142–3
Dohmen, Christoph 52n.48, 178n.44, 263n.78
Dold, Alban 32, 35nn.61–62, 36nn.63–65, 38nn.66–67, 39–40, 39nn.68–69, 64n.80, 159n.10, 179n.51
Dotan, Aron 16n.3
Dozeman, Thomas B. 52n.48, 70n.16, 106n.24, 123n.84, 134n.12, 144n.38, 265–6
Driver, Samuel R. 70n.15, 123n.84
Dubrovský, Peter 15n.1, 82n.48
Dunkelgrün, Theodor 269n.1

Edelman, Diana 143n.36
Ehrlich, Arnold B. 55n.52, 137n.17, 232nn.70, 71, 263n.76
Eichler, Raanan 53n.50, 105n.15
Elden, Stuart 7n.26
Elliger, Karl 123n.81, 196n.17, 202n.34, 217–19, 221n.31, 227n.58, 232n.70, 235n.82
Elliott, J. Keith 26n.40

304 AUTHOR INDEX

Elliott, Mark W. 214n.2
Erder, Yoram 207n.47
Erickson, Nancy 250n.31

Fauth, Wolfgang 115n.52
Feldman, Liane Marquis 6, 200–1, 202n.34,
  205–6, 211n.57, 219n.21
Fernández Marcos, Natalio 60n.73, 113n.48
Findlay, James D. 200n.31
Finn, A. H. 49–51
Fischer, Bonifatius 30–1, 30n.52
Fishbane, Michael A. 216n.8
Fleming, Daniel E. 5n.20, 138, 197n.24
Flusser, David 214n.2
Foucault, Michel 6–9
Freedman, David Noel 16n.2
Fretheim, Terence E. 102
Frevel, Christian 3, 4n.15, 103n.9, 123n.84,
  124n.87, 204–5, 220nn.25–26, 221n.34,
  232n.72, 251n.33, 274
Fried, Lisbeth S. 2, 3n.14, 6, 210n.55
Fritz, Volkmar 86n.59

Gallagher, Edmond L. 23n.27
Galling, Kurt 68n.7, 123n.81
Gane, Roy E. 202n.34, 226n.51
Gennep, Arnold van 188
George, Mark K. 5–6, 104n.14, 105n.20
Gertz, Jan Christian 127n.97
Gilders, William K. 145n.42, 190n.6, 191n.8,
  198n.27, 203, 253n.41, 254n.44, 262–3
Ginsburg, Christian D. 16n.3
Gitin, Seymour 143n.37, 262n.70
Goldingay, John 266n.87
Gooding, David W. 49–51, 52n.48, 55n.51, 57–9,
  62n.74, 70n.16, 179nn.50, 52
Gordon, Robert P. 139n.25, 195n.16,
  207n.48, 211n.56
Görg, Manfred 86n.59, 111n.41, 123n.79
Gorman, Frank H. 195n.15
Grabbe, Lester L. 2n.3
Gramsci, Antonio 9
Graupner, Axel 258n.57
Gray, George Buchanan 242–3, 248n.25, 250n.31
Greenstein, Edward L. 214–16
Grenz, Jesse R. 26n.39, 27n.42
Gross, Andrew 45n.28, 46n.31
Guggenheimer, Heinrich W. 114n.51
Guillaume, Philippe 123n.80
Gurtner, Daniel M. 26nn.39, 41

Hachlili, Rachel 106n.23, 107n.27
Haran, Menahem 5, 63n.77, 74n.27, 107n.28,
  109–12, 159n.9

Harrington, D. J. 208n.51
Hartley, John E. 235n.83
Haugaard, Mark 7n.25
Hawkes, Jane 269n.2
Hays, Nathan 234–5
Heger, Paul 146n.46
Hendel, Ronald S. 262n.72
Hill, Charles Evan 26n.39, 27n.42
Himbaza, Innocent 130n.2
Hirsch, Samuel Raphael 22n.19
Holzinger, H. 68n.6, 116nn.56–57, 144n.40
Homan, Michael M. 5n.20, 103n.7
Houtman, Cornelis 52n.48, 63n.77, 86n.64,
  103n.10, 107n.26, 122n.78, 125, 125n.90,
  143n.35, 146n.43, 149n.54, 155nn.2–3, 176n.41
Hundley, Michael B. 110n.35
Hunt, Alice 219n.18
Hurowitz, Victor 85n.58, 103n.8, 112–13, 112n.44
Hutzli, Jürg 86n.62

Imes, Carmen Joy 113n.47, 118n.61, 119n.66

Jacob, Benno 166n.15
Jacobson, Howard 208n.51, 209n.52
Janowski, Bernd 115n.52, 132n.8, 254n.45
Japhet, Sara 111n.39
Jenson, Philip Peter 5n.21
Johnstone, William 109n.32
Jürgens, Benedikt 230nn.66, 68

Kahle, Paul 60–1
Kartveit, Magnar 48n.36
Kearney, Peter J. 20n.17, 87n.67
Keel, Othmar 118n.61, 119n.64, 123n.79
Kellermann, Diether 236n.90, 242–3
Kennedy, A.R.S. 108
Khan, Geoffrey 16–17
Kim, Angela Y. 45nn.26–27
Kim, Kyung-Rae 49n.38
Kirschner, Robert 214n.2
Kiuchi, Nobuyoshi 198n.27, 203n.37,
  216n.8, 235n.83
Klingbeil, Gerald A. 198n.26
Klostermann, August 25n.32
Knierim, Rolf P. 245n.16, 246n.19, 247n.24
Knohl, Israel 82n.50, 93, 126n.96, 174n.37
Koch, Klaus 115n.52, 217–18, 219n.21
Kogman-Appel, Katrin 269n.1
Konkel, Michael 81n.47
Kratz, Reinhard Gregor 87n.67
Kreps, David 9n.35
Kuenen, Abraham 67–8, 68n.7, 70–1, 83,
  218n.13, 246–7, 251
Kutsch, Ernst 262n.69

AUTHOR INDEX 305

de Lagarde, Paul 60–1
Laird, Donna 3n.14
Lange, Armin 30n.51, 41–2, 42n.9, 43n.14,
  45n.26, 47n.32
Le Boulluec, Alain, 29n.49, 57n.56, 63n.78, 77n.38
Lehming, Sigo 225n.48
Levine, Baruch A. 168n.18, 197nn.21, 24,
  211n.59, 237n.93, 242–3, 245n.16, 246,
  250n.31, 252n.37, 253, 254n.43
Lewis, Theodore J. 262n.70
Liss, Hanna 119n.62, 274
Lo Sardo, Domenico 5n.18, 49n.40, 59n.67, 60,
  64n.81, 74n.27, 101n.2, 179n.48
Lohfink, Norbert 218n.14
Longacre, Drew, 26n.38, 42–4, 43n.13, 45n.26
Longacre, Robert E. 18n.13, 104n.13

MacDonald, John 263n.76
MacDonald, Nathan 10n.37, 82nn.48, 49,
  116n.57, 192n.13, 219n.18, 235n.86, 238n.96,
  252n.38, 254n.45
Magen, Yitzhak 109n.34
Magrini, Sabina 270n.3
Maier, Johann 46n.29
Mandell, Alice 126–7
Margalith, Othniel 63n.75
Mastnjak, Nathan 107n.29
Mazar, Amihai 110n.35
McCrory, Jefferson Harrell 68n.10
McKane, William 1n.1
McNeile, A.H. 70n.15
Meshel, Naphtali S. 221n.35, 222n.40
Meyers, Carol L. 47n.33, 106n.23
Meyvaert, Paul 270n.3
Milgrom, Jacob 106n.25, 115nn.52, 53, 130n.2,
  131n.5, 168n.18, 171n.26, 187n.1, 189n.4,
  190n.5, 192n.12, 199, 202n.34, 205–6,
  211–12, 216, 226–7, 228n.63, 229–31,
  232nn.70, 71, 233–4, 235n.82, 236n.90,
  238n.94, 242–3, 248n.27, 249n.30,
  252n.37, 253n.40
Milik, Jozef T. 41n.1, 42nn.4–5
Milstein, Sara J. 139n.27
Mirguet, Françoise 227n.55
Mizrahi, Noam 129n.1
Müller, Reinhard 260n.64

Namdar, Dvory 146n.47
Nelson, Russell David 52n.47
Nicholson, Ernest Wilson 256n.48
Nielsen, Eduard 258n.56
Nielsen, Kjeld 146n.46, 149n.54
Nihan, Christophe 59–60, 70–1, 84–6, 87n.65,
  88, 88n.68, 115n.52, 119n.64, 120–2, 123n.84,

  131n.4, 147n.51, 149, 181n.53, 191–3, 196,
  197n.24, 198n.27, 202n.34, 203n.38, 215–20,
  221nn.31–33, 222n.41, 223, 224nn.46, 47,
  226n.52, 227, 230n.67, 232n.72, 234nn.77, 80,
  235nn.82, 85, 238n.95
Nöldeke, Theodor 68n.3
Noonan, Benjamin J. 107n.29
Noth, Martin 84–5, 109n.31, 116n.55, 119n.63,
  123n.81, 131n.3, 137n.16, 138, 150n.56,
  192n.11, 202n.34, 218n.16, 221n.33, 227n.57,
  234–5, 235n.85, 252n.37

O'Conner, M. 143n.35
Oesch, Josef M. 17n.10
Olyan, Saul M. 82n.50
O'Reilly, Jennifer 270n.6
Oswald, Wolfgang 3n.8, 101n.1
Otto, Eckart 167n.16, 222n.43, 258n.56, 259n.59
Outhwaite, Ben 17n.9
Owczarek, Susanne 80n.43, 87n.65, 123n.81

Paul, Shalom M. 266n.87
Peckham, Brian 263n.76
Perkins, Larry 75n.32
Perlitt, Lothar 258–60, 263n.77
Perrot, Anthony 42
Péter, René 190n.5
Podella, Thomas 120n.71, 123n.84
Pola, Thomas 87, 102n.5, 220n.26
Popper, Julius 48n.34, 51–2, 63n.79, 67, 68n.9,
  70–1, 77n.39
Porzig, Peter 86n.63, 105n.15, 168n.17
Pralon, Didier 214n.2
Propp, William Henry 52n.48, 63n.77, 70n.16,
  88n.70, 101n.1, 109, 119n.63, 121n.72, 132,
  138n.18, 146n.43, 149n.54, 155nn.3, 4,
  166n.15, 173, 187n.1, 207–8, 248n.28, 264n.80
Pummer, Reinhard 23n.23, 269n.1
Purvis, J.D. 269n.1
de Pury, Albert 225n.48
Pyschny, Katharina 3n.12, 4n.15, 89n.71,
  120n.70, 224n.47

Quick, Laura 126n.95, 178

von Rad, Gerhard 4n.17, 68n.7, 90nn.75, 76,
  123n.81, 218n.14
Ranke, Ernest 30n.52
Reif, Stefan C. 245n.15
Rendtorff, Rolf 202, 203n.37, 214, 221n.37, 227,
  227n.55, 232nn.70, 71, 235n.84, 260nn.64–65
Rhyder, Julia 59–60, 90, 91n.78, 92n.79, 120–2,
  123n.84, 159nn.11–12, 161, 168–9
Richey, Madadh 5n.20

AUTHOR INDEX

Roberts, Ulysses 30n.51
Robertson, Edward 23n.26
Röhrig, Meike J. 196, 198nn.28, 29, 203n.37, 222n.41, 235n.85
Römer, Thomas 260
Rooke, Deborah W. 2, 3n.10, 4n.16, 6, 112n.45, 138n.24
Rosen, Baruch 146n.47
Rouse, Joseph 8n.31
Ruwe, Andreas 217n.12

Samuel, Harald 81n.44, 181n.53, 244n.13
Sanderson, Judith E. 42nn.6, 10, 43n.17, 44n.21
Sandevoir, Pierre 29n.49, 45n.26, 57n.56, 63n.78, 77n.38
Sarna, Nahum M. 46n.29, 109n.33, 133n.10
Schaper, Joachim 3n.8
Schenker, Adrian 16n.4, 60n.71, 119n.68, 257
Schiffman, Lawrence H. 44n.24, 45nn.28–29, 208n.50
Schmidt, Ludwig 222n.43, 257, 260n.64
Schorch, Stefan 23nn.20–24, 43n.18, 260n.65
Schottroff, Willy 122n.75
Schulz, Sarah 3nn.10–13, 120n.70
Schwartz, Baruch J. 258n.57
Seebass, Horst 236n.90, 252n.37
Segal, Michael 44nn.24–25, 48n.37
Seow, C.L. 106
Sharon, Diane M. 216n.8
Shectman, Sarah 174–5, 178n.44
Shinan, Avigdor 214n.2
Ska, Jean-Louis 259n.62, 264nn.80, 82, 265n.85
Skehan, Patrick W. 23n.21, 42n.6 n.10, 43n.17
Smith, William Robertson 262n.71
Sommer, Benjamin 5n.18, 74n.27
Stackert, Jeffrey 82n.50, 258n.57
Stavrakopoulou, Francesca 191n.7
Steins, Georg 19n.14, 85n.54, 104n.12, 120n.71, 264nn.81–83
Steuernagel, Carl 258, 262–3
Stökl, Jonathan 250n.31, 251n.35
Strommenger, Eva 112–13
Sturdy, John 242n.7

Talmon, Shemaryahu 144n.39, 211n.57
Talshir, Zipora 210n.55
de Tarragon, J.-M. 86n.63
Tigay, Jeffrey H. 122
Tov, Emanuel 24n.28, 44n.24, 45n.26, 47n.32, 48n.36, 49n.39, 113n.48

Trebolle Barrera, Julio 30n.51, 46n.29, 59–60
Tucker, Paavo N.82

Ulrich, Eugene 42nn.6, 10, 43nn.12, 15–17, 48n.35, 52n.47, 81n.44
Utzschneider, Helmut 82n.51, 104n.13, 105n.19, 134n.12

Van Dam, Cornelis 122n.78
VanderKam, James C. 3nn.9, 13, 44n.24, 113n.48
de Vaux, R. 41n.1, 42nn.4–5
Vercellone, Carlo 30n.52
Voss, Jens 106n.23

de Waard, Henk 1n.1
Wade, Martha 49n.40, 51–2, 58, 58nn.59, 63, 70n.16
Wagner, Thomas 222n.42
Walkenhorst, Karl-Heinz 196n.17
Waltke, Bruce K. 143n.35
Watts, James W. 106n.25, 195n.15, 202n.34, 215–17, 220, 223n.45, 225, 227n.56, 230n.64, 233–4, 234n.78, 236n.91, 237n.92
Weeks, Stuart 47n.33
Weimar, Peter 86n.61, 102n.6, 218n.14
Wellhausen, Julius 4–5, 67–8, 70–1, 76n.33, 83, 110–11, 146–7, 198n.25, 217–18, 251–2, 256n.47
Wenham, Gordon J. 195n.16, 200–1, 211n.56, 230n.64, 235n.84, 243–4
Wevers, John William 17n.6, 26, 27n.44, 27.45, 28nn.46–47, 29n.49, 49–51, 53n.49, 55n.51, 57–9, 58nn.59–61, 71n.18, 73n.20, 75n.31, 85n.58, 89n.73, 92n.80, 101n.2, 119n.65, 123n.86, 134n.11, 144n.38, 156nn.6, 7, 158n.8, 173n.32, 179n.49, 193n.14, 264n.79
Wildberger, Hans 235–6
Wilhelm, Gernot 115n.52
Williamson, H. G. M. 210n.55, 214n.1
Willis, Timothy M. 220n.30
Winter, Urs 179n.48
Wöhrle, Jakob 2n.3, 67n.2
Wright, David P. 190n.5, 262n.70
Würthwein, Ernst 169n.22

Zahn, Molly M. 25n.33, 44nn.22, 24, 48n.35
Ziegler, Leo 16n.5, 31–2, 35n.62, 36nn.63–65
Zwickel, Wolfgang 146n.46